Pro Silverlight 2 in C# 2008

■ ■ ■

Matthew MacDonald

Apress®

Pro Silverlight 2 in C# 2008

Copyright © 2009 by Matthew MacDonald

ISBN-13 (paperback): 978-1-59059-949-5

ISBN-13 (electronic): 978-1-4302-0564-7

Printed and bound in the United States of America 9 8 7 6 5 4 3 2

Trademarked names may appear in this book. Rather than use a trademark symbol with every occurrence of a trademarked name, we use the names only in an editorial fashion and to the benefit of the trademark owner, with no intention of infringement of the trademark.

Lead Editor: Ewan Buckingham
Technical Reviewer: Fabio Claudio Ferracchiati
Editorial Board: Clay Andres, Steve Anglin, Mark Beckner, Ewan Buckingham, Tony Campbell,
    Gary Cornell, Jonathan Gennick, Michelle Lowman, Matthew Moodie, Jeffrey Pepper,
    Frank Pohlmann, Ben Renow-Clarke, Dominic Shakeshaft, Matt Wade, Tom Welsh
Project Manager: Sofia Marchant
Copy Editor: Ami Knox
Associate Production Director: Kari Brooks-Copony
Production Editor: Ellie Fountain
Compositor: Dina Quan
Proofreaders: Nancy Bell and Nancy Riddiough
Indexer: Broccoli Information Management
Artist: Kinetic Publishing Services, LLC
Cover Designer: Kurt Krames
Manufacturing Director: Tom Debolski

Distributed to the book trade worldwide by Springer-Verlag New York, Inc., 233 Spring Street, 6th Floor, New York, NY 10013. Phone 1-800-SPRINGER, fax 201-348-4505, e-mail orders-ny@springer-sbm.com, or visit http://www.springeronline.com.

For information on translations, please contact Apress directly at 2855 Telegraph Avenue, Suite 600, Berkeley, CA 94705. Phone 510-549-5930, fax 510-549-5939, e-mail info@apress.com, or visit http://www.apress.com.

Apress and friends of ED books may be purchased in bulk for academic, corporate, or promotional use. eBook versions and licenses are also available for most titles. For more information, reference our Special Bulk Sales–eBook Licensing web page at http://www.apress.com/info/bulksales.

The source code for this book is available to readers at http://www.apress.com.

For my family

Contents at a Glance

Contents

About the Author

MATTHEW MACDONALD is an author, educator, and Microsoft MVP in Windows Client Development. He's a regular contributor to programming journals and the author of more than a dozen books about .NET programming, including *Pro WPF in C# 2008* (Apress, 2008), *Pro .NET 2.0 Windows Forms and Custom Controls in C#* (Apress, 2005), and *Pro ASP.NET 3.5 in C# 2008* (Apress, 2007). He lives in Toronto with his wife and two daughters.

About the Technical Reviewer

FABIO CLAUDIO FERRACCHIATI is a prolific writer on cutting-edge technologies and has contributed to more than a dozen books on .NET, C#, Visual Basic, and ASP.NET. He is a .NET MCSD and lives in Milan, Italy.

Acknowledgments

No author can complete a book without a small army of helpful individuals. I'm deeply indebted to the whole Apress team, including Sofia Marchant and Ellie Fountain, who shepherded this book through its many stages; Ami Knox, who speedily performed the copy edit; Fabio Ferracchiati, who hunted down errors in tech review; and many other individuals who worked behind the scenes indexing pages, drawing figures, and proofreading the final copy. I also owe a special thanks to Gary Cornell, who always offers invaluable advice about projects and the publishing world.

Finally, I'd never write any book without the support of my wife and these special individuals: Nora, Razia, Paul, and Hamid. Thanks everyone!

Introduction

Silverlight is a framework for building rich, browser-hosted applications that run on a variety of operating systems. Silverlight works its magic through a *browser plug-in*. When you surf to a web page that includes some Silverlight content, this browser plug-in runs, executes the code, and renders that content in a specifically designated region of the page. The important part is that the Silverlight plug-in provides a far richer environment than the traditional blend of HTML and JavaScript that powers ordinary web pages. Used carefully and artfully, you can create Silverlight pages that have interactive graphics, use vector animations, and play video and sound files.

If this all sounds eerily familiar, it's because the same trick has been tried before. Several other technologies use a plug-in to stretch the bounds of the browser, including Java, ActiveX, Shockwave, and (most successfully) Adobe Flash. Although all these alternatives are still in use, none of them has become the single, dominant platform for rich web development. Many of them suffer from a number of problems, including installation headaches, poor development tools, and insufficient compatibility with the full range of browsers and operating systems. The only technology that's been able to avoid these pitfalls is Flash, which boasts excellent cross-platform support and widespread adoption. However, Flash has only recently evolved from a spunky multimedia player into a set of dynamic programming tools. It still offers far less than a modern programming environment like .NET.

That's where Silverlight fits into the picture. Silverlight aims to combine the raw power and cross-platform support of Flash with a first-class programming platform that incorporates the fundamental concepts of .NET. At the moment, Flash has the edge over Silverlight because of its widespread adoption and its maturity. However, Silverlight boasts a few architectural features that Flash can't match—most importantly, the fact that it's based on a scaled-down version of .NET's common language runtime (CLR) and allows developers to write client-side code using pure C#.

Understanding Silverlight

Silverlight uses a familiar technique to go beyond the capabilities of standard web pages: a lightweight browser plug-in.

The advantage of the plug-in model is that the user needs to install just a single component to see content created by a range of different people and companies. Installing the plug-in requires a small download and forces the user to confirm the operation in at least one security dialog box. It takes a short but definite amount of time, and it's an obvious inconvenience. However, once the plug-in is installed, the browser can process any content that uses the plug-in seamlessly, with no further prompting.

▮**Note** Silverlight is designed to overcome the limitations of ordinary HTML to allow developers to create more graphical and interactive applications. However, Silverlight isn't a way for developers to break out of the browser's security sandbox. For the most part, Silverlight applications are limited in equivalent ways to ordinary web pages. For example, a Silverlight application is allowed to create and access files, but only those files that are stored in a special walled-off *isolated storage* area (described in Chapter 15). Conceptually, isolated storage works like the cookies in an ordinary web page. Files are separated by website and the current user, and size is limited.

Figure 1 shows two views of a page with Silverlight content. At the top is the page you'll see if you *don't* have the Silverlight plug-in installed. At this point, you can click the Get Microsoft Silverlight picture to be taken to Microsoft's website, where you'll be prompted to install the plug-in and then sent back to the original page. On the bottom is the page you'll see once the Silverlight plug-in is installed.

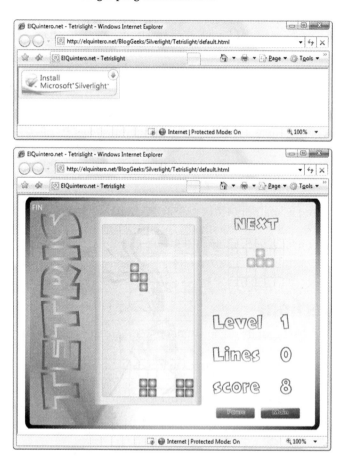

Figure 1. *Installing the Silverlight plug-in*

Silverlight System Requirements

With any Web-centric technology, it's keenly important to have compatibility with the widest possible range of computers and devices. Although Silverlight is still evolving, it already stacks up fairly well in this department:

- **Windows computers.** Silverlight 2 works on PCs with Windows Vista and Windows XP. The minimum browser versions that Silverlight 2 supports are Internet Explorer 6 and Firefox 1.5. Silverlight 2 will also work in Windows 2000, but only with Internet Explorer 6.

- **Mac computers.** Silverlight works on Mac computers with OS X 10.4.8 or later, provided they have Intel hardware (as opposed to the older PowerPC hardware). The minimum browser versions that Silverlight 2 supports are Firefox 1.5 and Safari.

- **Linux computers.** Although Silverlight 2 doesn't currently work on Linux, the Mono team is creating an open-source Linux implementation of Silverlight 1 and Silverlight 2. This project is known as Moonlight, and it's being developed with key support from Microsoft. To learn more, visit http://www.mono-project.com/Moonlight.

Note The system requirements for Silverlight may change as Microsoft releases plug-ins for other browsers. For example, the Opera browser currently works on PCs through an unsupported hack, but better support is planned in the future. To see the latest system requirements, check http://www.microsoft.com/silverlight/resources/install.aspx.

Installing Silverlight requires a small-sized setup (less than 5 MB) that's easy to download. That allows it to provide an all-important "frictionless" setup experience, much like Flash (but quite different from Java).

Silverlight vs. Flash

The most successful browser plug-in is Adobe Flash, which is installed on over 90 percent of the world's web browsers. Flash has a long history that spans more than ten years, beginning as a straightforward tool for adding animated graphics and gradually evolving into a platform for developing interactive content.

It's perfectly reasonable for .NET developers to create websites that use Flash content. However, doing so requires a separate design tool, and a completely different programming language (ActionScript) and programming environment (Flex). Furthermore, there's no straightforward way to integrate Flash content with server-side .NET code. For example, creating Flash applications that call .NET components is awkward at best. Using server-side .NET code to render Flash content (for example, a custom ASP.NET control that spits out a Flash content region) is far more difficult.

▪**Note** There are some third-party solutions that help break down the barrier between ASP.NET and Flash. One example is the innovative SWFSource.NET (http://www.activehead.com/SWFSource.aspx), which provides a set of .NET classes that allow you to dynamically generate Flash (.swf) files. However, these tools work at a relatively low level. They fall far short of a full development platform.

Silverlight aims to give .NET developers a better option for creating rich web content. Silverlight provides a browser plug-in with many similar features to Flash, but one that's designed from the ground up for .NET. Silverlight natively supports the C# language and embraces a range of .NET concepts. As a result, developers can write client-side code for Silverlight in the same language they use for server-side code (such as C# and VB), and use many of the same abstractions (including streams, controls, collections, generics, and LINQ).

The Silverlight plug-in has an impressive list of features, some of which are shared in common with Flash, and a few of which are entirely new and even revolutionary. Here are some highlights:

- **2-D drawing.** Silverlight provides a rich model for 2-D drawing. Best of all, the content you draw is defined as shapes and paths, so you can manipulate this content on the client side. You can even respond to events (like a mouse click on a portion of a graphic), which makes it easy to add interactivity to anything you draw.

- **Controls.** Developers don't want to reinvent the wheel, so Silverlight is stocked with a few essentials, including buttons, text boxes, lists, and a grid. Best of all, these basic building blocks can be restyled with custom visuals if you want all of the functionality but none of the stock look.

- **Animation.** Silverlight has a time-based animation model that lets you define what should happen and how long it should take. The Silverlight plug-in handles the sticky details, like interpolating intermediary values and calculating the frame rate.

- **Media.** Silverlight provides playback of Windows Media Audio (WMA), Windows Media Video (WMV7–9), MP3 audio, and VC-1 (which supports high definition). You aren't tied to the Windows Media Player ActiveX control or browser plug-in—instead, you can create any front-end you want, and you can even show video in full-screen mode. Microsoft also provides a free companion hosting service (at http://silverlight.live.com) that gives you space to store media files. Currently, it offers a generous 10 GB.

- **The common language runtime.** Most impressively, Silverlight includes a scaled-down version of the CLR, complete with an essential set of core classes, a garbage collector, a JIT (just-in-time) compiler, support for generics, threading, and so on. In many cases, developers can take code written for the full .NET CLR and use it in a Silverlight application with only moderate changes.

- **Networking.** Silverlight applications can call old-style ASP.NET web services (.asmx) or WCF (Windows Communication Foundation) web services. They can also send manually created XML requests over HTTP and even open direct socket connections for fast two-way communication. This gives developers a great way to combine rich client-side code with secure server-side routines.

- **Data binding.** Although it's not as capable as its big brother, WPF, Silverlight data binding provides a convenient way to display large amounts of data with minimal code. You can pull your data from XML or in-memory objects, giving you the ability to call a web service, receive a collection of objects, and display their data in a web page—often with just a couple of lines of code.

Of course, it's just as important to note what Silverlight *doesn't* include. Silverlight is a new technology that's evolving rapidly, and it's full of stumbling blocks for developers who are used to relying on .NET's rich libraries of prebuilt functionality. Prominent gaps include a lack of database support (there's no ADO.NET), no support for 3-D drawing, no printing, no command model, and few rich controls like trees and menus (although many developers and component companies are building their own). All of these features are available in Windows-centric WPF applications, and they may someday migrate to the Silverlight universe—or not.

Silverlight 1 and 2

Silverlight exists in two versions:

- The first version, Silverlight 1, is a relatively modest technology. It includes the 2-D drawing features and the media playback features. However, it doesn't include the CLR engine or support for .NET languages, so any code you write must use JavaScript.

- The second version, Silverlight 2, adds the .NET-powered features that have generated the most developer excitement. It includes the CLR, a subset of .NET Framework classes, and a user interface model based on WPF (as described in the next section, "Silverlight and WPF").

Many developers consider Silverlight 2 to be the first *real* first release of the Silverlight platform. It's the only version you'll consider in this book.

Note At present, Silverlight is only on a fraction of computers. However, Microsoft is convinced that if compelling content exists for Silverlight, users will download the plug-in. There are a number of factors that support this argument. Flash grew dramatically in a short space of time, and Microsoft has obvious experience with other web-based applications that have started small and eventually gained wide adoption. (Windows Messenger comes to mind, along with numerous ActiveX plug-ins for tasks ranging from multiuser coordination on MSN Games to Windows verification on MSDN.)

Silverlight and WPF

One of the most interesting aspects of Silverlight is the fact that it borrows the model WPF uses for rich, client-side user interfaces.

WPF is a next-generation technology for creating Windows applications. It was introduced in .NET 3.0 as the successor to Windows Forms. WPF is notable because it not only simplifies development with a powerful set of high-level features, it also increases performance by rendering everything through the DirectX pipeline. To learn about WPF, you can refer to *Pro WPF in C# 2008* (Apress, 2008).

Silverlight obviously can't duplicate the features of WPF, because many of them rely deeply on the capabilities of the operating system, including Windows-specific display drivers and DirectX technology. However, rather than invent an entirely new set of controls and classes for client-side development, Silverlight uses a subset of the WPF model. If you've had any experience with WPF, you'll be surprised to see how closely Silverlight resembles its big brother. Here are a few common details:

- To define a Silverlight user interface (the collection of elements that makes up a Silverlight content region), you use XAML markup, just as you do with WPF. You can even map data to your display using the same data-binding syntax.

- Silverlight borrows many of the same basic controls from WPF, along with the same styling system (for standardizing and reusing formatting), and a similar templating mechanism (for changing the appearance of standard controls).

- To draw 2-D graphics in Silverlight, you use shapes, paths, transforms, geometries, and brushes, all of which closely match their WPF equivalents.

- Silverlight provides a declarative animation model that's based on storyboards, and works in the same way as WPF's animation system.

- To show video or play audio files, you use the MediaElement class, as you do in WPF.

Microsoft has made no secret about its intention to continue to expand the capabilities of Silverlight by drawing from the full WPF model. In future Silverlight releases, you're likely to find that Silverlight borrows more and more features from WPF. This trend is already on display with the shift from Silverlight 1 to Silverlight 2.

▪**Note** WPF is not completely cut off from the easy deployment world of the Web. WPF allows developers to create browser-hosted applications called XBAPs (XAML Browser Applications). These applications are downloaded seamlessly, cached locally, and run directly inside the browser window, all without security prompts. However, although XBAPs run in Internet Explorer and Firefox, they are still a Windows-only technology, unlike Silverlight.

THE LIMITATIONS OF SILVERLIGHT

Silverlight compares well to any browser-based technology, with a full suite of modern features and some remarkable innovations. However, Silverlight can't offer all the power of a dedicated rich client technology like WPF, which is designed explicitly for the Windows platform and the DirectX libraries.

Here are some of the WPF features that you *won't* get in Silverlight—at least not now:

- **3-D graphics.** You can draw 3-D shapes using the 2-D drawing primitives that Silverlight offers. However, that leaves you with a lot of custom code to write and a huge amount of math to crunch. True 3-D drawing support, like that offered in WPF, takes care of issues like rotation, lighting, occlusion, and hit testing.

- **Hardware acceleration.** Silverlight will never reach the blistering speed of WPF, because it's designed for widespread compatibility, not native hardware. However, its performance is still impressive, and it offers a serious challenge to other browser-based technologies, like Flash.

- **Documents.** WPF has a rich flow model for showing large amounts of text content, with intelligent line breaking and justification algorithms. Silverlight doesn't.

- **Printing.** Silverlight doesn't provide any way for you to print with the client's printer.

- **Commands.** WPF uses a command model that allows you to define higher-level tasks that can be wired to different user interface controls. Silverlight doesn't include this abstraction—although you could build your own.

- **Triggers.** Silverlight control templates are vastly different than WPF control templates, because they don't support *triggers*, a tool for declaratively mapping events to state changes and animations. The solution is something called the Visual State Manager, which you'll study in Chapter 11.

- **Styles.** *Styles* are a way of reusing formatting on multiple elements. Silverlight supports styles, but in a limited fashion. Notably, it doesn't let you change styles after applying them (which limits some potential designs for skinnable applications), and it doesn't include a mechanism for applying styles to certain types of elements automatically.

- **Custom routed events.** Silverlight supports the concept of routed events—events that occur in one element and then bubble up the element hierarchy, giving you the opportunity to handle them in a containing element (as you'll see in Chapter 4). However, Silverlight imposes severe restrictions, including preventing you from using routed events in your own custom controls.

- **Offline mode.** Silverlight applications are downloaded to the client and executed in the browser. Although this model lends itself to the possibility of caching applications on the client's hard drive and executing them later, perhaps even outside the browser, Silverlight doesn't include this feature.

Expect to see at least some of these features appear in future versions of Silverlight.

About This Book

This book is an in-depth exploration of Silverlight for professional developers who know the .NET platform, the C# language, and the Visual Studio development environment.

■Tip Previous experience with WPF—the Windows-based big brother of Silverlight—isn't required. However, if you've programmed with WPF before, you'll breeze through many of Silverlight basics. When useful, this book points out the key differences between Silverlight and the WPF platform.

What You Need to Use This Book

In order to *run* Silverlight applications, you simply need the Silverlight browser plug-in, which is available at http://silverlight.net. In order to *create* Silverlight applications (and open the sample projects included with this book), you need Visual Studio 2008. You'll also need the Visual Studio extensions that allow you to create Silverlight projects (known as the Silverlight Tools for Visual Studio), which are available at http://silverlight.net/GetStarted. The Silverlight Tools for Visual Studio include both the Silverlight 2 runtime and the Silverlight 2 SDK, so a single download is all you need.

There's one other option. Instead of using any version of Visual Studio, you can use Expression Blend 2.5—a graphically oriented design tool—to build and test Silverlight applications. Overall, Expression Blend is intended for graphic designers who spend their time creating serious eye candy, while Visual Studio is ideal for code-heavy application programmers. This book assumes you're using Visual Studio. If you'd like to learn more about Expression Blend, you can consult one of many dedicated books on the subject.

Code Samples

It's a good idea to check the Apress website or http://www.prosetech.com to download the up-to-date code samples. You'll need to do this to test most of the more sophisticated code examples described in this book because the less significant details are usually left out. This book focuses on the most important sections so that you don't need to wade through needless extra pages to understand a concept.

To download the source code, surf to http://www.prosetech.com and look for the page for this book.

Feedback

This book has the ambitious goal of being the best tutorial and reference for programming Silverlight. Toward that end, your comments and suggestions are extremely helpful. You can send complaints, adulation, and everything in between directly to apress@prosetech.com. I can't solve your Silverlight problems or critique your code, but I will benefit from information about what this book did right and wrong (or what it may have done in an utterly confusing way).

The Last Word

As you've seen, Silverlight is a .NET-based Flash competitor. It aims to compete with Flash today, but provide a path to far more features in the future. Unlike the Flash development model, which is limited in several ways due to how it's evolved over the years, Silverlight is a starting-from-scratch attempt that's thoroughly based on .NET and WPF, and will therefore allow .NET developers to be far more productive. In many ways, Silverlight is the culmination of two trends: the drive to extend web pages to incorporate more and more rich-client features, and the drive to give the .NET Framework a broader reach. It's also a new direction that will only get more interesting in the months ahead.

■■■

CHAPTER 1

Introducing Silverlight

In the introduction, you learned about the overall goals and design philosophy that underpin Silverlight. Now, you're ready to get your hands dirty and create your first Silverlight application.

The most practical approach for building Silverlight applications is to use Visual Studio, Microsoft's premiere coding tool. In this chapter, you'll see how to create, compile, and deploy a Silverlight application using Visual Studio 2008. Along the way, you'll get a quick look at how Silverlight controls respond to events, you'll see how Silverlight applications are compiled and packaged for the Web, and you'll consider the two options for hosting Silverlight content: either in an ordinary HTML web page or in an ASP.NET web form.

Silverlight and Visual Studio

Although it's technically possible to create the files you need for a Silverlight application by hand, professional developers always use a development tool. If you're a graphic designer, that tool is likely to be Microsoft Expression Blend 2.5, which provides a full complement of features for designing visually rich user interfaces. If you're a developer, you'll probably use Visual Studio 2008, which includes well-rounded tools for coding, testing, and debugging.

Because both tools are equally at home with the Silverlight application model, you can easily create a workflow that incorporates both of them. For example, a developer could create a basic user interface with Visual Studio and then hand it off to a crack design team, who would polish it up with custom graphics in Expression Blend. When the facelift is finished, they would deliver the project back to the developer, who could then continue writing and refining its code in Visual Studio.

Note In this book, you'll focus your attention on Visual Studio. But before you can use Visual Studio 2008 to create Silverlight applications, you need to install a set of extensions for Silverlight development. For complete instructions, see the introduction of this book or the readme.txt file included with the sample code.

Understanding Silverlight Websites

There are two types of Silverlight websites that you can create in Visual Studio:

- **An ordinary website with HTML pages.** In this case, the entry point to your Silverlight application is a basic HTML file that includes a Silverlight content region.

- **ASP.NET website.** In this case, Visual Studio creates two projects—one to contain the Silverlight application files, and one to hold the server-side ASP.NET website that will be deployed alongside your Silverlight files. The entry point to your Silverlight application can be an ordinary HTML file, or it can be an ASP.NET web form that includes server-generated content.

So which approach is best? No matter which option you choose, your Silverlight application will run the same way—the client browser will receive an HTML document, that HTML document will include a Silverlight content region, and the Silverlight code will run on the local computer, *not* the web server. However, the ASP.NET web approach makes it easier to mix ASP.NET and Silverlight content. This is usually a better approach in the following cases:

- You want to create a website that contains both ASP.NET web pages and Silverlight-enhanced pages.

- You want to generate Silverlight content indirectly, using ASP.NET web controls.

- You want to create a Silverlight application that calls a web service, and you want to design the web service at the same time (and deploy it to the same web server).

On the other hand, if you don't need to write any server-side code, there's little point in creating a full-fledged ASP.NET website. Many of the Silverlight applications you'll see in this book use basic HTML-only websites. The examples only include ASP.NET websites when they need specific server-side features. For example, the examples in Chapter 14 use an ASP.NET website that includes a web service. This web service allows the Silverlight application to retrieve data from a database on the web server, a feat that would be impossible without server-side code.

ADDING SILVERLIGHT CONTENT TO AN EXISTING WEBSITE

A key point to keep in mind when considering the Silverlight development model is that in many cases you'll use Silverlight to *augment* the existing content of your website, which will still include generous amounts of HTML, CSS, and JavaScript. For example, you might add a Silverlight content region that shows an advertisement or allows an enhanced experience for a portion of a website (such as playing a game, completing a survey, interacting with a product, taking a virtual tour, and so on). You may use Silverlight-enhanced pages to present content that's already available in your website in a more engaging way, or to provide a value-added feature for users who have the Silverlight plug-in.

Of course, it's also possible to create a Silverlight-only website, which is a somewhat more daring approach. The key drawback is that Silverlight is still relatively new, and it doesn't support legacy clients (most notably, it has no support for users of Windows ME and Windows 98, and Internet Explorer–only support for Windows 2000). As a result, Silverlight doesn't have nearly the same reach as ordinary HTML. Many businesses that are adopting Silverlight are using it to distinguish themselves from other online competitors with cutting-edge content, but they aren't abandoning their traditional websites.

Creating a Stand-Alone Silverlight Project

The easiest way to start using Silverlight is to create an ordinary website with HTML pages and no server-side code. Here's how:

1. Select File ➤ New ➤ Project in Visual Studio, choose the Visual C# group of project types, and select the Silverlight Application template. As usual, you need to pick a project name and a location on your hard drive before clicking OK to create the project.

2. At this point, Visual Studio will prompt you to choose whether you want to create a full-fledged ASP.NET website that can run server-side code or an ordinary website with HTML pages (see Figure 1-1). For now, choose the second option ("Automatically generates a test page") to create an ordinary website and click OK.

Figure 1-1. *Choosing the type of website*

Every Silverlight project starts with a small set of essential files, as shown in Figure 1-2. All the files that end with the extension .xaml use a flexible markup standard called XAML, which you'll dissect in the next chapter. All the files that end with the extension .cs hold the C# source code that powers your application.

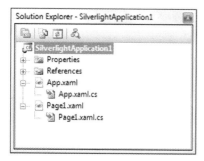

Figure 1-2. *A Silverlight project*

Here's a rundown of the files shown in Figure 1-2:

- **App.xaml and App.xaml.cs.** These files allow you to configure your Silverlight application. They allow you to define resources that will be made available to all the pages in your application (see Chapter 2), and they allow you react to application events such as startup, shutdown, and error conditions (see Chapter 6). In a newly generated project, the startup code in the App.xaml.cs file specifies that your application should begin by showing Page.xaml.

- **Page.xaml.** This file defines the user interface (the collection of controls, images, and text) that will be shown for your first page. Technically, Silverlight pages are *user controls*—custom classes that derive from UserControl. A Silverlight application can contain as many pages as you need—to add more, simply choose Project ➤ Add New Item, pick the Silverlight User Control template, choose a file name, and click Add.

- **Page.xaml.cs.** This file includes the code that underpins your first page, including the event handlers that react to user actions.

Along with these four essential files, there are a few more ingredients that you'll only find if you dig around. Under the Properties node in the Solution Explorer, you'll find a file named AppManifest.xml, which lists the assemblies that your application uses. You'll also find a file named AssemblyInfo.cs, which contains information about your project (such as its name, version, and publisher) that's embedded into your Silverlight assembly when it's compiled. Neither of these files should be edited by hand—instead, they're modified by Visual Studio when you add references or set projects properties.

Lastly, the gateway to your Silverlight application is an automatically generated but hidden HTML file named TestPage.html (see Figure 1-3). To see this file, make sure you've compiled your application at least once. Then, click the Show All Files button at the top of the Solution Explorer, and expand the Bin\Debug folder (which is where your application is compiled). You'll take a closer look at the content of the TestPage.html file a bit later in this chapter.

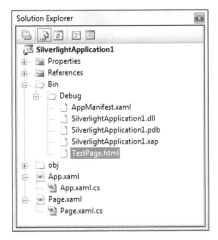

Figure 1-3. *The HTML test page*

Creating a Simple Silverlight Page

As you've already learned, every Silverlight page includes a markup portion that defines the visual appearance (the XAML file) and a source code file that contains event handlers. To customize your first Silverlight application, you simply need to open the Page.xaml file and begin adding markup.

Visual Studio gives you two ways to look at every XAML file—as a visual preview (known as the *design surface*) or the underlying markup (known as the *source view*). By default, Visual Studio shows both parts, stacked one on the other. Figure 1-4 shows this view and points out the buttons you can use to change your vantage point.

Drag this slider to change the zoom used to display the design surface

Double-click the Design tab or the XAML tab to see just that portion of the window (and collapse the other)

Switch the position of the two panes

Choose between a vertical or horizontal layout (also restores the split view if one part is collapsed)

Collapse the bottom pane

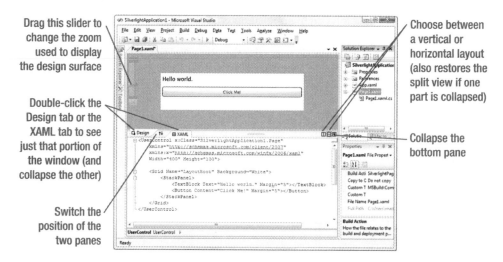

Figure 1-4. *Viewing XAML pages*

As you've no doubt guessed, you can start designing your XAML page by dragging controls from the Toolbox and dropping them onto the design surface. However, this convenience won't save you from learning the full intricacies of XAML. In order to organize your elements into the right layout containers, change their properties, wire up event handlers, and use Silverlight features like animation, styles, templates, and data binding, you'll need to edit the XAML markup by hand.

To get started, you can try creating the page shown here, which defines a block of text and a button. The portions in bold have been added to the basic page template that Visual Studio generated when you created the project.

```
<UserControl x:Class="SilverlightApplication1.Page"
    xmlns="http://schemas.microsoft.com/client/2007"
    xmlns:x="http://schemas.microsoft.com/winfx/2006/xaml"
    Width="400" Height="100">

    <Grid x:Name="LayoutRoot" Background="White">
        <StackPanel>
            <TextBlock x:Name="lblMessage" Text="Hello world."
             Margin="5"></TextBlock>
            <Button x:Name="cmdClickMe" Content="Click Me!" Margin="5"></Button>
        </StackPanel>
    </Grid>
</UserControl>
```

This creates a page that has a stacked arrangement of two elements. On the top is a block of text with a simple message. Underneath it is a button.

Note In Silverlight terminology, each graphical widget that meets these criteria (appears in a window and is represented by a .NET class) is called an *element*. The term *control* is generally reserved for elements that receive focus and allow user interaction. For example, a TextBox is a control, but the TextBlock is not.

Adding Event Handling Code

You attach event handlers to the elements in your page using attributes, which is the same approach that developers take in WPF, ASP.NET, and JavaScript. For example, the Button element exposes an event named Click that fires when the button is triggered with the mouse or keyboard. To react to this event, you add the Click attribute to the Button element, and set it to the name of a method in your code:

```
<Button x:Name="cmdClickMe" Click="cmdClickMe_Click" Content="Click Me!"
 Margin="5"></Button>
```

Tip Although it's not required, it's a common convention to name event handler methods in the form ElementName_EventName. If the element doesn't have a defined name (presumably because you don't need to interact with it in any other place in your code), consider using the name it *would* have.

This example assumes that you've created an event handling method named cmd-ClickMe_Click. Here's what it looks like in the Page.xaml.cs file:

```
private void cmdClickMe_Click(object sender, RoutedEventArgs e)
{
    lblMessage.Text = "Goodbye, cruel world.";
}
```

You can't coax Visual Studio into creating an event handler by double-clicking an element or using the Properties window (as you can in other types of projects). However, once you've added the event handler, you can use IntelliSense to quickly assign it to the right event. Begin by typing in the attribute name, followed by the equal sign. At this point, Visual Studio will pop up a menu that lists all the methods that have the right syntax to handle this event, and currently exist in your code behind class, as shown in Figure 1-5. Simply choose the right event handling method.

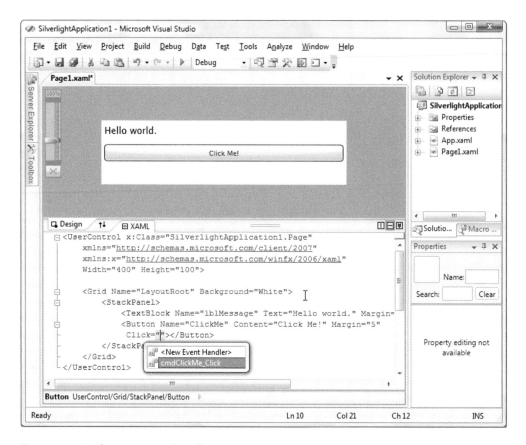

Figure 1-5. *Attaching an event handler*

It's possible to use Visual Studio to create and assign an event handler in one step by adding an event attribute and choosing the <New Event Handler> option in the menu.

Tip To jump quickly from the XAML to your event handling code, right-click the appropriate event attribute in your markup and choose Navigate to Event Handler.

You can also connect an event with code. The place to do it is the constructor for your page, after the call to InitializeComponent(), which initializes all your controls. Here's the code equivalent of the XAML markup shown previously:

```
public Page()
{
    InitializeComponent();
    cmdClickMe.Click += cmdClickMe_Click;
}
```

The code approach is useful if you need to dynamically create a control and attach an event handler at some point during the lifetime of your window. By comparison, the events you hook up in XAML are always attached when the window object is first instantiated. The code approach also allows you to keep your XAML simpler and more streamlined, which is perfect if you plan to share it with non-programmers, such as a design artist. The drawback is a significant amount of boilerplate code that will clutter up your code files.

If you want to detach an event handler, code is your only option. You can use the -= operator, as shown here:

```
cmdClickMe.Click -= cmdClickMe_Click;
```

It is technically possible to connect the same event handler to the same event more than once. This is almost always the result of a coding mistake. (In this case, the event handler will be triggered multiple times.) If you attempt to remove an event handler that's been connected twice, the event will still trigger the event handler, but just once.

Browsing the Silverlight Class Libraries

In order to write practical code, you need to know quite a bit about the classes you have to work with. That means acquiring a thorough knowledge of the core class libraries that ship with Silverlight.

Silverlight includes a subset of the classes from the full .NET Framework. Although it would be impossible to cram the entire .NET Framework into Silverlight—after all, it's a 4MB download that needs to support a variety of browsers and operating systems—Silverlight includes a remarkable amount of functionality.

The Silverlight version of the .NET Framework is simplified in two ways. First, it doesn't provide the sheer number of types you'll find in the full .NET Framework. Second, the classes that it does include often don't provide the full complement of constructors, methods, properties, and events. Instead, Silverlight keeps only the most practical members of the most important classes, which leaves it with enough functionality to create surprisingly compelling code.

Note The Silverlight classes are designed to have public interfaces that resemble their full-fledged counterparts in the .NET Framework. However, the actual plumbing of these classes is quite different. All the Silverlight classes have been rewritten from the ground up to be as streamlined and efficient as possible.

Before you start doing any serious Silverlight programming, you might like to browse the Silverlight version of the .NET Framework. One way to do so is to open a Silverlight project, and then show the Object Browser in Visual Studio (choose View ➤ Object Browser). Along with the assembly for the code in your project, you'll see the following Silverlight assemblies (shown in Figure 1-6):

- **mscorlib.dll.** This assembly is the Silverlight equivalent of the mscorlib.dll assembly that includes the most fundamental parts of the .NET Framework. The Silverlight version includes core data types, exceptions, and interfaces in the System namespace; ordinary and generic collections; file management classes; and support for globalization, reflection, resources, debugging, and multithreading.

- **System.dll.** This assembly contains additional generic collections, classes for dealing with URIs, and classes for dealing with regular expressions.

- **System.Core.dll.** This assembly contains support for LINQ. The name of the assembly matches the full .NET Framework, which implements new .NET 3.5 features in an assembly named System.Core.dll.

- **System.Net.dll.** This assembly contains classes that support networking, allowing you to download web pages and create socket-based connections.

- **System.Windows.dll.** This assembly includes many of the classes for building Silverlight user interfaces, including basic elements, shapes and brushes, classes that support animation and data binding, and a version of the OpenFileDialog that works with isolated storage.

- **System.Windows.Browser.dll.** This assembly contains classes for interacting with HTML elements.

- **System.Xml.dll.** This assembly includes the bare minimum classes you need for XML processing: XmlReader and XmlWriter.

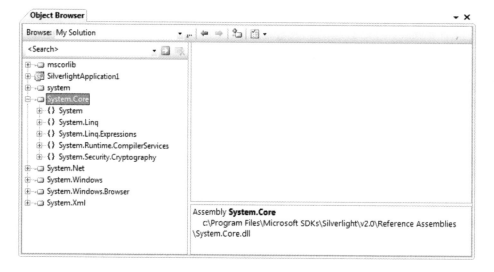

Figure 1-6. *Silverlight assemblies in the Object Browser*

▎**Note** Some of the members in the Silverlight assemblies are only available to .NET Framework code, and aren't callable from your code. These members are marked with the SecurityCritical attribute. However, this attribute does not appear in the Object Browser, so you won't be able to determine whether a specific feature is usable in a Silverlight application until you try to use it. (If you attempt to use a member that has the SecurityCritical attribute, you'll get a SecurityException.) For example, Silverlight applications are only allowed to access the file system through the isolated storage API or the OpenFileDialog class. For that reason, the constructor for the FileStream class is decorated with the SecurityCritical attribute.

SILVERLIGHT'S ADD-ON ASSEMBLIES

The architects of Silverlight have set out to keep the core framework as small as possible. This design makes the initial Silverlight plug-in small to download and quick to install—an obvious selling point to web surfers everywhere.

To achieve this lean-and-mean goal, the Silverlight designers have removed some functionality from the core Silverlight runtime and placed it in separate add-on assemblies. These assemblies are still considered to be part of the Silverlight platform, but if you want to use them, you'll need to package them with your application. This represents an obvious trade-off, because it will increase the download size of your application. (The effect is mitigated by Silverlight's built-in compression, which you'll learn about later in this chapter.)

You'll learn about Silverlight's add-on assemblies throughout this book. Two commonly used ones are:

- **System.Windows.Controls.dll.** This assembly contains a few new controls, including the Calendar, DatePicker, TabControl, and GridSplitter.

- **System.Windows.Controls.Data.dll.** This assembly has Silverlight's new built-from-scratch DataGrid.

Both of these assemblies add new controls to your Silverlight toolkit. In the near future, Microsoft plans to make many more add-on controls available. Eventually, the number of add-on controls will dwarf the number of core controls.

When you drag a control from an add-on assembly onto a Silverlight page, Visual Studio automatically adds the assembly reference you need. If you select that reference and look in the Properties window, you'll see that the Copy Local property is set to true, which is different from the other assemblies that make up the core Silverlight runtime. As a result, when you compile your application, the assembly will be embedded in the final package. Visual Studio is intelligent enough to recognize assemblies that aren't a part of the core Silverlight runtime—even if you add them by hand, it automatically sets Copy Local to true.

Testing a Silverlight Application

You now have enough to test your Silverlight project. When you run a Silverlight application, Visual Studio launches your default web browser and navigates to the hidden browser test page, named TestPage.html. The test page creates a new Silverlight control and initializes it using the markup in Page.xaml.

Note Visual Studio sets TestPage.html to be the start page for your project. As a result, when you launch your project, this page will be loaded in the browser. You can choose a different start page by right-clicking an HTML file in the Solution Explorer and choosing Set As Start Page.

Figure 1-7 shows the previous example at work. When you click the button, the event handling code runs and the text changes. This process happens entirely on the client—there is no need to contact the server or post back the page, as there is in a server-side programming framework like ASP.NET. All the Silverlight code is executed on the client side by the scaled-down version of .NET that's embedded in the Silverlight plug-in.

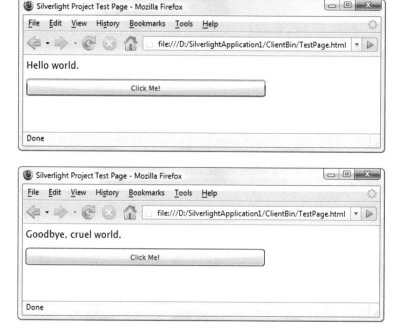

Figure 1-7. Running a Silverlight application (in Firefox)

If you're hosting your host Silverlight content in an ordinary website (with no server-side ASP.NET), Visual Studio won't use its integrated web server during the testing process. Instead, it simply opens the HTML test page directly from the file system. (You can see this in the address bar in Figure 1-7.)

In some situations, this behavior could cause discrepancies between your test environment and your deployed environment, which will use a full-fledged web server that serves pages over HTTP. The most obvious difference is the security context—in other words, you could configure your web browser to allow local web pages to perform actions that remote web content can't. In practice, this isn't often a problem, because Silverlight always executes in a stripped-down security context, and doesn't include any extra functionality for trusted locations. This simplifies the Silverlight development model, and ensures that features won't work in certain environments and break in others. However, when production testing a Silverlight application, it's best to create an ASP.NET test website (as described at the end of this chapter) or—even better—deploy your Silverlight application to a test web server.

Silverlight Compilation and Deployment

Now that you've seen how to create a basic Silverlight project, add a page with elements and code, and run your application, it's time to dig a bit deeper. In this section, you'll see how your Silverlight is transformed from a collection of XAML files and source code into a rich browser-based application.

Compiling a Silverlight Application

When you compile a Silverlight project, Visual Studio uses the same csc.exe compiler that you use for full-fledged .NET applications. However, it references a different set of assemblies and it passes in the command-line argument *nostdlib*, which prevents the C# compiler from using the standard library (the core parts of the .NET Framework that are defined in mscorlib.dll). In other words, Silverlight applications can be compiled like normal .NET applications written in standard C#, just with a more limited set of class libraries to draw on. The Silverlight compilation model has a number of advantages, including easy deployment and vastly improved performance when compared to ordinary JavaScript.

Your compiled Silverlight assembly includes the compiled code *and* the XAML documents for every page in your application, which are embedded in the assembly as resources. This ensures that there's no way for your event handling code to become separated from the user interface markup it needs. Incidentally, the XAML is not compiled in any way (unlike WPF, which converts it into a more optimized format called BAML).

Your Silverlight project is compiled into a DLL file named after your project. For example, if you have a project named SilverlightApplication1, the csc.exe compiler will create the file SilverlightApplication1.dll. The project assembly is dumped into a Bin\Debug folder in your project directory, along with a few other important files:

- **A PDB file.** This file contains information required for Visual Studio debugging. It's named after your project assembly (for example, SilverlightApplication1.pdb).

- **AppManifest.xaml.** This file lists assembly dependencies.

- **Dependent assemblies.** The Bin\Debug folder contains the assemblies that your Silverlight project uses, provided these assemblies have the Copy Local property set to true. Assemblies that are a core part of Silverlight have Copy Local set to false, because they don't need to be deployed with your application. (You can change the Copy Local setting by expanding the References node in the Solution Explorer, selecting the assembly, and using the Properties window.)

- **TestPage.html.** This is the entry page that the user requests to start your Silverlight application.

- **A XAP file.** This is a Silverlight package that contains everything you need to deploy your Silverlight application, including the application manifest, the project assembly, and any other assemblies that your application uses.

Of course, you can change the assembly name, the default namespace (which is used when you add new code files), and the XAP file name using the Visual Studio project properties (Figure 1-8). Just double-click the Properties node in the Solution Explorer.

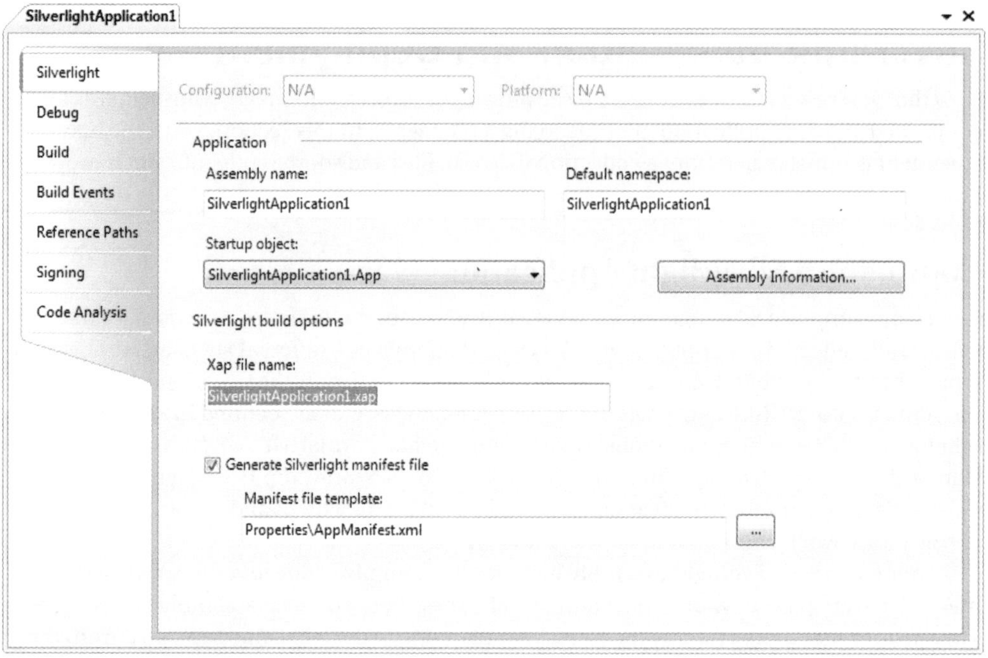

Figure 1-8. *Project properties in Visual Studio*

Deploying a Silverlight Application

Once you understand the Silverlight compilation model, it's a short step to understanding the deployment model. The XAP file is the key piece. It wraps the units of your application (the application manifest and the assemblies) into one neat container.

Technically, the XAP file is a ZIP archive. To verify this, rename a XAP file like Silverlight-Application1.xap to SilverlightApplication1.xap.zip. You can then open the archive and view the files inside. Figure 1-9 shows the contents of the XAP file for the simple example shown earlier in this chapter. Currently, it includes the application manifest and the application assembly. If your application uses add-on assemblies like System.Windows.Controls.dll, you'll find them in the XAP file as well.

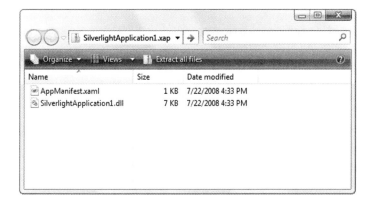

Figure 1-9. *The contents of a XAP file*

The XAP file system has two obvious benefits.

- **It compresses your content.** Because this content isn't decompressed until it reaches the client, it reduces the time required to download your application. This is particularly important if your application contains large static resources (see Chapter 6), like images or blocks of text.

- **It simplifies deployment.** When you're ready to take your Silverlight application live, you simply need to copy the XAP file to the web server, along with TestPage.html or a similar HTML file that includes a Silverlight content region. You don't need to worry about keeping track of the assemblies and resources.

Thanks to the XAP model, there's not much to think about when deploying a simple Silverlight application. Hosting a Silverlight application simply involves making the appropriate XAP file available, so the clients can download it through the browser and run it on their local machines.

■**Tip** Microsoft provides a free hosting solution that offers an impressive 10GB of space for Silverlight applications. To sign up, see `http://silverlight.live.com`.

However, there's one potential stumbling block. When hosting a Silverlight application, your web server must be configured to allow requests for the XAP file type. This file type is included by default in IIS 7, provided you're using Windows Server 2008 or Windows Vista with Service Pack 1. If you have Windows Vista without Service Pack 1, you have an earlier version of IIS, or you have another type of web server, you'll need to add a file type that maps the .xap extension to the MIME type application/x-silverlight-app. For IIS instructions, see `http://learn.iis.net/page.aspx/262/silverlight`.

■**Tip** In some situations, you may want to optimize startup times by splitting your Silverlight application into pieces that can be downloaded separately. In Chapter 6, you'll learn how to use this advanced technique to go beyond the basic single-XAP deployment model.

The HTML Test Page

The last ingredient in the deployment picture is the HTML test page. This page is the entry point into your Silverlight content—in other words, the page the user requests in the web browser. Visual Studio names this file TestPage.html (in a Silverlight-only solution), although you'll probably want to rename it to something more appropriate.

The HTML test page doesn't actually contain Silverlight markup or code. Instead, it simply sets up the content region for the Silverlight plug-in, using a small amount of JavaScript. (For this reason, browsers that have JavaScript disabled won't be able to see Silverlight content.) Here's a slightly shortened version of the HTML test page that preserves the key details:

```
<html xmlns="http://www.w3.org/1999/xhtml" >
<!-- saved from url=(0014)about:internet -->
<head>
    <title>Silverlight Project Test Page</title>

    <style type="text/css">
        ...
    </style>

    <script type="text/javascript">
        ...
    </script>
</head>

<body>
    <!-- Runtime errors from Silverlight will be displayed here. -->
    <div id='errorLocation' style="font-size: small;color: Gray;"></div>

    <!-- Silverlight content will be displayed here. -->
    <div id="silverlightControlHost">
        <object data="data:application/x-silverlight,"
          type="application/x-silverlight-2" width="100%" height="100%">
            <param name="source" value="SilverlightApplication1.xap"/>
            <param name="onerror" value="onSilverlightError" />
            <param name="background" value="white" />

            <a href="http://go.microsoft.com/fwlink/?LinkID=108182">
              <img src="http://go.microsoft.com/fwlink/?LinkId=108181"
               alt="Get Microsoft Silverlight" style="border-style: none"/>
```

```
            </a>
        </object>
        <iframe style='visibility:hidden;height:0;width:0;border:0px'></iframe>
    </div>
</body>
</html>
```

The key details in this markup are the two highlighted <div> elements. Both of these <div> elements are placeholders that are initially left empty. The first <div> element is reserved for error messages. If the Silverlight plug-in is launched but the Silverlight assembly fails to load successfully, an error message will be shown here, thanks to this JavaScript code, which is featured earlier in the page:

```
<script type="text/javascript">
    function onSilverlightError(sender, args) {
        if (args.errorType == "InitializeError")  {
            var errorDiv = document.getElementById("errorLocation");
            if (errorDiv != null)
                errorDiv.innerHTML = args.errorType + "- " + args.errorMessage;
        }
    }
</script>
```

Tip The error display is a debugging convenience. When you're ready to deploy the application, you should remove the <div> element and error handling code so sensitive information won't be shown to the user (who isn't in a position to correct the problem anyway).

This second <div> element is more interesting. It represents the Silverlight content region. It contains an <object> element that loads the Silverlight plug-in and an <iframe> element that's used to display it in certain browsers. The <object> element includes four key attributes: data (which identifies it as a Silverlight content region), type (which indicates the required Silverlight version), and height and width (which determine the dimensions of the Silverlight content region).

```
<object data="data:application/x-silverlight,"
  type="application/x-silverlight-2" width="100%" height="100%">
    ...
</object>
```

Sizing the Silverlight Content Region

By default, the Silverlight content region is given a width and height of 100%, so the Silverlight content can consume all the available space in the browser window. You can constrain the size of Silverlight content region by hard-coding pixel sizes for the height and width (which is limiting and usually avoided). Or, you can place the <div> element that holds the Silverlight content region in a more restrictive place on the page—for example, in a cell in a table, in another fixed-sized element, or between other <div> elements in a multicolumn layout.

Even though the default test page sizes the Silverlight content region to fit the available space in the browser window, your XAML pages may include hard-coded dimensions. By default, Visual Studio assigns every new Silverlight page a width of 400 pixels and a height of 300 pixels, and the example you saw earlier in this chapter limited the page to 400×100 pixels. If the browser window is larger than the hard-coded page size, the extra space won't be used. If the browser window is smaller than the hard-coded page size, part of the page may fall outside the visible area of the window.

Hard-coded sizes make sense when you have a graphically rich layout with absolute positioning and little flexibility. If you don't, you might prefer to remove the Width and Height attributes from the <UserControl> start tag. That way, the page will be sized to match the Silverlight content region, which in turn is sized to fit the browser window, and your Silverlight content will always fit itself into the currently available space.

To get a better understanding of the actual dimensions of the Silverlight content region, you can add a border around it by adding a simple style rule to the <div>, like this:

```
<div id="silverlightControlHost" style="border: 1px red solid">
```

You'll create resizable and scalable Silverlight pages in Chapter 3, when you explore layout in more detail.

Configuring the Silverlight Content Region

The <object> element contains a series of <param> elements that specify additional options to the Silverlight plug-in. Here are three of the options in the standard test page that Visual Studio generates:

```
<param name="source" value="SilverlightApplication1.xap"/>
<param name="onerror" value="onSilverlightError" />
<param name="background" value="white" />
```

Table 1-1 lists all the parameters that you can use. You'll use several of these parameters in examples throughout this book, as you delve into features like HTML access, splash screens, transparency, and animation.

Table 1-1. *Parameters for the Silverlight Plug-In*

Name	Value
source	A URI that points to the XAP file for your Silverlight application. This parameter is required.
background	The color that's used to paint the background of the Silverlight content region, behind any content that you display (but in front of any HTML content that occupies the same space). If you set the Background property of a page, it's painted over this background.

Name	Value
enableHtmlAccess	A Boolean that specifies whether the Silverlight plug-in has access to the HTML object model. Use true if you want to be able to interact with the HTML elements on the test page through your Silverlight code (as demonstrated in Chapter 12).
initParams	A string that you can use to pass custom initialization information. This technique (which is described in Chapter 6) is useful if you plan to use the same Silverlight application in different ways on different pages.
maxFramerate	The desired frame rate for animations. Higher frame rates result in smoother animations, but the system load and processing power of the current computer may mean that a high frame rate can't be honored. The value is 60 (for 60 frames per second). Animation is discussed in Chapter 9.
splashScreenSource	The location of a XAML splash screen to show while the XAP file is downloading. You'll learn how to use this technique in Chapter 6.
windowless	A Boolean that specifies whether the plug-in renders in windowed mode (the default) or windowless mode. If you set this true, the HTML content underneath your Silverlight content region can show through. This is ideal if you're planning to create a shaped Silverlight control that integrates with HTML content, and you'll see how to use it in Chapter 12.
onSourceDownloadProgressChanged	A JavaScript event handler that's triggered when a piece of the XAP file has been downloaded. You can use this event handler to build a startup progress bar, as in Chapter 6.
onSourceDownloadComplete	A JavaScript event handler that's triggered when the entire XAP file has been downloaded.
onLoad	A JavaScript event handler that's triggered when the markup in the XAP file has been processed and your first page has been loaded.
onResize	A JavaScript event handler that's triggered when the size of a Silverlight content region has changed.
onError	A JavaScript event handler that's triggered when a unhandled error occurs in the Silverlight plug-in or in your code).

Note By convention, all of these parameter names should be written completely in lowercase (for example, splashscreensource rather than splashScreenSource). However, they're shown with mixed case here for better readability.

Alternative Content

The <div> element also has some HTML markup that will be shown if the <object> tag isn't understood or the plug-in isn't available. In the standard test page, this markup consists of a "Get Silverlight" picture, which is wrapped in a hyperlink that, when clicked, takes the user to the Silverlight download page.

```
<a href="http://go.microsoft.com/fwlink/?LinkID=108182">
  <img src="http://go.microsoft.com/fwlink/?LinkId=108181"
  alt="Get Microsoft Silverlight" style="border-style: none"/>
</a>
```

The Mark of the Web

One of the stranger details in the HTML test page is the following comment, which appears in the second line:

```
<!-- saved from url=(0014)about:internet -->
```

Although this comment appears to be little more than an automatically generated stamp that the browser ignores, it actually has an effect on the way you debug your application. This comment is known as the *mark of the web*, and it's a specialized flag that forces Internet Explorer to run pages in a more restrictive security zone than it would normally use.

Ordinarily, the mark of the web indicates the website from which a locally stored page was originally downloaded. But in this case, Visual Studio has no way of knowing where your Silverlight application will eventually be deployed. It falls back on the URL about:internet, which simply signals that the page is from some arbitrary location on the public Internet. The number (14) simply indicates the number of characters in this URL. For a more detailed description of the mark of the web and its standard uses, see http://msdn.microsoft.com/en-us/library/ms537628(VS.85).aspx.

All of this raises an obvious question—namely, why is Visual Studio adding a marker that's typically reserved for downloaded pages? The reason is that without the mark of the web, Internet Explorer will load your page with the relaxed security settings of the local machine zone. This wouldn't cause a problem, except for the fact that Internet Explorer also includes a safeguard that disables scripts and ActiveX controls in this situation. As a result, if you run a test page that's stored on your local hard drive, and this test page doesn't have the mark of the web, you'll see the irritating warning message shown in Figure 1-10, and you'll need to explicitly allow the blocked content. Worst of all, you'll need to repeat this process every time you open the page.

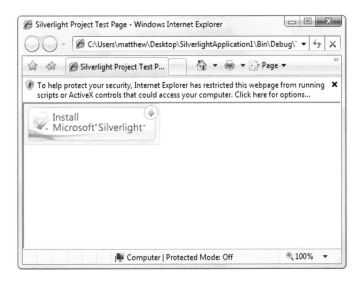

Figure 1-10. *A page with disabled Silverlight content*

This problem will disappear when you deploy the web page to a real website, but it's a significant inconvenience while testing. To avoid headaches like these, make sure you add a similar mark of the web comment if you design your own custom test pages.

CHANGING THE TEST PAGE

Visual Studio generates the test page each time you run the project. As a result, any changes you make to it will be discarded. If you want to customize the test page, the easiest solution is to create a new test page for your project. Here's how:

1. Run your project at least once to create the test page.

2. Click the Show All Files icon at the top of the Solution Explorer.

3. Expand the Bin\Debug folder in the Solution Explorer.

4. Find the TestPage.html file, right-click it, and choose Copy. Then right-click the Bin\Debug folder and choose Paste. This duplicate will be your custom test page. Right-click the new file and choose Rename to give it a better name.

5. To make the custom test page a part of your project, right-click it and choose Include in Project.

6. To tell Visual Studio to navigate to your test page when you run the project, right-click your test page and choose Set As Start Page.

The Application Manifest

As you've seen, the Silverlight execution model is quite straightforward. First, the client requests the HTML test page (such as TestPage.html). At this point, the browser downloads the HTML file and processes its markup. When it reaches the <object> element, it loads the Silverlight plug-in and creates the Silverlight content region. After this step, the client-side plug-in takes over. First, it downloads the linked XAP file (which is identified by the source parameter inside the <object> element). Then, it looks at the AppManifest.xaml file to decide what to do next.

Here's the content of the AppManifest.xaml for a newly generated Visual Studio project, which also matches the AppManifest.xaml in the simple example you saw earlier in this chapter:

```
<Deployment xmlns="http://schemas.microsoft.com/client/2007/deployment"
 xmlns:x="http://schemas.microsoft.com/winfx/2006/xaml"
 EntryPointAssembly="SilverlightApplication1"
 EntryPointType="SilverlightApplication1.App" RuntimeVersion="2.0.30904.0">
  <Deployment.Parts>
    <AssemblyPart x:Name="SilverlightApplication1"
    Source="SilverlightApplication1.dll" />
  </Deployment.Parts>
</Deployment>
```

The EntryPointAssembly and EntryPointType attributes are the key details that determine what code the Silverlight plug-in will execute next. EntryPointAssembly indicates the name of the DLL that has your compiled Silverlight code (without the .dll extension). EntryPointType indicates the name of the application class in that assembly. When the Silverlight plug-in sees the AppManifest.xaml shown here, it loads the SilverlightApplication1.dll assembly, and then creates the App object inside. The App object triggers a Startup event, which runs this code, creating the first page:

```
private void Application_Startup(object sender, StartupEventArgs e)
{
    // Load the main control.
    this.RootVisual = new Page();
}
```

If you've added a different user control to your application, and you want to show it as the first page, simply edit the App.xaml.cs file, and replace the Page class with the name of your custom class:

```
this.RootVisual = new CustomPage();
```

There's one other setting that you can add to the AppManifest.xaml file—the External-CallersFromCrossDomain setting. To understand the purpose it plays, you need to realize that Silverlight supports *cross-domain* deployment. This means Silverlight allows you to place your XAP file on one web server and your HTML or ASP.NET entry page on another. In this situation, you'll obviously need to edit the test page and modify the source parameter in the <object> element so that it points to the remote XAP file. However, there's one catch. To defeat certain types of attacks, Silverlight doesn't allow the hosting web page and your Silverlight code to interact if they're on different servers. If you do need this ability (which is described in Chapter 12), you need to set the ExternalCallersFromCrossDomain setting like this:

```
<Deployment xmlns="http://schemas.microsoft.com/client/2007/deployment"
 xmlns:x="http://schemas.microsoft.com/winfx/2006/xaml"
 ExternalCallersFromsCrossDomain="ScriptableOnly" ...>
```

The only value you can use other than ScriptableOnly is NoAccess.

SILVERLIGHT DECOMPILATION

Now that you understand the infrastructure that underpins a Silverlight project, it's easy to see how you can decompile any existing application to learn more about how it works. Here's how:

1. Surf to the entry page.

2. View the source for the web page, and look for the <param> element that points to the XAP file.

3. Type a request for the XAP file into your browser's address bar. (Keep the same domain, but replace the page name with the partial path that points to the XAP file.)

4. Choose Save As to save the XAP file locally.

5. Rename the XAP file to add the .zip extension. Then, open it and extract the project assembly. This assembly is essentially the same as the assemblies you build for ordinary .NET applications. Like ordinary .NET assemblies, it contains IL (Intermediate Language) code.

6. Open the project assembly in a tool like Reflector (`http://www.red-gate.com/products/reflector`) to view the IL and embedded resources. Using the right plug-in, you can even decompile the IL to C# syntax.

Of course, many Silverlight developers don't condone this sort of behavior (much as many .NET developers don't encourage end users to decompile their rich client applications). However, it's an unavoidable side effect of the Silverlight compilation model.

Because IL code can be easily decompiled or reverse engineered, it's not an appropriate place to store secrets (like encryption keys, proprietary algorithms, and so on). If you need to perform a task that uses sensitive code, consider calling a web service from your Silverlight application. If you just want to prevent other hotshots from reading your code and copying your style, you may be interested in raising the bar with an *obfuscation* tool that uses a number of tricks to scramble the structure and names in your compiled code without changing its behavior. Visual Studio ships with a scaled-down obfuscation tool named Dotfuscator, and many more are available commercially.

Creating an ASP.NET-Hosted Silverlight Project

Although Silverlight does perfectly well on its own, you can also develop, test, and deploy it as part of an ASP.NET website. Here's how to create a Silverlight project and an ASP.NET website that uses it in the same solution:

1. Select File ➤ New ➤ Project in Visual Studio, choose the Visual C# group of project types, and select the Silverlight Application template. It's a good idea to use the "Create directory for solution" option, so you can group together the two projects that Visual Studio will create—one for the Silverlight assembly and one for ASP.NET website.

2. Once you've picked the solution name and project name, click OK to create it.

3. When asked whether you want to create a test web, choose the first option, "Add a new Web." You'll also need to supply a project name for the ASP.NET website. By default, it's your project name with the added word Web at the end, as shown in Figure 1-11.

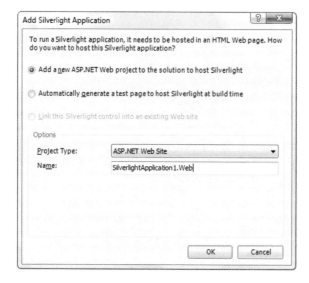

Figure 1-11. *Creating an ASP.NET website to host Silverlight content*

4. In the Project Type box, choose the way you want Visual Studio to manage your project—either as a web project or a website. The choice has no effect on how Silverlight works. If you choose a web project, Visual Studio uses a project file to track the contents of your web application and compiles your web page code into a single assembly before you run it. If you choose a website, Visual Studio simply assumes everything in the application folder is a part of your web application. Your web page code will be compiled the first time a user requests a page (or when you use the pre-compilation tool aspnet_compiler.exe).

■**Tip** For more information about the difference between web projects and projectless websites, and other ASP.NET basics, refer to *Pro ASP.NET 3.5 in C# 2008*.

5. Finally, click OK to create the solution.

■**Note** If you create an ordinary HTML-only website, you can host it on any web server. In this scenario, the web server has an easy job—it simply needs to send along your HTML files when a browser requests them. If you decide to create an ASP.NET website, your application's requirements change. Although the Silverlight portion of your application will still run on the client, any ASP.NET content you include will run on the web server, which must have the ASP.NET engine installed.

There are two ways to integrate Silverlight content into an ASP.NET application:

- **Create HTML files with Silverlight content.** You place these files in your ASP.NET website folder, just as you would with any other ordinary HTML file. The only limitation of this approach is that your HTML file obviously can't include ASP.NET controls, because it won't be processed on the server.

- **Place Silverlight content inside an ASP.NET web form.** To pull this trick off, you need the help of the Silverlight web control. You can also add other ASP.NET controls to different regions of the page. The only disadvantage to this approach is that the page is always processed on the server. If you aren't actually using any server-side ASP.NET content, this creates an extra bit of overhead that you don't need when the page is first requested.

Of course, you're also free to mingle both of these approaches, and use Silverlight content in dedicated HTML pages and inside ASP.NET web pages in the same site. When you create a Silverlight project with an ASP.NET website, you'll start with both. For example, if your Silverlight project is named SilverlightApplication1, you can use SilverlightApplication1Test-Page.html or SilverlightApplication1TestPage.aspx.

The HTML file is identical to the test page in the ordinary Silverlight-only solution you saw earlier. The only difference is that the page is generated once, when the ASP.NET website is first created, not every time you build the project. As a result, you can modify the HTML page without worrying that your changes will be overridden.

The .aspx file is an ASP.NET web form that uses ASP.NET's Silverlight web control to show your Silverlight application. The end result is the same as the HTML test page, but there's a key difference—the Silverlight control creates the test page markup dynamically, when it's processed on the server. This extra step gives you a chance to use your own server-side code to perform other tasks when the page is initially requested, before the Silverlight application is downloaded and launched. You'll explore the Silverlight web control in Chapter 13.

Figure 1-12 shows how a Silverlight and ASP.NET solution starts out. Along with the two test pages, the ASP.NET website also includes a Default.aspx page (which can be used as the entry point to your ASP.NET website) and web.config (which allows you to configure various website settings).

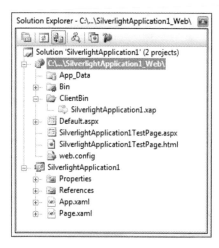

Figure 1-12. *Creating an ASP.NET website to host Silverlight content*

The Silverlight and ASP.NET option provides essentially the same debugging experience as a Silverlight-only solution. When you run the solution, Visual Studio compiles both projects, and copies the Silverlight assembly to the ClientBin folder in the ASP.NET website. (This is similar to assembly references—if an ASP.NET website references a private DLL, Visual Studio automatically copies this DLL to the Bin folder.)

Once both projects are compiled, Visual Studio looks to the startup project (which is the ASP.NET website) and looks for the currently selected page. It then launches the default browser and navigates to that page. The difference is that it doesn't request the start page directly from the file system. Instead, it communicates with its built-in test web server. This web server automatically loads up on a randomly chosen port. It acts like a scaled-down version of IIS, but accepts requests only from the local computer. This gives you the ease of debugging without needing to configure IIS virtual directories. Figure 1-13 shows the same Silverlight application you considered earlier, but hosted by ASP.NET.

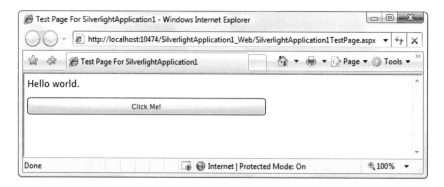

Figure 1-13. *An ASP.NET page*

To navigate to a different page from the ASP.NET project, you can type in the address bar of the browser.

Note Remember, when building a Silverlight and ASP.NET solution, you add all your Silverlight files and code to the Silverlight project. The ASP.NET website consumes the final, compiled Silverlight assembly, and makes it available through one or more of its web pages.

The Last Word

In this chapter, you took your first look at the Silverlight application model. You saw how to create a Silverlight project in Visual Studio, add a simple event handler, and test it. You also peered behind the scenes to explore how a Silverlight application is compiled and deployed.

In the following chapters, you'll learn much more about the full capabilities of the Silverlight platform. Sometimes, you might need to remind yourself that you're coding inside a lightweight browser-hosted framework, because much of Silverlight coding feels like the full .NET platform, despite the fact that it's built on only a few megabytes of compressed code. Out of all of Silverlight's many features, its ability to pack a miniature modern programming framework into a slim 4MB download is surely its most impressive.

CHAPTER 2

■■■

XAML

XAML (short for Extensible Application Markup Language, and pronounced "zammel") is a markup language used to instantiate .NET objects. Although XAML is a technology that can be applied to many different problem domains, it was initially designed as a part of Windows Presentation Foundation (WPF), where it allows Windows developers to construct rich user interfaces. When building user interfaces for Silverlight applications, you use the same standard.

Conceptually, XAML plays a role that's a lot like HTML, and is even closer to its stricter cousin, XHTML. XHTML allows you to define the elements that make up an ordinary web page. Similarly, XAML allows you to define the elements that make up a XAML content region. To manipulate XHTML elements, you can use client-side JavaScript. To manipulate XAML elements, you write client-side C# code. Finally, XAML and XHTML share many of the same syntax conventions. Like XHTML, XAML is an XML-based language that consists of elements that can be nested in any arrangement you like.

In this chapter, you'll get a detailed introduction to XAML. Once you understand the broad rules of XAML, you'll know what is and isn't possible in a Silverlight user interface—and how to make changes by hand. By exploring the tags in a Silverlight XAML document, you'll also learn more about the object model that underpins Silverlight user interfaces and get ready for the deeper exploration to come.

■**Note** Although XAML was created for WPF and reused for Silverlight, it has a few other high-profile roles. It's also used to define workflows for Windows Workflow Foundation (WF) and it's used to create XML Paper Specification (XPS) documents.

XAML Basics

The XAML standard is quite straightforward once you understand a few ground rules:

- Every element in a XAML document maps to an instance of a Silverlight class. The name of the element matches the name of the class *exactly*. For example, the element <Button> instructs Silverlight to create a Button object.

- As with any XML document, you can nest one element inside another. As you'll see, XAML gives every class the flexibility to decide how it handles this situation. However, nesting is usually a way to express *containment*—in other words, if you find a Button element inside a Grid element, your user interface probably includes a Grid that contains a Button inside.

- You can set the properties of each class through attributes. However, in some situations an attribute isn't powerful enough to handle the job. In these cases, you'll use nested tags with a special syntax.

■Tip If you're completely new to XML, you'll probably find it easier to review the basics before you tackle XAML. To get up to speed quickly, try the free web-based tutorial at http://www.w3schools.com/xml.

Before continuing, take a look at this bare-bones XAML document, which represents a blank page (as created by Visual Studio). The lines have been numbered for easy reference:

```
1   <UserControl x:Class="SilverlightApplication1.Page"
2       xmlns="http://schemas.microsoft.com/client/2007"
3       xmlns:x="http://schemas.microsoft.com/winfx/2006/xaml"
4       Width="400" Height="300">
5
6       <Grid x:Name="LayoutRoot" Background="White">
7       </Grid>
8   </UserControl>
```

This document includes only two elements—the top-level UserControl element, which wraps all the Silverlight content on the page, and the Grid, in which you can place all your elements.

As in all XML documents, there can only be one top-level element. In the previous example, that means that as soon as you close the UserControl element with the </UserControl> tag, you end the document. No more content can follow.

Looking at the start tag for the UserControl element, you'll find several interesting attributes, including a class name and two XML namespaces (described in the following sections). You'll also find the three properties shown here:

```
4       Width="400" Height="300">
```

Each attribute corresponds to a separate property of the UserControl class. In this case, the Width and Height properties tell Silverlight to create a region that's 400 by 300 pixels large. Similar markup sets the Background property of the Grid, ensuring that a white background appears under your content.

XAML Namespaces

When you use an element like <UserControl> in a XAML file, the Silverlight parser recognizes that you want to create an instance of the UserControl class. However, it doesn't necessarily know *what* UserControl class to use. After all, even if the Silverlight namespaces only include a single class with that name, there's no guarantee that you won't create a similarly named class of your own. Clearly, you need a way to indicate the Silverlight namespace information in order to use an element.

In Silverlight, classes are resolved by mapping XML namespaces to Silverlight namespaces. In the sample document shown earlier, two namespaces are defined:

```
2      xmlns="http://schemas.microsoft.com/client/2007"
3      xmlns:x="http://schemas.microsoft.com/winfx/2006/xaml"
```

■**Note** XML namespaces are declared using attributes. These attributes can be placed inside any element start tag. However, convention dictates that all the namespaces you need to use in a document should be declared in the very first tag, as they are in this example. Once a namespace is declared, it can be used anywhere in the document.

The xmlns attribute is a specialized attribute in the world of XML that's reserved for declaring namespaces. This snippet of markup declares two namespaces that you'll find in every Silverlight XAML document you create:

- **http://schemas.microsoft.com/client/2007** is the core Silverlight 2.0 namespace. It encompasses all the Silverlight 2.0 classes, including the UserControl and Grid. Ordinarily, this namespace is declared without a namespace prefix, so it becomes the default namespace for the entire document. In other words, every element is automatically placed in this namespace unless you specify otherwise.

- **http://schemas.microsoft.com/winfx/2006/xaml** is the XAML namespace. It includes various XAML utility features that allow you to influence how your document is interpreted. This namespace is mapped to the prefix *x*. That means you can apply it by placing the namespace prefix before the element name (as in <**x:**ElementName>).

The namespace information allows the XAML parser to find the right class. For example, when it looks at the UserControl and Grid elements, it sees that they are placed in the default http://schemas.microsoft.com/client/2007 namespace. It then searches the corresponding Silverlight namespaces, until it finds the matching classes System.Windows.UserControl and System.Windows.Controls.Grid.

XML NAMESPACES AND SILVERLIGHT NAMESPACES

The XML namespace name doesn't match a single Silverlight namespace. Instead, all the Silverlight namespaces share the same XML namespace. There are a couple of reasons the creators of XAML chose this design. By convention, XML namespaces are often URIs (as they are here). These URIs look like they point to a location on the Web, but they don't. The URI format is used because it makes it unlikely that different organizations will inadvertently create different XML-based languages with the same namespace. Because the domain schemas.microsoft.com is owned by Microsoft, only Microsoft will use it in an XML namespace name.

The other reason that there isn't a one-to-one mapping between the XML namespaces used in XAML and Silverlight namespaces is because it would significantly complicate your XAML documents. If each Silverlight namespace had a different XML namespace, you'd need to specify the right namespace for each and every control you use, which would quickly get messy. Instead, the creators of Silverlight chose to map all the Silverlight namespaces that include user interface elements to a single XML namespace. This works because within the different Silverlight namespaces, no two classes share the same name.

In many situations, you'll want to have access to your own namespaces in a XAML file. The most common example is if you want to use a custom Silverlight control that you (or another developer) have created. In this case, you need to define a new XML namespace prefix and map it to your assembly. Here's the syntax you need:

```
<UserControl x:Class="SilverlightApplication1.Page"
  xmlns:w="clr-namespace:Widgets;assembly=WidgetLibrary"
  ...
```

The XML namespace declaration sets three pieces of information:

- **The XML namespace prefix.** You'll use the namespace prefix to refer to the namespace in your XAML page. In this example, that's *w*, although you can choose anything you want that doesn't conflict with another namespace prefix.

- **The .NET namespace.** In this case, the classes are located in the Widgets namespace. If you have classes that you want to use in multiple namespaces, you can map them to different XML namespaces or to the same XML namespace (as long as there aren't any conflicting class names).

- **The assembly.** In this case, the classes are part of the WidgetLibrary.dll assembly. (You don't include the .dll extension when naming the assembly.) Silverlight will look for that assembly in the same XAP package where your project assembly is placed.

Note Remember, Silverlight uses a lean, stripped-down version of the CLR. For that reason, a Silverlight application can't use a full .NET class library assembly. Instead, it needs to use a Silverlight class library. You can easily create a Silverlight class library in Visual Studio by choosing the Silverlight Class Library project template.

Once you've mapped your .NET namespace to an XML namespace, you can use it anywhere in your XAML document. For example, if the Widgets namespace contains a control named HotButton, you could create an instance like this:

```
<w:HotButton Text="Click Me!" Click="DoSomething"></w:HotButton>
```

The Code-Behind Class

XAML allows you to construct a user interface, but in order to make a functioning application, you need a way to connect the event handlers that contain your application code. XAML makes this easy using the Class attribute that's shown here:

```
1  <UserControl x:Class="SilverlightApplication1.Page"
```

The *x* namespace prefix places the Class attribute in the XAML namespace, which means this is a more general part of the XAML language, not a specific Silverlight ingredient.

In fact, the Class attribute tells the Silverlight parser to generate a new class with the specified name. That class derives from the class that's named by the XML element. In other words, this example creates a new class named SilverlightProject1.Page, which derives from the User-Control class. The automatically generated portion of this class is merged with the code you've supplied in the code-behind file.

Usually, every XAML file will have a corresponding code-behind class with client-side C# code. Visual Studio creates a code-behind class for the Page.xaml file named Page.xaml.cs. Here's what you'll see in the Page.xaml.cs file:

```
using System;
using System.Collections.Generic;
using System.Linq;
using System.Windows;
using System.Windows.Controls;
using System.Windows.Documents;
using System.Windows.Input;
using System.Windows.Media;
using System.Windows.Media.Animation;
using System.Windows.Shapes;

namespace SilverlightApplication1
{
    public partial class Page : UserControl
    {
        public Page()
        {
            InitializeComponent();
        }
    }
}
```

Currently, the Page class code doesn't include any real functionality. However, it does include one important detail—the default constructor, which calls InitializeComponent() when you create an instance of the class. This parses your markup, creates the corresponding objects, sets their properties, and attaches any event handlers you've defined.

Note The InitializeComponent() method plays a key role in Silverlight content. For that reason, you should never delete the InitializeComponent() call from the constructor. Similarly, if you add another constructor to your page, make sure it also calls InitializeComponent().

Naming Elements

There's one more detail to consider. In your code-behind class, you'll often want to manipulate elements programmatically. For example, you might want to read or change properties or attach and detach event handlers on the fly. To make this possible, the control must include a XAML Name attribute. In the previous example, the Grid control already includes the Name attribute, so you can manipulate it in your code-behind file.

```
6       <Grid x:Name="LayoutRoot" Background="White">
7       </Grid>
```

The Name attribute tells the XAML parser to add a field like this to the automatically generated portion of the Window1 class:

```
private System.Windows.Controls.Grid LayoutRoot;
```

Now you can interact with the grid in your page class code by using the name LayoutRoot.
The Name property shown previously is part of the XAML language, and it's used to help integrate your code-behind class. Somewhat confusingly, many classes define their own Name property. (One example is the base FrameworkElement class from which all Silverlight elements derive.) In this case, the name you specify is used in the automatically generated code file *and* it's used to set the Name property.

Tip In a traditional Windows Forms application, every control has a name. In a Silverlight application, there's no such requirement. If you don't want to interact with an element in your code, you're free to remove its Name attribute from the markup. The examples in this book usually omit element names when they aren't needed, which makes the markup more concise.

Properties and Events in XAML

So far, you've considered a relatively unexciting example—a blank page that hosts an empty Grid control. Before going any further, it's worth introducing a more realistic page that includes several elements. Figure 2-1 shows an example with an automatic question answerer.

Figure 2-1. *Ask the eight ball and all will be revealed*

The eight ball page includes four elements: a Grid (the most common tool for arranging layout in Silverlight), two TextBox objects, and a Button. The markup that's required to arrange and configure these elements is significantly longer than the previous examples. Here's an abbreviated listing that replaces some of the details with an ellipsis (…) to expose the overall structure:

```
<UserControl x:Class="EightBall.Page"
 xmlns="http://schemas.microsoft.com/client/2007"
 xmlns:x="http://schemas.microsoft.com/winfx/2006/xaml"
 Width="400" Height="300">
  <Grid x:Name="grid1">
    <Grid.Background>
      ...
    </Grid.Background>
    <Grid.RowDefinitions>
      ...
    </Grid.RowDefinitions>

    <TextBox x:Name="txtQuestion" ... >
      ...
    </TextBox>

    <Button x:Name="cmdAnswer" ... >
      ...
    </Button>
```

```
    <TextBox x:Name="txtAnswer" ... >
      ...
    </TextBox>
  </Grid>
</Window>
```

In the following sections, you'll explore the parts of this document—and learn the syntax of XAML along the way.

Simple Properties and Type Converters

As you've already seen, the attributes of an element set the properties of the corresponding object. For example, the text boxes in the eight ball example configure the alignment, margin, and font:

```
<TextBox x:Name="txtQuestion"
 VerticalAlignment="Stretch" HorizontalAlignment="Stretch"
 FontFamily="Verdana" FontSize="24" Foreground="Green" ... >
```

In order for this to work, the System.Windows.Controls.TextBox class must provide the following properties: VerticalAlignment, HorizontalAlignment, FontFamily, FontSize, and Foreground. You'll learn the specific meaning for each of these properties in the following chapters.

■**Tip** There are three special characters that can't be entered directly into an attribute string: the quotation mark and the two angle brackets. To use these values, you must replace them with the equivalent XML character entity. That's " for a quotation mark, < for the < (less than) character, and > for the > (greater than) character. Of course, this limitation is a XAML detail and it won't affect you if you set a property in code.

To make the property system work, the XAML parser needs to perform a bit more work than you might initially realize. The value in an XML attribute is always a plain text string. However, object properties can be any .NET type. In the previous example, there are two properties that use enumerations (VerticalAlignment and HorizontalAlignment), one string (FontFamily), one integer (FontSize), and one Brush object (Foreground).

In order to bridge the gap between string values and non-string properties, the XAML parser needs to perform a conversion. The conversion is performed by *type converters*, a basic piece of infrastructure that's borrowed from the full .NET Framework.

Essentially, a type converter has one role in life—it provides utility methods that can convert a specific .NET data type to and from any other .NET type, such as a string representation in this case. The XAML parser follows two steps to find a type converter:

1. It examines the property declaration, looking for a TypeConverter attribute. (If present, the TypeConverter attribute indicates what class can perform the conversion.) For example, when you use a property such as Foreground, .NET checks the declaration of the Foreground property.

2. If there's no TypeConverter attribute on the property declaration, the XAML parser checks the class declaration of the corresponding data type. For example, the Foreground property uses a Brush object. The Brush class (and its derivatives) use the BrushConverter because the Brush class is decorated with the TypeConverter (typeof(BrushConverter)) attribute declaration.

If there's no associated type converter on the property declaration or the class declaration, the XAML parser generates an error.

This system is simple but flexible. If you set a type converter at the class level, that converter applies to every property that uses that class. On the other hand, if you want to fine-tune the way type conversion works for a particular property, you can use the TypeConverter attribute on the property declaration instead.

It's technically possible to use type converters in code, but the syntax is a bit convoluted. It's almost always better to set a property directly—not only is it faster; it also avoids potential errors from mistyping strings, which won't be caught until runtime. (This problem doesn't affect XAML, because the XAML is parsed and validated at compile time.)

■**Note** XAML, like all XML-based languages, is *case-sensitive*. That means you can't substitute <button> for <Button>. However, type converters usually aren't case-sensitive, which means both Foreground= "White" and Foreground="white" have the same result.

Complex Properties

As handy as type converters are, they aren't practical for all scenarios. For example, some properties are full-fledged objects with their own set of properties. Although it's possible to create a string representation that the type converter could use, that syntax might be difficult to use and prone to error.

Fortunately, XAML provides another option: *property-element syntax*. With property-element syntax, you add a child element with a name in the form Parent.PropertyName. For example, the Grid has a Background property that allows you to supply a brush that's used to paint the area behind the elements. If you want to use a complex brush—one more advanced than a solid color fill—you'll need to add a child tag named Grid.Background, as shown here:

```
<Grid x:Name="grid1">
  <Grid.Background>
    ...
  </Grid.Background>
  ...
</Grid>
```

The key detail that makes this work is the period (.) in the element name. This distinguishes properties from other types of nested content.

This still leaves one detail—namely, once you've identified the complex property you want to configure, how do you set it? Here's the trick. Inside the nested element, you can add another tag to instantiate a specific class. In the eight ball example (shown in Figure 2-1), the background is filled with a gradient. To define the gradient you want, you need to create a LinearGradientBrush object.

Using the rules of XAML, you can create the LinearGradientBrush object using an element with the name LinearGradientBrush:

```
<Grid x:Name="grid1">
  <Grid.Background>
    <LinearGradientBrush>
    </LinearGradientBrush>
  </Grid.Background>
  ...
</Grid>
```

The LinearGradientBrush is part of the Silverlight set of namespaces, so you can keep using the default XML namespace for your tags.

However, it's not enough to simply create the LinearGradientBrush—you also need to specify the colors in that gradient. You do this by filling the LinearGradientBrush.Gradient-Stops property with a collection of GradientStop objects. Once again, the GradientStops property is too complex to be set with an attribute value alone. Instead, you need to rely on the property-element syntax:

```
<Grid x:Name="grid1">
  <Grid.Background>
    <LinearGradientBrush>
      <LinearGradientBrush.GradientStops>
      </LinearGradientBrush.GradientStops>
    </LinearGradientBrush>
  </Grid.Background>
  ...
</Grid>
```

Finally, you can fill the GradientStops collection with a series of GradientStop objects. Each GradientStop object has an Offset and Color property. You can supply these two values using the ordinary property-attribute syntax:

```
<Grid x:Name="grid1">
  <Grid.Background>
    <LinearGradientBrush>
      <LinearGradientBrush.GradientStops>
        <GradientStop Offset="0.00" Color="Yellow" />
        <GradientStop Offset="0.50" Color="White" />
        <GradientStop Offset="1.00" Color="Purple" />
      </LinearGradientBrush.GradientStops>
```

```
    </LinearGradientBrush>
  </Grid.Background>
  ...
</Grid>
```

Note You can use property-element syntax for any property. But usually you'll use the simpler property-attribute approach if the property has a suitable type converter. Doing so results in more compact code.

Any set of XAML tags can be replaced with a set of code statements that performs the same task. The tags shown previously, which fill the background with a gradient of your choice, are equivalent to the following code:

```
LinearGradientBrush brush = new LinearGradientBrush();

GradientStop gradientStop1 = new GradientStop();
gradientStop1.Offset = 0;
gradientStop1.Color = Colors.Yellow;
brush.GradientStops.Add(gradientStop1);

GradientStop gradientStop2 = new GradientStop();
gradientStop2.Offset = 0.5;
gradientStop2.Color = Colors.White;
brush.GradientStops.Add(gradientStop2);

GradientStop gradientStop3 = new GradientStop();
gradientStop3.Offset = 1;
gradientStop3.Color = Colors.Purple;
brush.GradientStops.Add(gradientStop3);

grid1.Background = brush;
```

Attached Properties

Along with ordinary properties, XAML also includes the concept of *attached properties*—properties that may apply to several elements but are defined in a different class. In Silverlight, attached properties are frequently used to control layout.

Here's how it works. Every control has its own set of intrinsic properties. (For example, a text box has a specific font, text color, and text content as dictated by properties such as Font-Family, Foreground, and Text.) When you place a control inside a container, it gains additional features, depending on the type of container. (For example, if you place a text box inside a grid, you need to be able to choose the grid cell where it's positioned.) These additional details are set using attached properties.

Attached properties always use a two-part name in this form: DefiningType.Property-Name. This two-part naming syntax allows the XAML parser to distinguish between a normal property and an attached property.

In the eight ball example, attached properties allow the individual elements to place themselves on separate rows in the (invisible) grid:

```
<TextBox ... Grid.Row="0">
  [Place question here.]
</TextBox>

<Button ... Grid.Row="1">
  Ask the Eight Ball
</Button>

<TextBox ... Grid.Row="2">
  [Answer will appear here.]
</TextBox>
```

Attached properties aren't really properties at all. They're actually translated into method calls. The XAML parser calls the static method that has this form: *DefiningType*.Set*Property-Name*(). For example, in the previous XAML snippet, the defining type is the Grid class, and the property is Row, so the parser calls Grid.SetRow().

When calling SetPropertyName(), the parser passes two parameters: the object that's being modified, and the property value that's specified. For example, when you set the Grid.Row property on the TextBox control, the XAML parser executes this code:

```
Grid.SetRow(txtQuestion, 0);
```

This pattern (calling a static method of the defining type) is a convenience that conceals what's really taking place. To the casual eye, this code implies that the row number is stored in the Grid object. However, the row number is actually stored in the object that it *applies to*—in this case, the TextBox object.

This sleight of hand works because the TextBox derives from the DependencyObject base class, as do all Silverlight elements. The DependencyObject is designed to store a virtually unlimited collection of dependency properties (and attached properties are one type of dependency property).

In fact, the Grid.SetRow() method is actually a shortcut that's equivalent to calling the DependencyObject.SetValue() method, as shown here:

```
txtQuestion.SetValue(Grid.RowProperty, 0);
```

Attached properties are a core ingredient of Silverlight. They act as an all-purpose extensibility system. For example, by defining the Row property as an attached property, you guarantee that it's usable with any control. The other option, making it a part of a base class such as FrameworkElement, complicates life. Not only would it clutter the public interface with properties that only have meaning in certain circumstances (in this case, when an element is being used inside a Grid), it also makes it impossible to add new types of containers that require new properties.

Nesting Elements

As you've seen, XAML documents are arranged as a heavily nested tree of elements. In the current example, a Window element contains a Grid element, which contains TextBox and Button elements.

XAML allows each element to decide how it deals with nested elements. This interaction is mediated through one of three mechanisms that are evaluated in this order:

- If the parent implements IList<T>, the parser calls the IList<T>.Add() method and passes in the child.

- If the parent implements IDictionary<T>, the parser calls IDictionary<T>.Add() and passes in the child. When using a dictionary collection, you must also set the x:Key attribute to give a key name to each item.

- If the parent is decorated with the ContentProperty attribute, the parser uses the child to set that property.

For example, earlier in this chapter you saw how a LinearGradientBrush can hold a collection of GradientStop objects using syntax like this:

```
<LinearGradientBrush>
  <LinearGradientBrush.GradientStops>
    <GradientStop Offset="0.00" Color="Red" />
    <GradientStop Offset="0.50" Color="Indigo" />
    <GradientStop Offset="1.00" Color="Violet" />
  </LinearGradientBrush.GradientStops>
</LinearGradientBrush>
```

The XAML parser recognizes the LinearGradientBrush.GradientStops element is a complex property because it includes a period. However, it needs to process the tags inside (the three GradientStop elements) a little differently. In this case, the parser recognizes that the GradientStops property returns a GradientStopCollection object, and the GradientStop-Collection implements the IList interface. Thus, it assumes (quite rightly) that each Gradient-Stop should be added to the collection using the IList.Add() method:

```
GradientStop gradientStop1 = new GradientStop();
gradientStop1.Offset = 0;
gradientStop1.Color = Colors.Red;
IList list = brush.GradientStops;
list.Add(gradientStop1);
```

Some properties might support more than one type of collection. In this case, you need to add a tag that specifies the collection class, like this:

```
<LinearGradientBrush>
  <LinearGradientBrush.GradientStops>
    <GradientStopCollection>
      <GradientStop Offset="0.00" Color="Red" />
      <GradientStop Offset="0.50" Color="Indigo" />
      <GradientStop Offset="1.00" Color="Violet" />
```

```
    </GradientStopCollection>
  </LinearGradientBrush.GradientStops>
</LinearGradientBrush>
```

■**Note** If the collection defaults to null, you need to include the tag that specifies the collection class, thereby creating the collection object. If there's a default instance of the collection and you simply need to fill it, you can omit that part.

Nested content doesn't always indicate a collection. For example, consider the Grid element, which contains several other elements:

```
<Grid x:Name="grid1">
  ...
  <TextBox x:Name="txtQuestion" ... >
    ...
  </TextBox>
  <Button x:Name="cmdAnswer" ... >
    ...
  </Button>
  <TextBox x:Name="txtAnswer" ... >
    ...
  </TextBox>
</Grid>
```

These nested tags don't correspond to complex properties because they don't include the period. Furthermore, the Grid control isn't a collection and so it doesn't implement IList or IDictionary. What the Grid *does* support is the ContentProperty attribute, which indicates the property that should receive any nested content. Technically, the ContentProperty attribute is applied to the Panel class, from which the Grid derives, and looks like this:

```
[ContentPropertyAttribute("Children")]
public abstract class Panel : FrameworkElement
```

This indicates that any nested elements should be used to set the Children property. The XAML parser treats the content property differently depending on whether or not it's a collection property (in which case it implements the IList or IDictionary interface). Because the Panel.Children property returns a UIElementCollection, and because UIElementCollection implements IList, the parser uses the IList.Add() method to add nested content to the grid.

In other words, when the XAML parser meets the previous markup, it creates an instance of each nested element and passes it to the Grid using the Grid.Children.Add() method:

```
txtQuestion = new TextBox();
...
grid1.Children.Add(txtQuestion);
```

```
cmdAnswer = new Button();
...
grid1.Children.Add(cmdAnswer);

txtAnswer = new TextBox();
...
grid1.Children.Add(txtAnswer);
```

What happens next depends entirely on how the control implements the content property. The Grid displays all the elements it holds in an invisible layout of rows and columns, as you'll see in Chapter 3.

BROWSING NESTED ELEMENTS WITH VISUALTREEHELPER

Silverlight provides a VisualTreeHelper class that allows you to walk through the hierarchy elements. The VisualTreeHelper class provides three static methods: GetParent(), which returns the element that contains a specified element; GetChildrenCount(), which indicates how many elements are nested inside the specified element; and GetChild(),which retrieves one of the nested elements, by its index number position.

The advantage of VisualTreeHelper is that it works in a generic way that supports all Silverlight elements, no matter what content model they use. For example, you may know that list controls expose items through an Items property, layout containers provide their children through a Children property, and content controls expose the nested content element through a Content property, but only the VisualTreeHelper can dig through all three with the same seamless code.

The disadvantage to using the VisualTreeHelper is that it gets every detail of an element's visual composition, including some that aren't important to its function. For example, when you use VisualTreeHelper to browse through a ListBox, you'll come across a few low-level details that probably don't interest you, such as the Border that outlines it, the ScrollViewer that makes it scrollable, and the Grid that lays out items in discrete rows. For this reason, the only practical way to use the VisualTreeHelper is with recursive code—in essence, you keep digging through the tree until you find the type of element you're interested in, and then you act on it. The following example uses this technique to clear all the text boxes in a hierarchy of elements:

```
private void Clear(DependencyObject element)
{
    // If this is a text box, clear the text.
    TextBox txt = element as TextBox;
    if (txt != null) txt.Text = "";

    // Check for nested children.
    int children = VisualTreeHelper.GetChildrenCount(element);
    for (int i = 0; i < children; i++)
    {
        DependencyObject child = VisualTreeHelper.GetChild(element, i);
        Clear(child);
    }
}
```

> To set it in motion, call the Clear() method with the topmost object you want to examine. Here's how to dissect the entire current page:
>
> ```
> Clear(this);
> ```

Events

So far, all the attributes you've seen map to properties. However, attributes can also be used to attach event handlers. The syntax for this is EventName="EventHandlerMethodName".

For example, the Button control provides a Click event. You can attach an event handler like this:

```
<Button ... Click="cmdAnswer_Click">
```

This assumes that there is a method with the name cmdAnswer_Click in the code-behind class. The event handler must have the correct signature (that is, it must match the delegate for the Click event). Here's the method that does the trick:

```
private void cmdAnswer_Click(object sender, RoutedEventArgs e)
{
    AnswerGenerator generator = new AnswerGenerator();
    txtAnswer.Text = generator.GetRandomAnswer(txtQuestion.Text);
}
```

In many situations, you'll use attributes to set properties and attach event handlers on the same element. Silverlight always follows the same sequence: first it sets the Name property (if set), then it attaches any event handlers, and lastly it sets the properties. This means that any event handlers that respond to property changes will fire when the property is set for the first time.

The Full Eight Ball Example

Now that you've considered the fundamentals of XAML, you know enough to walk through the definition for the page in Figure 2-1. Here's the complete XAML markup:

```
<UserControl x:Class="EightBall.Page"
 xmlns="http://schemas.microsoft.com/client/2007"
 xmlns:x="http://schemas.microsoft.com/winfx/2006/xaml"
 Width="400" Height="300">
  <Grid x:Name="grid1">
    <Grid.RowDefinitions>
      <RowDefinition Height="*" />
      <RowDefinition Height="Auto" />
      <RowDefinition Height="*" />
    </Grid.RowDefinitions>
    <TextBox VerticalAlignment="Stretch" HorizontalAlignment="Stretch"
```

```
  Margin="10,10,13,10" x:Name="txtQuestion"
  TextWrapping="Wrap" FontFamily="Verdana" FontSize="24"
  Grid.Row="0">
    [Place question here.]
</TextBox>
<Button VerticalAlignment="Top" HorizontalAlignment="Left"
  Margin="10,0,0,20" Width="127" Height="23" x:Name="cmdAnswer"
  Click="cmdAnswer_Click" Grid.Row="1">
    Ask the Eight Ball
</Button>
<TextBox VerticalAlignment="Stretch" HorizontalAlignment="Stretch"
  Margin="10,10,13,10" x:Name="txtAnswer" TextWrapping="Wrap"
  IsReadOnly="True" FontFamily="Verdana" FontSize="24" Foreground="Green"
  Grid.Row="2">
    [Answer will appear here.]
</TextBox>

<Grid.Background>
  <LinearGradientBrush>
    <LinearGradientBrush.GradientStops>
      <GradientStop Offset="0.00" Color="Yellow" />
      <GradientStop Offset="0.50" Color="White" />
      <GradientStop Offset="1.00" Color="Purple" />
    </LinearGradientBrush.GradientStops>
  </LinearGradientBrush>
</Grid.Background>
  </Grid>
</Window>
```

Remember, you probably won't write the XAML for a graphically rich user interface by hand—doing so would be unbearably tedious. However, you might have good reason to edit the XAML code to make a change that would be awkward to accomplish in the designer. You might also find yourself reviewing XAML to get a better idea of how a page works.

Resources

Silverlight includes a resource system that integrates closely with XAML. Using resources, you can

- **Create non-visual objects.** This is useful if other elements use these objects. For example, you could create a data object as a resource and then use data binding to display its information in several elements.

- **Reuse objects.** Once you define a resource, several elements can draw upon it. For example, you can define a single brush that's used to color in several shapes. Later in this book, you'll use resources to define styles and templates that are reused among elements.

• **Centralize details.** Sometimes, it's easier to pull frequently changed information into one place (a resources section) rather than scatter it through a complex markup file, where it's more difficult to track down and change.

The resource system shouldn't be confused with *assembly resources*, which are blocks of data that you can embed in your compiled Silverlight assembly. (For example, the XAML files you add to your project are embedded as assembly resources.) You'll learn more about assembly resources in Chapter 6.

The Resources Collection

Every element includes a Resources property, which stores a dictionary collection of resources. The resources collection can hold any type of object, indexed by string.

Although every element includes the Resources property, the most common way to define resources is at the page level. That's because every element has access to the resources in its own resource collection and the resources in all of its parents' resource collections. So if you define a resource in the page, all the elements on the page can use it.

For example, consider the eight ball example. Currently, the GradientBrush that paints the background of the Grid is defined inline (in other words, it's defined and set in the same place). However, you might choose to pull the brush out of the Grid markup and place it in the resources collection instead:

```
<UserControl x:Class="EightBall.Page"
 xmlns="http://schemas.microsoft.com/client/2007"
 xmlns:x="http://schemas.microsoft.com/winfx/2006/xaml"
 Width="400" Height="300">
  <UserControl.Resources>
    <LinearGradientBrush x:Key="BackgroundBrush">
      <LinearGradientBrush.GradientStops>
        <GradientStop Offset="0.00" Color="Yellow" />
        <GradientStop Offset="0.50" Color="White" />
        <GradientStop Offset="1.00" Color="Purple" />
      </LinearGradientBrush.GradientStops>
    </LinearGradientBrush>
  </UserControl.Resources>
  ...
</UserControl>
```

The only important new detail is the Key attribute that's been added to the brush (and preceded by the x: namespace prefix, which puts it in the XAML namespace rather than the Silverlight namespace). The Key attribute assigns the name under which the brush will be indexed in the resources collection. You can use whatever you want, so long as you use the same name when you need to retrieve the resource. It's a good idea to name resources based on their function (which won't change) rather than the specific details of their implementation (which might). For that reason, BackgroundBrush is a better name than LinearGradientBrush or ThreeColorBrush.

> ■**Note** You can instantiate any .NET class in the resources section (including your own custom classes), as long as it's XAML-friendly. That means it needs to have a few basic characteristics, such as a public zero-argument constructor and writeable properties.

To use a resource in your XAML markup, you need a way to refer to it. This is accomplished using a *markup extension*—a specialized type of syntax that sets a property in a nonstandard way. Markup extensions extend the XAML language and can be recognized by their curly braces. To use a resource, you use a markup extension named StaticResource:

```
<Grid x:Name="grid1" Background="{StaticResource BackgroundBrush}">
```

This refactoring doesn't shorten the markup you need for the eight ball example. However, if you need to use the same brush in multiple elements, the resource approach is the best way to avoid duplicating the same details. And even if you don't use the brush more than once, you might still prefer this approach if your user interface includes a number of graphical details that are likely to change. For example, by placing all the brushes front and center in the resources collection, you'll have an easier time finding them and changing them. Some developers use the resources collection for virtually every complex object they create to set a property in XAML.

> ■**Note** The word *static* stems from the fact that WPF has two types of resources, static and dynamic. However, Silverlight only includes static resources.

The Hierarchy of Resources

Every element has its own resource collection, and Silverlight performs a recursive search up your element tree to find the resource you want. For example, imagine you have the following markup:

```
<UserControl x:Class="Resources.ResourceHierarchy"
 xmlns="http://schemas.microsoft.com/client/2007"
 xmlns:x="http://schemas.microsoft.com/winfx/2006/xaml"
 Width="400" Height="300">
  <Grid x:Name="LayoutRoot" Background="White">
    <StackPanel>
      <StackPanel.Resources>
        <LinearGradientBrush x:Key="ButtonFace">
          <GradientStop Offset="0.00" Color="Yellow" />
          <GradientStop Offset="0.50" Color="White" />
          <GradientStop Offset="1.00" Color="Purple" />
        </LinearGradientBrush>
      </StackPanel.Resources>
```

```
      <Button Content="Click Me First" Margin="5"
       Background="{StaticResource ButtonFace}"></Button>
       <Button Content="Click Me Next" Margin="5"
       Background="{StaticResource ButtonFace}"></Button>
    </StackPanel>
  </Grid>
</UserControl>
```

Figure 2-2 shows the page this markup creates.

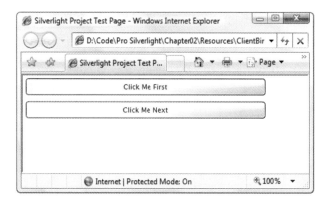

Figure 2-2. *Using one brush to color two buttons*

Here, both buttons set their backgrounds to the same resource. When encountering this markup, Silverlight will check the resources collection of the button itself, and then the Stack-Panel (where it's defined). If the StackPanel didn't include the right resource, Silverlight would continue its search with the resources collection of the Grid and then the UserControl. If it still hasn't found a resource with the right name, Silverlight will end by checking the application resources that are defined in the <Application.Resources> section of the App.xaml file. Thus, application resources give you a great way to reuse an object across an entire application. In this example, it's a good choice if you plan to use the brush in more than one page.

Note Before creating an application resource, consider the trade-off between complexity and reuse. Adding an application resource gives you better reuse, but it adds complexity because it's not immediately clear which pages use a given resource. (It's conceptually the same as an old-style C++ program with too many global variables.) A good guideline is to use application resources if your object is reused widely (for example, in many pages). If it's used in just two or three, consider defining the resource in each page.

Order is important when defining a resource in markup. The rule of thumb is that a resource must appear before you refer to it in your markup. That means that even though it's perfectly valid (from a markup perspective) to put the <StackPanel.Resources> section after the markup that declares the buttons, this change will break the current example. When the XAML parser encounters a reference to a resource it doesn't know, it throws an exception.

Interestingly, resource names can be reused as long as you don't use the same resource name more than once in the same collection. In this case, Silverlight uses the resource it finds first. For example, if you add a brush with the same name to the <UserControls.Resources> section in the previous example, it will be ignored.

Accessing Resources in Code

Usually, you'll define and use resources in your markup. However, if the need arises, you can work with the resources collection in code. The most straightforward approach is to look up the resource you need in the appropriate collection by name. For example, if you store a LinearGradientBrush in the <UserControl.Resources> section with the key name ButtonFace, you could use code like this:

```
LinearGradientBrush brush = (LinearGradientBrush)this.Resources["ButtonFace"];

// Swap the color order.
Color color = brush.GradientStops[0].Color;
brush.GradientStops[0].Color = brush.GradientStops[2].Color;
brush.GradientStops[2].Color = color;
```

When you change a resource in this way, every element that uses the resource updates itself automatically (see Figure 2-3). In other words, if you have four buttons using the Button-Face brush, they will all get the reversed colors when this code runs.

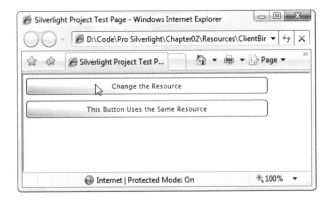

Figure 2-3. *Altering a resource*

However, there's one limitation. Because Silverlight doesn't support dynamic resources, you aren't allowed to change the resource reference. That means you can't replace a resource with a new object. Here's an example of code that breaks this rule, and will generate a runtime error:

```
SolidColorBrush brush = new SolidColorBrush(Colors.Yellow);
this.Resources["ButtonFace"] = brush;
```

Rather than dig through the resources collection to find the object you want, you can give your resource a name by adding the Name attribute. You can then access it directly by name in your code. However, you can't set both a name and a key on the same object, and the Static-Resource markup extension only recognizes keys. Thus, if you create a named resource, you won't be able to use it in your markup with a StaticResource reference. For that reason, it's more common to use keys.

The Last Word

In this chapter, you took a tour through a simple XAML file and learned the syntax rules of XAML at the same time. When you're designing an application, you don't need to write all your XAML by hand. Instead, you can use a tool like Visual Studio to drag and drop your pages into existence. Based on that fact, you might wonder whether it's worth spending so much time studying the syntax of XAML.

The answer is a resounding *yes*. Understanding XAML is critical to Silverlight application design. Understanding XAML will help you learn key Silverlight concepts, and ensure that you get the markup you really want. More importantly, there is a host of tasks that are only possible—or are far easier to accomplish—with handwritten XAML. They include wiring up event handlers, defining resources, creating control templates, writing data binding expressions, and defining animations.

In the future, most Silverlight developers will probably use a combination of techniques, laying out some of their user interface with a design tool (Visual Studio or Expression Blend) and then fine-tuning it by editing the XAML markup by hand. However, the support for Silverlight in the current generation of design tools is limited and changing rapidly. As a result, you'll probably find yourself using tools to create key content (for example, complex graphics), while adding the markup for most of the controls by hand.

CHAPTER 3

■■■

Layout

Half the battle in user interface design is organizing the content in a way that's attractive, practical, and flexible. In a browser-hosted application, this is a particularly tricky task, because your application may be used on a wide range of different computers and devices (all with different display hardware), and you have no control over the size of the browser window in which your Silverlight content is placed.

Fortunately, Silverlight inherits the most important part of WPF's extremely flexible layout model. Using the layout model, you organize your content in a set of different layout *containers*. Each container has its own layout logic—one stacks elements, another arranges them in a grid of invisible cells, and another uses a hard-coded coordinate system. If you're ambitious, you can even create your own containers with custom layout logic.

In this chapter, you'll learn how to use layout containers to create the visual skeleton for a Silverlight page. You'll spend most of your time exploring Silverlight's three core layout containers: the StackPanel, Grid, and Canvas. Once you've mastered these basics, you'll see how to extend your possibilities by creating new layout containers with custom layout logic. You'll also see how you can create an application that breaks out of the browser window and uses the full screen, and one that uses navigation to transition between pages.

The Layout Containers

A Silverlight window can hold only a single element. To fit in more than one element and create a more practical user interface, you need to place a container in your page and then add other elements to that container. Your layout is determined by the container that you use.

All the Silverlight layout containers are panels that derive from the abstract System. Windows.Controls.Panel class (see Figure 3-1).

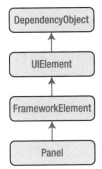

Figure 3-1. *The hierarchy of the Panel class*

The Panel class adds two public properties: Background and Children. Background is the brush that's used to paint the panel background. Children is the collection of items that's stored in the panel. (This is the first level of elements—in other words, these elements may themselves contain more elements.) The Panel class also has a bit of internal plumbing you can use to create your own layout container, as you'll learn later in this chapter.

On its own, the base Panel class is nothing but a starting point for other more specialized classes. Silverlight provides three Panel-derived classes that you can use to arrange layout, which are listed in Table 3-1. As with all Silverlight controls and most visual elements, these classes are found in the System.Windows.Controls namespace.

Table 3-1. *Core Layout Panels*

Name	Description
StackPanel	Places elements in a horizontal or vertical stack. This layout container is typically used for small sections of a larger, more complex page.
Grid	Arranges elements in rows and columns according to an invisible table. This is one of the most flexible and commonly used layout containers.
Canvas	Allows elements to be positioned absolutely using fixed coordinates. This layout container is the simplest but least flexible.

Layout containers can be nested. A typical user interface begins with the Grid, Silverlight's most capable container, and contains other layout containers that arrange smaller groups of elements, such as captioned text boxes, items in a list, icons on a toolbar, a column of buttons, and so on.

The Panel Background

All Panel elements introduce the concept of a background by adding a Background property. It's natural to expect that the Background property would use some sort of color object. However, the Background property actually uses something much more versatile: a Brush object. This design gives you the flexibility to fill your background and foreground content with a solid color (by using the SolidColorBrush) or something more exotic (for example, a gradient or a bitmap, by using a LinearGradientBrush or ImageBrush). In this section, you'll consider only the simple solid-color fills provided by the SolidColorBrush, but you'll try fancier brushwork in Chapter 8.

■**Note** All of Silverlight's Brush classes are found in the System.Windows.Media namespace.

For example, if you want to give your entire page a light blue background, you could adjust the background of the root panel. Here's the code that does the trick:

```
layoutRoot.Background = new SolidColorBrush(Colors.AliceBlue);
```

This code creates a new SolidColorBrush using a ready-made color via a static property of the handy Colors class. (The names are based on the color names supported by most web browsers.) It then sets the brush as the background brush for the button, which causes its background to be painted a light shade of blue.

The Colors class offers handy shortcuts, but it's not the only way to set a color. You can also create a Color object by supplying the red, green, and blue (R, G, B) values. Each one of these values is a number from 0 to 255:

```
int red = 0; int green = 255; int blue = 0;
layoutRoot.Background = new SolidColorBrush(Color.FromRgb(red, green, blue));
```

You can also make a color partly transparent by supplying an alpha value when calling the Color.FromArgb() method. An alpha value of 255 is completely opaque, while 0 is completely transparent.

Often, you'll set colors in XAML rather than in code. Here, you can use a helpful shortcut. Rather than define a Brush object, you can supply a color name or color value. The type converter for the Background property will automatically create a SolidColorBrush object using the color you specify. Here's an example that uses a color name:

```
<Grid x:Name="layoutRoot" Background="Red">
```

It's equivalent to this more verbose syntax:

```
<Grid x:Name="layoutRoot">
  <Grid.Background>
    <SolidColorBrush Color="Red" />
  </Grid.Background>
</Grid>
```

You need to use the longer form if you want to create a different type of brush, such as a LinearGradientBrush, and use that to paint the background.

If you want to use a color code, you need to use a slightly less convenient syntax that puts the R, G, and B values in hexadecimal notation. You can use one of two formats—either #rrggbb or #aarrggbb (the difference being that the latter includes the alpha value). You need only two digits to supply the A, R, G, and B values because they're all in hexadecimal notation. Here's an example that creates the same color as in the previous code snippets using #aarrggbb notation:

```
<Grid x:Name="layoutRoot" Background="#FFFF0000">
```

Here the alpha value is FF (255), the red value is FF (255), and the green and blue values are 0.

By default, the Background of a layout panel is set to a null reference, which is equivalent to this:

```
<Grid x:Name="layoutRoot" Background="{x:Null}">
```

When your panel has a null background, any content underneath will show through (similar to if you set a fully transparent background color). However, there's an important difference—the layout container won't be able to receive mouse events.

Note Brushes support automatic change notification. In other words, if you attach a brush to a control and change the brush, the control updates itself accordingly.

Borders

The layout containers allow you to paint a background, but not a border outline. However, there's an element that fills in the gap—the Border.

The Border class is pure simplicity. It takes a single piece of nested content (which is often a layout panel) and adds a background or border around it. To master the Border, you need nothing more than the properties listed in Table 3-2.

Table 3-2. *Properties of the Border Class*

Name	Description
Background	Sets a background that appears behind all the content in the border using a Brush object. You can use a solid color or something more exotic.
BorderBrush	Sets the fill of the border that appears around the edge of the Border object, using a Brush object. The most straightforward approach is to use a SolidColorBrush to create a solid border.
BorderThickness	Sets the width (in pixels) of the border on each side. The BorderThickness property holds an instance of the System.Windows.Thickness structure, with separate components for the top, bottom, left, and right edges.
CornerRadius	Allows you to gracefully round the corners of your border. The greater the CornerRadius, the more dramatic the rounding effect is.
Padding	Adds spacing between the border and the content inside. (By contrast, margin adds spacing outside the border.)

Here's a straightforward, slightly rounded border around a basic button:

```
<Border Margin="25" Padding="8" Background="LightYellow"
 BorderBrush="SteelBlue" BorderThickness="8" CornerRadius="15">
  <Button Margin="3" Content="Click  Me"></Button>
</Border>
```

Figure 3-2 shows the result.

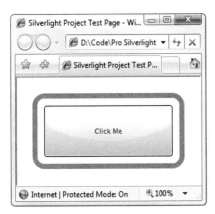

Figure 3-2. *A basic border*

Simple Layout with the StackPanel

The StackPanel is one of the simplest layout containers. It simply stacks its children in a single row or column. These elements are arranged based on their order.

For example, consider this page, which contains a stack with one TextBlock and four buttons:

```
<UserControl x:Class="Layout.SimpleStack"
 xmlns="http://schemas.microsoft.com/client/2007"
 xmlns:x="http://schemas.microsoft.com/winfx/2006/xaml">
  <StackPanel Background="White">
    <TextBlock Text="A Button Stack"></TextBlock>
    <Button Content="Button 1"></Button>
    <Button Content="Button 2"></Button>
    <Button Content="Button 3"></Button>
    <Button Content="Button 4"></Button>
  </StackPanel>
</UserControl>
```

Figure 3-3 shows the result.

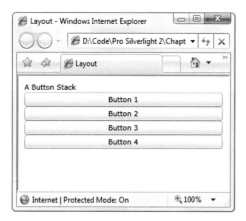

Figure 3-3. *The StackPanel in action*

By default, a StackPanel arranges elements from top to bottom, making each one as tall as is necessary to display its content. In this example, that means the TextBlock and buttons are sized just large enough to comfortably accommodate the text inside. All the elements are then stretched to the full width of the StackPanel, which is the width of your page.

In this example, the Height and Width properties of the page are not set. As a result, the page grows to fit the full Silverlight content region (in this case, the complete browser window). Most of the examples in this chapter use this approach, because it makes it easier to experiment with the different layout containers. You can then see how a layout container resizes itself to fit different page sizes simply by resizing the browser window.

■**Note** Once you've examined all the layout containers, you'll take a closer look at the issue of page sizes, and you'll learn about your different options for dealing content that doesn't fit in the browser window.

The StackPanel can also be used to arrange elements horizontally by setting the Orientation property:

```
<StackPanel Orientation="Horizontal" Background="White">
```

Now elements are given their minimum width (wide enough to fit their text) and are stretched to the full height of the containing panel (see Figure 3-4).

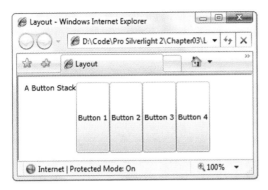

Figure 3-4. *The StackPanel with horizontal orientation*

Clearly, this doesn't provide the flexibility real applications need. Fortunately, you can fine-tune the way the StackPanel and other layout containers work using layout properties, as described next.

Layout Properties

Although layout is determined by the container, the child elements can still get their say. In fact, layout panels work in concert with their children by respecting a small set of layout properties, as listed in Table 3-3.

Table 3-3. *Layout Properties*

Name	Description
HorizontalAlignment	Determines how a child is positioned inside a layout container when there's extra horizontal space available. You can choose Center, Left, Right, or Stretch.
VerticalAlignment	Determines how a child is positioned inside a layout container when there's extra vertical space available. You can choose Center, Top, Bottom, or Stretch.
Margin	Adds a bit of breathing room around an element. The Margin property holds an instance of the System.Windows.Thickness structure, with separate components for the top, bottom, left, and right edges.
MinWidth and MinHeight	Sets the minimum dimensions of an element. If an element is too large for its layout container, it will be cropped to fit.
MaxWidth and MaxHeight	Sets the maximum dimensions of an element. If the container has more room available, the element won't be enlarged beyond these bounds, even if the HorizontalAlignment and VerticalAlignment properties are set to Stretch.
Width and Height	Explicitly sets the size of an element. This setting overrides a Stretch value for the HorizontalAlignment or VerticalAlignment properties. However, this size won't be honored if it's outside of the bounds set by the MinWidth, MinHeight, MaxWidth, and MaxHeight.

All of these properties are inherited from the base FrameworkElement class and are therefore supported by all the graphical widgets you can use in a Silverlight page.

Note As you learned in Chapter 2, different layout containers can provide *attached properties* to their children. For example, all the children of a Grid object gain Row and Column properties that allow them to choose the cell where they're placed. Attached properties allow you to set information that's specific to a particular layout container. However, the layout properties in Table 3-3 are generic enough that they apply to many layout panels. Thus, these properties are defined as part of the base FrameworkElement class.

Alignment

To understand how these properties work, take another look at the simple StackPanel shown in Figure 3-3. In this example—a StackPanel with vertical orientation—the VerticalAlignment property has no effect because each element is given as much height as it needs and no more. However, the HorizontalAlignment *is* important. It determines where each element is placed in its row.

Ordinarily, the default HorizontalAlignment is Left for a label and Stretch for a Button. That's why every button takes the full column width. However, you can change these details:

```
<StackPanel Background="White">
  <TextBlock HorizontalAlignment="Center" Text="A Button Stack"></TextBlock>
  <Button HorizontalAlignment="Left" Content="Button 1"></Button>
  <Button HorizontalAlignment="Right" Content="Button 2"></Button>
  <Button Content="Button 3"></Button>
  <Button Content="Button 4"></Button>
</StackPanel>
```

Figure 3-5 shows the result. The first two buttons are given their minimum sizes and aligned accordingly, while the bottom two buttons are stretched over the entire StackPanel. If you resize the page, you'll see that the label remains in the middle and the first two buttons stay stuck to either side.

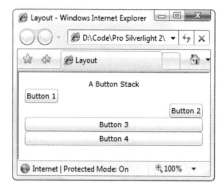

Figure 3-5. *A StackPanel with aligned buttons*

■**Note** The StackPanel also has its own HorizontalAlignment and VerticalAlignment properties. By default, both of these are set to Stretch, and so the StackPanel fills its container completely. In this example, that means the StackPanel fills the page. If you use a different value for VerticalAlignment, the StackPanel will be made just large enough to fit the widest control.

Margins

There's an obvious problem with the StackPanel example in its current form. A well-designed page doesn't just contain elements—it also includes a bit of extra space in between the elements. To introduce this extra space and make the StackPanel example less cramped, you can set control margins.

When setting margins, you can set a single width for all sides, like this:

```
<Button Margin="5" Content="Button 3"></Button>
```

Alternatively, you can set different margins for each side of a control in the order *left, top, right, bottom*:

```
<Button Margin="5,10,5,10" Content="Button 3"></Button>
```

In code, you can set margins using the Thickness structure:

```
cmd.Margin = new Thickness(5);
```

Getting the right control margins is a bit of an art because you need to consider how the margin settings of adjacent controls influence one another. For example, if you have two buttons stacked on top of each other, and the topmost button has a bottom margin of 5, and the bottommost button has a top margin of 5, you have a total of 10 pixels of space between the two buttons.

Ideally, you'll be able to keep different margin settings as consistent as possible and avoid setting distinct values for the different margin sides. For instance, in the StackPanel example it makes sense to use the same margins on the buttons and on the panel itself, as shown here:

```
<StackPanel Margin="3" Background="White">
  <TextBlock Margin="3" HorizontalAlignment="Center"
   Text="A Button Stack"></TextBlock>
  <Button Margin="3" HorizontalAlignment="Left" Content="Button 1"></Button>
  <Button Margin="3" HorizontalAlignment="Right" Content="Button 2"></Button>
  <Button Margin="3" Content="Button 3"></Button>
  <Button Margin="3" Content="Button 4"></Button>
</StackPanel>
```

This way, the total space between two buttons (the sum of the two button margins) is the same as the total space between the button at the edge of the page (the sum of the button margin and the StackPanel margin). Figure 3-6 shows this more respectable page, and Figure 3-7 shows how the margin settings break down.

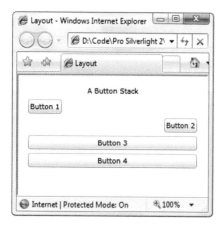

Figure 3-6. *Adding margins between elements*

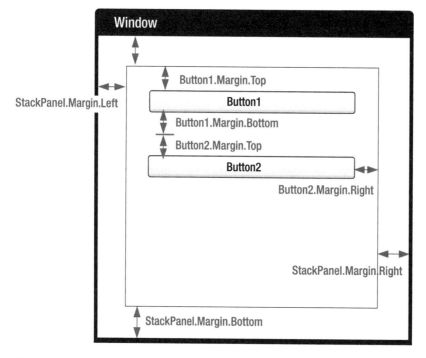

Figure 3-7. *How margins are combined*

Minimum, Maximum, and Explicit Sizes

Finally, every element includes Height and Width properties that allow you to give it an explicit size. However, just because you can set explicit sizes doesn't mean you *should*. In most cases, it's better to let elements grow to fit their content. For example, a button expands as you add more text. You can lock your elements into a range of acceptable sizes by setting a maximum and minimum size, if necessary. If you do add size information, you risk creating a more brittle layout that can't adapt to changes and (at worst) truncates content that doesn't fit.

For example, you might decide that the buttons in your StackPanel should stretch to fit the StackPanel but be made no larger than 200 pixels wide and no smaller than 100 pixels wide. (By default, buttons start with a minimum width of 75 pixels.) Here's the markup you need:

```
<StackPanel Margin="3">
  <TextBlock Margin="3" HorizontalAlignment="Center"
   Text="A Button Stack"></TextBlock>
  <Button Margin="3" MaxWidth="200" MinWidth="100" Content="Button 1"></Button>
  <Button Margin="3" MaxWidth="200" MinWidth="100" Content="Button 2"></Button>
  <Button Margin="3" MaxWidth="200" MinWidth="100" Content="Button 3"></Button>
  <Button Margin="3" MaxWidth="200" MinWidth="100" Content="Button 4"></Button>
</StackPanel>
```

■**Tip** At this point, you might be wondering if there's an easier way to set properties that are standardized across several elements, such as the button margins in this example. The answer is *styles*—a feature that allows you to reuse property settings. You'll learn about styles in Chapter 11.

When the StackPanel sizes a button that doesn't have a hard-coded size, it considers several pieces of information:

- **The minimum size.** Each button will always be at least as large as the minimum size.

- **The maximum size.** Each button will always be smaller than the maximum size (unless you've incorrectly set the maximum size to be smaller than the minimum size).

- **The content.** If the content inside the button requires a greater width, the StackPanel will attempt to enlarge the button.

- **The size of the container.** If the minimum width is larger than the width of the Stack-Panel, a portion of the button will be cut off. Otherwise, the button will not be allowed to grow wider than the StackPanel, even if it can't fit all its text on the button surface.

- **The horizontal alignment.** Because the button uses a HorizontalAlignment of Stretch (the default), the StackPanel will attempt to enlarge the button to fill the full width of the StackPanel.

The trick to understanding this process is to realize that the minimum and maximum size set the absolute bounds. Within those bounds, the StackPanel tries to respect the button's desired size (to fit its content) and its alignment settings.

Figure 3-8 sheds some light on how this works with the StackPanel. On the left is the page at its minimum size. The buttons are 200 pixels each, and the page cannot be resized to be narrower. If you shrink the page from this point, the right side of each button will be clipped off. (You can deal with this situation using scrolling, as discussed later in this chapter.)

As you enlarge the page, the buttons grow with it until they reach their maximum of 300 pixels. From this point on, if you make the page any larger, the extra space is added to either side of the button (as shown on the right).

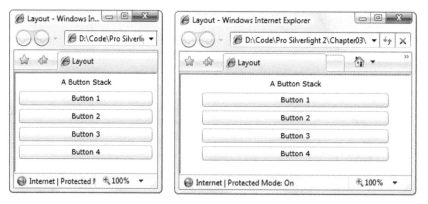

Figure 3-8. *Constrained button sizing*

▪**Note** In some situations, you might want to use code that checks how large an element is in a page. The Height and Width properties are no help because they indicate your desired size settings, which might not correspond to the actual rendered size. In an ideal scenario, you'll let your elements size to fit their content, and the Height and Width properties won't be set at all. However, you can find out the actual size used to render an element by reading the ActualHeight and ActualWidth properties. But remember, these values may change when the page is resized or the content inside it changes.

The Grid

The Grid is the most powerful layout container in Silverlight. In fact, the Grid is so useful that when you add a new XAML document for a page in Visual Studio, it automatically adds the Grid tags as the first-level container, nested inside the root UserControl element.

The Grid separates elements into an invisible grid of rows and columns. Although more than one element can be placed in a single cell (in which case they overlap), it generally makes sense to place just a single element per cell. Of course, that element may itself be another lay-out container that organizes its own group of contained controls.

▪**Tip** Although the Grid is designed to be invisible, you can set the Grid.ShowGridLines property to true to take a closer look. This feature isn't really intended for prettying up a page. Instead, it's a debugging conven-ience that's designed to help you understand how the Grid has subdivided itself into smaller regions. This feature is important because you have the ability to control exactly how the Grid chooses column widths and row heights.

Creating a Grid-based layout is a two-step process. First, you choose the number of columns and rows that you want. Next, you assign the appropriate row and column to each contained element, thereby placing it in just the right spot.

You create grids and rows by filling the Grid.ColumnDefinitions and Grid.RowDefinitions collections with objects. For example, if you decide you need two rows and three columns, you'd add the following tags:

```
<Grid ShowGridLines="True" Background="White">
  <Grid.RowDefinitions>
    <RowDefinition></RowDefinition>
    <RowDefinition></RowDefinition>
  </Grid.RowDefinitions>
  <Grid.ColumnDefinitions>
    <ColumnDefinition></ColumnDefinition>
    <ColumnDefinition></ColumnDefinition>
    <ColumnDefinition></ColumnDefinition>
  </Grid.ColumnDefinitions>

  ...
</Grid>
```

As this example shows, it's not necessary to supply any information in a RowDefinition or ColumnDefinition element. If you leave them empty (as shown here), the Grid will share the space evenly between all rows and columns. In this example, each cell will be exactly the same size, depending on the size of the containing page.

To place individual elements into a cell, you use the attached Row and Column properties. Both these properties take 0-based index numbers. For example, here's how you could create a partially filled grid of buttons:

```
<Grid ShowGridLines="True" Background="White">
  ...

  <Button Grid.Row="0" Grid.Column="0" Content="Top Left"></Button>
  <Button Grid.Row="0" Grid.Column="1" Content="Middle Left"></Button>
  <Button Grid.Row="1" Grid.Column="2" Content="Bottom Right"></Button>
  <Button Grid.Row="1" Grid.Column="1" Content="Bottom Middle"></Button>
</Grid>
```

Each element must be placed into its cell explicitly. This allows you to place more than one element into a cell (which rarely makes sense) or leave certain cells blank (which is often useful). It also means you can declare your elements out of order, as with the final two buttons in this example. However, it makes for clearer markup if you define your controls row by row, and from right to left in each row.

There is one exception. If you don't specify the Grid.Row property, the Grid assumes that it's 0. The same behavior applies to the Grid.Column property. Thus, you leave both attributes off of an element to place it in the first cell of the Grid.

Figure 3-9 shows how this simple grid appears at two different sizes. Notice that the ShowGridLines property is set to true so that you can see the separation between each column and row.

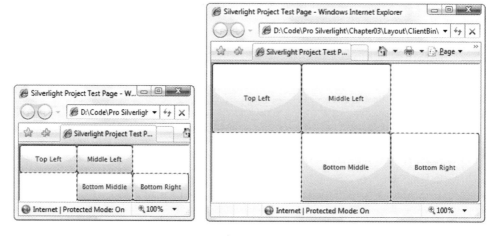

Figure 3-9. *A simple grid*

As you would expect, the Grid honors the basic set of layout properties listed in Table 3-3. That means you can add margins around the content in a cell, you can change the sizing mode so an element doesn't grow to fill the entire cell, and you can align an item along one of the edges of a cell. If you force an element to have a size that's larger than the cell can accommodate, part of the content will be chopped off.

Fine-Tuning Rows and Columns

As you've seen, the Grid gives you the ability to create a proportionately sized collection of rows and columns, which is often quite useful. However, to unlock the full potential of the Grid, you can change the way each row and column is sized.

The Grid supports three sizing strategies:

- **Absolute sizes.** You choose the exact size using pixels. This is the least useful strategy because it's not flexible enough to deal with changing content size, changing container size, or localization.

- **Automatic sizes.** Each row or column is given exactly the amount of space it needs, and no more. This is one of the most useful sizing modes.

- **Proportional sizes.** Space is divided between a group of rows or columns. This is the standard setting for all rows and columns. For example, in Figure 3-9 you can see that all cells increase in size proportionately as the Grid expands.

For maximum flexibility, you can mix and match these different sizing modes. For example, it's often useful to create several automatically sized rows and then let one or two remaining rows get the leftover space through proportional sizing.

You set the sizing mode using the Width property of the ColumnDefinition object or the Height property of the RowDefinition object to a number. For example, here's how you set an absolute width of 100 pixels:

```
<ColumnDefinition Width="100"></ColumnDefinition>
```

To use automatic sizing, you use a value of Auto:

```
<ColumnDefinition Width="Auto"></ColumnDefinition>
```

Finally, to use proportional sizing, you use an asterisk (*):

```
<ColumnDefinition Width="*"></ColumnDefinition>
```

This syntax stems from the world of the Web, where it's used with HTML frames pages. If you use a mix of proportional sizing and other sizing modes, the proportionally sized rows or columns get whatever space is left over.

If you want to divide the remaining space unequally, you can assign a *weight*, which you must place before the asterisk. For example, if you have two proportionately sized rows and you want the first to be half as high as the second, you could share the remaining space like this:

```
<RowDefinition Height="*"></RowDefinition>
<RowDefinition Height="2*"></RowDefinition>
```

This tells the Grid that the height of the second row should be twice the height of the first row. You can use whatever numbers you like to portion out the extra space.

Note It's easy to interact with ColumnDefinition and RowDefinition objects programmatically. You simply need to know that the Width and Height properties are GridLength objects. To create a GridLength that represents a specific size, just pass the appropriate value to the GridLength constructor. To create a GridLength that represents a proportional (*) size, pass the number to the GridLength constructor, and pass GridUnitType.Star as the second constructor argument. To indicate automatic sizing, use the static property GridLength.Auto.

Nesting Layout Containers

The Grid is impressive on its own, but most realistic user interfaces combine several layout containers. They may use an arrangement with more than one Grid, or mix the Grid with other layout containers like the StackPanel.

The following markup presents a simple example of this principle. It creates a basic dialog box with an OK and Cancel button in the bottom right-hand corner, and a large content region that's sized to fit its content (the text in a TextBlock). The entire package is centered in the middle of the page by setting the alignment properties on the Grid.

```
<Grid ShowGridLines="True" Background="SteelBlue"
 HorizontalAlignment="Center" VerticalAlignment="Center">
  <Grid.RowDefinitions>
    <RowDefinition Height="*"></RowDefinition>
    <RowDefinition Height="Auto"></RowDefinition>
  </Grid.RowDefinitions>

  <TextBlock Margin="10" Grid.Row="0" Foreground="White"
   Text="This is simply a test of nested containers."></TextBlock>
  <StackPanel Grid.Row="1" HorizontalAlignment="Right" Orientation="Horizontal">
    <Button Margin="10,10,2,10" Padding="3" Content="OK"></Button>
    <Button Margin="2,10,10,10" Padding="3" Content="Cancel"></Button>
  </StackPanel>
</Grid>
```

You'll notice that this Grid doesn't declare any columns. This is a shortcut you can take if your grid uses just one column and that column is proportionately sized (so it fills the entire width of the Grid). Figure 3-10 shows the rather pedestrian dialog box this markup creates.

■ **Note** In this example, the Padding adds some minimum space between the button border and the content inside (the word "OK" or "Cancel"). You'll learn more about Padding when you consider content controls in Chapter 5.

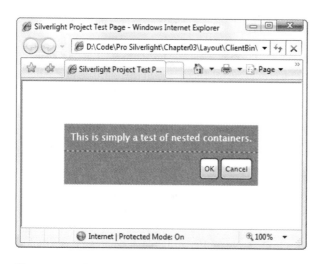

Figure 3-10. *A basic dialog box*

At first glance, nesting layout containers seems like a fair bit more work than placing controls in precise positions using coordinates. And in many cases, it is. However, the longer setup time is compensated by the ease with which you can change the user interface in the future.

For example, if you decide you want the OK and Cancel buttons to be centered at the bottom of the page, you simply need to change the alignment of the StackPanel that contains them:

```
<StackPanel Grid.Row="1" HorizontalAlignment="Center" ... >
```

Similarly, if you need to change the amount of content in the first row, the entire Grid will be enlarged to fit and the buttons will move obligingly out of the way. And if you add a dash of styles to this page (Chapter 11), you can improve it even further and remove other extraneous details (such as the margin settings) to create cleaner and more compact markup.

Tip If you have a densely nested tree of elements, it's easy to lose sight of the overall structure. Visual Studio provides a handy feature that shows you a tree representation of your elements and allows you to click your way down to the element you want to look at (or modify). This feature is the Document Outline window, and you can show it by choosing View ➤ Other Windows ➤ Document Outline from the menu.

Spanning Rows and Columns

You've already seen how to place elements in cells using the Row and Column attached properties. You can also use two more attached properties to make an element stretch over several cells: RowSpan and ColumnSpan. These properties take the number of rows or columns that the element should occupy.

For example, this button will take all the space that's available in the first and second cell of the first row:

```
<Button Grid.Row="0" Grid.Column="0" Grid.RowSpan="2" Content="Span Button">
</Button>
```

And this button will stretch over four cells in total by spanning two columns and two rows:

```
<Button Grid.Row="0" Grid.Column="0" Grid.RowSpan="2" Grid.ColumnSpan="2"
 Content="Span Button"></Button>
```

Row and column spanning can achieve some interesting effects and is particularly handy when you need to fit elements in a tabular structure that's broken up by dividers or longer sections of content.

Using column spanning, you could rewrite the simple dialog box example from Figure 3-10 using just a single Grid. This Grid divides the page into three columns, spreads the text box over all three, and uses the last two columns to align the OK and Cancel buttons.

```
<Grid ShowGridLines="True" Background="SteelBlue"
 HorizontalAlignment="Center" VerticalAlignment="Center">
  <Grid.RowDefinitions>
    <RowDefinition Height="*"></RowDefinition>
    <RowDefinition Height="Auto"></RowDefinition>
  </Grid.RowDefinitions>
```

```
<Grid.ColumnDefinitions>
  <ColumnDefinition Width="*"></ColumnDefinition>
  <ColumnDefinition Width="Auto"></ColumnDefinition>
  <ColumnDefinition Width="Auto"></ColumnDefinition>
</Grid.ColumnDefinitions>
<TextBlock Margin="10" Grid.Row="0" Grid.Column="0" Grid.ColumnSpan="3"
 Foreground="White"
 Text="This is simply a test of nested containers."></TextBlock>

<Button Margin="10,10,2,10" Padding="3"
  Grid.Row="1" Grid.Column="1" Content="OK"></Button>
<Button Margin="2,10,10,10" Padding="3"
  Grid.Row="1" Grid.Column="2" Content="Cancel"></Button>
</Grid>
```

Most developers will agree that this layout isn't clear or sensible. The column widths are determined by the size of the two buttons at the bottom of the page, which makes it difficult to add new content into the existing Grid structure. If you make even a minor addition to this page, you'll probably be forced to create a new set of columns.

As this shows, when you choose the layout containers for a page, you aren't simply interested in getting the correct layout behavior—you also want to build a layout structure that's easy to maintain and enhance in the future. A good rule of thumb is to use smaller layout containers such as the StackPanel for one-off layout tasks, such as arranging a group of buttons. On the other hand, if you need to apply a consistent structure to more than one area of your page, the Grid is an indispensable tool for standardizing your layout.

The GridSplitter

Every Windows user has seen *splitter bars*—draggable dividers that separate one section of a window from another. For example, when you use Windows Explorer, you're presented with a list of folders (on the left) and a list of files (on the right). You can drag the splitter bar in between to determine what proportion of the window is given to each pane.

In Silverlight, you can create a similar design and give the user the ability to resize rows or columns by adding a splitter bar to a Grid. Figure 3-11 shows a window where a GridSplitter sits between two columns. By dragging the splitter bar, the user can change the relative widths of both columns.

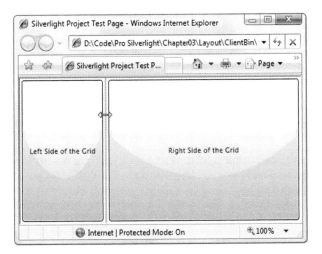

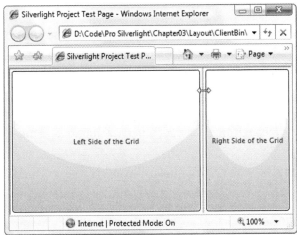

Figure 3-11. *Moving a splitter bar*

Before you can use the GridSplitter, you need to add a reference to the System.Windows.Controls.dll assembly where it's defined. Then, you need to map the namespace so it's available in your markup, as shown here:

```
<UserControl x:Class="Layout.SplitGrid" ...
 xmlns:basics=
 "clr-namespace:System.Windows.Controls;assembly=System.Windows.Controls">
```

You can now define a GridSplitter using the namespace prefix *basics*:

```
<basics:GridSplitter ...></basics:GridSplitter>
```

■**Note** As you learned in Chapter 1, the System.Windows.Controls.dll assembly isn't a part of the core Silverlight runtime. As a result, the assembly needs to be distributed with your application. When you add a reference to System.Windows.Controls.dll manually or by dragging a GridSplitter onto a page, Visual Studio will automatically set the Copy Local property of the reference to true. This ensures that it's packaged in the compiled XAP file.

To use the GridSplitter effectively, you need to know a little bit more about how it works. Although the GridSplitter serves a straightforward purpose, it can be awkward at first. To get the result you want, follow these guidelines:

- The GridSplitter must be placed in a Grid cell. You can place the GridSplitter in a cell with existing content, in which case you need to adjust the margin settings so it doesn't overlap. A better approach is to reserve a dedicated column or row for the GridSplitter, with a Height or Width value of Auto.

- The GridSplitter always resizes entire rows or columns (not single cells). To make the appearance of the GridSplitter consistent with this behavior, you should stretch the GridSplitter across an entire row or column, rather than limit it to a single cell. To accomplish this, you use the RowSpan or ColumnSpan properties you considered earlier. For example, the GridSplitter in Figure 3-11 has a RowSpan of 2. As a result, it stretches over the entire column. If you didn't add this setting, it would only appear in the top row (where it's placed), *even though* dragging the splitter bar would resize the entire column.

- Initially, the GridSplitter is invisibly small. To make it usable, you need to give it a minimum size. In the case of a vertical splitter bar (like the one in Figure 3-11), you need to set the VerticalAlignment to Stretch (so it fills the whole height of the available area) and the Width to a fixed size (such as 10 pixels). In the case of a horizontal splitter bar, you need to set HorizontalAlignment to Stretch, and Height to a fixed size.

- The GridSplitter alignment also determines whether the splitter bar is horizontal (used to resize rows) or vertical (used to resize columns). In the case of a horizontal splitter bar, you would set VerticalAlignment to Center (which is the default value) to indicate that dragging the splitter resizes the rows that are above and below. In the case of a vertical splitter bar (like the one in Figure 3-11), you would set HorizontalAlignment to Center to resize the columns on either side.

- To actually see the GridSplitter, you need to set the Background property. Otherwise, the GridSplitter remains transparent until you click on it (at which point a light blue focus rectangle appears around its edges).

- The GridSplitter respects minimum and maximum sizes, if you've set them on your ColumnDefinition or RowDefinition objects. The user won't be allowed to enlarge or shrink a column or row outside of its allowed size range.

To reinforce these rules, it helps to take a look at the actual markup for the example shown in Figure 3-11. In the following listing, the GridSplitter details are highlighted:

```
<Grid Background="White">
  <Grid.ColumnDefinitions>
    <ColumnDefinition MinWidth="100"></ColumnDefinition>
    <ColumnDefinition Width="Auto"></ColumnDefinition>
    <ColumnDefinition MinWidth="50"></ColumnDefinition>
  </Grid.ColumnDefinitions>

  <Button Grid.Column="0" Margin="3" Content="Left Side of the Grid"></Button>
  <basics:GridSplitter Grid.Column="1" Grid.RowSpan="2"
    Width="3" VerticalAlignment="Stretch" HorizontalAlignment="Center"
    Background="LightGray"ShowsPreview="False"></basics:GridSplitter>
  <Button Grid.Column="2" Margin="3" Content="Right Side of the Grid"></Button>
</Grid>
```

Tip Remember, if a Grid has just a single row or column, you can leave out the RowDefinitions section. Also, elements that don't have their row position explicitly set are assumed to have a Grid.Row value of 0 and are placed in the first row. The same holds true for elements that don't supply a Grid.Column value.

This markup includes one additional detail. When the GridSplitter is declared, the ShowsPreview property is set to false (which is the default value). As a result, when the splitter bar is dragged from one side to another, the columns are resized immediately. But if you set ShowsPreview to true, when you drag you'll see a gray shadow follow your mouse pointer to show you where the split will be. The columns won't be resized until you release the mouse button. You can also change the fill that's used for the GridSplitter so that it isn't just a shaded gray rectangle. The trick is to set the Background property.

A Grid usually contains no more than a single GridSplitter. However, you can nest one Grid inside another, and if you do, each Grid may have its own GridSplitter. This allows you to create a page that's split into two regions (for example, a left and right pane), and then further subdivide one of these regions (say, the pane on the right) into more sections (such as a resizable top and bottom portion). Figure 3-12 shows an example.

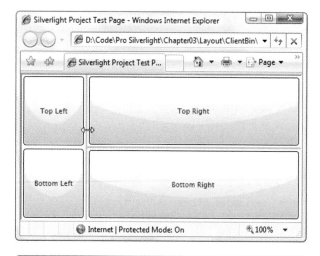

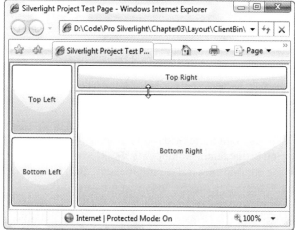

Figure 3-12. *Resizing a window with two splits*

Creating this page is fairly straightforward, although it's a chore to keep track of the three Grid containers that are involved: the overall Grid, the nested Grid on the left, and the nested Grid on the right. The only trick is to make sure the GridSplitter is placed in the correct cell and given the correct alignment. Here's the complete markup:

```
<!-- This is the Grid for the entire page. -->
<Grid Background="White">
  <Grid.ColumnDefinitions>
    <ColumnDefinition></ColumnDefinition>
    <ColumnDefinition Width="Auto"></ColumnDefinition>
    <ColumnDefinition></ColumnDefinition>
  </Grid.ColumnDefinitions>
```

```
<!-- This is the nested Grid on the left.
     It isn't subdivided further with a splitter. -->
<Grid Grid.Column="0" VerticalAlignment="Stretch">
  <Grid.RowDefinitions>
    <RowDefinition></RowDefinition>
    <RowDefinition></RowDefinition>
  </Grid.RowDefinitions>
  <Button Margin="3" Grid.Row="0" Content="Top Left"></Button>
  <Button Margin="3" Grid.Row="1" Content="Bottom Left"></Button>
</Grid>

<!-- This is the vertical splitter that sits between the two nested
     (left and right) grids. -->
<basics:GridSplitter Grid.Column="1" Background="LightGray"
 Width="3" HorizontalAlignment="Center" VerticalAlignment="Stretch">
</basics:GridSplitter>

<!-- This is the nested Grid on the right. -->
<Grid Grid.Column="2">
  <Grid.RowDefinitions>
    <RowDefinition></RowDefinition>
    <RowDefinition Height="Auto"></RowDefinition>
    <RowDefinition></RowDefinition>
  </Grid.RowDefinitions>

  <Button Grid.Row="0" Margin="3" Content="Top Right"></Button>
  <Button Grid.Row="2" Margin="3" Content="Bottom Right"></Button>

  <!-- This is the horizontal splitter that subdivides it into
       a top and bottom region.. -->
  <basics:GridSplitter Grid.Row="1" Background="LightGray"
   Height="3" VerticalAlignment="Center" HorizontalAlignment="Stretch"
   ShowsPreview="False"></basics:GridSplitter>
</Grid>
</Grid>
```

Coordinate-Based Layout with the Canvas

The only layout container you haven't considered yet is the Canvas. It allows you to place elements using exact coordinates, which is a poor choice for designing rich data-driven forms and standard dialog boxes, but a valuable tool if you need to build something a little different (such as a drawing surface for a diagramming tool). The Canvas is also the most lightweight of the layout containers. That's because it doesn't include any complex layout logic to negotiate the sizing preferences of its children. Instead, it simply lays them all out at the position they specify, with the exact size they want.

To position an element on the Canvas, you set the attached Canvas.Left and Canvas.Top properties. Canvas.Left sets the number of pixels between the left edge of your element and the left edge of the Canvas. Canvas.Top sets the number of pixels between the top of your element and the top of the Canvas.

Optionally, you can size your element explicitly using its Width and Height properties. This is more common when using the Canvas than it is in other panels because the Canvas has no layout logic of its own. (And often, you'll use the Canvas when you need precise control over how a combination of elements is arranged.) If you don't set the Width and Height properties, your element will get its desired size—in other words, it will grow just large enough to fit its content. If you change the size of the Canvas, it has no effect on the Controls inside.

Here's a simple Canvas that includes four buttons:

```
<Canvas Background="White">
  <Button Canvas.Left="10" Canvas.Top="10" Content="(10,10)"></Button>
  <Button Canvas.Left="120" Canvas.Top="30" Content="(120,30)"></Button>
  <Button Canvas.Left="60" Canvas.Top="80" Width="50" Height="50"
  Content="(60,80)"></Button>
  <Button Canvas.Left="70" Canvas.Top="120" Width="100" Height="50"
  Content="(70,120)"></Button>
</Canvas>
```

Figure 3-13 shows the result.

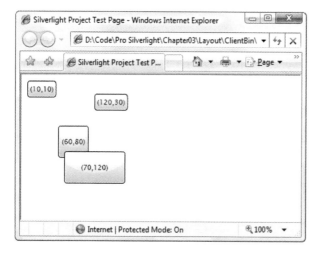

Figure 3-13. *Explicitly positioned buttons in a Canvas*

Like any other layout container, the Canvas can be nested inside a user interface. That means you can use the Canvas to draw some detailed content in a portion of your page, while using more standard Silverlight panels for the rest of your elements.

Layering with ZIndex

If you have more than one overlapping element, you can set the attached Canvas.ZIndex property to control how they are layered.

Ordinarily, all the elements you add have the same ZIndex—0. When elements have the same ZIndex, they're displayed in the same order that they exist in the Canvas.Children collection, which is based on the order that they're defined in the XAML markup. Elements declared later in the markup—such as button (70,120)—are displayed overtop of elements that are declared earlier—such as button (120,30).

However, you can promote any element to a higher level by increasing its ZIndex. That's because higher ZIndex elements *always* appear over lower ZIndex elements. Using this technique, you could reverse the layering in the previous example:

```
<Button Canvas.Left="60" Canvas.Top="80" Canvas.ZIndex="1" Width="50" Height="50"
  Content="(60,80)"></Button>
<Button Canvas.Left="70" Canvas.Top="120" Width="100" Height="50"
  Content="(70,120)"></Button>
```

Note The actual values you use for the Canvas.ZIndex property have no meaning. The important detail is how the ZIndex value of one element compares to the ZIndex value of another. You can set the ZIndex using any positive or negative integer.

The ZIndex property is particularly useful if you need to change the position of an element programmatically. Just call Canvas.SetZIndex() and pass in the element you want to modify and the new ZIndex you want to apply. Unfortunately, there is no BringToFront() or SendToBack() method—it's up to you to keep track of the highest and lowest ZIndex values if you want to implement this behavior.

Clipping

There's one aspect of the Canvas that's counterintuitive. In most layout containers, the contents are limited to the space that's available in that container. For example, if you create a StackPanel with a height of 100 pixels and place a tall column of buttons inside, those that don't fit will be chopped off the bottom. However, the Canvas doesn't follow this common-sense rule. Instead, it draws all its children, even if they fall outside its bounds. That means you could replace the earlier example with a Canvas that has a 0-pixel height and a 0-pixel width, and the result wouldn't change.

The Canvas works this way for performance reasons—quite simply, it's more efficient for the Canvas to draw all its children then check whether each one falls insides its bounds. However, this isn't always the behavior you want. For example, Chapter 9 includes an animated game that sends bombs flying off the edge of the playing area, which is a Canvas. In this situation, the bombs must only be visible inside the Canvas—when they leave, they should disappear under the Canvas border, not drift overtop of other elements.

Fortunately, the Canvas has support for *clipping*, which ensures that elements (or the portions of an element) that aren't inside a specified area are cut off, in much the same way as elements that extend beyond the edges of a StackPanel or Grid. The only inconvenience is that you need to set the shape of the clipping area manually using the Canvas.Clip property.

Technically, the Clip property takes a Geometry object, which is a useful object you'll consider in more detail when you tackle drawing in Chapter 7. Silverlight has different Geometry-derived classes for different types of shapes, including squares and rectangles (RectangleGeometry), circles and ellipses (EllipseGeometry), and more complex shapes (PathGeometry). Here's an example that sets the clipping region to a rectangular area that matches the bounds of the Canvas:

```
<Canvas x:Name="canvas" Width="200" Height="500" Background="AliceBlue">
  <Canvas.Clip>
    <RectangleGeometry Rect="0,0 200,500"></RectangleGeometry>
  </Canvas.Clip>
  ...
<Canvas>
```

In this example, the clipping region can be described as a rectangle with its top left at point (0, 0) and its bottom corner at point (200, 500). These coordinates are relative to the Canvas itself, so you must always have a top-left corner of (0,0) unless you want to leave out some of the content in the upper or left region of the Canvas.

Setting the clipping region in markup isn't always the best approach. It's particularly problematic if your Canvas is sized dynamically to fit a resizable container or the browser window. In this situation, it's far more effective to set the clipping region programmatically. Fortunately, all you need is a simple event handler that changes the clipping region when the Canvas is resized:

```
private void canva_SizeChanged(object sender, SizeChangedEventArgs e)
{
    RectangleGeometry rect = new RectangleGeometry();
    rect.Rect = new Rect(0, 0, canvas.ActualWidth, canvas.ActualHeight);
    canvasBackground.Clip = rect;
}
```

You can attach that event handler like so:

```
<Canvas x:Name="canvas" SizeChanged="canvas_SizeChanged" Background="AliceBlue">
```

You'll see this technique in action with the bomb-dropping game in Chapter 9.

CHOOSING THE RIGHT LAYOUT CONTAINER

As a general rule of thumb, the Grid and StackPanel are best when dealing with business-style applications (for example, when displaying data entry forms or documents). They deal well with changing window sizes and dynamic content (for example, blocks of text that can grow or shrink depending on the information at hand). They also make it easier to modify, localize, and re-skin the application, because adjacent elements will bump each other out of the way as they change size. The Grid and StackPanel are also closest to the way ordinary HTML pages work.

The Canvas is dramatically different. Because all of its children are arranged using fixed coordinates, you need to go to more work to position them (and even more work if you want to tweak the layout later on in response to new elements or new formatting.) However, the Canvas makes sense in certain types of graphically rich applications, such as games. In these applications, you need fine-grained control, text and graphics often overlap, and you often change coordinates programmatically. Here, the emphasis isn't on flexibility, but on achieving a specific visual appearance, and the Canvas makes more sense.

Custom Layout Containers

If you've programmed with WPF before, you've probably noticed that Silverlight includes fewer layout containers. Although it includes the commonly used StackPanel and the all-purpose Grid, it lacks a few more specialized containers such as the WrapPanel, DockPanel, and UniformGrid. It's not that these containers aren't possible—it's that they just aren't important enough. The developers of Silverlight left them out to keep the size of the Silverlight download as small as possible.

However, there's no reason you can't re-create some of the more specialized layout containers that exist in the WPF world. You simply need to derive a custom class from Panel and supply the appropriate layout logic. In the following sections, you'll see how to build a custom layout container that wraps elements over multiple lines. However, if you're ambitious, you can combine the layout logic of a panel with other Silverlight features. For example, you can create a panel that handles mouse-over events to provide automatic drag support for the elements inside (like the circling dragging example shown in Chapter 4), or you can create a panel that displays its children with an animated effect.

The Two-Step Layout Process

Every panel uses the same plumbing: a two-step process that's responsible for sizing and arranging children. The first stage is the *measure* pass, and it's at this point that the panel determines how large its children want to be. The second stage is the *layout* pass, and it's at this point that each control is assigned its bounds. Two steps are required because the panel might need to take into account the desires of all its children before it decides how to partition the available space.

You add the logic for these two steps by overriding the oddly named MeasureOverride() and ArrangeOverride() methods, which are defined in the FrameworkElement class as part of the Silverlight layout system. The odd names represent that the MeasureOverride() and ArrangeOverride() methods replace the logic that's defined in the MeasureCore() and ArrangeCore() methods that are defined in the UIElement class. These methods are *not* overridable.

MeasureOverride()

The first step is to determine how much space each child wants using the MeasureOverride() method. However, even in the MeasureOverride() method, children aren't given unlimited room. At a bare minimum, children are confined to fit in the space that's available to the panel. Optionally, you might want to limit them more stringently. For example, a Grid with two proportionally sized rows will give children half the available height. A StackPanel will offer the first element all the space that's available, and then offer the second element whatever's left, and so on.

Every MeasureOverride() implementation is responsible for looping through the collection of children and calling the Measure() method of each one. When you call the Measure() method, you supply the bounding box—a Size object that determines the maximum available space for the child control. At the end of the MeasureOverride() method, the panel returns the space it needs to display all its children and their desired sizes.

Here's the basic structure of the MeasureOverride() method, without the specific sizing details:

```
protected override Size MeasureOverride(Size constraint)
{
    // Examine all the children.
    foreach (UIElement element in this.Children)
    {
        // Ask each child how much space it would like, given the
        // availableSize constraint.
        Size availableSize = new Size(...);
        element.Measure(availableSize);
        // (You can now read element.DesiredSize to get the requested size.)
    }

    // Indicate how much space this panel requires.
    // This will be used to set the DesiredSize property of the panel.
    return new Size(...);
}
```

The Measure() method doesn't return a value. After you call Measure() on a child, that child's DesiredSize property provides the requested size. You can use this information in your calculations for future children (and to determine the total space required for the panel).

You *must* call Measure() on each child, even if you don't want to constrain the child's size or use the DesiredSize property. Many elements will not render themselves until you've called Measure(). If you want to give a child free rein to take all the space it wants, pass a Size object with a value of Double.PositiveInfinity for both dimensions. (The ScrollViewer is one element that uses this strategy, because it can handle any amount of content.) The child will then return the space it needs for all its content. Otherwise, the child will normally return the space it needs for its content or the space that's available—whichever is smaller.

At the end of the measuring process, the layout container must return its desired size. In a simple panel, you might calculate the panel's desired size by combining the desired size of every child.

> **Note** You can't simply return the constraint that's passed to the MeasureOverride() method for the desired size of your panel. Although this seems like a good way to take all the available size, it runs into trouble if the container passes in a Size object with Double.PositiveInfinity for one or both dimensions (which means "take all the space you want"). Although an infinite size is allowed as a sizing constraint, it's not allowed as a sizing result, because Silverlight won't be able to figure out how large your element should be. Furthermore, you really shouldn't take more space than you need. Doing so can cause extra whitespace and force elements that occur after your layout panel to be bumped farther down the window.

Attentive readers may have noticed that there's a close similarity between the Measure() method that's called on each child and the MeasureOverride() method that defines the first step of the panel's layout logic. In fact, the Measure() method triggers the MeasureOverride() method. Thus, if you place one layout container inside another, when you call Measure(), you'll get the total size required for the layout container and all its children.

One reason the measuring process goes through two steps (a Measure() method that triggers the MeasureOverride() method) is to deal with margins. When you call Measure(), you pass in the total available space. When Silverlight calls the MeasureOverride() method, it automatically reduces the available space to take margin space into account (unless you've passed in an infinite size).

ArrangeOverride()

Once every element has been measured, it's time to lay them out in the space that's available. The layout system calls the ArrangeOverride() method of your panel, and the panel calls the Arrange() method of each child to tell it how much space it's been allotted. (As you can probably guess, the Arrange() method triggers the ArrangeOverride() method, much as the Measure() method triggers the MeasureOverride() method.)

When measuring items with the Measure() method, you pass in a Size object that defines the bounds of the available space. When placing an item with the Arrange() method, you pass in a System.Windows.Rect object that defines the size *and* position of the item. At this point, it's as though every element is placed with Canvas-style X and Y coordinates that determine the distance between the top-left corner of your layout container and the element.

Here's the basic structure of the ArrangeOverride() method, without the specific sizing details:

```
protected override Size ArrangeOverride(Size arrangeSize)
{
    // Examine all the children.
    foreach (UIElement element in this.Children)
    {
        // Assign the child its bounds.
        Rect bounds = new Rect(...);
        element.Arrange(bounds);
        // (You can now read element.ActualHeight and element.ActualWidth
        //  to find out the size it used.)
    }
```

```
        // Indicate how much space this panel occupies.
        // This will be used to set the ActualHeight and ActualWidth properties
        // of the panel.
        return arrangeSize;
}
```

When arranging elements, you can't pass infinite sizes. However, you can give an element its desired size by passing in the value from its DesiredSize property. You can also give an element *more* space than it requires. In fact, this happens frequently. For example, a vertical StackPanel gives a child as much height as it requests but gives it the full width of the panel itself. Similarly, a Grid might use fixed or proportionally sized rows that are larger than the desired size of the element inside. And even if you've placed an element in a size-to-content container, that element can still be enlarged if an explicit size has been set using the Height and Width properties.

When an element is made larger than its desired size, the HorizontalAlignment and VerticalAlignment properties come into play. The element content is placed somewhere inside the bounds that it has been given.

Because the ArrangeOverride() method always receives a defined size (not an infinite size), you can return the Size object that's passed in to set the final size of your panel. In fact, many layout containers take this step to occupy all the space that's been given. (You aren't in danger of taking up space that could be needed for another control, because the measure step of the layout system ensures that you won't be given more space than you need unless that space is available.)

A Wrapping Panel

Now that you've examined the panel system in a fair bit of detail, it's worth creating your own layout container that adds something you can't get with the basic set of Silverlight panels. In this section, you'll see an example straight from the WPF world: a WrapPanel that allows you to flow elements over multiple lines, much like an HTML document in a browser.

```
public class WrapPanel : System.Windows.Controls.Panel
{ ... }
```

Conceptually, the WrapPanel is quite simple. It lays out its children one after the other, moving to the next line once the width in the current line is used up. The WrapPanel is occasionally useful for displaying a long list of items. (For example, you could tile images like a picture browsing tool.) The WrapPanel is also useful when dealing with dynamic content, because it will seamlessly reflow its content to fit the available space when an element is hidden or removed.

The MeasureOverride() method of the WrapPanel needs to lay its contents out on an imaginary surface in order to calculate the panel's final size. The first step is to walk through the collection of items, measuring each one:

```
protected override Size MeasureOverride(Size constraint)
{
    Size currentLineSize = new Size();
    Size panelSize = new Size();

    // Examine all the elements in this panel.
    foreach (UIElement element in this.Children)
    {
        // Get the desired size of the element.
        element.Measure(constraint);
        Size desiredSize = element.DesiredSize;
        ...
```

Then, the code checks if the item can fit on the current line. If it doesn't fit, the panel moves to the next line. If it does fit, the panel bumps right to the next free space in the line:

```
        ...
        if (currentLineSize.Width + desiredSize.Width > constraint.Width)
        {
            // Switch to a new line because space has run out.
            panelSize.Height += currentLineSize.Height;
            panelSize.Width = Math.Max(currentLineSize.Width, panelSize.Width);
            currentLineSize = desiredSize;

            // If the element is too wide to fit using the maximum width of
            // the line, just give it a separate line.
            if (desiredSize.Width > constraint.Width)
            {
                // Make the width of the element the new desired width.
                panelSize.Width = Math.Max(desiredSize.Width, panelSize.Width);
            }
        }
        else
        {
            // Add the element to the current line.
            currentLineSize.Width += desiredSize.Width;

            // Make sure the line is as tall as its tallest element.
            currentLineSize.Height = Math.Max(desiredSize.Height,
              currentLineSize.Height);
        }
    }
    ...
```

Finally, the MeasureOverride() method returns the final calculated size. Ordinarily, the final size is a region that has the width of the constraint, and the height that's required to fit all the elements. However, if the panel contains an element that's wider than the constraint width, the panel will use the width of that element as the desired width.

```
    ...
    panelSize.Width = Math.Max(currentLineSize.Width, panelSize.Width);
    panelSize.Height += currentLineSize.Height;
    return panelSize;
}
```

The ArrangeOverride() code has a similar task. However, it's no longer measuring the children. Instead, it's taking note of their desired sizes and physically placing them in the correct position using the Arrange() method.

```
protected override Size ArrangeOverride(Size arrangeBounds)
{
    Size currentLineSize = new Size();
    double totalHeight = 0;

    // Examine all the elements in this panel.
    foreach (UIElement element in this.Children)
    {
        Size desiredSize = element.DesiredSize;

        if (currentLineSize.Width + desiredSize.Width > arrangeBounds.Width)
        {
            // Switch to a new line because space has run out.
            totalHeight += currentLineSize.Height;
            currentLineSize = new Size();
        }

        // Make sure the line is as tall as its tallest element.
        currentLineSize.Height = Math.Max(desiredSize.Height,
          currentLineSize.Height);

        // Place the element on the line, giving it its desired size.
        element.Arrange(new Rect(currentLineSize.Width, totalHeight,
        element.DesiredSize.Width, element.DesiredSize.Height));

        // Move over for the next element.
        currentLineSize.Width += desiredSize.Width;
    }
```

```
    // Return the size this panel actually occupies.
    totalHeight += currentLineSize.Height;
    return new Size(arrangeBounds.Width, totalHeight);
}
```

In this example, the ArrangeOverride() method gives each element its desired size. However, there are other possibilities. If a line is taller than an element's desired size (because it contains another taller element somewhere on the line), you can choose to give the extra space to every element on the line. In the downloadable code for this chapter, there's an alternate implementation of the WrapPanel that does exactly that. Alternatively, you could read the element's VerticalAlignment property and use that to place the element when there's extra space available.

Using the WrapPanel is easy. You simply need to map the namespace in your XAML markup and then define the WrapPanel in the same way you define any other layout container. Here's an example that places the WrapPanel in a StackPanel with some text content. This allows you to verify that the size of the WrapPanel is correctly calculated, and the content that follows it is bumped out of the way:

```
<UserControl x:Class="Layout.WrapPanelTest"
 xmlns="http://schemas.microsoft.com/winfx/2006/xaml/presentation"
 xmlns:x="http://schemas.microsoft.com/winfx/2006/xaml"
 xmlns:local="clr-namespace:Layout" >
  <StackPanel Background="White">
    <TextBlock Margin="5" Text="Content above the WrapPanel."></TextBlock>

    <local:WrapPanel Margin="5" Background="LawnGreen">
      <Button Width="50" Content="Button"></Button>
      <Button Width="150" Content="Wide Button"></Button>
      <TextBlock Margin="5" Text="Text in the WrapPanel"></TextBlock>
      <Button Width="100" Height="50" Content="Tall Button"></Button>
      <Button Width="50" Content="Button"></Button>
      <Button Width="150" Content="Wide Button"></Button>
      <Button Width="50" Content="Button"></Button>
    </local:WrapPanel>
    <TextBlock Margin="5" Text="Content below the WrapPanel."></TextBlock>
  </StackPanel>
</UserControl>
```

Figure 3-14 shows how this markup is displayed at two different window sizes.

Figure 3-14. *The WrapPanel*

Sizing Pages

So far, you've taken an extensive look at the different layout containers Silverlight offers, and how you can use them to arrange groups of elements. However, there's one important part of the equation that you haven't considered yet—the top-level page that holds your entire user interface.

As you've already seen, the top-level container for each Silverlight page is a custom class that derives from UserControl. The UserControl class adds a single property, named Content, to Silverlight's basic element infrastructure. The Content property accepts a single element, which becomes the content of that user control.

User controls don't include any special functionality—they're simply a convenient way to group together a block of related elements. However, the way you size your user control can affect the appearance of your entire user interface, so it's worth taking a closer look.

You've already seen how you can use different layout containers with a variety of layout properties to control whether your elements size to fit their content, the available space, or hard-coded dimensions. Many of the same options are available when you're sizing a page, including

- **Fixed size.** Set the Width and Height properties of the user control to give your page an exact size. If you have controls inside the page that exceed these dimensions, they will be truncated. When using a fixed-size window, it's common to change the Horizontal-Alignment and VerticalAlignment properties of the user control to Center, so it floats in the center of the browser window rather than being locked into the top-left corner.

- **Browser size.** Remove the Width and Height properties to let your page take the full space allocated to it in the Silverlight content region. By default, Visual Studio creates an entry page that sizes the Silverlight content region to take 100% of the browser window. If you use this approach, it's still possible to create elements that stretch off the bounds of the display region, but the user can now observe the problem and resize the browser window to see the missing content. If you want to preserve some blank space between your page and the browser window when using this approach, you can set the user control's Margin property.

- **Constrained size.** Remove the Width and Height properties but use the MaxWidth, MaxHeight, MinWidth, and MinHeight properties instead. Now the user control will resize itself to fit the browser windows within a sensible range, and it will stop resizing when the window reaches very large or very small dimensions, ensuring it's never scrambled beyond recognition.

- **Unlimited size.** In some cases it makes sense to let your Silverlight content region take more than the full browser window. In this situation, the browser will add scroll bars, much as it does with a long HTML page. To get this effect, you need to remove the Width and Height properties and edit the entry page (TestPage.html). In the entry page, remove the width="100%" and height="100%" attributes in the <object> element. This way, the Silverlight content region will be allowed to grow to fit the size of your user control.

All of these approaches are reasonable choices. It simply depends on the type of user interface that you're building. When you use a non-fixed-size page, your application can take advantage of the extra space in the browser window by reflowing its layout to fit. The disadvantage is that extremely large or small windows may make your content more difficult to read or use. You can design for these issues, but it takes more work. On the other hand, the disadvantage of hard-coded sizes it that your application will be forever locked in a specific window size no matter what the browser window looks like. This can lead to oceans of empty space (if you've hard-coded a size that's smaller than the browser window) or make the application unusable (if you've hard-coded a size that's bigger than the browser window).

As a general rule of thumb, resizable pages are more flexible and preferred where possible. They're usually the best choice for business applications and applications with a more traditional user interface that isn't too heavy on the graphics. On the other hand, graphically rich applications and games often need more precise control over what's taking place in the page, and are more likely to use fixed page sizes.

Tip If you're testing out different approaches, it helps to make the bounds of the page more obvious. One easy way to do so is to apply a non-white background to the top-level content element. (For example, setting the Background property of a Grid to Yellow.) You can't set the Background property on the user control itself, because the UserControl class doesn't provide it. Another option is to use a Border element as your top-level element, which allows you to outline the page region.

There are also a few more specialized sizing options that you'll learn about in the following sections: scrollable interfaces, scalable interfaces, and full-screen interfaces.

Scrolling

None of the containers you've seen have provided support for *scrolling*, which is a key feature for fitting large amounts of content in a limited amount of space. In Silverlight, scrolling support is easy to get, but it requires another ingredient—the ScrollViewer content control.

In order to get scrolling support, you need to wrap the content you want to scroll inside a ScrollViewer. Although the ScrollViewer can hold anything, you'll typically use it to wrap a layout container. For example, here's a two-column grid of text boxes and buttons that's made scrollable. The page is sized to the full browser area, but it adds a margin to help distinguish the scroll bar from the browser window that surrounds it.

```
<UserControl x:Class="Layout.Scrolling"
 xmlns="http://schemas.microsoft.com/client/2007"
 xmlns:x="http://schemas.microsoft.com/winfx/2006/xaml"
 Margin="20">
  <ScrollViewer Background="AliceBlue">
    <Grid Margin="3,3,10,3">
      <Grid.RowDefinitions>
        <RowDefinition Height="Auto"></RowDefinition>
        ...
      </Grid.RowDefinitions>
      <Grid.ColumnDefinitions>
        <ColumnDefinition Width="*"></ColumnDefinition>
        <ColumnDefinition Width="Auto"></ColumnDefinition>
      </Grid.ColumnDefinitions>

      <TextBox Grid.Row="0" Grid.Column="0" Margin="3"
       Height="Auto" VerticalAlignment="Center"></TextBox>
      <Button Grid.Row="0" Grid.Column="1" Margin="3" Padding="2"
       Content="Browse"></Button>
      ...
    </Grid>
  </ScrollViewer>
</UserControl>
```

The result is shown in Figure 3-15.

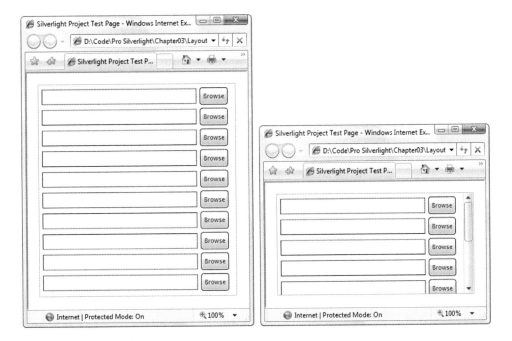

Figure 3-15. *A scrollable page*

If you resize the page in this example so that it's large enough to fit all its content, the scroll bar becomes disabled. However, the scroll bar will still be visible. You can control this behavior by setting the VerticalScrollBarVisibility property, which takes a value from the ScrollBarVisibility enumeration. The default value of Visible makes sure the vertical scroll bar is always present. Use Auto if you want the scroll bar to appear when it's needed and disappear when it's not. Or use Disabled if you don't want the scroll bar to appear at all.

■**Note** You can also use Hidden, which is similar to Disabled but subtly different. First, content with a hidden scroll bar is still scrollable. (For example, you can scroll through the content using the arrow keys.) Second, the content in a ScrollViewer is laid out differently. When you use Disabled, you tell the content in the ScrollViewer that it has only as much space as the ScrollViewer itself. On the other hand, if you use Hidden you tell the content that it has an infinite amount of space. That means it can overflow and stretch off into the scrollable region.

The ScrollViewer also supports horizontal scrolling. However, the HorizontalScrollBarVisibility property is Hidden by default. To use horizontal scrolling, you need to change this value to Visible or Auto.

Scaling

Earlier in this chapter, you saw how the Grid can use proportional sizing to make sure your elements take all the available space. Thus, the Grid is a great tool for building resizable interfaces that grow and shrink to fit the browser window.

Although this resizing behavior is usually what you want, it isn't always suitable. Changing the dimensions of controls changes the amount of content they can accommodate, and can have subtle layout-shifting effects. In graphically rich applications, you might need more precise control to keep your elements perfectly aligned. However, that doesn't mean you need to use fixed-size pages. Instead, you can use another trick, called *scaling*.

Essentially, scaling resizes the entire visual appearance of the control, not just its outside bounds. No matter what the scale, a control can hold the same content—it just looks different. Conceptually, it's like changing the zoom level.

Figure 3-16 compares the difference. On the left is a window at its normal size. In the middle is the window enlarged, using traditional resizing. On the right is the same expanded window using scaling.

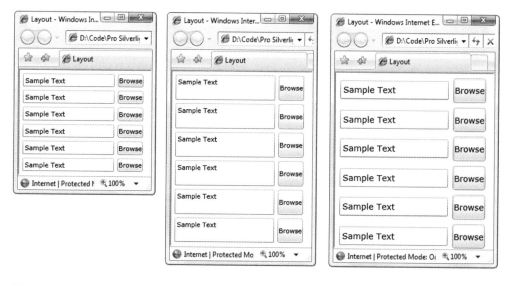

Figure 3-16. *Resizing (middle) versus rescaling (right)*

To use scaling, you need to use a *transform*. As you'll discover in Chapter 8, transforms are a key part of Silverlight's flexible 2-D drawing framework. They allow you to rescale, skew, rotate, and otherwise change the appearance of any element. In this example, you need the help of a ScaleTransform to change the scale of your page.

You apply a transform to an element by setting its RenderTransform property. When you transform an element, all its contained elements are also affected. Thus, the easiest way to ensure that you can change a large block of content is to change the RenderTransform of the top-level element—the UserControl.

Before you can write the rescaling code that you need, you need to make sure your markup is configured correctly. Here are a few rules you must follow to use this trick:

- Your user control can't be explicitly sized—instead, it needs to be able to grow to fill the browser window.

- In order to rescale a window to the right dimensions, you need to know its ideal size. These are the dimensions that exactly fit all of its content. Although these dimensions won't be set in your markup, they'll be used for the scaling calculations in your code.

- Your top-level container must be a Canvas. This lets you place your content precisely in the ideal, unscaled window. But just because you're using a canvas, it doesn't mean you're forced into the limiting world of fixed layout. There's no reason you can't fill your Canvas with an explicitly sized Grid or StackPanel layout container, which can then use the standard layout rules to arrange its child elements.

The following markup uses a Grid that has an ideal size of 200×225 pixels, and contains the stack of text boxes and buttons shown in Figure 3-16:

```
<UserControl x:Class="Layout.Page"
 xmlns="http://schemas.microsoft.com/client/2007"
 xmlns:x="http://schemas.microsoft.com/winfx/2006/xaml">

  <!-- This container is required for rescaling. -->
  <Canvas>
    <!-- This container is the layout root of your ordinary user interface. -->
    <Grid Canvas.Left="0" Canvas.Top="0"  Background="White"
     Width="200" Height="225" Margin="3,3,10,3">
      <Grid.RowDefinitions>

        ...
      </Grid.RowDefinitions>
      <Grid.ColumnDefinitions>
        <ColumnDefinition Width="*"></ColumnDefinition>
        <ColumnDefinition Width="Auto"></ColumnDefinition>
      </Grid.ColumnDefinitions>

      <TextBox Grid.Row="0" Grid.Column="0" Margin="3"
       Height="Auto" VerticalAlignment="Center" Text="Sample Text"></TextBox>
      <Button Grid.Row="0" Grid.Column="1" Margin="3" Padding="2"
       Content="Browse"></Button>

      ...

    </Grid>
  </Canvas>
</UserControl>
```

To implement the rescaling, you need to react to the UserControl.SizeChanged event. (Be careful—if you accidentally give the user control a hard-coded Width and Height, its size will never change, and the SizeChanged event won't fire.) You can attach the event handler you need in the constructor for your page:

```
public Page()
{
    InitializeComponent();
    this.SizeChanged += new SizeChangedEventHandler(Page_SizeChanged);
}
```

To change the scale of the page, you simply need to create a ScaleTransform object, set its X and Y scaling, and assign the ScaleTransform to the UserControl.RenderTransform property of your page.

The X and Y scaling factors are set by two properties of the ScaleTransform class, ScaleX and ScaleY. Both are ratios, so 1 is 100% scaling (no change), 0.5 is 50% scaling (which shrinks the page to half size), and 2 is 200% scaling (which expands the page to twice its normal size). To calculate the right scaling factors, you need to compare the current dimensions of the page (as reflected by the ActualWidth and ActualHeight properties of the user control) with the ideal page size (in this example, 200×225). Here's the code that does it:

```
private Size idealPageSize = new Size(200, 225);

private void Page_SizeChanged(object sender, SizeChangedEventArgs e)
{
    // Compare the current window to the ideal dimensions.
    double heightRatio = this.ActualHeight / idealPageSize.Height;
    double widthRatio = this.ActualWidth / idealPageSize.Width;

    // Create the transform.
    ScaleTransform scale = new ScaleTransform();

    // Determine the smallest dimension.
    // This preserves the aspect ratio.
    if (heightRatio < widthRatio)
    {
        scale.ScaleX = heightRatio;
        scale.ScaleY = heightRatio;
    }
    else
    {
        scale.ScaleX = widthRatio;
        scale.ScaleY = widthRatio;
    }

    // Apply the transform.
    this.RenderTransform = scale;
}
```

Although you calculate the X and Y scaling separately, you should only apply the smallest ratio. By doing so, you ensure that the rescaled page will always fit the window and never be skewed into a different aspect ratio. If the X and Y scaling factors don't match, your page will appear stretched in one direction.

Full Screen

Silverlight applications also have the capability to enter a full-screen mode, which allows them to break out of the browser window altogether. In full-screen mode, the Silverlight plug-in fills the whole display area, and is shown overtop of all other applications, including the browser.

Full-screen mode has some serious limitations:

- **You can only switch into full-screen mode when responding to a user input event.** In other words, you can switch into full-screen mode when the user clicks a button or hits a key. However, you can't switch into full-screen mode as soon as your application loads up. (If you attempt to do so, your code will simply be ignored.) This limitation is designed to prevent a Silverlight application from fooling a user into thinking it's actually another local application or a system window.

- **While in full-screen mode, keyboard access is limited.** Your code will still respond to the following keys: Tab, Enter, Home, End, Page Up, Page Down, Space, and the arrow keys. All other keys are ignored. This means that you can build a simple full-screen arcade game, but you can't use text boxes or other input controls. This limitation is designed to prevent password spoofing—for example, tricking the user into entering a password by mimicking a Windows dialog box.

Note Full-screen mode was primarily designed for showing video content in a large window. In Silverlight 1.0, full-screen mode does not allow any keyboard input. In Silverlight 2.0, select keys are allowed—just enough to build simple graphical applications (for example, a photo browser) and games. To handle key presses outside of an input control, you simply handle the standard KeyPress event. (For example, you can add a KeyPress event handler to your root layout container to capture every key press that takes place.) Chapter 4 has more information about keyboard handling.

Here's an event handler that responds to a button press by switching into full-screen mode:

```
private void Button_Click(object sender, RoutedEventArgs e)
{
    Application.Current.Host.Content.IsFullScreen = true;
}
```

When your application enters full-screen mode, it displays a message like the one shown in Figure 3-17. This message includes the Web domain where the application is situated. (If you're using an ASP.NET website and the built-in Visual Studio web server, you'll see the domain http://localhost. If you're hosting your application with an HTML test page that's stored on your hard drive, you'll see the domain file://.) The message also informs users that they can exit full-screen mode by pressing the Esc key, as shown in Figure 3-17. Alternatively, you can set the IsFullScreen property to false to exit full-screen mode.

Figure 3-17. *The full-screen mode message*

In order for your application to take advantage of full-screen mode, your top-level user control should not have a fixed Height or Width. That way, it can grow to fit the available space. You can also use the scaling technique described in the previous section to scale the elements in your application to larger sizes with a render transform when you enter full-screen mode.

Navigation

With the know-how you've picked up in this chapter, you're ready to create pages that use a variety of different layouts. However, there's still something missing—the ability to transition from one page to another. After all, traditional rich client applications are usually built around different windows that encapsulate distinct tasks.

The short answer is a bit disappointing. Surprisingly, Silverlight doesn't give you any built-in navigation capability. Although you can add multiple user controls to your project, there's no automated way to jump from one to another. Silverlight does include a HyperlinkButton control (which you'll consider in Chapter 5), but it's designed to navigate between HTML pages. In other words, when a user clicks a HyperlinkButton control, the current Silverlight application is abandoned and the browser requests a new URL. The new page may or may not have its own Silverlight application—but if it does, that application needs to be downloaded to the client and will start from scratch.

The lack of navigation in Silverlight is a clear drawback. However, there are several commonly used techniques to compensate for this limitation, as you'll see in the following sections.

> **Note** If you don't need the ability to show different pages, but you want to show some sort of title screen before your application gets under way, you may want to use the built-in splash screen feature that's discussed in Chapter 6.

Loading Child User Controls

One approach is to create a central page that acts as the main window for your application for its entire lifetime. However, this page can change itself by loading new user controls into its hierarchy of elements.

One example of this design is the menu page that's used for most of the sample projects that accompany this book. This page uses a Grid to divide itself into two main sections (separated by a horizontal grid splitter). At the top is a list of all the pages you can visit. When you select one of the times from this list, it's loaded into the larger content region underneath, as shown in Figure 3-18.

Figure 3-18. *A window that loads user controls dynamically*

Dynamically loading a user control is easy—you simply need to create an instance of the appropriate class and then add it to a suitable container, such as a Border, ScrollViewer, Stack-Panel, or Grid.

The example shown previously uses the Border element, which is a content control that adds the ability to paint a border around its edges using the BorderBrush and BorderThickness properties. Here's the markup (without the list of items in the ListBox):

```
<UserControl x:Class="Resources.MenuPage"
 xmlns="http://schemas.microsoft.com/client/2007"
 xmlns:x="http://schemas.microsoft.com/winfx/2006/xaml"
 xmlns:basics=
 "clr-namespace:System.Windows.Controls;assembly=System.Windows.Controls">
  <Grid x:Name="LayoutRoot" Background="White" Margin="5">
    <Grid.RowDefinitions>
      <RowDefinition Height="*"></RowDefinition>
      <RowDefinition Height="Auto"></RowDefinition>
      <RowDefinition Height="3*"></RowDefinition>
    </Grid.RowDefinitions>

    <ListBox SelectionChanged="lstPages_SelectionChanged">
      ...
    </ListBox>
```

```
    <basics:GridSplitter Grid.Row="1" Margin="0 3" HorizontalAlignment="Stretch"
    Height="2"></basics:GridSplitter>

    <Border Grid.Row="2" BorderBrush="SlateGray" BorderThickness="1"
    x:Name="borderPlaceholder" Background="AliceBlue"></Border>
  </Grid>
</UserControl>
```

In this example, the Border is named borderPlaceholder. Here's how you might display a new custom user control named Page2 in the borderPlaceholder region:

```
Page2 newPage = new Page2();
borderPlaceholder.Child = newPage;
```

If you're using a different container, you may need to set a different property instead. For example, Silverlight's layout panels can hold multiple controls, and so provide a Children collection. You need to clear this collection and then add the new control to it. Here's an example that duplicates the previous code, assuming you've replaced the Border with a single-celled Grid:

```
Page2 newPage = new Page2();
gridPlaceholder.Children.Clear();
gridPlaceholder.Children.Add(newPage);
```

If you create a Grid without declaring any rows or columns, the Grid will have a single proportionately sized cell that fits all the available space. Thus, adding a control to that Grid produces the same result as adding it to a Border.

The actual code that's used in the examples is a bit different, because it needs to work for all buttons. To determine which type of user control to create, the code examines the ListBox-Item that was just clicked. It then uses reflection to create the corresponding user control object:

```
private void lstPages_SelectionChanged(object sender, SelectionChangedEventArgs e)
{
    // Get the selected item.
    string newPageName = ((ListBoxItem)e.AddedItems[0]).Content.ToString();

    // Create an instance of the page named
    // by the current button.
    Type type = this.GetType();
    Assembly assembly = type.Assembly;
    UserControl newPage = (UserControl)assembly.CreateInstance(
      type.Namespace + "." + newPageName);

    // Show the page.
    pagePlaceholder.Child = newPage;
}
```

The process of *showing* the newly created user control—that is, setting the Border.Child property—is exactly the same.

The technique shown here is quite common, but it's not suited for all scenarios. Its key drawback is that it slots new content into an existing layout. In the previous example, that means the ListBox always remains fixed at the top of the page. This is handy if you're trying to create a toolbar that always remains accessible, but not as convenient if you want to switch to an entirely different task.

An alternative approach is to change the entire page from one control to another. The basic technique is to use a simple layout container as your application's root visual. You can then load user controls into the root visual when required, and unload them after. (The root visual itself can never be replaced once the application has started.) This useful technique is described in Chapter 6.

Hiding Elements

Out of the two patterns you've seen here, the first approach (creating a dynamic page that adds and removes subsections) is more commonly used than the second approach (removing all the content of a page and loading a different one). If you decide to create a dynamic page, it's important to realize that you aren't limited to adding and removing content. You can also temporarily hide it. The trick is to set the Visibility property, which is defined in the base UIElement class and inherited by all elements.

```
panel.Visibility = Visibility.Hidden;
```

The Visibility property uses an enumeration that provides just two values, Visible and Hidden. WPF included a third value, Collapsed, which is not supported in Silverlight. Although you can set the Visibility property of individual elements, usually you'll show and hide entire containers (Border, StackPanel, or Grid objects) at once.

When an element is hidden, it takes no space in the page and doesn't receive any input events. The rest of your interface will resize itself to fill the available space (unless you've positioned your other elements with fixed coordinates using a layout container like the Canvas).

Tip Many applications use panels that collapse or slide out of the way. To create this effect, you can combine this code with a dash of Silverlight animation. The animation will change the elements you want to hide—for example, shrinking, compressing, or moving it. You'll see how to use this technique in Chapter 9.

The Last Word

In this chapter, you took a detailed tour of the new Silverlight layout model and learned how to place elements in stacks, grids, and other arrangements. You built more complex layouts using nested combinations of the layout containers, and you threw the GridSplitter into the mix to make resizable split pages. You even considered how to build your own layout containers to get custom effects. Finally, you saw how to take control of the top-level user control that hosts your entire layout by resizing it, rescaling it, and changing it to show the content from different user controls.

■ ■ ■

CHAPTER 4

Dependency Properties and Routed Events

At this point, you're probably itching to dive into a realistic, practical example of Silverlight coding. But before you can get started, you need to understand a few more fundamentals. In this chapter, you'll get a whirlwind tour of two key Silverlight concepts: *dependency properties* and *routed events*.

Both of these concepts first appeared in Silverlight's big brother technology, WPF. They came as quite a surprise to most developers—after all, few expected a user interface technology to retool core parts of .NET's object abstraction. However, WPF's changes weren't designed to improve .NET but to support key WPF features. The new property model allowed WPF elements to plug into services such as data binding, animation, and styles. The new event model allowed WPF to adopt a layered content model (as described in the next chapter) without horribly complicating the task of responding to user actions like mouse clicks and key presses.

Silverlight borrows both concepts, albeit in a streamlined form. In this chapter, you'll see how they work.

■**Note** If you're an experienced WPF programmer, you're probably well versed in the intricacies of dependency properties and routed events, and you'll be able to quickly skim through this chapter. However, the Silverlight implementation of dependency properties and routed events is much simpler than that of WPF, because Silverlight is designed to be more compact, more streamlined, and more easily ported to different computing platforms. Dependency properties do not support the extensive metadata that WPF uses, and routed events are able to bubble but not tunnel—and even then, the bubbling only applies to a small set of built-in input events and is supported by just a few basic elements.

Dependency Properties

Essentially, a dependency property is a property that can be set directly (for example, by your code) or by one of Silverlight's services (such as data binding, styles, or animation). The key feature of this system is the way that these different property providers are *prioritized*. For example, an animation will take precedence over all other services while it's running. These overlapping factors make for a very flexible system. They also give dependency properties their name—in essence, a dependency property *depends* on multiple property providers, each with its own level of precedence.

Most of the properties that are exposed by Silverlight elements are dependency properties. For example, the Text property of the TextBlock, the Content property of the Button, and the Background property of the Grid—all of which you saw in the simple example in Chapter 1— are all dependency properties. This hints at an important principle of Silverlight dependency properties—they're designed to be consumed in the same way as normal properties. That's because the dependency properties in the Silverlight libraries are always wrapped by ordinary property definitions.

Although dependency features can be read and set in code like normal properties, they're implemented quite differently behind the scenes. The simple reason why is performance. If the designers of Silverlight simply added extra features on top of the .NET property system, they'd need to create a complex, bulky layer for your code to travel through. Ordinary properties could not support all the features of dependency properties without this extra overhead.

Tip As a general rule, you don't need to know that a property is a dependency property in order to use it. However, some Silverlight features are limited to dependency properties. Furthermore, you'll need to understand dependency properties in order to define them in your own classes.

Defining and Registering a Dependency Property

You'll spend much more time using dependency properties than creating them. However, there are still many reasons that you'll need to create your own dependency properties. Obviously, they're a key ingredient if you're designing a custom Silverlight element. They're also required in some cases if you want to add data binding, animation, or another Silverlight feature to a portion of code that wouldn't otherwise support it.

Creating a dependency property isn't difficult, but the syntax takes a little getting used to. It's thoroughly different than creating an ordinary .NET property.

The first step is to define an object that *represents* your property. This is an instance of the DependencyProperty class (which is found in the System.Windows namespace). The information about your property needs to be available all the time. For that reason, your Dependency-Property object must be defined as a static field in the associated class.

For example, consider the FrameworkElement class from which all Silverlight elements inherit. FrameworkElement defines a Margin dependency property that all elements share. It's defined like this:

```
public class FrameworkElement: UIElement
{
    public static readonly DependencyProperty MarginProperty;

    ...
}
```

By convention, the field that defines a dependency property has the name of the ordinary property, plus the word *Property* at the end. That way, you can separate the dependency property definition from the name of the actual property. The field is defined with the readonly keyword, which means it can only be set in the static constructor for the FrameworkElement.

Note Silverlight does not support WPF's system of property sharing—in other words, defining a dependency property in one class and reusing it in another. However, dependency properties follow the normal rules of inheritance, which means that a dependency property like Margin that's defined in the FrameworkElement class applies to all Silverlight elements, because all Silverlight elements derive from FrameworkElement.

Defining the DependencyProperty object is just the first step. In order for it to become usable, you need to register your dependency property with Silverlight. This step needs to be completed before any code uses the property, so it must be performed in a static constructor for the associated class.

Silverlight ensures that DependencyProperty objects can't be instantiated directly, because the DependencyObject class has no public constructor. Instead, a DependencyObject instance can be created only using the static DependencyProperty.Register() method. Silverlight also ensures that DependencyProperty objects can't be changed after they're created, because all DependencyProperty members are read-only. Instead, their values must be supplied as arguments to the Register() method.

The following code shows an example of how a DependencyPropery must be created. Here, the FrameworkElement class uses a static constructor to initialize the MarginProperty:

```
static FrameworkElement()
{
    MarginProperty = DependencyProperty.Register("Margin",
        typeof(Thickness), typeof(FrameworkElement), null);
    ...
}
```

The DependencyProperty.Register() method accepts the following arguments:

- The property name (Margin in this example).

- The data type used by the property (the Thickness structure in this example).

- The type that owns this property (the FrameworkElement class in this example).

- A PropertyMetadata object that provides additional information. Currently, Silverlight uses the PropertyMetadata to store just optional pieces of information: a default value for the property, and a callback that will be triggered when the property is changed. If you don't need to use either feature, supply a null value, as in this example.

Note To see a dependency property that uses the PropertyMetadata object to set a default value, refer to the WrapPanel example later in this chapter.

With these details in place, you're able to register a new dependency property so that it's available for use. However, whereas typical property procedures retrieve or set the value of a private field, the property procedures for a Silverlight property use the GetValue() and Set-Value() methods that are defined in the base DependencyObject class. Here's an example:

```
public Thickness Margin
{
    get { return (Thickness)GetValue(MarginProperty); }
    set { SetValue(MarginProperty, value); }
}
```

When you create the property wrapper, you should include nothing more than a call to SetValue() and a call to GetValue(), as in the previous example. You should *not* add any extra code to validate values, raise events, and so on. That's because other features in Silverlight may bypass the property wrapper and call SetValue() and GetValue() directly. (One example is when the Silverlight parser reads your XAML markup and uses it to initialize your user interface.)

You now have a fully functioning dependency property, which you can set just like any other .NET property using the property wrapper:

```
myElement.Margin = new Thickness(5);
```

There's one extra detail. Dependency properties follow strict rules of precedence to determine their current value. Even if you don't set a dependency property directly, it may already have a value—perhaps one that's applied by a binding or a style, or one that's inherited through the element tree. (You'll learn more about these rules of precedence a bit later in the next section.) However, as soon as you set the value directly, it overrides these other influences.

At some point later, you may want to remove your local value setting and let the property value be determined as though you never set it. Obviously, you can't accomplish this by setting a new value. Instead, you need to use another method that's inherited from Dependency-Object: the ClearValue() method. Here's how it works:

```
myElement.ClearValue(FrameworkElement.MarginProperty);
```

This tells Silverlight to treat the value as though you never set it.

Dynamic Value Resolution

As you've already learned, dependency properties depend on multiple different services, called property providers. To determine the current value of a property, Silverlight has to decide which one takes precedence. This process is called *dynamic value resolution*.

When evaluating a property, Silverlight considers the following factors, arranged from highest to lowest precedence:

1. **Animations.** If an animation is currently running, and that animation is changing the property value, Silverlight uses the animated value.

2. **Local value.** If you've explicitly set a value in XAML or in code, Silverlight uses the local value. Remember, you can set a value using the SetValue() method or the property wrapper. If you set a property using a data binding (Chapter 14) or a resource (Chapter 2), it's considered to be a locally set value.

3. **Styles.** Silverlight styles (Chapter 11) allow you to configure multiple controls with one rule. If you've set a style that applies to this control, it comes into play now.

4. **Property value inheritance.** Silverlight uses *property value inheritance* with a small set of control properties, including Foreground, FontFamily, FontSize, FontStretch, FontStyle, and FontWeight. That means if you set these properties in a higher level container (like a Button or a ContentControl), they cascade down to the contained content elements (like the TextBlock that actually holds the text inside).

Note The limitation with property value inheritance is that the container must provide the property you want to use. For example, you might want to specify a standard font for an entire page by setting the Font-Family property on the root Grid. However, this won't work because the Grid doesn't derive from Control, and so it doesn't provide the FontFamily property. (One solution is to wrap your elements in a ContentControl, which includes all the properties that use property value inheritance but has no built-in visual appearance.)

---

5. **Default value.** If no other property setter is at work, the dependency property gets its default value. The default value is set with the PropertyMetadata object when the dependency property is first created, as explained in the previous section.

One of the advantages of this system is that it's very economical. For example, if the value of a property has not been set locally, Silverlight will retrieve its value from the template or a style. In this case, no additional memory is required to store the value. Another advantage is that different property providers may override one another, but they don't *overwrite* each other. For example, if you set a local value and then trigger an animation, the animation temporarily takes control. However, your local value is retained and when the animation ends it comes back into effect.

Attached Properties

Chapter 2 introduced a special type of dependency property called an *attached property*. An attached property is a full-fledged dependency property and, like all dependency properties, it's managed by the Silverlight property system. The difference is that an attached property applies to a class other than the one where it's defined.

The most common example of attached properties is found in the layout containers you saw in Chapter 3. For example, the Grid class defines the attached properties Row and Column, which you set on the contained elements to indicate where they should be positioned.

Similarly, the Canvas defines the attached properties Left and Top that let you place elements using absolute coordinates.

To define an attached property, you use the DependencyProperty.RegisterAttached() method instead of Register(). Here's an example that registers the Grid.Row property:

```
Grid.RowProperty = DependencyProperty.RegisterAttached(
  "Row", typeof(int), typeof(Grid), null);
```

The properties are exactly the same for the RegisterAttached() method as they are for the Register() method.

When creating an attached property, you don't define the .NET property wrapper. That's because attached properties can be set on *any* dependency object. For example, the Grid.Row property may be set on a Grid object (if you have one Grid nested inside another) or on some other element. In fact, the Grid.Row property can be set on an element even if that element isn't in a Grid—and even if there isn't a single Grid object in your element tree.

Instead of using a .NET property wrapper, attached properties require a pair of static methods that can be called to set and get the property value. These methods use the familiar SetValue() and GetValue() methods (inherited from the DependencyObject class). The static methods should be named Set*PropertyName*() and Get*PropertyName*().

Here are the static methods that implement the Grid.Row attached property:

```
public static int GetRow(UIElement element)
{
    return (int)element.GetValue(Grid.RowProperty);
}

public static void SetRow(UIElement element, int value)
{
    element.SetValue(Grid.RowProperty, value);
}
```

And here's an example that positions an element in the first row of a Grid using code:

```
Grid.SetRow(txtElement, 0);
```

This sets the Grid.Row property to 0 on the txtElement object, which is a TextBox. Because Grid.Row is an attached property, Silverlight allows you to apply it to any other element.

The WrapPanel Example

Now that you understand the theory behind dependency properties, it's time to ground your knowledge in a realistic example. In Chapter 3, you saw how to create a custom layout container called the WrapPanel, which flows elements over multiple lines to fit the available space. By adding properties to the WrapPanel, you can customize the way it works. Because the WrapPanel is a Silverlight element, its properties should almost always be dependency properties, which gives them the flexibility to be used with other Silverlight features like data binding and animation.

For example, it makes sense to give the WrapPanel an orientation property like its distant relative, the StackPanel. That way, you could support displays that need to flow elements into multiple columns. Here's the code you need to add to the WrapPanel class to define an Orientation property that uses the data type System.Windows.Controls.Orientation:

```
public static readonly DependencyProperty OrientationProperty =
  DependencyProperty.Register("Orientation", typeof(Orientation),
  typeof(WrapPanel), new PropertyMetadata(Orientation.Horizontal));
```

This code uses one minor time-saver. Rather than define the DependencyProperty and register it with code in a static constructor, this definition takes care of the definition and registration (and the compiled code doesn't change). It also sets the default value to Orientation.Horizontal.

Next, you need to add the property wrapper, which is perfectly straightforward:

```
public Orientation Orientation
{
    get { return (Orientation)GetValue(OrientationProperty); }
    set { SetValue(OrientationProperty, value); }
}
```

Finally, you can add code to the WrapPanel that actually uses the Orientation property. In this case, you need code in the MeasureOverride() and ArrangeOverride() methods that performs the different types of layout:

```
protected override Size MeasureOverride(Size constraint)
{
    Size currentLineSize = new Size();
    Size panelSize = new Size();

    if (Orientation != Orientation.Horizontal)
    { ... }
    else
    { ... }
}
```

When using the WrapPanel in a Silverlight page, you can set the Orientation property as you set any other property:

```
<local:WrapPanel Margin="5" Orientation="Horizontal">
  ...
</local:WrapPanel>
```

A more interesting experiment is to create a version of the WrapPanel that uses an attached property. As you've already learned, attached properties are particularly useful in layout containers, because they allow children to pass along extra layout information (such as row positioning in the Grid or coordinates and layering in the Canvas).

With the WrapPanel, it would be useful for an element to be able to force a line break. That way, you can ensure that a specific element begins on a new line, no matter what width the WrapPanel has. To implement this, you can create an attached property named LineBreak-Before, as shown here:

```
public static DependencyProperty LineBreakBeforeProperty =
  DependencyProperty.RegisterAttached("LineBreakBefore", typeof(bool),
  typeof(WrapPanel), null);
```

To implement the LineBreakBefore property, you need to create the static get and set methods that call GetValue() and SetValue() on the element:

```
public static bool GetLineBreakBefore(UIElement element)
{
    return (bool)element.GetValue(LineBreakBeforeProperty);
}


public static void SetLineBreakBefore(UIElement element, bool value)
{
    element.SetValue(LineBreakBeforeProperty, value);
}
```

You can then modify the MeasureOverride() and ArrangeOverride() methods to check for forced breaks, as shown here:

```
// Check if the element fits in the line, or if a line break was requested.
if ((currentLineSize.Width + desiredSize.Width > constraint.Width) ||
  (WrapPanel.GetLineBreakBefore(element)))
{ ... }
```

To use this functionality, you simply need to add the LineBreakBefore property to an element, as shown here:

```
<local:WrapPanel Margin="5" Background="LawnGreen">
  <Button Width="50" Content="Button"></Button>
  <Button Width="150" Content="Wide Button"></Button>
  <Button Width="50" Content="Button"></Button>
  <Button Width="150" Content="Button with a Break"
   local:WrapPanel.LineBreakBefore="True" FontWeight="Bold"></Button>
  <Button Width="150" Content="Wide Button"></Button>
  <Button Width="50" Content="Button"></Button>
</local:WrapPanel>
```

Figure 4-1 shows the result.

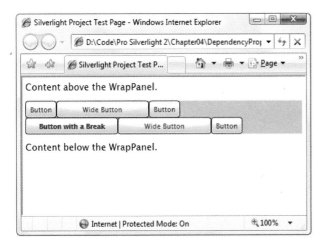

Figure 4-1. *A WrapPanel that supports forced line breaks*

Routed Events

Every .NET developer is familiar with the idea of *events*—messages that are sent by an object (such as a Silverlight element) to notify your code when something significant occurs. WPF enhanced the .NET event model with a new concept of *event routing*, which allows an event to originate in one element but be raised by another one. For example, event routing allows a click that begins in a shape to rise up to that shape's container and then to the containing page before it's handled by your code.

Silverlight borrows some of WPF's routed event model, but in a dramatically simplified form. While WPF supports several types of routed events, Silverlight only allows one: *bubbled events* that rise up the containment hierarchy from deeply nested elements to their containers. Furthermore, Silverlight's event bubbling is linked to a few keyboard and mouse input events (like MouseMove and KeyDown) and it's supported by just a few low-level elements. As you'll see, Silverlight doesn't use event bubbling for higher-level control events (like Click), and you can't use event routing with the events in your own custom controls.

The Core Element Events

Elements inherit their basic set of events from two core classes: UIElement and FrameworkElement. As Figure 4-2 shows, all Silverlight elements derive from these elements.

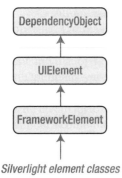

Silverlight element classes

Figure 4-2. *The hierarchy of Silverlight elements*

The UIElement class defines the most important events for handling user input and the only events that use event bubbling. Table 4-1 provides a list of all the UIElement events.

Table 4-1. *The UIElement Events*

Event	Bubbles	Description
KeyDown	Yes	Occurs when a key is pressed.
KeyUp	Yes	Occurs when a key is released.
GotFocus	Yes	Occurs when the focus changes to this element (when the user clicks it or tabs to it). The element that has focus is the control that will receive keyboard events first.
LostFocus	Yes	Occurs when the focus leaves this element.
MouseLeftButtonDown	Yes	Occurs when the left mouse button is pressed while the mouse pointer is positioned over the element. Silverlight does not provide events for other mouse events, like mouse wheeling scrolling or right-button clicking. (When the right mouse button is clicked over the Silverlight window, a Silverlight system menu pops up with one option: Silverlight Configuration.)
MouseLeftButtonUp	Yes	Occurs when a mouse button is released.
MouseEnter	No	Occurs when the mouse pointer first moves onto an element. This event doesn't bubble, but if you have several nested elements, they'll all fire MouseEnter events as you move to the most deeply nested element, passing over the bounding line that delineates the others.
MouseLeave	No	Occurs when the mouse pointer moves off of an element.
MouseMove	No	Occurs when the mouse moves while over an element. The MouseMove event is fired frequently—for example, if the user slowly moves the mouse pointer across the face of a button, you'll quickly receive hundreds of MouseMove events. For that reason, you shouldn't perform time-consuming tasks when reacting to this event.

In some cases, higher-level events may effectively replace some of the UIElement events. For example, the Button class provides a Click event that's triggered when the user presses and releases the mouse button, or when the button has focus and the user hits the space bar. Thus, when handling button clicks, you should always respond to the Click event, not MouseLeft-ButtonDown or MouseLeftButtonUp (which it suppresses). Similarly, the TextBox provides a TextChanged event which fires when the text is changed by any mechanism in addition to the basic KeyDown and KeyUp events.

The FrameworkElement class adds just a few more events to this model, as detailed in Table 4-2. None of these events use event bubbling.

Table 4-2. *The FrameworkElement Events*

Event	Description
Loaded	Occurs after an element has been created, configured, and arranged in the window for the first time. After this point, you may want to perform additional customization to the element in code.
SizeChanged	Occurs after the size of an element changes. As you saw in Chapter 3, you can react to this event to implement scaling.
LayoutUpdated	Occurs after the layout inside an element changes. For example, if you create a page that's uses no fixed size (and so fits the browser window), and you resize the browser window, the controls will be rearrange to fit the new dimensions, and the LayoutUpdated event will fire for your top-level layout container.
BindingValidationError	Occurs if a bound data object throws an exception when the user attempts to change a property. You'll learn how to use the Binding-ValidationError event to implement validation in Chapter 14.

Event Bubbling

Bubbling events are events that travel *up* the containment hierarchy. For example, MouseLeft-ButtonDown is a bubbling event. It's raised first by the element that is clicked. Next, it's raised by that element's parent, and then by *that* element's parent, and so on, until Silverlight reaches the top of the element tree.

Event bubbling is designed to support composition—in other words, to let you build more complex controls out of simpler ingredients. One example is Silverlight's *content controls*, which are controls that have the ability to hold a single nested element as content. (These controls are usually identified by the fact that they provide a property named Content.) For example, the button is a content control. Rather than displaying a line of text, you can fill it with a StackPanel that contains a whole group of elements, like this:

```
<Button BorderBrush="Black" BorderThickness="1" Click="cmd_Click">
  <StackPanel>
    <TextBlock Margin="3" Text="Image and text label"></TextBlock>
    <Image Source="happyface.jpg" Stretch="None"></Image>
    <TextBlock Margin="3" Text="Courtesy of the StackPanel"></TextBlock>
  </StackPanel>
</Button>
```

Here, the content element is a StackPanel that holds two pieces of text and an image. Figure 4-3 shows the fancy button that this markup creates.

Figure 4-3. *A button with contained elements*

In this situation, it's important that the button reacts to the mouse events of its contained elements. In other words, the Button.Click event should fire when the user clicks the image, some of the text, or part of the blank space inside the button border. In every case, you'd like to respond with the same code.

Of course, you could wire up the same event handler to the MouseLeftButtonDown or MouseLeftButtonUp event of each element inside the button, but that would result in a significant amount of clutter and it would make your markup more difficult to maintain. Event bubbling provides a better solution.

When the happy face is clicked, the MouseLeftButtonDown event fires first for the Image, then for the StackPanel, and then for the containing button. The button then reacts to the MouseLeftButtonDown by firing its own Click event, to which your code responds (with its cmd_Click event handler).

■**Note** The Button.Click event does not use event bubbling. This is a dramatic difference from WPF. In the world of Silverlight, only a small set of basic infrastructure events support event bubbling. Higher-level control events cannot use event bubbling. However, the button *uses* the bubbling nature of the MouseLeft-ButtonDown event to make sure it captures clicks on any contained elements.

Handled (Suppressed) Events

When the button in Figure 4-3 receives the MouseLeftButtonDown event, it takes an extra step and marks the event as *handled*. This prevents the event from bubbling up the control hierarchy any further. Most Silverlight controls use this handling technique to suppress MouseLeftButtonDown and MouseLeftButtonUp so they can replace them with more useful, higher-level events like Click.

However, there are a few elements that don't handle MouseLeftButtonDown and Mouse-LeftButtonUp:

- The Image class used to display bitmaps

- The TextBlock class used to show test

- The MediaElement class used to display video

- The shape classes used for 2D drawing (Line, Rectangle, Ellipse, Polygon, Polyline, Path)

- The layout containers used for arranging elements (Canvas, StackPanel, and Grid) and the Border class

These exceptions allow you to use these elements in content controls like the button without any limitations. For example, if you place a TextBlock in a button, when you click the TextBlock, the MouseLeftButtonUp event will bubble up to the button, which will then fire its Click event. However, if you take a control that isn't in the preceding list and place it inside the button—say, a list box, check box, or another button—you'll get different behavior. When you click that nested element, the MouseLeftButtonUp event won't bubble to the containing button, and the button won't register a click.

Note MouseLeftButtonDown and MouseLeftButtonUp are the only events that controls suppress. The bubbling key events (KeyUp, KeyDown, LostFocus, and GotFocus) aren't suppressed by any controls.

An Event Bubbling Example

To understand event bubbling and handled events, it helps to create a simple example, like the one shown in Figure 4-4. Here, as in the example you saw previously, the MouseLeft-ButtonDown event starts in a TextBlock or Image, and travels through the element hierarchy.

In this example, you can watch the MouseLeftButtonDown event bubble by attaching event handlers to multiple elements. As the event is intercepted at different levels, the event sequence is displayed in a list box. Figure 4-4 shows the display immediately after clicking the happy face image in the button. As you can see, the MouseLeftButtownDown event fires in the image, then in the containing StackPanel, and is finally intercepted by the button, which handles it. The button does not fire the MouseLeftButtonDown event, and therefore the MouseLeftButtonDown event does not bubble up to the Grid that holds the button.

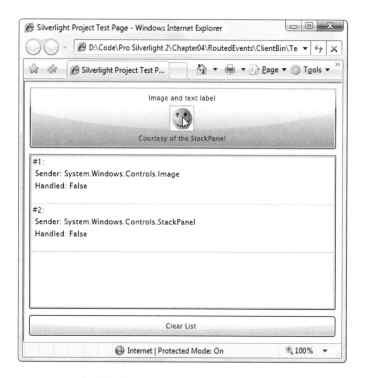

Figure 4-4. *A bubbled image click*

To create this test form, the image and every element above it in the element hierarchy are wired up to the same event handler—a method named SomethingClicked(). Here's the XAML that does it:

```
<UserControl x:Class="RoutedEvents.EventBubbling"
 xmlns="http://schemas.microsoft.com/client/2007"
 xmlns:x="http://schemas.microsoft.com/winfx/2006/xaml">

  <Grid Margin="3" MouseLeftButtonDown="SomethingClicked">
    <Grid.RowDefinitions>
      <RowDefinition Height="Auto"></RowDefinition>
      <RowDefinition Height="*"></RowDefinition>
      <RowDefinition Height="Auto"></RowDefinition>
      <RowDefinition Height="Auto"></RowDefinition>
    </Grid.RowDefinitions>

    <Button Margin="5" Grid.Row="0" MouseLeftButtonDown="SomethingClicked">
      <StackPanel MouseLeftButtonDown="SomethingClicked">
        <TextBlock Margin="3" MouseLeftButtonDown="SomethingClicked"
        HorizontalAlignment="Center" Text="Image and text label"></TextBlock>
        <Image Source="happyface.jpg" Stretch="None"
        MouseLeftButtonDown="SomethingClicked"></Image>
```

```
        <TextBlock Margin="3" HorizontalAlignment="Center"
          MouseLeftButtonDown="SomethingClicked"
          Text="Courtesy of the StackPanel"></TextBlock>
      </StackPanel>
    </Button>

    <ListBox Grid.Row="1" Margin="5" x:Name="lstMessages"></ListBox>

    <Button Grid.Row="3" Margin="5" Padding="3" x:Name="cmdClear"
      Click="cmdClear_Click" Content="Clear List"></Button>
  </Grid>
</UserControl>
```

The SomethingClicked() method simply examines the properties of the RoutedEventArgs object and adds a message to the list box:

```
protected int eventCounter = 0;

private void SomethingClicked(object sender, MouseButtonEventArgs e)
{
    eventCounter++;
    string message = "#" + eventCounter.ToString() + ":\r\n" +
      " Sender: " + sender.ToString() + "\r\n";
    lstMessages.Items.Add(message);
}

private void cmdClear_Click(object sender, RoutedEventArgs e)
{
    lstMessages.Items.Clear();
}
```

When dealing with a bubbled event like MouseLeftButtonDown, the sender parameter that's passed to your event handler always provides a reference to the last link in the chain. For example, if an event bubbles up from an image to a StackPanel before you handle it, the sender parameter references the StackPanel object.

In some cases, you'll want to determine where the event originally took place. The event arguments object for a bubbled event provides a Source property that tells you the specific element that originally raised the event. In the case of a keyboard event, this is the control that had focus when the event occurred (for example, when the key was pressed). In the case of a mouse event, this is the topmost element under the mouse pointer when the event occurred (for example, when a mouse button was clicked). However, the Source property can get a bit more detailed than you want—for example, if you click the blank space that forms the background of a button, the Source property will provide a reference to the Shape or Path object that actually draws the part of background you clicked.

Along with Source, the event arguments object for a bubbled event also provides a Boolean property named Handled, which allows you to suppress the event. For example, if you handle the MouseLeftButtonDown event in the StackPanel and set Handled to true, the StackPanel will not fire the MouseLeftButtonDown event. As a result, when you click the

StackPanel (or one of the elements inside), the MouseLeftButtonDown event will not reach the button, and the Click event will never fire. You can use this technique when building custom controls if you've taken care of a user action like a button click, and you don't want higher-level elements to get involved,

---

■**Note** WPF provides a back door that allows code to receive events that are marked handled (and would ordinarily be ignored). Silverlight does not provide this capability.

Mouse Movements

Along with the obvious mouse clicking events (MouseLeftButtonDown and MouseLeftButtonUp), Silverlight also provides mouse events that fire when the mouse pointer is moved. These events include MouseEnter (which fires when the mouse pointer moves over the element), MouseLeave (which fires when the mouse pointer moves away), and MouseMove (which fires at every point in between).

All of these events provide your code with the same information: a MouseEventArgs object. The MouseEventArgs object includes one important ingredient: a GetPosition() method that tells you the coordinates of the mouse in relation to an element of your choosing. Here's an example that displays the position of the mouse pointer:

```
private void MouseMoved(object sender, MouseEventArgs e)
{
    Point pt = e.GetPosition(this);
    lblInfo.Text =
        String.Format("You are at ({0},{1}) in page coordinates",
        pt.X, pt.Y);
}
```

In this case, the coordinates are measured from the top-left corner of the page area (just below the title bar of the browser).

■**Tip** In order to receive mouse events in a layout container, the Background property must be set to a non-null value—for example, a solid white fill.

Capturing the Mouse

Ordinarily, every time an element receives a mouse button "down" event, it will receive a corresponding mouse button "up" event shortly thereafter. However, this isn't always the case. For example, if you click an element, hold down the mouse, and then move the mouse pointer off the element, the element won't receive the mouse up event.

In some situations, you may want to have a notification of mouse up events, even if they occur after the mouse has moved off your element. To do so, you need to *capture* the mouse by calling the MouseCapture() method of the appropriate element. (MouseCapture() is defined by the base UIElement class, so it's supported by all Silverlight elements.) From that point on, your element will receive the MouseLeftButtonDown and MouseLeftButtonUp event until it loses the mouse capture. There are two ways to lose the mouse capture. First, you can give it up willingly by calling Mouse.Capture() again and passing in a null reference. Second, the user can click outside of your application—on another program, on the browser menu, on HTML content on the same web page.

While the mouse has been captured by an element, other elements won't receive mouse events. That means the user won't be able to click buttons elsewhere in the page, click inside text boxes, and so on. Mouse capturing is sometimes used to implement draggable and resizable elements.

A Mouse Event Example

You can put all these mouse input concepts together (and learn a bit about dynamic control creation) by reviewing a simple example.

Figure 4-5 shows a Silverlight application that allows you to draw small circles on a Canvas and move them around. Every time you click the Canvas, a red circle appears. To move a circle, you simply click and drag it to a new position. When you click a circle, it changes color from red to green. Finally, when you release your circle, it changes color to orange. There's no limit to how many circles you can add or how many times you can move them around your drawing surface.

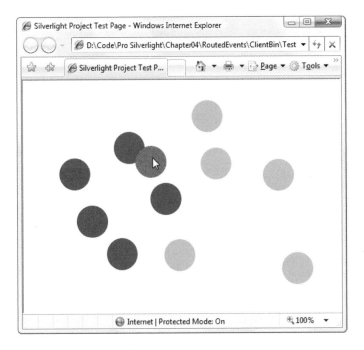

Figure 4-5. *Dragging shapes*

Each circle is an instance of the Ellipse element, which is simply a colored shape that's a basic ingredient in 2-D drawing. Obviously, you can't define all the ellipses you need in your XAML markup. Instead, you need a way to generate the Ellipse objects dynamically each time the user clicks the Canvas.

Creating an Ellipse object isn't terribly difficult—after all, you can instantiate it like any other .NET object, set its properties, and attach event handlers. You can even use the Set-Value() method to set attached properties to place it in the correct location in the Canvas. However, there's one more detail to take care of—you need a way to place the Ellipse in the Canvas. This is easy enough, as the Canvas class exposes a Children collection that holds all the child elements. Once you've added an element to this collection, it will appear in the Canvas.

The XAML page for this example uses a single event handler for the Canvas.MouseLeft-ButtonDown event. No other elements are defined.

```
<Canvas x:Name="parentCanvas" MouseLeftButtonDown="canvas_Click">
</Canvas>
```

In the code-behind class, you need two member variables to keep track of whether or not an ellipse-dragging operation is currently taking place:

```
// Keep track of when an ellipse is being dragged.
private bool isDragging = false;

// When an ellipse is clicked, record the exact position
// where the click is made.
private Point mouseOffset;
```

Here's the event-handling code that creates an ellipse when the Canvas is clicked:

```
private void canvas_Click(object sender, MouseButtonEventArgs e)
{
    // Create an ellipse (unless the user is in the process
    // of dragging another one).
    if (!isDragging)
    {
        // Give the ellipse a 50-pixel diameter and a red fill.
        Ellipse ellipse = new Ellipse();
        ellipse.Fill = new SolidColorBrush(Colors.Red);
        ellipse.Width = 50;
        ellipse.Height = 50;

        // Use the current mouse position for the center of
        // the ellipse.
        Point point = e.GetPosition(this);
        ellipse.SetValue(Canvas.TopProperty, point.Y - ellipse.Height/2);
        ellipse.SetValue(Canvas.LeftProperty, point.X - ellipse.Width/2);
```

```
        // Watch for left-button clicks.
        ellipse.MouseLeftButtonDown += ellipse_MouseDown;

        // Add the ellipse to the Canvas.
        parentCanvas.Children.Add(ellipse);
    }
}
```

Not only does this code create the ellipse, it also connects an event handler that responds when the ellipse is clicked. This event handler changes the ellipse color and initiates the ellipse-dragging operation:

```
private void ellipse_MouseDown(object sender, MouseButtonEventArgs e)
{
    // Dragging mode begins.
    isDragging = true;
    Ellipse ellipse = (Ellipse)sender;

    // Get the position of the click relative to the ellipse
    // so the top-left corner of the ellipse is (0,0).
    mouseOffset = e.GetPosition(ellipse);

    // Change the ellipse color.
    ellipse.Fill = new SolidColorBrush(Colors.Green);

    // Watch this ellipse for more mouse events.
    ellipse.MouseMove += ellipse_MouseMove;
    ellipse.MouseLeftButtonUp += ellipse_MouseUp;

    // Capture the mouse. This way you'll keep receiving
    // the MouseMove event even if the user jerks the mouse
    // off the ellipse.
    ellipse.CaptureMouse();
}
```

The ellipse isn't actually moved until the MouseMove event occurs. At this point, the Canvas.Left and Canvas.Top attached properties are set on the ellipse to move it to its new position. The coordinates are set based on the current position of the mouse, taking into account the point where the user initially clicked. This ellipse then moves seamlessly with the mouse, until the left mouse button is released.

```
private void ellipse_MouseMove(object sender, MouseEventArgs e)
{
    if (isDragging)
    {
        Ellipse ellipse = (Ellipse)sender;
```

```
        // Get the position of the ellipse relative to the Canvas.
        Point point = e.GetPosition(this);

        // Move the ellipse.
        ellipse.SetValue(Canvas.TopProperty, point.Y - mouseOffset.Y);
        ellipse.SetValue(Canvas.LeftProperty, point.X - mouseOffset.X);
    }
}
```

When the left mouse button is released, the code changes the color of the ellipse, releases the mouse capture, and stops listening for the MouseMove and MouseUp events. The user can click the ellipse again to start the whole process over.

```
private void ellipse_MouseUp(object sender, MouseButtonEventArgs e)
{
    if (isDragging)
    {
        Ellipse ellipse = (Ellipse)sender;

        // Change the ellipse color.
        ellipse.Fill = new SolidColorBrush(Colors.Orange);

        // Don't watch the mouse events any longer.
        ellipse.MouseMove -= ellipse_MouseMove;
        ellipse.MouseLeftButtonUp -= ellipse_MouseUp;
        ellipse.ReleaseMouseCapture();

        isDragging = false;
    }
}
```

Mouse Cursors

A common task in any application is to adjust the mouse cursor to show when the application is busy or to indicate how different controls work. You can set the mouse pointer for any element using the Cursor property, which is inherited from the FrameworkElement class.

Every cursor is represented by a System.Windows.Input.Cursor object. The easiest way to get a Cursor object is to use the static properties of the Cursors class (from the System.Windows.Input namespace). They include all the standard Windows cursors, such as the hourglass, the hand, resizing arrows, and so on. Here's an example that sets the hourglass for the current page:

```
this.Cursor = Cursors.Wait;
```

Now when you move the mouse over the current page, the mouse pointer changes to the familiar hourglass icon (in Windows XP) or the swirl (in Windows Vista).

Note The properties of the Cursors class draw on the cursors that are defined on the computer. If the user has customized the set of standard cursors, the application you create will use those customized cursors.

If you set the cursor in XAML, you don't need to use the Cursors class directly. That's because the type converter for the Cursor property is able to recognize the property names and retrieve the corresponding Cursor object from the Cursors class. That means you can write markup like this to show the "help" cursor (a combination of an arrow and a question mark) when the mouse is positioned over a button:

```
<Button Cursor="Help" Content="Help Me"></Button>
```

It's possible to have overlapping cursor settings. In this case, the most specific cursor wins. For example, you could set a different cursor on a button and on the page that contains the button. The button's cursor will be shown when you move the mouse over the button, and the page's cursor will be used for every other region in the page.

Tip Unlike WPF, Silverlight does not support custom mouse cursors. However, you can hide the mouse cursor (set it to Cursors.None) and then make a small image follow the mouse pointer using code like that shown in the previous section.

Key Presses

As you saw in Table 4-1, Silverlight elements use KeyDown and KeyUp events to notify you when a key is pressed. These events use bubbling, so they travel up from the element that currently has focus to the containing elements.

When you react to a key press event, you receive a KeyEventArgs object that provides two additional pieces of information: Key and PlatformKeyCode. Key indicates the key that was pressed as a value from the System.Windows.Input.Key enumeration (for example, Key.S is the S key). PlatformKeyCode is an integer value that must be interpreted based on the hardware and operating system that's being used on the client computer. For example, a non-standard key that Silverlight can't recognize will return a Key.Unknown value for the Key property, but will provide a PlatformKeyCode that's up to you to interpret. An example of a platform-specific key is Scroll Lock on Microsoft Windows computers.

Note In general, it's best to avoid any platform-specific coding. But if you really do need to evaluate a non-standard key, you can use the BrowserInformation class from the System.Windows.Browser namespace to get more information about the client computer where your application is running.

The best way to understand the key events is to use a sample program such as the one shown in Figure 4-6 a little later in this chapter. It monitors a text box for three events: Key-Down, KeyUp, and the higher-level TextChanged event (which is raised by the TextBox control), using this markup:

```
<TextBox KeyDown="txt_KeyDown" KeyUp="txt_KeyUp"
 TextChanged="txt_TextChanged"></TextBox>
```

Here, the TextBox handles the KeyDown, KeyUp, and TextChanged events explicitly. However, the KeyDown and KeyUp events bubble, which means you can handle them at a higher level. For example, you can attach KeyDown and KeyUp event handlers on the root Grid to receive key presses that are made anywhere in the page.

Here are the event handlers that react to these events:

```
private void txt_KeyUp(object sender, KeyEventArgs e)
{
    string message =
      "KeyUp " +
      " Key: " + e.Key;
      lstMessages.Items.Add(message);
}

private void txt_KeyDown(object sender, KeyEventArgs e)
{
    string message =
      "KeyDown " +
      " Key: " + e.Key;
    lstMessages.Items.Add(message);
}

private void txt_TextChanged(object sender, TextChangedEventArgs e)
{
    string message = "TextChanged";
    lstMessages.Items.Add(message);
}
```

Figure 4-6 shows the result of typing a lowercase *S* in the text box.

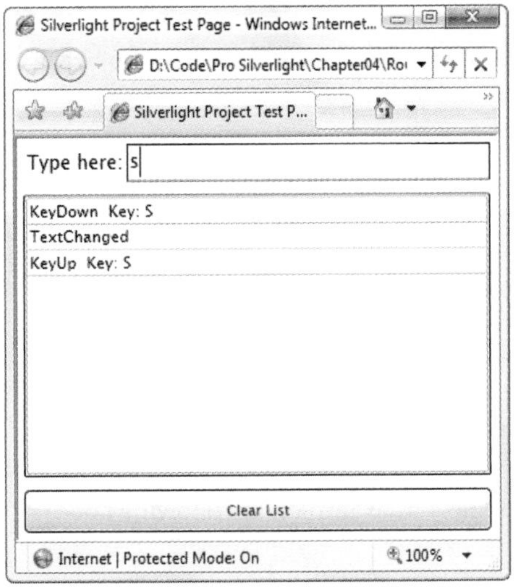

Figure 4-6. *Watching the keyboard*

Typing a single character may involve multiple key presses. For example, if you want to type a *capital* letter *S*, you must first press the Shift key, and then the *S* key. On most computers, keys that are pressed for longer than a brief moment start generating repeated key presses. For that reason, if you type a capital *S*, you're likely to see a series of KeyDown events for the Shift key, as shown in Figure 4-7. However, you'll only key two KeyUp events (for the *S* and for the Shift key), and just one TextChanged event.

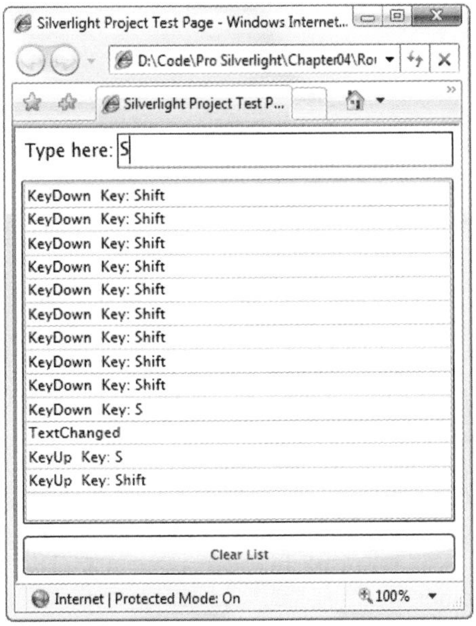

Figure 4-7. *Repeated keys*

■**Note** Controls like the TextBox aren't designed for low-level keyboard handling. When dealing with a text entry control, you should only react to its higher-level keyboard events (like TextChanged).

Key Modifiers

When a key press occurs, you often need to know more than just what key was pressed. It's also important to find out what other keys were held down at the same time. That means you might want to investigate the state of other keys, particularly modifiers such as Shift and Ctrl, both of which are supported on all platforms. Although you can handle the events for these keys separately and keep track of them in that way, it's much easier to use the static Modifiers property of the Keyboard class.

To test for a Keyboard.Modifier, you use bitwise logic. For example, the following code checks if the Ctrl key is currently pressed.

```
if ((Keyboard.Modifiers & ModifierKeys.Control) == ModifierKeys.Control)
{
    message += "You are holding the Control key.";
}
```

■**Note** The browser is free to intercept keystrokes. For example, in Internet Explorer you won't see the KeyDown event for the Alt key, because the browser intercepts it. The Alt key opens the Internet Explorer menu (when used alone) or triggers a shortcut (when used with another key).

Focus

In the Windows world, a user works with one control at a time. The control that is currently receiving the user's key presses is the control that has *focus*. Sometimes this control is drawn slightly differently. For example, the Silverlight button uses blue shading to show that it has the focus.

To move the focus from one element to another, the user can click the mouse or use the Tab and arrow keys. In previous development frameworks, programmers have been forced to take great care to make sure that the Tab key moves focus in a logical manner (generally from left to right and then down the window) and that the right control has focus when the window first appears. In Silverlight, this extra work is seldom necessary because Silverlight uses the hierarchical layout of your elements to implement a tabbing sequence. Essentially, when you press the Tab key you'll move to the first child in the current element or, if the current element has no children, to the next child at the same level. For example, if you tab through a window with two StackPanel containers, you'll move through all the controls in the first StackPanel and then through all the controls in the second container.

If you want to take control of tab sequence, you can set the TabIndex property for each control to place it in numerical order. The control with a TabIndex of 0 gets the focus first, followed by the next highest TabIndex value (for example, 1, then 2, then 3, and so on). If more than one element has the same TabIndex value, Silverlight uses the automatic tab sequence, which means it jumps to the nearest subsequent element.

Tip By default, the TabIndex property for all controls is set to 1. That means you can designate a specific control as the starting point for a window by setting its TabIndex to 0 but rely on automatic navigation to guide the user through the rest of the window from that starting point, according to the order that your elements are defined.

The TabIndex property is defined in the Control class, along with an IsTabStop property. You can set IsTabStop to false to prevent a control from being included in the tab sequence. A control that has IsTabStop set to false can still get the focus in another way—either programmatically (when your code calls its Focus() method) or by a mouse click.

Controls that are invisible or disabled ("grayed out") are skipped in the tab order and are not activated regardless of the TabIndex and IsTabStop settings. To hide or disable a control, you set the Visibility and IsEnabled properties, respectively.

The Last Word

In this chapter, you took a deep look at Silverlight dependency properties and routed events. First, you saw how dependency properties are defined and registered and how they plug into other Silverlight services. Next, you explored event bubbling and saw how it allows an event to travel up the element hierarchy. Finally, you considered the basic set of mouse and keyboard events that all elements provide.

Tip One of the best ways to learn more about the internals of Silverlight is to browse the code for basic Silverlight elements, such as Button, UIElement, and FrameworkElement. One of the best tools to perform this browsing is Reflector, which is available at http://www.red-gate.com/products/reflector. Using Reflector, you can see the definitions for dependency properties and routed events, browse through the static constructor code that initializes them, and even explore how the properties and events are used in the class code.

CHAPTER 5

■ ■ ■

Elements

Now that you've learned the fundamentals of XAML, layout, and mouse and keyboard handling, you're ready to consider the elements that allow you to build both simple and complex user interfaces.

In this chapter, you'll get an overview of Silverlight's core elements, and you'll explore many elements that you haven't studied yet. First, you'll learn how to display wrapped, formatted text with the TextBlock and how to show images with the Image element. Next, you'll consider content controls, including Silverlight's many different flavors of button and the ToolTip control. Finally, you'll take a look at several more specialized elements, such as Silverlight's list, text-entry, range, and date controls. By the time you finish this chapter, you'll have a solid overview of the essential ingredients that make up Silverlight pages.

The Silverlight Elements

You've already met quite a few of Silverlight's core elements, such as the layout containers in Chapter 3. Some of the more specialized elements, such as the ones used for drawing 2-D graphics, displaying Deep Zoom images, and playing video, won't be covered until later in this book. But this chapter deals with all the basics—fundamental widgets like buttons, text boxes, lists, and checkboxes.

Table 5-1 provides an at-a-glance look at all the elements that Silverlight includes, and points you to the part of this book where they're described. The list is ordered alphabetically, to match the order of elements in the Visual Studio Toolbox.

Table 5-1. *Silverlight Elements*

Class	Description	Place in This Book	Assembly (If Not a Core Element)
Border	A rectangular or rounded border that's drawn around a single, contained element.	Chapter 3	
Button	The familiar button, complete with a shaded gray background, which the user clicks to launch a task.	This chapter	

Continued

Table 5-1. *Continued*

Class	Description	Place in This Book	Assembly (If Not a Core Element)
Calendar	A one-month-at-a-time calendar view that allows the user to select a single date.	This chapter	System.Windows. Controls.dll
Canvas	A layout container that allows you to lay out elements with precise coordinates.	Chapter 3	
CheckBox	A box that can be checked or unchecked, with optional content displayed next to it.	This chapter	
ComboBox	A drop-down list of items, out of which a single one can be selected.	This chapter	
DataGrid	A multicolumn, multirow list filled with a collection of data objects.	Chapter 14	System.Windows. Controls.Data.dll
DatePicker	A text box for date entry, with a drop-down calendar for easy selection.	This chapter	System.Windows. Controls.dll
Ellipse	A shape drawing element that represents an ellipse.	Chapter 7	
Grid	A layout container that places children in an invisible grid of cells.	Chapter 3	
GridSplitter	A resizing bar that allows users to change the height or adjacent rows or width of adjacent columns in a Grid.	Chapter 3	System.Windows. Controls.dll
HyperlinkButton	A link that directs the user to another web page.	This chapter	
Image	An element that displays a supported image file.	This chapter	
Line	A shape drawing element that represents a line.	Chapter 7	
ListBox	A list of items, out of which a single one can be selected.	This chapter	
MediaElement	A media file, such as a video window.	Chapter 10	
MultiScaleImage	An element that supports Silverlight's Deep Zoom feature, and allows the user to zoom into a precise location in a massive image.	Chapter 10	
PasswordBox	A text box that masks the text the user enters.	This chapter	

Class	Description	Place in This Book	Assembly (If Not a Core Element)
ProgressBar	A colored bar that indicates the percent completion of a given task.	This chapter	
RadioButton	A small circle that represents one choice out of a group of options, with optional content displayed next to it.	This chapter	
Rectangle	A shape drawing element that represents a rectangle.	Chapter 7	
ScrollViewer	A container that holds any large content and makes it scrollable.	Chapter 3	
Slider	An input control that lets the user set a numeric value by dragging a thumb along a track.	This chapter	
StackPanel	A layout container that stacks items from top to bottom or left to right.	Chapter 3	
TabControl	A container that places items into separate tabs, and allows the user to view just one tab at a time.	This chapter	System.Windows.Controls.dll
TextBlock	An all-purpose text display control that includes the ability to give different formatting to multiple pieces of inline text.	This chapter	
TextBox	The familiar text-entry control.	This chapter	
ToggleButton	A button that has two states, on or off, and can be switched from one to another by clicking (like the CheckBox control).	This chapter	

In Chapter 1, you learned that Silverlight includes some non-core controls that—if used—must be included with your deployed XAP archive. As you can see in Table 5-1, this doesn't apply to most Silverlight controls, and even some highly specialized controls like the MultiScaleImage are part of the standard Silverlight package. However, you will need to include an assembly if you use the Calendar, DatePicker, DataGrid, GridSplitter, or TabControl.

In the following sections, you'll take a closer look at many of the controls from Table 5-1, and you'll learn how to customize them in your own applications.

Static Text

Silverlight doesn't include a Label control. The lynchpin for text display is the TextBlock element, which you've seen at work in many of the examples over the past four chapters.

The TextBlock element is refreshingly straightforward. It provides a Text property, which accepts a string with the text you want to display.

```
<TextBlock Text="This is the content."></TextBlock>
```

Alternatively, you can supply the text as nested content:

```
<TextBlock>This is the content.</TextBlock>
```

The chief advantage of this approach is that you can add line breaks and tabs to make large sections of text more readable in your code. Silverlight follows the standard rules of XML, which means it *collapses* whitespace. Thus a series of spaces, tabs, and hard returns is rendered using a single space character. If you really do want to split text over lines at an explicit position, you need to use separate TextBlock elements, or use a LineBreak inside the TextBlock element, as shown here:

```
<TextBlock>
    This is line 1.<LineBreak/>
    This is line 2.
</TextBlock>
```

■**Note** When using inline text, you can't use the < and > characters, because these have a specific XML meaning. Instead, you need to replace the angled brackets with the character entities < (for the less than symbol) and > (for the greater than symbol), which will be rendered as < and >.

Unsurprisingly, text is colored black by default. You can change the color of your text using the Foreground property. You can set it using a color name in XAML:

```
<TextBlock x:Name="txt" Text="Hello World" Foreground="Red"></TextBlock>
```

or in code:

```
txt.Foreground = new SolidColorBrush(Colors.Red);
```

Instead of using a color name, you can use RGB values. You can also use partially transparent colors that allow the background to show through. Both topics are covered in Chapter 3 when discussing how to paint the background of a panel.

■**Tip** Ordinarily, you'll use a solid color brush to fill in text. (The default is obviously a black brush.) However, you can create more exotic effects by filling in your text with gradients and tiled patterns using the fancy brushes discussed in Chapter 8.

The TextBlock also provides a TextAlignment property (which allows you to center or right-justify text), a Padding property (which sets the space between the text and the outer edges of the TextBlock), and a few more properties for controlling fonts, inline formatting, and text wrapping. You'll consider these properties in the following sections.

Font Properties

The TextBlock class defines font properties that determine how text appears in a control. These properties are outlined in Table 5-2.

Table 5-2. *Font-Related Properties of the Control Class*

Name	Description
FontFamily	The name of the font you want to use. Because Silverlight is a client-side technology, it's limited to just nine built-in fonts (Arial, Arial Black, Comic Sans MS, Courier New, Georgia, Lucida, Times New Roman, Trebuchet MS, and Verdana). However, you can also distribute custom fonts by going to a bit more work and packing them up with your project assembly.
FontSize	The size of the font in pixels. Ordinary Windows applications measure fonts using *points*, which are assumed to be 1/72 of an inch on a standard PC monitor, while pixels are assumed to be 1/96 of an inch. Thus, if you want to turn a Silverlight font size into a more familiar point size, you can use a handy trick—just multiply by 3/4. For example, a 20-pixel FontSize is equivalent to a traditional 15-point font size.
FontStyle	The angling of the text, as represented as a FontStyle object. You get the FontStyle preset you need from the static properties of the FontStyles class, which includes Normal and Italic lettering. If you apply italic lettering to a font that doesn't provide an italic variant, Silverlight will simply slant the letters. However, this behavior only gives a crude approximation of a true italic typeface.
FontWeight	The heaviness of text, as represented as a FontWeight object. You get the FontWeight preset you need from the static properties of the FontWeights class. Normal and Bold are the most obvious of these, but some typefaces provide other variations such as Heavy, Light, ExtraBold, and so on. If you use Bold on a font that doesn't provide a bold variant, Silverlight will paint a thicker border around the letters, thereby simulating a bold font.
FontStretch	The amount that text is stretched or compressed, as represented by a FontStretch object. You get the FontStretch preset you need from the static properties of the FontStretches class. For example, UltraCondensed reduces fonts to 50% of their normal width, while UltraExpanded expands them to 200%. Font stretching is an OpenType feature that is not supported by many typefaces. The built-in Silverlight fonts don't support any of these variants.

Obviously, the most important of these properties is FontFamily. A *font family* is a collection of related typefaces—for example, Arial Regular, Arial Bold, Arial Italic, and Arial Bold Italic are all part of the Arial font family. Although the typographic rules and characters for each variation are defined separately, the operating system realizes they're related. As a result, you can configure an element to use Arial Regular, set the FontWeight property to Bold, and be confident that Silverlight will switch over to the Arial Bold typeface.

When choosing a font, you must supply the full family name, as shown here:

```
<TextBlock x:Name="txt" FontFamily="Times New Roman" FontSize="18">
 Some Bold Text</TextBlock>
```

It's much the same in code:

```
txt.FontFamily = "Times New Roman";
txt.FontSize = "18";
```

When identifying a FontFamily, a shortened string is not enough. That means you can't substitute Times or Times New instead of the full name Times New Roman.

Optionally, you can use the full name of a typeface to get italic or bold, as shown here:

```
<TextBlock FontFamily="Times New Roman Bold">A Button</TextBlock >
```

However, it's clearer and more flexible to use just the family name and set other properties (such as FontStyle and FontWeight) to get the variant you want. For example, the following markup sets the FontFamily to Times New Roman and sets the FontWeight to FontWeights.Bold:

```
<TextBlock FontFamily="Times New Roman" FontWeight="Bold">A Button</TextBlock >
```

Standard Fonts

Silverlight supports nine core fonts, which are guaranteed to render correctly on any browser and operating system that supports Silverlight. They're shown in Figure 5-1.

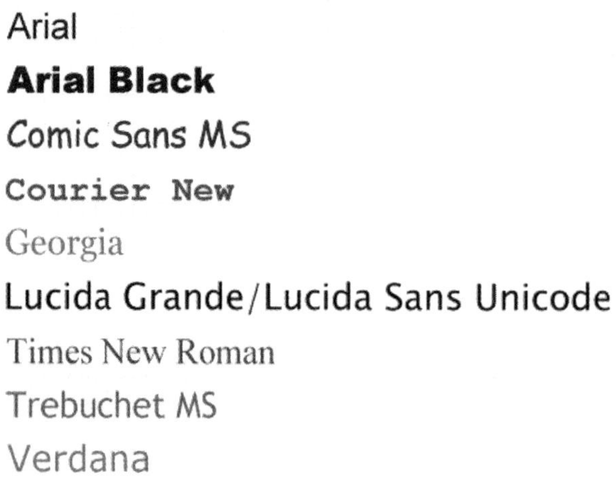

Arial

Arial Black

Comic Sans MS

Courier New

Georgia

Lucida Grande/Lucida Sans Unicode

Times New Roman

Trebuchet MS

Verdana

Figure 5-1. *Silverlight's built-in fonts*

In the case of Lucida, there are two variants with slightly different names. Lucida Sans Unicode is included with Windows, while Lucida Grande is an almost identical font that's included with Mac OS X. To allow this system to work, the FontFamily property supports font fallback—in other words, you can supply a comma-separated list of font names and Silverlight will used the first supported font. The default TextBlock font is equivalent to setting the Font-Family property to the string "Lucida Sans Unicode, Lucida Grande."

You might think that you can use more specialized fonts, which may or may not be present on the client's computer. However, Silverlight doesn't allow this. If you specify a font that isn't one of the nine built-in fonts, and it isn't included with your application assembly (more on that in the next section), your font setting will be ignored. This happens regardless of whether the client has an installed font with the appropriate name. This makes sense—after all, using a font that's only supported on some systems could lead to an application that's mangled or completely unreadable on others, which is an easy mistake to make.

Font Embedding

If you want to use non-standard fonts in your application, you can embed them in your application assembly. That way, your application never has a problem finding the font you want to use.

The embedding process is simple. First, you add the font file (typically, a file with the extension .ttf) to your application and set the Build Action to Resource. (You can do this in Visual Studio by selecting the font file in the Solution Explorer and changing its Build Action in the Properties page.)

Next, when you set the FontFamily property, you need to use this format:

FontFileName#FontName

For example, if you have a font file named BayernFont.ttf, and that includes a font named Bayern, you would use markup like this:

```
<TextBlock FontFamily="BayernFont.ttf#Bayern">This is an embedded font</TextBlock>
```

Figure 5-2 shows the result.

Figure 5-2. *Using an embedded font*

Alternatively, you can set the font using a stream that contains the font file. In this case, you need to set the TextBlock.FontSource property with the font file stream, and then set the TextBlock.FontFamily property with the font name. For example, if you've added the BayernFont.ttf file as a resource to a project named FontTest, you can retrieve it programmatically using this code:

```
StreamResourceInfo sri = Application.GetResourceStream(
  new Uri("FontTest;component/BayernFont.ttf", UriKind.Relative));

lbl.FontSource = new FontSource(sri.Stream);
lbl.FontFamily = new FontFamily("Bayern");
```

To pull the resource out of the current assembly, this code uses the Application.Get-ResourceStream() method and the URI syntax you learned about in Chapter 6.

No matter which approach, the process of using a custom font is fairly easy. However, font embedding raises obvious licensing concerns. Most font vendors allow their fonts to be embedded in documents (such as PDF files) but not applications (such as Silverlight assemblies). The problem is obvious—users can download the XAP file by hand, unzip it, retrieve the font resource, and then access it on their local computers. Silverlight doesn't make any attempt to enforce font licensing, but you should make sure you're on solid legal ground before you redistribute a font.

You can check a font's embedding permissions using Microsoft's free font properties extension utility, which is available at `http://www.microsoft.com/typography/TrueTypeProperty21.mspx`. Once you install this utility, right-click any font file, and choose Properties to see more detailed information about it. In particular, check the Embedding tab for information about the allowed embedding for this font. Fonts marked with Installed Embedding Allowed are suitable for Silverlight applications, while fonts with Editable Embedding Allowed may not be. Consult with the font vendor for licensing information about a specific font.

Note If all else fails, you can get around licensing issues by changing your fonts to graphics. This works for small pieces of graphical text (for example, headings), but isn't appropriate for large blocks of text. You can save graphical text as a bitmap in your favorite drawing program, or you can convert text to a series of shapes using Silverlight's Path element (which is discussed in Chapter 7). You can convert graphical text to a path using Expression Designer or Expression Blend (simply select the TextBlock and choose Object ➤ Path ➤ Convert to Path). Interestingly, Silverlight also allows you to perform the same trick through code. Surf to `http://tinyurl.com/69f74v` to see an example in which a Silverlight application calls a web service that dynamically generates a path for non-Western text. The web service returns the path data to the Silverlight application, which displays it seamlessly.

Underlining

You can add underlining to any font by setting the TextDecorations property to Underline:

```
<TextBlock TextDecorations="Underline">Underlined text</TextBlock>
```

In WPF, there are several types of text decorations, including overlines and strikethrough. However, at present Silverlight only includes underlining.

If you want to underline an individual word in a block of text, you'll need to use inline elements, as described in the next section.

Runs

In many situations, you'll want to format individual bits of text, but keep them together in a single paragraph in a TextBlock. To accomplish this, you need to use a Run object inside the TextBlock element. Here's an example that formats several words differently (see Figure 5-3):

```
<TextBlock FontFamily="Georgia" FontSize="20" >
  This <Run FontStyle="Italic" Foreground="YellowGreen">is</Run> a
  <Run FontFamily="Comic Sans MS" Foreground="Red" FontSize="40">test.</Run>
</TextBlock>
```

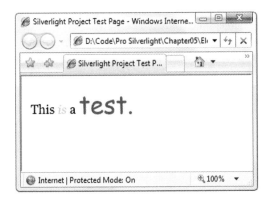

Figure 5-3. *Formatting text with runs*

A run supports the same key formatting properties as the TextBlock, including Foreground, TextDecorations, and the five font properties (FontFamily, FontSize, FontStyle, FontWeight, and FontStretch).

Technically, a Run object is not a true element. Instead, it's an *inline*. Silverlight provides just two types of inlines—the LineBreak class that you saw earlier and the Run object. You can interact with the runs in your TextBlock through the TextBlock.Inlines collection. In fact, the TextBlock actually has two overlapping content models. You can set text through the simple Text property, or you can supply it through the Inlines collection. However, the changes you make in one affect the other, so if you set the Text property, you'll wipe out the current collection of inlines.

■**Note** The inline Run and LineBreak classes are the only part of WPF's document model that survives in Silverlight.

Wrapping Text

To wrap text over several lines, you use the TextWrapping property. Ordinarily, TextWrapping is set to TextWrapping.NoWrap, and content is truncated if it extends past the right edge of the containing element. If you use TextWrapping.Wrap, your content will be wrapped over multiple lines when the width of the TextBlock element is constrained in some way. (For example, you place it into a proportionately sized or fixed-width Grid cell.) When wrapping, the TextBlock splits lines at the nearest space. If you have a word that is longer than the available line width, the TextBlock will split that word wherever it can to make it fit.

When wrapping text, the LineHeight and LineStackingStrategy properties become important. The LineHeight property can set a fixed height (in pixels) that will be used for every line. However, the LineHeight can only be used to increase the line height—if you specify a height that's smaller than what's required to show the text, your setting will be ignored. The LineStackingStrategy determines what the TextBlock will do when dealing with multiline content that uses different fonts. You can choose to use the standard behavior, MaxHeight, which makes each line as high as it needs to be to fit the tallest piece of text it contains, or you can use BlockLineHeight, which sets the lines to one fixed height—the height set by the LineHeight property. Shorter text will then have extra space, and taller text will overlap with other lines. Figure 5-4 compares the different options.

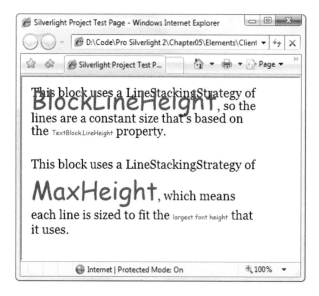

Figure 5-4. *Two different ways to calculate line height*

Images

Displaying an image is one of the easier tasks in Silverlight. You simply need to add an Image element and set its Source property. However, there are some limitations that you need to understand.

The most obvious limitation is that the Image element supports just two image formats. It has full support for JPEG, and fairly broad support for PNG (although it doesn't support PNG files that use 64-bit color or grayscale). The Image element does *not* support GIF files. There are two reasons for this omission—it allows the Silverlight download to remain that much slimmer, and it avoids potential confusion between the Silverlight animation model and the much more basic (and unsupported) animated GIF feature that's used on the Web.

It's also important to recognize that the Image.Source property is set with a relative or absolute URI. Usually, you'll use a relative URI to display an image that you've added to your project as a resource. For example, if you add a new image named grandpiano.jpg to your project, Visual Studio will automatically configure it to be a resource, and it will embed that resource in the compiled assembly as a block of binary data. At runtime, you can retrieve that image using its resource name (which is the file name it has in the Solution Explorer). Here's how:

```
<Image Source="grandpiano.jpg"></Image>
```

Alternatively, you can construct the URI in code and set the Image.Source property programmatically:

```
img.Source = new BitmapImage(new Uri("grandpiano.jpg", UriKind.Relative));
```

You can also use image URIs to point to images that aren't embedded in your application. You can show images that are located on the same website as your Silverlight application, or images that exist on separate websites.

```
<Image Source="http://www.mysite.com/Images/grandpiano.jpg"></Image>
```

However, there's one catch. When testing a file-based website (one that doesn't use an ASP.NET website and the Visual Studio test web server), you won't be able to use absolute URLs. This limitation is a security restriction that results from the mismatch between the way you're running your application (from the file system) and the way you want to retrieve your images (from the Web, over HTTP).

For more information, and to see a few examples that demonstrate your different options for using URIs and managing resources, refer to Chapter 6.

■**Tip** Interestingly, Silverlight uses bitmap caching to reduce the number of URI requests it makes. That means you can link to an image file on a website multiple times, but your application will only download it once.

Image Sizing

Images can be resized in two ways. First, you can set an explicit size for your image using the Height and Width properties. Second, you can place your Image element in a container that uses resizing, such as a proportionately-sized cell in a Grid. If neither of these factors comes into play—in other words, you don't set the Height and Width properties and you place your Image in a simple layout container like the Canvas—your image will be displayed using the native size that's defined in the image file.

To control this behavior, you can use the Stretch property. The Stretch property determines how an image is resized when the dimensions of the Image element don't match the native dimensions of the image file. Table 5-3 lists the values you can use for the Stretch property, and Figure 5-5 compares them.

Table 5-3. *Values for the Stretch Enumeration*

Name	Description
Fill	Your image is stretched in width and height to fit the Image element dimensions exactly. (If you set an explicit height and width, this setting has no effect.)
None	The image keeps its native size.
Uniform	The image is given the largest possible size that fits in the Image element and doesn't change its aspect ratio. This is the default value.
UniformToFill	The width and height of the image are sized proportionately until the image fills all the available height and width. For example, if you place a picture with this stretch setting into an Image element that's 100×200 pixels, you'll get a 200×200 picture, and part of it will be clipped off.

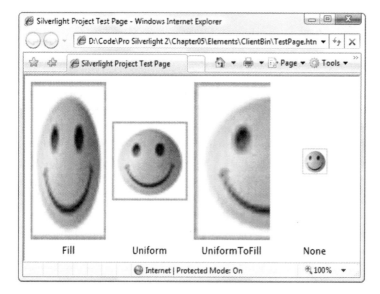

Figure 5-5. *Four different ways to size an image*

Image Errors

Several factors can cause an image not to appear, such as using a URI to a nonexistent file or trying to display an image in an unsupported format. In these situations, the Image element raises the ImageFailed event. You can react to this event to determine the problem and take alternative actions. (For example, if a large image is not available from the Web, you can substitute a small placeholder that's embedded in your application assembly.)

Image errors are not fatal, and your application will continue running even if it can't display an image. In this situation, the Image element will remain blank. Your image will also be blank if the image data takes a significant amount of time to download. Silverlight will perform the image request asynchronously, and render the rest of the layout in your page while waiting.

Content Controls

Content controls are a specialized type of controls that are designed to hold (and display) a piece of content. Technically, a content control is a control that can contain a *single* nested element. The one-child limit is what differentiates content controls from layout containers, which can hold as many nested elements as you want.

As you learned in Chapter 3, all Silverlight layout containers derive from the Panel class, which gives the support for holding multiple elements. Similarly, all content controls derive from the ContentControl class. Figure 5-6 shows the class hierarchy.

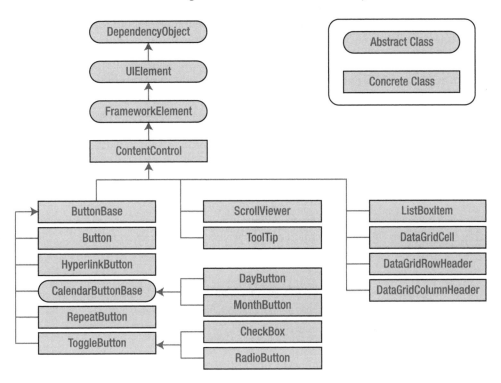

Figure 5-6. *The hierarchy of content controls*

As Figure 5-6 shows, several common controls are actually content controls, including the Tooltip, Button, RadioButton, and the CheckBox. There are also a few more specialized content controls, such as ScrollViewer (which you used in Chapter 3 to create a scrollable panel), and some controls that are designed for being used with another, specific control. (For example, the ListBox control holds ListBoxItem content controls; the Calendar requires the DayButton and MonthButton; and the DataGrid uses the DataGridCell, DataGridRowHeader, and DataColumnHeader).

The Content Property

Whereas the Panel class adds the Children collection to hold nested elements, the Content-Control class adds a Content property, which accepts a single object. The Content property supports any type of object. It gives you three ways to show content:

- **Elements.** If you use an object that derives from UIElement for the content of a content control, that element will be rendered.

- **Other objects.** If you place a non-element object into a content control, the control will simply call ToString() to get the text representation for that control. For some types of objects, ToString() produces a reasonable text representation. For others, it simply returns the fully qualified class name of the object, which is the default implementation.

- **Other objects, with a data template.** If you place a non-element object into a content control, and you set the ContentTemplate property with a data template, the content control will render the data template and use the expressions it contains to pull information out of the properties of your object. This approach is particularly useful when dealing with collections of data objects, and you'll see how it works in Chapter 14.

To understand how this works, consider the humble button. An ordinary button may just use a simple string object to generate its content:

```
<Button Margin="3" Content="Text content"></Button>
```

This string is set as the button content and displayed on the button surface.

Tip When filling a button with unformatted text, you may want to use the font-related properties that the Button class inherits from Control, which duplicate the TextBlock properties listed in Table 5-2.

However, you can get more ambitious by placing other elements inside the button. For example, you can place an image inside using the Image class:

```
<Button Margin="3">
  <Image Source="happyface.jpg"></Image>
</Button>
```

Or you could combine text and images by wrapping them all in a layout container like the StackPanel, as you saw in Chapter 3:

```
<Button Margin="3">
  <StackPanel>
    <TextBlock Margin="3" Text="Image and text button"></TextBlock>
    <Image Source="happyface.jpg" />
    <TextBlock Margin="3" Text="Courtesy of the StackPanel"></TextBlock>
  </StackPanel>
</Button>
```

If you want to create a truly exotic button, you could even place other content controls such as text boxes and buttons inside (and nest still elements inside these). It's doubtful that such an interface would make much sense, but it is possible.

At this point, you might be wondering if the Silverlight content model is really worth all the trouble. After all, you might choose to place an image inside a button, but you're unlikely to embed other controls and entire layout panels. However, there are a few important advantages to the content model.

For example, the previous markup placed a bitmap into a button. However, this approach isn't as flexible as creating a vector drawing out of Silverlight shapes. Using a vector drawing, you can create a button image that's rescalable and can be changed programmatically (for example, with different colors, a transform, or an animation). Using a vector-based button opens you up to the possibility of creating a dynamic interface that responds to state changes and user actions.

In Chapter 7, you'll consider how you can begin building vector images in Silverlight. However, the key fact you should understand now is that the vector drawing model integrates seamlessly with content controls because they have the ability to hold any element. For example, this markup creates a simple graphical button that contains two diamond shapes (as shown in Figure 5-7):

```
<Button Margin="3" Height="70" Width="215">
  <Grid Margin="5">
    <Polygon Points="100,25 125,0 200,25 125,50"
     Fill="LightSteelBlue" />
    <Polygon Points="100,25 75,0 0,25 75,50"
     Fill="White"/>
  </Grid>
</Button>
```

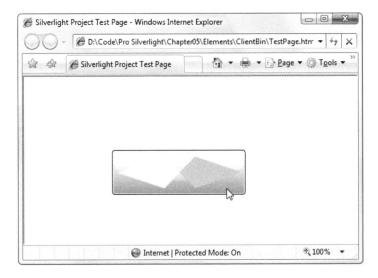

Figure 5-7. A button with shape content

Clearly, in this case the nested content model is simpler than adding extra properties to the Button class to support the different types of content. Not only is the nested content model more flexible, it also allows the Button class to expose a simpler interface. And because all content controls support content nesting in the same way, there's no need to add different content properties to multiple classes.

In essence, the nested content model is a trade. It simplifies the class model for elements because there's no need to use additional layers of inheritance to add properties for different types of content. However, you need to use a slightly more complex *object* model—elements that can be built out of other nested elements.

Note You can't always get the effect you want by changing the content of a control. For example, even though you can place any content in a button, a few details never change, such as the button's shaded background, its rounded border, and the mouse-over effect that makes it glow when you move the mouse pointer over it. However, there's another way to change these built-in details—by applying a new control template. Chapter 11 shows how you can change all aspects of a control's look and feel using a control template.

Aligning Content

In Chapter 3, you learned how to align different controls in a container using the Horizontal-Alignment and VerticalAlignment properties, which are defined in the base Framework-Element class. However, once a control contains content, there's another level of organization to think about. You need to decide how the content inside your content control is aligned with its borders. This is accomplished using the HorizontalContentAlignment and VerticalContent-Alignment properties.

HorizontalContentAlignment and VerticalContentAlignment support the same values as HorizontalAlignment and VerticalAlignment. That means you can line content up on the inside of any edge (Top, Bottom, Left, or Right), you can center it (Center), or you can stretch it to fill the available space (Stretch). These settings are applied directly to the nested content element, but you can use multiple levels of nesting to create a sophisticated layout. For example, if you nest a StackPanel in a Button element, the Button.HorizontalContentAlignment determines where the StackPanel is placed, but the alignment and sizing options of the Stack-Panel and its children will determine the rest of the layout.

In Chapter 3, you also learned about the Margin property, which allows you to add white-space between adjacent elements. Content controls use a complementary property named Padding, which inserts space between the edges of the control and the edges of the content. To see the difference, compare the following two buttons:

```
<Button Content="Absolutely No Padding"></Button>
<Button Padding="3" Content="Well Padded"></Button>
```

The button that has no padding (the default) has its text crowded up against the button edge. The button that has a padding of 3 pixels on each side gets a more respectable amount of breathing space.

■**Note** The HorizontalContentAlignment, VerticalContentAlignment, and Padding properties are all defined as part of the Control class, not the more specific ContentControl class. That's because there may be controls that aren't content controls but still have some sort of content. One example is the TextBox—its contained text (stored in the Text property) is adjusted using the alignment and padding settings you've applied.

Buttons

Silverlight recognizes three types of button controls: the familiar Button, the CheckBox, and the RadioButton. All of these controls are content controls that derive from ButtonBase.

The ButtonBase class includes only a few members. It defines the obviously important Click event and adds the IsFocused, IsMouseOver, and IsPressed read-only properties. Finally, the ButtonBase class adds a ClickMode property, which determines when a button fires its Click event in response to mouse actions. The default value is ClickMode.Release, which means the Click event fires when the mouse is clicked and released. However, you can also choose to fire the Click event mouse when the mouse button is first pressed (ClickMode.Press) or, oddly enough, whenever the mouse moves over the button and pauses there (ClickMode.Hover).

You've already seen how to use the ordinary button. In the following sections, you'll take a quick look at the more specialized alternatives that Silverlight provides.

The HyperlinkButton

The ordinary Button control is simple enough—you click it and it fires a Click event that you handle in code. But what about the other variants that Silverlight offers?

One of the simplest is the HyperlinkButton. When clicked, it directs the browser to another web page, effectively ending the current Silverlight application. The HyperlinkButton class adds two properties: NavigateUri (a relative or absolute path that points to a web page) and TargetName (which, optionally, identifies a bookmark in that page).

```
<HyperlinkButton Content="Buy Now" NavigateUri="shopping.aspx"></HyperlinkButton>
```

The HyperlinkButton doesn't draw the standard button background. Instead, it simply renders the content that you supply. If you use text in the HyperlinkButton, it appears blue by default, but it's not underlined. (Use the TextDecorations property if you want that effect.)

When you move the mouse over a HyperlinkButton, the mouse cursor changes to the pointing hand. You can override this effect by setting the Cursor property.

The ToggleButton and RepeatButton

Alongside Button and HyperlinkButton, three more classes derive from ButtonBase. These include the following:

- CalendarButtonBase, which is used to build the clickable month and day buttons in the Calendar control.

- RepeatButton, which fires Click events continuously, as long as the button is held down. Ordinary buttons fire one Click event per user click.

- ToggleButton, which represents a button that has two states (pushed or unpushed). When you click a ToggleButton, it stays in its pushed state until you click it again to release it. This is sometimes described as "sticky click" behavior.

Both RepeatButton and ToggleButton are defined in the System.Windows.Controls.Primitives namespace, which indicates they aren't often used on their own. Instead, they're used to build more complex controls by composition, or extended with features through inheritance. For example, the RepeatButton is used to build the higher-level ScrollBar control (which, ultimately, is a part of the even higher-level ScrollViewer). The RepeatButton gives the arrow buttons at the ends of the scroll bar their trademark behavior—scrolling continues as long as you hold it down. Similarly, the ToggleButton is used to derive the more useful CheckBox and RadioButton classes described next. However, neither the RepeatButton nor the ToggleButton is an abstract class, so you can use both of them directly in your user interfaces or to build custom controls if the need arises.

The CheckBox

Both the CheckBox and the RadioButton are buttons of a different sort. They derive from ToggleButton, which means they can be switched on or off by the user, hence their "toggle" behavior. In the case of the CheckBox, switching the control "on" means placing a checkmark in it.

The CheckBox class doesn't add any members, so the basic CheckBox interface is defined in the ToggleButton class. Most important, ToggleButton adds an IsChecked property. IsChecked is a nullable Boolean, which means it can be set to true, false, or a null value. Obviously, true represents a checked box, while false represents an empty one. The null value is a little trickier—it represents an indeterminate state, which is displayed as a shaded box. The indeterminate state is commonly used to represent values that haven't been set or areas where some discrepancy exists. For example, if you have a checkbox that allows you to apply bold formatting in a text application and the current selection includes both bold and regular text, you might set the checkbox to null to show an indeterminate state.

To assign a null value in Silverlight markup, you need to use the null markup extension, as shown here:

```
<CheckBox IsChecked="{x:Null}" Content="A check box in indeterminate state">
</CheckBox>
```

Along with the IsChecked property, the ToggleButton class adds a property named IsThreeState, which determines whether the user is able to place the checkbox into an indeterminate state. If IsThreeState is false (the default), clicking the checkbox alternates its state between checked and unchecked, and the only way to place it in an indeterminate state is through code. If IsThreeState is true, clicking the checkbox cycles through all three possible states.

The ToggleButton class also defines three events that fire when the checkbox enters specific states: Checked, Unchecked, and Indeterminate. In most cases, it's easier to consolidate this logic into one event handler by handling the Click event that's inherited from ButtonBase. The Click event fires whenever the button changes state.

The RadioButton

The RadioButton also derives from ToggleButton and uses the same IsChecked property and the same Checked, Unchecked, and Indeterminate events. Along with these, the RadioButton adds a single property named GroupName, which allows you to control how radio buttons are placed into groups.

Ordinarily, radio buttons are grouped by their container. That means if you place three RadioButton controls in a single StackPanel, they form a group from which you can select just one of the three. On the other hand, if you place a combination of radio buttons in two separate StackPanel controls, you have two independent groups on your hands.

The GroupName property allows you to override this behavior. You can use it to create more than one group in the same container or to create a single group that spans multiple containers. Either way, the trick is simple—just give all the radio buttons that belong together the same group name.

Consider this example:

```
<StackPanel>
  <Border Margin="5" Padding="5" BorderBrush="Yellow" BorderThickness="1"
   CornerRadius="5">
    <StackPanel>
      <RadioButton Content="Group 1"></RadioButton>
      <RadioButton Content="Group 1"></RadioButton>
      <RadioButton Content="Group 1"></RadioButton>
      <RadioButton GroupName="Group2" Content="Group 2"></RadioButton>
    </StackPanel>
  </Border>
  <Border Margin="5" Padding="5" BorderBrush="Yellow" BorderThickness="1"
   CornerRadius="5">
    <StackPanel>
      <RadioButton Content="Group 3"></RadioButton>
      <RadioButton Content="Group 3"></RadioButton>
      <RadioButton Content="Group 3"></RadioButton>
      <RadioButton GroupName="Group2" Content="Group 2"></RadioButton>
    </StackPanel>
  </Border>
</StackPanel>
```

Here, there are two containers holding radio buttons, but three groups (see Figure 5-8). The final radio button at the bottom of each group box is part of a third group. In this example, it makes for a confusing design, but there may be some scenarios where you want to separate a specific radio button from the pack in a subtle way without causing it to lose its group membership.

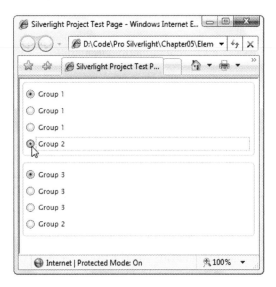

Figure 5-8. *Grouping radio buttons*

Tooltips and Pop-Ups

Silverlight has a flexible model for *tooltips* (those infamous yellow boxes that pop up when you hover over something interesting). Because tooltips in Silverlight are content controls, you can place virtually anything inside a tooltip. You can also tweak various timing settings to control how quickly tooltips appear and disappear.

Tooltips are represented by the ToolTip content control. However, you don't add the ToolTip element to your markup directly. Instead, you use the ToolTipService to configure a tooltip for an existing element, by setting attached properties. Silverlight will then create the ToolTip automatically and display it when it's needed.

The simplest example is a text-only tooltip. You can create a text-only tooltip by setting the ToolTipService.ToolTip property on another element, as shown here:

```
<Button ToolTipService.ToolTip="This is my tooltip">
 Content="I have a tooltip"></Button>
```

When you hover over this button, the text "This is my tooltip" appears in a gray pop-up box.

Customized ToolTips

If you want to supply more ambitious tooltip content, such as a combination of nested elements, you need to break the ToolTipService.ToolTip property out into a separate element. Here's an example that sets the ToolTip property of a button using more complex nested content:

```
<Button Content="I have a fancy tooltip">
  <ToolTipService.ToolTip>
    <StackPanel>
      <TextBlock Margin="3" Text="Image and text"></TextBlock>
      <Image Source="happyface.jpg"></Image>
      <TextBlock Margin="3" Text="Image and text"></TextBlock>
    </StackPanel>
  </ToolTipService.ToolTip>
</Button>
```

As in the previous example, Silverlight implicitly creates a ToolTip element. The difference is that in this case the ToolTip object contains a StackPanel rather than a simple string. Figure 5-9 shows the result.

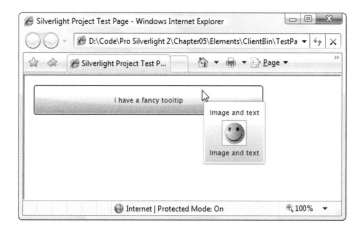

Figure 5-9. *A fancy tooltip*

■ **Note** Don't put user-interactive controls in a tooltip because the ToolTip page can't accept focus. For example, if you place a button in a ToolTip, the button will appear, but it isn't clickable. (If you attempt to click it, your mouse click will just pass through to the page underneath.) If you want a tooltip-like page that can hold other controls, consider using the Popup control instead, which is discussed shortly, in the section named "The Popup."

At this point, you might be wondering if you can customize other aspects of the tooltip's appearance, such as the standard gray background. You can get a bit more control by explicitly defining the ToolTip element when setting the ToolTipService.ToolTip property. Because the ToolTip is a content control, it provides a number of useful properties. You can adjust size and alignment properties (like Width, Height, MaxWidth, HoriztontalContentAlignment, Padding, and so on), font (FontFamily, FontSize, FontStyle, and so on), and color (Background and Foreground). You can also use the HorizontalOffset and VerticalOffset properties to nudge the tooltip away from the mouse pointer and into the position you want, with negative or positive values.

Using the ToolTip properties, the following markup creates a tooltip that uses a red background and makes the text inside white by default:

```
<Button Content="I have a fancy tooltip">
  <Button.ToolTip>
    <ToolTip Background="DarkRed" Foreground="White">
      <StackPanel>
        <TextBlock Margin="3" Text="Image and text"></TextBlock>
        <Image Source="happyface.jpg"></Image>
        <TextBlock Margin="3" Text="Image and text"></TextBlock>
      </StackPanel>
    </ToolTip>
  </Button.ToolTip>
</Button>
```

If you assign a name to your tooltip, you can also interact with it programmatically. For example, you can use the IsEnabled property to temporarily disable a ToolTip and IsOpen to programmatically show or hide a tooltip (or just check whether the tooltip is open). You can also handle its Opened and Closed events, which is useful if you want to generate the content for a tooltip dynamically, just as it opens.

Tip If you still want more control over the appearance of a tooltip—for example, you want to remove the black border or change its shape—you simply need to substitute a new control template with the visuals you prefer. Chapter 11 has the details.

The Popup

The Popup control has a great deal in common with the ToolTip control, although neither one derives from the other.

Like the ToolTip, the Popup can hold a single piece of content, which can include any Silverlight element. (This content is stored in the Popup.Child property, rather than the ToolTip.Content property.) Also, like the ToolTip, the content in the Popup can extend beyond the bounds of the page. Lastly, the Popup can be placed using the same placement properties and shown or hidden using the same IsOpen property.

The differences between the Popup and ToolTip are more important. They include the following:

- **The Popup is never shown automatically.** You must set the IsOpen property for it to appear. The Popup does not disappear until you explicitly set its IsOpen property to false.

- **The Popup can accept focus.** Thus, you can place user-interactive controls in it, such as a Button. This functionality is one of the key reasons to use the Popup instead of the ToolTip.

Because the Popup must be shown manually, you may choose to create it entirely in code. However, you can define it just as easily in XAML markup—just make sure to include the Name property so you can manipulate it in code. The placement of the Popup in your markup isn't important, because its top left will always be aligned with the top-left corner of the Silverlight content region.

```
<StackPanel Margin="20">
  <TextBlock TextWrapping="Wrap" MouseLeftButtonDown="txt_MouseLeftButtonDown"
   Text="Click here to open the PopUp."></TextBlock>

  <Popup x:Name="popUp" MaxWidth="200">
    <Border Background="Lime" MouseLeftButtonDown="popUp_MouseLeftButtonDown">
      <TextBlock Margin="10" Text="This is the PopUp."></TextBlock>
    </Border>
  </Popup>
</StackPanel>
```

The only remaining detail is the relatively trivial code that shows the Popup when the user clicks it, and the code that hides the Popup when it's clicked:

```
private void txt_MouseLeftButtonDown(object sender, MouseButtonEventArgs e)
{
    popUp.IsOpen = true;
}

private void popUp_MouseLeftButtonDown(object sender, MouseButtonEventArgs e)
{
    popUp.IsOpen = false;
}
```

Figure 5-10 shows the Popup in action.

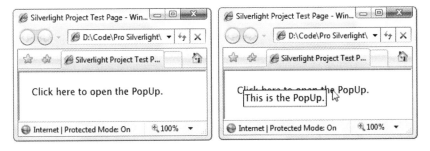

Figure 5-10. *A tooltip-like effect with the Popup*

Tip If you plan to create an extravagantly detailed Popup, you may want to consider creating a custom user control for the Popup content. You can then place an instance of that custom user control inside your pop-up. The end result is the same, but this technique simplifies your markup dramatically.

Items Controls

Controls that wrap collections of items generally derive from the ItemsControl class. Silverlight provides just three list-based controls: the ListBox, the ComboBox, and the TabControl.

The ItemsControl class fills in the basic plumbing that's used by all list-based controls. Notably, it gives you two ways to fill the list of items. The most straightforward approach is to add them directly to the Items collection, using code or XAML. This is the approach you'll see in this chapter. However, if you need to display a dynamic list, it's more common to use data binding. In this case, you set the ItemsSource property to the object that has the collection of data items you want to display. This process is covered in Chapter 14.

The ListBox

To add items to the ListBox, you can nest ListBoxItem elements inside the ListBox element. For example, here's a ListBox that contains a list of colors:

```
<ListBox>
  <ListBoxItem Content="Green"></ListBoxItem>
  <ListBoxItem Content="Blue"></ListBoxItem>
  <ListBoxItem Content="Yellow"></ListBoxItem>
  <ListBoxItem Content="Red"></ListBoxItem>
</ListBox>
```

As you'll remember from Chapter 2, different controls treat their nested content in different ways. The ListBox stores each nested object in its Items collection.

Note Unlike WPF (and HTML forms), the Silverlight ListBox does not support multiple selection. It provides a SelectionMode property for future use, but currently the only possible value is Single.

The ListBox is a remarkably flexible control. Not only can it hold ListBoxItem objects, but it can also host any arbitrary element. This works because the ListBoxItem class derives from ContentControl, which gives it the ability to hold a single piece of nested content. If that piece of content is a UIElement-derived class, it will be rendered in the ListBox. If it's some other type of object, the ListBoxItem will call ToString() and display the resulting text.

For example, if you decided you want to create a list with images, you could create markup like this:

```
<ListBox>
  <ListBoxItem>
    <Image Source="happyface.jpg"></Image>
  </ListBoxItem>
  <ListBoxItem>
    <Image Source="happyface.jpg"></Image>
  </ListBoxItem>
</ListBox>
```

The ListBox is actually intelligent enough to create the ListBoxItem objects it needs implicitly. That means you can place your objects directly inside the ListBox element. Here's a more ambitious example that uses nested StackPanel objects to combine text and image content:

```
<ListBox>
  <StackPanel Orientation="Horizontal">
    <Image Source="happyface.jpg"  Width="30" Height="30"></Image>
    <TextBlock VerticalAlignment="Center" Text="A happy face"></TextBlock>
  </StackPanel>
  <StackPanel Orientation="Horizontal">
    <Image Source="redx.jpg" Width="30" Height="30"></Image>
    <TextBlock VerticalAlignment="Center" Text="A warning sign"></TextBlock>
  </StackPanel>
  <StackPanel Orientation="Horizontal">
    <Image Source="happyface.jpg"  Width="30" Height="30"></Image>
    <TextBlock VerticalAlignment="Center" Text="A happy face"></TextBlock>
  </StackPanel>
</ListBox>
```

In this example, the StackPanel becomes the item that's wrapped by the ListBoxItem. This markup creates the list shown in Figure 5-11.

Figure 5-11. *A list of images*

This ability to nest arbitrary elements inside list box items allows you to create a variety of list-based controls without needing to use specialized classes. For example, you can display a checkbox next to every item by nesting the CheckBox element inside the ListBox.

There's one caveat to be aware of when you use a list with different elements inside. When you read the SelectedItem value (and the SelectedItems and Items collections), you won't see ListBoxItem objects—instead, you'll see whatever objects you placed in the list. In the previous example, that means SelectedItem provides a StackPanel object.

When manually placing items in a list, it's up to you whether you want to place the items in directly or explicitly wrap each one in a ListBoxItem object. The second approach is often cleaner, albeit more tedious. The most important consideration is to be consistent. For example, if you place StackPanel objects in your list, the ListBox.SelectedItem object will be a StackPanel. If you place StackPanel objects wrapped by ListBoxItem objects, the ListBox.SelectedItem object will be a ListBoxItem, so code accordingly. And there's a third option—you can place data objects inside your ListBox and use a data template to display the properties you want. Chapter 14 has more about this technique.

The ListBoxItem offers a little bit of extra functionality from what you get with directly nested objects. Namely, it defines an IsSelected property that you can read (or set) and a Selected and Unselected event that tells you when that item is highlighted. However, you can get similar functionality using the members of the ListBox class, such as the SelectedItem and SelectedIndex properties and the SelectionChanged event.

The ComboBox

The ComboBox is similar to the ListBox control. It holds a collection of ComboBoxItem objects, which are created either implicitly or explicitly. As with the ListBoxItem, the ComboBoxItem is a content control that can contain any nested element. Unlike combo boxes in the Windows world, you can't type in the Silverlight ComboBox control to select an item or edit the selected value. Instead, you must use the arrow keys or the mouse to pick from the list.

The key difference between the ComboBox and ListBox classes is the way they render themselves in a window. The ComboBox control uses a drop-down list, which means only one item can be selected at a time.

One ComboBox quirk is the way it sizes itself when you use automatic sizing. The ComboBox widens itself to fit its content, which means that it changes size as you move from one item to the next. Unfortunately, there's no easy way to tell the ComboBox to take the size of its largest contained item. Instead, you may need to supply a hard-coded value for the Width property, which isn't ideal.

The TabControl

You're no doubt familiar with the TabControl, a handy container that condenses a large amount of user interface into a set of tabbed pages. In Silverlight, the TabControl is an items control that holds one or more TabItem elements.

Like several of Silverlight's more specialized controls, the TabControl is defined in a separate assembly. When you add it to a page, Visual Studio will add a reference to the System.Windows.Controls.dll assembly, and map a new XML namespace, like this one:

```
<UserControl xmlns:basics=
 "clr-namespace:System.Windows.Controls;assembly=System.Windows.Controls"
 ... >
```

To use the TabControl, you must fill it with one or more TabItem elements. Each TabItem represents a separate page. Because the TabItem is a content control, it can hold another Silverlight element (like a layout container).

Here's an example of a TabControl that includes two tabs. The first tab holds a StackPanel with three checkboxes:

```
<basics:TabControl>
  <basics:TabItem Header="Tab One">
    <StackPanel Margin="3">
      <CheckBox Margin="3" Content="Setting 1"></CheckBox>
      <CheckBox Margin="3" Content="Setting 2"></CheckBox>
      <CheckBox Margin="3" Content="Setting 3"></CheckBox>
    </StackPanel>
  </basics:TabItem>
  <basics:TabItem  Header="Tab Two">
    ...
  </basics:TabItem>
</basics:TabControl>
```

The TabItem holds its content (in this example, a StackPanel) in the TabItem.Content property. Interestingly, the TabItem also has another property that can hold arbitrary content—the Header. In the previous example, the Header holds a simple text string. However, you just as readily fill it with graphical content or a layout container that holds a whole host of elements, as shown here:

```
<basics:TabControl>
  <basics:TabItem>
    <basics:TabItem.Header>
      <StackPanel>
        <TextBlock Margin="3">Image and Text Tab Title</TextBlock>
        <Image Source="happyface.jpg" Stretch="None" />
      </StackPanel>
    </basics:TabItem.Header>

    <StackPanel Margin="3">
      <CheckBox Margin="3" Content="Setting 1"></CheckBox>
      <CheckBox Margin="3" Content="Setting 2"></CheckBox>
      <CheckBox Margin="3" Content="Setting 3"></CheckBox>
    </StackPanel>
  </basics:TabItem>
  <basics:TabItem  Header="Tab Two">
    ...
  </basics:TabItem>
</basics:TabControl>
```

Figure 5-12 shows the somewhat garish result.

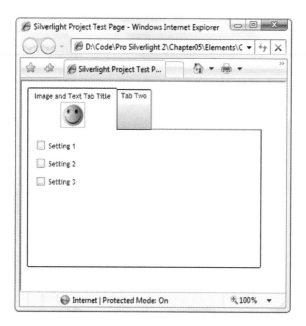

Figure 5-12. *An exotic tab title*

Like the ListBox, the TabControl includes a SelectionChanged event that fires when the visible tab changes, and a SelectedIndex and SelectedItem property, which allow you to determine or set the current tab. The TabControl also adds a TabStripPlacement property, which allows you to make the tabs appear on the side or bottom of the tab control, rather than their normal location at the top.

Text Controls

Silverlight includes a standard text box that supports any of the features of its counterpart in the Windows world, including scrolling, text wrapping, clipboard cut-and-paste, and selection.

A text box always stores a string, which is provided by the Text property. You can change the alignment of that text using the TextAlignment property, and you can use all the properties listed in Table 5-2 to control the font of the text inside the text box.

Ordinarily, the TextBox control stores a single line of text. (You can limit the allowed number of characters by setting the MaxLength property.) However, you can allow text to span multiple lines in two ways. First, you can enable wrapping using the TextWrapping property. Second, you can allow the user to insert line breaks with the Enter key by setting the AcceptsReturn property to true.

Sometimes, you'll create a text box purely for the purpose of displaying text. In this case, set the IsReadOnly property to true to prevent editing. This is preferable to disabling the text box by setting IsEnabled to false because a disabled text box shows grayed-out text (which is more difficult to read) and does not support selection (or copying to the clipboard).

Text Selection

As you already know, you can select text in any text box by clicking and dragging with the mouse or holding down Shift while you move through the text with the arrow keys. The TextBox class also gives you the ability to determine or change the currently selected text programmatically, using the SelectionStart, SelectionLength, and SelectedText properties.

SelectionStart identifies the zero-based position where the selection begins. For example, if you set this property to 10, the first selected character is the 11th character in the text box. The Selection Length indicates the total number of selected characters. (A value of 0 indicates no selected characters.) Finally, the SelectedText property allows you to quickly examine or change the selected text in the text box.

You can react to the selection being changed by handling the SelectionChanged event. Here's an example that reacts to this event and displays the current selection information:

```
private void txt_SelectionChanged(object sender, RoutedEventArgs e)
{
    if (txtSelection == null) return;

    txtSelection.Text = String.Format(
        "Selection from {0} to {1} is \"{2}\"",
        txt.SelectionStart, txt.SelectionLength, txt.SelectedText);
}
```

Figure 5-13 shows the result.

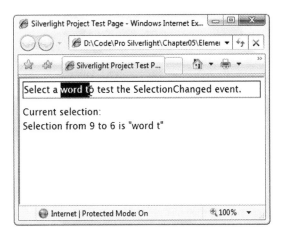

Figure 5-13. *Selecting text*

The PasswordBox

Silverlight includes a separate control called the PasswordBox to deal with password entry. The PasswordBox looks like a TextBox, but it displays a string of circle symbols to mask the characters inside. You can choose a different mask character by setting the PasswordChar property, and you can set (or retrieve) the text inside through the Password property. The PasswordBox does not provide a Text property.

Additionally, the PasswordBox does not support the clipboard. This means the user can't copy the text it contains using shortcut keys, and your code can't use properties like Selected-Text.

Note The WPF PasswordBox uses in-memory encryption, to ensure that passwords can't be retrieved in certain types of exploits (like memory dumps). The Silverlight Password box doesn't include this feature. It stores its contents in the same way as the ordinary TextBox.

Range-Based Controls

Silverlight includes two controls that use the concept of a *range*. These controls take a numeric value that falls in between a specific minimum and maximum value. These controls—ScrollBar, Slider, and ProgressBar—derive from the RangeBase class (which itself derives from the Control class). The RangeBase class adds a ValueChanged event, a Tooltip property, and the range properties shown in Table 5-4.

Table 5-4. *Properties of the RangeBase Class*

Name	Description
Value	This is the current value of the control (which must fall between the minimum and maximum). By default, it starts at 0. Contrary to what you might expect, Value isn't an integer—it's a double, so it accepts fractional values. You can react to the ValueChanged event if you want to be notified when the value is changed.
Maximum	This is the upper limit (the largest allowed value).
Minimum	This is the lower limit (the smallest allowed value).
SmallChange	This is the amount the Value property is adjusted up or down for a "small change." The meaning of a small change depends on the control (and may not be used at all). For the ScrollBar and Slider, this is the amount the value changes when you use the arrow keys. For the ScrollBar, you can also use the arrow buttons at either end of the bar.
LargeChange	This is the amount the Value property is adjusted up or down for a "large change." The meaning of a large change depends on the control (and may not be used at all). For the ScrollBar and Slider, this is the amount the value changes when you use the Page Up and Page Down keys or when you click the bar on either side of the thumb (which indicates the current position).

Ordinarily, there's no need to use the ScrollBar control directly. The higher-level Scroll-Viewer control, which wraps two ScrollBar controls, is typically much more useful. (The ScrollViewer was covered in Chapter 3.) However, the Slider and ProgressBar are more useful on their own.

The Slider

The Slider is a specialized control that's occasionally useful. You might use it to set numeric values in situations where the number itself isn't particularly significant. For example, it makes sense to set the volume in a media player by dragging the thumb in a slider bar from side to side. The general position of the thumb indicates the relative loudness (normal, quiet, loud), but the underlying number has no meaning to the user.

Here's an example that creates the horizontal slider shown in Figure 5-14:

```
<Slider Orientation="Horizontal" Minimum="0" Maximum="10" Width="100" />
```

Figure 5-14. *A basic slider*

Unlike WPF, the Silverlight slider doesn't provide any properties for adding tick marks. However, as with any control, you can change its appearance while leaving its functionality intact using the control templating feature described in Chapter 11.

The ProgressBar

The ProgressBar indicates the progress of a long-running task. Unlike the slider, the Progress-Bar isn't user interactive. Instead, it's up to your code to periodically increment the Value property. By default, the Minimum value of a ProgressBar is 0, and the Maximum value is 100, so the Value corresponds to the percentage of work done. You'll see an example with the Pro-gressBar in Chapter 6, with a page that downloads a file from the Web and shows its progress on the way.

One neat trick that you can perform with the ProgressBar is using it to show a long-running status indicator, even if you don't know how long the task will take. You do this by setting the IsIndeterminate property to true:

```
<ProgressBar Height="18" Width="200" IsIndeterminate="True"></ProgressBar>
```

When setting IsIndeterminate, you no longer use the Minimum, Maximum, and Value properties. No matter what values these properties have, the ProgressBar will show a hatched pattern that travels continuously from left to right. This pattern indicates that there's work in progress, but it doesn't provide any information about how much progress has been made so far.

Date Controls

Silverlight adds two date controls, neither of which exists in the WPF control library. Both are designed to allow the user to choose a single date.

The Calendar control displays a calendar that's similar to what you see in the Windows operating system (for example, when you configure the system date). It shows a single month at a time, and allows you to step through from month to month (by clicking the arrow buttons), or jump to a specific month (by clicking the month header to view an entire year, and then clicking the month).

The DateTimePicker requires less space. It's modeled after a simple text box, which holds a date string in long or short date format. However, the DateTimePicker provides a drop-down arrow that, when clicked, pops open a full calendar view that's identical to that shown by the Calendar control. This pop-up is displayed over top of any other content, just like a drop-down combo box.

Figure 5-15 shows the two display modes that the Calendar supports, and the two date formats that the DateTimePicker allows.

Figure 5-15. *The Calendar and DatePicker*

The Calendar and DateTimePicker include properties that allow you to determine which dates are shown and which dates are selectable (provided they fall in a contiguous range). Table 5-5 lists the properties you can use.

Table 5-5. *Properties of the Calendar and DateTimePicker Classes*

Property	Description
DisplayDateStart and DisplayDateEnd	Sets the range of dates that are displayed in the view from the first, earliest date to the last, oldest date (DisplayDateEnd). The user won't be able to navigate to months that don't have any displayable dates. To show all dates, set DisplayDateStart to DateTime.MinValue and DisplayDateEnd to DateTime.MaxValue.
BlackoutDates	Holds a collection of dates that will be disabled in the calendar, and won't be selectable. (If these dates are not in the range of displayed dates, or if one of these dates is already selected, you'll receive an exception.) To prevent selection of any date in the past, call the Calendar.BlackoutDates.AddDatesInPast() method.
SelectedDate	Provides the selected date as a DateTime object (or a null value if no date is selected). It can be set programmatically, by the user clicking the date in the calendar, or by the user typing in a date string (in the DatePicker). The Calendar also provides a SelectedDates property, which is useful if you change the SelectionMode property to allow multiple date selection.
DisplayDate	Determines what month is shown in the calendar view. If null, the month of the SelectedDate is shown. If DisplayDate and SelectedDate are both null, the current month is used.
FirstDayOfWeek	Determines the day of the week that will be displayed at the start of each calendar row, in the leftmost position.
IsTodayHighlighted	Determines whether the calendar view uses highlighting to point out the current date.
DisplayMode (Calendar only)	Determines the initial display month of the calendar. If set to Month, the Calendar shows the standard single-month view. If set to Year, the Calendar shows the months in the current year (similar to when the user clicks the month header). Once the user clicks a month, the Calendar shows the full calendar view for that month.
SelectionMode (Calendar only)	Determines what type of date selections are allowed. The default is SingleDate, which allows a single date to be selected. Other options include None (selection is disabled entirely), SingleRange (a contiguous group of dates can be selected), and MultipleRange (any combination of dates can be selected). In SingleRange or MultipleRange modes, the user can drag to select multiple dates, or click while holding down the Ctrl key. You can use the SelectedDates property to get a collection with all the selected dates.
IsDropDownOpen (DatePicker only)	Determines whether the calendar view drop-down is open in the DatePicker. You can set this property programmatically to show or hide the calendar.

Continued

Table 5-5. *Continued*

Property	Description
SelectedDateFormat (DatePicker only)	Determines how the selected date will be displayed in the text part of the DatePicker. You can choose Short or Long. The actual display format is based on the client computer's regional settings. For example, if you use Short, the date might be rendered in the yyyy/mm/dd format or dd/mm/yyyy. The long format generally includes the month and day names.

■ **Note** Don't rely on the AreDatesInPastSelectable, SelectableDateStart, and SelectableDateEnd properties to prevent all invalid input. They use the clock on the client computer, which could be inaccurate.

The date controls also provide a few different events. Most useful is SelectedDateChanged (in the DatePicker) or the very similar SelectedDatesChanged (in the Calendar), which adds support for multiple date selection. You can react to these events to reject specific date selections, such as dates that fall on a weekend:

```
private void Calendar_SelectedDatesChanged (object sender,
  CalendarDateChangedEventArgs e)
{
    // Check all the newly added items.
    foreach (DateTime selectedDate in e.AddedItems)
    {
        if ((selectedDate.DayOfWeek == DayOfWeek.Saturday) ||
          (selectedDate.DayOfWeek == DayOfWeek.Sunday))
        {
            lblError.Text = "Weekends are not allowed";

            // Remove the selected date.
            ((Calendar)sender).SelectedDates.Remove(selectedDate);
        }
    }
}
```

You can try this out with a Calendar that supports single or multiple selection. If it supports multiple selection, try dragging the mouse over an entire week of dates. All the dates will remain highlighted except for the disallowed weekend dates, which will be unselected automatically.

The Calendar also adds a DisplayDateChanged event (when the user browses to a new month). The DateTimePicker adds a CalendarOpened and CalendarClosed event (which fire when the calendar drop-down is displayed and closed) and a DateValidationError event (which fires when the user types a value in the text entry portion that can't be interpreted as a valid date). Ordinarily, invalid values are discarded when the user opens the calendar view, but here's an option that fills in some text to alert the user of the problem:

```
private void DatePicker_DateValidationError(object sender,
  DatePickerDateValidationErrorEventArgs e)
{
    lblError.Text = "'" + e.Text +
      "' is not a valid value because " + e.Exception.Message;
}
```

The Last Word

In this chapter, you saw all the fundamental Silverlight elements. You considered several categories:

- The TextBlock, which allows you to display richly formatted text using built-in and custom fonts

- The Image, which allows you to show JPEG and PNG images

- Content controls that can contain nested elements, including various types of buttons and the ToolTip

- List controls that contain a collection of items, such as the ListBox, ComboBox, and TabControl

- The TextBox, which provides basic text editing

- Range-based controls that take a numeric value from a range, such as the Slider

- The date controls, which allow the user to select one or more dates from a calendar display

Although you haven't had an exhaustive look at every detail of XAML markup, you've learned enough to reap all its benefits. Now, your attention can shift to the Silverlight technology itself, which holds some of the most interesting surprises. In the next chapter, you'll start out by considering the core of the Silverlight application model: the Application class.

CHAPTER 6

■■■

The Application Model

Over the past five chapters, you've taken a detailed look at the different types of visual elements you can put inside Silverlight pages. You've learned how to use layout containers and common controls, and how to respond to mouse and keyboard events. Now it's time to take a second look at the Silverlight application model, which shapes how your application is deployed and hosted.

In this chapter, you'll consider the application events that allow you to respond when your application is created, unloaded, or runs into trouble with an unhandled exception. Along the way, you'll see how to use initialization parameters, how to navigate from one page to another, and how to show a custom splash screen. Next, you'll take a detailed look at the many options Silverlight provides for retrieving resources, including large files (like images and video) and dependent assemblies. You'll learn how to include essential resources in your application package for easy deployment or download them on-demand to streamline performance.

Application Events

In Chapter 1, you took your first look at the life cycle of a Silverlight application. Here's a quick review:

1. The user requests the HTML entry page in the browser.

2. The Silverlight plug-in is loaded. It downloads the XAP file with your application.

3. The Silverlight plug-in reads the AppManifest.xml file from the XAP to find out what assemblies your application uses. It creates the Silverlight runtime environment and then loads your application assembly (and any dependencies).

4. The Silverlight plug-in creates an instance of your custom application class (which is defined in the App.xaml and App.xaml.cs files).

5. The default constructor of the application class raises the Startup event.

6. Your application handles the Startup event and creates the root visual.

From this point on, your page code takes over, until it encounters an unhandled error (UnhandledException) or finally ends (Exit). These events—Startup, UnhandledException, and Exit—are the only events that the Application class provides.

If you look at the contents of the App.xaml.cs file, you'll see that in Visual Studio there's some pre-generated code in the application constructor. This code attaches an event handler to the three application events:

```
public App()
{
    this.Startup += this.Application_Startup;
    this.Exit += this.Application_Exit;
    this.UnhandledException += this.Application_UnhandledException;

    InitializeComponent();
}
```

As with the page and element events you've considered in earlier chapters, there are actually two ways to attach application event handlers. Instead of using code, you could add event attributes to the XAML markup, as shown here:

```
<Application ... x:Class="SilverlightApplication1.App"
 Startup="Application_Startup" >
```

There's no reason to prefer one approach to the other. By default, Visual Studio uses the code approach shown earlier.

In the following sections, you'll see how you can write code that plugs into the application events.

Application Startup

By default, the Application_Startup method simply creates the first page and assigns it to the Application.RootVisual property, ensuring that it becomes the main application element.

```
private void Application_Startup(object sender, StartupEventArgs e)
{
    this.RootVisual = new Page();
}
```

Although you can change the root visual by adding or removing elements, you can't reassign the RootVisual property. After the application starts, it's essentially read-only. However, you'll learn how to manipulate the root visual to simulate the effect of changing pages in the "Changing the Page" section later in this chapter.

Application Shutdown

At some point, your Silverlight application ends. Most commonly, this occurs when the user surfs to another page in the web browser or closes the browser window. It also occurs if the users refreshes the page (effectively abandoning the current instance of the application and launching a new one), if the page runs JavaScript code that removes the Silverlight content region or changes its source, or an unhandled exception derails your code.

Just before the application is released from memory, Silverlight gives you the chance to run some code by responding to the Application.Exit event. This event is commonly used to store user-specific information locally in isolated storage (see Chapter 15), so it's available the next time the user runs your application.

The Exit event doesn't provide any additional information in its event arguments.

Unhandled Exceptions

Although you should use disciplined exception handling code in situations where errors are possible (for example, when reading a file, downloading web content, or accessing a web service), it's not always possible to anticipate all sources of error. If your application encounters an error that isn't handled, it will end, and the Silverlight content region will revert to a blank space. If you've included JavaScript code that reacts to potential errors from the Silverlight plug-in (as described in Chapter 1), that code will run. Otherwise, you won't receive any indication about the error that's just occurred.

The Application.UnhandledException event gives you a last-ditch chance to respond to an exception before it reaches the Silverlight plug-in and terminates your application. This code is notably different than the JavaScript error-handling code that you may add to the page, because it has the ability to mark an exception as handled. Doing so effectively neutralizes the exception, preventing it from rising to the plug-in and ending your application.

Here's an example that checks the exception type and decides whether to allow the application to continue:

```
public void Application_UnhandledException(object sender,
  ApplicationUnhandledExceptionEventArgs e)
{
    if (e.ExceptionObject is FileNotFoundException)
    {
        // Suppress the exception and allow the application to continue.
        e.Handled = true;
    }
}
```

Ideally, an exception like this will be handled closer to where it occurs—for example, in your page code, when you're performing a task that may result in a FileNotFoundException. Application-level error handling isn't ideal, because it's difficult to identify the original process that caused the problem and it's awkward to notify the user about what went wrong. But application-level error handling does occasionally offer a simpler and more streamlined way to handle certain scenarios—for example, when a certain type of exception crops up in numerous places.

Once you've neutralized the error, it makes sense to notify the user. One option is to call a custom method in your root visual. For example, this code calls a custom ReportError() method in the Page1 class, which is the root visual for the application:

```
Page1 rootPage = (Page1)this.RootVisual;
rootPage.ReportError(e.ExceptionObject);
```

Now the Page1.ReportError() method can examine the exception object and display the appropriate message in an element on the page.

In an effort to make your applications a little more resilient, Visual Studio adds a bit of boilerplate error-handling code to every new Silverlight application. This code checks if a debugger is currently attached (which indicates that the application is running in the Visual Studio debug environment). If there's no debugger, the code handles the error (rendering it harmless), and uses the HTML interoperability features you'll learn about in Chapter 12 to raise a JavaScript error in its place. Here's the slightly shortened code that shows how the process works:

```
public void Application_UnhandledException(object sender,
  ApplicationUnhandledExceptionEventArgs e)
{
    if (!System.Diagnostics.Debugger.IsAttached)
    {
        // Suppress the exception and allow the application to continue.
        e.Handled = true;

        try
        {
            // Build an error message.
            string errorMsg = e.ExceptionObject.Message +
              e.ExceptionObject.StackTrace;
            errorMsg = errorMsg.Replace('"', '\'').Replace("\r\n", @"\n");

            // Use the Window.Eval() method to run a line of JavaScript code that
            // will raise an error with the error message.
            HtmlPage.Window.Eval(
              "throw new Error(\"Unhandled Error in Silverlight 2 Application " +
              errorMsg + "\");");
        }
        catch {}
    }
}
```

Essentially, this code converts a fatal Silverlight error to a relatively harmless JavaScript error. The way the JavaScript error is dealt with depends on the browser. In Internet Explorer, a yellow alert icon will appear in the status bar. (Double-click the alert icon to get the full error details, as shown in Figure 6-1.) In Firefox, a script error message will appear. Either way, the error won't stop your application from continuing.

When you finish developing your application, you'll need to tweak the automatically generated error-handling code. That's because it just isn't acceptable to indiscriminately ignore all errors—doing so allows bugs to flourish and cause other usability problems or data errors further down the road. Instead, consider selectively ignoring errors that correspond to known error conditions and signaling the problem to the user.

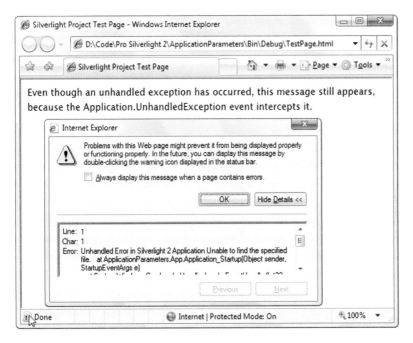

Figure 6-1. *A JavaScript error that represents an unhandled Silverlight exception*

■**Caution** It's easy to forget that you need to tweak the Application.UnhandledException event handler, because it only springs into action when you run your Silverlight application without a debugger. When you're testing your application in Visual Studio, you won't see this behavior—instead, any unhandled exception will end the application immediately.

XAML Resources

Although the most important part of your application is the logic in the code-behind file (App.xaml.cs), there is one ingredient you'll want to add to the application markup (App.xaml)—*application resources*.

In Chapter 2, you learned how XAML allows you to define objects in a resources collection and then use them in your markup. Resources allow you to centralize changing details (like vector drawings and formatting preferences), and they make it easier to reuse them throughout your markup.

Resources use a hierarchical lookup system. In other words, when you use a resource in an element, Silverlight checks the resources in that element, then that element's container, and so on, eventually ending up at the resources collection of the top-level user control that represents your page. However, resource lookup doesn't stop there. It continues for one more level, to the application resources collection, which is defined in the App.xaml collection. For instance, here's an example that defines a brush in the application resources collection:

```
<Application xmlns="http://schemas.microsoft.com/client/2007"
 xmlns:x="http://schemas.microsoft.com/winfx/2006/xaml"
 x:Class="SilverlightApplication1.App">
  <Application.Resources>
    <LinearGradientBrush x:Key="PageBackgroundBrush">
      <LinearGradientBrush.GradientStops>
        <GradientStop Offset="0.00" Color="Yellow" />
        <GradientStop Offset="0.50" Color="White" />
        <GradientStop Offset="1.00" Color="Purple" />
      </LinearGradientBrush.GradientStops>
    </LinearGradientBrush>
  </Application.Resources>
</Application>
```

The advantage of placing resources in the application collection is that they're completely removed from the markup in your page, and they can be reused in all the pages in your application:

```
<Grid x:Name="grid1" Background="{StaticResource PageBackgroundBrush}">
```

Furthermore, pages can selectively override a resource by defining a replacement with the same name in their resource collections.

Unfortunately, Silverlight doesn't currently allow you to merge resource dictionaries, which means there's no way to split your application resources into separate files and then merge them into your application (which is possible in WPF).

Note XAML resources shouldn't be confused with the binary resources you'll explore later in this chapter. XAML resources are objects that are declared in your markup. Binary resources are non-executable files that are inserted into your assembly or XAP file when your project is compiled.

Application Tasks

Now that you understand the lifetime of a Silverlight application, and the content of the App.xaml and App.xaml.cs files, you're ready to take a look at a few common scenarios. In the following sections, you'll consider how you can process initialization parameters, support page navigation, and show a splash screen while your application is loading.

Accessing the Current Application

You can retrieve a reference to the application object at any time, at any point in your code, using the static Application.Current property. However, the application object is typed as a System.Windows.Application object. To use any custom properties or methods that you've added to your derived application class, you must cast the reference to the App type:

```
((App)Application.Current).DoSomething()
```

Along with the static Current property, the Application class also provides several more important members, as described in Table 6-1.

Table 6-1. *Members of the Application Class*

Member	Description
Host	This property allows you to interact with the browser, and through it the rest of the HTML content on the web page. It's discussed in Chapter 12.
Resources	This property provides access to the collection of XAML resources that are declared in App.xaml, as shown earlier.
RootVisual	This property provides access to the root visual for your application— typically, the user control that's created when your application first starts. Once set, the root visual can't be changed, although you can manipulate the root visual to give the impression that the user is moving from one page to another, as demonstrated later in this chapter, in the section "Changing the Page."
GetResourceStream()	This static method is used to retrieve resources in code. You'll see how to use it later in this chapter in the "Resources" section.
LoadComponent()	This static method accepts a XAML file and instantiates the corresponding elements (much as Silverlight does automatically when you create a page class and the constructor calls the InitializeComponent() method).

Initialization Parameters

The Startup event passes in a StartupEventArgs object, which includes one additional detail— initialization parameters. This mechanism allows the page that hosts the Silverlight control to pass in custom information. This is particularly useful if you host the same Silverlight application on different pages, or you want the Silverlight application to vary based on user-specific or session-specific information. For example, you might customize the application's view depending on whether users are entering from the customer page or the employees page. Or, you might choose to load up different information based on the product that the user is currently viewing. Just remember that the initialization parameters come from the tags of the HTML entry page, and a malicious user can alter them.

▌Note For more detailed interaction between the HTML and your Silverlight application—for example, to pass information back and forth while your Silverlight application is running—see Chapter 12.

For example, imagine you want to pass a ViewMode parameter that has two possible values: Customer or Employee, as represented by this enumeration:

```
public enum ViewMode
{
    Customer, Employee
}
```

You'll need to change a variety of details based on this information, so it makes sense to store it somewhere that's accessible throughout your application. The logical choice is to add a property to your custom application class, as shown here:

```
private ViewMode viewMode = ViewMode.Customer;
public ViewMode ViewMode
{
    get { return viewMode; }
}
```

This property defaults to customer view, so it only needs to be changed if the web page specifically requests the employee view.

To pass the parameter into your Silverlight application, you need to add a <param> element to the markup in the Silverlight content region. This parameter must have the name initParams. Its value is a comma-separated list of name-value pairs that set your custom parameters. For example, to add a parameter named view mode, you would add the following line (shown in bold) to your markup:

```
<div id="silverlightControlHost">
  <object data="data:application/x-silverlight,"
   type="application/x-silverlight-2" width="100%" height="100%">
    <param name="source" value="TransparentSilverlight.xap"/>
    <param name="onerror" value="onSilverlightError" />
    <param name="background" value="white" />
    <param name="initParams" value=" viewMode=Customer" />

    ...
  </object>
  <iframe style='visibility:hidden;height:0;width:0;border:0px'></iframe>
</div>
```

Then, you can retrieve this from the StartupEventArgs.InitParams collection. However, you must check first that it exists:

```
private void Application_Startup(object sender, StartupEventArgs e)
{
    // Take the view mode setting, and store in an application property.
    if (e.InitParams.ContainsKey("viewMode"))
    {
        string view = e.InitParams["viewMode"];
        if (view == "Employee") this.view = ViewMode.Employee;
    }

    // Create the root page.
    this.RootVisual = new Page();
}
```

If you have many possible values, you can use the following leaner code to convert the string to the corresponding enumeration value, assuming the text matches exactly:

```
string view = e.InitParams["viewMode"];
try
{
    this.viewMode = (ViewMode)Enum.Parse(typeof(ViewMode), view, true);
}
catch { }
```

Now, different pages are free to pass in a different parameter and launch your application with different view settings. Because the view information is stored as a property in the custom application class (named App), you can retrieve it anywhere in your application:

```
lblViewMode.Text = "Current view mode: " +
  ((App)Application.Current).ViewMode.ToString();
```

Figure 6-2 shows what you'll see when you run the test page that uses the Customer view mode.

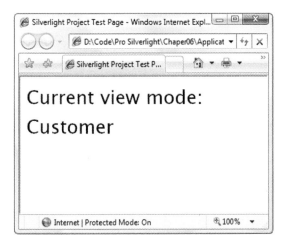

Figure 6-2. *Displaying an initialization parameter*

If you have more than one initialization parameter, simply pass them all in one comma-delimited string. Initialization values should be made up of alphanumeric characters. There's currently no support for escaping special characters like commas in parameter values.

```
<param name="initParams" value="startPage=Page1,viewMode=Customer" />
```

Now the event handler for the Startup event can retrieve the StartPage value and use it to choose the application's root page. You can load the correct page using a block of conditional logic that distinguishes between the available choices, or you can write a more general solution that uses reflection to attempt to create the class with the requested name, as shown here:

```
UserControl startPage = null;
if (e.InitParams.ContainsKey("startPage"))
{
    try
```

```
    {
        // Create an instance of the page.
        Type type = this.GetType();
        Assembly assembly = type.Assembly;
        startPage = (UserControl)assembly.CreateInstance(
            type.Namespace + "." + startPageName);
    }
    catch
    {
        startPage = null;
    }
}
// If no parameter was supplied or the class couldn't be created, use a default.
if (startPage == null) startPage = new MenuPage();

this.RootVisual = startPage;
```

Changing the Page

Once you've set the RootVisual property and your application has finished loading up, you can't change it. That means there's no way to unload a page and replace it with a new one. However, you can achieve much the same effect by changing what you use for your root visual. Instead of setting it with a custom user control, you can use something a bit more flexible—a simple container like the Border or layout panel like the Grid. Here's an example of the latter approach:

```
// This Grid will host your pages.
private Grid rootVisual = new Grid();

private void Application_Startup(object sender, StartupEventArgs e)
{
    // Load the first page.
    this.RootVisual = rootVisual;
    rootVisual.Children.Add(new Page());
}
```

Now, you can switch to another page by removing the first page from the Grid and adding a different one. To make this process relatively straightforward, you can add a static method like this to the App class:

```
public static void Navigate(UserControl newPage)
{
    // Get the current application object and cast it to
    // an instance of the custom (derived) App class.
    App currentApp = (App)Application.Current;
```

```
    // Change the currently displayed page.
    currentApp.rootVisual.Children.Clear();
    currentApp.rootVisual.Children.Add(newPage);
}
```

Now you can navigate at any point using code like this:

```
App.Navigate(new Page2());
```

Retaining Page State

If you plan to allow the user to navigate frequently between complex pages, it makes more sense to create them once and keep the page instance in memory until later. (This also has the sometimes-important side effect of maintaining that page's current state, including all the values in any input controls.) To implement this pattern, you first need a system to identify pages. You could fall back on string names, but an enumeration gives you better error prevention:

```
public enum Pages
{
    MainWindow, ReviewPage, AboutPage
}
```

You can then store the pages of your application in private fields in your custom application class. Here's a simple dictionary that does the trick:

```
private static Dictionary<Pages, UserControl> pageCache =
  new Dictionary<Pages,UserControl>();
```

In your Navigate() method, create the page only if it needs to be created—in other words, the corresponding object doesn't exist in the collection of cached pages.

```
public static void Navigate(Pages newPage)
{
    // Get the current application object and cast it to
    // an instance of the custom (derived) App class.
    App currentApp = (App)Application.Current;

    // Check if the page has been created before.
    if (!pageCache.ContainsKey(newPage))
    {
        // Create the first instance of the page,
        // and cache it for future use.
        Type type = currentApp.GetType();
        Assembly assembly = type.Assembly;
        pageCache[newPage] = (UserControl)assembly.CreateInstance(
          type.Namespace + "." + newPage.ToString());
    }
```

```
// Change the currently displayed page.
currentApp.rootVisual.Children.Clear();
currentApp.rootVisual.Children.Add(pageCache[newPage]);
}
```

Now you can navigate by indicating the page you want with the Pages enumeration:

```
App.Navigate(Pages.MainWindow);
```

Because there's only one version of the page ever created, and it's kept in memory over the lifetime of the application, all the page's state remains intact when you navigate away and back again (see Figure 6-3).

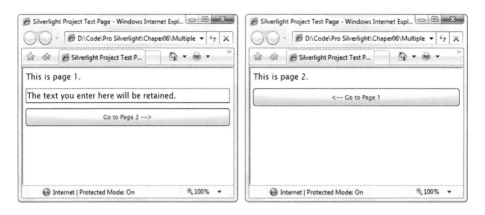

Figure 6-3. *Moving from one page to another*

Browser History

The only limitation with the navigation methods described in this section is the fact that the browser has no idea you've changed from one page to another. If you want to allow the user to go back, it's up to you to add the controls that do it. The browser's Back button will only send you to the previous HTML page (thereby exiting your Silverlight application). If you want to create an application that integrates more effectively with the browser and supports the Back button, it is possible—but you'll need to use Silverlight's HTML interaction support. Chapter 12 provides a complete example that demonstrates this technique.

■**Tip** You can add a dash of Silverlight animation and graphics to create a more pleasing transition between pages, such as a gentle fade or wipe. You'll learn how to perform this technique in Chapter 9.

Splash Screens

If a Silverlight application is small, it will be downloaded quickly and appear in the browser. If a Silverlight application is large, it may take a few seconds to download. As long as your application takes longer than 500 milliseconds to download, Silverlight will show an animated splash screen.

The built-in splash screen isn't too exciting—it simply displays a ring of blinking circles and the percentage of the application that's been downloaded so far (see Figure 6-4).

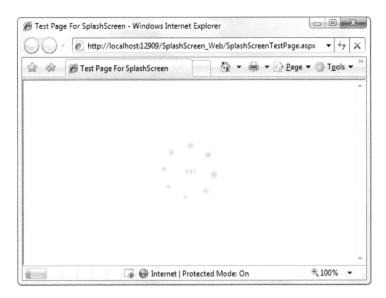

Figure 6-4. *The built-in Silverlight splash screen*

If you don't like the stock splash screen, you can easily create your own (see Figure 6-5). Essentially, a custom splash screen is a XAML file with the graphical content you want to display, and a dash of JavaScript code that updates the splash screen as the application is downloaded. You can't use C# code at this point, because the management Silverlight programming environment hasn't been initialized yet. However, this isn't a major setback, because the code you need is relatively straightforward. It lives in one or two event handling functions that are triggered as content is being downloaded and once it's finished, respectively. And because JavaScript is syntactically similar to C#, you won't have much trouble putting together the code you need.

Furthermore, the XAML file for your splash screen can't be a part of your Silverlight XAP file. That's because the splash screen needs to be shown while the XAP file is still in the process of being downloaded. For that reason, the splash screen XAML must be a separate file that's placed alongside your XAP file at the same web location.

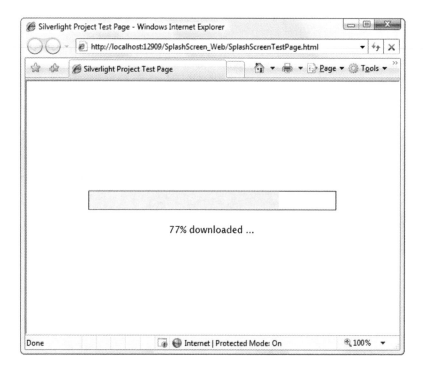

Figure 6-5. *A custom splash screen*

■**Note** Testing a custom splash screen requires a bit of work. Ordinarily, you won't see the splash screen while testing because the application is sent to the browser too quickly. To slow down your application enough to see the splash screen, you need to first ensure that you're using an ASP.NET test website, which ensures that your Silverlight application is hosted by Visual Studio test web server (as described in Chapter 1). Then, you need to add multiple large resource files to your Silverlight project—say, a handful of MP3 files— and set the build action of each one to Resource so it's added to the XAP file. Another trick is to temporarily remove the line of code in the Application_Startup() method that sets the root visual for your application. This way, once your application has been completely downloaded, it won't actually display anything. Instead, the splash screen will remain visible, displaying a progress percentage of 100%.

To create the example shown in Figure 6-5, begin by creating a new Silverlight project with an ASP.NET test website, as described in Chapter 1. Then, add a new XAML file to your ASP.NET website (not the Silverlight project). To do so, select the ASP.NET website in the Solution Explorer and choose Website ➤ Add New Item. Choose the Silverlight JScript page template, enter a name, and click Add. This XAML file will hold the markup for your splash screen.

When you add a new XAML file, Visual Studio will create a basic XAML skeleton that defines a Canvas. That's because Visual Studio assumes you're building a Silverlight 1.0 application, which supports a much smaller set of elements and doesn't include any of the more advanced layout containers. However, you can use any of the core Silverlight 2.0 elements—that is, elements that are in the built-in assemblies and don't require a separate download. You can't use elements that are defined in the add-on System.Windows.Controls.dll assembly, or those in any other assembly that needs to be packaged in the XAP and downloaded by the client.

Tip The easiest way to build a simple splash screen is to create it in your Silverlight project and then copy the markup into the splash screen file on your website. This way, you can take advantage of the Visual Studio design surface and XAML IntelliSense, which won't be available if you write the markup directly in your ASP.NET website.

Here's the XAML for the simple splash screen shown in Figure 6-5. It includes a Grid with a TextBlock and two Rectangle objects. (The Rectangle is a shape-drawing element you'll learn about in Chapter 7.) The first Rectangle paints the background of the progress bar, while the second paints the foreground. The two Rectangle objects are placed together in a single-celled Grid, so that the one rectangle is superimposed over the other.

```
<Grid xmlns="http://schemas.microsoft.com/client/2007"
 xmlns:x="http://schemas.microsoft.com/winfx/2006/xaml">
  <StackPanel VerticalAlignment="Center">
    <Grid>
      <Rectangle x:Name="progressBarBackground" Fill="White" Stroke="Black"
       StrokeThickness="1" Height="30" Width="200"></Rectangle>
      <Rectangle x:Name="progressBar" Fill="Yellow" Height="28" Width="0">
      </Rectangle>
    </Grid>
    <TextBlock x:Name="progressText" HorizontalAlignment="Center"
     Text="0% downloaded ..."></TextBlock>
  </StackPanel>
</Grid>
```

Next, you need to add a JavaScript function to your HTML entry page or ASP.NET test page. (If you plan on using both, place the JavaScript function in a separate file and then link to it in both files using the source attribute of the script block.) The JavaScript code can look up named elements on the page using the sender.findName() method, and manipulate their properties. It can also determine the current progress using the eventArgs.progress property. In this example, the event handling code simply updates the text and widens the progress bar based on the current progress percentage:

```
<script type="text/javascript">
  function onSourceDownloadProgressChanged(sender, eventArgs)
  {
      sender.findName("progressText").Text =
        Math.round((eventArgs.progress * 100)) + "% downloaded ...";
      sender.findName("progressBar").Width =
```

```
        eventArgs.progress * sender.findName("progressBarBackground").Width;
   }
</script>
```

■**Note** The splash screen example that's included with the downloadable code uses a slightly more advanced technique that draws on a transform, a concept you'll explore in Chapter 8. This approach allows you to create a progress bar effect without hard-coding the maximum width, so the progress bar is sized to fit the current browser window.

To use this splash screen, you need to add the splashscreensource parameter to identify your XAML splash screen and the onsourcedownloadprogresschanged parameter to hook up your JavaScript event handler. If you want to react when the download is finished, you can hook up a different JavaScript event handler using the onsourcedownloadcomplete parameter.

```
<object data="data:application/x-silverlight," type="application/x-silverlight-2"
 width="100%" height="100%">
  <param name="source" value="ClientBin/SplashScreen.xap"/>
  <param name="onerror" value="onSilverlightError" />
  <param name="background" value="white" />
  <param name="splashscreensource" value="SplashScreen.xaml" />
  <param name="onsourcedownloadprogresschanged"
   value="onSourceDownloadProgressChanged" />
  ...
</object>
```

If you're using an ASP.NET page to host your Silverlight application, you don't directly define the <object> element for the Silverlight content region. Instead, you work with the Silverlight web control, which is described in Chapter 13. This control provides three equivalent properties named SplashScreenSource, OnSourceDownloadProgressChanged, and OnSourceDownloadComplete. You set them in the same way as you would set the parameters in the HTML test page:

```
<asp:Silverlight ID="silverlightControl" runat="server"
 Source="~/ClientBin/MyApp.xap" Version="2.0" Width="800" Height="500"
 SplashScreenSource="~/SplashScreen.xaml"
 OnSourceDownloadProgressChanged="onSourceDownloadProgressChanged" />
```

Expert designers can craft elaborate splash screens. This tradition is well-established with Flash applications. To see a taste of what's possible, visit http://www.smashingmagazine.com/2008/03/13/showcase-of-creative-flash-preloaders. You can duplicate many of these effects with an ordinary Silverlight splash screen, like the one described here. However, some are extremely difficult. Most would be far easier to achieve *after* you've downloaded your application, such as code-heavy animations.

If you want more flexibility to create an eye-catching splash screen, you'll need to use a completely different technique. First, make your application as small as possible. Move its functionality to class library assemblies, and place large resources (like graphics and videos) in separate files or in separate class library assemblies. Now that your application is stripped down to a hollow shell, it can be downloaded quite quickly. Once downloaded, your application can show its fancy preloader and start the real work—programmatically downloading the resources and assemblies it needs to function.

Designing an application this way takes more work, but you'll get all the information you need to perform dynamic downloads in the following sections. Pay particular attention to the last section in this chapter, "Downloading Assemblies on Demand."

Resources

As you learned in Chapter 1, a Silverlight application is actually a package of files that's archived using ZIP compression and stored as a single file, with the extension .xap. In a simple application, the XAP file has little more than a manifest (which list the files your project uses) and your application assembly. However, there's something else you can place in the XAP file—resources.

A XAP resource is a distinct file that you want to make available to your compiled application. Common examples include graphical *assets*—images, sounds, and video files that you want to display in your user interface.

However, using resources can be unnecessarily complicated because of the wealth of different options Silverlight provides for storing them. Here's a quick roundup of your options:

- **In the application assembly.** The resource file is embedded in the compiled DLL file for your project, such as SilverlightApplication1.dll. This is the default approach.

- **In the application package.** The resource file is placed in the XAP file alongside your application assembly. It's still just as easy to deploy, but now it's a bit easier to manage, because you replace or modify your assets by editing the XAP file, without compiling your application.

- **On the site of origin.** The resource file is placed on the website alongside your XAP file. Now you have more deployment headaches, because you need to make sure you deploy both the XAP file and the resource file. However, you gain the ability to use your resource in other ways—for example, you can use images in ordinary HTML web pages, or make videos available for easy downloading. You can reduce the size of the initial XAP download, which is important if the resources are large.

These aren't all your options. As you'll see later in this chapter in the "Class Library Assemblies" section, you can also place resources in other assemblies that your application uses. (This approach gives you more advanced options for controlling the way you share content between different Silverlight applications.) However, before tackling that topic, it's worth taking a closer look at the more common options outlined previously. In the following sections, you'll explore each approach.

Placing Resources in the Application Assembly

This is the standard approach, and it's similar to the approach used in other types of .NET applications (such as WPF applications). For example, if you want to show an image in Silverlight's Image element, begin by adding the image file to your project. By default, Visual Studio will give image files the Resource build action, as shown in Figure 6-6. (To change the build action of an existing file, select it in the Solution Explorer, and make a new selection in the Build Action box in the Properties pane.)

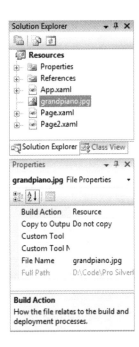

Figure 6-6. *An application resource*

■**Note** Don't confuse the build action of Resource with Embedded Resource. Although both do the same thing (embed a resource in the assembly as a block of binary data), Silverlight does not support the Embedded Resource approach, and you won't be able to reference files that are stored in this way using URIs.

Now, when you compile your application, the resource will be embedded in the project assembly, and the project assembly will be placed in the XAP file.

> **Note** Although the resource option makes it most difficult for a user to extract a resource file from your application, it's still possible. To retrieve a resource, the user needs to download the XAP file, unzip it, and decompile the DLL file. Tools like Reflector (`http://www.aisto.com/roeder/dotnet`) provide plug-ins that can extract and save embedded resources from an assembly.

Using an embedded resource is easy, because of the way Silverlight uses URIs. If you use a relative URI with the Image (for graphics) or MediaElement (for sound and video files), Silverlight checks the assembly for a resource with the right name. That means this is all you need to use the resource shown in Figure 6-6:

```
<Image x:Name="img" Source="grandpiano.jpg"></Image>
```

Using Subfolders

It's possible to use the folders to group resource files in your project. This changes how the resource is named. For example, consider Figure 6-7, which puts the grandpiano.jpg file in a subfolder named Images.

Figure 6-7. *A resource in a subfolder*

Now you need to use this URI:

```
<Image Source="Images/grandpiano.jpg"></Image>
```

Programmatically Retrieving a Resource

Using resources is easy when you have an element that supports Silverlight's URI standard, such as the Image and MediaElement. However, in some situations you'll need to manipulate your resource in code before handing it off to an element, or you might not want to use an element at all. For example, you might have some static data in a text or binary file that's stored as a resource. In your code, you want to retrieve this file and process its data.

To perform this task, you need the help of the Application.GetResourceStream(). It allows you to retrieve the data for a specific resource, which you indicate by supplying the correct URI. The trick is that you need to use the following URI format:

```
/AssemblyName;component/ResourceFileName
```

For example, if you have a resource named ProductList.bin in a project named Silverlight-Application1, you would use this line of code:

```
StreamResourceInfo sri = Application.GetResourceStream(
  new Uri("SilverlightApplication1;component/ProductList.bin", UriKind.Relative));
```

The GetResourceStream() method doesn't retrieve a stream. Instead, it gets a System.Windows.Resources.StreamResourceInfo object, which wraps a Stream property (with the underlying stream) and a ContentType property (with the MIME type). Here's the code that creates a BinaryReader for the stream:

```
BinaryReader reader = new BinaryReader(sri.Stream);
```

You can now use the methods of the binary reader to pull each piece of data out of the file. The same approach works with the StreamReader (for text-based data) or the XmlReader (for XML data). However, there's a slightly easier option when XML data is involved, because the XmlReader.Create() method accepts either a stream or a URI string that points to a resource. So if you have a resource named ProductList.xml, this code works:

```
StreamResourceInfo sri = Application.GetResourceStream(
  new Uri("SilverlightApplication1;component/ProductList.xml", UriKind.Relative));
XmlReader reader = XmlReader.Create(sri.Stream, new XmlReaderSettings());
```

and so does this more streamlined approach:

```
XmlReader reader = XmlReader.Create("ProductList.xml")
```

Placing Resources in the Application Package

Your second option for resource storage is to place it in the XAP file where your application assembly is stored. To do this, you simply need to add the appropriate file to your project and change the build action to Content. Best of all, you can use almost the same URLs. You simply need to precede them with a forward slash, as shown here:

```
<Image Source="/grandpiano.jpg"></Image>
```

Similarly, here's a resource in a subfolder in the XAP:

```
<Image Source="/Images/grandpiano.jpg"></Image>
```

The leading slash represents the root of the XAP file.

If you add the extension .zip to your XAP file, you can open it up and verify that the resource file is stored inside, as shown in Figure 6-8.

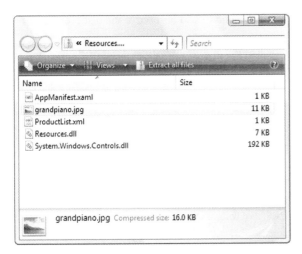

Figure 6-8. *A resource in a XAP file*

Placing resources in the XAP file gives you the same easy deployment as embedding them in the assembly. However, it adds a slight bit of flexibility. If you're willing to go to a bit more work, you can manipulate the files in the XAP file (for example, updating a graphic), without recompiling the application. Furthermore, if you have several class library assemblies in the same XAP file, they can all use the same resource files in the XAP. (This is an unlikely arrangement, but a possible one.) Overall, placing resources in the application package is a similar approach to embedding them in the assembly.

Placing Resources on the Web

Your third option is to remove resource files from your application completely, but make them available on the Web. That way, your application can download them when needed. Thanks to Silverlight's URI support, you can usually use this scenario without writing any extra code to deal with the download process.

The simplest option when deploying resources on the Web is to place them in the same web location as your Silverlight assembly. If you're using an ASP.NET test website, you can easily add the files to the test website—just place them in the ClientBin folder where the XAP file is placed. If you're using an HTML test page, you'll need to add the file to your Silverlight project and explicitly tell Visual Studio what to do with it. First, select the resource file and choose None for the build action. Then, set the Copy to Output Directory setting to Copy Always. It's still up to you to remember to copy the resource files with the XAP file when you deploy the application.

When using web resources, you use the same URIs as when placing resources in the application package. These are relative URIs prefaced with a forward slash. Here's an example:

```
<Image Source="/grandpiano.jpg"></Image>
```

Silverlight will check the XAP file first, and then check the folder where the XAP file is located. Thus, you can freely switch between the XAP file approach and the website approach after you've compiled an application—you simply need to add or remove the resource files in the XAP file.

Web-deployed resources don't need to be located at the same site as your XAP file, although that's the most common approach. If you use an absolute URL, you can show an image from any location:

```
<Image Source="http://www.mysite.com/Images/grandpiano.jpg"></Image>
```

■**Note** When testing an application that uses images with absolute URLs, a small glitch can creep in. The problem is that the Image element can't perform cross-scheme access, which means if you're running Silverlight directly from your hard drive using a simple HTML test page, you won't be able to retrieve an image from the Web. To resolve this problem, add an ASP.NET test website to your project, as described in Chapter 1.

Web-deployed resources are treated in a significantly different way in your application. Because they aren't in the XAP file (either directly or indirectly, as part of the assembly), they aren't compressed. If you have a large, easily compressed file (say, XML data), this means that the web-deployed option will result in longer download times, at least for some users. More significant is the fact the web-deployed resources are downloaded on demand, when they're referenced in your application. Thus, if you have a significant number of large resources, web deployment is often much better—it trades a long delay on startup for many smaller delays when individual resources are accessed.

■**Note** The obvious disadvantage with all of these resource-storing approaches is that they require fixed, unchanging data. In other words, there's no way for your application to modify the resource file and then save the modified version in the assembly, XAP file, or website. (In theory, the last one—website uploading—could be made possible, but it would create an obvious security hole.) The best solution when you need to change data is to use isolated storage (if storing the changed data locally is a good enough solution) or a web service (if you need a way to submit changes to the server). These approaches are discussed in Chapter 15 and Chapter 13, respectively.

Failing to Download Resources

When you use web-deployed resources, you introduce the possibility that your resources won't be where you expect them to be, and you won't be able to download them successfully. Elements that use the URI system often provide events to notify when a download can't be completed, such as ImageFailed for the ImageElement and MediaFailed for the MediaElement.

Failing to download a resource is not considered a critical error. For example, if the Image element fails to find the right picture, it simply remains blank. However, you can react to the corresponding failure event to update your user interface.

Downloading Resources with WebClient

Web-deployed resources can't be accessed using the handy Application.GetResourceStream()
method. As a result, if you want to use the data from a web-deployed resource and you don't
have an element that uses Silverlight URIs, you'll need to go to a bit more work.

In this situation, you need to use the System.Net.WebClient class to download the resource.
The WebClient class provides three key methods. OpenReadAsync() is the most useful—it
downloads a file as blob of binary data, which is then exposed as a stream. By comparison,
DownloadStringAsync() downloads the contents into a single string. Finally, CancelAsync()
halts any download that's currently underway.

The WebClient does its work asynchronously. You can respond to the DownloadProgress-
Changed event while the download is underway to find out how many bytes have been retrieved
so far. When the download is complete, you can respond to the OpenReadCompleted or
DownloadStringCompleted event, depending on which operation you're using, and then
retrieve your content.

The WebClient has two important limitations:

- The WebClient does not support "downloading" from the file system. Thus, in order to
  use the WebClient class, you must be running your application through a web server.
  The easiest way to do this in Visual Studio is to let Visual Studio create an ASP.NET website, which will then be hosted by the integrated web server (as described in Chapter 1).
  If you open your Silverlight page directly from the file system, you'll get an exception
  when you attempt to use the downloading methods in the WebClient.

- The WebClient doesn't support relative URIs. To get the right URI, you can determine
  the URI of the current page and then add the relative URI that points to your resource.

- The WebClient only allows one download at a time. If you attempt to start a second
  request while the first is still underway, you'll receive a NotSupportedException.

■**Note** There's one other issue—Silverlight's security model. If you plan to use WebClient to download a
file from another web server (not the web server where your application is hosted), you'll need to make sure
that web server explicitly allows cross-domain calls. Chapter 13 discusses this issue in detail.

Here's an example that puts the pieces together. It reads binary data from the Product-
List.bin file, just as you saw earlier. However, in this example ProductList.bin is hosted on the
website and isn't a part of the XAP file or project assembly. (When testing this example using
an ASP.NET website, you need to add the ProductList.bin file to the ASP.NET website, not the
Silverlight project. To see the correct setup, refer to the downloadable examples for this
chapter.)

When a button is clicked, the downloading process starts. Notice that there's a bit of string
processing at work with the URI. To get the right path, you need to create a fully qualified URI
using the current address of the entry page, which can be retrieved from the Application.Host
property.

```
private void cmdRetrieveResource_Click(object sender, RoutedEventArgs e)
{
    // Construct the fully qualified URI.
    // Assume the file is in the website root, one level above the ClientBin
    // folder. (In other words, the file has been added to the root level
    // of the ASP.NET website.)
    string uri = Application.Current.Host.Source.AbsoluteUri;
    int index = uri.IndexOf("/ClientBin");
    uri = uri.Substring(0, index) + "/ProductList.bin";

    // Begin the download.
    WebClient webClient = new WebClient();
    webClient.OpenReadCompleted += webClient_OpenReadCompleted;
    webClient.OpenReadAsync(new Uri(uri));
}
```

Now, you can respond when the file has been completed and manipulate the downloaded data as a stream.

```
private void webClient_OpenReadCompleted(object sender,
  OpenReadCompletedEventArgs e)
{
    if (e.Error != null)
    {
        // (Add code to display error or downgrade gracefully.)
    }
    else
    {
        Stream stream = e.Result;
        BinaryReader reader = new BinaryReader(stream);
        // (Now process the contents of the resource.)
        reader.Close();
    }
}
```

For simplicity's sake, this code retrieves the resource every time you click the button. However, a more efficient approach is to store the retrieved data in memory so it doesn't need to be downloaded more than once.

The OpenReadCompletedEventArgs provides several pieces of information along with the Result property. To determine if the operation was cancelled using the CancelAsync() method, you can check the Cancelled property, and if an error occurred you can get the exception object from the Error property. (In this situation, attempting to read the other properties of the OpenReadCompletedEventArgs object will result in a TargetInvocationException.) You can also use an overloaded version of the OpenReadAsync() method that accepts a custom object, which you can then retrieve from the UserState property. However, this is of limited use, because the WebClient only allows one download at a time.

When downloading a large file, it's often worth showing a progress indicator to inform the user of what's taking place. To do so, attach an event handler to the DownloadProgressChanged event:

```
webClient.DownloadProgressChanged += webClient_DownloadProgressChanged;
```

Here's the code that calculates the percentage that's been downloaded and uses it to set the value of a progress bar and a text label:

```
private void webClient_DownloadProgressChanged(object sender,
  DownloadProgressChangedEventArgs e)
{
    lblProgress.Text = e.ProgressPercentage.ToString() + " % downloaded.";
    progressBar.Value = e.ProgressPercentage
}
```

Class Library Assemblies

So far, all the examples you've seen in this book have placed all their code into a single assembly. For a small or modest-sized Silverlight application, this straightforward design makes good sense. However, it's not hard to imagine that you might want to factor out certain functionality and place it in a separate class library assembly. Usually, you'll take this step because you want to reuse that functionality with more than one Silverlight application. Alternatively, you might just want to separate it so it can be coded, compiled, debugged, and revised separately, which is particularly important if that code is being created by a different development team.

Creating a Silverlight class library is easy. In fact, it's essentially the same process you follow to create and use class library assemblies in ordinary .NET applications. First, create a new project in Visual Studio using the Silverlight Class Library project template. Then, add a reference in your Silverlight application that points to that project or assembly. The dependent assembly will be copied into the XAP package when you build your application.

Using Resources in an Assembly

Class libraries give you a handy way to share resources between applications. You can embed a resource in a class library and then retrieve it in your application. In fact, this technique is easy—the only trick is constructing the right URIs. To pull a resource out of a library, you need to use a URI that includes the application in this format:

```
/ClassLibraryName;component/ResourceFileName
```

This is the same format you learned about earlier, in the section "Programmatically Retrieving a Resource," but with one addition. Now, the URI begins with a leading slash, which represents the root of the XAP file. This URI points to the dependent assembly in that file, and then indicates a resource in that assembly.

For example, consider the ResourceClassLibrary assembly in Figure 6-9. It includes a resource named happyface.jpg, and that file has a build action of Resource.

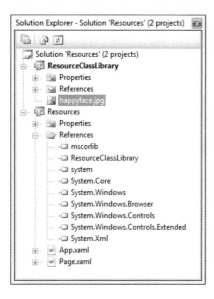

Figure 6-9. *A resource in a XAP file*

Here's an image file that uses the resource from the class library:

```
<Image Source="/ResourceClassLibrary;component/happyface.jpg"></Image>
```

Downloading Assemblies on Demand

In some situations, the code in a class library is used infrequently, or perhaps not at all for certain users. However, if the class library contains a significant amount of code or (more likely) has large embedded resources like graphics, including it with your application will increase the size of your XAP file and lengthen download times needlessly. In this case, you might want to create a separate component assembly—one that isn't downloaded until you need it. This scenario is similar to on-demand resource downloading. You place the separate resource in a separate file outside of the XAP file, but on the same website.

Before you use assembly downloading, you need to make sure that the dependent assembly won't be placed in the XAP file. To do so, select the project reference that points to the assembly. In the Properties window, set Copy Local to false. Next, make sure the assembly is copied to the same location as your website. If you're using an ASP.NET test website, that means you must add the assembly to the ClientBin folder in the test website. (You can't try this example with a simple HTML test page, because the WebClient doesn't work when you run a Silverlight application from the file system.)

To implement on-demand downloading of assemblies, you need to use the WebClient you saw earlier, in conjunction with the AssemblyPart class. The WebClient retrieves the assembly, and the assembly makes it available for downloading.

```
string uri = Application.Current.Host.Source.AbsoluteUri;
int index = uri.IndexOf("/ClientBin");
// In this example, the URI includes the /ClientBin portion, because we've
// decided to place the DLL in the ClientBin folder.
uri = uri.Substring(0, index) + "/ClientBin/ResourceClassLibrary.dll";

// Begin the download.
WebClient webClient = new WebClient();
webClient.OpenReadCompleted += webClient_OpenReadCompleted;
webClient.OpenReadAsync(new Uri(uri));
```

When the assembly is downloaded, you use the AssemblyPart.Load() method to load it into the current application domain:

```
private void webClient_OpenReadCompleted(object sender,
  OpenReadCompletedEventArgs e)
{
    if (e.Error != null)
    {
        // (Add code to display error or downgrade gracefully.)
    }
    else
    {
        AssemblyPart assemblypart = new AssemblyPart();
        assemblypart.Load(e.Result);
    }
}
```

Once you've performed this step, you can retrieve resources from your assembly and instantiate types from it. It's as though your assembly had been a part of the XAP file from the start. You can try a demonstration of this technique with the sample code for this chapter.

Once again, it's important to keep track of whether you've downloaded an assembly, so you don't attempt to download it more than once. Some applications "daisy chain" assemblies, so one application downloads other dependent assemblies on demand, and these assemblies download additional assemblies when *they* need them.

Tip If you attempt to use an assembly that hasn't been downloaded, you'll receive an exception. However, the exception won't be raised to the code that is attempting to use the assembly. Instead, that code will be aborted, and the exception will pass to the event handler for the Application.UnhandledException event. The actual exception is a FileNotFoundException object, and the message includes the name of the missing assembly.

The Last Word

In this chapter, you explored the Silverlight application model in detail. You reexamined the application object, and considered how you can react to application events and store application resources. Next, you considered practical techniques that depend on the application class, such as passing initialization parameters from different web pages, moving from one page to another in your Silverlight application, and displaying a splash screen while your application is being downloaded. Finally, you explored the resource system that Silverlight uses, and considered the many options for deploying resources and class libraries, from placing them alongside your assembly to downloading them only when needed.

CHAPTER 7

■ ■ ■

Shapes and Geometries

Silverlight's 2-D drawing support is the basic foundation for many of its more sophisticated features, such as custom-drawn controls, interactive graphics, and animation. Even if you don't plan to create customized art for your application, you need to have a solid understanding of Silverlight's drawing fundamentals. You'll use it to add professional yet straightforward touches, like reflection effects. You'll also need it to add interactivity to your graphics—for example, to make shapes move or change in response to user actions.

Silverlight supports a surprisingly large subset of the drawing features from WPF, its more capable sibling. In this chapter, you'll explore the shape model, which allows you to construct graphics out of rectangles, ellipses, lines, and curves. You'll also see how you can convert existing vector art to the XAML format you need, which allows you to reuse existing graphics rather than build them from scratch.

Basic Shapes

The simplest way to draw 2-D graphical content in a Silverlight user interface is to use *shapes*: dedicated classes that represent simple lines, ellipses, rectangles, and polygons. Technically, shapes are known as drawing *primitives*. You can combine these basic ingredients to create more complex graphics.

The most important detail about shapes in Silverlight is the fact that they all derive from FrameworkElement. As a result, shapes *are* elements. This has a number of important consequences:

- **Shapes draw themselves.** You don't need to manage the invalidation and painting process. For example, you don't need to manually repaint a shape when content moves, the page is resized, or the shape's properties change.

- **Shapes are organized in the same way as other elements.** In other words, you can place a shape in any of the layout containers you learned about in Chapter 3. (Although the Canvas is obviously the most useful container because it allows you to place shapes at specific coordinates, which is important when you're building a complex drawing out of multiple pieces.)

- **Shapes support the same events as other elements.** That means you don't need to go to any extra work to deal with key presses, mouse movements, and mouse clicks. You can use the same set of events you'd use with any element.

Silverlight uses a number of optimizations to make 2-D drawing as fast as possible. For example, because shapes often overlap in complex drawings, Silverlight uses sophisticated algorithms to determine when part of a shape won't be visible, and thereby avoid the overhead of rendering and then overwriting it with another shape.

The Shape Classes

Every shape derives from the abstract System.Windows.Shapes.Shape class. Figure 7-1 shows the inheritance hierarchy for shapes.

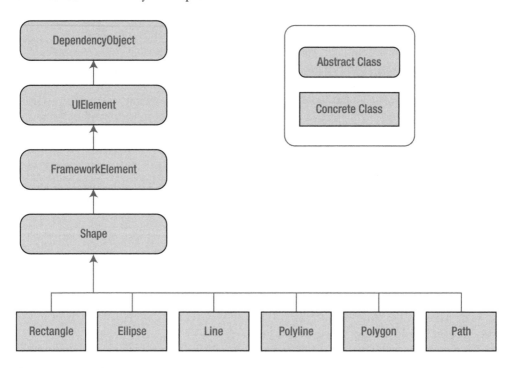

Figure 7-1. *The Silverlight shape classes*

As you can see, there's a relatively small set of classes that derive from the Shape class. Line, Ellipse, and Rectangle are all straightforward, while Polyline is a connected series of straight lines, and Polygon is a closed shape made up of a connected series of straight lines. Finally, the Path class is an all-in-one superpower that can combine basic shapes in a single element.

Although the Shape class can't do anything on its own, it defines a small set of important properties, which are listed in Table 7-1.

Table 7-1. *Shape Properties*

Name	Description
Fill	Sets the brush object that paints the surface of the shape (everything inside its borders).
Stroke	Sets the brush object that paints the edge of the shape (its border).
StrokeThickness	Sets the thickness of the border, in pixels.
StrokeStartLineCap and StrokeEndLineCap	Determine the contour of the edge of the beginning and end of the line. These properties only have an effect for the Line, the Polyline, and (sometimes) the Path shapes. All other shapes are closed, and so have no starting and ending point.
StrokeDashArray, StrokeDashOffset, and StrokeDashCap	Allow you to create a dashed border around a shape. You can control the size and frequency of the dashes and how the edge where each dash line begins and ends is contoured.
StrokeLineJoin and StrokeMiterLimit	Determine the contour of the corners of a shape. Technically, these properties affect the *vertices* where different lines meet, such as the corners of a Rectangle. These properties have no effect for shapes without corners, such as Line and Ellipse.
Stretch	Determines how a shape fills its available space. You can use this property to create a shape that expands to fit its container. However, you'll rarely set the Stretch property, because each shape uses the default value that makes most sense for it.
GeometryTransform	Allows you to apply a transform object that changes the coordinate system that's used to draw a shape. This allows you to skew, rotate, or displace a shape. Transforms are particularly useful when animating graphics. You'll learn about transforms in Chapter 8.

Rectangle and Ellipse

The Rectangle and Ellipse are the two simplest shapes. To create either one, set the familiar Height and Width properties (inherited from FrameworkElement) to define the size of your shape, and then set the Fill or Stroke property (or both) to make the shape visible. You're also free to use properties such as MinHeight, MinWidth, HorizontalAlignment, VerticalAlignment, and Margin.

■**Note** If you fail to supply a brush for the Stroke or Fill property, your shape won't appear at all.

Here's a simple example that stacks an ellipse on a rectangle (see Figure 7-2) using a StackPanel:

```
<StackPanel>
  <Ellipse Fill="Yellow" Stroke="Blue"
   Height="50" Width="100" Margin="5" HorizontalAlignment="Left"></Ellipse>
  <Rectangle Fill="Yellow" Stroke="Blue"
   Height="50" Width="100" Margin="5" HorizontalAlignment="Left"></Rectangle>
</StackPanel>
```

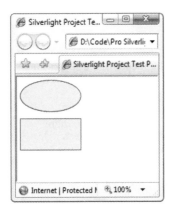

Figure 7-2. *Two simple shapes*

The Ellipse class doesn't add any properties. The Rectangle class adds just two: RadiusX and RadiusY. When set to nonzero values, these properties allow you to create nicely rounded corners.

You can think of RadiusX and RadiusY as describing an ellipse that's used just to fill in the corners of the rectangle. For example, if you set both properties to 10, Silverlight draws your corners using the edge of a circle that's 10 pixels wide. As you make your radius larger, more of your rectangle will be rounded off. If you increase RadiusY more than RadiusX, your corners will round off more gradually along the left and right sides and more sharply along the top and bottom edge. If you increase the RadiusX property to match your rectangle's width, and increase RadiusY to match its height, you'll end up converting your rectangle into an ordinary ellipse.

Figure 7-3 shows a few rectangles with rounded corners.

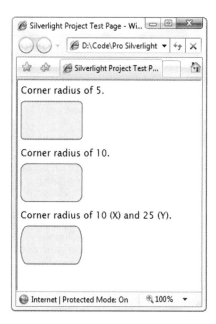

Figure 7-3. *Rounded corners*

Sizing and Placing Shapes

As you already know, hard-coded sizes are usually not the ideal approach to creating user interfaces. They limit your ability to handle dynamic content, and they make it more difficult to localize your application into other languages.

When drawing shapes, these concerns don't always apply. Often, you'll need tighter control over shape placement. However, there are many cases where you can make your design a little more flexible. Both the Ellipse and the Rectangle have the ability to size themselves to fill the available space.

If you don't supply the Height and Width properties, the shape is sized based on its container. For example, if you use the proportional row-sizing behavior of the Grid, you can create an ellipse that fills a page with this stripped-down markup:

```
<Grid>
  <Ellipse Fill="Yellow" Stroke="Blue"></Ellipse>
</Grid>
```

Here, the Grid fills the entire page. The Grid contains a single proportionately sized row, which fills the entire Grid. Finally, the ellipse fills the entire row.

This sizing behavior depends on the value of the Stretch property (which is defined in the Shape class). By default, it's set to Fill, which stretches a shape to fill its container if an explicit size isn't indicated. Table 7-2 lists all your possibilities.

Table 7-2. *Values for the Stretch Enumeration*

Name	Description
Fill	Your shape is stretched in width and height to fit its container exactly. (If you set an explicit height and width, this setting has no effect.)
None	The shape is not stretched. Unless you set a nonzero width and height (using the Height and Width or MinHeight and MinWidth properties), your shape won't appear.
Uniform	The width and height are sized up proportionately until the shape reaches the edge of the container. If you use this with an ellipse, you'll end up with the biggest circle that fits in the container. If you use it with a rectangle, you'll get the biggest possible square. (If you set an explicit height and width, your shape is sized within those bounds. For example, if you set a Width of 10 and a Height of 100 for a rectangle, you'll only get a 10×10 square.)
UniformToFill	The width and height are sized proportionately until the shape fills all the available height and width. For example, if you place a rectangle with this stretch setting into a page that's 100×200 pixels, you'll get a 200×200 rectangle, and part of it will be clipped off. (If you set an explicit height and width, your shape is sized within those bounds. For example, if you set a Width of 10 and a Height of 100 for a rectangle, you'll get a 100×100 rectangle that's clipped to fit a 10×100 box.)

Figure 7-4 shows the difference between Fill, Uniform, and UniformToFill.

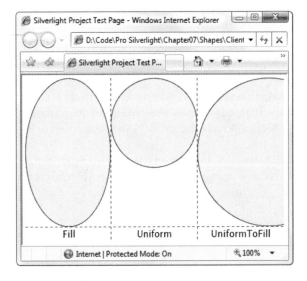

Figure 7-4. *Filling three cells in a Grid*

Usually, a Stretch value of Fill is the same as setting both HorizontalAlignment and VerticalAlignment to Stretch. The difference occurs if you choose to set a fixed Width or Height on your shape. In this case, the HorizontalAlignment and VerticalAlignment values are simply ignored. However, the Stretch setting still has an effect—it determines how your shape content is sized within the bounds you've given it.

■**Tip** In most cases, you'll size a shape explicitly or allow it to stretch to fit. You won't combine both approaches.

So far, you've seen how to size a Rectangle and an Ellipse, but what about placing them exactly where you want them? Silverlight shapes use the same layout system as any other element. However, some layout containers aren't as appropriate. For example, the StackPanel, DockPanel, and WrapPanel often aren't what you want because they're designed to separate elements. The Grid is a bit more flexible because it allows you to place as many elements as you want in the same cell (although it doesn't let you position them in different parts of that cell). The ideal container is the Canvas, which forces you to specify the coordinates of each shape using the attached Left, Top, Right, or Bottom properties. This gives you complete control over how shapes overlap:

```
<Canvas>
  <Ellipse Fill="Yellow" Stroke="Blue" Canvas.Left="100" Canvas.Top="50"
    Width="100" Height="50"></Ellipse>
    <Rectangle Fill="Yellow" Stroke="Blue" Canvas.Left="30" Canvas.Top="40"
      Width="100" Height="50"></Rectangle>
</Canvas>
```

With a Canvas, the order of your tags is important. In the previous example, the rectangle is superimposed on the ellipse because the ellipse appears first in the list, and so is drawn first (see Figure 7-5). If this isn't what you want, you can rearrange the markup or use the Canvas.ZIndex attached property to move an element to a specific layer.

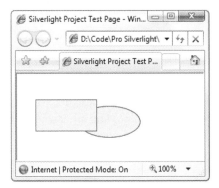

Figure 7-5. *Overlapping shapes in a Canvas*

Remember, a Canvas doesn't need to occupy an entire page. For example, there's no reason why you can't create a Grid that uses a Canvas in one of its cells. This gives you the perfect way to lock down fixed bits of drawing logic in a dynamic, free-flowing user interface.

Line

The Line shape represents a straight line that connects one point to another. The starting and ending points are set by four properties: X1 and Y1 (for the first point) and X2 and Y2 (for the second). For example, here's a line that stretches from (0, 0) to (10, 100):

```
<Line Stroke="Blue" X1="0" Y1="0" X2="10" Y2="100"></Line>
```

The Fill property has no effect for a line. You must set the Stroke property.

The coordinates you use in a line are relative to the top-left corner where the line is placed. For example, if you place the previous line in a StackPanel, the coordinate (0, 0) points to wherever that item in the StackPanel is placed. It might be the top-left corner of the page, but it probably isn't. If the StackPanel uses a nonzero Margin, or if the line is preceded by other elements, the line will begin at a point (0, 0) some distance down from the top of the page.

However, it's perfectly reasonable to use negative coordinates for a line. In fact, you can use coordinates that take your line out of its allocated space and draw overtop of any other part of the page. This isn't possible with the Rectangle and Ellipse shapes you've seen so far. However, there's also a drawback to this behavior—namely, lines can't use the flow content model. That means there's no point setting properties such as Margin, HorizontalAlignment, and VerticalAlignment on a line, as they won't have any effect. The same limitation applies to the Polyline and Polygon shapes.

If you place a Line in a Canvas, the attached position properties (such as Top and Left) still apply. They determine the starting position of the line. In other words, the two line coordinates are offset by that amount. Consider this line:

```
<Line Stroke="Blue" X1="0" Y1="0" X2="10" Y2="100"
 Canvas.Left="5" Canvas.Top="100"></Line>
```

It stretches from (0, 0) to (10, 100), using a coordinate system that treats the point (5, 100) on the Canvas as (0, 0). That makes it equivalent to this line that doesn't use the Top and Left properties:

```
<Line Stroke="Blue" X1="5" Y1="100" X2="15" Y2="200"></Line>
```

It's up to you whether you use the position properties when you place a Line on a Canvas. Often you can simplify your line drawing by picking a good starting point. You also make it easier to move parts of your drawing. For example, if you draw several lines and other shapes at a specific position in a Canvas, it's a good idea to draw them relative to a nearby point (by using the same Top and Left coordinates). That way, you can shift that entire part of your drawing to a new position as needed.

Note There's no way to create a curved line with Line or Polyline shapes. Instead, you need the more advanced Path class described later in this chapter.

Polyline

The Polyline class allows you to draw a sequence of connected straight lines. You simply supply a list of X and Y coordinates using the Points property. Technically, the Points property requires a PointCollection object, but you fill this collection in XAML using a lean string-based syntax. You simply need to supply a list of points and add a space or a comma between each coordinate.

A Polyline can have as few as two points. For example, here's a Polyline that duplicates the first line you saw in this section, which stretches from (5, 100) to (15, 200):

```
<Polyline Stroke="Blue" Points="5 100 15 200"></Polyline>
```

For better readability, use commas in between each X and Y coordinate:

```
<Polyline Stroke="Blue" Points="5,100 15,200"></Polyline>
```

And here's a more complex PolyLine that begins at (10, 150). The points move steadily to the right, oscillating between higher Y values such as (50, 160) and lower ones such as (70, 130):

```
<Canvas>
  <Polyline Stroke="Blue" StrokeThickness="5" Points="10,150 30,140 50,160 70,130
90,170 110,120 130,180 150,110 170,190 190,100 210,240" >
  </Polyline>
</Canvas>
```

Figure 7-6 shows the final line.

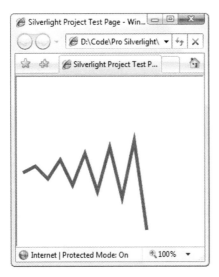

Figure 7-6. *A line with several segments*

At this point, it might occur to you that it would be easier to fill the Points collection programmatically, using some sort of loop that automatically increments X and Y values accordingly. This is true if you need to create highly dynamic graphics—for example, a chart that varies its appearance based on a set of data you extract from a database. But if you simply want to build a fixed piece of graphical content, you won't want to worry about the specific coordinates of your shapes at all. Instead, you (or a designer) will use another tool, such as Expression Design, to draw the appropriate graphics, and then export them to XAML.

Polygon

The Polygon is virtually the same as the Polyline. Like the Polyline class, the Polygon class has a Points collection that takes a list of coordinates. The only difference is that the Polygon adds a final line segment that connects the final point to the starting point. (If your final point is already the same as the first point, the Polygon class has no difference.) You can fill the interior of this shape using the Fill brush. Figure 7-7 shows the previous Polyline as a Polygon with a yellow fill.

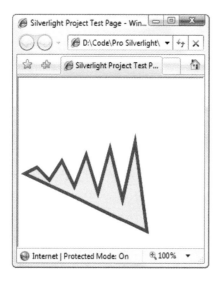

Figure 7-7. *A filled polygon*

Note Technically, you can set the Fill property of a Polyline as well. In this situation, the Polyline fills itself as though it were a Polygon—in other words, as though it has an invisible line segment connecting the last point to the first point. This effect is of limited use.

In a simple shape where the lines never cross, it's easy to fill the interior. However, sometimes you'll have a more complex Polygon where it's not necessarily obvious what portions are "inside" the shape (and should be filled) and what portions are outside.

For example, consider Figure 7-8, which features a line that crosses more than one other line, leaving an irregular region at the center that you may or may not want to fill. Obviously, you can control exactly what gets filled by breaking this drawing down into smaller shapes. But you may not need to.

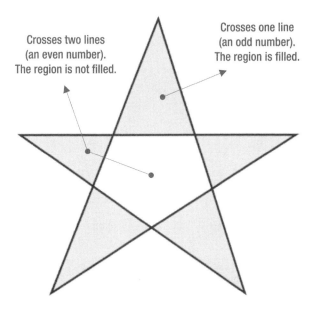

Crosses two lines
(an even number).
The region is not filled.

Crosses one line
(an odd number).
The region is filled.

Figure 7-8. *Determining fill areas when FillRule is EvenOdd*

Every Polygon and Polyline includes a FillRule property that lets you choose between two different approaches for filling in regions. By default, Fill Rule is set to EvenOdd. In order to decide whether to fill a region, Silverlight counts the number of lines that must be crossed to reach the outside of the shape. If this number is odd, the region is filled in; if it's even, the region isn't filled. In the center area of Figure 7-8, you must cross two lines to get out of the shape, so it's not filled.

Silverlight also supports the Nonzero fill rule, which is a little trickier. Essentially, with Nonzero, Silverlight follows the same line-counting process as EvenOdd, but it takes into account the direction that each line flows. If the number of lines going in one direction (say, left to right) is equal to the number going in the opposite direction (right to left), the region is not filled. If the difference between these two counts is not zero, the region is filled. In the shape from the previous example, the interior region is filled if you set the FillRule to Nonzero. Figure 7-9 shows why. (In this example, the points are numbered in the order they are drawn, and arrows show the direction in which each line is drawn.)

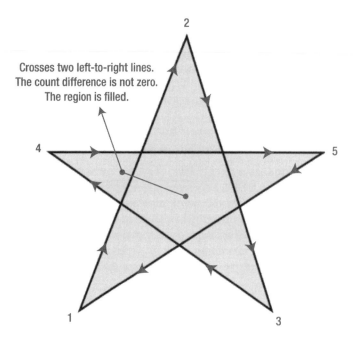

Crosses two left-to-right lines.
The count difference is not zero.
The region is filled.

Figure 7-9. *Determining fill areas when FillRule is Nonzero*

Note If there are an odd number of lines, the difference between the two counts can't be zero. Thus, the Nonzero fill rule always fills at least as much as the EvenOdd rule, plus possibly a bit more.

The tricky part about Nonzero is that its fill settings depend on *how* you draw the shape, not what the shape itself looks like. For example, you could draw the same shape in such a way that the center isn't filled (although it's much more awkward, you'd begin by drawing the inner region and then draw the outside spikes in the reverse direction).

Here's the markup that draws the star shown in Figure 7-10:

```
<Polygon Stroke="Blue" StrokeThickness="1" Fill="Yellow"
 Canvas.Left="10" Canvas.Top="175" FillRule="Nonzero"
 Points="15,200 68,70 110,200 0,125 135,125">
</Polygon>
```

Line Caps and Line Joins

When drawing with the Line and Polyline shapes, you can choose how the starting and ending edge of the line is drawn using the StartLineCap and EndLineCap properties. (These properties have no effect on other shapes because they're closed.)

Ordinarily, both StartLineCap and EndLineCap are set to Flat, which means the line ends immediately at its final coordinate. Your other choices are Round (which rounds the corner off gently), Triangle (which draws the two sides of the line together in a point), and Square (which ends the line with a sharp edge). All of these values add length to the line—in other words, they take it beyond the position where it would otherwise end. The extra distance is half the thickness of the line.

Note The only difference between Flat and Square is the fact that the Square-edged line extends this extra distance. In all other respects, the edge looks the same.

Figure 7-10 shows different line caps at the end of a line.

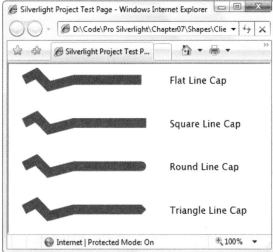

Figure 7-10. *Line caps*

All shape classes except Line allow you to tweak how their corners are shaped using the StrokeLineJoin property. You have three choices. The default value, Miter, uses sharp edges, while Bevel cuts off the point edge, and Round rounds it out gently. Figure 7-11 shows the difference.

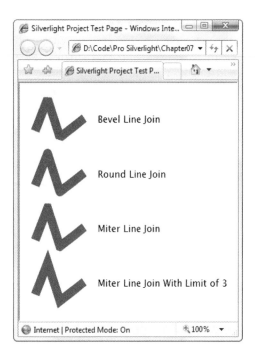

Figure 7-11. *Line joins*

When using mitered edges with thick lines and very small angles, the sharp corner can extend an impractically long distance. In this case, you can use Bevel or Round to pare down the corner. Or you could use the StrokeMiterLimit, which automatically bevels the edge when it reaches a certain maximum length. The StrokeMiterLimit is a ratio that compares the length used to miter the corner to half the thickness of the line. If you set this to 1 (which is the default value), you're allowing the corner to extend half the thickness of the line. If you set it to 3, you're allowing the corner to extend to 1.5 times the thickness of the line. The last line in Figure 7-11 uses a higher miter limit with a narrow corner.

Dashes

Instead of drawing boring solid lines for the borders of your shape, you can draw *dashed lines*—lines that are broken with spaces according to a pattern you specify.

When creating a dashed line in Silverlight, you aren't limited to specific presets. Instead, you choose the length of the solid segment of the line and the length of the broken (blank) segment by setting the StrokeDashArray property. For example, consider this line:

```
<Polyline Stroke="Blue" StrokeThickness="14" StrokeDashArray="1 2"
  Points="10,30 60,0 90,40 120,10 350,10">
</Polyline>
```

It has a line value of 1 and a gap value of 2. These values are interpreted relative to the thickness of the line. So if the line is 14 pixels thick (as in this example), the solid portion is

14 pixels, followed by a blank portion of 28 pixels. The line repeats this pattern for its entire length.

On the other hand, if you swap these values around like so:

```
StrokeDashArray="2 1"
```

you get a line that has 28-pixel solid portions broken by 7-pixel spaces. Figure 7-12 shows both lines. As you'll notice, when a very thick line segment falls on a corner, it may be broken unevenly.

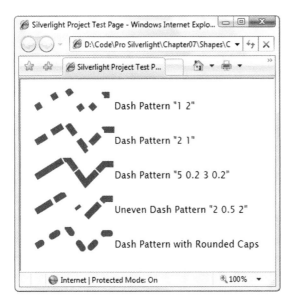

Figure 7-12. *Dashed lines*

There's no reason that you need to stick with whole number values. For example, this StrokeDashArray is perfectly reasonable:

```
StrokeDashArray="5 0.2 3 0.2"
```

It supplies a more complex sequence—a dashed line that's 5×14 length, then a 0.2×15 break, followed by a 3×14 length and another 0.2×14 length. At the end of this sequence, the line repeats the pattern from the beginning.

An interesting thing happens if you supply an odd number of values for the Stroke-DashArray. Take this one for example:

```
StrokeDashArray="3 0.5 2"
```

When drawing this line, Silverlight begins with a 3-times-thickness line, followed by a 0.5-times-thickness space, followed by a 2-times-thickness-line. But when it repeats the pattern it starts with a gap, meaning you get a 3-times-thickness *space*, followed by a 0.5-times-thickness line, and so on. Essentially, the dashed line alternates its pattern between line segments and spaces.

If you want to start midway into your pattern, you can use the StrokeDashOffset property, which is a 0-based index number that points to one of the values in your StrokeDashArray. For example, if you set StrokeDashOffset to 1 in the previous example, the line will begin with the 0.5-thickness space. Set it to 2, and the line begins with the 2-thickness segment.

Finally, you can control how the broken edges of your line are capped. Ordinarily, it's a straight edge, but you can set the StrokeDashCap to the Bevel, Square, and Triangle values you considered in the previous section. Remember, all of these settings add one half the line thickness to the end of your dash. If you don't take this into account, you might end up with dashes that overlap one another. The solution is to add extra space to compensate.

■**Tip** When using the StrokeDashCap property with a line (not a shape), it's often a good idea to set the StartLineCap and EndLineCap to the same values. This makes the line look consistent.

Paths and Geometries

So far, you've taken a look at a number of classes that derive from Shape, including Rectangle, Ellipse, Polygon, and Polyline. However, there's one Shape-derived class that you haven't considered yet, and it's the most powerful by far. The Path class has the ability to encompass any simple shape, groups of shapes, and more complex ingredients such as curves.

The Path class includes a single property, named Data, that accepts a Geometry object that defines the shape (or shapes) the path includes. You can't create a Geometry object directly because it's an abstract class. Instead, you need to use one of the derived classes listed in Table 7-3.

Table 7-3. *Geometry Classes*

Name	Description
LineGeometry	Represents a straight line. The geometry equivalent of the Line shape.
RectangleGeometry	Represents a rectangle (optionally with rounded corners). The geometry equivalent of the Rectangle shape.
EllipseGeometry	Represents an ellipse. The geometry equivalent of the Ellipse shape.
GeometryGroup	Adds any number of Geometry objects to a single path, using the EvenOdd or NonZero fill rule to determine what regions to fill.
PathGeometry	Represents a more complex figure that's composed of arcs, curves, and lines, and can be open or closed.

■**Note** Silverlight does not include all the geometry classes that WPF supports. Notably absent is the CombinedGeometry class, which allows two geometries to be fused together (although the effect can be duplicated with the more powerful PathGeometry class). Also missing is StreamGeometry, which provides a lightweight read-only equivalent to PathGeometry.

At this point you might be wondering what the difference is between a path and a geometry. The geometry *defines* a shape. A path allows you to *draw* the shape. Thus, the Geometry object defines details such as the coordinates and size of your shape, while the Path object supplies the Stroke and Fill brushes you'll use to paint it. The Path class also includes the features it inherits from the UIElement infrastructure, such as mouse and keyboard handling.

In the following sections, you'll explore all the classes that derive from Geometry.

Line, Rectangle, and Ellipse Geometries

The LineGeometry, RectangleGeometry, and EllipseGeometry classes map directly to the Line, Rectangle, and Ellipse shapes that you learned about in the first half of this chapter. For example, you can convert this markup that uses the Rectangle element:

```
<Rectangle Fill="Yellow" Stroke="Blue"
  Width="100" Height="50" ></Rectangle>
```

to this markup that uses the Path element:

```
<Path Fill="Yellow" Stroke="Blue">
  <Path.Data>
    <RectangleGeometry Rect="0,0 100,50"></RectangleGeometry>
  </Path.Data>
</Path>
```

The only real difference is that the Rectangle shape takes Height and Width values, while the RectangleGeometry takes four numbers that describe the size *and* location of the rectangle. The first two numbers describe the X and Y coordinates point where the top-left corner will be placed, while the last two numbers set the width and height of the rectangle. You can start the rectangle out at (0, 0) to get the same effect as an ordinary Rectangle element, or you can offset the rectangle using different values. The RectangleGeometry class also includes the RadiusX and RadiusY properties that let you round the corners (as described earlier).

Similarly, you can convert the following Line:

```
<Line Stroke="Blue" X1="0" Y1="0" X2="10" Y2="100"></Line>
```

to this LineGeometry:

```
<Path Fill="Yellow" Stroke="Blue">
  <Path.Data>
    <LineGeometry StartPoint="0,0" EndPoint="10,100"></LineGeometry>
  </Path.Data>
</Path>
```

and you can convert an Ellipse like this:

```
<Ellipse Fill="Yellow" Stroke="Blue"
  Width="100" Height="50" HorizontalAlignment="Left"></Ellipse>
```

to this EllipseGeometry:

```
<Path Fill="Yellow" Stroke="Blue">
  <Path.Data>
    <EllipseGeometry RadiusX="50" RadiusY="25" Center="50,25"></EllipseGeometry>
  </Path.Data>
</Path>
```

Notice that the two radius values are simply half of the width and height values. You can also use the Center property to offset the location of the ellipse. In this example, the center is placed in the exact middle of the ellipse bounding box, so that it's drawn in exactly the same way as the Ellipse shape.

Overall, these simple geometries work in exactly the same way as the corresponding shapes. You get the added ability to offset rectangles and ellipses, but that's not necessary if you're placing your shapes on a Canvas, which already gives you the ability to position your shapes at a specific position. In fact, if this were all you could do with geometries, you probably wouldn't bother to use the Path element. The difference appears when you decide to group more than one geometry in the same path and when you step up to more complex curves, as described in the following sections.

Combining Shapes with GeometryGroup

The simplest way to combine geometries is to use the GeometryGroup and nest the other Geometry-derived objects inside. Here's an example that places an ellipse next to a square:

```
<Path Fill="Yellow" Stroke="Blue" Margin="5" Canvas.Top="10" Canvas.Left="10" >
  <Path.Data>
    <GeometryGroup>
      <RectangleGeometry Rect="0,0 100,100"></RectangleGeometry>
      <EllipseGeometry Center="150,50" RadiusX="35" RadiusY="25"></EllipseGeometry>
    </GeometryGroup>
  </Path.Data>
</Path>
```

The effect of this markup is the same as if you supplied two Path elements, one with the RectangleGeometry and one with the EllipseGeometry (and that's the same as if you used a Rectangle and Ellipse shape instead). However, there's one advantage to this approach. You've replaced two elements with one, which means you've reduced the overhead of your user interface. In general, a page that uses a smaller number of elements with more complex geometries will perform faster than a page that has a large number of elements with simpler geometries. This effect won't be apparent in a page that has just a few dozen shapes, but it may become significant in one that requires hundreds or thousands.

Of course, there's also a drawback to combining geometries in a single Path element—namely, you won't be able to perform event handling of the different shapes separately. Instead, the Path element will fire all mouse events. And although Silverlight provides a way to perform hit testing to find out if a point is on an element (through the HitTest() method that's built into all elements), it doesn't include a way to hit test geometries.

However, even when you combine geometries you still have the ability to manipulate the nested RectangleGeometry and EllipseGeometry objects independently. For example, each geometry provides a Transform property that you can set to stretch, skew, or rotate that part of the path.

■ **Note** Unlike WPF, Silverlight does not allow you to reuse a single geometry object with more than one Path. If two objects share the same geometry, you must create a distinct copy for each one.

The GeometryGroup becomes more interesting when your shapes intersect. Rather than simply treating your drawing as a combination of solid shapes, the GeometryGroup uses its FillRule property (which can be EvenOdd or Nonzero, as described earlier) to decide what shapes to fill. Consider what happens if you alter the markup shown earlier like this, placing the ellipse over the square:

```
<Path Fill="Yellow" Stroke="Blue" Margin="5" Canvas.Top="10" Canvas.Left="10" >
  <Path.Data>
    <GeometryGroup>
      <RectangleGeometry Rect="0,0 100,100"></RectangleGeometry>
      <EllipseGeometry Center="50,50" RadiusX="35" RadiusY="25"></EllipseGeometry>
    </GeometryGroup>
  </Path.Data>
</Path>
```

Now this markup creates a square with an ellipse-shaped hole in it. If you change FillRule to Nonzero, you'll get a solid ellipse over a solid rectangle, both with the same yellow fill.

You could create the square-with-a-hole effect by simply superimposing a white-filled ellipse over your square. However, the GeometryGroup class becomes more useful if you have content underneath, which is typical in a complex drawing. Because the ellipse is treated as a hole in your shape (not another shape with a different fill), any content underneath shows through—for example, if you add this line of text:

```
<TextBlock Canvas.Top="50" Canvas.Left="20" FontSize="25" FontWeight="Bold">
  Hello There</TextBlock>
```

Now you'll get the result shown in Figure 7-13.

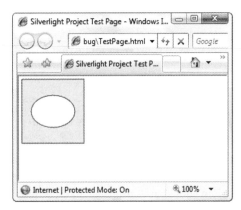

Figure 7-13. *A path that uses two shapes*

Curves and Lines with PathGeometry

PathGeometry is the superpower of geometries. It can draw anything that the other geometries can, and much more. The only drawback is a lengthier (and somewhat more complex) syntax.

Every PathGeometry object is built out of one or more PathFigure objects (which are stored in the PathGeometry.Figures collection). Each PathFigure is a continuous set of connected lines and curves that can be closed or open. The figure is closed if the end of the last line in the figure connects to the beginning of the first line.

The PathFigure class has four key properties, as described in Table 7-4.

Table 7-4. *PathFigure Properties*

Name	Description
StartPoint	This is a Point that indicates where the line for the figure begins.
Segments	This is a collection of PathSegment objects that are used to draw the figure.
IsClosed	If true, Silverlight adds a straight line to connect the starting and ending points (if they aren't the same).
IsFilled	If true, the area inside the figure is filled in using the Path.Fill brush.

So far, this all sounds fairly straightforward. The PathFigure is a shape that's drawn using an unbroken line that consists of a number of segments. However, the trick is that there are several type of segments, all of which derive from the PathSegment class. Some are simple, like the LineSegment that draws a straight line. Others, like the BezierSegment, draw curves and are correspondingly more complex.

You can mix and match different segments freely to build your figure. Table 7-5 lists the segment classes you can use.

Table 7-5. *PathSegment Classes*

Name	Description
LineSegment	Creates a straight line between two points.
ArcSegment	Creates an elliptical arc between two points.
BezierSegment	Creates a Bézier curve between two points.
QuadraticBezierSegment	Creates a simpler form of Bézier curve that has one control point instead of two, and is faster to calculate.
PolyLineSegment	Creates a series of straight lines. You can get the same effect using multiple LineSegment objects, but a single PolyLineSegment is more concise.
PolyBezierSegment	Creates a series of Bézier curves.
PolyQuadraticBezierSegment	Creates a series of simpler quadratic Bézier curves.

Straight Lines

It's easy enough to create simple lines using the LineSegment and PathGeometry classes. You simply set the StartPoint and add one LineSegment for each section of the line. The LineSegment.Point property identifies the end point of each segment.

For example, the following markup begins at (10, 100), draws a straight line to (100, 100), and then draws a line from that point to (100, 50). Because the PathFigure.IsClosed property is set to true, a final line segment is adding connection (100, 50) to (0, 0). The final result is a right-angled triangle:

```
<Path Stroke="Blue">
  <Path.Data>
    <PathGeometry>
      <PathFigure IsClosed="True" StartPoint="10,100">
        <LineSegment Point="100,100" />
        <LineSegment Point="100,50" />
      </PathFigure>
    </PathGeometry>
  </Path.Data>
</Path>
```

Silverlight allows you to manipulate figures in your code. For example, you can add or remove path segments, or you can dynamically warp a shape by modifying existing line segments or changing its start point. You could even use animation to modify the points in your path smoothly and incrementally, as described in Chapter 9.

■Note Remember, each PathGeometry can contain an unlimited number of PathFigure objects. That means you can create several separate open or closed figures that are all considered part of the same path.

Arcs

Arcs are a little more interesting than straight lines. You identify the end point of the line using the ArcSegment.Point property, just as you would with a LineSegment. However, the PathFigure draws a curved line from the starting point (or the end point of the previous segment) to the end point of your arc. This curved connecting line is actually a portion of the edge of an ellipse.

Obviously, the end point isn't enough information to draw the arc because there are many curves (some gentle, some more extreme) that could connect two points. You also need to indicate the size of the imaginary ellipse that's being used to draw the arc. You do this using the ArcSegment.Size property, which supplies the X radius and the Y radius of the ellipse. The larger the ellipse size of the imaginary ellipse, the more gradually its edge curves.

Note For any two points, there is a practical maximum and minimum size for the ellipse. The maximum occurs when you create an ellipse so large the line segment you're drawing appears straight. Increasing the size beyond this point has no effect. The minimum occurs when the ellipse is small enough that a full semi-circle connects the two points. Shrinking the size beyond this point also has no effect.

Here's an example that creates the gentle arc shown in Figure 7-14:

```
<Path Stroke="Blue" StrokeThickness="3">
  <Path.Data>
    <PathGeometry>
      <PathFigure IsClosed="False" StartPoint="10,100" >
        <ArcSegment Point="250,150" Size="200,300" />
      </PathFigure>
    </PathGeometry>
  </Path.Data>
</Path>
```

Figure 7-14. *A simple arc*

So far, arcs sound fairly straightforward. However, it turns out that even with the start and end point and the size of the ellipse, you still don't have all the information you need to draw your arc unambiguously. In the previous example, you're relying on two default values that may not be set to your liking.

To understand the problem, you need to consider the other ways that an arc can connect the same two points. If you picture two points on an ellipse, it's clear that you can connect them in two ways—by going around the short side, or by going around the long side. Figure 7-15 illustrates.

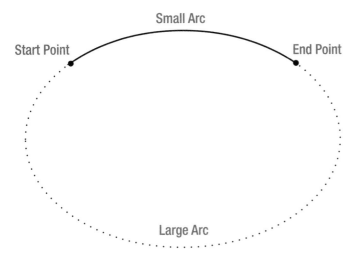

Figure 7-15. *Two ways to trace a curve along an ellipse*

You set the direction using the ArcSegment.IsLargeArc property, which can be true or false. The default value is false, which means you get the shorter of the two arcs.

Even once you've set the direction, there is still one point of ambiguity—where the ellipse is placed. For example, imagine you draw an arc that connects a point on the left with a point on the right, using the shortest possible arc. The curve that connects these two points could be stretched down and then up (as it does in Figure 7-14), or it could be flipped so that it curves up and then down. The arc you get depends on the order in which you define the two points in the arc and the ArcSegment.SweepDirection property, which can be Counterclockwise (the default) or Clockwise. Figure 7-16 shows the difference.

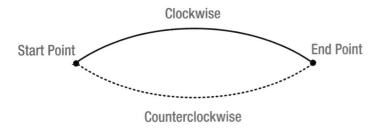

Figure 7-16. *Two ways to flip a curve*

Bézier Curves

Bézier curves connect two line segments using a complex mathematical formula that incorporates two *control points* that determine how the curve is shaped. Bézier curves are an ingredient in virtually every vector drawing application ever created because they're remarkably flexible. Using nothing more than start point, end point, and two control points, you can create a surprisingly wide variety of smooth curves (including loops). Figure 7-17 shows a classic Bézier curve. Two small circles indicate the control points, and a dashed line connects each control point to the end of the line it affects the most.

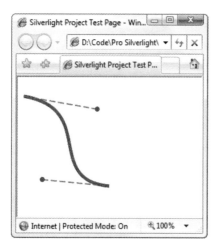

Figure 7-17. *A Bézier curve*

Even without understanding the math underpinnings, it's fairly easy to get the "feel" of how Bézier curves work. Essentially, the two control points do all the magic. They influence the curve in two ways:

- At the starting point, a Bézier curve runs parallel with the line that connects it to the first control point. At the ending point, the curve runs parallel with the line that connects it to the end point. (In between, it curves.)

- The degree of curvature is determined by the distance to the two control points. If one control point is farther away, it exerts a stronger "pull."

To define a Bézier curve in markup, you supply three points. The first two points (BezierSegment.Point1 and BezierSegment.Point2) are the control points. The third point (BezierSegment.Point3) is the end point of the curve. As always, the starting point is that starting point of the path or wherever the previous segment leaves off.

The example shown in Figure 14-7 includes three separate components, each of which uses a different stroke and thus requires a separate Path element. The first path creates the curve, the second adds the dashed lines, and the third applies the circles that indicate the control points. Here's the complete markup:

```
<Canvas>
  <Path Stroke="Blue" StrokeThickness="5" Canvas.Top="20">
    <Path.Data>
      <PathGeometry>
        <PathFigure StartPoint="10,10">
          <BezierSegment Point1="130,30" Point2="40,140"
            Point3="150,150"></BezierSegment>
        </PathFigure>
      </PathGeometry>
    </Path.Data>
  </Path>
  <Path Stroke="Green" StrokeThickness="2" StrokeDashArray="5 2" Canvas.Top="20">
    <Path.Data>
      <GeometryGroup>
        <LineGeometry StartPoint="10,10" EndPoint="130,30"></LineGeometry>
        <LineGeometry StartPoint="40,140" EndPoint="150,150"></LineGeometry>
      </GeometryGroup>
    </Path.Data>
  </Path>
  <Path Fill="Red" Stroke="Red" StrokeThickness="8"  Canvas.Top="20">
    <Path.Data>
      <GeometryGroup>
        <EllipseGeometry Center="130,30"></EllipseGeometry>
        <EllipseGeometry Center="40,140"></EllipseGeometry>
      </GeometryGroup>
    </Path.Data>
  </Path>
</Canvas>
```

Trying to code Bézier paths is a recipe for many thankless hours of trial-and-error computer coding. You're much more likely to draw your curves (and many other graphical elements) in a dedicated drawing program that has an export-to-XAML feature, or Microsoft Expression Blend.

■**Tip** To learn more about the algorithm that underlies the Bézier curve, you can read an informative Wikipedia article on the subject at http://en.wikipedia.org/wiki/Bezier_curve.

The Geometry Mini-Language

The geometries you've seen so far have been relatively concise, with only a few points. More complex geometries are conceptually the same but can easily require hundreds of segments. Defining each line, arc, and curve in a complex path is extremely verbose and unnecessary—after all, it's likely that complex paths will be generated by a design tool rather than written by hand, so the clarity of the markup isn't all that important. With this in mind, the creators of

Silverlight added a more concise alternative syntax for defining geometries that allows you to represent detailed figures with much smaller amounts of markup. This syntax is often described as the *geometry mini-language* (and sometimes the *path mini-language* due to its application with the Path element).

To understand the mini-language, you need to realize that it is essentially a long string holding a series of commands. These commands are read by a type converter that then creates the corresponding geometry. Each command is a single letter and is optionally followed by a few bits of numeric information (such as X and Y coordinates) separated by spaces. Each command is also separated from the previous command with a space.

For example, a bit earlier you created a basic triangle using a closed path with two line segments. Here's the markup that did the trick:

```
<Path Stroke="Blue">
  <Path.Data>
    <PathGeometry>
      <PathFigure IsClosed="True" StartPoint="10,100">
        <LineSegment Point="100,100" />
        <LineSegment Point="100,50" />
      </PathFigure>
    </PathGeometry>
  </Path.Data>
</Path>
```

To duplicate this figure using the mini-language, you'd write this:

```
<Path Stroke="Blue" Data="M 10,100 L 100,100 L 100,50 Z"/>
```

This path uses a sequence of four commands. The first command (M) creates the Path-Figure and sets the starting point to (10, 100). The following two commands (L) create line segments. The final command (Z) ends the PathFigure and sets the IsClosed property to true. The commas in this string are optional, as are the spaces between the command and its parameters, but you must leave at least one space between adjacent parameters and commands. That means you can reduce the syntax even further to this less-readable form:

```
<Path Stroke="Blue" Data="M10 100 L100 100 L100 50 Z"/>
```

The geometry mini-language is easy to grasp. It uses a fairly small set of commands, which are detailed in Table 7-6. Parameters are shown in italics.

Table 7-6. *Commands for the Geometry Mini-Language*

Command	Description
F *value*	Sets the Geometry.FillRule property. Use 0 for EvenOdd or 1 for NonZero. This command must appear at the beginning of the string (if you decide to use it).
M *x,y*	Creates a new PathFigure for the geometry and sets its start point. This command must be used before any other commands except F. However, you can also use it during your drawing sequence to move the origin of your coordinate system. (The M stands for *move*.)

Command	Description
L *x,y*	Creates a LineSegment to the specified point.
H *x*	Creates a horizontal LineSegment using the specified X value and keeping the Y value constant.
V *y*	Creates a vertical LineSegment using the specified Y value and keeping the X value constant.
A *radiusX, radiusY degrees isLargeArc, isClockwise x,y*	Creates an ArcSegment to the indicated point. You specify the radii of the ellipse that describes the arc, the number of degrees the arc is rotated, and Boolean flags that set the IsLargeArc and SweepDirection properties described earlier.
C *x1,y1 x2,y2 x,y*	Creates a BezierSegment to the indicated point, using control points at (*x1*, *y1*) and (*x2*, *y2*).
Q *x1, y1 x,y*	Creates a QuadraticBezierSegment to the indicated point, with one control point at (*x1*, *y1*).
S *x2,y2 x,y*	Creates a smooth BezierSegment by using the second control point from the previous BezierSegment as the first control point in the new BezierSegment.
Z	Ends the current PathFigure and sets IsClosed to true. You don't need to use this command if you don't want to set IsClosed to true—instead, simply use M if you want to start a new PathFigure or end the string.

Tip There's one more trick in the geometry mini-language. You can use a command in lowercase if you want its parameters to be evaluated relative to the previous point rather than using absolute coordinates.

Clipping with Geometry

As you've seen, geometries are the most powerful way to create a shape. However, geometries aren't limited to the Path element. They're also used anywhere you need to supply the abstract definition of a shape (rather than draw a real, concrete shape in a page).

Another place geometries are used is to set the Clip property, which is provided by all elements. The Clip property allows you to constrain the outer bounds of an element to fit a specific geometry. You can use the Clip property to create a number of exotic effects. Although it's commonly used to trim down image content in an Image element, you can use the Clip property with any element. The only limitation is that you'll need a closed geometry if you actually want to see anything—individual curves and line segments aren't of much use.

The following example uses the same geometry to clip two elements: an Image element that contains a bitmap, and a standard Button element. The results are shown in Figure 7-18.

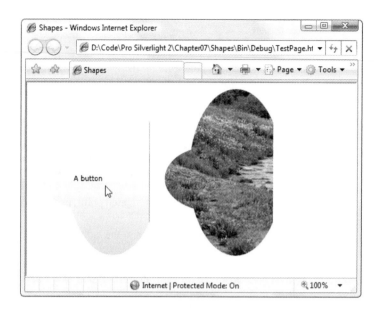

Figure 7-18. *Clipping two elements*

Here's the markup for this example:

```
<Grid>
  <Grid.ColumnDefinitions>
    <ColumnDefinition></ColumnDefinition>
    <ColumnDefinition></ColumnDefinition>
  </Grid.ColumnDefinitions>

  <Button Content="A button">
    <Button.Clip>
      <GeometryGroup FillRule="Nonzero">
        <EllipseGeometry RadiusX="75" RadiusY="50" Center="100,150" />
        <EllipseGeometry RadiusX="100" RadiusY="25" Center="200,150" />
        <EllipseGeometry RadiusX="75" RadiusY="130" Center="140,140" />
      </GeometryGroup>
    </Button.Clip>
  </Button>
  <Image Grid.Column="1" Stretch="None" Source="creek.jpg">
    <Image.Clip>
      <GeometryGroup FillRule="Nonzero">
        <EllipseGeometry RadiusX="75" RadiusY="50" Center="100,150" />
        <EllipseGeometry RadiusX="100" RadiusY="25" Center="200,150" />
        <EllipseGeometry RadiusX="75" RadiusY="130" Center="140,140" />
      </GeometryGroup>
    </Image.Clip>
  </Image>
</Grid>
```

The clipping you set doesn't take the size of the element into account. In this example, that means that if the button is enlarged, the clipped region will remain at the same position and show a different portion of the button.

Exporting Clip Art

In most cases, you won't create Silverlight art by hand. Instead, you (or a graphic designer) will use a design tool to create vector art, and then export it to XAML. The exported XAML document you'll end up with is essentially a Canvas that contains a combination of shape elements. You can place that Canvas inside an existing Canvas to show your artwork.

Although many drawing programs don't have built-in support for XAML export, there are still many options for getting the graphics you need. The following sections outline the options you can use to get vector art out of virtually any application.

Expression Design

Expression Design, Microsoft's illustration and graphic design program, has a built-in XAML export. In can read import a variety of vector art file formats, including Adobe Illustrator (.ai) files, and it can export to XAML.

When exporting to XAML, follow these steps:

1. Choose File ➤ Export from the menu.

2. In the Export dialog box, in the Save As Type list, choose XAML. Then, enter a file name and click Save. The Export XAML window will appear (see Figure 7-19), which shows you the image you are exporting and a preview of the XAML content it will create (click the XAML tab to see).

3. In the Document Format group of settings, click Silverlight to ensure you're creating a Silverlight-compatible XAML file. This ensures that XAML features that are supported in WPF but not in Silverlight won't be used.

Note Usually, the standard XAML export option (Canvas) will work with Silverlight applications, with minimal changes, such as manually removing a few unsupported attributes. However, the Resource Dictionary export option will create XAML files that won't work with Silverlight. That's because this option stores the graphic in a collection of DrawingBrush resources instead of a Canvas. This makes it easier to efficiently reuse the drawing in WPF, but it's useless in Silverlight, because Silverlight doesn't include the Drawing or DrawingBrush classes.

---

4. Click Export to save the file.

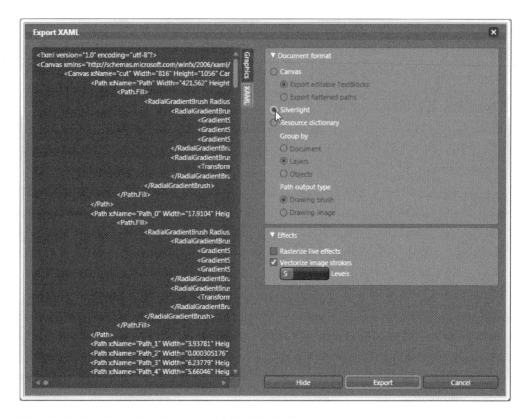

Figure 7-19. *Creating a Silverlight-compatible XAML file*

The generated XAML file includes a root-level Canvas element. Inside the Canvas, you'll find dozens of Path elements, each positioned at a specific place in the Canvas, and with its own data and brushes.

You can cut and paste this entire block of markup into any Silverlight page to reproduce the graphic. However, this approach is inconvenient if you have a page that includes a large number of complex graphics, or if you need to reuse a custom graphic in multiple places. If you use the cut-and-paste approach here, you'll clutter your markup beyond recognition and create duplicate sections that are much more difficult to debug or modify later on.

Ideally, you'd use the resources collection in the App.xaml file to share frequently used graphics. Unfortunately, this approach isn't possible, because Silverlight doesn't allow you to store and reuse entire elements (such as a Canvas with graphical content), and it doesn't provide a way to define drawings without using elements. The most common workaround is to create a separate user control for each important graphic. You can then insert these user controls into other pages, wherever you need them. You'll see this technique in action in Chapter 9, which presents a simple bomb-dropping game that uses dedicated user controls for its bomb graphic and its title logo.

Conversion

Microsoft Expression Design is one example of a design tool that supports XAML natively. However, plug-ins and conversion tools are available for many other popular formats. Mike Swanson, a Microsoft evangelist, maintains a page at `http://blogs.msdn.com/mswanson/articles/WPFToolsAndControls.aspx` with links to many free converters, including

- An Adobe Illustrator (.ai) to XAML converter

- A Flash (.swf) to XAML converter

- A Visio plug-in for exporting XAML

You can also find more non-free XAML conversion tools on the Web. These tools won't necessarily create XAML content that is completely compatible with Silverlight. However, in most cases it will take only minor edits to fix markup errors.

Save or Print to XPS

The XML Paper Specification (XPS) is a Microsoft standard for creating fixed, print-ready documents. It's similar to the Adobe PDF standard, and support is included in Office 2007 and Windows Vista. However, the XPS standard is based on XAML, which makes it possible to transfer content from an XPS document to a Silverlight page. If you're using Windows Vista, this gives you a back door to get graphic output from virtually any application.

For example, Figure 7-20 shows a document in Word 2007, after performing a clip-art search and dragging a vector image (a stack of money) onto the page. The easiest way to save this graphic as an XPS document is to use the free Save As PDF or XPS add-in that Microsoft provides at `http://tinyurl.com/y69y7g`. Then, you can save the document simply by choosing File ➤ Save As ➤ PDF or XPS. If you're using Windows Vista, you have another option that works with other non-Office programs. You can choose to print your document to the Microsoft XPS Document Writer print device.

Either way, you'll end up with a file that has the extension .xps. This file is actually a ZIP archive (somewhat like the XAP files that Silverlight uses). To extract the XAML inside, you need to begin by renaming the extension to .zip and opening the archive to view the files inside. Bitmaps will be included as separate files in the Resources folder. Vector art, like the money stack shown in Figure 7-20, will be defined in XAML inside a page in the Documents\1\Pages folder. There, you'll find a file for each page in your document, with file names in the format [PageNumber].fpage. For example, in the XPS file that's generated for the previous example, you'll find a single file named 1.fpage that defines the page with the money graphic.

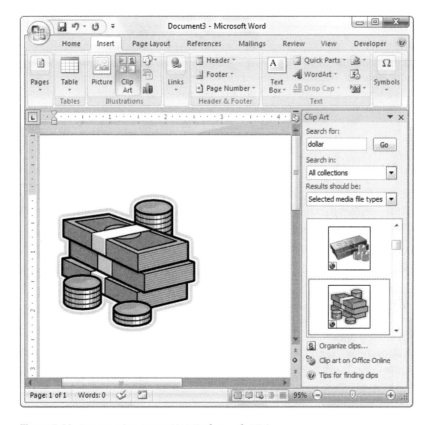

Figure 7-20. *Export pictures to XAML through XPS*

If you extract that file and open it in a text editor, you'll see that it's completely legitimate
XAML. The root element is named FixedPage, which is not recognized in Silverlight, but inside
that is an ordinary Canvas that you can cut and paste into a Silverlight window. For the example shown in Figure 7-20, you'll find that the Canvas holds a series of Path elements that define
the different parts of the shape. Once you paste it into a Silverlight page, you'll get a result like
the one shown in Figure 7-21.

Figure 7-21. *Content from an XPS document in Silverlight*

When you paste the XPS markup into a Silverlight page, you'll often need to make minor changes. Here are some examples:

- **Removing unsupported attributes.** When you attempt to compile your application, Visual Studio will point out any problems in your markup and flag them as compile errors.

- **Replacing the Glyphs element with a TextBlock.** The Glyphs element is a low-level way to show text. Unlike the TextBlock, when you use the Glyphs element you need to supply several details (including a font file) or your text won't appear at all. When you create an XPS document that includes text, it will use the Glyphs element. However, in order to make your text appear, you'll need to find the font file in your XPS archive, extract it, add it to your project, and change the Glyphs.FontUri property to match. An easier approach is to simply replace the Glyphs element with the higher-level TextBlock, and use the Glyphs.UnicodeString property to set the TextBlock.Text property.

- **Changing the transforms.** Sometimes, the exported art will use transforms to resize and position the graphic. (This is most common when you use the Save As XPS feature in Word rather than the XPS print driver in Windows Vista.) By removing or modifying these transforms, you can free the image from the printed layout so it can fit your Silverlight page perfectly. You'll learn all about transforms in Chapter 8.

The Last Word

In this chapter, you took a detailed look at Silverlight's support for basic 2-D drawing. You began by considering the simple shape classes, and continued the Path, the most sophisticated of the shape classes, which lets you add arcs and curves.

However, your journey is complete. In the next chapter, you'll consider how you can create better drawings by using the right brushes, controlling opacity, and applying with transforms.

CHAPTER 8

Brushes and Transforms

In the previous chapter, you started your exploration into Silverlight's 2-D drawing model. You considered how you can use Shape-derived classes like the Rectangle, Ellipse, Polygon, Polyline, and Path to create a variety of different drawings. However, shapes alone fall short of what you need to create detailed 2-D vector art for a graphically rich application. In this chapter, you'll pick up the missing pieces.

First, you'll learn about the more exotic Silverlight brushes that allow you to create gradients, tiled patterns, and bitmap fills in any shape. Next, you'll see how you can use Silverlight's effortless support for transparency to blend multiple images and elements together. Finally, you'll consider *transforms*—specialized objects that can change the visual appearance of any element by scaling, rotating, or skewing it. As you'll see, when you combine these features— for example, tossing together a dash of transparency with the warping effect of a transform— you can create popular effects, like reflections, glows, and shadows.

Brushes

As you know, brushes fill an area, whether it's the background, foreground, or border of an element, or the fill or stroke of a shape. For elements, you use brushes with the Foreground, Background, and BorderBrush properties. For shapes, you use the Fill and Stroke properties.

You've used brushes throughout this book, but so far you've done most of your work with the straightforward SolidColorBrush. Although SolidColorBrush is indisputably useful, there are several other classes that inherit from System.Windows.Media.Brush and give you more exotic effects. Table 8-1 lists them all.

Table 8-1. *Brush Classes*

Name	Description
SolidColorBrush	Paints an area using a solid single-color fill.
LinearGradientBrush	Paints an area using a gradient fill, a gradually shaded fill that changes from one color to another (and, optionally, to another and then another, and so on).
RadialGradientBrush	Paints an area using a radial gradient fill, which is similar to a linear gradient except it radiates out in a circular pattern starting from a center point.

Continued

Table 8-1. *Continued*

Name	Description
ImageBrush	Paints an area using an image that can be stretched, scaled, or tiled.
VideoBrush	Paints an area using a MediaElement (which gets its content from a video file). This allows you to play video in any shape or element.

In this chapter, you'll learn how to use the LinearGradientBrush, RadialGradientBrush, and ImageBrush. The VideoBrush is discussed in Chapter 10, when you explore Silverlight's media support.

The LinearGradientBrush

The LinearGradientBrush allows you to create a blended fill that changes from one color to another.

Here's the simplest possible gradient. It shades a rectangle diagonally from blue (in the top-left corner) to white (in the bottom-right corner):

```
<Rectangle Width="150" Height="100">
  <Rectangle.Fill>
    <LinearGradientBrush >
      <GradientStop Color="Blue" Offset="0"/>
      <GradientStop Color="White" Offset="1" />
    </LinearGradientBrush>
  </Rectangle.Fill>
</Rectangle>
```

The top gradient in Figure 8-1 shows the result.

To create the first gradient, you need to add one GradientStop for each color. You also need to place each color in your gradient using an Offset value from 0 to 1. In this example, the GradientStop for the blue color has an offset of 0, which means it's placed at the very beginning of the gradient. The GradientStop for the white color has an offset of 1, which places it at the end. If you change these values, you could adjust how quickly the gradient switches from one color to the other. For example, if you set the GradientStop for the white color to 0.5, the gradient would blend from blue (in the top-left corner) to white in the middle (the point between the two corners). The right side of the rectangle would be completely white. (The second gradient in Figure 8-1 shows this example.)

The previous markup creates a gradient with a diagonal fill that stretches from one corner to another. However, you might want to create a gradient that blends from top to bottom or side to side, or uses a different diagonal angle. You control these details using the StartPoint and EndPoint properties of the LinearGradientBrush. These properties allow you to choose the point where the first color begins to change and the point where the color change ends with the final color. (The area in between is blended gradually.) However, there's one quirk. The coordinates you use for the starting and ending point aren't real coordinates. Instead, the LinearGradientBrush assigns the point (0, 0) to the top-left corner and (1, 1) to the bottom-right corner of the area you want to fill, no matter how high and wide it actually is.

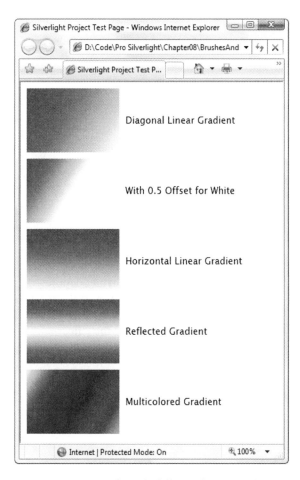

Figure 8-1. *A rectangle with different linear gradients*

To create a top-to-bottom horizontal fill, you can use a start point of (0, 0) for the top-left corner, and an end point of (0, 1), which represents the bottom-left corner. To create a side-to-side vertical fill (with no slant), you can use a start point of (0, 0) and an end point of (1, 0) for the bottom-left corner. Figure 8-1 shows a horizontal gradient (it's the third one).

You can get a little craftier by supplying start points and end points that aren't quite aligned with the corners of your gradient. For example, you could have a gradient stretch from (0, 0) to (0, 0.5), which is a point on the left edge, halfway down. This creates a compressed linear gradient—one color starts at the top, blending to the second color in the middle. The bottom half of the shape is filled with the second color. But wait—you can change this behavior using the LinearGradientBrush.SpreadMethod property. It's Pad by default (which means areas outside the gradient are given a solid fill with the appropriate color), but you can also use Reflect (to reverse the gradient, going from the second color back to the first) or Repeat (to duplicate the same color progression). Figure 8-1 shows the Reflect effect (it's the fourth gradient).

The LinearGradientBrush also allows you to create gradients with more than two colors by adding more than two GradientStop objects. For example, here's a gradient that moves through a rainbow of colors:

```
<Rectangle Width="150" Height="100">
  <Rectangle.Fill>
    <LinearGradientBrush StartPoint="0,0" EndPoint="1,1">
      <GradientStop Color="Yellow" Offset="0.0" />
      <GradientStop Color="Red" Offset="0.25" />
      <GradientStop Color="Blue" Offset="0.75" />
      <GradientStop Color="LimeGreen" Offset="1.0" />
    </LinearGradientBrush>
  </Rectangle.Fill>
</Rectangle>
```

The only trick is to set the appropriate offset for each GradientStop. For example, if you want to transition through five colors, you might give your first color an offset of 0, the second 0.25, the third 0.5, the fourth 0.75, and the fifth 1. Or if you want the colors to blend more quickly at the beginning and then end more gradually, you could give the offsets 0, 0.1, 0.2, 0.4, 0.6, and 1.

Remember, Brushes aren't limited to shape drawing. You can substitute the Linear-GradientBrush anytime you would use the SolidColorBrush—for example, when filling the background surface of an element (using the Background property), the foreground color of its text (using the Foreground property), or the fill of a border (using the BorderBrush property). Figure 8-2 shows an example of a gradient-filled TextBlock.

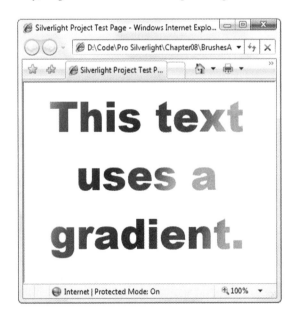

Figure 8-2. *Using the LinearGradientBrush to set the TextBlock.Foreground property*

The RadialGradientBrush

The RadialGradientBrush works similarly to the LinearGradientBrush. It also takes a sequence of colors with different offsets. As with the LinearGradientBrush, you can use as many colors as you want. The difference is how you place the gradient.

To identify the point where the first color in the gradient starts, you use the GradientOrigin property. By default, it's (0.5, 0.5), which represents the middle of the fill region.

Note As with the LinearGradientBrush, the RadialGradientBrush uses a proportional coordinate system that acts as though the top-left corner of your rectangular fill area is (0, 0) and the bottom-right corner is (1, 1). That means you can pick any coordinate from (0, 0) to (1, 1) to place the starting point of the gradient. In fact, you can even go beyond these limits if you want to locate the starting point outside the fill region.

The gradient radiates out from the starting point in a circular fashion. Eventually, your gradient reaches the edge of an inner gradient circle, where it ends. This center of this circle may or may not line up with the gradient origin, depending on the effect you want. The area beyond the edge of the inner gradient circle and the outermost edge of the fill region is given a solid fill using the last color that's defined in RadialGradientBrush.GradientStops collection, as Figure 8-3 illustrates.

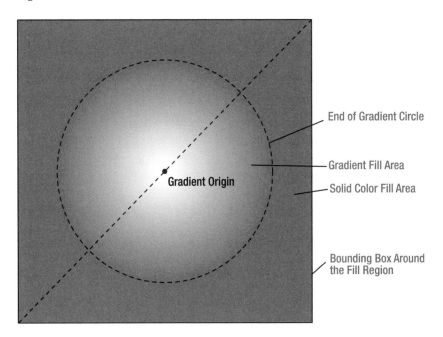

Figure 8-3. *How a radial gradient is filled*

You set the edge of the inner gradient circle using three properties: Center, RadiusX, and RadiusY. By default, the Center property is (0.5, 0.5), which places the center of the limiting circle in the middle of your fill region and in the same position as the gradient origin.

The RadiusX and RadiusY determine the size of the limiting circle, and by default they're both set to 0.5. These values can be a bit unintuitive—they're measured in relation to the *diagonal* span of your fill area (the length of an imaginary line stretching from the top-left corner to the bottom-right corner of your fill area). That means a radius of 0.5 defines a circle that has a radius that's half the length of this diagonal. If you have a square fill region, you can use a dash of Pythagoras to calculate that this is about 0.7 times the width (or height) of your region. Thus, if you're filling a square region with the default settings, the gradient begins in the center and stretches to its outermost edge at about 0.7 times the width of the square.

■**Note** If you trace the largest possible ellipse that fits in your fill area, that's the place where the gradient ends with your second color.

The radial gradient fill is a particularly good choice for filling rounded shapes and creating lighting effects. (Master artists use a combination of gradients to create buttons with a glow effect.) A common trick is to offset the GradientOrigin point slightly to create an illusion of depth in your shape. Here's an example:

```
<Ellipse Margin="5" Stroke="Black" StrokeThickness="1" Width="200" Height="200">
  <Ellipse.Fill>
    <RadialGradientBrush RadiusX="1" RadiusY="1" GradientOrigin="0.7,0.3">
      <GradientStop Color="White" Offset="0" />
      <GradientStop Color="Blue" Offset="1" />
    </RadialGradientBrush>
  </Ellipse.Fill>
</Ellipse>
```

Figure 8-4 shows this gradient, along with an ordinary radial gradient that has the standard GradientOrigin (0.5, 0.5).

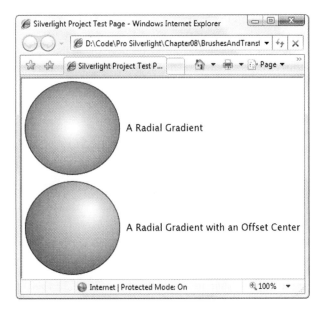

Figure 8-4. *Radial gradients*

The ImageBrush

The ImageBrush allows you to fill an area with a bitmap image using any file type that Silverlight supports (BMP, PNG, and JPEG files). You identify the image you want to use by setting the ImageSource property. For example, this brush paints the background of a Grid using an image named logo.jpg that's included in your project as a resource (and therefore embedded in your application's XAP file):

```
<Grid>
  <Grid.Background>
    <ImageBrush ImageSource="logo.jpg"></ImageBrush>
  </Grid.Background>
</Grid>
```

The ImageSource property of the ImageBrush works in the same way as the Source property of the Image element, which means you can also set it using a URI that points to an embedded file in your project or a web location.

■**Note** Silverlight respects any transparency information that it finds in an image. For example, Silverlight supports transparent areas in a PNG file.

In this example, the ImageBrush is used to paint the background of a cell. As a result, the image is stretched to fit the fill area. If the Grid is larger than the original size of the image, you may see resizing artifacts in your image (such as a general fuzziness). If the shape of the Grid doesn't match the aspect ratio of the picture, the picture will be distorted to fit. You can control this behavior by modifying the ImageBrush.Stretch property and assigning one of the values listed in Table 8-2.

Table 8-2. *Values for the Stretch Enumeration*

Name	Description
Fill	Your image is stretched in width and height to fit its container exactly. This is the default.
None	The image is not stretched. Its native size is used (and any part that won't fit is clipped).
Uniform	The width and height are sized up proportionately until the image reaches the edge of the container. The image's aspect ratio is preserved, but there may be extra blank space.
UniformToFill	The width and height are sized proportionately until the shape fills all the available height and width. The image's aspect ratio is preserved, but it may be clipped to fit the region.

■**Note** Even with a Stretch of None, your image may still be scaled. For example, if you've set your Windows system DPI setting to 120 dpi (also known as *large fonts*), Silverlight will scale up your bitmap proportionately. This may introduce some fuzziness, but it's a better solution than having your image sizes (and the alignment of your overall user interface) change on monitors with different dpi settings.

If the image is painted smaller than the fill region, the image is aligned according to the AlignmentX and AlignmentY properties. The unfilled area is left transparent. This occurs if you're using Uniform scaling and the region you're filling has a different shape (in which case you'll get blank bars on the top or the sides). It also occurs if you're using None and the fill region is larger than the image.

Transparency

In the examples you've considered so far, the shapes you've seen have been completely opaque. However, Silverlight supports true transparency. That means if you layer several elements on top of one another and give them all varying layers of transparency, you'll see exactly what you expect. At its simplest, this feature gives you the ability to create graphical backgrounds that "show through" the elements you place on top. At its most complex, this feature allows you to create multilayered animations and other effects.

There are several ways to make an element partly transparent:

- **Set the Opacity property of the element.** Opacity is a fractional value from 0 to 1, where 1 is completely solid (the default) and 0 is completely transparent. The Opacity property is defined in the UIElement class, so it applies to all elements.

- **Set the Opacity property of the brush.** Like elements, the various brush classes include an Opacity property that allows you to make their fill partially transparent. You can then use these brushes to paint part of with an element.

- **Use a semitransparent color.** Any color that has an alpha value less than 255 is semitransparent. You can use a semitransparent color when setting the foreground, background, or border of an element.

- **Set the OpacityMask property.** This allows you to make specific regions of an element transparent or partially transparent. For example, you can use it to fade a shape gradually into transparency.

Figure 8-5 shows an example that uses the first two approaches to create transparent elements.

Figure 8-5. *A page with several semitransparent elements*

In this example, the top-level layout container is a Grid that uses an ImageBrush that sets a picture for the background. The opacity of the StackPanel is reduced to 70%, allowing the solid color underneath to show through. (In this case, it's simply a white background, which lightens the image.)

```
<Grid Margin="5" Opacity="0.7">
  <Grid.Background>
    <ImageBrush ImageSource="celestial.jpg" />
  </Grid.Background>
  ...
</Grid>
```

The first element inside is a button, which uses a partially transparent red background color (set through the Foreground property). The image shows through in the button background, but the text is opaque. (Had the Opacity property been set, both the foreground and background would have become semitransparent.)

```
<Button Foreground="Green" Background="#60AA4030" FontSize="16" Margin="10"
 Padding="20" Content="A Semi-Transparent Button"></Button>
```

▍Note Silverlight supports the ARGB color standard, which uses four values to describe every color. These four values (each of which ranges from 0 to 255) record the alpha, red, green, and blue components, respectively. The *alpha* component is a measure of how transparent the color is—0 is fully transparent and 255 is fully opaque.

The next element is a TextBlock. By default, all TextBlock elements have a completely transparent background color, so the content underneath can show through. This example doesn't change that detail, but it does use the Opacity property to make the text partially transparent. The same effect could have been accomplished by setting a white color with a non-zero alpha value for the Foreground property.

```
<TextBlock Grid.Row="1" Margin="10" TextWrapping="Wrap"
 Foreground="White" Opacity="0.3" FontSize="38" FontFamily="Arial Black"
 Text="SEMI-TRANSPARENT TEXT"></TextBlock>
```

Last is a nested Grid that places two elements in the same cell, one over the other. (You could also use a Canvas to overlap two elements and control their positions more precisely.) On the bottom is a partially transparent Image element that shows a happy face. It also uses the Opacity property to allow the other image to show through underneath. Over that is a TextBlock element with partially transparent text. If you look carefully, you can see both backgrounds show through under some letters.

```
<Image Grid.Row="2" Margin="10" Source="happyface.jpg" Opacity="0.5" ></Image>
```

You could extend the layering, and tile multiple images or elements on top of each other, making each one partially transparent. Of course, if you add enough transparent layers, performance will suffer, particularly if your application uses dynamic effects like animation. Furthermore, you're unlikely to perceive the difference with more than two or three layers of transparency. However, Silverlight imposes no limits on how you use transparency.

Opacity Masks

You can use the OpacityMask property to make specific regions of an element transparent or partially transparent. The OpacityMask allows you to achieve a variety of common and exotic effects. For example, you can use it to fade a shape gradually into transparency.

The OpacityMask property accepts any brush. The alpha channel of the brush determines where the transparency occurs. For example, if you use a SolidColorBrush that's set to a transparent color for your OpacityMask, your entire element will disappear. If you use a Solid-ColorBrush that's set to use a nontransparent color, your element will remain completely visible. The other details of the color (the red, green, and blue components) aren't important and are ignored when you set the OpacityMask property.

Using the OpacityMask with a SolidColorBrush doesn't make much sense because you can accomplish the same effect more easily with the Opacity property. However, OpacityMask becomes more useful when you use more exotic types of brushes, such as the LinearGradient or RadialGradientBrush. Using a gradient that moves from a solid to a transparent color, you can create a transparency effect that fades in over the surface of your element, like the one used by this button:

```
<Button FontSize="14" FontWeight="Bold" Content="A Partially Transparent Button">
  <Button.OpacityMask>
    <LinearGradientBrush StartPoint="0,0" EndPoint="1,0">
      <GradientStop Offset="0" Color="Transparent"></GradientStop>
      <GradientStop Offset="0.8" Color="Black"></GradientStop>
    </LinearGradientBrush>
  </Button.OpacityMask>
</Button>
```

Figure 8-6 shows this button over a page that displays a picture of a grand piano.

Figure 8-6. *A button that fades from transparent (left) to solid (right)*

Making the Silverlight Control Transparent

So far, you've seen how to make different elements in a Silverlight region transparent. But there's one more transparency trick you can use—making the Silverlight content region *windowless*, so its background allows HTML content to show through.

To configure Silverlight to use windowless rendering, you need to follow several steps. First, you must edit your XAML to make sure that your markup doesn't set an opaque background. Ordinarily, when you create a new page with Visual Studio, it adds a single Grid container that fills the entire page. This Grid is the layout root for the page, and Visual Studio explicitly gives it a white background, as shown here:

```
<Grid x:Name="LayoutRoot" Background="White">
```

To make the page transparent, you'll need to remove the Background property setting, so the Grid can revert to its default transparent background.

Next, you need to edit your HTML entry page. Find the <div> element that holds the Silverlight content region. Now you need to make two changes. First, change the *background* parameter from White to Transparent. Next, add a *windowless* parameter with a value of true. Here's the modified HTML markup:

```
<div id="silverlightControlHost">
  <object data="data:application/x-silverlight,"
   type="application/x-silverlight-2" width="100%" height="100%">
    <param name="source" value="TransparentSilverlight.xap"/>
    <param name="onerror" value="onSilverlightError" />
    <param name="background" value="transparent" />
    <param name="windowless" value="true" />
    ...
  </object>
  <iframe style='visibility:hidden;height:0;width:0;border:0px'></iframe>
</div>
```

Figure 8-7 and Figure 8-8 show an example that places the Silverlight content region in the left column of a multicolumned page. Each column is represented by a <div> element with different style settings. Figure 8-7 shows the Silverlight control as it normally appears, with an opaque background. Figure 8-8 shows the same example with a windowless Silverlight content region. Because the Silverlight control is transparent, the tiled column background can show through.

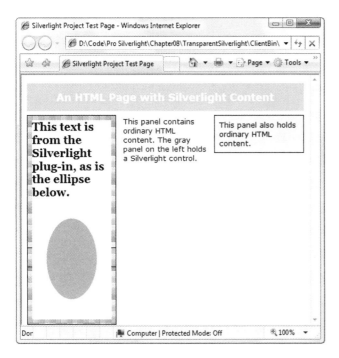

Figure 8-7. *Normal Silverlight content*

Figure 8-8. *A windowless Silverlight content region*

A windowless Silverlight content region has two important differences. Not only does it allow HTML content underneath to show through, it also allows HTML content above to overlap. Figure 8-8 demonstrates this fact with a small snippet of floating HTML that appears over the Silverlight content region and displays the message "This is HTML text."

To create this effect, two <div> elements are positioned using absolute coordinates on the left side of the page, using these two style classes:

```
.SilverlightLeftPanel
{
  background-image: url('tiles5x5.png');
  background-repeat:repeat;
  position: absolute;
  top: 70px;
  left: 10px;
  width: 142px;
  border-width: 1px;
  border-style: solid;
  border-color: black;
  padding: 8px;
}

.HtmlLeftPanel
{
  background-color: Transparent;
  position: absolute;
  top: 300px;
  left: 10px;
  width: 142px;
  font-weight: bold;
  border-width: 1px;
  border-style: solid;
  border-color: black;
  padding: 8px;
}
```

The first <div> element holds the Silverlight content region, and the second <div> holds the overlapping HTML content, as shown here:

```
<div class="SilverlightLeftPanel">
  <div id="silverlightControlHost">...</div>
</div>

<div class="HtmlLeftPanel" >
  <p>This is HTML text.</p>
</div>
```

To see the complete HTML for this page, refer to the downloadable code for this chapter.

Tip The most common reason to use a windowless Silverlight control is because you want non-rectangular Silverlight content to blend in seamlessly with the web page background underneath. However, you might also use a windowless Silverlight control to put HTML elements and Silverlight elements side by side. This is particularly useful if these elements interact (as described in Chapter 12). For example, if you want to create a Silverlight media player with HTML playback buttons, you'll probably use a windowless Silverlight control.

Only use a windowless Silverlight content region if you need it. It requires extra overhead, which can reduce the performance in applications that require frequent redrawing or use a large number of animations. When you aren't using a windowless content region, don't assume your Silverlight control will automatically get a solid white background. When running on Mac computers, Silverlight always uses windowless mode, regardless of the parameters you pass. That's why the default entry page explicitly sets the background parameter to white.

Transforms

A great deal of drawing tasks can be made simpler with the use of a *transform*—an object that alters the way a shape or element is drawn by secretly shifting the coordinate system it uses. In Silverlight, transforms are represented by classes that derive from the abstract System.Windows.Media.Transform class, as listed in Table 8-3.

Table 8-3. *Transform Classes*

Name	Description	Important Properties
TranslateTransform	Displaces your coordinate system by some amount. This transform is useful if you want to draw the same shape in different places.	X, Y
RotateTransform	Rotates your coordinate system. The shapes you draw normally are turned around a center point you choose.	Angle, CenterX, CenterY
ScaleTransform	Scales your coordinate system up or down, so that your shapes are drawn smaller or larger. You can apply different degrees of scaling in the X and Y dimensions, thereby stretching or compressing your shape. When a shape is resized, Silverlight resizes its inside area and its border proportionately. That means the larger your shape grows, the thicker its border will be.	ScaleX, ScaleY, CenterX, CenterY
SkewTransform	Warps your coordinate system by slanting it a number of degrees. For example, if you draw a square, it becomes a parallelogram.	AngleX, AngleY, CenterX, CenterX

Continued

Table 8-3. *Continued*

Name	Description	Important Properties
MatrixTransform	Modifies your coordinate system using matrix multiplication with the matrix you supply. This is the most complex option— it requires some mathematical skill.	Matrix
TransformGroup	Combines multiple transforms so they can all be applied at once. The order in which you apply transformations is important— it affects the final result. For example, rotating a shape (with RotateTransform) and then moving it (with TranslateTransform) sends the shape off in a different direction than if you move it and *then* rotate it.	N/A

Technically, all transforms use matrix math to alter the coordinates of your shape. However, using the prebuilt transforms such as TranslateTransform, RotateTransform, ScaleTransform, and SkewTransform is far simpler than using the MatrixTransform and trying to work out the right matrix for the operation you want to perform. When you perform a series of transforms with the TransformGroup, Silverlight fuses your transforms together into a single MatrixTransform, ensuring optimal performance.

■**Note** All transforms have automatic change notification support. If you change a transform that's being used in a shape, the shape will redraw itself immediately.

Transforms are one of those quirky concepts that turn out to be extremely useful in a variety of different contexts. Some examples include the following:

- **Angling a shape.** Using the RotateTransform, you can turn your coordinate system to create certain shapes more easily.

- **Repeating a shape.** Many drawings are built using a similar shape in several different places. Using a transform, you can take a shape and then move it, rotate it, resize it, and so on.

■**Tip** In order to use the same shape in multiple places, you'll need to duplicate the shape in your markup (which isn't ideal), use code (to create the shape programmatically), or use the Path shape described in Chapter 7. The Path shape accepts Geometry objects, and you can store a geometry object as a resource so it can be reused throughout your markup.

- **Dynamic effects and animation.** You can create a number of sophisticated effects with the help of a transform, such as rotating a shape, moving it from one place to another, and warping it dynamically.

You've already seen how transforms allow you to create scalable pages (Chapter 4). In Chapter 9, you'll use transforms to build powerful animations. But for now, you'll take a quick look at how transforms work by considering how you can apply a basic transform to an ordinary shape.

Transforming Shapes

To transform a shape, you assign the RenderTransform property to the transform object you want to use. Depending on the transform object you're using, you'll need to fill in different properties to configure it, as detailed in Table 8-3.

For example, if you're rotating a shape, you need to use the RotateTransform, and supply the angle in degrees. Here's an example that rotates a square by 25 degrees:

```
<Rectangle Width="80" Height="10" Stroke="Blue" Fill="Yellow"
  Canvas.Left="100" Canvas.Top="100">
  <Rectangle.RenderTransform>
    <RotateTransform Angle="25" />
  </Rectangle.RenderTransform>
</Rectangle>
```

When you rotate a shape in this way, you rotate it about the shape's origin (the top-left corner). Figure 8-9 illustrates this by rotating the same square 25, 50, 75, and then 100 degrees.

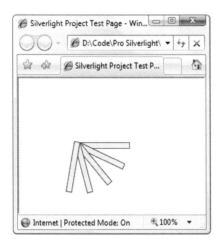

Figure 8-9. *Rotating a rectangle four times*

Sometimes you'll want to rotate a shape around a different point. The RotateTransform, like many other transform classes, provides a CenterX property and a CenterY property. You can use these properties to indicate the center point around which the rotation should be performed. Here's a rectangle that uses this approach to rotate itself 25 degrees around its center point:

```
<Rectangle Width="80" Height="10" Stroke="Blue" Fill="Yellow"
  Canvas.Left="100" Canvas.Top="100">
  <Rectangle.RenderTransform>
    <RotateTransform Angle="25" CenterX="45" CenterY="5" />
  </Rectangle.RenderTransform>
</Rectangle>
```

Figure 8-10 shows the result of performing the same sequence of rotations featured in Figure 8-9, but around the designated center point.

Figure 8-10. *Rotating a rectangle around its middle*

There's a clear limitation to using the CenterX and CenterY properties of the RotateTransform. These properties are defined using absolute coordinates, which means you need to know the exact center point of your content. If you're displaying dynamic content (for example, pictures of varying dimensions or elements that can be resized), this introduces a problem. Fortunately, Silverlight has a solution with the handy RenderTransformOrigin property, which is supported by all shapes. This property sets the center point using a proportional coordinate system that stretches from 0 to 1 in both dimensions. In other words, the point (0, 0) is designated as the top-left corner and (1, 1) is the bottom-right corner. (If the shape region isn't square, the coordinate system is stretched accordingly.)

With the help of the RenderTransformOrigin property, you can rotate any shape around its center point using markup like this:

```
<Rectangle Width="80" Height="10" Stroke="Blue" Fill="Yellow"
  Canvas.Left="100" Canvas.Top="100" RenderTransformOrigin="0.5,0.5">
  <Rectangle.RenderTransform>
    <RotateTransform Angle="25" />
  </Rectangle.RenderTransform>
</Rectangle>
```

This works because the point (0.5, 0.5) designates the center of the shape, regardless of its size. In practice, RenderTransformOrigin is generally more useful than the CenterX and CenterY properties, although you can use either one (or both) depending on your needs.

Tip You can use values greater than 1 or less than 0 when setting the RenderTransformOrigin property to designate a point that appears outside the bounding box of your shape. For example, you can use this technique with a RotateTransform to rotate a shape in a large arc around a very distant point, such as (5, 5).

Transforms and Layout Containers

The RenderTransform and RenderTransformOrigin properties aren't limited to shapes. In fact, the Shape class inherits them from the UIElement class, which means they're supported by all Silverlight elements, including buttons, text boxes, the TextBlock, entire layout containers full of content, and so on. Amazingly, you can rotate, skew, and scale any piece of Silverlight user interface (although in most cases you shouldn't).

It's important to note that when applying transforms to the elements in a layout container, the transforming is performed after the layout. For the simple Canvas, which uses coordinate-based layout, this distinction has no effect. But for other layout containers, which position elements *relatively* based on the placement and size of other elements, the effect is important. For instance, consider the example shown in Figure 8-11, which shows a Stack-Panel that contains a rotated button. Here, the StackPanel lays out the two buttons as though the first button is positioned normally, and the rotation happens just before the button is rendered. As a result, the rotated button overlaps the one underneath.

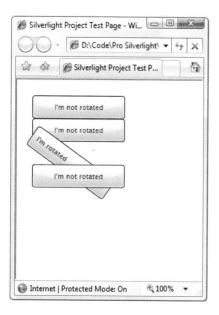

Figure 8-11. *Rotating buttons*

WPF also has the ability to use layout transforms, which are applied before the layout pass, which means the layout container uses the transformed dimensions of an element when positioning other elements. However, Silverlight does not provide this ability.

■**Tip** You can also use transforms to change a wide range of Silverlight ingredients, such as brushes, geometries, and clipping regions.

A Reflection Effect

Transforms are important for applying many types of effects. One example is a reflection effect, such as the one demonstrated in Figure 8-12.

Figure 8-12. *A reflection effect*

To create a reflection effect in Silverlight, you need to begin by explicitly duplicating the content that will use the effect. For example, to create the reflection shown in Figure 8-11, you need to begin with two identical Image elements—one of which shows the original image and the other which shows the reflected copy:

```
<Grid x:Name="LayoutRoot" Background="White">
  <Grid.RowDefinitions>
    <RowDefinition></RowDefinition>
    <RowDefinition></RowDefinition>
  </Grid.RowDefinitions>
  <Image Source=" harpsichord.jpg"></Image>
  <Image Grid.Row="1" Source=" harpsichord.jpg"></Image>
</Grid>
```

Because this technique forces you to duplicate your content, it generally isn't practical to add a reflection effect to controls. However, it is possible to create a reflection of a live video playback with the help of the VideoBrush, which is described in Chapter 10.

The second step is to modify the copy of your content to make it look more like a reflection. To accomplish this, you need to use a combination of two ingredients: a transform, which flips the image into place, and an opacity mask, which fades it gently out of sight.

```
<Image Grid.Row="1" Source="harpsichord.jpg" RenderTransformOrigin="0,0.4">
  <Image.RenderTransform>
    <ScaleTransform ScaleY="-0.8"></ScaleTransform>
  </Image.RenderTransform>
  <Image.OpacityMask>
    <LinearGradientBrush StartPoint="0,0" EndPoint="0,1">
      <GradientStop Offset="0" Color="Transparent"></GradientStop>
      <GradientStop Offset="1" Color="#44000000"></GradientStop>
    </LinearGradientBrush>
  </Image.OpacityMask>
</Image>
```

Here, a ScaleTransform flips the image over by using a negative value for ScaleY. To flip an image horizontally, you use –1. By using a fractional value (in this case, –0.8), the image is simultaneously flipped and compressed, so it's shorter than the original image. To make sure the flipped copy appears in the right place, you'll need to position it exactly (using a layout container like the Canvas) or use the RenderTransformOrigin property, as in this example. Here, the image is flipped around the point (0, 0.4). In other words, it keeps the same left alignment (x = 0), but is moved down (y = 0.4). Essentially, it's flipped around an imaginary horizontal line that's just a bit higher than the midpoint of the image.

This example uses a LinearGradientBrush that fades between a completely transparent color and a partially transparent color, to make the reflected content more faded. Because the image is upside down, the gradient stops must be defined in the reverse order.

Note Now that you understand the tools of Silverlight graphics, you can implement other effects, like glows and shadows, which use multiple layers of gradient fills. You can find one example at http://blogs.msdn.com/timrule/archive/2008/04/21/shadow-effect.aspx.

The Last Word

In this chapter, you delved deeper into Silverlight's 2-D drawing model. It's important to understand the plumbing behind 2-D graphics, because it makes it far easier for you to manipulate them. For example, you can alter a standard 2-D graphic by modifying the brushes used to paint various shapes, applying transforms to individual geometries, or altering the opacity or transform of an entire layer of shapes. More dramatically, you can add, remove, or alter individual geometries. These techniques can be easily combined with the animation skills you'll pick up in the next chapter. For example, it's easy to rotate a Geometry object by modifying the Angle property of a RotateTransform, fade a layer of shapes into existence using DrawingGroup.Opacity, or create a swirling gradient effect by animating a LinearGradient-Brush that paints the fill for a GeometryDrawing.

CHAPTER 9

■■■■

Animation

Animation allows you to create truly *dynamic* user interfaces. It's often used to apply effects—for example, icons that grow when you move over them, logos that spin, text that scrolls into view, and so on. Sometimes, these effects seem like excessive glitz. But used properly, animations can enhance an application in a number of ways. They can make an application seem more responsive, natural, and intuitive. (For example, a button that slides in when you click it feels like a real, physical button—not just another gray rectangle.) Animations can also draw attention to important elements and guide the user through transitions to new content. (For example, an application could advertise new content with a twinkling, blinking, or pulsing icon.)

Animations are a core part of the Silverlight model. That means you don't need to use timers and event handling code to put them into action. Instead, you can create them declaratively, configure them using one of a handful of classes, and put them into action without writing a single line of C# code. Animations also integrate themselves seamlessly into ordinary Silverlight pages. For example, if you animate a button so it drifts around the page, the button still behaves like a button. It can be styled, it can receive focus, and it can be clicked to fire off the typical event handling code. This is what separates animation from traditional media files, such as video. (In Chapter 10, you'll learn how to put a video page in your application. A video page is a completely separate region of your application—it's able to play video content, but it's not user interactive.)

In this chapter, you'll consider the set of animation classes that Silverlight provides. You'll see how to construct them with XAML and (more commonly) how to control them with code. Along the way, you'll see a wide range of animation examples, including page transitions and a simple catch-the-bombs game.

Note Silverlight animation is a scaled-down version of the WPF animation system. It keeps the same conceptual framework, the same model for defining animations with animation classes, and the same storyboard system. However, WPF developers will find some key differences, particularly in the way that animations are created and started in code. (For example, Silverlight elements lack the built-in Begin-Animation() method that they have in WPF.)

Understanding Silverlight Animation

Often, an animation is thought of as a series of frames. To perform the animation, these frames are shown one after the other, like a stop-motion video.

Silverlight animations use a dramatically different model. Essentially, a Silverlight animation is simply a way to modify the value of a dependency property over an interval of time. For example, to make a button that grows and shrinks, you can modify its Width property in an animation. To make it shimmer, you could change the properties of the LinearGradientBrush that it uses for its background. The secret to creating the right animation is determining what properties you need to modify.

If you want to make other changes that can't be made by modifying a property, you're out of luck. For example, you can't add or remove elements as part of an animation. Similarly, you can't ask Silverlight to perform a transition between a starting scene and an ending scene (although some crafty workarounds can simulate this effect). And finally, you can use animation only with a dependency property, because only dependency properties use the dynamic value resolution system (described in Chapter 4) that takes animations into account.

At first glance, the property-focused nature of Silverlight animations seems terribly limiting. However, as you work with Silverlight, you'll find that it's surprisingly capable. In fact, you can create a wide range of animated effects using common properties that every element supports. In this chapter, you'll even see how you can use it to build a simple game.

GOING BEYOND SILVERLIGHT ANIMATION

That said, there are some cases where the property-based animation system won't suit. As a rule of thumb, the property-based animation is a great way to add dynamic effects to an otherwise ordinary application (like buttons that glow, pictures that expand when you move over them, and so on). However, if you need to use animations as part of the core purpose of your application and you want them to continue running over the lifetime of your application, you may need something more flexible and more powerful. For example, if you're creating a complex arcade game or using physics calculations to model collisions, you'll need greater control over the animation.

Later in this chapter, you'll learn how to take a completely different approach with frame-based animations. In a frame-based animation, your code runs several times a second, and each time it runs you have a chance to modify the content of your window. For more information, see the section "Frame-Based Animation."

The Rules of Animation

In order to understand Silverlight animation, you need to understand the following key rules:

- **Silverlight animations are time-based.** Thus, you set the initial state, the final state, and the duration of your animation. Silverlight calculates the frame rate.

- **Animations act on properties.** That means a Silverlight animation can do only one thing: modify the value of a property over an interval of time. This sounds like a significant limitation (and it many ways, it is), but there's a surprisingly large range of effects you can create by simply modifying properties.

- **Every data type requires a different animation class.** For example, the Button.Width property uses the double data type. To animate it, you use the DoubleAnimation class. If you want to modify the color that's used to paint the background of your Canvas, you need to use the ColorAnimation class.

Silverlight has relatively few animation classes, so you're limited in the data types you can use. At present, you can use animations to modify properties with the following data types: double, object, Color, and Point. However, you can also craft your own animation classes that work for different data types—all you need to do is derive from System.Windows.Media.Animation and indicate how the value should change as time passes.

Many data types don't have a corresponding animation class because it wouldn't be practical. A prime example is enumerations. For example, you can control how an element is placed in a layout panel using the HorizontalAlignment property, which takes a value from the HorizontalAlignment enumeration. However, the HorizontalAlignment enumeration allows you to choose between only four values (Left, Right, Center, and Stretch), which greatly limits its use in an animation. Although you can swap between one orientation and another, you can't smoothly transition an element from one alignment to another. For that reason, there's no animation class for the HorizontalAlignment data type. You can build one yourself, but you're still constrained by the four values of the enumeration.

Reference types are not usually animated. However, their subproperties are. For example, all content controls sport a Background property that allows you to set a Brush object that's used to paint the background. It's rarely efficient to use animation to switch from one brush to another, but you can use animation to vary the properties of a brush. For example, you could vary the Color property of a SolidColorBrush (using the ColorAnimation class) or the Offset property of a GradientStop in a LinearGradientBrush (using the DoubleAnimation class). This extends the reach of Silverlight animation, allowing you to animate specific aspects of an element's appearance.

Tip As you'll see, the DoubleAnimation is by far the most useful of Silverlight's animation classes. Most of the properties you'll want to change are doubles, including the position of an element on a Canvas, its size, its opacity, and the properties of the transforms it uses.

Creating Simple Animations

Creating an animation is a multistep process. You need to create three separate ingredients: an animation object to perform your animation, a storyboard to manage your animation, and an event handler (an event trigger) to start your storyboard. In the following sections, you'll tackle each of these steps.

The Animation Class

There are actually two types of animation classes in Silverlight. Each type of animation uses a different strategy for varying a property value.

- **Linear interpolation.** With linear interpretation, the property value varies smoothly and continuously over the duration of the animation. Silverlight includes three such classes: DoubleAnimation, PointAnimation, and ColorAnimation.

- **Key frame animation.** With key frame animation, values can jump abruptly from one value to another, or they can combine jumps and periods of linear interpolation. Silverlight includes four such classes: ColorAnimationUsingKeyFrames, DoubleAnimationUsingKeyFrames, PointAnimationUsingKeyFrames, and ObjectAnimationUsingKeyFrames.

In this chapter, you'll begin by focusing on the indispensable DoubleAnimation, which uses linear interpolation to change a double from a starting value to its ending value.

Animations are defined using XAML markup. Although the animation classes aren't elements, they can still be created with the same XAML syntax. For example, here's the markup required to create a DoubleAnimation:

```
<DoubleAnimation From="160" To="300" Duration="0:0:5"></DoubleAnimation>
```

This animation lasts 5 seconds (as indicated by the Duration property, which takes a time value in the format Hours:Minutes:Seconds.FractionalSeconds). While the animation is running, it changes the target value from 160 to 300. Because the DoubleAnimation uses linear interpolation, this change takes place smoothly and continuously.

There's one important detail that's missing from this markup. The animation indicates how the property will be changed, but it doesn't indicate *what* property to use. This detail is supplied by another ingredient, which is represented by the Storyboard class.

The Storyboard Class

The storyboard manages the timeline of your animation. You can use a storyboard to group multiple animations, and it also has the ability to control the playback of animation—pausing it, stopping it, and changing its position. However, the most basic feature provided by the Storyboard class is its ability to point to a specific property and specific element using the TargetProperty and TargetName properties. In other words, the storyboard bridges the gap between your animation and the property you want to animate.

Here's how you might define a storyboard that applies a DoubleAnimation to the Width property of a button named cmdGrow:

```
<Storyboard x:Name="storyboard"
  Storyboard.TargetName="cmdGrow" Storyboard.TargetProperty="Width">
  <DoubleAnimation From="160" To="300" Duration="0:0:5"></DoubleAnimation>
</Storyboard>
```

The Storyboard.TargetProperty property identifies the property you want to change. (In the previous example, it's Width.) If you don't supply a class name, the storyboard uses the parent element. If you want to set an attached property (for example, Canvas.Left or Canvas.Top), you need to wrap the entire property in brackets, like this:

```
<Storyboard x:Name="storyboard"
  Storyboard.TargetName="cmdGrow" Storyboard.TargetProperty="(Canvas.Left)">
  ...
</Storyboard>
```

Both TargetName and TargetProperty are attached properties. That means you can apply them directly to the animation, as shown here:

```
<Storyboard x:Name="storyboard">
  <DoubleAnimation
   Storyboard.TargetName="cmdGrow" Storyboard.TargetProperty="Width"
   From="160" To="300" Duration="0:0:5"></DoubleAnimation>
</Storyboard>
```

This syntax is more common, because it allows you to put several animations in the same storyboard but allow each animation to act on a different element and property. Although you can't animate the same property at the same time with multiple animations, you can (and often will) animate different properties of the same element at once.

Starting an Animation with an Event Trigger

Defining a storyboard and an animation are the first steps to creating an animation. To actually put this storyboard into action, you need an event trigger. An event trigger responds to an event by performing a storyboard action. The only storyboard action that Silverlight currently supports is BeginStoryboard, which starts a storyboard (and hence all the animations it contains).

The following example uses the Triggers collection of a page to attach an animation to the Loaded event. When the Silverlight content is first rendered in the browser, and the page element is loaded, the button begins to grow. Five seconds later, its width has stretched from 160 pixels to 300.

```
<UserControl ... >
  <UserControl.Triggers>
    <EventTrigger>
      <EventTrigger.Actions>
        <BeginStoryboard>
          <Storyboard>
            <DoubleAnimation Storyboard.TargetName="cmdGrow"
              Storyboard.TargetProperty="Width"
              From="160" To="300" Duration="0:0:5"></DoubleAnimation>
          </Storyboard>
        </BeginStoryboard>
      </EventTrigger.Actions>
    </EventTrigger>
  </UserControl.Triggers>
```

```
<Grid x:Name="LayoutRoot" Background="White">
  <Button x:Name="cmdGrow" Width="160" Height="30"
   Content="This button grows"></Button>
</Grid>
</UserControl>
```

Unfortunately, Silverlight event triggers are dramatically limited, much more so than their WPF counterparts. Currently, Silverlight only allows event triggers to respond to the Loaded event when your page is first created. They can't react to other events, like clicks, key presses, and mouse movements. For those, you need the code described in the next section.

Starting an Animation with Code

You can start a Silverlight animation in response to any event using code that interacts with the storyboard. The first step is to move your storyboard out of the Triggers collection and place it in another collection of the same element: the Resources collection.

As you learned in Chapter 1, Silverlight elements provide a Resources property, which holds a collection where you can store miscellaneous objects. The primary purpose of the Resources collection is to allow you to define objects in XAML that aren't elements, and so can't be placed into the visual layout of your content region. For example, you might want to declare a Brush object as a resource so it can be used by more than one element. Resources can be retrieved in your code or used elsewhere in your markup.

Here's an example that defines the button-growing animation as a resource:

```
<UserControl ... >
  <UserControl.Resources>
    <Storyboard x:Name="storyboard">
      <DoubleAnimation
       Storyboard.TargetName="cmdGrow" Storyboard.TargetProperty="Width"
       From="160" To="300" Duration="0:0:5"></DoubleAnimation>
    </Storyboard>
  </UserControl.Resources>

  <Grid x:Name="LayoutRoot" Background="White">
    <Button x:Name="cmdGrow" Width="160" Height="30"
     Content="This button grows"></Button>
  </Grid>
</UserControl>
```

Notice that it's now given a name, so you can manipulate it in your code. (You can also add a name to the DoubleAnimation if you want to tweak its properties programmatically before launching the animation.) You'll also notice that you need to explicitly specify the Storyboard.TargetName property to connect it to the right element when you're using this approach.

Now you simply need to call the methods of the Storyboard object in an event handler in your Silverlight code-behind file. The methods you can use include Begin(), Stop(), Pause(), Resume(), and Seek(), all of which are fairly self-explanatory.

```
private void Button_Click(object sender, RoutedEventArgs e)
{
    storyboard.Begin();
}
```

Now, clicking the button launches the animation, and the button stretches from 160 to 300 pixels, as shown in Figure 9-1.

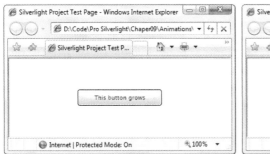

Figure 9-1. *Animating a button's width*

Configuring Animation Properties

To get the most out of your animations, you need to take a closer look at the seemingly simple animation class properties that were set in the previous example, including From, To, and Duration. As you'll see, there's a bit more subtlety—and a few more possibilities—than you might initially expect.

From

The From value is the starting value. In the previous example, the animation starts at 160 pixels. Thus, each time you click the button and start the animation, the Width is reset to 160 and the animation runs again. This is true even if you click the button while an animation is already underway.

■**Note** This example exposes another detail about Silverlight animations; namely, every dependency property can be acted on by only one animation at a time. If you start a second animation, the first one is discarded.

In many situations, you don't want an animation to begin at the original From value. There are two common reasons:

- **You have an animation that can be triggered multiple times in a row for a cumulative effect.** For example, you might want to create a button that grows a bit more each time it's clicked.

- **You have animations that may overlap.** For example, you might use the MouseEnter event to trigger an animation that expands a button and the MouseLeave event to trigger a complementary animation that shrinks it back. (This is often known as a "fisheye" effect.) If you move the mouse over and off this sort of button several times in quick succession, each new animation will interrupt the previous one, causing the button to "jump" back to the size that's set by the From property.

If you leave the From value out in the button-growing example, you can click the button multiple times without resetting its progress. Each time, a new animation will start, but it will continue from the current width. When the button reaches its maximum width, further clicks will have no effect, unless you add another animation to shrink it back.

```
<DoubleAnimation Storyboard.TargetName="cmdGrow"
 Storyboard.TargetProperty="Width" To="300" Duration="0:0:5"></DoubleAnimation>
```

There's one catch. For this technique to work, the property you're animating must have a previously set value. In this example, that means the button must have a hard-coded width (whether it's defined directly in the button tag or applied through a style setter). The problem is that in many layout containers, it's common not to specify a width and to allow the container to control it based on the element's alignment properties. In this case, the default width applies, which is the special value Double.NaN (where NaN stands for "not a number"). You can't animate a property that has this value using linear interpolation.

So, what's the solution? In many cases, the answer is to hard-code the button's width. As you'll see, animations often require a more fine-grained control of element sizing and positioning than you'd otherwise use. In fact, the most common layout container for "animatable" content is the Canvas, because it makes it easy to move content around (with possible overlap) and resize it. The Canvas is also the most lightweight layout container, because no extra layout work is needed when a property like Width is changed.

In the current example, there's another option. You could retrieve the current value of the button using its ActualWidth property, which indicates the current rendered width. You can't animate ActualWidth (it's read-only), but you can use it to set the From property of your animation programmatically, before you start the animation.

You need to be aware of another issue when you use the current value as a starting point for an animation—it may change the speed of your animation. That's because the duration isn't adjusted to take into account that there's a smaller spread between the initial value and the final value. For example, imagine you create a button that doesn't use the From value and instead animates from its current position. If you click the button when it has almost reached its maximum width, a new animation begins. This animation is configured to take five seconds (through the Duration property), even though there are only a few more pixels to go. As a result, the growth of the button will appear to slow down.

This effect appears only when you restart an animation that's almost complete. Although it's a bit odd, most developers don't bother trying to code around it. Instead, it's considered to be an acceptable quirk.

To

Just as you can omit the From property, you can omit the To property. In fact, you could leave out both the From and To properties to create an animation like this:

```
<DoubleAnimation Storyboard.TargetName="cmdGrow"
 Storyboard.TargetProperty="Width" Duration="0:0:5"></DoubleAnimation>
```

At first glance, this animation seems like a long-winded way to do nothing at all. It's logical to assume that because both the To and From properties are left out, they'll both use the same value. But there's a subtle and important difference.

When you leave out From, the animation uses the current value and takes animation into account. For example, if the button is midway through a grow operation, the From value uses the expanded width. However, when you leave out To, the animation uses the current value *without taking animation into account*. Essentially, that means the To value becomes the *original* value—whatever you last set in code, on the element tag, or through a style. (This works thanks to Silverlight's property resolution system, which is able to calculate a value for a property based on several overlapping property providers, without discarding any information. Chapter 4 describes this system in more detail.)

In the button example, that means if you start a grow animation and then interrupt it with the animation shown previously (perhaps by clicking another button), the button will shrink from its half-grown size until it reaches the original width that's set in the XAML markup. On the other hand, if you run this code while no other animation is underway, nothing will happen. That's because the From value (the animated width) and the To value (the original width) are the same.

By

Instead of using To, you can use the By property. The By property is used to create an animation that changes a value *by* a set amount, rather than *to* a specific target. For example, you could create an animation that enlarges a button by 10 pixels more than its current size, as shown here:

```
<DoubleAnimation Storyboard.TargetName="cmdGrow" By="10"
 Storyboard.TargetProperty="Width" Duration="0:0:5"></DoubleAnimation>
```

Clicking this button will always enlarge the button, no matter how many times you've run the animation and how large it's already grown.

The By property is not offered with all animation classes. For example, it doesn't make sense with non-numeric data types, such as a Color structure (as used by ColorAnimation).

Duration

The Duration property is straightforward enough—it takes the time interval (in milliseconds, minutes, hours, or whatever else you'd like to use) between the time the animation starts and the time it ends. Although the duration of the animations in the previous examples is set using a TimeSpan, the Duration property actually requires a Duration object. Fortunately, Duration and TimeSpan are quite similar, and the Duration structure defines an implicit cast that can convert System.TimeSpan to System.Windows.Duration as needed. That's why code like this is perfectly reasonable:

```
widthAnimation.Duration = TimeSpan.FromSeconds(5);
```

So, why bother introducing a whole new type? The Duration also includes two special values that can't be represented by a TimeSpan object—Duration.Automatic and Duration.Forever. Neither of these values is useful in the current example. Automatic simply sets the animation to a 1-second duration, and Forever makes the animation infinite in length, which prevents it from having any effect.

However, Duration.Forever becomes useful if you're creating a reversible animation. To do so, simply set the AutoReverse property to true. Now, the animation will play out in reverse once it's complete, reverting to the original value (and doubling the time the animation takes). Because a reversible animation returns to its initial state, Duration.Forever makes sense—it forces the animation to repeat endlessly.

Animation Lifetime

Technically, Silverlight animations are *temporary*, which means they don't actually change the value of the underlying property. While an animation is active, it simply overrides the property value. This is because of the way that dependency properties work (as described in Chapter 4), and it's an often overlooked detail that can cause significant confusion.

A one-way animation (like the button growing animation) remains active after it finishes running. That's because the animation needs to hold the button's width at the new size. This can lead to an unusual problem—namely, if you try to modify the value of the property using code after the animation has completed, your code will appear to have no effect. Your code simply assigns a new local value to the property, but the animated value still takes precedence.

You can solve this problem in several ways, depending on what you're trying to accomplish:

* Create an animation that resets your element to its original state. You do this by not setting the To property. For example, the button shrinking animation reduces the width of the button to its last set size, after which you can change it in your code.

* Create a reversible animation. You do this by setting the AutoReverse property to true. For example, when the button growing animation finishes widening the button, it will play out the animation in reverse, returning it to its original width. The total duration of your animation will be doubled.

* Change the FillBehavior property. Ordinarily, FillBehavior is set to HoldEnd, which means that when an animation ends, it continues to apply its final value to the target property. If you change FillBehavior to Stop, as soon as the animation ends the property reverts to its original value.

* Remove the animation object when the animation is complete by handling the Completed event of the animation object.

The first three options change the behavior of your animation. One way or another, they return the animated property to its original value. If this isn't what you want, you need to use the last option.

First, before you launch the animation, attach an event handler that reacts when the animation finishes. You can do this when the page first loads:

```
widthAnimation.Completed += animation_Completed;
```

When the Completed event fires, you can retrieve the storyboard that controls the animation and stop it:

```
private void storyboard_Completed(object sender, EventArgs e)
{
    Storyboard storyboard = (Storyboard)sender;
    storyboard.Stop();
}
```

When you call Storyboard.Stop(), the property returns to the value it had before the animation started. If this isn't what you want, you can take note of the current value that's being applied by the animation, remove the animation, and then manually set the new property, like so:

```
double currentWidth = cmdGrow.Width;
storyboard.Stop();
cmdGrow.Width = currentWidth;
```

Keep in mind that this changes the local value of the property. That may affect how other animations work. For example, if you animate this button with an animation that doesn't specify the From property, it uses this newly applied value as a starting point. In most cases, this is the behavior you want.

RepeatBehavior

The RepeatBehavior property allows you to control how an animation is repeated. If you want to repeat it a fixed number of times, indicate the number of times to repeat, followed by an *x*. For example, this animation repeats twice:

```
<DoubleAnimation Storyboard.TargetName="cmdGrow" RepeatBehavior="2x"
 Storyboard.TargetProperty="Width" To="300" Duration="0:0:5"></DoubleAnimation>
```

Or in code, pass the number of times to the RepeatBehavior constructor:

```
widthAnimation.RepeatBehavior = new RepeatBehavior(2);
```

When you run this animation, the button will increase in size (over five seconds), jump back to its original value, and then increase in size again (over five seconds), ending at the full width of the page. If you've set AutoReverse to true, the behavior is slightly different—the entire animation is completed forward and backward (meaning the button expands and then shrinks), and *then* it's repeated again.

Rather than using RepeatBehavior to set a repeat count, you can use it to set a repeat *interval*. To do so, simply set the RepeatBehavior property with a constructor. For example, the following animation repeats itself for 13 seconds:

```
<DoubleAnimation Storyboard.TargetName="cmdGrow" RepeatBehavior="0:0:13"
 Storyboard.TargetProperty="Width" To="300" Duration="0:0:5"></DoubleAnimation>
```

And here's the same change made in code:

```
widthAnimation.RepeatBehavior = new RepeatBehavior(TimeSpan.FromSeconds(13));
```

In this example, the Duration property specifies that the entire animation takes five seconds. As a result, the RepeatBehavior of 13 seconds will trigger two repeats and then leave the button halfway through a third repeat (at the three-second mark).

■**Tip** You can use RepeatBehavior to perform just part of an animation. To do so, use a fractional number of repetitions, or use a TimeSpan that's less than the duration.

Finally, you can cause an animation to repeat itself endlessly with the RepeatBehavior.Forever value:

```
<DoubleAnimation Storyboard.TargetName="cmdGrow" RepeatBehavior="Forever"
 Storyboard.TargetProperty="Width" To="300" Duration="0:0:5"></DoubleAnimation>
```

Simultaneous Animations

The Storyboard class has the ability to hold more than one animation. Best of all, these animations are managed as one group—meaning they're started at the same time.

To see an example, consider the following storyboard. It wraps two animations, one that acts on the Width property of a button and the other that acts on the Height property. Because the animations are grouped into one storyboard, they increment the button's dimensions in unison.

```
<Storyboard x:Name="storyboard" Storyboard.TargetName="cmdGrow">
  <DoubleAnimation Storyboard.TargetProperty="Width"
   To="300" Duration="0:0:5"></DoubleAnimation>
  <DoubleAnimation Storyboard.TargetProperty="Height"
   To="300" Duration="0:0:5"></DoubleAnimation>
</Storyboard>
```

In this example, both animations have the same duration, but this isn't a requirement. The only consideration with animations that end at different times is their FillBehavior. If an animation's FillBehavior property is set to HoldEnd (the default), it holds the value until all the animations in the storyboard are completed. At this point, the storyboard's FillBehavior comes into effect, either continuing to hold the values from both animations (HoldEnd) or reverting them to their initial values (Stop). On the other hand, if you have multiple animations and one of them has a FillBehavior of Stop, this animated property will revert to its initial value when the animation is complete, even if there are other animations in the storyboard that are still running.

When dealing with more than one simultaneous animation, there are two more animation class properties that become useful: BeginTime and SpeedRatio. Sets a delay that will be added before the animation starts (as a TimeSpan). This delay is added to the total time, so a 5-second animation with a 5-second delay takes 10 seconds. BeginTime is useful when synchronizing different animations that start at the same time but should apply their effects in sequence. SpeedRatio increases or decreases the speed of the animation. Ordinarily, SpeedRatio is 1. If you increase it, the animation completes more quickly (for example, a SpeedRatio of 5 completes five times faster). If you decrease it, the animation is slowed down (for example, a SpeedRatio of 0.5 takes twice as long). Although the overall effect is the same as changing the Duration property of your animation, setting the SpeedRatio makes it easier to control how simultaneous animations overlap.

Controlling Playback

You've already seen how to start an animation using the Storyboard.Begin() method. The Storyboard class also provides a few more methods that allow you to stop or pause an animation. You'll see them in action in the following example, shown in Figure 9-2. This page superimposes two Image elements in exactly the same position, using a grid. Initially, only the topmost image—which shows a day scene of a Toronto city landmark—is visible. But as the animation runs, it reduces the opacity from 1 to 0, eventually allowing the night scene to show through completely. The effect is as if the image is changing from day to night, like a sequence of time-lapse photography.

Figure 9-2. *A controllable animation*

Here's the markup that defines the Grid with its two images:

```
<Grid>
  <Image Source="night.jpg"></Image>
  <Image Source="day.jpg" x:Name="imgDay"></Image>
</Grid>
```

and here's the storyboard that fades from one to the other, which is placed in the Resources collection of the page:

```
<Storyboard x:Name="fadeStoryboard">
  <DoubleAnimation x:Name="fadeAnimation"
    Storyboard.TargetName="imgDay" Storyboard.TargetProperty="Opacity"
    From="1" To="0" Duration="0:0:10">
  </DoubleAnimation>
</Storyboard>
```

To make this example more interesting, it includes several buttons at the bottom that allow you to control the playback of this animation. Using these buttons, you can perform the typical media player actions, such as pausing, resuming, and stopping. The event handling code simply uses the appropriate methods of the Storyboard object, as shown here:

```
private void cmdStart_Click(object sender, RoutedEventArgs e)
{
    fadeStoryboard.Begin();
}

private void cmdPause_Click(object sender, RoutedEventArgs e)
{
    fadeStoryboard.Pause();
}

private void cmdResume_Click(object sender, RoutedEventArgs e)
{
    fadeStoryboard.Resume();
}

private void cmdStop_Click(object sender, RoutedEventArgs e)
{
    fadeStoryboard.Stop();
}

private void cmdMiddle_Click(object sender, RoutedEventArgs e)
{
    // Start the animation, in case it's not currently underway.
    fadeStoryboard.Begin();
```

```
    // Move to the time position that represents the middle of the animation.
    fadeStoryboard.Seek(
        TimeSpan.FromSeconds(fadeAnimation.Duration.TimeSpan.TotalSeconds/2));
}
```

Note Remember, stopping an animation is not equivalent to completing an animation (unless FillBehavior is set to Stop). That's because even when an animation reaches the end of its timeline, it continues to apply its final value. Similarly, when an animation is paused, it continues to apply the most recent intermediary value. However, when an animation is stopped, it no longer applies any value, and the property reverts to its preanimation value.

There's one more event handler that reacts when you drag the thumb on a Slider. It then takes the value of the slider (which ranges from 0 to 3) and uses it to apply a new speed ratio:

```
private void sldSpeed_ValueChanged(object sender, RoutedEventArgs e)
{
    // To nothing if the page is still being initialized.
    if (sldSpeed == null) return;

    // This also restarts the animation if it's currently underway.
    fadeStoryboard.SpeedRatio = sldSpeed.Value;
    lblSpeed.Text = sldSpeed.Value.ToString("0.0");
}
```

Unlike in WPF, the Storyboard class in Silverlight does not provide events that allow you to monitor the progress of an event. For example, there's no CurrentTimeInvalidated event to tell you the animation is ticking forward.

Desired Frame Rate

As you've already learned, the most common animation technique is linear interpolation, which modifies a property smoothly from its starting point to its end point. For example, if you set a starting value of 1 and an ending value of 10, your property might be rapidly changed from 1 to 1.1, 1.2, 1.3, and so on, until the value reaches 10.

At this point, you may be wondering how Silverlight determines the increments it will use when performing interpolation. Happily, this detail is taken care of automatically. Silverlight uses whatever increment it needs to ensure a smooth animation at the currently configured frame rate. The standard frame rate Silverlight uses is 60 frames per second. In other words, every 1/60th of a second Silverlight calculates all animated values and updates the corresponding properties. A rate of 60 frames per second ensures smooth, fluid animations from start to finish. (Of course, Silverlight might not be able to deliver on its intentions, depending on its performance and the client's hardware.)

Silverlight makes it possible for you to decrease the frame rate. You might choose to do this if you know your animation looks good at a lower frame rate, so you don't want to waste the extra CPU cycles. Or, you may find that your animation performs better on lesser powered computers when it runs at a slower frame rate. On the Web, many animations run at a more modest 15 frames per second.

To adjust the frame rate, you need to add the maxFramerate parameter to the entry page for your application, as shown here:

```
<div id="silverlightControlHost">
  <object data="data:application/x-silverlight,"
   type="application/x-silverlight-2" width="100%" height="100%">
  <param name="source" value="Animations.xap"/>
  <param name="onerror" value="onSilverlightError" />
  <param name="background" value="white" />
  <param name="maxFramerate" value="15" />
  ...
  </object>
  <iframe style='visibility:hidden;height:0;width:0;border:0px'></iframe>
</div>
```

■**Tip** For best animation performance, use transparency sparingly, avoid animating text size (because font smoothing and hinting slows down performance), and don't use the windowless setting discussed in Chapter 8 (which allows HTML elements to show through the Silverlight content region).

Animation Types Revisited

You now know the fundamentals of Silverlight's property animation system—how animations are defined, how they're connected to elements, and how you can control playback with a storyboard. Now is a good time to take a step back and take a closer look at the animation classes for different data types, and consider how you can use them to achieve the effect you want.

The first challenge in creating any animation is choosing the right property to animate. Making the leap between the result you want (for example, an element moving across the page) and the property you need to use (in this case, Canvas.Left and Canvas.Top) isn't always intuitive. Here are a few guidelines:

- If you want to use an animation to make an element appear or disappear, don't use the Visibility property (which allows you to switch only between completely visible or completely invisible). Instead, use the Opacity property to fade it in or out.

- If you want to animate the position of an element, consider using a Canvas. It provides the most direct properties (Canvas.Left and Canvas.Top) and requires the least overhead. Alternatively, you can get similar effects in other layout containers by animating properties such as Margin and Padding using the ThicknessAnimation class. You can also animate the MinWidth or MinHeight or a column or row in a Grid.

- The most common properties to animate are transforms. You can use them to move or flip an element (TranslateTransform), rotate it (RotateTransform), resize or stretch it (ScaleTransform), and more. Used carefully, they can sometimes allow you to avoid hard-coding sizes and positions in your animation. The TranslateTransform also allows you to move elements in layout containers like the Grid in much the same way you can position them in the Canvas.

- One good way to change the surface of an element through an animation is to modify the properties of the brush. You can use a ColorAnimation to change the color or another animation object to transform a property of a more complex brush, like the offset in a gradient.

The following examples demonstrate how to animate transforms and brushes and how to use a few more animation types. You'll also learn how to create multi-segmented animations with key frames.

Animating Transforms

Transforms offer one of the most powerful ways to customize an element. When you use transforms, you don't simply change the bounds of an element. Instead, the entire visual appearance of the element is moved, flipped, skewed, stretched, enlarged, shrunk, or rotated. For example, if you animate the size of a button using a ScaleTransform, the entire button is resized, including its border and its inner content. The effect is much more impressive than if you animate its Width and Height or the FontSize property that affects its text.

To use a transform in animation, the first step is to define the transform. (An animation can change an existing transform but not create a new one.) For example, imagine you want to allow a button to rotate. This requires the RotateTransform:

```
<Button Content="A Button">
  <Button.RenderTransform>
    <RotateTransform></RotateTransform>
  </Button.RenderTransform>
</Button>
```

■Tip You can easily use transforms in combination. In fact, it's easy—you simply need to use the TransformGroup to set the RenderTransform property. You can nest as many transforms as you need inside the TransformGroup. You'll see an example in the bomb game that's shown later in this chapter.

Now here's an animation that makes a button rotate when the mouse moves over it. It acts on the Button.RotateTransform object, and uses the target property Angle. The fact that the RenderTransform property can hold a variety of different transform objects, each with different properties, doesn't cause a problem. As long as you're using a transform that has an angle property, this animation will work.

```
<Storyboard x:Name="rotateStoryboard">
  <DoubleAnimation Storyboard.TargetElement="cmd.RenderTransform"
    Storyboard.TargetProperty="Angle"
    To="360" Duration="0:0:0.8" RepeatBehavior="Forever"></DoubleAnimation>
</Storyboard>
```

If you place this animation in the Resources collection of the page, you can trigger it when the user moves the mouse over the button:

```
private void cmd_MouseEnter(object sender, MouseEventArgs e)
{
    rotateStoryboard.Begin();
}
```

The button rotates one revolution every 0.8 seconds and continues rotating perpetually. While the button is rotating, it's still completely usable—for example, you can click it and handle the Click event.

To make sure the button rotates around its center point (not the top-left corner), you need to set the RenderTransformOrigin property as shown here:

```
<Button Content="One" Margin="5" RenderTransformOrigin="0.5,0.5"
 MouseEnter="cmd_MouseEnter">
  <Button.RenderTransform>
    <RotateTransform></RotateTransform>
  </Button.RenderTransform>
</Button>
```

Remember, the RenderTransformOrigin property uses relative units from 0 to 1, so 0.5 represents a midpoint.

To stop the rotation, you can react to the MouseLeave event. At this point, you could stop the storyboard that performs the rotation, but this causes the button to jump back to its original orientation in one step. A better approach is to start a second animation that replaces the first. This animation leaves out the From property, which allows it to seamlessly rotate the button from its current angle to its original orientation in a snappy 0.2 seconds:

```
<Storyboard x:Name="unrotateStoryboard">
  <DoubleAnimation Storyboard.TargetElement="cmd.RenderTransform"
    Storyboard.TargetProperty="Angle" Duration="0:0:0.2"></DoubleAnimation>
</Storyboard>
```

Here's the event handler:

```
private void cmd_MouseLeave(object sender, MouseEventArgs e)
{
    unrotateStoryboard.Begin();
}
```

With a little more work, you can make these two animations and the two event handlers work for a whole stack of rotatable buttons, like the one shown in Figure 9-3. The trick is to handle the events of all the buttons with the same code, and dynamically assign the target of the storyboard to the current button using the Storyboard.SetTarget() method:

```
private void cmd_MouseEnter(object sender, MouseEventArgs e)
{
    rotateStoryboard.Stop();
    Storyboard.SetTarget(rotateStoryboard, ((Button)sender).RenderTransform);
    rotateStoryboard.Begin();
}

private void cmd_MouseLeave(object sender, MouseEventArgs e)
{
    unrotateStoryboard.Stop();
    Storyboard.SetTarget(unrotateStoryboard, ((Button)sender).RenderTransform);
    unrotateStoryboard.Begin();
}
```

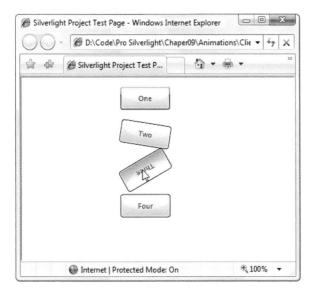

Figure 9-3. *Using a render transform*

There are two limitations to this approach. First, because the code reuses the same story-boards for all the buttons, there's no way to have two buttons rotating at once. For example, if you quickly slide the mouse over several buttons, the buttons you leave first might not rotate all the way back to their initial position, because the storyboard is commandeered by another button. If this behavior is a problem, you can code around it by creating the storyboards you need dynamically in code. You'll see how to implement this technique later in this chapter, when you consider the bomb game.

The other shortcoming in this example is the fact that you need a fair bit of markup to define the margins, event handlers, and transforms for all the buttons. You can streamline this markup by using styles to apply the same settings to various buttons (see Chapter 11) or by configuring the buttons programmatically.

Animating Brushes

Animating brushes is another common technique in Silverlight animations, and it's just as easy as animating transforms. Once again, the technique is to dig into the particular subprop-erty you want to change, using the appropriate animation type.

Figure 9-4 shows an example that tweaks a RadialGradientBrush. As the animation runs, the center point of the radial gradient drifts along the ellipse, giving it a three-dimensional effect. At the same time, the outer color of the gradient changes from blue to black.

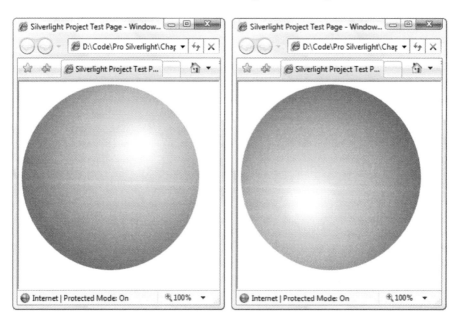

Figure 9-4. *Altering a radial gradient*

To perform this animation, you need to use two animation types that you haven't consid-ered yet. ColorAnimation blends gradually between two colors, creating a subtle color-shift effect. PointAnimation allows you to move a point from one location to another. (It's essen-tially the same as if you modified both the X coordinate and the Y coordinate using a separate

DoubleAnimation, with linear interpolation.) You can use a PointAnimation to deform a figure that you've constructed out of points or to change the location of the radial gradient's center point, as in this example.

Here's the markup that defines the ellipse and its brush:

```
<Ellipse x:Name="ellipse" Margin="5" Grid.Row="1" Stretch="Uniform">
  <Ellipse.Fill>
    <RadialGradientBrush x:Name="ellipseBrush"
     RadiusX="1" RadiusY="1" GradientOrigin="0.7,0.3">
        <GradientStop x:Name="ellipseBrushStop" Color="White"
         Offset="0"></GradientStop>
        <GradientStop Color="Blue" Offset="1"></GradientStop>
    </RadialGradientBrush>
  </Ellipse.Fill>
</Ellipse>
```

and here are the two animations that move the center point and change the second color in the gradient:

```
<Storyboard x:Name="ellipseStoryboard">
  <PointAnimation Storyboard.TargetName="ellipseBrush"
   Storyboard.TargetProperty="GradientOrigin"
   From="0.7,0.3" To="0.3,0.7" Duration="0:0:10" AutoReverse="True"
   RepeatBehavior="Forever">
  </PointAnimation>
  <ColorAnimation Storyboard.TargetName="ellipseBrushStop"
   Storyboard.TargetProperty="Color"
   To="Black" Duration="0:0:10" AutoReverse="True"
   RepeatBehavior="Forever">
  </ColorAnimation>
</Storyboard>
```

You can create a huge range of hypnotic effects by varying the colors and offsets in Linear-GradientBrush and RadialGradientBrush. And if that's not enough, gradient brushes also have their own RelativeTransform property that you can use to rotate, scale, stretch, and skew them. (The WPF team has a fun tool called Gradient Obsession for building gradient-based animations, most of which will work with Silverlight with some adjustment. You can find it at http://wpf.netfx3.com/files/folders/designer/entry7718.aspx.)

Key Frame Animation

All the animations you've seen so far have used linear interpolation to move from a starting point to an ending point. But what if you need to create an animation that has multiple segments and moves less regularly? For example, you might want to create an animation that slides an element into view quickly and then slowly moves it the rest of the way into place. You could achieve this effect by creating a sequence of two animations and using the BeginTime property to start the second animation after the first one. However, there's an easier approach—you can use a key frame animation.

A *key frame animation* is an animation that's made up of many short segments. Each segment represents an initial, final, or intermediary value in the animation. When you run the animation, it moves smoothly from one value to another.

For example, consider the Point animation that allowed you to move the center point of a RadialGradientBrush from one spot to another:

```
<PointAnimation Storyboard.TargetName="ellipseBrush"
 Storyboard.TargetProperty="GradientOrigin"
 From="0.7,0.3" To="0.3,0.7" Duration="0:0:10" AutoReverse="True"
 RepeatBehavior="Forever">
</PointAnimation>
```

You can replace this PointAnimation object with an equivalent PointAnimationUsingKeyFrames object, as shown here:

```
<PointAnimationUsingKeyFrames Storyboard.TargetName="ellipseBrush"
 Storyboard.TargetProperty="GradientOrigin"
 AutoReverse="True" RepeatBehavior="Forever" >
  <LinearPointKeyFrame Value="0.7,0.3" KeyTime="0:0:0"></LinearPointKeyFrame>
  <LinearPointKeyFrame Value="0.3,0.7" KeyTime="0:0:10"></LinearPointKeyFrame>
</PointAnimationUsingKeyFrames>
```

This animation includes two key frames. The first sets the Point value when the animation first starts. (If you want to use the current value that's set in the RadialGradientBrush, you can leave out this key frame.) The second key frame defines the end value, which is reached after ten seconds. The PointAnimationUsingKeyFrames object performs linear interpolation to move smoothly from the first key frame value to the second, just as the PointAnimation does with the From and To values.

Note Every key frame animation uses its own key frame animation object (like LinearPointKeyFrame). For the most point, these classes are the same—they include a Value property that stores the target value and a KeyTime property that indicates when the frame reaches the target value. The only difference is the data type of the Value property. In a LinearPointKeyFrame it's a Point, in a DoubleKeyFrame it's a double, and so on.

You can create a more interesting example using a series of key frames. The following animation walks the center point through a series of positions that are reached at different times. The speed that the center point moves will change depending on how long the duration is between key frames and how much distance needs to be covered.

```
<PointAnimationUsingKeyFrames Storyboard.TargetName="ellipseBrush"
 Storyboard.TargetProperty="GradientOrigin"
 RepeatBehavior="Forever" >
  <LinearPointKeyFrame Value="0.7,0.3" KeyTime="0:0:0"></LinearPointKeyFrame>
  <LinearPointKeyFrame Value="0.3,0.7" KeyTime="0:0:5"></LinearPointKeyFrame>
```

```
    <LinearPointKeyFrame Value="0.5,0.9" KeyTime="0:0:8"></LinearPointKeyFrame>
    <LinearPointKeyFrame Value="0.9,0.6" KeyTime="0:0:10"></LinearPointKeyFrame>
    <LinearPointKeyFrame Value="0.8,0.2" KeyTime="0:0:12"></LinearPointKeyFrame>
    <LinearPointKeyFrame Value="0.7,0.3" KeyTime="0:0:14"></LinearPointKeyFrame>
</PointAnimationUsingKeyFrames>
```

This animation isn't reversible, but it does repeat. To make sure there's no jump between the final value of one iteration and the starting value of the next iteration, the animation ends at the same center point that it began.

Discrete Key Frame Animations

The key frame animation you saw in the previous example uses *linear* key frames. As a result, it transitions smoothly between the key frame values. Another option is to use *discrete* key frames. In this case, no interpolation is performed. When the key time is reached, the property changes abruptly to the new value.

Linear key frame classes are named in the form Linear*DataType*KeyFrame. Discrete key frame classes are named in the form Discrete*DataType*KeyFrame. Here's a revised version of the RadialGradientBrush example that uses discrete key frames:

```
<PointAnimationUsingKeyFrames Storyboard.TargetName="ellipseBrush"
 Storyboard.TargetProperty="GradientOrigin"
 RepeatBehavior="Forever" >
  <DiscretePointKeyFrame Value="0.7,0.3" KeyTime="0:0:0"></DiscretePointKeyFrame>
  <DiscretePointKeyFrame Value="0.3,0.7" KeyTime="0:0:5"></DiscretePointKeyFrame>
  <DiscretePointKeyFrame Value="0.5,0.9" KeyTime="0:0:8"></DiscretePointKeyFrame>
  <DiscretePointKeyFrame Value="0.9,0.6" KeyTime="0:0:10"></DiscretePointKeyFrame>
  <DiscretePointKeyFrame Value="0.8,0.2" KeyTime="0:0:12"></DiscretePointKeyFrame>
  <DiscretePointKeyFrame Value="0.7,0.3" KeyTime="0:0:14"></DiscretePointKeyFrame>
</PointAnimationUsingKeyFrames>
```

When you run this animation, the center point will jump from one position to the next at the appropriate time. It's a dramatic (but jerky) effect.

All key frame animation classes support discrete key frames, but only some support linear key frames. It all depends on the data type. The data types that support linear key frames are the same ones that support linear interpolation and provide a *DataType*Animation class. These are Point, Color, and double. The only other animatable data type is object, which doesn't support linear interpolation. (Essentially, "animating" an object means replacing it with completely new values at specific times in a discrete key frame animation.)

■**Tip** You can combine both types of key frame—linear and discrete—in the same key frame animation, as long as they're both supported for that data type.

Spline Key Frame Animations

There's one more type of key frame: a *spline* key frame. Every class that supports linear key frames also supports spline key frames, and they're named in the form Spline*DataType*-KeyFrame.

Like linear key frames, spline key frames use interpolation to move smoothly from one key value to another. The difference is that every spline key frame sports a KeySpline property. Using the KeySpline property, you define a cubic Bézier curve that influences the way interpolation is performed. Although it's tricky to get the effect you want (at least without an advanced design tool to help you), this technique gives the ability to create more seamless acceleration and deceleration and more lifelike motion.

As you may remember from Chapter 7, a Bézier curve is defined by a start point, an end point, and two control points. In the case of a key spline, the start point is always (0,0), and the end point is always (1,1). You simply supply the two control points. The curve that you create describes the relationship between time (in the X axis) and the animated value (in the Y axis).

Here's an example that demonstrates a key spline animation by comparing the motion of two ellipses across a Canvas. The first ellipse uses a DoubleAnimation to move slowly and evenly across the page. The second ellipse uses a DoubleAnimationUsingKeyFrames with two SplineDoubleKeyFrame objects. It reaches the destination at the same times (after ten seconds), but it accelerates and decelerates during its travel, pulling ahead and dropping behind the other ellipse.

```
<DoubleAnimation Storyboard.TargetName="ellipse1"
 Storyboard.TargetProperty="(Canvas.Left)"
 To="500" Duration="0:0:10">
</DoubleAnimation>

<DoubleAnimationUsingKeyFrames Storyboard.TargetName="ellipse2"
 Storyboard.TargetProperty="(Canvas.Left)" >
  <SplineDoubleKeyFrame KeyTime="0:0:5" Value="250"
    KeySpline="0.25,0 0.5,0.7"></SplineDoubleKeyFrame>
  <SplineDoubleKeyFrame KeyTime="0:0:10" Value="500"
    KeySpline="0.25,0.8 0.2,0.4"></SplineDoubleKeyFrame>
</DoubleAnimationUsingKeyFrames>
```

The fastest acceleration occurs shortly after the five-second mark, when the second SplineDoubleKeyFrame kicks in. Its first control point matches a relatively large Y axis value, which represents the animation progress (0.8) against a correspondingly smaller X axis value, which represents the time. As a result, the ellipse increases its speed over a small distance, before slowing down again.

Figure 9-5 shows a graphical depiction of the two curves that control the movement of the ellipse. To interpret these curves, remember that they chart the progress of the animation from top to bottom. Looking at the first curve, you can see that it follows a fairly even progress downward, with a short pause at the beginning and a gradual leveling off at the end. However, the second curve plummets downward quite quickly, achieving the bulk of its progress, and then levels off for the remainder of the animation.

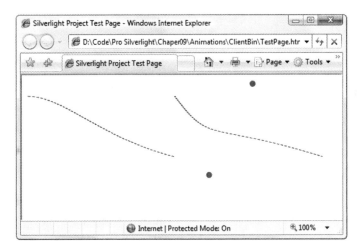

Figure 9-5. *Charting the progress of a key spline animation*

Animations in Code

Sometimes, you'll need to create every detail of an animation programmatically in code. In fact, this scenario is fairly common. It occurs any time you have multiple animations to deal with, and you don't know in advance how many animations there will be or how they should be configured. (This is the case with the simple bomb-dropping game you'll see in this section.) It also occurs if you want to use the same animation in different pages, or you simply want the flexibility to separate all the animation-related details from your markup for easier reuse. (This is the case with animation that's used for page transitions later in this chapter.)

It isn't difficult to create, configure, and launch an animation programmatically. You simple need to create the animation and storyboard objects, add the animations to the storyboard, and start the storyboard. You can perform any cleanup work after your animation ends by reacting to the Storyboard.Completed event.

In the following example, you'll see how to create the game shown in Figure 9-6. Here, a series of bombs are dropped at ever-increasing speeds. The player must click each bomb to diffuse it. When a set limit is reached—by default, five dropped bombs—the game ends.

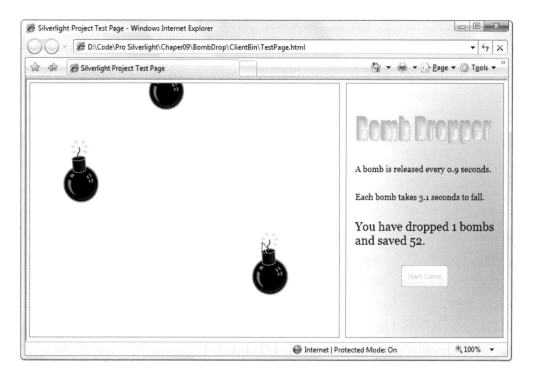

Figure 9-6. *Catching bombs*

In this example, every dropped bomb has its own storyboard with two animations. The first animation drops the bomb (by animating the Canvas.Top property), while the second animation rotates the bomb a slight bit back and forth, giving it a realistic "wiggle" effect. If the user clicks a bomb, these animations are halted and two more take place, to send the bomb careening harmlessly off the side of the Canvas. Finally, every time an animation ends the application checks to see if it represents a bomb that fell down or one that was saved, and updates the count accordingly.

In the following sections, you'll see how to create each part of this example.

The Main Page

The main page in the BombDropper example is fairly straightforward. It contains a two-column Grid. On the left side is a border, which contains the Canvas that represents the game surface:

```
<Border BorderBrush="SteelBlue" BorderThickness="1" Margin="5">
  <Grid>
    <Canvas x:Name="canvasBackground" SizeChanged="canvasBackground_SizeChanged"
      MinWidth="50">
      <Canvas.Background>
        <RadialGradientBrush>
          <GradientStop Color="AliceBlue" Offset="0"></GradientStop>
          <GradientStop Color="White" Offset="0.7"></GradientStop>
```

```
      </RadialGradientBrush>
    </Canvas.Background>
  </Canvas>
 </Grid>
</Border>
```

When the Canvas is sized for the first time or resized (when the user changes the size of the browser window), the following code runs and sets the clipping region:

```
private void canvasBackground_SizeChanged(object sender, SizeChangedEventArgs e)
{
    // Set the clipping region to match the current display region of the Canvas.
    RectangleGeometry rect = new RectangleGeometry();
    rect.Rect = new Rect(0, 0,
        canvasBackground.ActualWidth, canvasBackground.ActualHeight);
    canvasBackground.Clip = rect;
}
```

This is required because otherwise the Canvas draws its children even if they lie outside its display area. In the bomb-dropping game, this would cause the bombs to fly out of the box that delineates the Canvas.

▪ Note Because the user control is defined without explicit sizes, it's free to resize itself to match the browser window. The game logic uses the current window dimensions without attempting to compensate for them in any way. Thus, if you have a very wide window, bombs will be spread across a wide area, making the game more difficult. Similarly, if you have a very tall window, bombs will fall faster so they can complete their trajectory in the same interval of time. You could get around this issue by using a fixed-size region, which you could then center in the middle of your user control. However, a resizable window makes the example more adaptable and more interesting.

On the right side of the main window is a fixed-width panel that shows the game statistics, the current bomb dropped and saved count, and a button for starting the game:

```
<Border Grid.Column="2" BorderBrush="SteelBlue" BorderThickness="1" Margin="5">
  <Border.Background>
    <RadialGradientBrush GradientOrigin="1,0.7" Center="1,0.7"
     RadiusX="1" RadiusY="1">
      <GradientStop Color="Orange"  Offset="0"></GradientStop>
      <GradientStop Color="White" Offset="1"></GradientStop>
    </RadialGradientBrush>
  </Border.Background>

  <StackPanel Margin="15" VerticalAlignment="Center" HorizontalAlignment="Center">
    <bomb:Title></bomb:Title>
    <TextBlock x:Name="lblRate" Margin="0,30,0,0" TextWrapping="Wrap"
```

```
        FontFamily="Georgia" FontSize="14"></TextBlock>
      <TextBlock x:Name="lblSpeed" Margin="0,30" TextWrapping="Wrap"
       FontFamily="Georgia" FontSize="14"></TextBlock>
      <TextBlock x:Name="lblStatus" TextWrapping="Wrap"
       FontFamily="Georgia" FontSize="20">No bombs have dropped.</TextBlock>
      <Button x:Name="cmdStart" Padding="5" Margin="0,30" Width="80"
       Content="Start Game" Click="cmdStart_Click"></Button>
    </StackPanel>
</Border>
```

You'll notice that the right-side column contains one unusual ingredient—an element named Title. This is a custom user control that shows the BombDropper title in fiery orange letters. Technically, it's a piece of vector art. It was created in Microsoft Word using the WordArt feature, saved as an XPS file, and then exported to XAML using the technique described in Chapter 7. Although the markup for the BombDropper title could be inserted directly into the main page, defining it as a separate user control allows you to separate the title markup from the rest of the user interface.

To use the Title user control, you simply need to map your project namespace to an XML namespace, thereby making it available in your page (as described in Chapter 2). Assuming the project is named BombDropper, here's what you need to add:

```
<UserControl x:Class="BombDropper.Page"
    xmlns="http://schemas.microsoft.com/client/2007"
    xmlns:x="http://schemas.microsoft.com/winfx/2006/xaml"
    xmlns:bomb="clr-namespace:BombDropper;assembly=BombDropper">
```

Now you can use the XML prefix bomb to insert any custom controls from your project, including user controls:

```
<bomb:Title></bomb:Title>
```

The Bomb User Control

The next step is to create the graphical image of the bomb. Although you could use a static image (as long as it has a transparent background), it's always better to deal with more flexible Silverlight shapes. By using shapes, you gain the ability to resize the bomb without introducing distortion, and you can animate or alter individual parts of the drawing. The bomb shown in this example is drawn straight from Microsoft Word's online clipart collection. The bomb was converted to XAML by inserting it into a Word document and then saving that document as an XPS file, a process described in Chapter 7. The full XAML, which uses a combination of Path elements, isn't shown here. However, you can see it by downloading the BombDropper game along with the samples for this chapter.

The XAML for the Bomb class was then simplified slightly (by removing the unnecessary extra Canvas elements around it and the transforms for scaling it). The XAML was then inserted into a new user control named Bomb. This way, the main page can show a bomb simply by creating the Bomb user control and adding it to a layout container (like a Canvas).

Placing the graphic in a separate user control makes it easy to instantiate multiple copies of that graphic in your user interface. It also allows you to encapsulate related functionality, by adding to the user control's code. In the bomb dropping example, only one detail is added to the code—a Boolean property that tracks whether the bomb is currently falling:

```
public partial class Bomb : UserControl
{
    public Bomb()
    {
        InitializeComponent();
    }

    public bool IsFalling
    {
        get;
        set;
    }
}
```

The markup for the bomb includes a RotateTransform, which the animation code can use to give the bomb a realistic "wiggling" effect as it falls. Although this RotateTransform could be created and added programmatically, it makes more sense to define it in the XAML file for the bomb:

```
<UserControl x:Class="BombDrop.Bomb"
    xmlns="http://schemas.microsoft.com/client/2007"
    xmlns:x="http://schemas.microsoft.com/winfx/2006/xaml"
    >
  <UserControl.RenderTransform>
    <TransformGroup>
      <RotateTransform Angle="20" CenterX="50" CenterY="50"></RotateTransform>
      <ScaleTransform ScaleX="0.5" ScaleY="0.5"></ScaleTransform>
    </TransformGroup>
  </UserControl.RenderTransform>

  <Canvas>
    <!-- The Path elements that draw the bomb graphic are defined here. -->
  </Canvas>
</UserControl>
```

With this code in place, you could insert a bomb into your window using a <bomb:Bomb> element, much as the main window inserts the Title user control (as described in the previous section). However, in this case it makes far more sense to create the bombs programmatically.

Dropping the Bombs

To drop the bombs, the application uses a DispatcherTimer, a timer that plays nicely with Silverlight user interface because it triggers events on the user interface thread (saving you the effort of *marshalling* or *locking*, two multithreaded programming techniques that are described in Chapter 16). You choose a time interval, and then the DispatcherTimer fires a periodic Tick event at that interval.

```
private DispatcherTimer bombTimer = new DispatcherTimer();

public Page()
{
    InitializeComponent();
    bombTimer.Tick += bombTimer_Tick;
}
```

In the BombDropper game, the timer initially fires every 1.3 seconds. When the user clicks the button to start the game, the timer is started:

```
// Keep track of how many are dropped and stopped.
private int droppedCount = 0;
private int savedCount = 0;

// Initially, bombs fall every 1.3 seconds, and hit the ground after 3.5 seconds.
private double initialSecondsBetweenBombs = 1.3;
private double initialSecondsToFall = 3.5;
private double secondsBetweenBombs;
private double secondsToFall;

private void cmdStart_Click(object sender, RoutedEventArgs e)
{
    cmdStart.IsEnabled = false;

    // Reset the game.
    droppedCount = 0;
    savedCount = 0;
    secondsBetweenBombs = initialSecondsBetweenBombs;
    secondsToFall = initialSecondsToFall;

    // Start the bomb-dropping timer.
    bombTimer.Interval = TimeSpan.FromSeconds(secondsBetweenBombs);
    bombTimer.Start();
}
```

Every time the timer fires, the code creates a new Bomb object and sets its position on the Canvas. The bomb is placed just above the top edge of the Canvas, so it can fall seamlessly into view. It's given a random horizontal position that falls somewhere between the left and right sides:

```
private void bombTimer_Tick(object sender, EventArgs e)
{
    // Create the bomb.
    Bomb bomb = new Bomb();
    bomb.IsFalling = true;

    // Position the bomb.
    Random random = new Random();
    bomb.SetValue(Canvas.LeftProperty,
      (double)(random.Next(0, (int)(canvasBackground.ActualWidth - 50))));
    bomb.SetValue(Canvas.TopProperty, -100.0);

    // Add the bomb to the Canvas.
    canvasBackground.Children.Add(bomb);
    ...
```

The code then dynamically creates a storyboard to animate the bomb. Two animations
are used—one that drops the bomb by changing the attached Canvas.Top property, and one
that wiggles the bomb by changing the angle of its RotateTransform. Because Storyboard.Tar-
getElement and Storyboard.TargetProperty are attached properties, they must be set using the
Storyboard.SetTargetElement() and Storyboard.SetTargetProperty() methods.

```
    ...
    // Attach mouse click event (for defusing the bomb).
    bomb.MouseLeftButtonDown += bomb_MouseLeftButtonDown;

    // Create the animation for the falling bomb.
    Storyboard storyboard = new Storyboard();
    DoubleAnimation fallAnimation = new DoubleAnimation();
    fallAnimation.To = canvasBackground.ActualHeight;
    fallAnimation.Duration = TimeSpan.FromSeconds(secondsToFall);

    Storyboard.SetTarget(fallAnimation, bomb);
    Storyboard.SetTargetProperty(fallAnimation, new PropertyPath("(Canvas.Top)"));
    storyboard.Children.Add(fallAnimation);

    // Create the animation for the bomb "wiggle."
    DoubleAnimation wiggleAnimation = new DoubleAnimation();
    wiggleAnimation.To = 30;
    wiggleAnimation.Duration = TimeSpan.FromSeconds(0.2);
    wiggleAnimation.RepeatBehavior = RepeatBehavior.Forever;
    wiggleAnimation.AutoReverse = true;

    Storyboard.SetTarget(wiggleAnimation,
      ((TransformGroup)bomb.RenderTransform).Children[0]);
    Storyboard.SetTargetProperty(wiggleAnimation, new PropertyPath("Angle"));
    storyboard.Children.Add(wiggleAnimation);
    ...
```

The newly created bomb and storyboard are stored in two Dictionary collections so they can be retrieved easily in other event handlers. The collections are stored as fields in the main page class, and are defined like this:

```
// Make it possible to look up a bomb based on a storyboard, and vice versa.
private Dictionary<Bomb, Storyboard> storyboards =
  new Dictionary<Bomb, Storyboard>();
private Dictionary<Storyboard, Bomb> bombs = new Dictionary<Storyboard, Bomb>();
```

Here's the code that adds the bomb and storyboard to these two collections:

```
...
bombs.Add(storyboard, bomb);
storyboards.Add(bomb, storyboard);
...
```

Next, an event handler is attached that will react when the storyboard finishes the fall-Animation, which occurs when the bomb hits the ground. Finally, the storyboard is started and the animations are put in motion:

```
...
storyboard.Duration = fallAnimation.Duration;
storyboard.Completed += storyboard_Completed;
storyboard.Begin();
...
```

There's one last detail for the bomb-dropping code. As the game progresses, the game becomes more difficult. The timer begins to fire more frequently, the bombs begin to appear more closely together, and the fall time is reduced. To implement these changes, the timer code makes periodic adjustments whenever a set interval of time has passed. By default, the BombDropper makes an adjustment every 15 seconds. Here are the fields that control the adjustments:

```
// Perform an adjustment every 15 seconds.
private double secondsBetweenAdjustments = 15;
private DateTime lastAdjustmentTime = DateTime.MinValue;

// After every adjustment, shave 0.1 seconds off both.
private double secondsBetweenBombsReduction = 0.1;
private double secondsToFallReduction = 0.1;
```

And here's the code at the end of the DispatcherTimer.Tick event handler, which checks whether an adjustment is needed and makes the appropriate changes:

```
...
// Perform an "adjustment" when needed.
if ((DateTime.Now.Subtract(lastAdjustmentTime).TotalSeconds >
  secondsBetweenAdjustments))
{
    lastAdjustmentTime = DateTime.Now;
```

```
        secondsBetweenBombs -= secondsBetweenBombsReduction;
        secondsToFall -= secondsToFallReduction;

        // (Technically, you should check for 0 or negative values.
        // However, in practice these won't occur because the game will
        // always end first.)

        // Set the timer to drop the next bomb at the appropriate time.
        bombTimer.Interval = TimeSpan.FromSeconds(secondsBetweenBombs);

        // Update the status message.
        lblRate.Text = String.Format("A bomb is released every {0} seconds.",
          secondsBetweenBombs);
        lblSpeed.Text = String.Format("Each bomb takes {0} seconds to fall.",
          secondsToFall);
    }
}
```

With this code in place, there's enough functionality to drop bombs at an ever-increasing rate. However, the game still lacks the code that responds to dropped and saved bombs.

Intercepting a Bomb

The user saves a bomb by clicking it before it reaches the bottom of the Canvas and explodes. Because each bomb is a separate instance of the Bomb user control, intercepting mouse clicks is easy—all you need to do is handle the MouseLeftButtonDown event, which fires when any part of the bomb is clicked (but doesn't fire if you click somewhere in the background, such as around the edges of the bomb circle).

When a bomb is clicked, the first step is to get appropriate bomb object and set its IsFalling property to indicate that it's no longer falling. (The IsFalling property is used by the event handler that deals with completed animations.)

```
private void bomb_MouseLeftButtonDown(object sender, MouseButtonEventArgs e)
{
    // Get the bomb.
    Bomb bomb = (Bomb)sender;
    bomb.IsFalling = false;

    // Record the bomb's current (animated) position.
    double currentTop = Canvas.GetTop(bomb);
    ...
```

The next step is to find the storyboard that controls the animation for this bomb so it can be stopped. To find the storyboard, you simply need to look it up in the Dictionary collections this game uses for tracking. Currently, Silverlight doesn't include any standardized way to find the animations that are acting on a given element.

```
...
// Stop the bomb from falling.
Storyboard storyboard = storyboards[bomb];
storyboard.Stop();
...
```

After a button is clicked, another set of animations moves it off the screen, throwing it up and left or right (depending on which side is closest). Although you could create an entirely new storyboard to implement this effect, the BombDropper game simply clears the current storyboard that's being used for the bomb and adds new animations to it. When this process is completed, the new storyboard is started.

```
...
// Reuse the existing storyboard, but with new animations.
// Send the bomb on a new trajectory by animating Canvas.Top
// and Canvas.Left.
storyboard.Children.Clear();

DoubleAnimation riseAnimation = new DoubleAnimation();
riseAnimation.From = currentTop;
riseAnimation.To = 0;
riseAnimation.Duration = TimeSpan.FromSeconds(2);

Storyboard.SetTarget(riseAnimation, bomb);
Storyboard.SetTargetProperty(riseAnimation, new PropertyPath("(Canvas.Top)"));
storyboard.Children.Add(riseAnimation);

DoubleAnimation slideAnimation = new DoubleAnimation();
double currentLeft = Canvas.GetLeft(bomb);

// Throw the bomb off the closest side.
if (currentLeft < canvasBackground.ActualWidth / 2)
{
    slideAnimation.To = -100;
}
else
{
    slideAnimation.To = canvasBackground.ActualWidth + 100;
}
slideAnimation.Duration = TimeSpan.FromSeconds(1);
Storyboard.SetTarget(slideAnimation, bomb);
Storyboard.SetTargetProperty(slideAnimation, new PropertyPath("(Canvas.Left)"));
storyboard.Children.Add(slideAnimation);

// Start the new animation.
storyboard.Duration = slideAnimation.Duration;
storyboard.Begin();
}
```

Now the game has enough code to drop bombs and bounce them off the screen when the user saves them. However, to keep track of what bombs are saved and which ones are dropped, you need to react to the Storyboard.Completed event that fires at the end of an animation.

Counting Bombs and Cleaning Up

As you've seen, the BombDropper uses storyboards in two ways: to animate a falling bomb and to animate a defused bomb. You could handle the completion of these storyboards with different event handlers, but to keep things simple the BombDropper uses just one. It tells the difference between an exploded and a rescued bomb by examining the Bomb.IsFalling property.

```csharp
// End the game when 5 bombs have fallen.
private int maxDropped = 5;

private void storyboard_Completed(object sender, EventArgs e)
{
    Storyboard completedStoryboard = (Storyboard)sender;
    Bomb completedBomb = bombs[completedStoryboard];

    // Determine if a bomb fell or flew off the Canvas after being clicked.
    if (completedBomb.IsFalling)
    {
        droppedCount++;
    }
    else
    {
        savedCount++;
    }
    ...
```

Either way, the code then updates the display test to indicate how many bombs have been dropped and saved. It then performs some clean up, removing the bomb from the Canvas, and removing both the bomb and the storyboard from the Dictionary collections that are used for tracking.

```csharp
    ...
    // Update the display.
    lblStatus.Text = String.Format("You have dropped {0} bombs and saved {1}.",
      droppedCount, savedCount);

    // Clean up.
    completedStoryboard.Stop();
    canvasBackground.Children.Remove(completedBomb);
```

```
// Update the tracking collections.
storyboards.Remove(completedBomb);
bombs.Remove(completedStoryboard);
...
```

At this point, the code checks to see if the maximum number of dropped bombs has been reached. If it has, the game ends, the timer is stopped, and all the bombs and storyboards are removed.

```
...
// Check if it's game over.
if (droppedCount >= maxDropped)
{
    bombTimer.Stop();
    lblStatus.Text += "\r\n\r\nGame over.";

    // Find all the storyboards that are underway.
    foreach (KeyValuePair<Bomb, Storyboard> item in storyboards)
    {
        Storyboard storyboard = item.Value;
        Bomb bomb = item.Key;

        storyboard.Stop();
        canvasBackground.Children.Remove(bomb);
    }

    // Empty the tracking collections.
    storyboards.Clear();
    bombs.Clear();

    // Allow the user to start a new game.
    cmdStart.IsEnabled = true;
}
}
```

This completes the code for BombDropper game. However, there are plenty of refinements you can make. Some examples include the following:

- **Animate a bomb explosion effect.** This effect could make the flames around the bomb twinkle or send small pieces of shrapnel flying across the Canvas.

- **Animate the background.** This change is easy, and it adds pizzazz. For example, you could create a linear gradient that shifts up, creating an impression of movement, or one that transitions between two colors.

- **Add depth.** It's easier than you think. The basic technique is to give the bombs different sizes. Bombs that are bigger should have a higher ZIndex, ensuring they overlap smaller bombs, and should be given a shorter animation time, ensuring they fall faster. You could also make the bombs partially transparent, so as one falls the others behind them are visible.

- **Add sound effects.** In Chapter 10, you'll learn to use sound and other media in Silverlight. You can use well-timed sound effects to punctuate bomb explosions or rescued bombs.

- **Fine-tune the parameters.** Provide more dials to tweak behavior (for example, variables that set how the bomb times, trajectories, and frequencies are altered as the game processes). You can also inject more randomness (for example, allow saved bombs to bounce off the Canvas in slightly different ways).

You can find countless examples of Silverlight game programming on the Web. Microsoft's Silverlight community site includes game samples with full source code at http:// silverlight.net/themes/silverlight/community/gallerydetail.aspx?cat=6. You can also check out Andy Beaulieu's website, which provides Silverlight games and an impressive physics simulator, at http://www.andybeaulieu.com.

Encapsulating Animations

When you create animations dynamically in code, there's a fair bit of boilerplate code required to create the animations, set the storyboard properties, and handle the Completed event to clean up. For this reason, Silverlight developers often wrap animations in higher-level classes that take care of the low-level details.

For example, you might create an animation class named FadeElementEffect. You can then fade an element out of view using code like this:

```
FadeElementEffect fade = new FadeElementEffect();
fade.Animate(canvas);
```

Creating classes like this is fairly straightforward, although the exact design depends on the needs of your application. In the rest of this section, you'll consider one possible way to create animation helper classes that provide transitional animations when the user navigates between pages.

Page Transitions

In Chapter 6, you saw how to support page navigation in a Silverlight application. The basic technique is to use some sort of layout container as your application's root element. You can then add user controls to this container and remove them when needed. Navigating from one page to another consists of removing the user control for the current page and adding the user control for the next page.

With this framework in place, it takes just a bit more work to use an animation that switches between the two pages. For example, you can create an animation that fades in or slides in the new page. To make this work, you add both pages to the root visual at once, one over the other. (The easiest way to do this is to place both user controls in the same cell of a Grid, but a Canvas works equally well.) Then, you animate the properties of the topmost page. For example, you can change the Opacity to fade it in, alter the properties of a TranslateTransform to move it, and so on. You can even apply multiple effects at once—for example, to create a "blow up" effect that expands a page from the corner to fill the entire display area.

In the rest of this chapter, you'll learn how to use a simple "wipe" effect that unveils the new page overtop of the current one. Figure 9-7 shows the wipe in action.

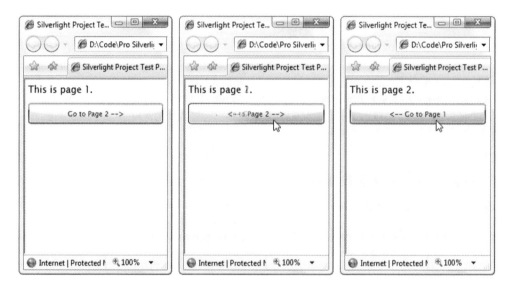

Figure 9-7. *Transitioning between pages with a wipe*

This example assumes the root element in your application is a Grid. In other words, your Application class requires code like this:

```
// This Grid will host your pages.
private Grid rootVisual = new Grid();

private void Application_Startup(object sender, StartupEventArgs e)
{
    // Load the first page.
    this.RootVisual = rootVisual;
    rootVisual.Children.Add(new Page());
}
```

This technique is discussed in Chapter 6.

The Base Class

The most straightforward way to animate a transition between pages is to code it directly in the App class, using a custom Navigate() method. However, it's far more flexible (and just a bit more effort) to place the animation code in a separate class. And if you standardize your animations with an abstract class or an interface, you'll gain far more flexibility to swap in the new effects.

In this example, all transitions inherit from an abstract class named PageTransitionBase. This class stores the storyboard, the previous page, and the new page as fields.

```csharp
public abstract class PageTransitionBase
{
    protected Storyboard storyboard = new Storyboard();
    protected UserControl oldPage;
    protected UserControl newPage;

    public PageTransitionBase()
    {
        storyboard.Completed += TransitionCompleted;
    }
    ...
```

The application calls the PageTransitionBase.Navigate() method to move from one page to another. The Navigate() method adds both pages to the Grid, calls a PrepareStoryboard() method to set up the animation, and then starts the storyboard:

```csharp
    ...
    public void Navigate(UserControl newPage)
    {
        // Set the pages.
        this.newPage = newPage;
        Grid grid = (Grid)Application.Current.RootVisual;
        oldPage = (UserControl)grid.Children[0];

        // Insert the new page first (so it lies "behind" the old page).
        grid.Children.Insert(0, newPage);

        // Prepared the animation.
        PrepareStoryboard();

        // Perform the animation.
        storyboard.Begin();
    }
    ...
```

The PrepareStoryboard() method is abstract. It must be overridden in derived classes, which will create the specific animation objects they want.

```
...
protected abstract void PrepareStoryboard();
...
```

The TransitionCompleted() event handler responds when the animation is complete. It removes the old page.

```
...
private void TransitionCompleted(object sender, EventArgs e)
{
    // Remove the old page, which is not needed any longer.
    Grid grid = (Grid)Application.Current.RootVisual;
    grid.Children.Remove(oldPage);
}
}
```

You can also use this method to perform clean up. However, in this example the animation acts on the old page, which is discarded after the navigation. No extra cleanup is needed.

The Wipe Transition

To actually use a page transition, you need at least one derived class that creates animations. In this section, you'll consider one example—a WipeTransition class that wipes away the old page, revealing the new one underneath.

The trick to creating a wipe effect is animating a brush that uses an opacity mask. (As you learned in Chapter 8, an opacity mask determines what portions of an image or element should be visible, and which ones should be transparent.) To use an animation as a page transition, you need to use a LinearGradientBrush for the opacity mask. As the animation progresses, you move the offsets in the opacity mask, gradually making more of the topmost element transparent and revealing more of the content underneath. In a page transition, the topmost element is the old page, and underneath is the new page. Wipes commonly work from left to right or top to bottom, but more creative effects are possible by using different opacity masks.

To perform its work, the WipeTransition class overrides the PrepareStoryboard() method. Its first task is to create the opacity mask and add it to the old page (which is topmost in the grid). This opacity mask uses a gradient that defines two gradient stops, Black (where the image will be completely visible) and Transparent (where the image will be completely transparent). Initially, both stops are positioned at the left edge of the image. Because the visible stop is declared last, it takes precedence, and the image will be completely opaque.

```
public class WipeTransition : PageTransitionBase
{
    protected override void PrepareStoryboard()
    {
        // Create the opacity mask.
        LinearGradientBrush mask = new LinearGradientBrush();
```

```
mask.StartPoint = new Point(0,0);
mask.EndPoint = new Point(1,0);

GradientStop transparentStop = new GradientStop();
transparentStop.Color = Colors.Transparent;
transparentStop.Offset = 0;
mask.GradientStops.Add(transparentStop);
GradientStop visibleStop = new GradientStop();
visibleStop.Color = Colors.Black;
visibleStop.Offset = 0;
mask.GradientStops.Add(visibleStop);

oldPage.OpacityMask = mask;
...
```

Next, you need to perform your animation on the offsets of the LinearGradientBrush. In this example, both offsets are moved from the left side to the right side, allowing the image underneath to appear. To make this example a bit fancier, the offsets don't occupy the same position while they move. Instead, the visible offset leads the way, followed by the transparent offset after a short delay of 0.2 seconds. This creates a blended fringe at the edge of the wipe while the animation is underway.

```
...
// Create the animations for the opacity mask.
DoubleAnimation visibleStopAnimation = new DoubleAnimation();
Storyboard.SetTarget(visibleStopAnimation, visibleStop);
Storyboard.SetTargetProperty(visibleStopAnimation,
  new PropertyPath("Offset"));
visibleStopAnimation.Duration = TimeSpan.FromSeconds(1.2);
visibleStopAnimation.From = 0;
visibleStopAnimation.To = 1.2;

DoubleAnimation transparentStopAnimation = new DoubleAnimation();
Storyboard.SetTarget(transparentStopAnimation, transparentStop);
Storyboard.SetTargetProperty(transparentStopAnimation,
  new PropertyPath("Offset"));
transparentStopAnimation.BeginTime = TimeSpan.FromSeconds(0.2);
transparentStopAnimation.From = 0;
transparentStopAnimation.To = 1;
transparentStopAnimation.Duration = TimeSpan.FromSeconds(1);
...
```

There's one odd detail here. The visible stop moves to 1.2 rather than simply 1, which denotes the right edge of the image. This ensures that both offsets move at the same speed, because the total distance each one must cover is proportional to the duration of its animation.

The final step is to add the animations to the storyboard. There's no need to start the storyboard, because the base PageTransitionBase class performs this step as soon as the PrepareStoryboard() method returns.

```
...
// Add the animations to the storyboard.
storyboard.Children.Add(transparentStopAnimation);
storyboard.Children.Add(visibleStopAnimation);
   }
}
```

Now you can use code like this to navigate between pages:

```
WipeTransition transition = new WipeTransition();
transition.Navigate(new Page2());
```

As with the BombDropper, there are plenty of imaginative ways to extend this example:

- **Add transition properties.** You could enhance the WipeTransition class with more possibilities, allowing a configurable wipe direction, a configurable wipe time, and so on.

- **Create more transitions.** Creating a new animated page transition is as simple as deriving a class from PageTransitionBase and overriding PrepareStoryboard().

- **Refactor the PageTransitionBase code.** The current example is designed to be as simple as possible. However, a more elaborate design would pull out the code that adds and removes pages, and place that in the custom application class. This opens up new possibilities. It allows you to use different layouts. (For example, you can use a transition animation in one panel rather than for the entire window.) It also allows the application class to add application services. (For example, you can keep pages alive in a cache once you navigate away from them, as described in Chapter 6. This allows you to retain the current state of all your elements.)

For an excellent example that picks up on some of these themes and demonstrates several additional transitions, see http://www.flawlesscode.com/post/2008/03/ Silverlight-2-Navigating-Between-Xaml-Pages.aspx.

Frame-Based Animation

Along with the property-based animation system, Silverlight provides a way to create frame-based animation using nothing but code. All you need to do is respond to the static CompositionTarget.Rendering event, which is fired to get the content for each frame. This is a far lower-level approach, which you won't want to tackle unless you're sure the standard property-based animation model won't work for your scenario (for example, if you're building a simple side-scrolling game, creating physics-based animations, or modeling particle effects such as fire, snow, and bubbles).

The basic technique for building a frame-based animation is easy. You simply need to attach an event handler to the static CompositionTarget.Rendering event. Once you do, Silverlight will begin calling this event handler continuously. (As long as your rendering code executes quickly enough, Silverlight will call it 60 times each second.) In the rendering event handler, it's up to you to create or adjust the elements in the window accordingly. In other words, you need to manage all the work yourself. When the animation has ended, detach the event handler.

Figure 9-9 shows a straightforward example. Here, a random number of circles fall from the top of a Canvas to the bottom. They fall at different speeds (based on a random starting velocity), but they accelerate downward at the same rate. The animation ends when all the circles reach the bottom.

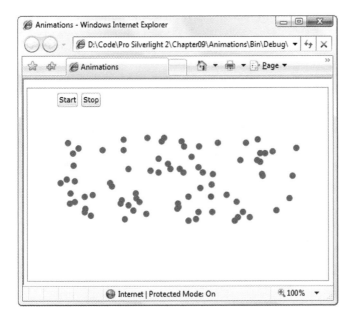

Figure 9-8. *A frame-based animation of falling circles*

In this example, each falling circle is represented by an Ellipse element. A custom class named EllipseInfo keeps a reference to the ellipse and tracks the details that are important for the physics model. In this case, there's only one piece of information—the velocity at which the ellipse is moving along the X axis. (You could easily extend this class to include a velocity along the Y axis, additional acceleration information, and so on.)

```
public class EllipseInfo
{
    public Ellipse Ellipse
    {
        get; set;
    }

    public double VelocityY
    {
        get; set;
    }
}
```

```
    public EllipseInfo(Ellipse ellipse, double velocityY)
    {
        VelocityY = velocityY;
        Ellipse = ellipse;
    }
}
```

The application keeps track of the EllipseInfo object for each ellipse using a collection. There are several more window-level fields, which record various details that are used when calculating the fall of the ellipse. You could easily make these details configurable.

```
private List<EllipseInfo> ellipses = new List<EllipseInfo>();

private double accelerationY = 0.1;
private int minStartingSpeed = 1;
private int maxStartingSpeed = 50;
private double speedRatio = 0.1;
private int minEllipses = 20;
private int maxEllipses = 100;
private int ellipseRadius = 10;
private SolidColorBrush ellipseBrush = new SolidColorBrush(Colors.Green);
```

When a button is clicked, the collection is cleared, and the event handler is attached to the CompositionTarget.Rendering event:

```
private bool rendering = false;

private void cmdStart_Clicked(object sender, RoutedEventArgs e)
{
    if (!rendering)
    {
        ellipses.Clear();
        canvas.Children.Clear();

        CompositionTarget.Rendering += RenderFrame;
        rendering = true;
    }
}
```

If the ellipses don't exist, the rendering code creates them automatically. It creates a random number of ellipses (currently, between 20 and 100) and gives each of them the same size and color. The ellipses are placed at the top of the Canvas, but they're offset randomly along the X axis.

```
private void RenderFrame(object sender, EventArgs e)
{
    if (ellipses.Count == 0)
    {
```

```
    // Animation just started. Create the ellipses.
    int halfCanvasWidth = (int)canvas.ActualWidth / 2;

    Random rand = new Random();
    int ellipseCount = rand.Next(minEllipses, maxEllipses+1);
    for (int i = 0; i < ellipseCount; i++)
    {
        // Create the ellipse.
        Ellipse ellipse = new Ellipse();
        ellipse.Fill = ellipseBrush;
        ellipse.Width = ellipseRadius;
        ellipse.Height = ellipseRadius;

        // Place the ellipse.
        Canvas.SetLeft(ellipse, halfCanvasWidth +
            rand.Next(-halfCanvasWidth, halfCanvasWidth));
        Canvas.SetTop(ellipse, 0);
        canvas.Children.Add(ellipse);

        // Track the ellipse.
        EllipseInfo info = new EllipseInfo(ellipse,
            speedRatio * rand.Next(minStartingSpeed, maxStartingSpeed));
        ellipses.Add(info);
    }
}
...
```

If the ellipses already exist, the code tackles the more interesting job of animating them. Each ellipse is moved slightly using the Canvas.SetTop() method. The amount of movement depends on the assigned velocity.

```
...
else
{
    for (int i = ellipses.Count-1; i >= 0; i--)
    {
        EllipseInfo info = ellipses[i];
        double top = Canvas.GetTop(info.Ellipse);
        Canvas.SetTop(info.Ellipse, top + 1 * info.VelocityY);
        ...
```

To improve performance, the ellipses are removed from the tracking collection as soon as they've reached the bottom of the Canvas. That way, you don't need to process them again. To allow this to work without causing you to lose your place while stepping through the collection, you need to iterate backward, from the end of the collection to the beginning.

If the ellipse hasn't yet reached the bottom of the Canvas, the code increases the velocity. (Alternatively, you could set the velocity based on how close the ellipse is to the bottom of the Canvas for a magnet-like effect.)

```
...
if (top >= (canvas.ActualHeight - ellipseRadius*2))
{
    // This circle has reached the bottom.
    // Stop animating it.
    ellipses.Remove(info);
}
else
{
    // Increase the velocity.
    info.VelocityY += accelerationY;
}
...
```

Finally, if all the ellipses have been removed from the collection, the event handler is removed, allowing the animation to end:

```
...
if (ellipses.Count == 0)
{
    // End the animation.
    // There's no reason to keep calling this method
    // if it has no work to do.
    CompositionTarget.Rendering -= RenderFrame;
    rendering = false;
}
        }
    }
}
```

Obviously, you could extend this animation to make the circles bounce, scatter, and so on. The technique is the same—you simply need to use more complex formulas to arrive at the velocity.

There's one caveat to consider when building frame-based animations: they aren't time-dependent. In other words, your animation may run faster on fast computers, because the frame rate will increase and your CompositionTarget.Rendering event will be called more frequently. To compensate for this effect, you need to write code that takes the current time into account.

The Last Word

In this chapter, you explored Silverlight's animation support in detail. Now that you've mastered the basics, you can spend more time with the art of animation—deciding what properties to animate and how to modify them to get the effect you want.

The animation model in Silverlight is surprisingly full-featured. However, getting the result you want isn't always easy. If you want to animate separate portions of your interface as part of a single animated "scene," you're forced to take care of a few tedious details, such as tracking animated objects and performing cleanup. Furthermore, none of the stock animation classes accept arguments in their parameters. As a result, the code required to programmatically build a new animation is often simple, but long. The future of Silverlight animation promises higher-level classes that are built on the basic plumbing you've learned about in this chapter. Ideally, you'll be able to plug animations into your application simply by using pre-built animation classes, wrapping your elements in specialized containers, and setting a few attached properties. The actual implementation that generates the effect you want—whether it's a smooth dissolve between two images or a series of animated fly-ins that builds a page—will be provided for you.

CHAPTER 10

■■■

Sound, Video, and Deep Zoom

In this chapter, you'll tackle one of Silverlight's most mature features: audio and video support.

Since version 1.0, Silverlight has distinguished itself as a technology that brings high-end multimedia support to the limited world of the browser. And though Silverlight can't support the full range of media codecs (as that would multiply the size of the Silverlight download and increase its licensing costs), Silverlight still gives you everything you need to incorporate high-quality audio and video in your applications. Even more remarkable is the way that Silverlight allows you to *use* multimedia, and particularly video. For example, you can use video to fill thousands of elements at once and combine it with other effects, such as animation, transforms, and transparency.

In this chapter, you'll learn how to incorporate ordinary audio and video into your applications, and you'll consider the best way to encode and host video files for Silverlight. Next, you'll see how Silverlight's VideoBrush allows you to create impressive effects like video-filled text and video reflections. Finally, you'll look at Deep Zoom—a different interactive multimedia technology that lets users zoom into massive images in real time.

Supported File Types

Because Silverlight needs to ensure compatibility on a number of different operating systems and browsers, it can't support the full range of media files that you'll find in a desktop application like Windows Media Player. Before you get started with Silverlight audio and video, you need to know exactly what media types it supports.

For audio, Silverlight supports the following:

- Windows Media Audio (WMA), versions 7, 8, and 9

- MP3, with fixed or variable bit rates from 8 to 320 kbps

Note Unlike WPF, Silverlight doesn't support simple WAV audio. Also, it can't play MIDI music files.

When it comes to video, Silverlight supports the follow standards:

- Windows Media Video 7 (WMV1)

- Windows Media Video 8 (WMV2)

- Windows Media Video 9 (WMV3)

- Windows Media Video Advanced Profile, non-VC-1 (WMVA)

- Windows Media Video Advanced Profile, VC-1 (WMVC1)

Often, you can recognize Windows Media Video by the file extension .wmv. Other video formats—for example, MPEG and QuickTime—need not apply.

Out of this list, the last option—WMVC1—is the one you'll use most often. It adheres to a video codec known as VC-1, which is a widely supported industry standard. (Notable examples where VC-1 is used include Blu-ray, HD DVD, and the Xbox 360. Of course, the VC-1 standard supports different bit rates and resolutions, so your Silverlight application isn't forced to include DVD-quality video just because it uses VC-1.)

Silverlight doesn't support other Windows Media formats (such as Windows Media Screen, Windows Media Audio Professional, and Windows Media Voice), nor does it support the combination of Windows Media Video with MP3 audio. Finally, it doesn't support video files that use frames with odd-number dimensions (dimensions that aren't divisible by 2), such as 127×135.

■Note Adding audio to a Silverlight application is fairly easy, because you can throw in just about any MP3 file. Using a video file is more work. Not only must you make sure you're using one of the supported WMV formats, but you also need to carefully consider the quality you need and the bandwidth your visitors can support. Later in this chapter, you'll consider how to encode video for a Silverlight application. But first, you'll consider how to add basic audio.

The MediaElement

In Silverlight, all the audio and video functionality is built into a single class: the MediaElement.

Like all elements, the MediaElement is placed directly in your user interface. If you're using the MediaElement to play audio, this fact isn't important, because the MediaElement remains invisible. If you're using the MediaElement for video, you place it where the video window should appear.

A simple MediaElement tag is all you need to play a sound. For example, add this markup to your user interface:

```
<MediaElement Source="test.mp3"></MediaElement>
```

Now, once the page is loaded, it will download the test.mp3 file and begin playing it automatically.

Of course, in order for this to work, your Silverlight application needs to be able to find the test.mp3 file. The MediaElement class uses the same URL system as the Image class. That means you can embed a media file in your XAP package or deploy it to the same website, alongside the XAP file. Generally, it's best to keep media files separate, unless they are extremely small. Otherwise, you will bloat the size of your application and lengthen the initial download time.

■**Note** When you first add a media file like test.mp3 to a project, Visual Studio sets its Build Action to None and its Copy To Output Directory setting to "Do not copy." To deploy your media file alongside your XAP file, you must change the Copy To Output Directory setting to "Copy always." To deploy your media file inside the XAP package, change Build Action to Resource. The downloadable code for this chapter uses the first of these two approaches.

Controlling Playback

The previous example starts playing an audio file immediately when the page with the Media-Element is loaded. Playback continues until the audio file is complete.

Although this example is straightforward, it's also a bit limiting. Usually, you'll want the ability to control playback more precisely. For example, you might want it to be triggered at a specific time, repeated indefinitely, and so on. One way to achieve this result is to use the methods of the MediaElement class at the appropriate time.

The startup behavior of the MediaElement is determined by its AutoPlay property. If set to false, the audio file will be loaded, but your code takes responsibility for starting the playback at the right time.

```
<MediaElement x:Name="media" Source="test.mp3" AutoPlay="False"></MediaElement>
```

When using this approach, you must make sure to give the MediaElement a name so that you can interact with it in code. Generally, interaction consists of calling the straightforward Play(), Pause(), and Stop() methods. You can also use the SetSource() method to load new media content from a stream (which is useful if you're downloading media files asynchronously using the WebClient, as described in Chapter 6), and you can change the Position property to move through the audio.

Here's a simple event handler that seeks to the beginning of the current audio file and then starts playback:

```
private void cmdPlay_Click(object sender, RoutedEventArgs e)
{
    media.Position = TimeSpan.Zero;
    media.Play();
}
```

If this code runs while playback is already underway, the first line will reset the position to the beginning, and playback will continue from that point. The second line will have no effect, because the media file is already being played.

Note Depending on the types of media files you support, you may want to check the CanPause and CanSeek properties before you attempt to pause playback or jump to a new position. Some types of streamed media files do not support pausing and seeking.

Handling Errors

The MediaElement doesn't throw an exception if it can't find or load a file. Instead, it's up to you to handle the MediaFailed event. Fortunately, this task is easy. First, tweak your Media-Element tag as shown here:

```
<MediaElement ... MediaFailed="media_MediaFailed"></MediaElement>
```

Then, in the event handler, you can use the ExceptionRoutedEventArgs.ErrorException property to get an exception object that describes the problem. Here's an example that simply displays the appropriate error message:

```
private void media_MediaFailed(object sender, ExceptionRoutedEventArgs e)
{
    lblErrorText.Content = e.ErrorException.Message;
}
```

Playing Multiple Sounds

The MediaElement is limited to playing a single media file. If you change the Source property (or call the SetSource() method), any playback that's currently taking place stops immediately. However, this limitation doesn't apply to Silverlight as a whole. In fact, Silverlight can quite easily play multiple media files at once, as long as each one has its own MediaElement.

There are two approaches you can use to creating an application with multiple sounds. First, you can create all the MediaElement objects you need at design time. This approach is useful if you plan to reuse the same two or three MediaElement objects.

For example, you might define two MediaElement objects and flip between them each time you play a new sound. (You can keep track of which object you used last using a Boolean variable in your page class.) To make this technique really effortless, you can store the audio file names in the Tag property of the appropriate element, so all your event handling code needs to do is read the file name from the Tag property, find the right MediaElement to use, set its Source property, and then call its Play() method. Because this example uses two Media-Element objects, you'll be limited to just two simultaneous sounds, which is a reasonable compromise if you don't think the user will be able pick out a third sound out over the din anyway.

Your other option is to create every MediaElement object you need dynamically. This approach requires more overhead, but the difference is minimal (unless you go overboard and play dozens of simultaneous media files). When creating a MediaElement in code, you need to remember to add it to a container in your application. Assuming you haven't changed the AutoPlay property, it will begin playing as soon as you add it. If you set AutoPlay to false, you'll need to use the Play() method. Finally, it's also a good idea to handle the MediaEnded event to remove the MediaElement once playback is finished.

Here's some code for a button that starts a new playback of the same sound file each time it's pressed:

```
private void cmdPlay_Click(object sender, RoutedEventArgs e)
{
    MediaElement media = new MediaElement();
    media.Source = new Uri("test.mp3", UriKind.Relative);
    media.MediaEnded += new RoutedEventHandler(media_MediaEnded);
    LayoutRoot.Children.Add(media);
}

private void media_MediaEnded(object sender, RoutedEventArgs e)
{
    LayoutRoot.Children.Remove((MediaElement)sender);
}
```

To make it easier to keep track of a batch of dynamically generated MediaElement objects, you can add them all to a designated container (for example, an invisible StackPanel). This allows you to quickly examine all the currently playing media files, and stop them all. Figure 10-1 shows an example that uses this approach, and displays the element count of the invisible StackPanel every time a MediaElement is inserted or removed.

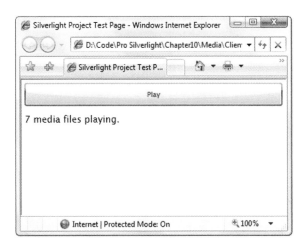

Figure 10-1. *Playing media files simultaneously*

Changing Volume, Balance, and Position

The MediaElement exposes a number of properties that allow you to control your playback. The most fundamental are:

- **Volume.** Sets the volume as a number from 0 (completely muted) to 1 (full volume). The default value is 0.5. To temporarily mute playback without pausing it or changing the volume setting, set IsMuted to true.

- **Balance.** Sets the balance between the left and right speaker as a number from –1 (left speaker only) to 1 (right speaker only).

- **CurrentState.** Indicates whether the player is currently playing, paused, stopped, downloading a media file (Opening), buffering it (Buffering), or acquiring a license for DRM content (AcquiringLicense). If no media file was supplied, the CurrentState will be Closed.

- **Position.** Provides a TimeSpan indicating the current location in the media file. You can set this property to skip to a specific time position.

Figure 10-2 shows a simple page that allows the user to control playback.

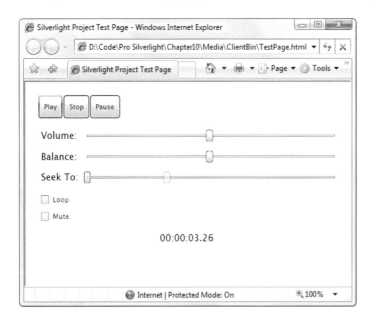

Figure 10-2. *Controlling more playback details*

At the top of the window are three buttons for controlling playback. They use rather unremarkable code—they simply call the Start(), Stop(), and Play() methods of the MediaElement when clicked.

Underneath are two sliders for adjusting volume and balance. These sliders are set to the appropriate ranges (0 to 1 and -1 to 1):

```
<Slider Grid.Column="1" x:Name="sliderVolume" Minimum="0" Maximum="1" Value="0.5"
  ValueChanged="sliderVolume_ValueChanged" ></Slider>

<Slider Grid.Row="1" Grid.Column="1" x:Name="sliderBalance" Minimum="-1" Maximum="1"
  ValueChanged="sliderBalance_ValueChanged"></Slider>
```

When the user drags the thumb in the slider, the change is applied to the MediaElement:

```
private void sliderVolume_ValueChanged(object sender,
  RoutedPropertyChangedEventArgs<double> e)
{
    media.Volume = sliderVolume.Value;
}

private void sliderBalance_ValueChanged(object sender,
  RoutedPropertyChangedEventArgs<double> e)
{
    media.Balance = sliderBalance.Value;
}
```

The third slider allows the user to jump to a new position. The code sets up the position slider by reading the full running time from the NaturalDuration property once the media file has been opened:

```
private void media_MediaOpened(object sender, RoutedEventArgs e)
{
    sliderPosition.Maximum = media.NaturalDuration.TimeSpan.TotalSeconds;
}
```

You can then jump to a specific position when the slider tab is moved:

```
private void sliderPosition_ValueChanged(object sender, RoutedEventArgs e)
{
    // Pausing the player before moving it reduces audio "glitches"
    // when the value changes several times in quick succession.
    media.Pause();
    media.Position = TimeSpan.FromSeconds(sliderPosition.Value);
    media.Play();
}
```

The third slider actually consists of two sliders that are superimposed on top of one another. The slider in the background (the one defined first) is the position slider that the user drags to jump to a new part of the audio file:

```
<Slider Minimum="0" Grid.Column="1" Grid.Row="2" x:Name="sliderPosition"
 ValueChanged="sliderPosition_ValueChanged" ></Slider>
```

In front is a slider that ignores mouse activity (because its IsHitTestVisible property is set to false) and is partially transparent (because its Opacity property is set to 0.5). The result is that the slider appears to be a faint image behind the position slider.

```
<Slider Minimum="0" Grid.Column="1" Grid.Row="2" x:Name="sliderPositionBackground"
 IsHitTestVisible="False" Opacity="0.5"></Slider>
```

This slider (sliderPositionBackground) represents the current position of the audio file. As the audio advances, the code moves the thumb in sliderPositionBackground along the track, to give the user a visual indication of how far playback has progressed. You could do much the same trick by moving the sliderPosition slider, but this could become problematic because your code would need to distinguish between user-initiated changes (when the user drags the slider, at which point your code should change the current position of the MediaElement) and playback synchronization (at which point your code should do nothing).

Incidentally, the MediaElement doesn't fire any sort of event to notify you that playback is underway. Thus, if you want to move the thumb for sliderPositionBackground along the track, or you want to update the TextBlock with the current time offset at the bottom of the page, you need to use a timer.

The DispatcherTimer is a perfect solution. You can create one when the page loads, use a short 0.1 second interval, and start and stop it along with your playback.

```
private DispatcherTimer timer = new DispatcherTimer();

public MediaPlayer()
{
    InitializeComponent();
    timer.Interval = TimeSpan.FromSeconds(0.1);
    timer.Tick += timer_Tick;
}
```

When the DispatcherTimer.Tick event fires, you can update your user interface like this:

```
private void timer_Tick(object sender, EventArgs e)
{
    lblStatus.Text = media.Position.ToString().TrimEnd(new char[]{'0'});
    sliderPositionBackground.Value = media.Position.TotalSeconds;
}
```

The two checkboxes on the page are the last ingredient in this media player, and one of the simplest details. The Mute checkbox simply sets the corresponding IsMuted property of the MediaElement:

```
private void chkMute_Click(object sender, RoutedEventArgs e)
{
    media.IsMuted = (bool)chkMute.IsChecked;
}
```

The MediaElement has no built-in support for looping playback. If the Loop checkbox is set, the code in the page simply restarts playback when the MediaEnded event fires:

```
private void media_MediaEnded(object sender, RoutedEventArgs e)
{
    if ((bool)chkLoop.IsChecked)
    {
        media.Position = TimeSpan.Zero;
        media.Play();
    }
    else
    {
```

```
        timer.Stop();
    }
}
```

Although relatively simple, this example could be the springboard for a more advanced player—all you need is a heavy dose of animation, transparency, and eye candy. You'll see some examples of more stylized media players that have mostly the same functionality when you consider Expression Encoder later in this chapter.

Playing Video

Everything you've learned about using the MediaElement class applies equally well when you use a video file instead of an audio file.

The key difference with video files is that the visual and layout-related properties of the MediaElement are suddenly important. The original size of the video is provided through the NaturalVideoHeight and NaturalVideoWidth properties of the MediaElement. You can also scale or stretch a video to fit different page sizes using the Stretch property. Use None to keep the native size (which is recommended for optimum performance), Uniform to stretch it to fit its container without changing its aspect ratio (which is the default), Fill to stretch it to fit its container in both dimensions (even if that means stretching the picture), and UniformToFill to resize the picture to fit the largest dimension of its container while preserving its aspect ratio (which guarantees that part of the video page will be clipped out if the container doesn't have the same aspect ratio as the video).

Tip The MediaElement's preferred size is based on the native video dimensions. For example, if you create a MediaElement with a Stretch value of Uniform (the default) and place it inside a Grid row with a Height value of Auto, the row will be sized just large enough to keep the video at its standard size, so no scaling is required.

Progressive Downloading and Streaming

Ordinarily, if you take no special steps, Silverlight plays media files using *progressive downloading*. This technique means that the client downloads media files one chunk at a time. Once it's accumulated enough of a buffer to provide for a few seconds of playback, it begins playing the media file, while it continues downloading the rest of the file in the background.

The overwhelming advantage of progressive downloading is the fact that the client can begin playing a media file almost immediately. In fact, the total length of the file has no effect on the initial playback delay. The only factor is the *bit rate*—in other words, how many bytes of data it takes to play 5 seconds of media.

Progressive downloading also has a second not-so-trivial advantage: it doesn't require any special server software, because the client handles all the work of buffering. Thus, the client can use progressive downloading with any web server. And if you want to ensure scalability on the web server, you simply need to set a maximum transfer rate using *bit rate throttling*, as described in the sidebar on this page.

BIT RATE THROTTLING

Bit rate throttling is a feature in the IIS web server that allows you to limit what users can download to certain types of content. With video content, bit rate throttling prevents people with good connections from downloading the video file really quickly, which could swamp the server if a large number of people request the file simultaneously. Bit rate throttling also saves bandwidth overall. That's because most web surfers won't watch a video form start to finish. In fact, it's estimated that 80% of users navigate to a new page before finishing a video, effectively throwing away any extra unwatched video data they've downloaded in advance.

Typically, when using bit rate throttling you'll configure IIS to begin by sending a burst of content when a video file is requested. This ensures that the user can start playback as fast as possible. However, after this burst—for example, after the user has downloaded 10 seconds of video—the rest of the video data will be sent much more slowly. Limiting the transfer rate has no real effect on the client's ability to play the media, as long as the client can download the content faster than the application can play it. In other words, a 700KB/s transfer limit would be a disaster if you had a high-quality video with a bit rate over 700KB/s.

To use bit rate throttling, you need to download the IIS 7 Media Pack, which Microsoft provides as a free download at `http://www.iis.net/default.aspx?tabid=22`. You can also find a full walkthrough that shows you how to configure bit rate throttling at `http://learn.iis.net/page.aspx/148/bit-rate-throttling-configuration-walkthrough`.

For all its advantages, progressive downloading isn't perfect. It also has a few notable disadvantages, which are remedied by a technology called *streaming*. When streaming, the client doesn't perform an ordinary download—instead, it communicates with web server continuously. Furthermore, the client doesn't need to manage the buffering, because the web server sends just the content that's required.

Streaming has the instant playback ability of progressive downloading, along with the following advantages:

- **Scalability.** Although bandwidth throttling ensures respectable server scalability, streaming is still far more efficient. Although there are numerous factors, switching from progressive downloading to streaming could net your web server a two or three times improvement in scalability—in other words, it may be able to serve the same video content to three times as many simultaneous users. This is the reason that streaming is usually adopted.

- **Control over seeking.** With streaming, each chunk of video data is discarded once it's been displayed. This prevents users from saving the complete video file on their hard disk. You also have the choice of whether or not to allow seeking. You can index your content so that the user can freely jump around to new positions, with little lag, or you can restrict seeking in some video content so that the user is forced to watch it from beginning to end—and annoying but practical technique if you're displaying an advertisement before the real video content that the user wants to watch.

* **Adaptability.** Different clients have different connection speeds, and can support different bit rates. When providing progressive downloads, many websites deal with this issue by including lower-quality videos that are more likely to be supported, or by giving users the choice of different versions of the same file, each of which is encoded at a different bit rate. The first technique gives you a poorer viewing experience, and the second option has its own problems—it's time-consuming, average users don't always know their bandwidth, and the amount of video data a computer can handle can be influenced by other factors, such as the current CPU load or the quality of a wireless connection. When you use streaming server, you can opt into a more powerful solution called *adaptive streaming*. With adaptive streaming, the web server customizes the bit rate of the media file to suit the client. If the situation changes—for example, the network starts to slow down—the server deals with the issue seamlessly, automatically adjusting the bit rate down, and bringing it back up again when the connection improves. The player won't have to stop and refill its buffer, as it would with a progressive download.

Streaming also has one significant disadvantage. Namely, it needs the dedicated server-side software known as Windows Media Services. Windows Media Services is included with Windows Server 2003, and available as a free download for Windows Server 2008.

■**Note** If you use the MediaElement with a URL that starts with http:// or https://, Silverlight begins a progressive download. If you use the MediaElement with a URL that starts with mms://, Silverlight attempts to stream it, and falls back on a progressive download if streaming fails.

So what's the bottom line for a developer when creating a media-rich Silverlight application? First, determine whether you'll be deploying your application to a web server that supports streaming. That will determine the best way to encode your video files (as described in the next section). Currently, about 65% of all web content is delivered by progressive download, with YouTube leading the way as the single most popular deliverer of video content. For a deeper look at the technical differences between streaming servers and progressive download, check out `http://learn.iis.net/page.aspx/454/windows-media-server-or-web-server`.

If you don't want the complexity of configuring and maintaining a server with Windows Media Services, or you use a web host that doesn't provide this service, your applications will use progressive downloading. You'll get the most out of progressive downloading if you follow these best practices:

* **Consider providing multiple versions of the same media file.** If you have huge media files and you need to support users with a wide range of connection speeds, consider including an option in your application where users can specify their bandwidth. If a user specifies a low-speed bandwidth, you can seamlessly load smaller media files into the MediaElement. (Alternatively, consider encoding your video with a lower bit rate. If the tradeoff in quality is acceptable, you'll simplify your code.)

- **Adjust the BufferingTime property on the MediaElement.** You can control how much content Silverlight buffers in a progressive download by setting the BufferingTime property of the MediaElement. The default is 5 seconds of playback, but higher-quality videos that will be played over lower-bandwidth connections will need different rates. A longer BufferingTime property won't allow a slow connection to play a high–bit rate video file (unless you buffer virtually the entire file), but it will smooth over unreliable connections and give a bit more breathing room.

- **Keep the user informed about the download.** It's often useful to show the client how much of a particular media file has been downloaded. For example, websites like YouTube and players like Media Player use a progress bar that has a shaded background, indicating how much of the file is available. To create a similar effect in a Silverlight application, you can use the DownloadProgressChanged event. It fires each time Silverlight crosses a 5% download threshold (for example, when it downloads the first 5%, when it reaches 10%, when it reaches 15%, and so on). It also fires again when the file is completely downloaded. When the DownloadProgressChanged event fires, you can read the DownloadProgress property to determine how much of the file is currently available (as a value from 0 to 1). Use this information to set the width of a Rectangle, and you're well on the way to creating a download progress bar.

- **Consider informing the user about the buffer.** You can react as the buffer is filled using the BufferingProgressChanged and read the BufferingProgress property to find out how much content is in the buffer (as a value from 0 to 1). For example, with a Buffering-Time of 5 seconds, a BufferingProgress of 1 means the client has its full 5 seconds of media, while a BufferingProgress of 0.5 means the buffer is half full, with just 2.5 seconds available. This might be too much information to display, or it might be useful to the user to see why a media file can't be buffered successfully over the current connection.

- **Use bit rate throttling.** If you own the web server, you may want to ensure the best possible scalability by limiting the speed at which users can download content. Choose a limit that's slightly above the bit rate of your videos, but not extreme (for example, 500KB/s).

It's worth noting that the word *streaming* isn't always used in the technical sense described here. For example, Microsoft provides a fantastic free Silverlight hosting service called Silverlight Streaming. It provides 10GB of hosting space for Silverlight applications and media files. But despite its name, Silverlight Streaming doesn't use streaming—instead, it simply serves video files and allows the client to perform progressive downloading.

■**Tip** If you're looking for an efficient way to host large media files with your Silverlight application, be sure to consider Silverlight Streaming (`http://silverlight.live.com`). It's free, has no advertisements or annoying branding requirements, and offers a staggering 5 terabytes per month of bandwidth for video viewing.

Client-Side Playlists

Silverlight also supports Windows Media metafiles, which are essentially playlists that point to one or more other media files. Windows Media metafiles typically have the file extension .wax, .wvx, .wmx, .wpl, or .asx. Certain features of these files are not supported and will cause errors if used, such as script commands. For the full list of unsupported features, refer to the Silverlight documentation.

Here's a basic playlist that refers to two video files:

```
<asx version="3.0">
  <title>Two Video Playlist</title>
    <entry>
    <title>Video 1</title>
      <ref href="Video1.wmv" />
  </entry>
  <entry>
    <title>Video 2</title>
    <ref href="Video2.wmv" />
  </entry>
</asx>
```

If you point the Source property of the MediaElement to this file, it will begin playing Video1.wmv (assuming it exists) and then play Video2.wmv immediately after.

Typically, .asx files are used with .asf streaming files. In this case, the .asx file includes a link to the .asf streaming file.

Server-Side Playlists

If you're streaming video using Windows Media Services, you can also create a server-side playlist. Server-side playlists allow you to combine more than one video into a single stream, without revealing the source of each video to the user. Server-side playlists offer one technique for integrating advertisements into your video stream—simply create a server-side playlist that places an ad before the requested video.

Server-side playlists often have the file extension .wsx. As with client-side playlists, they contain XML markup:

```
<?wsx version="1.0"?>
<smil>
  <seq id="sq1">
    <media id="video2" src="Video1.wmv" />
    <media id="video1" src="Advertisement.wmv" />
    <media id="video2" src="Video2.wmv" />
  <seq>
</smil>
```

The root element is <smil>. Here, the <smil> element contains an ordered sequence of video files represented by the <seq> element, with each video represented by the <media> element. More sophisticated server-side playlists can repeat videos, play clips of longer videos, and specify videos that will be played in the event of an error. For more information about the standard for .wsx files (and the elements that are supported and unsupported in Silverlight 2), see `http://msdn.microsoft.com/en-us/library/cc645037(VS.95).aspx`.

Advanced Video Playback

You now know enough to play audio and video in a Silverlight application. However, there are a few finer details that can help you get the result you want when dealing with video. First, you need to start with the right type of video—that means a file in the right format and with the right dimensions and bit rate (the number of bytes of data it requires per second). You may also want to consider a streamed video file for optimum network efficiency. Next, you may be interested in additional features like markers. And finally, some of the most dazzling Silverlight effects depend on an artful use of the VideoBrush, which allows you to paint an ordinary Silverlight element with live video. You'll explore all of these topics in the following sections.

Video Encoding

To get the best results, you should prepare your files with Silverlight in mind. For example, you should use video files that won't overwhelm the bandwidth of your visitors. This is particularly true if you plan to use large media files (for example, to display a thirty-minute lecture).

Typically, the WMV files that you use in your Silverlight application will be a final product based on larger, higher-quality original video files. Often, the original files will be in a non-WMV format. However, this detail isn't terribly important, because you'll need to re-encode them anyway to reduce their size and quality to web-friendly proportions.

To get the right results when preparing video for the Web, you need the right tool. Microsoft provides three options:

- **Windows Movie Maker.** Included with recent versions of Windows (such as Windows Vista), and aimed squarely at the home user, Windows Movie Maker is too limiting for professional use. Although it can work in a pinch, its lack of control and its basic features makes it more suitable for authoring home movies than preparing web video content.

- **Windows Media Encoder.** Available as a free download at `http://www.microsoft.com/windows/windowsmedia/forpros/encoder/default.mspx`, Windows Media is a straightforward tool for video conversion. It's the best choice for those who don't have Expression Encoder.

- **Expression Encoder.** Available as a premium part of Microsoft's Expression Suite, Expression Encoder boasts some heavyweight features. Best of all, it's designed for Silverlight, which allows it to provide valuable features like automatic generation of custom-skinned Silverlight video pages. You can learn more, see training video, and download a free trial at `http://www.microsoft.com/expression/products/Overview.aspx?key=encoder`.

■**Note** Both Windows Media Encoder and Expression Encoder offer a different set of features, and neither one has all the capabilities of the other. The most obvious missing feature in Expression Encoder is support for creating files with multiple bit rates, which you need to use adaptive streaming.

In this chapter, you'll see how to use Windows Media Encoder and Expression Encoder to take care of one common task with video files—adding markers. You'll also see how to use Expression Encoder to generate beautifully customized Silverlight video pages. However, Expression Encoder has a significant limitation. At the time of this writing, the current version is Expression Encoder 2, which is designed for Silverlight 1.0. Although you can create media files that will work just as well with Silverlight 2.0, any video pages you generated will use the Silverlight 1.0 plug-in, and JavaScript code instead of C#.

To learn more about video encoding, you can browse the product documentation, website articles, or a dedicated book. The following sections outline the absolute basics to get you started with Windows Media Encoder or Expression Encoder.

Encoding in Windows Media Encoder

Silverlight doesn't support all the variations of video that the Windows Media Encoder can create. To make sure your files are compatible, it's easiest to use the ready-made profiles that you can download at `http://dev.live.com/silverlight/downloads/profiles.zip`. Unzip them to the Windows Media Encoder Profiles folder, which is typically C:\Program Files\Windows Media Components\Encoder\Profiles.

To use the profiles, follow these steps:

1. Start a new session. (If the New Session window isn't already open, click the New Session button in the toolbar now.)

2. In the Wizards tab, choose the Custom session option and click OK. When Windows Media Encoder creates a custom session, it opens the Session Properties panel, where you can configure a slew of properties.

3. In the Session Properties panel, choose the Sources tab, and specify your source. Usually, you'll be converting another file, which means you should click the File option and then click Browse to find it. Windows Media Encoder also has the ability to capture from other hardware devices (for example, a connected video camera) and the current screen.

4. Choose the Output tab. Clear the other checkboxes (for saving your output directly on a web server), and switch on the Archive to file setting instead. Then, supply the location and name of the output file you want to create (as shown in Figure 10-3).

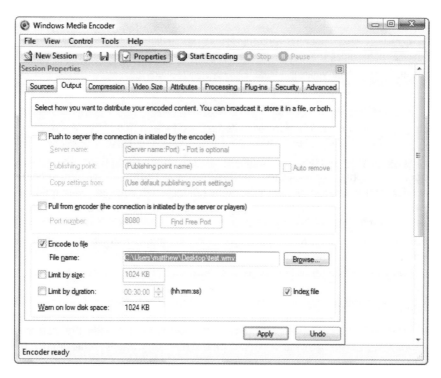

Figure 10-3. *Specifying the output file*

5. Choose the Compression tab. Here's where you'll need to use one of the custom profiles. Next to Destination, click Edit. The Custom Encoding Settings dialog box will appear.

6. In the Custom Encoding Settings dialog box, click Import. You'll see the profiles you downloaded earlier (see Figure 10-4). Choose the profile that matches the way you plan to deploy your Silverlight content. For example, if you plan to place your video file on your Silverlight website, you might choose VC-1 Web Server 256k DSL. If you suspect your users will have faster connections, you can step up to VC-1 Web Server 512k DSL or VC-1 Web Server Broadband. If you plan to use streaming with Windows Media Services, there's a similar range of profiles to choose from, such as VC-1 Streaming 256k DSL. (Once you choose a specific profile and click Open, you'll see the corresponding technical details appear in the Custom Encoding Settings dialog box.)

Figure 10-4. *Choosing an encoding profile*

SILVERLIGHT COMPRESSION: CBR AND VBR

Depending on whether you're planning to use streaming or simple progressive downloads, Silverlight chooses between two compression modes.

- **Constant Bit-Rate Encoding (CBR).** This is the best choice if you plan to allow video streaming. With CBR encoding, the average bit rate and the peak bit rate are the same, which means the data flow remains relatively constant at all times. Another way of looking at this is that the quality of the encoding may vary in order to preserve a constant bit rate, ensuring that the user will get smooth playback. (This isn't necessary if your application is using progressive downloading, because then it will cache as much of the media file as it can.)

- **Variable Bit-Rate Encoding (VBR).** This is the best choice if you plan to use progressive downloading. With VBR encoding, the bit rate varies throughout the file depending on the complexity of the video, meaning more complex content will be encoded with a higher bit rate. In other words, the quality remains constant, but the bit rate is allowed to change. Video files are usually limited by their worst parts, so a VBR-encoded file generally requires a smaller total file size to achieve the same quality as a CBR-encoded file. When using VBR encoding with Silverlight, the maximum bit rate is still constrained. For example, if you choose the VC-1 Web Server 512k DSL profile, you'll create encoded video with an average bit rate of 350KB/s (well within the range of the 512KB/s connection) and a maximum bit rate of 750KB/s.

When you import a profile, you'll see what standard you're using, and you'll get the technical information with the exact average and peak bit rates for audio and video encoding.

There's one twist. If you're using adaptive streaming (a feature that allows a server with Windows Media Services to intelligently switch to the best bandwidth based on the current connection speed and client capabilities), you need to use Multiple Bit-Rate Encoding (MBR). An MBR file includes multiple streams of data in the same file. Each of these streams uses CBR, but has a different bit rate. For example, an MBR file might combine a 700KB/s, 500KB/s, and 300KB/s stream. The web server can then choose the best CBR stream during playback.

Although creating and playing CBR files is out of the scope of this chapter, you can start experimenting in Windows Media Encoder. Choose the Compression tab, in the Destination list pick "Windows media server (streaming)," and in the Video list choose "Multiple bit rates video (CBR)." You can then add a checkmark next to each bit rate you want to use in "Bit rates" list underneath. For more technical information about adaptive streaming, see `http://www.microsoft.com/windows/windowsmedia/howto/articles/intstreaming.aspx`.

7. Click OK to close the Custom Encoding Settings dialog box.

8. At the bottom of the Session Properties pane, click Apply.

9. Click the Start Encoding button in the toolbar. When the process is finished, the Encoding Results dialog box will appear.

10. Click Close in the Encoding Results. If you want, you can save your custom session now to reuse its settings later (perhaps with a different file).

Encoding in Expression Encoder

Expression Encoder gives you the same encoding ability of Windows Media Encoder, with a few nifty extra features that this chapter won't cover:

- **Simple video editing.** You can cut out sections of video, insert a lead-in, and perform other minor edits.

- **Overlays.** You can watermark videos with a still or animated logo that stays superimposed over the video for as long as you want it to.

- **A/B compare.** To test the effect of a change or a new encoding, you can play the original and preview the converted video at the same time. Expression Encoder keeps both videos synchronized, so you can get a quick sense of quality differences.

- **Silverlight-ready.** Expression Encoder ships with suitable profiles for a Silverlight application. (They're the same ones you can download for Windows Media Encoder.) Additionally, Expression Encoder allows you to create a fully skinned Silverlight video player, complete with nifty features like image thumbnails. Unfortunately, Expression Encoder 2.0 creates Silverlight 1.0 pages, and you'll need to wait for Expression Encoder 2.5 to generate a Silverlight 2.0 application.

To encode a video file in Expression Encoder, follow these steps:

1. To specify the source file, choose File ➤ Import. Browse to the appropriate media file, selected it, and click Open. There will be a short delay while Expression Encoder analyzes it before it appears in the list in the Media Content panel at the bottom-left of the window. At this point, you can perform any other edits you want, such as trimming out unwanted video, inserting a lead-in, or adding an overlay. (All these changes are made through the Enhance tab on the right side of the window.)

2. To specify the destination file, look at the group of tabs on the right side of the window, and select the Output tab. In the Job Output section you can specify the directory where the new file will be placed, and its name.

3. To choose the encoding rate, click the Encode tab and make a selection from the Video list (see Figure 10-5). If you're using progressive downloads, you'll want a format that begins with the words "Web Server" (for example, Web Server 512k DSL). If you're using streaming with Windows Media Services, you'll choose one that starts with the word "Streaming" (for example, Streaming 512k DSL). These options determine whether Expression Encoder will use CBR or VBR encoding, as described earlier in the sidebar "Silverlight Compression: CBR and VBR."

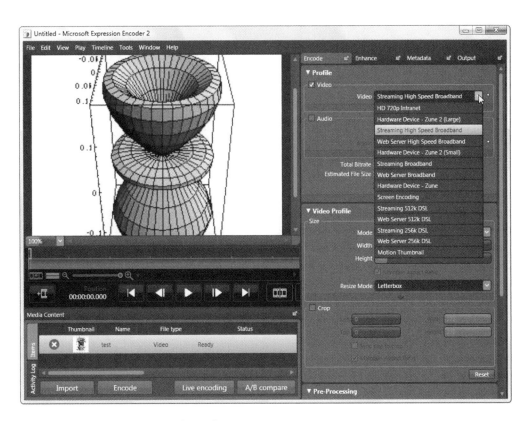

Figure 10-5. *Choosing the type of encoding*

4. Once you choose an encoding, you'll see the relevant information appear in the other sections of the Encode tab. Now, before you perform the encoding, you can tweak these details. For example, you can adjust the dimensions of the video output using the Size box. You can also preview what the file will look like by playing it in the video window on the left.

5. Click the Encode button at the bottom of the window, in the Media Content panel. If you want, you can save your job when the encoding is finished so you can reuse its settings later (perhaps to encode an updated version of the same file).

Markers

Markers are text annotations that are embedded in a media file and linked to a particular time. Technically, the WMV format supports text markers and script commands (used to do things like launch web pages while playback is underway), but Silverlight treats both of these the same, as timed bookmarks with a bit of text.

Markers provide some interesting possibilities for creating smarter Silverlight-based media players. For example, you could embed captions as a set of markers, and display them at the appropriate times. (You could even use this technique to build a poor man's subtitling system.) Or, you could embed other types of instructions, which your application could then read and act upon.

While it's up to you to write the code that reacts to markers, Silverlight gives you two tools: a MarkerReached event and the Markers collection in the MediaElement. But before you can investigate these details, you first need to consider how to add markers to your media file in the first place.

Adding Markers with Windows Media File Editor

Windows Media Encoder doesn't give you the ability to add markers. However, when you install Windows Media Encoder you also get a few utilities. One of these utilities, Windows Media File Editor, lets you add markers with ease. You'll find it in the Start menu, in the Windows Media ➤ Utilities group.

To add markers to a video file with Windows Media File Editor, follow these steps:

1. Choose File ➤ Open, pick your file, and click Open. You'll see your video appear in a small Media Player window.

2. Using the position bar in the Media Player widow, move to the spot where you want to place the marker, as shown in Figure 10-6. (Or, start playback, and hit pause when you get there.)

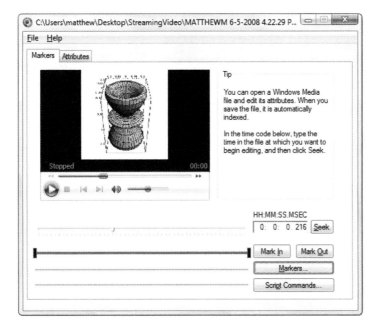

Figure 10-6. *Opening a video in Windows Media File Editor*

3. Click the Markers button.

4. In the Markers dialog box, click Add.

5. Enter the text for your marker in the Name box (see Figure 10-7). If necessary, adjust the marker time, which is shown in the Time box.

Figure 10-7. *Adding a new marker in Windows Media File Editor*

6. Click OK to add the marker and then OK to close the Markers dialog box.

7. Repeat the process (starting at step 2) to add more markers. You can also use the Markers dialog box to rename or remove existing markers.

8. When you're finished, save a new file with the marker information by choosing File ➤ Save As and Index. Then, close Windows Media File Editor.

Adding Markers with Expression Encoder

Expression Encoder has a built-in feature for adding markers. Here's how to use it:

1. After you've imported a media file, choose the Metadata tab at the left of the window.

2. Drag the playback bar under the video file to the position where you want to place the marker.

3. In the Metadata tab, find the Markers box. At the bottom of the Markers box, click the Add button to create a new marker, which will be added to the list (see Figure 10-8).

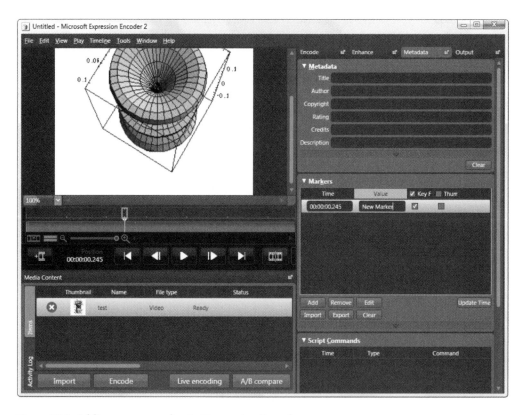

Figure 10-8. *Adding a new marker in Expression Encoder*

4. Adjust the time if necessary and supply the marker text in the Value column.

5. If you want to use a marker for indexed navigation, you may want to check the Key Frame and Thumbnail checkboxes next to your new marker. If you create a key frame at this location, playback will be able to resume at precisely this location with minimal delay. If you create a thumbnail, you can show that thumbnail to the user. The user can click that thumbnail to tell your application to seek to the corresponding marker location. Both of these features really only apply if you use Expression Encoder to generate a Silverlight video page, although you can build similar features on your own.

Note If you want to build a complete Silverlight video application from inside Expression Encoder, and you aren't put off by the fact that your video page will use Silverlight 1.0, here's what to do. Choose the Output tab at the far left, find the Job Output box, and choose an item from the Template list. The template determines the visual skin that the Silverlight player page uses—you'll see a thumbnail preview when you make your selection. If you choose (None), Expression Encoder will not create a Silverlight video player. This feature is an impressive single-click way to create a jazzed up multimedia player, and it will get a lot more interesting in Expression Encoder 2.5 with support for Silverlight 2.0.

---

6. Return to step 2 and repeat to add more markers. You can also edit existing markers, and click Remove to delete the currently selected marker.

7. When you're finished, click Encode to start encoding your video.

Using Markers in a Silverlight Application

The easiest way to show marker information is to handle the MarkerReached event of the MediaElement. The TimelineMarkerRoutedEventArgs object will provide the text of the marker and (through the TimelineMarker object), the exact time where it's placed.

Here's a simple event handler that copies the text from a marker to a TextBlock in the Silverlight page, as shown in Figure 10-9:

```
private void media_MarkerReached(object sender, TimelineMarkerRoutedEventArgs e)
{
    lblMarker.Text = e.Marker.Text + " at " + e.Marker.Time.TotalSeconds +
      " seconds";
}
```

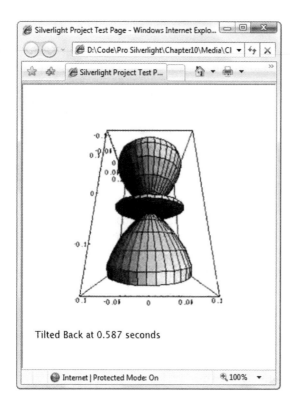

Figure 10-9. *Displaying a marker*

Rather than setting text, you could examine it and then determine the appropriate action to perform.

Instead of waiting for the MarkerReached event, you can examine the Markers collection of the MediaElement. This technique is particularly useful if you want to use markers for navigation. For example, you could react to the MediaOpened event (at which point the Markers collection has been populated), and then display the marker information in a list:

```csharp
private void media_MediaOpened(object sender, RoutedEventArgs e)
{
    foreach (TimelineMarker marker in media.Markers)
    {
        lstMarkers.Items.Add(marker.Text + " (" + marker.Time.Minutes + ":" +
            marker.Time.Seconds + ":" + marker.Time.Milliseconds + ")");
    }
}
```

■**Note** If your media file includes separate-stream script commands, they won't appear in the Markers collection. That's because this type of marker information can exist anywhere in the stream, and it may not have been downloaded when the MediaOpened event fires. To prevent inconsistent behavior, these types of markers are never added to the Markers collection. However, the MediaElement will still detect them and fire the MarkerReached event at the appropriate time. If this isn't the behavior you want, use the more common header-embedded script commands, which place them in the header (which *will* be read before MediaOpened fires).

You can also use the TimelineMarker.Time property to perform navigation:

```
media.Position = selectedMarker.Time;
media.Play();
```

Figure 10-10 shows the result.

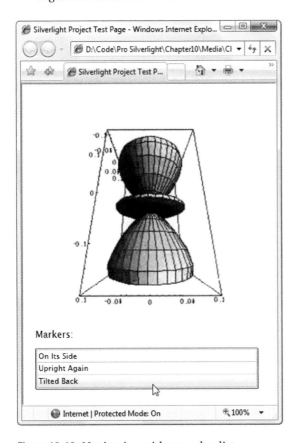

Figure 10-10. *Navigating with a marker list*

In this example, the code reads the markers from the media file. You can also create TimelineMarker objects programmatically and add them to the Markers collection once the media file has been loaded and the MediaOpened event has fired. In this case, the marker will act as a normal marker in all respects—for example, the MediaElement will fire the Marker-Reached event when it's reached. However, the marker won't be persisted in the video file when you close and reload it. This behavior gives you the ability to load marker information from another source, like a text file.

■**Note** Expression Encoder includes a feature that allows you to create image thumbnails for your markers. These images are embedded in your video file or linked to it in any way. If you use this feature, it's up to you to show the images in your page and use code to navigate to the right position. If you look at the code for the video player application that Expression Encoder can create, you'll find that it hard-codes the image file names and the marker positions, which is a suitable approach for automatically generated code, but not as good an idea in application code that you need to maintain.

VideoBrush

The VideoBrush is a Silverlight brush that paints an area with the video content that's currently playing in a specified MediaElement. Like other Silverlight brushes, you can use the VideoBrush to fill anything from a basic shape to a complex path or element.

The basic approach to using a VideoBrush is straightforward. First, create a Media-Element for the file you want to play:

```
<MediaElement x:Name="fireMovie" Source="fire.wmv"
 Height="0" Width="0"></MediaElement>
```

Notice that this example sets the Height and Width of the MediaElement to 0. This way, the original video window won't appear at all, and it won't take up any space in your layout. The only video that will appear is the video that's being painted by the VideoBrush. You can't get the same result by setting the Visibility property—in fact, if you hide the MediaElement by setting its Visibility to Collapsed, you'll also end up hiding the content that the VideoBrush is painting.

■**Tip** In some situations, you might want to display the original video window (which is shown in the MediaElement) *and* the video content that's painted by the VideoBrush. For example, you'll want the original video window to remain visible if you're using the VideoBrush to create a reflection effect.

The next step is to choose the element you want to paint with the VideoBrush. You can use the VideoBrush anywhere an element expects a brush. If you're dealing with the shape elements, you'll look to set properties like Fill and Stroke. If you're dealing with other elements, you'll look for properties like Foreground and Background. The following example uses the VideoBrush to fill the text in a large TextBlock:

```
<TextBlock Text="Fiery Letters" FontFamily="Arial Black" FontSize="80">
  <TextBlock.Foreground>
    <VideoBrush SourceName="fireMovie"></VideoBrush>
  </TextBlock.Foreground>
</TextBlock>
```

The SourceName property links the VideoBrush to the corresponding MediaElement. Figure 10-11 shows the result—text that's filled with roaring flames.

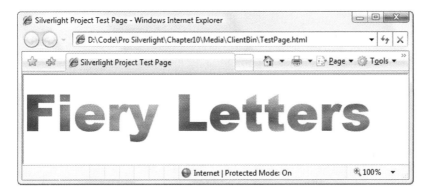

Figure 10-11. *Using video to fill text*

When using the VideoBrush, playback is still controlled through the MediaElement. In the current example, the video file begins to play automatically, because AutoPlay is true by default. Alternatively, you can set AutoPlay to false and control playback using the familiar Play(), Stop(), and Pause() methods of the MediaElement, and its Position property.

It's also worth noting that certain details can be set in the MediaElement without affecting the VideoBrush. Properties that affect the visual appearance of the MediaElement, such as Height, Width, Opacity, Stretch, RenderTransform, and Clip, have no effect on the VideoBrush. (The obvious exception is Visibility.) Instead, if you want to alter the video output, you can modify similar properties of the VideoBrush or the element that you're painting with the VideoBrush.

Video Effects

Because the MediaElement works like any other Silverlight element, and the VideoBrush works like any other Silverlight brush, you have the ability to manipulate video in some surprising ways. Here are some examples:

- You can use a MediaElement as the content inside a content control, such as a button.

- You can set the content for thousands of content controls at once with multiple Media-Element objects—although the client's CPU might not bear up very well under the strain.

- You can also combine video with transformations through the RenderTransform property. This allows you to move your video page, stretch it, skew it, or rotate it.

- You can set the Clipping property of the MediaElement to cut down the video page to a specific shape or path and show only a portion of the full frame.

- You can set the Opacity property to allow other content to show through behind your video. In fact, you can even stack multiple semitransparent video pages on top of each other.

- You can use an animation to change a property of the MediaElement (or one of its transforms) dynamically.

- You can copy the current content of the video page to another place in your user interface using a VideoBrush, which allows you to create specific effects like reflection.

- You can also use the same VideoBrush to paint multiple elements (or create multiple VideoBrush objects that use the same MediaElement). Both of these techniques allow you to fill multiple objects with the same video, or transformed versions of the same video.

For example, Figure 10-12 shows a video with a reflection effect underneath. It does so by creating a Grid with two rows. The top row holds a MediaElement that plays a video file. The bottom row holds a Rectangle that's painted with a VideoBrush. The video content is then flipped over by using the RelativeTransform property and then faded out gradually toward the bottom using an OpacityMask gradient.

```
<Grid Margin="15" HorizontalAlignment="Center">
  <Grid.RowDefinitions>
    <RowDefinition></RowDefinition>
    <RowDefinition></RowDefinition>
  </Grid.RowDefinitions>

  <MediaElement x:Name="media" Source="test.wmv"
   Stretch="Uniform"></MediaElement>

  <Rectangle Grid.Row="1" Stretch="Uniform">
    <Rectangle.Fill>
      <VideoBrush SourceName="media">
        <VideoBrush.RelativeTransform>
          <ScaleTransform ScaleY="-1" CenterY="0.5"></ScaleTransform>
        </VideoBrush.RelativeTransform>
      </VideoBrush>
    </Rectangle.Fill>

    <Rectangle.OpacityMask>
      <LinearGradientBrush StartPoint="0,0" EndPoint="0,1">
        <GradientStop Color="Black" Offset="0"></GradientStop>
        <GradientStop Color="Transparent" Offset="0.6"></GradientStop>
```

```
            </LinearGradientBrush>
          </Rectangle.OpacityMask>
      </Rectangle>
  </Grid>
```

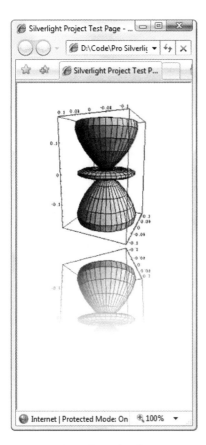

Figure 10-12. *Reflected video*

This example performs fairly well. Each frame must be copied to the lower rectangle, and each frame needs to be flipped and faded to create the reflection effect. (Silverlight uses an intermediary rendering surface to perform these transformations.) But the work required to download and decode the frame of video is performed just once, and on a modern computer, the extra overhead is barely noticeable.

One of the most impressive effects in the early days of Silverlight development was a video puzzle. It took a high-resolution video file and split it into a grid of interlocking puzzle pieces, which the user could then drag apart. The effect—separate puzzle pieces, each playing a completely synchronized portion of a single video—was stunning.

With the help of the VideoBrush, creating an effect like this is almost trivial. The following example shows a slightly simplified version of the original puzzle demonstration. It starts with a single window of puzzle pieces that's divided into a configurable number of squares. When the user clicks a square in the video window, an animation moves it to a random position (as shown in Figure 10-13). Several clicks later, the video image is completely scrambled, but all the pieces are still playing the synchronized video.

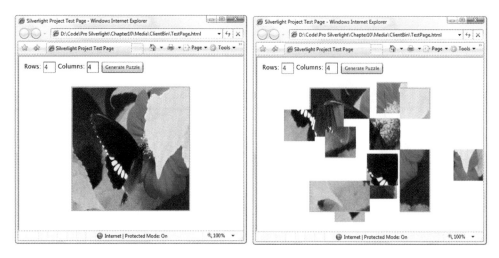

Figure 10-13. *Scrambling a video while it's playing*

To create this example, you first need the MediaElement that plays the video. Because all the puzzle pieces are showing portions of the same video, and you want the playback synchronized, you need just one MediaElement. It's given a Height and Width of 0 to make it invisible, so it will only appear when used through the VideoBrush.

```
<MediaElement x:Name="videoClip" Source="Butterfly.wmv" Height="0" Width="0"
 MediaEnded="videoClip_MediaEnded"></MediaElement>
```

When the media ends, it's started again, providing a looping playback:

```
private void videoClip_MediaEnded(object sender, RoutedEventArgs e)
{
    videoClip.Stop();
    videoClip.Play();
}
```

Next, you need a layout container that will hold the puzzle pieces. In this case, a Canvas makes most sense because the animation needs to move the pieces around the page when they're clicked.

```
<Canvas Margin="20" x:Name="puzzleSurface" Width="300" Height="300"
 Background="White" HorizontalAlignment="Center" VerticalAlignment="Center">
</Canvas>
```

The most interesting code happens when the Generate Puzzle button is clicked. This code calculates the size of rectangle needed to make a puzzle piece, and then dynamically creates each piece as a simple Rectangle element. Here's the code that starts it off:

```
private void cmdGeneratePuzzle_Click(object sender, RoutedEventArgs e)
{
    // Get the requested dimensions.
    int rows; int cols;
    Int32.TryParse(txtRows.Text, out rows);
    Int32.TryParse(txtCols.Text, out cols);

    if ((rows < 1) || (cols <1))
        return;

    // Clear the surface.
    puzzleSurface.Children.Clear();

    // Determine the rectangle size.
    double squareWidth = puzzleSurface.ActualWidth / cols;
    double squareHeight = puzzleSurface.ActualHeight / rows;

    // Create the brush for the MediaElement named videoClip.
    VideoBrush brush = new VideoBrush();
    brush.SetSource(videoClip);

    // Create the rectangles.
    double top = 0; double left = 0;
    for (int row = 0; row < rows; row++)
    {
        for (int col = 0; col < cols; col++)
        {
            ...
```

The next step is to make sure that each Rectangle only shows the region that's assigned to it. You could accomplish this by applying a transform to the VideoBrush, but then you'd need to use a different VideoBrush object for each square. An alternate approach is to tweak the clipping region of rectangle. In this case, each rectangle gets the size of the full video window, but it's clipped to show just the appropriate region. Here's the code that creates the rectangles and sets the clipping:

```
            ...
            // Create the rectangle. Every rectangle is sized to match the Canvas.
            Rectangle rect = new Rectangle();
            rect.Width = puzzleSurface.ActualWidth;
            rect.Height = puzzleSurface.ActualHeight;

            rect.Fill = brush;
            SolidColorBrush rectBrush = new SolidColorBrush(Colors.Blue);
            rect.StrokeThickness = 3;
            rect.Stroke = rectBrush;
```

```
            // Clip the rectangle to fit its portion of the puzzle.
            RectangleGeometry clip = new RectangleGeometry();
            // A 1-pixel correction factor ensures there are never lines in between.
            clip.Rect = new Rect(left, top, squareWidth+1, squareHeight+1);
            rect.Clip = clip;

            // Handle rectangle clicks.
            rect.MouseLeftButtonDown += rect_MouseLeftButtonDown;

            puzzleSurface.Children.Add(rect);

            // Go to the next column.
            left += squareWidth;
        }
        // Go to the next row.
        left = 0;
        top += squareHeight;
    }
    // (If the video is not already playing, you can start it now.)
}
```

When a rectangle is clicked, the code responds by starting two animations that move it to a new, random position. Although you could create these animations manually, it's even easier to define them in the resources collection. That's because the application requires just two animations, and can reuse them for whatever square is clicked.

Here are the two animations. The animation that shifts the rectangle sideways takes 0.25 seconds, while the animation that moves it up or down takes 0.15 seconds:

```
<UserControl.Resources>
  <Storyboard x:Name="squareMoveStoryboard">
    <DoubleAnimation x:Name="leftAnimation" Duration="0:0:0.25"
     Storyboard.TargetProperty="(Canvas.Left)"></DoubleAnimation>
    <DoubleAnimation x:Name="topAnimation" Duration="0:0:0.15"
     Storyboard.TargetProperty="(Canvas.Top)"></DoubleAnimation>
  </Storyboard>
</UserControl.Resources>
```

You'll notice that this code uses a single storyboard for all its animations. You must take extra care when reusing this storyboard. Before you can start a new animation, you must manually place the current square to its new position, and then stop the storyboard. The alternative is to dynamically create a new storyboard every time a square is clicked. (You saw this technique in action in Chapter 9, with the bomb dropping game.)

Here's the code that manages the storyboard and moves the square when it's clicked, sending it drifting to a new, random location.

```
private Rectangle previousRectangle;

private void rect_MouseLeftButtonDown(object sender, MouseButtonEventArgs e)
{
    // Get the square.
    Rectangle rectangle = (Rectangle)sender;

    // Stop the current animation.
    if (previousRectangle != null)
    {
        double left = Canvas.GetLeft(rectangle);
        double top = Canvas.GetTop(rectangle);
        squareMoveStoryboard.Stop();
        Canvas.SetLeft(rectangle, left);
        Canvas.SetTop(rectangle, top);
    }

    // Attach the animation.
    squareMoveStoryboard.Stop();

    // Attach the animation.
    Storyboard.SetTarget(squareMoveStoryboard, rectangle);

    // Choose a random direction and movement amount.
    Random rand = new Random();
    int sign = 1;
    if (rand.Next(0, 2) == 0) sign = -1;
    leftAnimation.To = Canvas.GetLeft(rectangle) + rand.Next(60,150) * sign;
    topAnimation.To = Canvas.GetTop(rectangle) + rand.Next(60, 150) * sign;

    // Store a reference to the square that's being animated.
    previousRectangle = rectangle;

    // Start the animation.
    squareMoveStoryboard.Begin();
}
```

This is all the code you need to complete the example, combining video, interactivity, and a rather dramatic effect that's leagues beyond other browser-based application platforms.

Deep Zoom

Now that you've explored the fine details of Silverlight's audio and video support, it's time to branch out to a very different type of multimedia: Silverlight's new Deep Zoom feature.

The idea behind Deep Zoom is to present a "zoom-able" interface for huge images. The typical Deep Zoom image is far too large to be shown on screen at once at its native resolution.

Initially, the Deep Zoom image is shown at a greatly reduced size, so that the user gets a bird's eye view of the entire picture. The user can then click to zoom in on a specific spot. As the user clicks, Silverlight zooms in more and more, eventually enlarging the selected area of the image to its native resolution (and beyond), and exposing the fine details that weren't initially visible.

Figure 10-14 shows the Deep Zoom process. At the top is the initial zoomed out view of a beach scene. At the bottom is the waste basket that you can see after zooming in on one small region at the right of the image.

Figure 10-14. *Using Deep Zoom to explore a panoramic image*

Usually, Deep Zoom images are stitched together from dozens or hundreds of smaller images to create a seamless panorama. However, Deep Zoom can also work with a quilt of distinct images. One example is the Hard Rock Memorabilia website (`http://memorabilia.hardrock.com`), which uses Deep Zoom to allow visitors to examine different relics, which are tiled together into one huge picture.

Note Deep Zoom is not a new idea. There are already many competitors that implement the same feature. One popular example is Zoomify, which is built using Adobe Flash. However, Deep Zoom feels surprisingly mature. It provides notably smooth zooming (rather than simply jumping between differently sized images) and fast performance that outdoes many more established competitors.

It's easy to create a Silverlight application that uses Deep Zoom, provided you have the right tools. The most important is the free Deep Zoom Composer tool. (To download, search for it at `http://www.microsoft.com/downloads`). The Deep Zoom Composer allows you to convert a large image into the tiled groups of images that Deep Zoom needs for its zooming interface. It can also generate a ready-made Silverlight 2 project that uses this image set, and it allows you to tile together smaller images to create a large image that's suitable for Deep Zoom. However, if you want to seamlessly stitch together a large picture, you'll probably want to use more specialized stitching software, which is able to adjust geometry and lighting for a truly seamless effect. Image stitching software can often save a huge amount of work by automatically matching image tiles to create the stitched image. Examples of stitching software include Windows Live Photo Gallery and the more powerful Autopano Pro.

Tip If you simply want to try out the Deep Zoom feature, you have several options for getting the large image you need. Some dedicated photo stitchers post extremely large pictures to photo sharing sites like Flickr. (Obviously, you'll need to ask for permission if you want to use the picture for anything other than a test on your local computer.) You can also grab huge satellite images from NASA's Visible Earth website (`http://visibleearth.nasa.gov`).

Once you have the Deep Zoom Composer software and a suitable image (or images), you're ready to get to work.

Creating a Deep Zoom Image Set

To get started, load Deep Zoom Composer and click New Project.

There are three steps to building a Deep Zoom image set with Deep Zoom composer. First, you import the picture (or pictures) you plan to use. Next, you arrange the pictures. If you have a single picture, this won't take long. If you have multiple pictures, this is when you tile them together by hand. Finally, you export the Deep Zoom image set and create the Silverlight project.

You can switch from one step to another using the three tab buttons at the top of the Deep Zoom Composer window. Initially, you begin in the Import tab. Here's what to do:

1. To get the pictures you want, click the Import button in the right-side panel, browse to the right file, and click OK. Importing large pictures can be slow, so be prepared to wait.

2. Repeat step 1 until you've imported all the pictures you need.

3. Click the Compose button. Here, you start off with a blank design surface where you can lay out your pictures (see Figure 10-15).

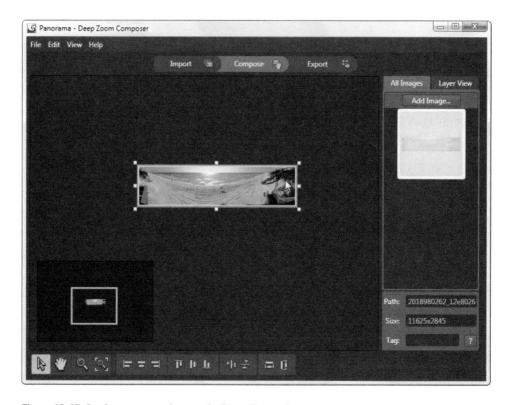

Figure 10-15. *Laying out your images in Deep Zoom Composer*

4. To add a picture to the design surface, drag it from the right-side panel. If you have several pictures, you must drag, position, and size each one. Images can overlap, but it's up to you to line them up correctly by hand. In general, this ability to arrange multiple pictures is only useful if you're creating a Deep Zoom image set that's made up of distinctly separate images (like the tiled items in the Hard Rock Memorabilia display). If you want to create the illusion of a single huge picture, you'll need to use dedicated photo stitching software instead.

5. Click the Export button. You have two export options: you can export your image set to PhotoZoom (a new Microsoft service for displaying Deep Zoom image sets), or, more practically, you can create a Silverlight project that you can then edit and deploy to your own web server.

6. To create a Silverlight project, click the Silverlight Export tab in the right-side panel. Then, fill in the required information.

7. In the Name text box, enter a name for your project. If you want to export it to a different folder, change the path in the Export Location text box.

8. In the Image Format list, choose either PNG or JPEG. PNG is the default, and it offers better quality through lossless compression. However, JPEG gives you the option to reduce the image quality, which will decrease the size of your image files and thereby increase performance.

9. In the Output Type box, choose Export Images and Silverlight Project. Alternatively, you can choose Export Images to export the Deep Zoom image set without the Silverlight project files. However, the exported project includes some genuinely useful code that allows the user to zoom by clicking or using the mouse wheel. If you create your project from scratch, you'll need to write your own code to make the page interactive.

10. Click Export to create the image set and Silverlight project. This process may take some time. When it's finished, a window will appear with several options (see Figure 10-16), allowing you to preview the Silverlight project in your browser, or browse to the image folder or project folder.

Figure 10-16. *Completing an export*

Using a Deep Zoom Image Set in Silverlight

As you work with Deep Zoom Composer, it creates two folders in your initial project location. One folder, named Working Data, holds temporary files. The second folder, named Source Images, holds the original, imported pictures. It also holds subfolders with the final result of the exporting process.

For example, if you create a Deep Zoom project named Panorama, and you use it to export a Silverlight project, your files will end up in the folder Panorama\Source Images\ OutputSdi\PanoramaProject (see Figure 10-17). This is where you go to find the .sln solution file, which you can use to open the project in Visual Studio.

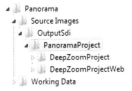

Figure 10-17. *The generated Silverlight project for Panorama*

Inside the project folder, you'll find two more folders: one with the Silverlight application, and one with the hosting website, which is a local website that uses an ordinary HTML test page, not an ASP.NET website. These folders are named according to the Silverlight project name you picked in step 7. For example, if you chose DeepZoomProject, you'll see a folder named DeepZoomProject with the Silverlight application and another named DeepZoom-ProjectWeb with the test page and all the generated images.

At this point, you're probably wondering where you'll find the generated Deep Zoom images. They're placed, logically enough, in a website subfolder named GeneratedImages (see Figure 10-18). Thus, when you deploy your Silverlight application, you'll need to include the GeneratedImages folder, complete with all its contents (including XML files that describe the image set, multiple subfolders, and the image tiles).

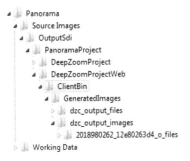

Figure 10-18. *The website folder (ClientBin) and the Deep Zoom image set (GeneratedImages)*

Now that you've oriented yourself, it's worth checking out the actual code. To show a Deep Zoom image, you simply need to use the MultiScaleImage element. Here's what it looks like in the automatically generated project:

```
<UserControl x:Class="DeepZoomProject.Page"
 xmlns="http://schemas.microsoft.com/winfx/2006/xaml/presentation"
 xmlns:x="http://schemas.microsoft.com/winfx/2006/xaml"
 Width="800" Height="600">
  <Grid x:Name="LayoutRoot" Background="White">
    <Border BorderBrush="#FF727272" BorderThickness="1,1,1,1">
      <MultiScaleImage Height="600" x:Name="msi" Width="800"/>
    </Border>
  </Grid>
</UserControl>
```

The source for the MultiScaleImage is an XML file that defines the Deep Zoom image set. Although you could set the source for the MultiScaleImage in markup, the automatically generated project uses code, as shown here:

```
msi.Source = new DeepZoomImageTileSource(
  new Uri("GeneratedImages/dzc_output.xml", UriKind.Relative));
```

This URL points to the GeneratedImages subfolder you saw in Figure 10-18.

The MultiScaleImage has three key methods, which are detailed in Table 10-1.

Table 10-1. *Methods of the MultiScaleImage*

Method	Description
ElementToLogicalPoint()	This method converts a physical on-screen point in the MultiScaleImage element to a logical point in the large, virtual image. This translation process allows you to zoom into a specific area.
LogicalToElementPoint()	This method converts a logical point in the virtual image to a physical location in the MultiScaleImage where that point is currently being displayed.
ZoomAboutLogicalPoint()	This method zooms in or out, using a logical center point you specify and a zoom factor. The zoom factor is a number greater than 0. Use 1 to fit the available space precisely. Numbers greater than 1 zoom in (for example, 3 zooms in to three times magnification) and numbers less than 1 zoom out (for example, 0.5 zooms out to half magnification).

The automatically generated project uses these methods to control zooming. The lynchpin is a simple Zoom() method that translates a point in the element to logical coordinates, and then zooms to that point.

```
public void Zoom(double zoom, Point pointToZoom)
{
    Point logicalPoint = msi.ElementToLogicalPoint(pointToZoom);
    msi.ZoomAboutLogicalPoint(zoom, logicalPoint.X, logicalPoint.Y);
}
```

Using this method, you can programmatically zoom in on the center point, like this:

```
Zoom(1.2, new Point(this.ActualWidth / 2, this.ActualHeight / 2));
```

or zoom out, like this:

```
Zoom(.8, new Point(this.ActualWidth / 2, this.ActualHeight / 2));
```

The code in the automatically generated project goes a bit further. It allows the user to drag the image around the viewing area (using code that's similar to the dragging circle example in Chapter 4). It also allows the user to zoom in by clicking or turning the scroll wheel on the mouse. First, every time the mouse moves, its position is recorded:

```
this.lastMousePos = e.GetPosition(this.msi);
```

Then, when the user clicks, the image is zoomed in (or zoomed out if the Shift key is held down):

```
bool shiftDown = (Keyboard.Modifiers & ModifierKeys.Shift) == ModifierKeys.Shift;

if (shiftDown)
    ZoomFactor = 0.5;
else
    ZoomFactor = 2.0;

Zoom(ZoomFactor, this.lastMousePos);
```

The scroll wheel has much the same effect, but the zoom amount is less:

```
if (e.Delta > 0)
    ZoomFactor = 1.2;
else
    ZoomFactor = .80;

Zoom(ZoomFactor, this.lastMousePos);
```

Most Silverlight applications that use Deep Zoom will include this code. However, you're free to extend it to suit your needs. For example, the Hard Rock Memorabilia website checks the clicked point to determine what item is in that location. It then zooms and displays a panel with information about the selected item next to the image.

The Last Word

In this example, you explored how to integrate sound and video into a Silverlight application. You also considered the best practices for dealing with video and ensuring optimum playback performance in the client and scalability on the server.

Microsoft has placed a great deal of emphasis on Silverlight's multimedia capabilities (particularly in version 1.0). In fact, multimedia is one area where Silverlight is gaining features that haven't appeared in the WPF world. For example, WPF has no VideoBrush (although it provides another way to accomplish the same effect with the VisualBrush). Furthermore, its version of the MediaElement lacks a few properties that Silverlight applications use to control buffering and interact with markers. Finally, WPF has no implementation of the Deep Zoom technology—so if you want a similar capability in a rich client application, you'll be forced to build it yourself.

■ ■ ■

CHAPTER 11

Styles, Templates, and Custom Controls

Silverlight applications would be a drab bunch if you were limited to the plain, gray look of ordinary buttons and other common controls. Fortunately, Silverlight has several features that allow you to inject some flair into basic elements, and standardize the look-and-feel of your application. In this chapter, you'll learn about the two most important: styles and templates.

Styles are an essential tool for organizing and reusing for formatting choices. Rather than fill your XAML with repetitive markup to set details like margins, padding, colors, and fonts, you can create a set of well-encapsulated styles. You can then apply the styles where you need them by setting a single property.

Templates give you a more ambitious tool to change the visual "face" of any common control. In other words, if you can't get the custom appearance you want by tweaking properties alone (and often you can't), you can almost certainly get it by applying a new template. And while creating custom templates is more work than just setting control properties, it's still far simpler and more flexible than developing an entirely new custom control (which many other programming frameworks will force you to do).

Despite the power of styles and templates, you'll occasionally choose to create your own control. Usually, you'll take this step because you need functionality that's not offered by the core Silverlight controls. In this chapter, you'll learn how to use the template model in your custom control, so you (and other developers) can change every aspect of its appearance without losing any part of its behavior.

■**Note** Styles and templates are noticeably less featured than their WPF counterparts. However, these limitations won't stop you from fulfilling their original goal—completing customizing the visuals of a control without disturbing the way it works.

Styles

A *style* is a collection of property values that you can apply to an element in one step. In Silverlight, styles allow you to streamline your XAML markup by pulling repetitive formatting details out of your element tags.

The Silverlight style system plays a similar role to the cascading style sheet (CSS) standard in HTML markup. Like CSS, Silverlight styles allow you to define a common set of formatting characteristics and apply them throughout your application to ensure consistency. However, Silverlight styles have a few key limitations—for example, you won't be able to share styles between different elements or apply styles automatically. For these reason, styles seem a bit clumsy in Silverlight, even though they still rank as a key feature. In the following sections, you'll see how to use them.

WPF STYLES VS. SILVERLIGHT STYLES

If you've used styles in WPF, you'll find that Silverlight styles are dramatically scaled back. Here are some things that you can do with WPF styles but not with Silverlight styles:

- Apply styles to element types automatically (for example, style all the buttons in a window).

- Use style triggers to change the style of a control when another property changes.

- Apply the same style to different types of elements (for example, buttons and TextBlock elements).

- Use style to attach event handlers.

- Create styles that inherit from other styles.

- Dynamically change the style that a control uses at runtime (which is useful if you want to build a user-selectable "skinning" feature).

Although some of these limitations are not trivial, the Silverlight style system is still useful. You'll almost certainly use it to standardize and reuse formatting throughout an application.

Defining a Style

For example, imagine you need to standardize the font and foreground color that's used in the buttons of a page. The first step is to define a Style object that wraps all the properties you want to set. You'll store this Style object as a resource, typically in the UserControl.Resources collection that holds resources for the entire page:

```
<UserControl.Resources>
  <Style x:Key="BigButtonStyle" TargetType="Button">
    ...
  </Style>
</UserControl.Resources>
```

Like all resources, the style has a key name so you can pull it out of the collection when needed. In this case, the key name is BigButtonStyle. (By convention, the key names for styles usually end with "Style.") Additionally, every Silverlight style requires a TargetType, which is the type of element on which you apply the style. In this case, the style is being built to format buttons.

This style object holds a Setters collection with three Setter objects, one for each property you want to set. Each Setter object sets a single property in an element. The only limitation is that a setter can only change a dependency property—other properties can't be modified. In practice, this isn't much a limitation, because Silverlight elements consist almost entirely of dependency properties. The property setters can act on any dependency property, even ones that govern behavior rather than appearance. For example, if you're applying a style to a text box, you might choose AcceptsReturn and IsReadOnly.

Here's a style that gives buttons large, white text using Georgia font on a dark background:

```
<UserControl.Resources>
  <Style x:Key="BigButtonStyle" TargetType="Button">
    <Setter Property="FontFamily" Value="Georgia" />
    <Setter Property="FontSize" Value="40" />
    <Setter Property="Foreground" Value="SlateGray" />
    <Setter Property="Background" Value="Black" />
    <Setter Property="Padding" Value="20" />
    <Setter Property="Margin" Value="10" />
  </Style>
</UserControl.Resources>
```

In some cases, you won't be able to set the property value using a simple attribute string. For example, you can create a complex brush like the LinearGradientBrush or ImageBrush with a simple string. In this situation, you can use the familiar XAML trick of replacing the attribute with a nested element. Here's an example:

```
<Style x:Key="BigButtonStyle" TargetType="Button">
  <Setter Property="Background">
    <Setter.Value>
      <LinearGradientBrush StartPoint="0,0" EndPoint="1,0">
        <GradientStop Color="Blue"></GradientStop>
        <GradientStop Color="Yellow" Offset="1"></GradientStop>
      </LinearGradientBrush>
    </Setter.Value>
  </Setter>
  ...
</Style>
```

Applying a Style

Every Silverlight element can use a single style (or no style). The style plugs into an element through the element's Style property (which is defined in the base FrameworkElement class). For example, to configure a button to use the style you created previously, you'd point the button to the style resource like this:

```
<Button Style="{StaticResource BigButtonStyle}"
  Content="A Customized Button"></Button>
```

Styles set the initial appearance of an element, but you're free to override the characteristics they set. For example, if you apply the BigButtonStyle style and set the FontSize property explicitly, the FontSize setting in the button tag overrides the style. Ideally, you won't rely on this behavior—instead, create more styles so that you can set as many details as possible at the style level. This gives you more flexibility to adjust your user interface in the future with minimum disruption.

Figure 11-1 shows a page with two buttons that use the BigButtonStyle.

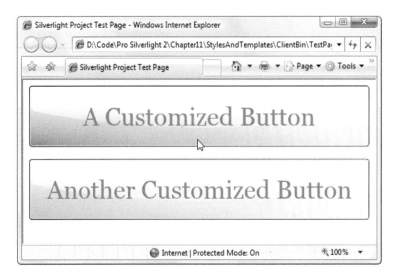

Figure 11-1. *Reusing button settings with a style*

The style system adds many benefits. Not only does it allow you to create groups of settings that are clearly related, it also streamlines your markup by making it easier to apply these settings. Best of all, you can apply a style without worrying about what properties it sets. In the previous example the font settings were organized into a style named BigButtonStyle. If you decide later that your big-font buttons also need more padding and margin space, you can add setters for the Padding and Margin properties as well. All the buttons that use the style automatically acquire the new style settings.

Note Technically, it is possible to set a style programmatically. However, this step can only be performed once. If you attempt to style a button that's already been styled, you'll receive an exception.

Organizing Styles

In the previous example, the style object is defined at the page level and then reused in two buttons inside that page. Although that's a common design, it's certainly not your only choice.

Strictly speaking, you don't need to use styles and resources together. For example, you could define the style of a particular button by filling its Style collection directly, as shown here:

```
<Button Content="A Customized Button">
  <Button.Style>
    <Style TargetType="Button">
      <Setter Property="FontFamily" Value="Georgia" />
      <Setter Property="FontSize" Value="40" />
      <Setter Property="Foreground" Value="White" />
      <Setter Property="Background" Value="Black" />
    </Style>
  </Button.Style>
</Button>
```

This works, but it's obviously a lot less useful. Now there's no way to share this style with other elements.

More usefully, you may want to define styles in different resource collections. If you want to create more finely targeted styles, you could define them using the resources collection of their container, such as a StackPanel or a Grid. It's even possible for the same style to be defined at multiple levels (in a StackPanel containing a button and in the page that holds the StackPanel). In this situation, Silverlight follows the standard resource resolution process you learned about in Chapter 2—namely, it searches in the resources collection of the current element first, then the containing element, then its container, and so on, until it finds a style with the matching name. If you want to reuse styles across an application, you should define them using the resources collection of your application (in the App.xaml file), which is the last place Silverlight checks.

Template Basics

Styles allow you to change the appearance of an element. However, styles are limited to setting properties that are defined in the element class. For example, there are various visual details about a button that you can't change because they aren't exposed through properties. Examples include the shading in a button's background to the way it highlights itself when you click down on it with the mouse.

However, Silverlight has another, much more radical customization tool called *templates*. While styles can be used with any Silverlight element, templates are limited to Silverlight controls—in other words, elements that inherit from the Control class in the System.Windows. Controls namespace. These elements acquire a property named Template, which you can set to apply a custom template, effectively overriding the control's standard visuals.

For example, by changing the template used by a Button object, you can create many exotic types of buttons that would be unthinkable with styles alone. You can create buttons that use round or shaped borders, and buttons that use eye-catching mouse-over effects (like glowing, enlarging, or twinkling). All you need to do is draw upon the drawing smarts you picked up in Chapter 7 and Chapter 8, and the animation techniques you learned in Chapter 9 when you build your custom template.

In the following sections, you'll peer into the templates used by common controls, and see how to craft custom templates.

WPF TEMPLATES VS. SILVERLIGHT TEMPLATES

Templates are one of WPF's most complex features, so it's no surprise that the Silverlight version lacks a few features. What's more surprising is the fact that the lack of a few features forces Silverlight controls to use a new set of standards and best practices for template design.

In WPF, templates make heavy use of *triggers*. Triggers react when a property changes—for example, when IsMouseOver becomes true in a button, a trigger reacts and changes the button's shading. Often, there's no need to write any code to implement this change—the trigger in the control template simply modifies another property (such as the background brush or the visibility of a specific shape in the control template). You can even use triggers to fire off animations that are completely defined in XAML markup.

Silverlight doesn't support triggers, so it needs to do more work in code. Most Silverlight controls are designed to look for specific, hard-coded animations in their templates, and fire them up at the right time. For example, move your mouse over a button, and you'll trigger a behind-the-scenes event handler that launches an animation to change the button. You can get the same functionality as triggers, but the control needs to take charge.

Silverlight architects suggest that future versions of Silverlight will add support for triggers. However, that doesn't mean the new template-building techniques will be replaced. They point out that the new template model (which you'll explore in this chapter) has some advantages—although it can be a bit tedious, it has a clear structure. In fact, done properly it's often easier to see how to customize the template of a Silverlight control than a WPF control, because it's easier to understand how that control works by reading the template. WPF architects tell us that the new template model will also be enhanced in the future, so it isn't a dead-end for development.

Lastly, it's important to understand the bottom-line compatibility goals for the Silverlight template model. If you've created custom templates in WPF templates, they almost certainly won't work in Silverlight. Similarly, the templates you create for a standard Silverlight control (like the Button class) won't work for the WPF equivalent. However, Microsoft is working to bring the two models closer together. This involves adding missing features to future versions of Silverlight (such as triggers) and adding support for the "parts and states" model in WPF.

Creating a Template

Every control has a built-in recipe that determines how it should be rendered (as a group of more fundamental elements). That recipe is called a *control template*. It's defined using a block of XAML markup, and applied to a control through the Template property.

For example, consider the basic button. Perhaps you want to get more control over the shading and animation effects that a button provides by creating a custom template. In this case, the first step is to try replacing the button's default template with one of your own devising.

To create a template for a basic button, you need to draw your own border and background and then place the content inside the button. There are several possible candidates for drawing the border, depending on the root element you choose:

- **The Border.** This element does double-duty—it holds a single element inside (say, a TextBlock with the button caption), and draws a border around it.

- **The Grid.** By placing multiple elements in the same place, you can create a bordered button. Use a Silverlight shape element (such as a Rectangle or Path) and place a TextBlock in the same cell. Make sure the TextBlock is defined after the shape in XAML, so that appears superimposed over the shape background. One advantage of the Grid is that it supports automatic sizing, so you can make sure your control is made only as large as its content requires.

- **The Canvas.** The Canvas can place elements more precisely using coordinates. It's usually overkill, but it may be a good choice if you need to position a cluster of shapes in specific positions relative to each other, as part of a more complex button graphic.

The following example uses the Border class to combine a rounded orange outline with an eye-catching red background and white text:

```
<Button Content="A Custom Button Template">
  <Button.Template>
    <ControlTemplate TargetType="Button" >
      <Border BorderBrush="Orange" BorderThickness="3" CornerRadius="10"
        Background="Red">
        <TextBlock Foreground="White" Text="A Custom Template"></TextBlock>
      </Border>
    </ControlTemplate>
  </Button.Template>
</Button>
```

Figure 11-2 shows the result.

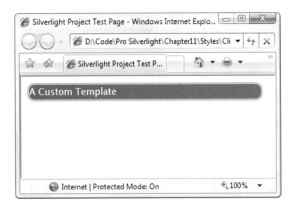

Figure 11-2. *A very basic new look for a button*

If you try this button out, you'll find it's a pretty poor template. It loses many of the button features (such as changing appearance when the button is clicked). It also ignores virtually every property you set on the button, including the fundamentally important Content property. (Instead, it displays some hard-coded text.) However, this template is actually on its way to becoming a much better button template, and you'll begin refining it in the following sections.

■**Note** At this point, you might be wondering why you've started building a custom button template without seeing the default button template. That's because default templates are extremely detailed. In fact, a simple button has a control template that's four printed pages long. But once you understand how a template is built, you'll be able to make your way through all the details in the default template.

Reusing Control Templates

In the previous example, the template definition is nested inside the element. However, it's much more common to set the template of a control through a style. That's because you'll almost always want to reuse your template to skin multiple instances of the same control.

To accommodate this design, you need to define your control template as a resource:

```
<UserControl.Resources>
  <ControlTemplate x:Key="ButtonTemplate" TargetType="Button" >
    <Border BorderBrush="Orange" BorderThickness="3" CornerRadius="10"
      Background="Red">
      <TextBlock Foreground="White" Text="A Custom Template"></TextBlock>
    </Border>
  </ControlTemplate>
</UserControl.Resources>
```

You can then refer to it using a StaticResource reference, as shown here:

```
<Button Template="{StaticResource ButtonTemplate}" ... ></Button>
```

Not only does this approach make it easier to create a whole host of customized buttons, it also gives you the flexibility to modify your control template later without disrupting the rest of your application's user interface.

There's one more option—you can define your template as part of a style. The advantage to this approach is that your style can combine setters that adjust other properties, as well as a setter that applies the new control template. When you set the Style property of your button, all the setters will come into action, giving your button a new template and adjusting any other related properties.

Note There are a few more considerations that apply if you're creating a whole set of related styles that will replace the standard Silverlight controls to give your application a custom "skinned" look. In this situation, you should define all your styles in the App.xaml file, and you should place commonly used details in separate resources. For example, if all of your controls use the same highlighting effect when selected (which is a good idea for visual consistency), create a resource named HighlightBrush, and use that resource in your control templates.

The ContentPresenter

The previous example creates a rather unhelpful button that displays hard-coded text. What you really want to do is take the value of the Button.Content property and display it in your custom template. To pull this off, you need a specially designed placeholder called Content-Presenter.

The ContentPresenter is required for all content controls—it's the "insert content here" marker that tells Silverlight where to stuff the content. Here's how you can add it to the current example:

```
<ControlTemplate x:Key="ButtonTemplate" TargetType="Button">
  <Border BorderBrush="Orange" BorderThickness="3" CornerRadius="10"
    Background="Red">
    <ContentPresenter></ContentPresenter>
  </Border>
</ControlTemplate>
```

Note ContentPresenter isn't the only placeholder that you will use when developing custom templates, although it's the most common. Controls that represent lists and use ItemsControl will use an ItemsPresenter in their control templates, which indicates where the panel that contains the list of items will be placed. Scrollable content inside a ScrollViewer control is represented by a ScrollContentPresenter.

Template Bindings

Although the revised button template respects the content of the button, it ignores most other properties. For example, consider this instance that uses the template:

```
<Button Template="{StaticResource ButtonTemplate}" Content="A Templated Button"
 Margin="10" Padding="20"></Button>
```

This markup gives the button a Margin value of 10 and a Padding of 20. The element that holds the button is responsible for paying attention to the Margin property. However, the Padding property is ignored, leaving the contents of your button scrunched up against the sides. The problem here is the fact that the Padding property doesn't have any effect unless you specifically use it in your template. In other words, it's up to your template to retrieve the padding value and use it to insert some extra space around your content.

Fortunately, Silverlight has a feature that's designed exactly for this purpose: *template bindings*. By using a template binding, your control template can pull out a value from the control to which you're applying the template. In this example, you can use a template binding to retrieve the value of the Padding property and use it to create a margin around the ContentPresenter:

```
<ControlTemplate x:Key="ButtonTemplate" TargetType="Button">
  <Border BorderBrush="Orange" BorderThickness="3" CornerRadius="10"
   Background="Red">
    <ContentPresenter Margin="{TemplateBinding Padding}">
    </ContentPresenter>
  </Border>
</ControlTemplate>
```

This achieves the desired effect of adding some space between the border and the content. Figure 11-3 shows your modest new button.

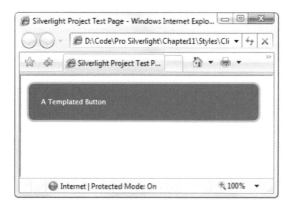

Figure 11-3. *A button with a customized control template*

■**Note** Template bindings are similar to ordinary data bindings (which you'll consider in Chapter 14), but they're lighter weight because they're specifically designed for use in a control template. They only support one-way data binding (in other words, they can pass information from the control to the template but not the other way around).

It turns out that there are quite a few details that you need to set in the ContentPresenter if you want to fully respect the properties of the Button class. For example, you need additional bindings if you want to get details like text alignment, text wrapping, and so on. In fact, buttons use a default control template that includes a ContentPresenter like this:

```
<ContentPresenter
 Content="{TemplateBinding Content}"
 ContentTemplate="{TemplateBinding ContentTemplate}"
 HorizontalContentAlignment="{TemplateBinding HorizontalContentAlignment}"
 Padding="{TemplateBinding Padding}"
 TextAlignment="{TemplateBinding TextAlignment}"
 TextDecorations="{TemplateBinding TextDecorations}"
 TextWrapping="{TemplateBinding TextWrapping}"
 VerticalContentAlignment="{TemplateBinding VerticalContentAlignment}"
 Margin="4,5,4,4">
</ContentPresenter>
```

The template binding for the Content property plays a key role—it extracts the content from the control and displays it in the ContentPresenter. However, this template binding is set implicitly. For that reason, you don't need to include it in your markup.

The only way you can anticipate what template bindings are needed is to check the default control template, as you'll see a bit later in this chapter (in the section "The Parts and States Model"). But in many cases, leaving out template bindings isn't a problem. In fact, you don't need to bind a property if you don't plan to use it or don't want it to change your template.

■ **Note** Template bindings support the Silverlight change-monitoring infrastructure that's built into all dependency properties. That means that if you modify a property in a control, the template takes it into account automatically. This detail is particularly useful when you're using animations that change a property value repeatedly in a short space of time.

Setting Templates Through Styles

Template bindings aren't limited to the ContentPresenter. In fact, you can use them anywhere in a control template. Consider the current button example, which hard-codes the red background in the Border element. Here's how you would use a template binding to set this detail:

```
<Border BorderBrush="Orange" BorderThickness="3" CornerRadius="10"
 Background="{TemplateBinding Background}">
```

This raises an obvious design question. Is it better to hard-code the color to preserve the default appearance of your customized button, or use a template binding to make it more flexible?

In this case, there's a compromise that lets you do both—you can combine templates with styles. The basic idea is to use style rules to set your template *and* set default values. Here's an example:

```
<Style x:Key="ButtonStyle" TargetType="Button">
  <Setter Property="Background" Value="Red"></Setter>
  <Setter Property="Template">
```

```
        <Setter.Value>
          <ControlTemplate TargetType="Button">
            <Border BorderBrush="Orange" BorderThickness="3" CornerRadius="10"
            Background="{TemplateBinding Background}">
              <ContentPresenter Margin="{TemplateBinding Padding}">
              </ContentPresenter>
            </Border>
          </ControlTemplate>
        </Setter.Value>
      </Setter>
</Style>
```

It's up to you whether you define the ControlTemplate inline (as in this example), or as a separate resource, as shown here:

```
<Style x:Key="ButtonStyle" TargetType="Button">
  <Setter Property="Background" Value="Red"></Setter>
  <Setter Property="Template" Value="{StaticResource ButtonTemplate}"></Setter>
</Style>
```

It's also useful to combine styles and templates if you need to set properties that aren't exposed by the ContentPresenter or the container elements in your control template. In the current example, you'll notice that there are no bindings that pass along the foreground color or font details of the button. That's because these properties (Foreground, FontFamily, Font-Size, FontWeight, and so on) support *property inheritance*. When you set those values on a higher-level element (like the Button class) they cascade down to contained elements (like the TextBlock inside the button). The ContentPresenter itself doesn't provide any of these proper-ties, because it doesn't need to. They flow from the control to the content inside, skipping right over the ContentPresenter.

In some cases you'll want to change the inherited property values to better suit your cus-tom control template. For instance, in the current example it's important to set white as the foreground color, because white text stands out better against the button's colored back-ground. However, the standard font color is inherited from the containing Silverlight page, and it's black. Furthermore, you can't set the color through the ContentPresenter, because it doesn't offer the Foreground property. The solution is to combine the control template with a style setter that applies the white text:

```
<Style x:Key="ButtonStyle" TargetType="Button">
  <Setter Property="Foreground" Value="White"></Setter>
  <Setter Property="Background" Value="Red"></Setter>
  <Setter Property="Template" Value="{StaticResource ButtonTemplate}"></Setter>
</Style>
```

This approach gives you convenience and flexibility. If you take no extra steps, you auto-matically get the customized red background and white text. However, you also have the flexibility to create a new style that changes the color scheme but uses the existing control template, which can save a great deal of work.

Reusing Colors

As you've seen, flexible control templates can be influenced by control properties, which can be set through style rules. However, Silverlight applications rarely change just a single control at a time. Most use an entire set of custom control templates to change the appearance of all Silverlight's common controls. In this situation, you need a way to share certain details (such as colors) between the controls.

The easiest way to implement this sharing is to pull hard-coded values out of styles and control templates and define them as separate resources, like this:

```
<SolidColorBrush x:Key="BackgroundBrush" Color="Red"></SolidColorBrush>
```

You can then use these resources in your styles and control templates.

```
<Style x:Key="ButtonStyle" TargetType="Button">
  <Setter Property="Foreground" Value="White"></Setter>
  <Setter Property="Background" Value="{StaticResource BackgroundBrush}"></Setter>
  <Setter Property="Template" Value="{StaticResource ButtonTemplate}"></Setter>
</Style>
```

This allows you to keep the same template, but use a different border color simply by adding a resource with the right name. However, the drawback is that this approach can complicate your design.

For even greater flexibility, you can define your colors as separate resources, and then use them in brush resources, as shown here:

```
<Color x:Key="BackgroundColor">#FF800000</Color>
<SolidColorBrush x:Key="ButtonBorderBrush"
 Color="{StaticResource BackgroundColor"></SolidColorBrush>
```

This two-step approach allows you to reuse a color scheme in a variety of different ways (for example, in solid fills and in gradient brushes), without duplicating the color information in your markup. If you apply this pattern carefully, you'll be able to change the color scheme of your entire application by modifying a single set of color resources.

■ **Note** When defining a color as a resource, the content inside must be a color name or a hexadecimal HTML color code (as shown in the previous example). Unfortunately, you can't declare a color in XAML using the red, green, and blue components.

The Parts and States Model

If you try out the button that you created in the previous section, you'll find it's a major disappointment. Essentially, it's nothing more than a rounded red rectangle—as you move the mouse over it or click it, there's no visual feedback. The button simply lies there inert. (Of course, the Click event still fires when you click it, but that's small consolation.) In WPF, you'd fix this problem with triggers. But in Silverlight triggers aren't supported, and you need to include specially named elements and animations in your control template.

To understand how to make a template that can plug into the back-end code that a control uses, you need to study the Silverlight documentation. Online, you can view http://msdn.microsoft.com/en-us/library/cc278075(VS.95).aspx, which takes you to the Control Styles and Templates section. In this topic, you'll find a separate section that details the default templates for each control. There's one problem—the templates are intimidatingly huge.

To break a template down into manageable pieces, you need to understand the parts and states model, which is how Silverlight templates are organized. *Parts* are the named elements that a control expects to find in a template. *States* are the named animations that are applied at specific times.

If your control template lacks a specific part or state, it usually won't cause an error. Instead, best design practices state that the control should degrade gracefully, and ignore the missing information. However, if that part or state represents a key ingredient that's required for some part of the control's core functionality, the control may not work as expected (or at all). For example, this is why you lose the mouse-over behavior in the super-simple button template shown in the previous example.

The obvious question is this: How do you know what parts and states your control template needs to supply? There are two avenues. First, you can look at the documentation that was described in the previous section. Each control-specific page lists the parts and states that are required for that template, in two separate tables. Figure 11-4 shows an example for the Button control. Like many controls, the Button requires certain states but no specific named parts, so you'll see just one table.

Figure 11-4. *The named states for the Button class*

Your other option is to use reflection in code to examine the control class. Each part is represented with a separate TemplatePart attribute applied to the class declaration. Each state is represented with a separate TemplateVisualState attribute. You'll take a closer look at these attributes in the following sections.

Understanding States with the Button Control

If you look at the declaration for the Button class (or the documentation shown in Figure 11-4), you'll discover that you need to supply six states to create a complete, well-rounded button:

Here are the six states for the Button class:

```
[TemplateVisualState(Name="Normal", GroupName="CommonStates")]
[TemplateVisualState(Name="MouseOver", GroupName="CommonStates")]
[TemplateVisualState(Name="Pressed", GroupName="CommonStates")]
[TemplateVisualState(Name="Disabled", GroupName="CommonStates")]
[TemplateVisualState(Name="Unfocused", GroupName="FocusStates")]
[TemplateVisualState(Name="Focused", GroupName="FocusStates")]
public class Button : ButtonBase
{ ... }
```

States are placed together in *groups*. Groups are mutually exclusive, which means a control has one state in each group. For example, the button has two state groups: CommonStates and FocusStates. At any given time, the button has one of the states from the CommonStates group *and* one of the states from the FocusStates group.

For example, if you tab over to the button, its states will be Normal (from CommonStates) and Focused (from FocusStates). If you then move the mouse over the button, its states will be MouseOver (from CommonStates) and Focused (from FocusStates). Without state groups, you'd have trouble dealing with this situation. You'd either be forced to make some states dominate over others (so a button in the MouseOver state would lose its focus indicator) or you'd need to create many more states (like FocusedNormal, UnfocusedNormal, Focused-MouseOver, UnfocusedMouseOver, and so on).

To define state groups, you must add a VisualStateManager.VisualStates group in the root element of your control template, as shown here:

```
<ControlTemplate x:Key="ButtonTemplate" TargetType="Button">
  <Grid>
    <VisualStateManager.VisualStateGroups>
      ...
    </VisualStateManager.VisualStateGroups>

    <Border x:Name="ButtonBorder" BorderBrush="Orange" BorderThickness="3"
     CornerRadius="15">

      <Border.Background>
        <SolidColorBrush x:Name="ButtonBackgroundBrush" Color="Red" />
      </Border.Background>
```

```
        <ContentPresenter ... />
      </Border>
  </Grid>
</ControlTemplate>
```

In order to add the VisualStateManager element to your template, you need to use a layout panel. This layout panel will hold both the visuals for your control and the VisualState-Manager, which is invisible. Like the resources you first learned about in Chapter 2, the VisualStateManager simply defines objects—in this case, storyboards with animations—that the control can use at the appropriate time.

Usually, you'll add a Grid at the root level of your template. In the button example, a Grid holds the VisualStateManager element and the Border element that renders the actual button.

Inside the VisualStateGroups element, you can create the state groups using appropriately named VisualStateGroup elements. In the case of the button, there are two state groups:

```
<VisualStateManager.VisualStateGroups>
  <VisualStateGroup x:Name="CommonStates">
    ...
  </VisualStateGroup>

  <VisualStateGroup x:Name="FocusStates">
    ...
  </VisualStateGroup>
</VisualStateManager.VisualStateGroups>
```

Once you've added the VisualStateManager and the VisualStateGroup elements, you're ready to add a VisualState element for each state. You can add all the states that the control supports (as identified by the documentation and the TemplateVisualState attributes), or you can supply only those that you choose to use. For example, if you want to create a button that provides a mouse-over effect, you simply need to add the MouseOver state (which applies the effect) and the Normal state (which returns the button to its normal appearance). Here's an example that defines these two states:

```
<VisualStateManager.VisualStateGroups>
  <VisualStateGroup x:Name="CommonStates">
    <VisualState x:Name="MouseOver">
      ...
    </VisualState>

    <VisualState x:Name="Normal">
      ...
    </VisualState>
  </VisualStateGroup>

  <VisualStateGroup x:Name="FocusStates">
    ...
  </VisualStateGroup>
</VisualStateManager.VisualStateGroups>
```

Each state corresponds to a storyboard with one or more animations. If these storyboards exist, they're triggered at the appropriate times. For example, when the user moves the mouse over the button, you might want to use an animation to perform one of the following tasks:

- **Show a new visual.** To do this, you need to change the Opacity property of an element in the control template so it springs into view.

- **Change the shape or position.** You can use a TranslateTransform to tweak the positioning of an element (for example, offsetting it slightly to give the impression that the button's been pressed). You can use the ScaleTransform or RotateTransform to twiddle the element's appearance slightly as the user moves the mouse over it.

- **Change the lighting or coloration.** To do this, you need an animation that acts on the brush that you use to paint the background. You can use a ColorAnimation to simply change colors in a SolidBrush, but more advanced effects are possible by animating more complex brushes. For example, you can change one of the colors in a Linear-GradientBrush (which is what the default button control template does), or you can shift the center point of a RadialGradientBrush.

Tip Some advanced lighting effects use multiple layers of transparent elements. In this case, your animation simply modifies the opacity of one layer to let other layers show through.

Figure 11-5 shows an example of a button that uses customized state animations to change its background color when the user moves the mouse over it.

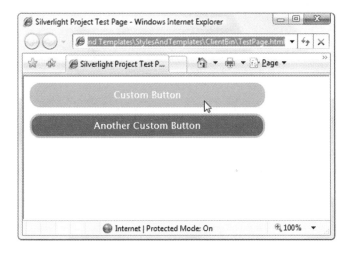

Figure 11-5. *Animated effects in a custom button template*

Here's the markup that does the trick:

```
<VisualStateManager.VisualStateGroups>
  <VisualStateGroup x:Name="CommonStates">
    <VisualState x:Name="MouseOver">
      <Storyboard>
        <ColorAnimation Duration="0:0:0"
          Storyboard.TargetName="ButtonBackgroundBrush"
          Storyboard.TargetProperty="Color" To="Orange" />
      </Storyboard>
    </VisualState>

    <VisualState x:Name="Normal">
      <Storyboard>
        <ColorAnimation Duration="0:0:0"
          Storyboard.TargetName="ButtonBackgroundBrush"
          Storyboard.TargetProperty="Color" />
      </Storyboard>
    </VisualState>
  </VisualStateGroup>
</VisualStateManager.VisualStateGroups>
```

Here, the MouseOver state applies a new, hard-coded color using a ColorAnimation. The Normal state uses a ColorAnimation with no set color, which means the animation simply reverts to the color that was set initially.

HARD-CODING ANIMATION VALUES

You'll notice that this example has a hard-coded background color (Orange). It's also possible to pull details out of other properties and apply them to your animations using the TemplateBinding extension you saw earlier. However, this refactoring isn't necessary. As a general rule of thumb, it's acceptable for a customized control template to have hard-coded details like colors, fonts, and margins, because each template represents a specific, customized visual "look."

When you create the default control template for a new custom control, it's much more important to make sure that the template is flexible. In this situation, control consumers should be able to customize the control's appearance by setting properties, and they shouldn't be forced to supply a whole new control template if only minor modifications are required. You'll learn more about creating a default control template later in this chapter, in the section "Creating Templates for Custom Controls."

Showing a Focus Cue

In the previous example, you used the Normal and MouseOver states from the CommonStates group to control how the button looks when the mouse moves overtop. You can also add the Pressed and Disabled states to customize your other two alternatives. These four states are mutually exclusive—if the button is pressed, the MouseOver state no longer applies, and if the button is disabled, all the other states are ignored no matter what the user does with the mouse. (There's a quirk here. If you don't supply a state animation, the previous animation will keep working. For example, if you don't supply a Pressed state animation, the MouseOver state animation will stay active when the button is pressed.)

As you saw earlier, the button actually has two groups of states. Along with the four CommonStates are two FocusStates, which allows the button to be focused or unfocused. The CommonStates and FocusStates are independent, which means the buttons can be focused or unfocused no matter what's taking place with the mouse. Of course, there may be exceptions depending on the internal logic in the control. For example, a disabled button won't ever get the keyboard focus, so the Focused state will never apply when the common state is Disabled.

Many controls use a focus cue to indicate when they have focus. In the control template for the button, the focus cue is a Rectangle with a dotted border. The focus cue is placed over-top of the button surface using a Grid, which holds both the focus cue and the button border in the same cell. The animations in the FocusStates group simply show or hide the focus rectangle by adjusting its Opacity.

```
<Grid>
  <VisualStateManager.VisualStateGroups>
    <VisualStateGroup x:Name="FocusStates">
      <VisualState x:Name="Focused">
        <Storyboard>
          <DoubleAnimation Duration="0" Storyboard.TargetName="FocusVisualElement"
            Storyboard.TargetProperty="Opacity" To="1" />
        </Storyboard>
      </VisualState>

      <VisualState x:Name="Unfocused">
        <Storyboard>
          <DoubleAnimation Duration="0" Storyboard.TargetName="FocusVisualElement"
            Storyboard.TargetProperty="Opacity" To="0" />
        </Storyboard>
      </VisualState>
    </VisualStateGroup>
    ...
  </VisualStateManager.VisualStateGroups>

  <Border x:Name="ButtonBorder" ...>
    <ContentPresenter ... />
  </Border>

  <Rectangle x:Name="FocusVisualElement" Stroke="Black" Margin="8" Opacity="0"
    StrokeThickness="1" StrokeDashArray="1 2"></Rectangle>
</Grid>
```

Now the button will show the focus cue when it has the keyboard focus. Figure 11-6 shows an example with two buttons that use the same control template. The first button shows the focus cue.

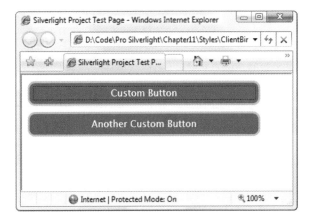

Figure 11-6. *Focus in a custom button template*

You should take care to avoid animating the same properties in different state groups. For example, if you animate the background color in the MouseOver state (which is in the CommonStates group), you should not animate the background color in the Focused state (which is in the FocusStates group). If you do, the result will depend on the order that the control applies its states. For example, if the button applies the state from the FocusStates group first and then the state from the CommonStates group, your Focused state animation will be active for just a split second before being replaced by the competing MouseOver state.

Transitions

The button shown in the previous example uses zero-length state animations. As a result, the color change happens instantly when the mouse moves overtop.

You could lengthen the duration to create a more gradual color blending effect. Here's an example that fades the new color in over a snappy 0.2 seconds:

```
<VisualStateManager.VisualStateGroups>
  <VisualStateGroup x:Name="CommonStates">
    <VisualState x:Name="MouseOver">
      <Storyboard>
        <ColorAnimation Duration="0:0:0.2" ... />
      </Storyboard>
    </VisualState>

    ...
  </VisualStateGroup>
</VisualStateManager.VisualStateGroups>
```

Although this works, the concept isn't quite right. Technically, each visual state is meant to represent the appearance of the control while it's in that state (not including the transition that's used to get *into* that state). Ideally, a visual state animation should be either a zero-length animation like the ones shown earlier or a *steady-state* animation—an animation that repeats itself one or more times. For example, a button that glimmers when you move the mouse over it uses a steady-state animation.

If you want an animated effect to signal when the control switches from one state to another, you should use a *transition* instead. A transition is simply an animation that starts from the current state and ends at the new state. One of the advantages of the transition model is that you don't need to create the storyboard for this animation. Instead, Silverlight creates the animation you need automatically.

■**Note** Controls are smart enough to skip transition animations when the controls begin in a certain state. For example, consider the CheckBox control, which has an Unchecked state and a Checked state. You might decide to use an animation to fade the checkmark in gracefully when the checkbox is checked. If you add the fade-in effect to the Checked state animation, it will apply when you show a checked checkbox for the first time. (For example, if you have a page with three checked checkboxes, all three checkmarks will fade in when the page first appears.) However, if you add the fade-in effect through a transition, it will only be used when the user clicks the checkbox to change its state. It won't apply when the control is shown for the first time, which makes more sense.

The Default Transition

Transitions apply to state groups. When defining a transition, you must add it to the Visual-StateGroup.Transitions collection. The simplest type of transition is a *default transition*, which applies to all the state changes for that group. To create the default transition, you simply need to add a VisualTransition element and set the GeneratedDuration property to set the length of the transition effect. Here's an example:

```
<VisualStateManager.VisualStateGroups>
  <VisualStateGroup x:Name="CommonStates">
    <VisualStateGroup.Transitions>
      <VisualTransition GeneratedDuration="0:0:0.2" />
    </VisualStateGroup.Transitions>

    <VisualState x:Name="MouseOver">
      <Storyboard>
        <ColorAnimation Duration="0:0:0"
         Storyboard.TargetName="ButtonBackgroundBrush"
         Storyboard.TargetProperty="Color" To="Orange" />
      </Storyboard>
    </VisualState>

    <VisualState x:Name="Normal">
      <Storyboard>
        <ColorAnimation Duration="0:0:0"
```

```
            Storyboard.TargetName="ButtonBackgroundBrush"
            Storyboard.TargetProperty="Color" />
        </Storyboard>
    </VisualStateGroup>
</VisualStateManager.VisualStateGroups>
```

Now, whenever the button changes from one of the common states to another, the default 0.2 second transition kicks in. That means when the user moves the mouse over the button and it enters the MouseOver state, the new color will fade in over 0.2 seconds, even though the MouseOver state animation has a zero length. Similarly, when the user moves the mouse off the button, it will blend back to its original color over 0.2 seconds.

Essentially, a transition is an animation that takes you from one state to another. The VisualStateManager can create a transition animation as long as your state animations use one of the following types:

- ColorAnimation or ColorAnimationUsingKeyFrames

- PointAnimation or PointAnimationUsingKeyFrames

- DoubleAnimation or DoubleAnimationUsingKeyFrames

The button example works because the Normal and MouseOver states use a color animation, which is one of the supported types. If you used something else—say, an ObjectAnimationUsingKeyFrames—the transition won't have any effect. Instead, the old value will stay in place, the transition will run out its duration, and then the new value will snap in.

Note In some cases, you'll have a state that uses several animations. In this situation, all the animations that use supported types will be animated by the transition. Any unsupported types will snap in at the end of the transition.

From and To Transitions

A default transition is convenient, but it's a one-size-fits-all solution that's not always suitable. For example, you might want a button to transition to the MouseOver state over 0.2 seconds, but return instantly to the Normal state when the mouse moves away. To set this up, you need to define multiple transitions, and you need to set the From and To properties to specify when the transition will come into effect.

For example, if you have these transitions:

```
<VisualStateGroup x:Name="CommonStates">
  <VisualStateGroup.Transitions>
    <VisualTransition To="MouseOver" GeneratedDuration="0:0:0.5" />
    <VisualTransition From="MouseOver" GeneratedDuration="0:0:0.1" />
  </VisualStateGroup.Transitions>
```

the button will switch into the MouseOver state in 0.5 seconds, and it will leave the Mouse-Over state in 0.1 seconds. There is no default transition, so any other state changes will happen instantly.

This example shows transitions that apply when entering specific states and transitions that apply when leaving specific states. You can also use the To and From properties in conjunction to create even more specific transitions that only apply when moving between two specific states. When applying transitions, Silverlight looks through the collection of transitions to find the most specific one that applies, and uses only that one. For example, when the mouse moves over a button the VisualStateManager, it searches for states in this order, stopping when it finds a match:

1. A transition with `From="Normal"` and `To="MouseOver"`

2. A transition with `To="MouseOver"`

3. A transition with `From="Normal"`

4. The default transition

If there's no default transition, it switches between the two states immediately.

Transitioning to a Steady State

So far, you've seen how transitions work with zero-length state animations. However, it's equally possible to create a control template that uses transitions to move between steady-state animations—looping animations that are repeated multiple times. To understand what happens, you simply need to realize that a transition to a steady-state animation will move from the current property value to the *starting* property value of the steady-state animation.

For example, imagine you want to create a button that pulses steadily when the mouse is overtop. As with all steady-state animations, you need to set the RepeatBehavior property to a number of repetitions you want, or use Forever to loop indefinitely (as in this example). Depending on the data type, you may also need to set the AutoReverse property to true. For example, with a color animation you need to use automatic reversal to return to the original color before repeating the animation. With a key frame animation, this extra step isn't necessary because you can animate from the last key frame at the end of the animation to the first key frame of a new iteration.

Here's the steady-state animation for the pulsing button:

```
<VisualState x:Name="MouseOver">
  <Storyboard>
    <ColorAnimation Duration="0:0:0.4" Storyboard.TargetName="ButtonBackgroundBrush"
      Storyboard.TargetProperty="Color" From="DarkOrange" To="Orange"
      RepeatBehavior="Forever" AutoReverse="True" />
  </Storyboard>
</VisualState>
```

It's not necessary to use a transition with this button—after all, you might want the pulsing effect to kick in immediately. But if you do want to provide a transition, it will occur before the pulsing begins. Consider a standard transition like this one:

```
<VisualStateGroup.Transitions>
  <VisualTransition From="Normal" To="MouseOver" GeneratedDuration="0:0:1" />
</VisualStateGroup.Transitions>
```

This takes the button from its current color (Red) to the starting color of the steady-state animation (DarkOrange) using a 1-second animation. After that, the pulsing begins.

Custom Transition

All the previous examples have used automatically generated transition animations. They change a property smoothly from its current value to the value set by the new state. However, you might want to define customized transitions that work differently. You may even choose to mix standard transitions with custom transitions that apply only to specific state changes.

To define a custom animation, you simply place a storyboard with one or more animations inside the VisualTransition element. Here's an example that creates an elastic compression effect when the user moves the mouse off a button:

```
<VisualStateGroup.Transitions>
  <VisualTransition To="Normal" From="MouseOver" GeneratedDuration="0:0:0.7">
    <Storyboard>
      <DoubleAnimationUsingKeyFrames Storyboard.TargetName="ScaleTransform"
       Storyboard.TargetProperty="ScaleX">
        <LinearDoubleKeyFrame KeyTime="0:0:0.5" Value="0" />
        <LinearDoubleKeyFrame KeyTime="0:0:0.7" Value="1" />
      </DoubleAnimationUsingKeyFrames>
    </Storyboard>
  </VisualTransition>
</VisualStateGroup.Transitions>
```

Note When using a custom transition, you must still set the VisualTransition.GeneratedDuration property to match the duration of your animation. Without this detail, the VisualStateManager won't be able to use your transition, and it will apply the new state immediately.

This transition uses a key frame animation. The first key frame compresses the button horizontally until it disappears from view, while the second key frame causes it to spring back into sight over a shorter interval of time. The transition animation works by adjusting the scale of this ScaleTransform object, which is defined in the control template:

```
<Grid RenderTransformOrigin="0.5,0.5">
  <Grid.RenderTransform>
    <ScaleTransform x:Name="ScaleTransform" ScaleX="1" />
  </Grid.RenderTransform>
  ...
</Grid>
```

When the transition is complete, the transition animation is stopped, and the animated properties return to their original values (or the values that are set by the current state animation). In this example, the animation returns the ScaleTransform to its initial ScaleX value of 1, so you don't notice any change when the transition animation ends.

It's logical to assume that a custom transition animation like this one replaces the automatically generated transition that the VisualStateManager would otherwise use. However, this isn't necessarily the case. Instead, it all depends whether your custom transition animates the same properties as the VisualStateManager.

If your transition animates the same properties as the new state animation, your transition replaces the automatically generated transition. In the current example, the transition bridges the gap between the MouseOver state and the Normal state. The new state, Normal, uses a zero-length animation to change the button's background color. Thus, if you don't supply a custom animation for your transition, the VisualStateManager will create an animation that smoothly shifts the background color from the old state to the new state.

So what happens if you throw a custom transition into the mix? If you create a custom transition animation that targets the background color, the VisualStateManager will use your animation instead of its default transition animation. However, that's not what happens in this example. Here, the custom transition doesn't modify the color—instead, it animates a transform. For that reason, the VisualStateManager will still generate an automatic animation to change the background color. It will use its automatically generated animation in addition to your custom transition animation, and it will run them both at the same time, giving both the duration that's set on the corresponding VisualTransition object. In this example, that means the new color fades in over 0.7 seconds, and at the same time the custom transition animation is applying the compression effect.

Understanding Parts with the Slider Control

In the parts and states model, the states dominate. Many controls, like the Button, use templates that define multiple state groups but no parts. But in other controls, like the Slider, parts allow you to wire up elements in the control template to key pieces of control functionality.

To understand how parts work, you need to consider a control that uses them. Often parts are found in controls that contain small "working parts." For example, the DatePicker uses parts to identify the drop-down button that opens the calendar display and the text box that shows the currently selected date. The ScrollBar uses parts to delineate the draggable thumb, the track, and the scroll buttons. The Slider uses much the same set of parts, although its scroll buttons are placed over the track, and they're invisible. This allows the user to move the slider by clicking on either side of the track.

A control indicates that it uses a specific part with the TemplatePart attribute. Here are the TemplatePart attributes that decorate the Slider control:

```
[TemplatePart(Name="HorizontalTemplate", Type=typeof(FrameworkElement))]
[TemplatePart(Name="HorizontalTrackLargeChangeIncreaseRepeatButton",
 Type=typeof(RepeatButton))]
[TemplatePart(Name="HorizontalTrackLargeChangeDecreaseRepeatButton",
 Type=typeof(RepeatButton))]
[TemplatePart(Name="HorizontalThumb", Type=typeof(Thumb))]
```

```
[TemplatePart(Name="VerticalTemplate", Type=typeof(FrameworkElement))]
[TemplatePart(Name="VerticalTrackLargeChangeIncreaseRepeatButton",
Type=typeof(RepeatButton))]
[TemplatePart(Name="VerticalTrackLargeChangeDecreaseRepeatButton",
Type=typeof(RepeatButton))]
[TemplatePart(Name="VerticalThumb", Type=typeof(Thumb))]
[TemplateVisualState(Name="Disabled", GroupName="CommonStates")]
[TemplateVisualState(Name="Unfocused", GroupName="FocusStates")]
[TemplateVisualState(Name="MouseOver", GroupName="CommonStates")]
[TemplateVisualState(Name="Focused", GroupName="FocusStates")]
[TemplateVisualState(Name="Normal", GroupName="CommonStates")]
public class Slider : RangeBase
{ ... }
```

The Slider is complicated by the fact that it can be used in two different orientations, which require two separate templates that are coded side by side. Here's the basic structure:

```
<ControlTemplate TargetType="Slider">
  <!-- This Grid groups the two orientations together in the same template.-->
  <Grid>

    <!-- This Grid is used for the horizontal orientation. -->
    <Grid x:Name="HorizontalTemplate">

      ...
    </Grid>

    <!-- This Grid is used for the vertical orientation. -->
    <Grid x:Name="VerticalTemplate">

      ...
    </Grid>


  </Grid>
</ControlTemplate>
```

If Slider.Orientation is Horizontal, the Slider will show the HorizontalTemplate element and hide the VerticalTemplate element (if it exists). Usually, both of these elements are layout containers. In this example, each one is a Grid that contains the rest of the markup for that orientation.

Once you understand that there are two distinct layouts embedded in one control template, you'll realize that there are two sets of template parts to match. In this example, you'll consider a Slider that's always used in horizontal orientation, and so only provides the corresponding horizontal parts—namely, HorizontalTemplate, HorizontalTrackLargeChange-IncreaseRepeatButton, HorizontalTrackLargeChangeDecreaseRepeatButton, and Horizontal-Thumb.

Figure 11-7 shows how these parts work together. Essentially, the thumb sits in the middle, on the track. On the left and right are two invisible buttons that allow you to quickly scroll the thumb to a new value by clicking on one side of the track and holding down the mouse button.

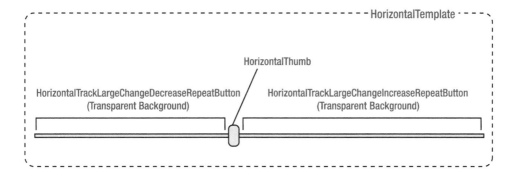

Figure 11-7. *The named parts in the HorizontalTemplate for the Slider*

The TemplatePart attribute indicates the name that the element must have, which is critical because the control code will search for that element by name. It also indicates the element type, which may be something very specific (such as Thumb, in the case of the HorizontalThumb part) or something much more general (for example, FrameworkElement, in the case of the HorizontalTemplate part, which allows you to use any element).

The fact that an element is used as a part in a control template tells you nothing about *how* that element is used. However, there are a few common patterns:

- The control handles events from a part. For example, the Slider code searches for the Thumb when it's initialized and attaches event handlers that react when the Thumb is clicked and dragged.

- The control changes the visibility of a part. For example, depending on the orientation, the Slider shows or hides the HorizontalTemplate and VerticalTemplate.

- If a part is not present, the control will not raise an exception. Depending on the importance of the part, the control may continue to work (if at all possible) or an important part of its functionality may be missing. For example, when dealing with the Slider, you can safely omit the HorizontalTrackLargeChangeIncreaseRepeatButton and Horizontal-TrackLargeChangeDecreaseRepeatButton. Even without these parts, you can still set the Slider value by dragging the thumb. However, if you omit the HorizontalThumb element, you'll end up with a much less useful slider.

Figure 11-8 shows a customized Slider control. Here, a custom control template changes the appearance of the track (using a gently rounded Rectangle element) and the thumb (using a semi-transparent circle).

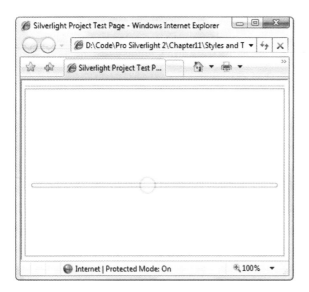

Figure 11-8. *A customized Slider*

To create this effect, your custom template must supply a HorizontalTemplate. In that HorizontalTemplate, you must also include the HorizontalThumb. The TemplatePart attribute makes it clear that you can't replace the Thumb control with another element. However, you can customize the control template of the Thumb to modify its visual appearance, as in this example.

Here's the complete custom control template:

```
<ControlTemplate TargetType="Slider">
  <Grid>
    <Grid x:Name="HorizontalTemplate">
      <Grid.ColumnDefinitions>
        <ColumnDefinition Width="Auto" />
        <ColumnDefinition Width="Auto" />
        <ColumnDefinition Width="*" />
      </Grid.ColumnDefinitions>

      <!-- The track -->
      <Rectangle Stroke="SteelBlue" StrokeThickness="1" Fill="AliceBlue"
        Grid.Column="0" Grid.ColumnSpan="3" Height="7" RadiusX="3" RadiusY="3" />

      <!-- The left RepeatButton, Thumb, and right RepeatButton -->
      <RepeatButton x:Name="HorizontalTrackLargeChangeDecreaseRepeatButton"
        Grid.Column="0" Background="Transparent" Opacity="0"  IsTabStop="False" />

      <Thumb x:Name="HorizontalThumb" Height="28" Width="28" Grid.Column="1">
        <Thumb.Template>
          <ControlTemplate TargetType="Thumb">
```

```
            <Ellipse x:Name="Thumb" Opacity="0.3"  Fill="AliceBlue"
              Stroke="SteelBlue" StrokeThickness="3" Stretch="Fill"></Ellipse>
          </ControlTemplate>
        </Thumb.Template>
      </Thumb>

      <RepeatButton x:Name="HorizontalTrackLargeChangeIncreaseRepeatButton"
        Grid.Column="2" Background="Transparent" Opacity="0"  IsTabStop="False" />

    </Grid>
    <!-- Add VerticalTemplate here if desired. -->
  </Grid>
</ControlTemplate>
```

CREATING SLICK CONTROL SKINS

The examples you've seen in this chapter demonstrate everything you need to know about the parts and states model. However, they lack one thing—eye candy. For example, although you now understand the concepts you need to create a customized button and Slider control, you haven't seen how to *design* the graphics that make a truly attractive control. And though the simple animated effects you've seen here— color changing, pulsing, and scaling—are respectable, they certainly aren't eye-catching. To get more dramatic results, you need to get creative with the graphics and animation skills you've picked up in earlier chapters.

To get an idea of what's possible, you should check out the Silverlight control examples that are available on the Web, including the many different glass and glow buttons that developers have created. You can find one example at http://blogs.msdn.com/corrinab, which provides three different control template sets that address all the common Silverlight controls. After all, if you're going to start restyling one control, it's probably worth adjusting them all to get the consistent, themed look that you want.

Creating Templates for Custom Controls

As you've seen, every Silverlight control is designed to be *lookless*, which means that its visuals (the "look") can be completely redefined. What doesn't change is the control's behavior, which is hardwired into the control class. When you choose to use a control like the Button, you choose it because you want button-like behavior—in other words, an element that presents content and can be clicked to trigger an action.

In some cases, you'll want different behavior, which means you'll need to create a custom control. As with all controls, your custom control will be lookless. Although it will provide a default control template, it won't force you to use that template. Instead, it will allow the control consumer to replace the default template with a fine-tuned custom template.

In the rest of this chapter, you'll learn how you can create a template-driven custom control. This custom control will allow control consumers to supply different visuals, just like the standard Silverlight controls you've used up to this point.

CONTROL CUSTOMIZATION

Custom control development is less common in Silverlight than in many other rich client platforms. That's because Silverlight provides so many other avenues for customization, such as

- **Content controls.** Any control that derives from ContentControl supports nested content. Using content controls, you can quickly create compound controls that aggregate other elements. (For example, you can transform a button into an image button or a list box into an image list.)

- **Styles and control templates.** You can use a style to painlessly reuse a combination of control properties. This means there's no reason to derive a custom control just to set a standard, built-in appearance. Templates go even further, giving you the ability to revamp every aspect of a control's visual appearance.

- **Control templates.** All WPF controls are *lookless*, which means they have hardwired functionality but the appearance is defined separately through the control template. Replace the default template with something new, and you can revamp basic controls such as buttons, checkboxes, radio buttons, and even windows.

- **Data templates.** Silverlight's list controls support data templates, which allow you to create a rich list representation of some type of data object. Using the right data template, you can display each item using a combination of text, images, and even editable controls, all in a layout container of your choosing. You'll learn how in Chapter 14.

If possible, you should pursue these avenues before you decide to create a custom control or another type of custom element. That's because these solutions are simpler, easier to implement, and often easier to reuse.

So, when *should* you create a custom element? Custom elements aren't the best choice when you want to fine-tune the appearance of an element, but they do make sense when you want to change its underlying functionality or design a control that has its own distinct set of properties, methods, and events.

Planning the Expander

One notable omission in Silverlight's control family is the Expander, a basic WPF control that acts like a collapsible panel. When collapsed, the Expander shows nothing more than a header region and an arrow. When the arrow is clicked, the Expander expands to its full size, and reveals a content region inside.

Building an Expander is refreshingly easy (particularly if you follow the WPF example). You need to create a control with two regions (the header and the collapsible content), along with animations that expand and collapse the content region. Ideally, you'll create a carefully structured control template that allows others to restyle the custom Expander with different visuals.

Figure 11-9 shows the Expander that's developed in the following sections.

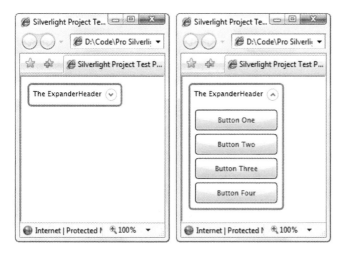

Figure 11-9. *Expanding and collapsing a content region*

Creating the Solution

Although you can develop a custom Silverlight control in the same assembly that holds your application, it's better to place it in a separate assembly. This approach allows you to refine, revise, and debug your control without affecting the application. It also gives you the option of using the same control with different Silverlight applications.

As you learned in Chapter 6, you can create Silverlight class library applications in much the same way that you create class library applications for the full .NET Framework. To add a Silverlight class library project to an existing solution that already holds a Silverlight application, choose File ➤ Add ➤ New Project. Then, choose the Silverlight Class Library project, choose the name and location, and click OK. Now you're ready to begin designing your custom control.

Starting the Expander Class

When stripped down to its bare bones, the Expander is surprisingly simple. It's made up of a collapsible content region and a header region that's displayed above the content (although the exact placement of the header region is configurable if you supply a new template). The user can fill the content and header region with any element (including a layout container that contains an assortment of elements). Additionally, the header region contains the all-important button that allows the user to collapse the content out of sight or expand it into view.

Although you could create the control by deriving directly from the base Control class, the ContentControl gives a bit of a head start. The ContentControl is designed to hold one piece of arbitrary content, and it already includes the Content property, which the Expander can use for its expandable content region:

```
public class Expander : ContentControl
{...}
```

However, it's up to you to add a similar Header property that can hold the element that will be placed in the header region. As with almost all of the properties in a Silverlight element, the Header property must be declared as a dependency property.

As you learned in Chapter 4, defining a dependency property is a two-part process. First, you need a static definition that records some metadata about the property—namely, its name, its type, the type of the containing class, and an optional callback that will be triggered when the property changes. Here's what the Expander uses to define its HeaderContent property:

```
public static readonly DependencyProperty HeaderContentProperty =
  DependencyProperty.Register("HeaderContent", typeof(object),
  typeof(Expander), null);
```

Next, you need to add a traditional .NET property procedure that calls the base GetValue() and SetValue() methods to actually change the dependency property. Here's the property procedure implementation for the HeaderContent property:

```
public object HeaderContent
{
    get { return (object)GetValue(HeaderContentProperty); }
    set { SetValue(HeaderContentProperty, value); }
}
```

There's just one more essential property to add: IsExpanded. This property keeps track of the current state of the content region (collapsed or visible), and allows the control consumer to expand or collapse it programmatically.

```
public static readonly DependencyProperty IsExpandedProperty =
  DependencyProperty.Register("IsExpanded", typeof(bool), typeof(Expander),
  new PropertyMetadata(true));

public bool IsExpanded
{
    get { return (bool)GetValue(IsExpandedProperty); }
    set {
        SetValue(IsExpandedProperty, value);
    }
}
```

The Expander doesn't need many more properties, because it inherits virtually everything it needs from the ContentControl class. One exception is the CornerRadius property. Although the ContentControl includes BorderBrush and BorderThickness properties, which you can use to draw a border around the Expander, it lacks the CornerRadius property for rounding square edges into a gentler curve, as the Border element does. Implementing the same effect in the Expander is easy, provided you add the CornerRadius property and use it to configure a Border element in the Expander's default control template.

```
public static readonly DependencyProperty CornerRadiusProperty =
  DependencyProperty.Register("CornerRadius", typeof(CornerRadius),
  typeof(Expander), null);

public CornerRadius CornerRadius
{
    get { return (CornerRadius)GetValue(CornerRadiusProperty); }
    set { SetValue(CornerRadiusProperty, value); }
}
```

Adding the Default Style with Generic.xaml

Custom controls suffer from a chicken-and-egg and dilemma. You can't write the code in the control class without thinking about the type of control template you'll use. But you can't create the control template until you know how your control works.

The solution is to build both the control class and the default control template at the same time. The control class can be placed in any code file template in your Silverlight class library. The control template must be placed in a file named *generic.xaml*. If your class library contains multiple controls, all of their default templates must be placed in the same generic.xaml file. To add it, follow these steps:

1. Right-click the class library project in the Solution Explorer and choose Add ➤ New Folder.

2. Name the new folder Themes.

3. Right-click the Themes folder and choose Add ➤ New Item.

4. In the Add New Item dialog box, pick the XML file template, enter the name generic.xaml, and click Add.

The generic.xaml file holds a resource dictionary with styles for your custom controls. You must add one style for each custom control. And as you've probably guessed, the style must set the Template property of the corresponding control to apply the default control template.

■**Note** The generic.xaml file is placed in a folder named Themes for consistency with WPF, which takes the Windows theme settings into account. Silverlight keeps the Themes folder, even though it does not have a similar mechanism.

For example, consider the Silverlight project and class library combination shown in Figure 11-10. The ExpanderControl project is the class library with the custom control, and the ExpanderTest project is the Silverlight application that uses it.

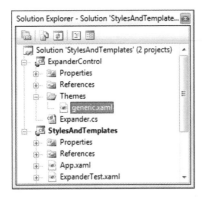

Figure 11-10. *A Silverlight application and class library*

In the generic.xaml file, you need to declare a resource dictionary. You then need to map the project namespace to an XML namespace prefix, so you can access your custom control in your markup (as you first saw in Chapter 2). In this example, the project namespace is ExpanderControl and the assembly is named ExpanderControl.dll (as you would expect based on the project name).

```
<ResourceDictionary
 xmlns="http://schemas.microsoft.com/client/2007"
 xmlns:x="http://schemas.microsoft.com/winfx/2006/xaml"
 xmlns:local="clr-namespace:ExpanderControl;assembly=ExpanderControl">
  ...
</ResourceDictionary>
```

Notice that when you map the control namespace, you need to include both the project namespace *and* the project assembly name, which isn't the case when you use custom classes inside a Silverlight application. That's because the custom control will be used in other applications, and if you don't specify an assembly, Silverlight will assume that the application assembly is the one that you want.

Inside the resource dictionary, you can define a style for your control. Here's an example:

```
<Style TargetType="local:Expander">
  <Setter Property="Template">
    <Setter.Value>
      <ControlTemplate TargetType="local:Expander">
        ...
      </ControlTemplate>
    </Setter.Value>
  </Setter>
</Style>
```

There's one last detail. In order to tell your control to pick up the default style from the generic.xaml file, you need to set the control's DefaultStyleKey property in the constructor:

```
public Expander()
{
    DefaultStyleKey = typeof(Expander);
}
```

The DefaultStyleKey indicates the type that will be used to look up the style. In this case, the style is defined with the TargetType of Expander, so the DefaultStyleKey must also use the Expander type. In most cases, this is the pattern you'll follow. The only exception is when you are deriving a more specialized control from an existing control class. In this case, you have the option of keeping the original constructor logic, and inheriting the standard style from the base class. For example, if you create a customized Button-derived class with additional functionality, you can use the standard button style and save the trouble of creating a new style. On the other hand, if you do want a different style and a different default control template, you simply need to add the style using the TargetType of the new class, and write a new constructor that sets the DefaultStyleKey property accordingly.

Choosing Parts and States

Now that you have the basic structure in place, you're ready to identify the parts and states that you'll use in the control template.

Clearly, the Expander requires two states:

- **Collapsed.** This is the storyboard that collapses the content region out of sight.

- **Expanded.** This is the storyboard that expands the content region back into view.

In addition, you need two parts:

- **ExpandCollapseButton.** This is the button that, when clicked, expands or collapses the content region. The Expander provides this service by handling the events of the ExpandCollapseButton.

- **Content.** This is the element that contains the collapsible content region.

Strictly speaking, the Expander control doesn't need to manipulate the content element, and you don't need to include it as a named part. Instead, the state animations can do all the work you need. However, defining the content as a part allows you to go one step further and interact with the content element programmatically. Most usefully, this allows you to explicitly hide the content region when the state changes to Collapsed and show it when the state changes to Expanded. This way, the control will work even if no state animations are defined, in which case the content region will simply pop in and out of existence with no animation.

Explicitly hiding the content element is also useful if your template uses animations that change the appearance of the content region but don't change the amount of space it occupies. For example, imagine you have an animation that crushes the content out of view with a ScaleTransform (as demonstrated later, in the section "Defining the State Animations"). Although this gives the impression that your content is collapsing, the overall size of the Expander won't change, which means it will be left with the original dimensions and some extra blank space. There are two possible solutions to this dilemma. First, you could add a second animation that changes the Height of the Expander at the same time that the content region is being scaled down. This approach works, but it forces you to hard-code pixel sizes in your animations, which isn't very flexible. The alternative solution is to let the Expander solve the problem by explicitly hiding the content region when the collapsing animation is complete. At this point, the Expander will shrink to fit just the header region, the extra space will be reclaimed, and any elements underneath will be bumped up the page.

To advertise the fact that the Expander uses these parts and states, you should apply the TemplatePart attribute to your control class, as shown here:

```
[TemplateVisualState(Name = "Collapsed", GroupName="ViewStates")]
[TemplateVisualState(Name = "Expanded", GroupName = "ViewStates")]
[TemplatePart(Name = "Content", Type = typeof(FrameworkElement))]
[TemplatePart(Name = "ExpandCollapseButton", Type = typeof(ToggleButton))]
public class Expander : ContentControl
{ ... }
```

The content element is defined using the FrameworkElement type, which means you can use any Silverlight element for these ingredients. The OpenCloseButtonElement is more restricted—it can only be a ToggleButton or an instance of a ToggleButton-derived class. (As you may remember from Chapter 5, the ToggleButton is a clickable button that can be in one of two states. In the case of the Expander control, the ToggleButton states will correspond to an open or closed content region.)

Tip In order to ensure the best, most flexible template support, use the least-specialized element type that you can. For example, it's better to use FrameworkElement than ContentControl, unless you need some property or behavior that ContentControl provides.

NAMING CONVENTIONS FOR STATES, PARTS, AND STATE GROUPS

The naming conventions for parts and states are fairly straightforward. When naming a part or state, do not include a prefix or suffix—for example, use Collapsed and Content rather than CollapsedState, ContentPart, or ContentElement. The exception is state groups, which should always end with the word *States*, as in View-States.

It also helps to look at similar controls in the Silverlight framework and use the same names. This is especially true if you need to use the states that are commonly defined in the CommonStates group (Normal, MouseOver, Pressed, and Disabled) or the FocusStates group (Focused and Unfocused). Remember, the control consumer must use the exact name. If you create a button-like control that breaks with convention and uses a Clicked state instead of a Pressed state, and the control consumer inadvertently defines a Pressed state, its animation will be quietly ignored.

Starting the Default Control Template

Now you can slot these pieces into the default control template. The root element is a two-row Grid that holds the header area (in the top row) and the content area (in the bottom row). The header area is further subdivided into two columns using a nested Grid. On the left is the actual header content, and on the right is the button for expanding and collapsing the Grid.

To fill in the header and content region, the Expander uses the ContentPresenter. This technique is virtually the same as in the custom button example, except you need two ContentPresenter elements, one for each region in the Grid.

Here's the basic skeleton for the default control template. The named parts are in bold.

```
<ControlTemplate TargetType="local:Expander">
  <Grid>
    <VisualStateManager.VisualStateGroups>
      <!-- Place state animations here. -->
    </VisualStateManager.VisualStateGroups>

    <Border BorderBrush="{TemplateBinding BorderBrush}"
      BorderThickness="{TemplateBinding BorderThickness}"
      CornerRadius="{TemplateBinding CornerRadius}"
      Background="{TemplateBinding Background}">

      <Grid>
        <Grid.RowDefinitions>
          <RowDefinition Height="Auto"></RowDefinition>
          <RowDefinition Height="Auto"></RowDefinition>
        </Grid.RowDefinitions>

        <!-- This the header. -->
        <Grid Margin="3">
          <Grid.ColumnDefinitions>
            <ColumnDefinition Width="Auto"></ColumnDefinition>
            <ColumnDefinition Width="Auto"></ColumnDefinition>
          </Grid.ColumnDefinitions>

          <ContentPresenter
            Content="{TemplateBinding HeaderContent}" Margin="3"></ContentPresenter>

          <ToggleButton Grid.Column="1" x:Name="ExpandCollapseButton"
            Margin="3"></ToggleButton>
        </Grid>

        <!-- This is the content. -->
        <ContentPresenter Grid.Row="1" x:Name="Content"
          Content="{TemplateBinding Content}" Margin="5"></ContentPresenter>
```

```
      </Grid>
    </Border>
  </Grid>
</ControlTemplate>
```

When creating a default control template, it's best to avoid hard-coding details that the control consumer might want to customize. Instead, you need to use template binding expressions. In this example, several properties are set using template binding expressions: BorderBrush, BorderThickness, CornerRadius, Background, HeaderContent, and Content. To set the default value for these properties (and thereby ensure you get the right visual even if the control consumer doesn't set them), you must add additional setters to your control's default style.

The Expand or Collapse Button

The control template shown in the previous example includes a ToggleButton. However, it uses the ToggleButton's default appearance, which makes the ToggleButton look like an ordinary button, complete with the traditional shaded background. This just isn't suitable for the Expander.

Although you can place any content you want inside the ToggleButton, the Expander requires a bit more. It needs to do away with the standard background, and change the appearance of the elements inside depending on the state of the ToggleButton. As you can see earlier in Figure 11-9, the ToggleButton points down when the content region is collapsed, and points up when the content region is expanded, which makes its purpose clearer.

To create this effect, you need to design a custom control template for the ToggleButton. This control template can include the shape elements that draw the arrow you need. In this example, the ToggleButton is drawn with an Ellipse for the circle and a Path for the arrow, both of which are placed in a single-cell Grid.

```
<ToggleButton Grid.Column="1" x:Name="ExpandCollapseButton" Margin="3">
  <ToggleButton.Template>
    <ControlTemplate>
      <Grid>
        <Ellipse Stroke="#FFA9A9A9"  Fill="AliceBlue"  Width="19" Height="19"  />
        <Path RenderTransformOrigin="0.5,0.5" Data="M1,1.5L4.5,5 8,1.5"
         Stroke="#FF666666" StrokeThickness="2"
         HorizontalAlignment="Center" VerticalAlignment="Center">
          <Path.RenderTransform>
            <RotateTransform x:Name="RotateButtonAnimation"></RotateTransform>
          </Path.RenderTransform>
        </Path>
      </Grid>
    </ControlTemplate>
  </ToggleButton.Template>
</ToggleButton>
```

Defining the State Animations

The state animations are the most interesting part of the control template. They're the ingredient that gives the expanding or collapsing behavior. They're also the details that are most likely to be changed if a developer creates a custom template for the Expander.

In the default control template, the animations change the size of the content region, squashing it out of sight when the user clicks the collapse button. There's more than one way to make this happen, but the most obvious approach—modifying the Height of the content element—isn't ideal. It forces you to hard-code pixel sizes, and it gives a graphically unimpressive result.

In Chapter 9, you learned that the solution to many animation challenges is to use a transform, and the Expander is another example of this rule. Rather than shrinking the content region, you can add a ScaleTransform, and shrink that:

```
<ContentPresenter Grid.Row="1" x:Name="Content"
 Content="{TemplateBinding Content}" Margin="5">
  <ContentPresenter.RenderTransform>
    <ScaleTransform x:Name="ContentScaleTransform"></ScaleTransform>
  </ContentPresenter.RenderTransform>
</ContentPresenter>
```

The advantage of this approach is that you'll always know how to restore the Expander to its initial state—you simply need to return the ScaleTransform dimensions to 1.

The content region isn't the only part of the Expander that you need to animate. You must also add a RotateTransform to the Path inside the ToggleButton so that you can rotate the arrow to point up when the content is collapsed:

```
<Path ... >
  <Path.RenderTransform>
    <RotateTransform x:Name="RotateButtonAnimation"></RotateTransform>
  </Path.RenderTransform>
</Path>
```

Here are the animations that shrink and expand the content region and rotate the Toggle-Button arrow:

```
<VisualStateManager.VisualStateGroups>
  <VisualStateGroup x:Name="ViewStates">
    <VisualStateGroup.Transitions>
      <VisualTransition GeneratedDuration="0:0:0.5">
        <!-- This transition bridges the gap between states using an
             automatically generated 0.5 second animation. -->
      </VisualTransition>
    </VisualStateGroup.Transitions>

    <VisualState x:Name="Expanded">
      <Storyboard>
        <DoubleAnimation Storyboard.TargetName="ContentScaleTransform"
         Storyboard.TargetProperty="ScaleY" To="1" Duration="0"></DoubleAnimation>
```

```
            <DoubleAnimation Storyboard.TargetName="RotateButtonTransform"
              Storyboard.TargetProperty="Angle" Duration="0" To="180"></DoubleAnimation>
          </Storyboard>
        </VisualState>

        <VisualState x:Name="Collapsed">
          <Storyboard>
            <DoubleAnimation Storyboard.TargetName="ContentScaleTransform"
              Storyboard.TargetProperty="ScaleY" To="0" Duration="0"></DoubleAnimation>
            <DoubleAnimation Storyboard.TargetName="RotateButtonTransform"
              Storyboard.TargetProperty="Angle" Duration="0" To="0"></DoubleAnimation>
          </Storyboard>
        </VisualState>
      </VisualStateGroup>
```

Notice that all the animations are performed through transitions, which is the correct approach. For example, the Collapsed state uses a zero-length animation to change the ScaleY property to 0 and rotate the arrow 180 degrees. When the Expander switches to the Collapsed state, the default transition applies both of these effects smoothly and gradually over a 0.5-second interval.

Wiring Up the Elements in the Template

Now that you've polished off a respectable control template, you need to fill in the plumbing in the Expander control to make it work.

The trick is a protected method named OnApplyTemplate(), which is defined in the base Control class. This method is called when the control is being initialized. This is the point where the control needs to examine its template and fish out the elements it needs. The exact action a control performs with an element varies—it may set a property, attach an event handler, or store a reference for future use.

To use the template in a custom control, you override the OnApplyTemplate() method. To find an element with a specific name, you call the GetTemplateChild() method (which is inherited from FrameworkElement along with the OnApplyTemplate() method). If you don't find an element that you want to work with, the recommended pattern is to do nothing. Optionally, you can add code that checks that the element, if present, is the correct type and raises an exception if it isn't. (The thinking here is that a missing element represents a conscious opting out of a specific feature, whereas an incorrect element type represents a mistake.)

The OnApplyTemplate() method for the Expander retrieves the ToggleButton and content element, and stores references to them for later use. It also attaches an event handler to the ToggleButton, so it can react when the user clicks to expand or collapse the control, and another event handler to the Completed event at the end of the Collapsed animation, so it can hide the content region completely and reclaim the empty space. Finally, the OnApplyTemplate() method ends by calling a custom method named ChangeVisualState(), which ensures that the control's visuals match its current state.

```
// Keep track of elements you need to manipulate later.
private ToggleButton cmdExpandOrCollapse;
private FrameworkElement contentElement;

public override void OnApplyTemplate()
{
    base.OnApplyTemplate();

    // Look for the ToggleButton.
    cmdExpandOrCollapse = GetTemplateChild("ExpandCollapseButton") as ToggleButton;
    if (cmdExpandOrCollapse != null)
    {
        // Attach an event handler that expands or collapses the content region.
        cmdExpandOrCollapse.Click += cmdExpandCollapseButton_Click;
    }

    // Look for the content element.
    contentElement = GetTemplateChild("Content") as FrameworkElement;
    if (contentElement != null)
    {
        // If there's a Collapsed state animation, attach an event handler that
        // hides the content region when the animation ends.
        VisualState collapsedState = GetTemplateChild("Collapsed") as VisualState;
        if ((collapsedState != null) && (collapsedState.Storyboard != null))
        {
            collapsedState.Storyboard.Completed += collapsedStoryboard_Completed;
        }
    }

    // Update the control to make sure it's in the right state.
    ChangeVisualState(false);
}
```

Tip When calling GetTemplateChild(), you need to indicate the string name of the element you want. To avoid possible errors, you can declare this string as a constant in your control. You can then use that constant in the TemplatePart attribute and when calling GetTemplateChild().

Here's the event handler that allows the user to click the ToggleButton and collapse or expand the content inside the Expander:

```
private void cmdExpandCollapseButton_Click(object sender, RoutedEventArgs e)
{
    IsExpanded = !IsExpanded;
    cmdExpandOrCollapse.IsChecked = IsExpanded;
```

```
    // Change the appearance of the control to match the new state.
    ChangeVisualState(useTransitions);
}
```

And here's the event handler that neatens up when the Expander has finished collapsing, and reclaims any extra space:

```
private void collapsedStoryboard_Completed(object sender, EventArgs e)
{
    contentElement.Visibility = Visibility.Collapsed;
}
```

Fortunately, you don't need to manually trigger the state animations. Nor do you need to create or trigger the transition animations. Instead, to change from one state to another, you simply need to call the static VisualStateManager.GoToState() method. When you do, you pass in a reference to the control object that's changing state, the name of the new state, and a Boolean value that determines whether a transition is shown. This value should be true when it's a user-initiated change (for example, when the user clicks the ToggleButton), but false when it's a property setting (for example, if the markup for your page sets the initial value of the IsExpanded property).

Dealing with all the different states a control supports can become messy. To avoid scattering GoToState() calls throughout your control code, most controls add a custom method like the ChangeVisualState() method in the Expander. This method has the responsibility of applying the correct state in each state group. The code inside uses one if block (or switch statement) to apply the current state in each state group. This approach works because it's completely acceptable to call GoToState() with the name of the current state. In this situation, when the current state and the requested state are the same, nothing happens.

Here's the code for the Expander's version of the ChangeVisualState() method:

```
private void ChangeVisualState(bool useTransitions)
{
    //  Apply the current state from the ViewStates group.
    if (IsExpanded)
    {
        if (contentElement != null) contentElement.Visibility = Visibility.Visible;
        VisualStateManager.GoToState(this, "Expanded", useTransitions);
    }
    else
    {
        VisualStateManager.GoToState(this, "Collapsed", useTransitions);
        if (collapsedState == null)
        {
            // There is no state animation, so just hide the content region
            // immediately.
            if (contentElement != null)
              contentElement.Visibility = Visibility.Collapsed;
        }
    }
}
```

```
    // (If there were other state groups, you would set them now.)
}
```

Usually, you'll call the ChangeVisualState() method (or your equivalent) in the following places:

- After initializing the control at the end of the OnApplyTemplate() method

- When reacting to an event that represents a state change, such as a mouse movement or a click of the ToggleButton

- When reacting to a property change or a method that's triggered through code

Because none of the parts or states are required, the Expander control is remarkably flexible. For example, you can use it without a ToggleButton, and collapse it programmatically (perhaps when the user clicks a different control). Or, you can use the Expander without any animations, and the content region will simply be collapsed and revealed immediately when the Expander sets the Visibility property of the content element.

Using the Expander

Now that you've completed the control template and code for the Expander, you're ready to use it in an application. Assuming you've added the necessary assembly reference, you can then map an XML prefix to the namespace that holds your custom control:

```
<UserControl x:Class="ExpanderTest.Page"
  xmlns:lib="clr-namespace:ExpanderControl;assembly=ExpanderControl" ... >
```

Now you can add instances of the Expander to your page. Here's an example that supplies a simple string for the header (although a full-fledge element is allowed) and uses a StackPanel full of elements for the content region:

```
<lib:Expander Margin="10" HeaderContent="The Expander Header" >
  <lib:Expander.Content>
    <StackPanel>
      <Button Margin="3" Padding="3" Content="Button One"></Button>
      <Button Margin="3" Padding="3" Content="Button Two"></Button>
      <Button Margin="3" Padding="3" Content="Button Three"></Button>
      <Button Margin="3" Padding="3" Content="Button Four"></Button>
    </StackPanel>
  </lib:Expander.Content>
</lib:Expander>
```

This creates the Expander example shown previously in Figure 11-9.

Using a Different Control Template

Custom controls that have been designed properly are extremely flexible. In the case of the Expander, you can supply a new template to change the appearance of the ToggleButton, the placement of the header element and content element animation relative to one another, and the animated effects that are used when collapsing and expanding the content region.

Figure 11-11 shows one such example. Here, the expand button is placed underneath the header, and is drawn as a solid triangle in a square. There's no border around the element, and the content region isn't squashed out of the way when you collapse the Expander—instead, it fades away. Similarly, the arrow above doesn't rotate; it flips around a center line.

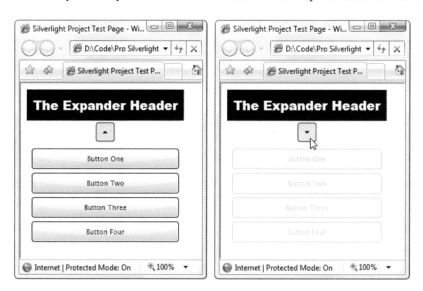

Figure 11-11. *The Expander with a different control template*

Here's the control template used to create Figure 11-11. The ToggleButton details are similar to the previous example, and are omitted. (For the complete markup, refer to the download examples for this chapter.)

```
<ControlTemplate TargetType="lib:Expander">
  <Grid>
    <VisualStateManager.VisualStateGroups>
      <VisualStateGroup x:Name="ViewStates">
        <VisualStateGroup.Transitions>
          <VisualTransition GeneratedDuration="0:0:0.5"></VisualTransition>
        </VisualStateGroup.Transitions>

        <VisualState x:Name="Expanded">
          <Storyboard >
            <DoubleAnimation Storyboard.TargetName="Content"
              Storyboard.TargetProperty="Opacity" To="1" Duration="0:0:0" />
            <DoubleAnimation Storyboard.TargetName="ScaleArrowTransform"
              Storyboard.TargetProperty="ScaleY" Duration="0" To="1" />
          </Storyboard>
        </VisualState>
```

```xml
      <VisualState x:Name="Collapsed">
        <Storyboard>
          <DoubleAnimation Storyboard.TargetName="Content"
            Storyboard.TargetProperty="Opacity" To="0" Duration="0:0:0" />
          <DoubleAnimation Storyboard.TargetName="ScaleArrowTransform"
            Storyboard.TargetProperty="ScaleY" Duration="0" To="-1" />
        </Storyboard>
      </VisualState>
    </VisualStateGroup>
  </VisualStateManager.VisualStateGroups>

  <Grid.RowDefinitions>
    <RowDefinition Height="Auto"></RowDefinition>
    <RowDefinition Height="Auto"></RowDefinition>
    <RowDefinition Height="Auto"></RowDefinition>
  </Grid.RowDefinitions>

  <!-- Header -->
  <Grid Background="Black">
    <ContentControl>
      <ContentControl.Style>
        <Style TargetType="ContentControl">
          <Setter Property="Foreground" Value="White" />
          <Setter Property="FontFamily" Value="Arial Black" />
          <Setter Property="FontSize" Value="20" />
        </Style>
      </ContentControl.Style>

      <ContentPresenter x:Name="HeaderElement" Margin="10"
        Content="{TemplateBinding HeaderContent}"></ContentPresenter>
    </ContentControl>
  </Grid>

  <ToggleButton Grid.Row="1" x:Name="ExpandCollapseButtonElement" Margin="3"
    HorizontalAlignment="Center" Width="30" Height="30">...</ToggleButton>

  <!-- Content -->
  <ContentPresenter Grid.Row="2" x:Name="Content"
    Content="{TemplateBinding Content}" Margin="5"></ContentPresenter>

  </Grid>
</ControlTemplate>
```

Although you could place a formatted TextBlock directly in the header of the Expander, this control template keeps all the formatting details in the control template. That way, your content remains clean, simple, and streamlined. However, in order to get the desired result this example needs one new trick. It wraps the ContentPresenter for the header in two containers. First, a Grid element applies the black background. Then, a ContentControl provides the style that passes the font formatting down to the header text. This is a crafty workaround, because you can't set the font properties directly on the Grid or ContentPresenter, and the ContentControl doesn't have any built-in visuals of its own.

The Last Word

In this chapter, you saw how to use styles to reuse formatting and control templates to make more radical changes. You used the parts and states model to customize a Silverlight control, and saw how you could create a respectable button without being forced to reimplement any core button functionality. These custom buttons support all the normal button behavior—you can tab from one to the next, you can click them to fire an event, and so on. Best of all, you can reuse your button template throughout your application and still replace it with a whole new design at a moment's notice.

So what more do you need to know before you can skin all the Silverlight controls? In order to get the snazzy look you probably want, you might need to spend more time studying the details of Silverlight drawing ad animation. Using the shapes, brushes, and transforms that you've already learned about, you can build sophisticated controls with glass-style blurs and soft glow effects. The secret is in combining multiple layers of shapes, each with a different gradient brush. The best way to get this sort of effect is to learn from the control template examples others have created.

You may also be interested in third-party controls. One impressive example is GOA WinForms, which provides Silverlight elements that duplicate the basic controls from Windows Forms development. (There's also a version of GOA WinForms that provides the same set of controls for Flash applications.) You can find out more at http://community.netikatech.com/demos. Many third-party component developers are also creating their own suites of Silverlight controls (one example is Sapphire by ComponentOne, at http://labs.componentone.com/Sapphire), and many developers are releasing their own open source experiments.

CHAPTER 12

■ ■ ■

Browser Integration

Because Silverlight applications run in their own carefully designed environment, you're insulated from the quirks and cross-platform headaches that traditionally confront developers when they attempt to build rich browser-based applications. This is a tremendous advantage. It means that you can work with an efficient mix of C# code and XAML markup, rather than struggle through a quagmire of HTML, JavaScript, and browser compatibility issues.

However, there are some cases when you'll need to create a web page that isn't just a thin shell around a Silverlight application. Instead, you might want to add Silverlight content to an existing page, and allow the HTML and Silverlight portions of your page to interact.

There are several reasons you might choose to blend the classic browser world with the managed Silverlight environment. Here are some possibilities:

- **Compatibility.** You can't be sure that your visitors will have the Silverlight plug-in installed. If you're building a core part of your website, your need to ensure broad compatibility (with HTML) may trump your desire to use the latest and greatest user interface frills (with Silverlight). In this situation, you might decide to include a Silverlight content region to show non-essential extras alongside the critical HTML content.

- **Legacy web pages.** If you have an existing web page that does exactly what you want, it makes more sense to extend it with a bit of Silverlight pizzazz than to replace it outright. Once again, the solution is to create a page that includes both HTML and Silverlight content.

- **Server-side features.** Some types of tasks require server-side code. For example, Silverlight is a poor fit for tasks that need to access server resources or require high security, which is why it makes far more sense to build a secure checkout process with a server-side programming framework like ASP.NET. However, you can still use Silverlight to display advertisements, video content, product visualizations, and other value-added features that you'll place in the same pages.

In this chapter, you'll consider how you can bridge the gap between Silverlight and the ordinary world of HTML. First, you'll consider how Silverlight can reach out to other HTML elements on the page and manipulate them. Next, you'll consider how Silverlight can fire off JavaScript code, and how JavaScript code can trigger a method in your Silverlight application. Finally, you'll consider an example that blends Silverlight and JavaScript to enhance the browser's Back button, and you'll look at a few more options for overlapping Silverlight content and ordinary HTML elements.

Interacting with HTML Elements

Silverlight includes a set of managed classes that replicate the HTML DOM (document object model) in managed code. These classes allow your Silverlight code to interact with the HTML content on the same page. Depending on the scenario, this interaction might involve reading a control value, updating text, or adding new HTML elements to the page.

The classes you need to perform all these feats are found in the System.Windows.Browser namespace, and are listed in Table 12-1. You'll learn about them in the following sections.

Table 12-1. *The Classes in the System.Windows.Browser Namespace*

Class	Description
HtmlPage	Represents the current HTML page (where the Silverlight control is placed). The HtmlPage class is a jumping-off point for most of the HTML interaction features. It provides members for exploring the HTML elements on the page (the Document property), retrieving browser information (the Browser-Information property), interacting with the current browser window (the Window property), and registering Silverlight methods that you want to make available to JavaScript (the RegisterCreatableType() and RegisterScriptableType() methods).
BrowserInformation	Provides some basic information about the browser that's being used to run your application, including the browser name, version, and operating system. You can retrieve an instance of the BrowserInformation class from the HtmlPage.Browser-Information property.
HtmlDocument	Represents a complete HTML document. You can get an instance of HtmlDocument that represents the current HTML page from the HtmlPage.Document property. You can then use the Html-Document to explore the structure and content of the page (as nested levels of HtmlElement objects).
HtmlElement	Represents any HTML element on the page. You can use methods like SetAttribute() and SetProperty() to manipulate that element. Usually, you'll look up HtmlElement objects in an Html-Document object.
HtmlWindow	Represents the browser window, and provides methods for navigating to a new page or to a different anchor in the current page. You can get an instance of HtmlWindow that holds the current page from the HtmlPage.Window property.
HttpUtility	Provides static methods for a few common HTML-related tasks, including HTML encoding and decoding (making text safe for display in a web page) and URL encoding and decoding (making text safe for use in a URL—for example, as a query string argument).
ScriptableTypeAttribute and ScriptableMemberAttribute	You can use these attributes to decorate classes and methods in your Silverlight application, which will then be callable from JavaScript.
ScriptObject	Represents a JavaScript function that's defined in the page, and allows you to invoke the function from your Silverlight application.

Getting Browser Information

Most of the time, you shouldn't worry about the specific browser that's being used to access your application. After all, one of the key advantages to Silverlight is that it saves the browser-compatibility hassles of ordinary web programming, and allows you to write code that will behave in the same way in every supported environment. However, there are scenarios when you may choose to take a closer look at the browser—for example, when diagnosing an unusual error that could be browser-related.

The browser information that's available in the BrowserInformation class is fairly modest. You're given four string properties that indicate the browser name, version, operating system, and user agent string—a long string that includes technical details about the browser (for example, in Internet Explorer it includes the currently installed versions of the .NET Framework). You can also use the Boolean CookiesEnabled property to determine if the current browser supports cookies and has them enabled (in which case it will be true). You can then read or change cookies through the HtmlPage class.

■**Note** The information you get from the BrowserInformation class depends on how the browser represents itself to the world, but it may not reflect the browser's true identity. Browsers can be configured to impersonate other browsers, and some use this technique by default to ensure broader compatibility. If you write any browser-specific code, make sure you test it with a range of browsers to verify that you're detecting the correct conditions.

Here's some straightforward code that displays all the available browser information:

```
BrowserInformation b = HtmlPage.BrowserInformation;
lblInfo.Text = "Name: " + b.Name;
lblInfo.Text += "\nBrowser Version: " + b.BrowserVersion.ToString();
lblInfo.Text += "\nPlatform: " + b.Platform;
lblInfo.Text += "\nCookies Enabled: " + b.CookiesEnabled;
lblInfo.Text += "\nUser Agent: " + b.UserAgent;
```

Figure 12-1 shows the result.

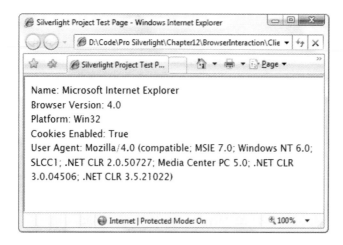

Figure 12-1. *Profiling the browser*

The HTML Window

Silverlight also gives you limited ability to control the browser through the HtmlWindow class. It provides two methods that allow you to trigger navigation: Navigate() and NavigateToBookmark().

Navigate() sends the browser to another page. You can use an overloaded version of the Navigate() method to specify a target frame. When you use Navigate(), you abandon the current Silverlight application. It's the same as if the user had typed in a new URL in the browser's address bar.

NavigateToBookmark() scrolls to a specific bookmark in the current page. A bookmark is an <a> element with an ID (or name), but no target:

```
<a id="myBookmark">...</a>
```

To navigate to a bookmark, you add the number sign (#) and bookmark name to the end of your URL:

```
<a href="page.html#myBookmark">Jump to bookmark</a>
```

The NavigateToBookmark() method raises an interesting possibility. You can use a bookmark to store some state information. Because this state information is part of the URL, it's preserved in the browser history and (if you bookmark a page with Silverlight content) the browser's favorites list.

To understand how you might use this technique, imagine you create a Silverlight application with multiple pages. If the user navigates to a different site and then clicks the Back button to return to the Silverlight page, the application starts from scratch. It makes no difference what page the user was at most recently, because the application will always start on the first page. Similarly, if the user bookmarks the Silverlight page and uses that bookmark to return later on, the user will begin in the same starting place, regardless of where the application was at when the bookmark was created.

One way around this is to store information about the current page as a bookmark. If you're using the navigation technique described in Chapter 6, which uses a static Navigate() method in the App class, you would use this point to store the page details. Here's an example that gets the fully qualified class name of the new user control and adds it to the URL as a bookmark just before the navigation is performed:

```
private Grid rootVisual = new Grid();

public static void Navigate(UserControl newPage)
{
    // Store the new page in the bookmark.
    HtmlPage.Window.NavigateToBookmark(newPage.GetType().FullName);

    // Change the currently displayed page.
    App currentApp = (App)Application.Current;
    currentApp.rootVisual.Children.Clear();
    currentApp.rootVisual.Children.Add(newPage);
}
```

Figure 12-2 shows the URL in the browser after navigating to the second page.

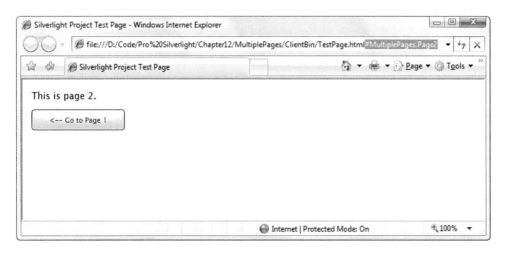

Figure 12-2. *Tracking the current Silverlight page in the URL*

Now, when the application starts up you can check for any information in the bookmark. If the class name is there, you can attempt to create the corresponding user control:

```
private void Application_Startup(object sender, StartupEventArgs e)
{
    this.RootVisual = rootVisual;

    if (String.IsNullOrEmpty(HtmlPage.Window.CurrentBookmark))
    {
        rootVisual.Children.Add(new Page());
```

```
    }
    else
    {
        try
        {
            Type type = this.GetType();
            Assembly assembly = type.Assembly;
            UserControl newPage = (UserControl)assembly.CreateInstance(
                HtmlPage.Window.CurrentBookmark);
            rootVisual.Children.Add(newPage);
        }
        catch
        {
            rootVisual.Children.Add(new Page());
        }
    }
}
```

Keep in mind that this approach assumes that your application doesn't need to prevent users from reaching certain pages at certain times. After all, once the startup page information is in the URL it's trivially easy for a user to change it by hand and cause an error or reach a different page. A more robust approach that requires a bit more code is to use the values from an enumeration to indicate supported startup pages, as described in Chapter 6.

Furthermore, this system doesn't make any attempt to integrate with the browser's history. When the user moves from one page to another in your Silverlight application and you call NavigateToBookmark(), the browser treats this as the same page, and it doesn't add any new items to the history list. If you want a single Silverlight application to create multiple entries in the browser history, you need to go to quite a bit more work. Later in this chapter, you'll see one possible approach.

Note When the user "returns" to a page through a URL bookmark, that page is created from scratch. Thus, this example won't capture other state details, such as any list selection, text box entries, and so on. If these details are important, you can respond to the Application.Exit event, which occurs when the user is leaving the Silverlight application, and use this point to store additional information in isolated storage, as described in Chapter 15.

Inspecting the HTML Document

Retrieving browser information and performing navigation are two relatively straightforward tasks. Life gets a whole lot more interesting when you start peering into the structure of the page that hosts your Silverlight content.

To start your exploration, you use one of two static properties from the HtmlPage class. The Plugin property provides a reference to the <object> element that represents the Silverlight control, as an HtmlElement object. The Document property provides something more interesting—an HtmlDocument object that represents the entire page, with the members set out in Table 12-2.

Table 12-2. *Members of the HtmlDocument Class*

Member	Description
DocumentUri	Returns the URL of the current document as a Uri object.
QueryString	Returns the query string portion of the URL as a single long string that you must parse.
DocumentElement	Provides an HtmlElement object that represents the top-level <html> element in the HTML page.
Body	Provides an HtmlElement object that represents the <body> element in the HTML page.
Cookies	Provides a collection of all the current HTTP cookies. You can read or set the values in these cookies. Cookies provide one easy, low-cost way to transfer information from server-side ASP.NET code to client-side Silverlight code. However, cookies aren't the best approach for storing small amounts of data on the client's computer—isolated storage, which is discussed in Chapter 15, provides a similar feature with better compatibility and programming support.
CurrentBookmark	Returns the optional bookmark portion of the URL string, which can point to a specific anchor on a page. You can use NavigateToBookmark() to move to a different bookmark.
IsReady	Returns true if the browser is idle, or false if it's still downloading the page.
CreateElement()	Creates a new HtmlElement object to represent a dynamically created HTML element, which you can then insert into the page.
AttachEvent() and DetachEvent()	Connects an event handler in your Silverlight application to a JavaScript event that's raised by the document.
Submit()	Submits the page, by posting a form and its data back to the server. This is useful if you're hosting your Silverlight control in an ASP.NET page, because it triggers a postback that allows server-side code to run.

Once you have the HtmlDocument object that represents the page, you can browse down through the element tree, starting at HtmlDocument.DocumentElement or HtmlDocument.Body. To step from one element to another, you use the Children property (to see the elements nested inside the current element) and the Parent property (to get the element that contains the current element).

Figure 12-3 shows an example—a Silverlight application that starts at the top-level <html> element and uses a recursive method to drill through the entire page. It displays the name and ID of each element.

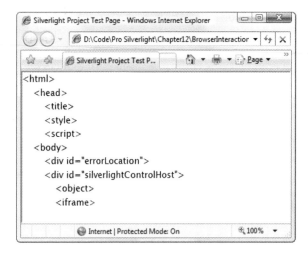

Figure 12-3. *Dissecting the current page*

Here's the code that creates this display when the page first loads:

```
private void UserControl_Loaded(object sender, RoutedEventArgs e)
{
    // Start processing the top-level <html> element.
    HtmlElement element = HtmlPage.Document.DocumentElement;
    ProcessElement(element, 0);
}

private void ProcessElement(HtmlElement element, int indent)
{
    // Ignore comments.
    if (element.TagName == "!") return;

    // Indent the element to help show different levels of nesting.
    lblElementTree.Text += new String(' ', indent * 4);

    // Display the tag name.
    lblElementTree.Text += "<" + element.TagName;

    // Only show the id attribute if it's set.
    if (element.Id != "") lblElementTree.Text += " id=\"" + element.Id + "\"";
    lblElementTree.Text += ">\n";

    // Process all the elements nested inside the current element.
    foreach (HtmlElement childElement in element.Children)
    {
        ProcessElement(childElement, indent + 1);
    }
}
```

The HtmlElement provides relatively few properties. Aside from the Children and Parent properties that allow you to navigate between elements, it also includes the TagName and Id demonstrated shown here, and a CssClass property that indicates the name of the CSS style that's set through the class attribute and used to configure the appearance of the current element. To get more information out of an element, you need to use one of the HtmlElement methods you'll learn about in the next section.

Manipulating an HTML Element

The Parent and Children properties aren't the only way to travel through an HtmlDocument object. You can also search for an element with a specific name using the GetElementByID() or GetElementsByTagName() method. Once you have the element you want, you can manipulate it using one of the methods described in Table 12-3.

Table 12-3. *Methods of the HtmlElement Class*

Method	Description
AppendChild()	Inserts a new HTML element as the last nested element inside the current element. To create the element, you must first use the HtmlDocument.CreateElement() method.
RemoveChild()	Removes the specified HtmlElement (which you supply as an argument). This HtmlElement must be one of the children that's nested in the current HtmlElement.
Focus()	Gives focus to the current element, so it will receive keyboard events.
GetAttribute(), SetAttribute(), and RemoveAttribute()	Allows you to retrieve the value of any attribute in the element, set the value (in which case the attribute will be added if it doesn't already exist), or remove the attribute altogether.
GetStyleAttribute(), SetStyleAttribute(), RemoveStyleAttribute()	Allows you to retrieve a value of a CSS style property, set the value, or remove the style attribute altogether. (As you no doubt know, CSS properties are the modern way to format HTML elements, and they allow you to control details like font, foreground and background color, spacing and positioning, and borders.)
GetProperty() and SetProperty()	Allows you to retrieve or set values that are defined as part of the HTML DOM. These are the values that are commonly manipulated in JavaScript code. For example, you can extract the text content of an element using the innerHTML property.
AttachEvent() and DetachEvent()	Connects an event handler in your Silverlight application to a JavaScript event that's raised by an HTML element.

For example, imagine that you have a <p> element just underneath your Silverlight content region (and your Silverlight content region doesn't fill the entire browser window). You want to manipulate the paragraph with your Silverlight application, so you assign it a unique ID like this:

```
<p id="paragraph">...</p>
```

You can retrieve an HtmlElement object that represents this paragraph in any Silverlight event handler. The following code retrieves the paragraph and changes the text inside:

```
HtmlElement element = HtmlPage.Document.GetElementById("paragraph");
element.SetProperty("innerHTML",
  "This HTML paragraph has been updated by Silverlight.");
```

This code works by calling the HtmlElement.SetProperty() method and setting the inner-HTML property. Long-time JavaScript developers will recognize innerHTML as one of the fundamental ingredients in the DOM.

■ **Note** When you use methods like SetProperty() and SetStyleAttribute(), you leave the predictable Silverlight environment and enter the quirky world of the browser. As a result, cross-platform considerations may come into play. For example, if you use the innerText property (which is similar to innerHTML, but performs automatic HTML escaping to ensure that special characters aren't interpreted as tags), you'll find that your code no longer works in Firefox, because Firefox doesn't support innerText.

Figure 12-4 shows a test page that demonstrates this code. At the top of the page is a Silverlight content region with a single button. When the button is clicked, the text is changed in the HTML element underneath (which is wrapped in a solid border to make it easy to spot).

Figure 12-4. *Changing HTML elements with Silverlight code*

You'll notice that the transition between Silverlight and the HTML DOM isn't quite perfect. Silverlight doesn't include a full HTML DOM, just a lightweight version that standardizes on a basic HtmlElement class. To manipulate this element in a meaningful way, you'll often need to set an HTML DOM property (such as innerHTML in the previous example) using the SetProperty() method and supply the name of the property as a string. If you plan to be doing a lot of work with specific HTML elements, you may want to wrap them in higher-level custom classes (for example, by creating a custom Paragraph class) and replace their DOM properties or CSS style properties with strongly typed properties. Many developers use this approach to prevent minor typographic errors in property names that won't be caught at compile time.

ESCAPING SPECIAL CHARACTERS

When you set the innerHTML property, your text is interpreted as raw HTML. That means you're free to use nested elements, like this:

```
element.SetProperty("innerHTML", "This <b>word</b> is bold.");
```

If you want to use an angle bracket that would otherwise be interpreted as a special character, you need to replace it with the < and > character entities, as shown here:

```
element.SetProperty("innerHTML", "To get bold text use the &lt;b&gt; element.");
```

If you have a string with many characters that need to be escaped, or you don't want reduce the readability of your code with character entities, you can use the static HttpUtility.HtmlEncode() method to do the work, as shown here:

```
element.SetProperty("innerHTML",
  HttpUtility.HtmlEncode("My favorite elements are <b>, <i>, <u>, and <p>."));
```

If you want to add extra spaces (rather than allow them to be collapsed to a single space character), you need to use the   character entity for a nonbreaking space.

Inserting and Removing Elements

The previous example modified an existing HTML element. It's just as easy to add or remove elements from an HTML page, using three methods: HtmlDocument.CreateElement(), HtmlElement.AppendChild(), and HtmlElement.RemoveChild().

For example, the following code assumes that the paragraph doesn't exist in the text page, and creates it:

```
HtmlElement element = HtmlPage.Document.CreateElement("p");
element.Id = "paragraph";
element.SetProperty("innerHTML",
  "This is a new element. Click to change its background color.");

HtmlPage.Document.Body.AppendChild(element);
```

In this example, the element is inserted as the last child of the <body> element, which means it's placed at the end of the document. If you have a place where you want to insert dynamic Silverlight content, it's easiest to define an empty <div> container with a unique ID. You can then retrieve the HtmlElement for that <div> and use AppendChild() to insert your new content.

Note You can execute this code more than once to add multiple paragraphs to the end of the HTML document. However, as it currently stands each paragraph will be given the same ID, which isn't strictly correct. If you use the GetElementById() method on a document like this, you'll only get the first matching element.

Ordinarily, the AppendChild() method always places the new element at the end of the collection of nested children. However, it's possible to position an element more precisely by using an overloaded version of the AppendChild() that accepts another HtmlElement to act as a reference. When you use this approach, the element is inserted just *before* the referenced element:

```
// Get a reference to the first element in the <body>.
HtmlElement referenceElement = HtmlPage.Document.Body.Children[0];

// Make the new element the very first child in the <body> element,
// before all other nested elements.
HtmlPage.Document.Body.AppendChild(element, referenceElement);
```

Incidentally, it's even easier to remove an element. The only trick is that you need to use the RemoveChild() method of the *parent*, not the actual element you want to remove.

Here's the code that removes the paragraph element if it exists:

```
HtmlElement element = HtmlPage.Document.GetElementById("paragraph");
if (element != null)
  element.Parent.RemoveChild(element);
```

Changing Style Properties

Setting style attributes is just as easy as setting DOM properties. You have essentially three options.

First, you can set the element to use an existing style class. To do this, you set the HtmlElement.CssClass property:

```
element.CssClass = "highlightedParagraph";
```

For this to work, the named style must be defined in the current HTML document or in a linked stylesheet. Here's an example that defines the highlightedParagraph style in the <head> of the HTML page:

```
<html xmlns="http://www.w3.org/1999/xhtml">
  <head>
    <style type="text/css">
        .highlightedParagraph
        {
            color: White;
            border: solid 1px black;
            background-color: Lime;
        }
        ...
    </style>
    ...
  </head>
  <body>...</body>
</html>
```

This approach requires the least code and keeps the formatting details in your HTML markup. However, it's an all or nothing approach—if you want to fine-tune individual style properties, you'll need to follow up with a different approach.

Another option is to set the element's style all at once. To do this, you use the HtmlElement.SetAttribute() method and set the style property. Here's an example:

```
element.SetAttribute("style",
    "color: White; border: solid 1px black; background-color: Lime;");
```

But a neater approach is to set the style properties separately using the SetStyleAttribute() method several times:

```
element.SetStyleAttribute("color", "White");
element.SetStyleAttribute("border", "solid 1px black");
element.SetStyleAttribute("background", "Lime");
```

You can use the SetStyleAttribute() at any point to change a single style property, regardless of how you set the style initially (or even if you haven't set any other style properties).

Tip For a review of the CSS properties you can use to configure elements, refer to
http://www.w3schools.com/Css/default.asp.

Handling JavaScript Events

Not only can you find, examine, and change HTML elements, you can also handle their events. Once again, you need to know the name of the HTML DOM event. In other words, you'll need to have your JavaScript skills handy in order to make the leap between Silverlight and HTML. Table 12-4 summarizes the most commonly used events.

Table 12-4. *Common HTML DOM Events*

Event	Description
onchange	Occurs when the user changes the value in an input control. In text controls, this event fires after the user changes focus to another control.
onclick	Occurs when the user clicks a control.
onmouseover	Occurs when the user moves the mouse pointer over a control.
onmouseout	Occurs when the user moves the mouse pointer away from a control.
onkeydown	Occurs when the user presses a key.
onkeyup	Occurs when the user releases a pressed key.
onselect	Occurs when the user selects a portion of text in an input control.
onfocus	Occurs when a control receives focus.
onblur	Occurs when focus leaves a control.
onabort	Occurs when the user cancels an image download.
onerror	Occurs when an image can't be downloaded (probably because of an incorrect URL).
onload	Occurs when a new page finishes downloading.
onunload	Occurs when a page is unloaded. (This typically occurs after a new URL has been entered or a link has been clicked. It fires just before the new page is downloaded.)

To attach your event handler, you use the HtmlElement.AttachEvent() method. You can call this method at any point, and use it with existing or newly created elements. Here's an example that watches for the onclick event in the paragraph:

```
element.AttachEvent("onclick", paragraph_Click);
```

Tip You can use HtmlElement.AttachEvent() to handle the events raised by any HTML element. You can also use HtmlWindow.AttachEvent() to deal with events raised by the browser window (the DOM window object), and HtmlDocument.AttachEvent() to handle the events raised by the top-level document (the DOM document object).

The event handler receives an HtmlEventArgs object that provides a fair bit of additional information. For mouse events you'll be able to check the exact coordinates of the mouse (relative to the element that raised the event) and the state of different mouse buttons.

In this example, the event handler simply changes the text and background color of the paragraph:

```
private void paragraph_Click(object sender, HtmlEventArgs e)
{
    HtmlElement element = (HtmlElement)sender;
    element.SetProperty("innerHTML",
```

```
            "You clicked this HTML element, and Silverlight handled it.");
        element.SetStyleAttribute("background", "#00ff00");
}
```

This technique achieves an impressive feat. Using Silverlight as an intermediary, you can script an HTML page with client-side C# code, instead of using the JavaScript that would normally be required.

Figure 12-5 shows this code in action.

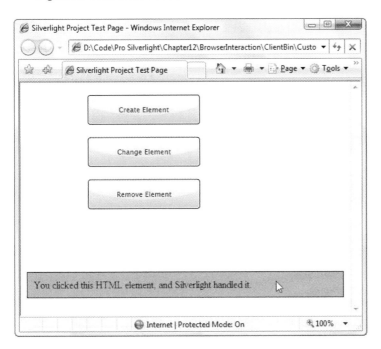

Figure 12-5. *Silverlight and HTML interaction*

Code Interaction

So far, you've seen how a Silverlight application can reach into the browser to perform navigation and manipulate HTML elements. The one weakness of this approach is that it creates tightly bound code—in other words, a Silverlight application that has hard-coded assumptions about the HTML elements on the current page and their unique IDs. Change these details in the HTML page, and the Silverlight code for interacting with them won't work anymore.

One alternative that addresses this issue is to allow interaction between *code*, not elements. For example, your Silverlight application could update the content of the HTML page by calling a JavaScript method that's in the page. Essentially, the JavaScript code creates an extra layer of flexibility in between the Silverlight code and HTML content. This way, if the HTML elements on the page are ever changed, the JavaScript method can be updated to match at the same time and the Silverlight application won't need to be recompiled. The same interaction can work in the reverse direction—for example, you can create JavaScript code that calls a Silverlight method that's written in managed C# code. In the following sections, you'll see an example of both techniques.

Calling Browser Script from Silverlight

Using the Silverlight classes in the System.Windows.Browser namespace, you can invoke a JavaScript function that's declared in a script block. This gives you a disciplined, carefully controlled way for Silverlight code to interact with a page. It's particularly useful if you already have a self-sufficient page with a full complement of JavaScript functions. Rather than duplicating the code that manipulates the elements in that page, you can simply call one of the existing methods.

For example, assume you have this function defined in the <head> section of your HTML page:

```
<script type="text/javascript">
    function changeParagraph(newText) {
        var element = document.getElementById("paragraph");
        element.innerHTML = newText;
    }
</script>
```

To call this method, you need to use the HtmlWindow.GetProperty() method and pass in the name of the function. You'll receive a ScriptObject, which you can execute at any time by calling InvokeSelf().

```
ScriptObject script = (ScriptObject)HtmlPage.Window.GetProperty("changeParagraph");
```

When you call InvokeSelf(), you pass in all the parameters. The changeParagraph() function requires a single string paragraph, so you can call it like this:

```
script.InvokeSelf("Changed through JavaScript.");
```

Calling Silverlight Methods from the Browser

Interestingly, Silverlight also has the complementary ability to let JavaScript code call a method written in managed code. This process is a bit more involved. In order to make it work, you need to take the following steps:

1. Create a public method in your Silverlight code that exposes the information or functionality you want the web page to use. You can place the method in your page class or in a separate class. You'll need to stick to simple data types, like strings, Boolean values, and numbers, unless you want to go through the additional work of serializing your objects to a simpler form.

2. Add the ScriptableMember attribute to the declaration of the method that you want to call from JavaScript.

3. Add the ScriptableType attribute to the declaration of the class that includes the scriptable method.

4. To expose your Silverlight method to JavaScript, call the HtmlPage.RegisterScriptable-Object() method.

Provided you take all these steps, your JavaScript code will be able to call your Silverlight method through the <object> element that represents the Silverlight content region. However, to make this task easier, it's important to give the <object> element a unique ID. By default, Visual Studio creates a test page that assigns a name to the <div> element that contains the <object> element (silverlightControlHost), but it doesn't give a name to the <object> element inside. Before continuing, you should create a test page that adds this detail, as shown here:

```
<div id="silverlightControlHost">
  <object data="data:application/x-silverlight,"
  type="application/x-silverlight-2-b1" width="400" height="300"
  id="silverlightControl">
    ...
  </object>
  <iframe style='visibility:hidden;height:0;width:0;border:0px'></iframe>
</div>
```

■ **Note** Remember, you can't modify the test page in a stand-alone Silverlight application, because it will be replaced when you rebuild your project. Instead, you need to create a new test page as described in Chapter 1. If you're using a solution that includes an ASP.NET test website, you can change the HTML test page directly. If you're using the server-side .aspx test page, you can simply change the ID of the server-side Silverlight control, which will be used when creating the client-side Silverlight control.

Once you've named the Silverlight control, you're ready to create the scriptable Silverlight method. Consider the example shown in Figure 12-6. Here, a Silverlight region (the area with the gradient background) includes a single TextBlock (left). Underneath is an HTML paragraph. When the user clicks the paragraph, a JavaScript event handler springs into action, and calls a method in the Silverlight application that updates the TextBlock (right).

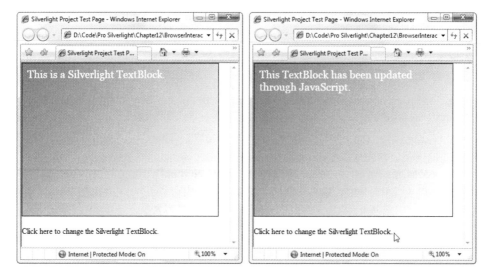

Figure 12-6. *Calling Silverlight code from JavaScript*

To create this example, you simply need the custom page class shown here. It includes a single scriptable method, which is registered when the page is first created.

```
[ScriptableType()]
public partial class ScriptableSilverlight : UserControl
{
    public ScriptableSilverlight()
    {
        InitializeComponent();

        HtmlPage.RegisterScriptableObject("Page", this);
    }

    [ScriptableMember()]
    public void ChangeText(string newText)
    {
        lbl.Text = newText;
    }
}
```

When registering a scriptable type, you need to specify a JavaScript object name and pass a reference to the appropriate object. Here, an instance of the ScriptableSilverlight class is registered with the name Page. This tells Silverlight to create a property named Page in the Silverlight control on the JavaScript page. Thus, to call this method, the JavaScript code needs to use the find the Silverlight control, get its content, and then call its Page.ChangeText() method.

Here's an example of a function that does exactly that:

```
<script type="text/javascript">
  function updateSilverlightText()
  {
      var control = document.getElementById("silverlightControl");
      control.content.Page.ChangeText(
        "This TextBlock has been updated through JavaScript.");
  }
</script>
```

You can trigger this JavaScript method at any time. Here's an example that fires it off when a paragraph is clicked:

```
<p onclick="updateSilverlightText()">Click here to change the Silverlight
 TextBlock.</p>
```

Now clicking the paragraph triggers the updateSilverlight() JavaScript function, which in turn calls the ChangeText () method that's a part of your ScriptableSilverlight class.

Instantiating Silverlight Objects in the Browser

The previous example demonstrated how you can call a Silverlight method for JavaScript code. Silverlight has one more trick for code interaction—it allows JavaScript code to instantiate a Silverlight object.

As before, you start with a scriptable type that includes scriptable methods. Here's an example of a very basic Silverlight class that returns random numbers:

```
[ScriptableType()]
public class RandomNumbers
{
    private Random random = new Random();

    [ScriptableMember()]
    public int GetRandomNumberInRange(int from, int to)
    {
        return random.Next(from, to+1);
    }
}
```

As with the previous example, you need to register this class to make it available to JavaScript code. However, instead of using the RegisterScriptableObject() method, you use the RegisterCreateableType() method, as shown here:

```
HtmlPage.RegisterCreateableType("RandomNumbers", typeof(RandomNumbers));
```

To create an instance of a registered type, you need to find the Silverlight control, use call its content.services.createObject() method. Here's an example with a JavaScript function that displays a random number from 1 to 6 using an instance of the Silverlight RandomNumbers class:

```
<script type="text/javascript">
  function getRandom1To6()
  {
      var control = document.getElementById("silverlightControl");
      var random = control.content.services.createObject("RandomNumbers");
      alert("Your number is: " + random.GetRandomNumberInRange(1, 6));
  }
</script>
```

The final detail is an HTML element that calls getRandom1To6():

```
<p onclick="getRandom1To6()">Click here to get a random number from 1 to 6.</p>
```

Figure 12-7 shows this code in action.

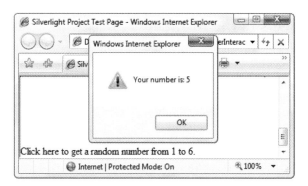

Figure 12-7. *Creating a Silverlight object from JavaScript*

A Browser History Example

Using the techniques you've just learned about, you can tackle a true Silverlight challenge—integrating your application with the history list in the web browser.

Ordinarily, Silverlight content exists inside a single page. Thus, no matter what takes place in that page the browser history list never changes. This can confuse users, who often expect that clicking the back button will bring them back to the previous visual in your Silverlight application, whereas it will actually *end* the current Silverlight application and bring them to the previous page.

Flash applications and HTML pages that make heavy use of Ajax features face the same problem. There are several known workarounds, although none are simple and many have subtle compatibility issues that prevent them from working with certain browsers. In this example, you'll see a reasonably robust solution that works with recent versions of Internet Explorer and Firefox. However, if you decided to use this code in a real-world application, you'd need to test and refine its code more thoroughly to make sure that it doesn't cause problems on less common browsers.

■ **Tip** There are several Ajax libraries that offer history list solutions. If you use one of these in other web development, you can probably integrate it into Silverlight uses the techniques explained in this section. Also, future versions of ASP.NET will include an Ajax-powered history management feature, which can also be adapted to work with a Silverlight application if you're hosting it in an ASP.NET website.

In the following sections, you'll study the solution piece by piece. Figure 12-8 shows the final result, in a simple application that allows you to move through a sequence of pages. On the left side, the user starts on the first page. After clicking ahead twice, the user moves to the third page. The browser history list shows the page names and allows the user to jump back to an earlier point.

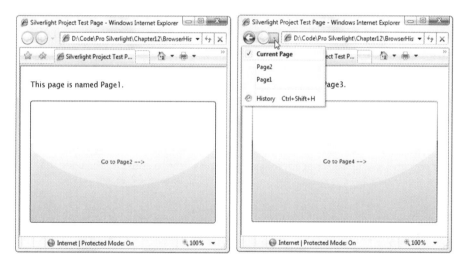

Figure 12-8. *Showing Silverlight pages in the browser history list*

The iframe Approach

The trick that makes this example work is the <iframe> element. As you no doubt know, the iframe allows you to create a frame that displays the content of another page. This content appears in a bordered, scrollable container inside the current page.

Browsers have an interesting way of dealing with iframe navigation. If you click a link inside the page in an iframe, the new page loads up inside the iframe, as you would expect. But what you might not realize is that the browser treats this as a normal page navigation, and it adds an entry to the history menu. If you click the Back button at this point, the current page won't change, but the iframe will load up *its* previous page. If you click Back again after you reach the first iframe page, you'll get the behavior you expect—namely, the browser will return to the previous visited page.

You can take advantage of this behavior to trick the browser into thinking you're navigating from page to page. All you need is a hidden iframe on your page. For example, if you load up a new user control in your Silverlight application, you could also redirect the iframe to a new page. The browser would notice the change, and add an entry to the history list. You can also take advantage of this behavior to let the user return to previously visited places in your Silverlight application. When the user clicks back, the browser will change the page in the iframe. You can react to this event by changing the display in your Silverlight page accordingly.

Although the user won't ever see the content of the iframe, you still need to load a valid HTML document to convince the browser to add a history item. However, you can leave these dummy pages blank, as long as they have the basic skeleton of a valid HTML page.

To build a navigation system, you need exactly two dummy pages. That way, your application can switch between these two pages endlessly. In the example shown in Figure 12-8, the pages are named Pager1.html and Pager2.html. As the user travels to different places in the application, the Silverlight application directs the iframe back and forth between these two pages.

Of course, you also need to track some sort of information about the user's navigation history, so that you can restore the right page when the user clicks the back button. The easiest approach is to add the information you need as a query string argument to the URL that the iframe uses. In this example, the query string argument is named StateKey. The value of the StateKey argument indicates the class name of the corresponding Silverlight page. For example, this URL points to the Silverlight user control named Page1:

```
Pager2.html?StateKey=Page1
```

From the point of view of your Silverlight application, it makes no different what page is shown in the iframe (Pager1.html or Pager2.html). Your code simply needs to heed the StateKey.

Now that you understand the concept that's at work, it's time to consider the code that implements it.

The Test Page

The test page requires relatively few changes. Somewhere on the page, you need to add an invisible iframe named Pager:

```
<iframe id="Pager" src="Pager2.html?StateKey=Page1"
 style='visibility:hidden;height:0;width:0;border:0px'></iframe>
```

Notice that the StateKey query string argument is set to Page1. That's because Page1 is the first page that's shown in the Silverlight application. In order for the history tracking code to work, you need to record this initial page.

There's one more change you need to make to the test page. Because you'll be calling Silverlight methods from JavaScript code, you need to make sure that you've given your Silverlight control a unique ID. If you're using an HTML test page, you need to add the id attribute, as shown here:

```
<object data="data:application/x-silverlight," type="application/x-silverlight-2-b1"
 width="100%" height="100%" id="silverlightControl">
```

Page Navigation

This Silverlight application uses page navigation code that's based on the approach you saw in Chapter 6. A static Navigate() method in the custom App class loads the right user control into the root visual, which is a Grid.

The one new detail is a call to a method named Pager.AddHistoryItem(). This method adds the previous page to the browser history list, using a custom Pager class that you haven't yet considered.

```
private Grid rootVisual = new Grid();
private Pager pager = new Pager();

public static void Navigate(UserControl newPage)
{
    App currentApp = (App)Application.Current;

    // Record the page the application is on.
    Type type = newPage.GetType();
    currentApp.pager.AddHistoryItem(type.Name);

    // Change the currently displayed page.
    currentApp.rootVisual.Children.Clear();
    currentApp.rootVisual.Children.Add(newPage);
}
```

As written, this code makes no attempt to store any state information. As a result, clicking the back button will load up a previously visited page but won't restore any changed control values. If you do want to store state, you can cache pages in memory using the slightly modified navigation code described in Chapter 6.

The custom Pager class has the heart of the page navigation code.

```
[ScriptableType()]
public class Pager
{...}
```

It plays two roles. First, it allows the application to add a page to the browser history using the AddHistoryItem() method. Second, it allows the HTML page to inform the Silverlight application when the user has clicked to another page in the history list, at which you'll want to load the corresponding user control into the Grid. You'll explore these two processes in the following sections.

Adding Items to the History List

To add items to the history list, the Navigate() method calls the Pager.AddHistoryItem() method. At this point, you need to find the iframe element and point it to a new page. But in order to know which page to use (Pager1.html or Pager2.html), you also need to know what page was used most recently. In this example, the Pager switches from one page to the other based on the value of a Boolean field named pageSwitch.

```
private bool pageSwitch = false;
```

The AddHistoryItem() also sets the page name in the URL using the StateKey query string argument. It keeps track of the most recent state key using a string field named current-StateKey. This is important, because the Pager uses the currentStateKey to determine when the user has clicked to another page through the browser history list.

```
private string currentStateKey;
```

There are two versions of the AddHistoryItem() method—one which allows you to specify the name of the <iframe> element, and the other which uses the default name Pager. Here's the complete code for both:

```
public void AddHistoryItem(string stateKey)
{
    AddHistoryItem(stateKey, "Pager");
}

public void AddHistoryItem(string stateKey, string pagerElementName)
{
    currentStateKey = stateKey;
    HtmlElement iframe = HtmlPage.Document.GetElementById(pagerElementName);
    pageSwitch = !pageSwitch;

    if (pageSwitch)
    {
        iframe.SetAttribute("src", "Pager1.html?StateKey=" + stateKey);
    }
    else
    {
        iframe.SetAttribute("src", "Pager2.html?StateKey=" + stateKey);
    }
}
```

The actual logic involved is quite simple. The code simply sets the new URL for the iframe by calling the familiar HtmlElement.SetAttribute() method on the src attribute.

Returning to Pages in the History List

Filling the history list is only half the problem. You also need to respond when the user picks an item out of the history list or clicks the Back or Forward button. If the iframe element fired a JavaScript event when navigation occurred, you could simply handle this event in your Silverlight code. Unfortunately, it doesn't. As a result, you need a slightly more long-winded approach.

Here's how it works. Both Pager1.html and Pager2.html handle the onload event. At this point, they run some JavaScript code to pass the information along to your Silverlight application. The information you need is simple—it's just the value of StateKey from the current URL.

As you've learned, to allow JavaScript code to call a Silverlight method, you need to register a scriptable type that contains at least one scriptable method. The Pager class is a scriptable type, and it registers itself in the constructor when it's first created:

```
public Pager()
{
    HtmlPage.RegisterScriptableObject("PagerScript", this);
}
```

The Pager class contains a scriptable method named Navigate(). The Navigate() method takes the StateKey value and checks if it corresponds to a new page. (This allows you to ignore the onload event that occurs when you call AddHistoryItem(), and the new page is loaded into the iframe for the first time. Other solutions are possible, but they require a bit more JavaScript code.) If it is a new page, the Navigate() method calls the RestorePage() method in the App class.

```
[ScriptableMember()]
public void Navigate(string stateKey)
{
    if (stateKey != currentStateKey)
    {
        App.RestorePage(stateKey);
        pageSwitch = !pageSwitch;
        currentStateKey = stateKey;
    }
}
```

The App.RestorePage() method uses reflection to create the right page and load it up:

```
public static void RestorePage(string pageClassName)
{
    App currentApp = (App)Application.Current;

    Type type = currentApp.GetType();
    Assembly assembly = type.Assembly;
    UserControl newPage = (UserControl)assembly.CreateInstance(
      type.Namespace + "." + pageClassName);

    currentApp.rootVisual.Children.Clear();
    currentApp.rootVisual.Children.Add( newPage);
}
```

The final ingredient is the code in Pager1.html and Pager2.html. This code needs to find the Silverlight control in the hosting page, and then call the Navigate() method to pass along the new StateKey.

Here's the complete markup for Pager1.html, with the important parts highlighted:

```
<html xmlns="http://www.w3.org/1999/xhtml" >
  <head>
    <script type="text/javascript">
      function Reloaded()
      {
          // Get the state key.
```

```
            var stateKey = document.URL.substring(
                document.URL.indexOf("?StateKey=") + 10);
            document.title = stateKey;

            // Tell the Silverlight application that the iframe page changed.
            var control = top.document.getElementById("silverlightControl");
            control.content.PagerScript.Navigate(stateKey);
        }
    </script>

    <title>BrowserInteraction</title>
  </head>

  <body onload="Reloaded()">
  </body>
</html>
```

You'll notice that the Reloaded() method takes one extra step. Before it calls Navigate(), it sets the document title. This ensures that the name that appears in the history list matches the state key, giving the helpful page names shown in Figure 12-8. Unfortunately, this trick doesn't work in Firefox. It uses the title of the page that contains the iframe, which means that all your entries in the page history will have the same name. (You could get around this by adding JavaScript code to dynamically change the top-level page title, but that gets a bit messier.)

You've now seen the complete example. Although the need to use a hidden iframe complicates the approach, the interaction between the Silverlight code and the HTML page works smoothly and seamlessly in both directions.

Combining Silverlight and HTML Content

In Chapter 8, you learned how to create a windowless Silverlight content region. You can then use a transparent background to allow your Silverlight elements to "sit" directly on your HTML page. You can even use partial transparency to let the HTML content show through underneath your Silverlight content.

This visual integration comes in quite handy when you use Silverlight code integration. For example, many developers have created custom-skinned media players using Silverlight's standard video window in conjunction with JavaScript-powered HTML element. These controls can control playback by calling the scriptable methods in your Silverlight application.

When you combine HTML elements and Silverlight elements in the same visual space, it can take a bit of work to get the right layout. Usually, the trick is to fiddle around with CSS styles. For example, to constrain Silverlight content to a specific region of your page, you can place it in a <div> container. That <div> can even be placed with absolute coordinates. Other <div> containers can be used to arrange blocks of HTML content alongside the Silverlight content. (You saw an example of this technique in Chapter 8, where a windowless Silverlight control was placed into a single column in a multicolumn layout.)

Occasionally, you'll want more layout control. For example, you may need to place or size your Silverlight control based on the current dimensions of the browser window or the location of other HTML elements. In the following sections, you'll see two examples that use Silverlight's HTML interoperability to place the Silverlight control dynamically.

Sizing the Silverlight Control to Fit Its Content

As you learned in Chapter 1, the default test page makes a Silverlight content region that fills the entire browser window. You can change this sizing, but you'll still be forced to assign an explicit size to your Silverlight control. If you don't, your Silverlight content will be arranged according to the size of the page, but the page will be truncated to fit a standard 200 by 200 pixel region, as shown in Figure 12-9.

Figure 12-9. *The default Silverlight control size*

Sometimes, it would be nice to have a way to make the Silverlight content region size itself to match the dimensions of Silverlight page. Ordinarily, this doesn't happen. However, you can put it in to practice with some simple code and Silverlight's HTML interoperability. In fact, it's easy. All you need to do is wait for your page to load up, find the corresponding <object> element on the page, and resize it to match the dimensions of the page.

Here's an event handler that does the trick. It sizes the Silverlight control using the width and height style properties.

```
private void Page_Loaded(object sender, RoutedEventArgs e)
{
    HtmlElement element = HtmlPage.Document.GetElementById("silverlightControl");
    element.SetStyleAttribute("width", this.Width + "px");
    element.SetStyleAttribute("height", this.Height + "px");
}
```

You can use this code once, to size the Silverlight content region when the application is first loaded and the first page appears, or you can resize the content region to correspond to the content you're currently displaying by using the same code in several pages. Figure 12-10 shows the result of this approach, as the user navigates from one page to another inside a Silverlight application.

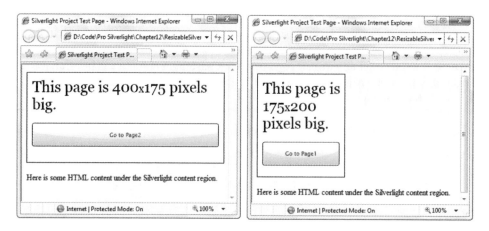

Figure 12-10. *Sizing the Silverlight control to fit the page*

Placing the Silverlight Control Next to an HTML Element

Much as you can resize the Silverlight control using style properties, you can also reposition it. The trick is to use a CSS style that specifies absolute positioning for the Silverlight control (or the <div> element that wraps it). You can then place the Silverlight control at the appropriate coordinates by setting the left and top style properties.

For example, in Figure 12-11 the goal is to pop up the Silverlight application in a floating window overtop of the page, but next to a specific HTML element (which is highlighted in yellow). The specific position of the highlighted HTML element changes depending on the size of the browser window. Thus, to put the Silverlight content in the right place you need to position it dynamically with code.

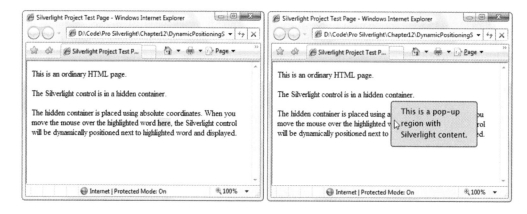

Figure 12-11. *Positioning Silverlight content next to an element*

To make this work, you must begin with a style that specifies absolute positioning for the Silverlight control. This style rule also sets the width and height to 0, so the control won't appear initially. (You could use the visibility style property to accomplish the same thing, but in this case the width and height will be set dynamically to match the Silverlight page size, so it may as well start at 0.)

```
#silverlightControlHost
{
    position: absolute;
    width: 0px;
    height: 0px;
}
```

The Silverlight content region won't appear until the user moves the mouse over the appropriate HTML element. In this example, the element is a <span> placed in a block of text.

```
<div>
  <p>This is an ordinary HTML page.</p>
  <p>The Silverlight control is in a hidden container.</p>
  <p>The hidden container is placed using absolute coordinates.
  When you move the mouse over the highlighted word <span id="target">here</span>,
  the Silverlight control will be dynamically positioned next to highlighted word
  and displayed.
</div>
```

This span is given a yellow background through another style:

```
#target
{
    background-color: Yellow;
}
```

When the Silverlight page loads, the code finds the target <span> element and attaches an event handler to the JavaScript onmouseover event:

```
private void Page_Loaded(object sender, RoutedEventArgs e)
{
    HtmlElement target = HtmlPage.Document.GetElementById("target");
    target.AttachEvent("onmouseover", element_MouseOver);
}
```

When the user moves the mouse over the element, the event handler finds its current position using the HTML DOM properties offsetLeft and offsetTop. It then places the Silverlight container in a nearby location using the left and top style properties.

```
private void element_MouseOver(object sender, HtmlEventArgs e)
{
    // Get the current position of the <span>.
    HtmlElement target = HtmlPage.Document.GetElementById("target");
    double targetLeft = Convert.ToDouble(target.GetProperty("offsetLeft")) - 20;
    double targetTop = Convert.ToDouble(target.GetProperty("offsetTop")) - 20;
```

```
    // Get the Silverlight container, and position it.
    HtmlElement silverlightControl =
      HtmlPage.Document.GetElementById("silverlightControlHost");
    silverlightControl.SetStyleAttribute("left", targetLeft.ToString() + "px");
    silverlightControl.SetStyleAttribute("top", targetTop.ToString() + "px");

    // Resize the Silverlight container to match the actual page size.
    silverlightControl.SetStyleAttribute("width", this.Width + "px");
    silverlightControl.SetStyleAttribute("height", this.Height + "px");
}
```

The Silverlight content region is hidden using an ordinary Silverlight event handler that reacts to the MouseLeave event of the top-level user control:

```
private void Page_MouseLeave(object sender, MouseEventArgs e)
{
    HtmlElement silverlightControl =
      HtmlPage.Document.GetElementById("silverlightControlHost");
    silverlightControl.SetStyleAttribute("width", "0px");
    silverlightControl.SetStyleAttribute("height", "0px");
}
```

To give this example just a bit more pizzazz, you can use an animation to fade the Silverlight content region into appearance. Here's an example that alternates the opacity of the top-level container from 0 to 1 over half a second:

```
<UserControl.Resources>
  <Storyboard x:Name="fadeUp">
    <DoubleAnimation Storyboard.TargetName="LayoutRoot"
     Storyboard.TargetProperty="Opacity"
     From="0" To="1" Duration="0:0:0.5" />
  </Storyboard>
</UserControl.Resources>
```

To use this animation, you simply need to add this statement to the end of the element_MouseOver() event handler:

```
fadeUp.Begin();
```

The Last Word

In this chapter, you saw how to build more advanced web pages by blending the boundaries between Silverlight and the containing HTML page. You learned how Silverlight can find and manipulate HTML elements directly, and how it can call JavaScript code routines. You also learned how to use the reverse trick, and let JavaScript call scriptable methods in your Silverlight application. On the way, you saw how to store state information in the URL and integrate more closely with the browser's history list.

CHAPTER 13

■■■

ASP.NET and Web Services

In Chapter 1, you learned that there were two ways to build a Silverlight project—in a stand-alone project with an HTML test page, or alongside an ASP.NET test website. So far, most of the examples you've seen have used the first approach, which assumes that your Silverlight application is a distinct piece of programming functionality. It may exist on the same page as some server-generated content, but it doesn't need to interact with server-side code.

This is often exactly the design you want. But sometimes, you do need to integrate some server-side processes with your client-side Silverlight application. For example, your application may need access to a server resource, like a database. Or, your application might need to take some information that the user has entered and pass it to a server-side process.

In this chapter, you'll start by exploring the small set of ASP.NET controls that use Silverlight. First, you'll learn how to customize the Silverlight control, which allows you to host Silverlight content in any ASP.NET page. Next, you'll consider the MediaPlayer control, which gives you a code-free way to create a Silverlight-powered media playback page.

In the second half of this chapter, you'll tackle an even more interesting topic—web services. With a bit of planning ahead, the web services you host in your ASP.NET website can provide a powerful server-side backend for your Silverlight application. For example, they can run queries and updates against a server-side database, as you'll see in Chapter 14. They can also allow your Silverlight application to tap into ASP.NET platform features. And if you create a *duplex* service, they can even perform two-way communication to notify your application when specific events occur on the web server.

■**Note** This chapter assumes you have basic familiarity with ASP.NET, although you don't necessarily need to know about the Windows Communication Foundation (WCF) technology used to build web services. For more information about server-side programming and ASP.NET, refer to *Beginning ASP.NET 3.5 in C# 2008* (Apress, 2007). Or, for a faster-paced introduction with more gritty details and less hand holding, read *Pro ASP.NET 3.5 in C# 2008* (Apress, 2007).

ASP.NET Controls That Use Silverlight

As you saw in Chapter 1, it's easy to build a simple ASP.NET web application that includes Silverlight content. You simply need to create a website that includes an HTML or an .aspx test page.

Although this approach allows you to place Silverlight and ASP.NET pages side by side on the same website, they aren't in any way integrated. You can navigate from one page to another (for example, use a link to send a user from an ASP.NET web form to a Silverlight entry page), but there's no interaction between the server-side and client-side code. In many situations, this design is completely reasonable, because the Silverlight application represents a distinct "applet" that's available in your website. In other scenarios, you might want to share part of your data model, or integrate server-side processing and client-side processing as part of a single task. This requires more planning.

The simplest type of interaction is for an ASP.NET control to generate some Silverlight content. In fact, this approach suits the Silverlight model quite well. Silverlight content is wrapped into a distinct element (usually, it's an <object> element that's placed in a <div>), which can coexist alongside other content. An ASP.NET control could render the markup for the <object> element in the same way it spits out simple HTML for standard web controls (like the Button) or a combination of HTML and JavaScript for more complex controls (like the Calendar and GridView). In fact, this is exactly how ASP.NET's new Silverlight controls work.

These controls are a part of the System.Web.Silverlight.dll assembly, which is part of the Silverlight 2 SDK. When you create a Silverlight and ASP.NET solution, a reference is automatically included for this assembly. But in order to use these controls in your pages, you need to register a control tag prefix for the System.Web.UI.SilverlightControls namespace (which is where the Silverlight controls are located). Here's the Register directive that you can add to a web page (just after the Page directive) to use the standard asp tag prefix with the new ASP.NET Futures controls:

```
<%@ Register Assembly="System.Web.Silverlight"
 Namespace="System.Web.UI.SilverlightControls" TagPrefix="asp" %>
```

This directive is automatically inserted in the .aspx test page (for example, Silverlight-Application1TestPage.aspx). It's also added to other web pages when you drag and drop a Silverlight control (from the Silverlight tab of the Toolbox) onto your web form.

Alternatively, you can register the control prefix in your web.config file so that it automatically applies to all pages:

```
<?xml version="1.0"?>
<configuration>
  ...
  <system.web>
    <pages>
      <controls>
        <add tagPrefix="asp" namespace=" System.Web.UI.SilverlightControls"
         assembly="System.Web.Silverlight" />
        ...
      </controls>
    </pages>
```

```
    ...
  </system.web>
  ...
</configuration>
```

Currently, ASP.NET includes just two Silverlight controls, which are named Silverlight and MediaPlayer. They appear in the Toolbox tab named Silverlight Controls.

Note To use the Silverlight controls, you also need an instance of the invisible ScriptManager control. The ScriptManager powers client-side JavaScript features—for example, it makes the createObject() function available so the Silverlight content region can be created. The ScriptManager control is automatically added to the .aspx test page, but if you create additional ASP.NET web pages that show Silverlight content, you'll need to add the ScriptManager from the Toolbox.

The Silverlight Control

As you learned earlier, the HTML entry page creates a Silverlight content region using a <div> placeholder that contains an <object> element. There's no reason you can't duplicate the same approach to place a Silverlight content region in an ASP.NET web form. However, there's a shortcut that you can use. Rather than adding the <object> element by hand, you can use the Silverlight control.

The Silverlight control has a single role in life—to create the Silverlight content region in an ASP.NET web page. The markup that the Silverlight control generates is slightly different than what you'll find in the standard HTML entry page. The Silverlight does render a <div> element, in which the Silverlight content is placed. However, it doesn't render a nested <object> element. Instead, it creates the Silverlight control using a custom JavaScript function named Sys.UI.Silverlight.Control.createObject(), which is part of the ASP.NET AJAX client-side JavaScript libraries. The createObject() function uses arguments to pass information to the Silverlight plug-in, much as the test page uses nested elements to supply the same details.

Here's the complete ASP.NET markup you'd use to show a XAML file named Page.xaml:

```
<%@ Page Language="C#" AutoEventWireup="true" %>

<%@ Register Assembly="System.Web.Silverlight"
  Namespace="System.Web.UI.SilverlightControls" TagPrefix="asp" %>

<html xmlns="http://www.w3.org/1999/xhtml" style="height:100%;">
<head>
    <title>Test Page For SilverlightApplication1</title>
</head>
<body style="height:100%;margin:0;">
    <form id="form1" runat="server" style="height:100%;">
        <asp:ScriptManager ID="ScriptManager1" runat="server"></asp:ScriptManager>
        <div style="height:100%;">
```

```
        <asp:Silverlight ID="Xaml1" runat="server"
          Source="~/ClientBin/SilverlightApplication1.xap" Version="2.0"
          Width="100%" Height="100%" />
      </div>
    </form>
  </body>
</html>
```

Here's what happens when this page is requested:

1. The server creates all the server-side objects (in this example, that includes the Script-Manager and Silverlight controls) and begins the page lifecycle.

2. After all the events have fired (and any event handling code has finished), the server renders the page to ordinary HTML, one web control at a time. At this point, the Silverlight control converts itself to a <span> placeholder inside the <div> element and generates the JavaScript code that calls createObject().

3. When the page is fully rendered, it's sent to the client. The server-side objects are released from memory.

4. When the browser receives the page, it begins processing it. It displays the HTML content and runs the JavaScript. In turn, the JavaScript calls createObject(), which launches the Silverlight application.

5. The browser initializes the Silverlight plug-in, downloads the XAP file for the Silverlight application (if it's not already present in the cache), and starts the application.

6. The Silverlight application runs in the client browser. No more server-side web page code will be executed, unless the user navigates to another page or refreshes the current page (both of which will shut down the current Silverlight application and restart the entire process). If the user interacts with an ASP.NET control elsewhere on the page, that control may post back the page (which will effectively end the currently running Silverlight application) or call back to the web server using ASP.NET AJAX (which won't disturb it). As you'll see later in this chapter, the Silverlight application also has the ability to trigger web server code by calling a web service.

You can set a number of properties on the Silverlight control to configure how the Silverlight content region will be created. Most of these properties correspond to parameters you can place inside the <object> element in an HTML-only test page. Table 13-1 lists the most important.

Table 13-1. *Properties of the Silverlight Web Control*

Member	Description
Source	Identifies the XAML source file or XAP file that represents your application. The Silverlight control will load this content.
Version	Indicates the minimum required Silverlight version. For example, if you use 2.0 (which is what ASP.NET uses in the test page), the Silverlight control will only attempt to load the plug-in if the user has Silverlight 2.0 installed. If the user doesn't have Silverlight or has an earlier version, they'll see the alternative HTML content.
EnableHtmlAccess	Determines whether the Silverlight control can access the HTML elements in the page. If true, you can write code that uses the HTML DOM, as described in Chapter 12.
Windowless	Determines whether the Silverlight control has a transparent background that shows the HTML content of the page underneath. It's false by default (for optimum performance), but can be set to true to create integrated effects that combine HTML and Silverlight, as described in Chapter 8.
InitParameters	Holds custom parameters that you can use to pass information from the hosting page to the Silverlight application, as demonstrated in Chapter 6.
PluginBackground	Sets the color that's used as the Silverlight background. If you are creating a windowless Silverlight control, this must be Transparent.
PluginNotInstalledTemplate	Specifies the HTML content that's shown in the Silverlight plug-in isn't installed on the client or isn't the right version. If you don't specify anything, the Silverlight control will use the default markup, which shows the Silverlight logo and provides a link to install the Silverlight plug-in.
MaxFrameRate	Sets the maximum frame rate for animation. Frame rates are discussed in Chapter 9.
EnableFrameRateCounter	Allows you to judge performance of your Silverlight animations with a frame rate counter. If you set this property to true, Internet Explorer shows the current frame rate in the browser's status bar. (This setting doesn't work for non-Internet Explorer browsers.) The frame rate counter is intended for testing purposes only.
EnableRedrawRegions	Allows you to analyze the performance of your Silverlight animations. If you set this property to true, each time Silverlight renders a new frame it paints a different color background behind the new content. This creates a flickering effect that highlights the areas of the window that are being changed frequently. With this information, you can identify animations that cause excessive repainting. This setting is for testing purposes only.
OnPluginError	Allows you to react to unhandled Silverlight errors with a Java-Script function. To use this feature, you must add the JavaScript function to the page, and then set OnPluginError to the name of that function.

Continued

Table 13-1. *Continued*

Member	Description
OnPluginFullScreenChanged	Allows you to react when the Silverlight plug-in enters or exits full-screen mode (as discussed in Chapter 3). To use this feature, you must add the JavaScript function to the page, and then set OnPluginFullScreenChanged to the name of that function.
OnPluginLoaded	Allows you to react when the Silverlight plug-in is initialized. To use this feature, you must add the JavaScript function to the page, and then set OnPluginLoaded to the name of that function.
OnPluginResized	Allows you to react when the Silverlight control is given a different size (for example, if it uses 100% sizing and the browser window is resized, or if the width and height style properties are set through code). To use this feature, you must add the JavaScript function to the page, and then set OnPluginResized to the name of that function.

The MediaPlayer Control

The MediaPlayer web control gives you a server-side abstraction over the MediaElement class from Silverlight, which you used in Chapter 10.

The obvious question is whether you should use the MediaElement or prefer the server-side MediaPlayer web control. They both amount to the same thing—after all, the server-side MediaPlayer web control renders a MediaElement, although it requires slightly more work on the server to do so. There are two key advantages to using the MediaPlayer web control:

- You have the chance to set some of its properties using server-side code. For example, you could set the media URL based on information from a server-side database.

- The MediaPlayer generates the MediaElement for playing the media (and showing video content) and also adds controls that allow the user to control playback. As you learned in Chapter 10, you can accomplish the same thing by adding your own controls and writing some fairly straightforward code. However, the MediaPlayer uses prebuilt skins to give your media player a slick look with no effort. It's similar to the video-page-generation feature in Expression Blend.

Here's an example of how you might define the MediaPlayer control:

```
<asp:MediaPlayer runat="server" ID="MediaPlayer1"
  MediaSource="~/Butterfly.wmv" Height="600" Width="700" />
```

This creates a Silverlight content region with a media player in it, as shown in Figure 13-1. The media player attempts to access the Butterfly.wmv file (in the root website folder) and begins playing it immediately. The user can control playback using buttons that have a similar style to Windows Media Player.

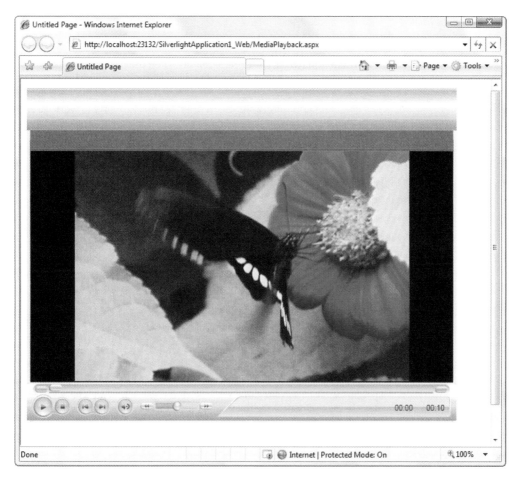

Figure 13-1. *The default skin of the Silverlight media player*

To get the most out of Silverlight's media playing ability, you need to take a closer look at the properties provided by the MediaPlayer control. Table 13-2 lists some of the most important.

Table 13-2. *Properties of the MediaPlayer Web Control*

Property	Description
MediaSource	Identifies the location of the media file as a URL. You can specify a relative path for a file on your web server, or you can supply a full URL that points to another location.
AutoLoad	Sets whether the media file is downloaded immediately when the page is initialized. The default is true. If false, the media file is downloaded when the user starts playback by clicking the play button.

Continued

Table 13-2. *Continued*

Property	Description
AutoPlay	Sets whether playback starts immediately when the page is initialized. The default is false, which means the user will need to use the playback controls to initiate playback.
EnableCaptions	Sets whether captions are shown. In order for this property to work, your media file must contain the embedded captions and your skin must include a display area for them.
Volume	Sets the volume as a value between 0 (silent) and 1 (the maximum volume).
Muted	Determines whether the audio should be muted initially. The default is false.
Height and Width	Sets the dimensions of the MediaPlayer. Unfortunately, you must explicitly size your playback window—there's no setting that allows the MediaPlayer to size itself to fit your skin or your video content.
ScaleMode	Sets whether the MediaPlayer's user interface should be resized to fit the Width and Height dimensions you specify. Your options include none (in which case the MediaPlayer is given the size that's specified in the corresponding skin file), Stretch (in which case the MediaPlayer is stretched in both dimensions to fit the specified bounds), and Zoom (in which case the MediaPlayer is enlarged as much as possible to fit the specified dimensions, without being stretched out of proportion). The default is Zoom. To get better control over the size of the video window (which is just one component of the MediaPlayer user interface), you need to modify the skin by hand.
PlaceholderImageUrl	Specifies a URL to a placeholder image that will be shown while the media file is being opened. Once the media file is opened, this image is replaced with the first frame of your video.

■**Tip** The MediaPlayer control derives from the Silverlight control. Thus, it also includes the properties listed in Table 13-1. Many of these are useful with the MediaPlayer, such as PluginBackground and PluginNotIn-stalledTemplate.

In addition to the properties listed here, the MediaPlayer also includes properties for setting the skin and dealing with chapters, which you'll consider in the following sections.

Lastly, the MediaPlayer has a set of On*Xxx* properties that allow you to connect JavaScript event handlers. (For example, you can use OnClientChapterSelected to connect a JavaScript event handler that reacts when the user chooses a new chapter.) In your JavaScript code, you can interact with the MediaPlayer object that's provided through ASP.NET AJAX. However, this technique is primarily of interest to ASP.NET developers who are already knee-deep in an ASP.NET AJAX application—otherwise, you'll find it's easier to build your own media player interface in Silverlight and write full-fledged Silverlight code in C#.

MediaPlayer Skins

With virtually no effort, you can transform the MediaPlayer's standard look. The trick is using MediaPlayer *skins*.

Technically, a MediaPlayer skin is a XAML file that defines the layout of the MediaElement and playback controls, complete with a full complement of animations that make the playback controls feel responsive and professional. The skin doesn't include any code. Instead, the MediaPlayer looks for elements that have predefined names (like PlayPauseButton and VolumeSlider) and wires up the appropriate functionality automatically. In this respect, a MediaPlayer skin works in a similar way to the control templates you learned about in Chapter 11.

Although you could create your own skin, it's easier to take an existing skin and modify it to suit your needs. The easiest way to pick the theme for your MediaPlayer is using the Visual Studio smart tag. While editing your ASP.NET page, switch to design mode or split mode (using the Design or Split buttons at the bottom of the document window). Then, find the box that represents the MediaPlayer on the page, select it, and click the tiny arrow that appears next to the top-right corner. Figure 13-2 shows the smart tag that appears, with a handful of options for configuring the MediaPlayer.

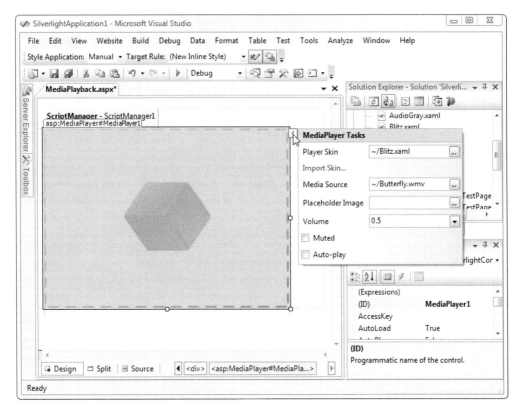

Figure 13-2. *Choosing a MediaPlayer skin*

Under the Player Skin text box, click the Import Skin link. Visual Studio will show an Open dialog box that's pointed to the location where the prebuilt skins are installed. (Typically, it's c:\Program Files\Microsoft SDKs\Silverlight\v2.0\Libraries\Server\MediaPlayerSkins.) Your options include AudioGray.xaml (a slimmed down interface without a video window, for audio only), Basic.xaml, Blitz.xaml, Classic.xaml, Console.xaml (themed to resemble the Xbox), Expression.xaml (themed to resemble Microsoft's Expression applications), Professional.xaml, and Simple.xaml.

Once you import a skin, the corresponding XAML file will be added to your web project and the MediaPlayer.SkinSource property will be set to point to it. You can then open the skin file and edit it by hand. If you do, you'll quickly see that the MediaPlayer uses the Canvas to organize elements, it uses the Path and Rectangle elements to build its playback controls, it includes a MediaElement for the video window, and it declares a long list of storyboards and animations for creating dynamic mouse-over and click effects. You can tweak any of these details using the layout, drawing, and animation skills you've picked up in earlier chapters.

Sizing the MediaPlayer

Although the MediaPlayer's standard skins seem quite self-sufficient at first glance, you may need to customize the ones you want to use. That's because all the included skins hard-code two important details: the size of the video window, and the size of the root Canvas that holds the entire user interface. When you set the Width and Height properties of the MediaPlayer web control (which you must), the entire skin will be scaled up or down to match.

This doesn't necessarily represent a problem—after all, the user interface that the Media-Player uses is composed of vector art, and so it can be resized to any size without sacrificing quality. Furthermore, the MediaElement that represents the video window in each skin uses the standard value for the Stretch property (Uniform), which means your video won't be squashed or otherwise mangled when it's resized. However, the scaling process isn't always ideal.

First, the hard-coded size for the root Canvas represents a best practices recommendation that ensures your playback controls are given a good, standard size. If you don't heed this size, you're forcing the MediaPlayer to scale up or scale down its entire user interface. It's better to open your skin, look at the Width and Height properties that are applied to the root Canvas element, and set the Width and Height of the MediaPlayer control to match.

Second, consider the size of the video window. Although the video window won't be stretched out of its proper aspect ratio, it may be scaled up (which can result in a loss of quality) or scaled down (which means you're throwing away some of the video data, and would be better off re-encoding your video at a smaller size). A better approach is to give your video window the exact dimensions you want. Every skin has a different hard-coded size for the video window. To check what the size is in your skin (and change the value to match your video exactly), look for the MediaElement named VideoWindow. However, you'll need to make sure you've also set the dimensions of the MediaPlayer to match the Height and Width properties of the root Canvas. Otherwise, the MediaPlayer will rescale its entire user interface, including the video window, thereby changing its dimensions.

Using Chapters

In Chapter 10, you learned how to add chapters to a media file, and use these chapters to react in your code or provide navigation points. These features still work with the MediaPlayer, although if you want to react to chapter navigation, you'll need to write a client-side JavaScript function to do it (and set the OnClientMarkerReached property). The navigation features of chapter marks are more interesting. That's because the MediaPlayer gives you a practical way to define chapter marks in your web form markup, complete with thumbnail images. These chapter marks will then be used by the MediaPlayer skin to provide navigation.

For each chapter, you need to add a MediaChapter element inside the MediaPlayer.Chapters collection. Each chapter requires a position, an image file, and a title. Here's an example with three chapters:

```
<asp:MediaPlayer runat="server" ID="MediaPlayer1"
 MediaSource="~/MyFile.wmv" Height="600" Width="700">
  <Chapters>
    <asp:MediaChapter Position="3"
     ThumbnailSource="~/Media/image1.jpg"
     Title="Chapter 1" />
    <asp:MediaChapter Position="5"
     ThumbnailSource="~/Media/image2.jpg"
     Title="Chapter 2" />
    <asp:MediaChapter Position="10"
     ThumbnailSource="~/Media/image3.jpg"
     Title="Chapter 3" />
  </Chapters>
</asp:MediaPlayer>
```

Different skins may display the chapter information in different ways. For example, the Blitz.xaml skin includes a button that, when clicked, shows the thumbnail list. On the other hand, the Professional.xaml skin pops up a panel with the thumbnail list when the mouse hovers just underneath the movie (see Figure 13-3). Either way, thumbnails are shown in a scrollable container, which means you can include as many as you need without affecting the layout of the MediaPlayer's user interface. To jump to a specific chapter, the user simply needs to click the appropriate thumbnail.

It's up to you to create the images for each chapter. If you use Microsoft Expression Encoder, you can create thumbnail images for any position in a video file, as described in Chapter 10. In fact, Expression Encoder even allows you to avoid writing the chapter markup altogether by generating a *media definition file*.

To create a media definition file, you need to use Expression Encoder's ability to generate a Silverlight video player page. That means you need to go to the Output pane, find the Job Output box, and choose a template from the list, as described in Chapter 10. When you encode your video, Expression Encoder will create an output directory that includes your Silverlight application (which you don't need), your video, and a media definition file named MediaDefinition.xml.

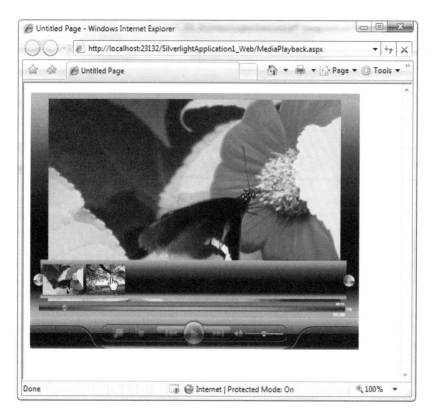

Figure 13-3. *Thumbnail images for chapters*

The media definition file is essentially a list of chapter information in XML format. Here's one that duplicates the previous example, and also defines the placeholder image:

```
<mediaDefinition>
  <mediaItems>
    <mediaItem mediaSource="MyFile.wmv" placeholderSource="image0.jpg">
      <chapters>
        <chapter position="3" thumbnailSource="image1.jpg" title="Chapter 1" />
        <chapter position="5" thumbnailSource="image1.jpg" title="Chapter 2" />
        <chapter position="10" thumbnailSource="image2.jpg" title="Chapter 3" />
      </chapters>
    </mediaItem>
  </mediaItems>
</mediaDefinition>
```

To use a media definition file, you simply add it to your ASP.NET website and set the MediaPlayer.MediaDefinition property with a URL that points to the media definition file:

```
<asp:MediaPlayer runat="server" ID="MediaPlayer1" MediaSource="~/MyFile.wmv"
 MediaDefinition="~/Media/MediaDefintion.xml" Height="600" Width="700"/>
```

Custom Controls

So far, you've seen how specialized ASP.NET server controls can bridge the gap between ASP.NET and Silverlight. The Silverlight control works by rendering the code needed to host a Silverlight application that you've prepared separately. The MediaPlayer control is more interesting—it renders a complete Silverlight application based on the properties you set.

By this point, it may have occurred to you that crafty ASP.NET developers can duplicate the technique that the MediaPlayer control uses by devising custom ASP.NET controls that render themselves into Silverlight applications. For example, you could build a Silverlight version of the ASP.NET AdRotator control that renders a Silverlight-powered ad bar, suitable for inclusion on an ordinary ASP.NET page.

Unfortunately, this model isn't quite as simple as it seems at first. One challenge is the fact that Silverlight applications depend on separate resources, like XAML files. These files can be embedded in your ASP.NET assembly and retrieved when needed using the ASP.NET web resources model, but this design complicates life. Furthermore, you need a way to customize the Silverlight content based on the properties of the custom control. For example, you may need to examine properties set on the server control and use that to change the details in the embedded XAML. ASP.NET AJAX has possible solutions for this sort of challenge, but they're fairly involved and out of the scope of this chapter.

In the future, developers will get better tools that make this scenario—building custom ASP.NET controls that generate Silverlight content—easier and more practical. In the meantime, cutting-edge developers who are planning to experiment can check out `http://msdn.microsoft.com/en-us/magazine/cc135987.aspx` for an example that works with Silverlight 1.0.

Hybrid Pages

Almost all of the examples you've seen in this book have used HTML-only test pages or ASP.NET test pages with very little ASP.NET content beyond the Silverlight control. However, more ambitious ASP.NET developers might use Silverlight to add new functionality (or just sugarcoat) existing ASP.NET pages. Examples include Silverlight-powered ad content, menu systems, and embedded applets (like calculators or games).

In Chapter 12, you considered a variation of this idea, and built Silverlight pages that broke down the barrier between Silverlight and HTML. When dealing with the interaction between Silverlight and ASP.NET, a few more considerations apply.

First, unlike the JavaScript code you saw in Chapter 12, all ASP.NET code runs on the web server. To get server-side code to run, ASP.NET controls use a postback mechanism that sends the current page back to the server. For example, this happens when you click an ASP.NET button. The problem is that when the page is posted back, the current Silverlight application ends. The web server code runs, a new version of the page is sent to the browser, and the browser loads this new page, at which point your Silverlight application restarts. Not only does this send the user back to the starting point, it also takes additional time because the Silverlight environment must be initialized all over again.

If you want to avoid this disruption, you can use ASP.NET AJAX techniques. A particularly useful tool is the UpdatePanel. The basic technique is to wrap the controls that would ordinarily trigger a postback and any other controls that they modify into one or more UpdatePanel controls. Then, when the user clicks a button, an asynchronous request is sent to the web server instead of a full postback. When the browser receives the reply, it updates the corresponding portions of the page, without disrupting the Silverlight content.

Figure 13-4 shows a simple demonstration of this technique. The page is carved into two regions—a top region with ASP.NET controls, and a bottom region that shows a Silverlight application. The ASP.NET section includes two buttons and a label. When either button is clicked, the label is updated with the current date and time, using exactly the same code:

```
protected void cmdUpdatePost_Click(object sender, EventArgs e)
{
    lbl.Text = "This label was refreshed at " + DateTime.Now.ToLongTimeString();
}

protected void cmdUpdateNoPost_Click(object sender, EventArgs e)
{
    lbl.Text = "This label was refreshed at " + DateTime.Now.ToLongTimeString();
}
```

However, there's a twist. The topmost button and the label are wrapped in an UpdatePanel. As a result, clicking that button results in a seamless refresh, while clicking the button below posts back the page. Here's the markup that makes this work:

```
<div style=
 "background-color: Lime; padding: 15px; font-family: Verdana; font-size: small">
  <p>This section is ASP.NET content.</p>
  <asp:UpdatePanel id="updatePanel1" runat="server">
    <ContentTemplate>
      <asp:Button ID="cmdUpdateNoPost" runat="server"
       Text="Update Label (no postback)" OnClick="cmdUpdateNoPost_Click" />
      <br /><br />
      <asp:Label ID="lbl" runat="server"></asp:Label>
    </ContentTemplate>
  </asp:UpdatePanel>

  <br />
  <asp:Button ID="cmdUpdatePost" runat="server"
   Text="Update Label (with postback)" OnClick="cmdUpdatePost_Click" />
  <br /><br />
</div>
<br />

<asp:Silverlight ID="Silverlight1" runat="server"
 Source="~/ClientBin/SilverlightApplication1.xap"
 BorderColor="SteelBlue" BorderStyle="Solid" BorderWidth="1"
 Height="150" Width="100%">
</asp:Silverlight>
```

You can see the difference in two ways. First, the full-page postback causes the page to flicker as it's refreshed. Second, the full-page postback causes the Silverlight application to restart itself. Each time it starts, it runs a similar piece of code to display the current time. Figure 13-4 shows the result of loading the page, waiting a few seconds, and then clicking the button in the UpdatePanel to perform a refresh without a postback.

Figure 13-4. *Updating an ASP.NET page without restarting a Silverlight application*

■**Tip** For a much more detailed exploration of the UpdatePanel, refer to *Pro ASP.NET 3.5 in C# 2008*.

In some cases, you may allow direct interaction between Silverlight and ASP.NET content. In this situation, you can use some of the techniques described in Chapter 12. For example, you use HTML interoperability to allow your Silverlight application to change the HTML that's generated for ASP.NET controls, although some headaches can occur.

If you want Silverlight to modify an element on a page, the easiest approach is to make it an HTML element rather than an ASP.NET control. If you need to modify an element on the client side (through Silverlight) and on the server side (through ASP.NET), the next best option is to use an HTML server control in ASP.NET. This way, you'll be absolutely clear what the rendered HTML will look like, and you'll know how to manipulate it in Silverlight. If you need to modify an ASP.NET web control with Silverlight, you can retrieve the rendered HTML element using the control name. However, you may need to do some digging through the generated HTML to determine exactly what that HTML element looks like and how you can interact with it. Some types of interactions are more problematic than others. Attempting to modify certain details in a complex control can cause problems with that control's view state and ASP.NET security features like event validation.

Building Web Services for Silverlight

Without a doubt, the most effective way for a Silverlight application to tap into server-side code is through web services. The basic idea is simple—you include a web service with your ASP.NET website, and your Silverlight application calls the methods in that web service. The web service code can perform server-side tasks, access server-side databases, and so on. With a little extra work, it can even use ASP.NET services like authentication and session state. Best of all, because the page isn't posted back, your Silverlight application continues running without interruption.

Silverlight applications can call traditional ASP.NET web services (.asmx services) as well as the WCF services, which are the newer standard. In the following sections, you'll learn how to build, call, and refine a WCF service. In Chapter 17, you'll consider how Silverlight applications can also call non-.NET web services, such as simpler REST services.

Creating a Web Service

To create a WCF service in Visual Studio, right-click your ASP.NET website in the Solution Explorer and choose Add New Item. Choose the "Silverlight-enabled WCF Service" template, enter a file name, and click Add.

When adding a new WCF service, Visual Studio creates two files (see Figure 13-5):

- **The service endpoint.** The service endpoint has the extension .svc, and is placed in your root website folder. For example, if you create a web service named TestService, you'll get a file named TestService.svc. When using the web service, the client will request a URL that points to the .svc file. However, the .svc file doesn't contain any code—it simply includes one line of markup that tells ASP.NET where to find the corresponding web service code.

- **The service code.** The service code is placed in the App_Code folder of your website. For example, if you create a web service named TestService, you'll get a code file named TestService.cs. It includes a class that implements the service interface and provides the actual code for your web service.

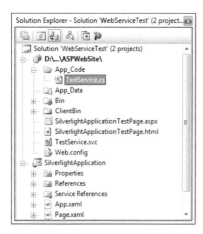

Figure 13-5. *An ASP.NET project with a WCF service*

The code file for your web service begins with two attributes. The ServiceContract attribute indicates that it defines a service contract—in other words, a set of methods that you plan to expose to remote callers as part of a service. The AspNetCompatibilityRequirements attribute indicates that it will have access to ASP.NET platform features like session state.

```
[ServiceContract]
[AspNetCompatibilityRequirements(RequirementsMode =
 AspNetCompatibilityRequirementsMode.Allowed)]
public class TestService
{ ... }
```

To add a new web service method, you simply add a new method to the code file, and make sure that it's decorated with the OperationContract attribute. For example, if you want to add a method that returns the current time on the server, you might modify the interface like this:

```
[ServiceContract]
[AspNetCompatibilityRequirements(RequirementsMode =
 AspNetCompatibilityRequirementsMode.Allowed)]
public class TestService
{
    [OperationContract]
    public DateTime GetServerTime()
    {
        return DateTime.Now;
    }
}
```

Consuming a Web Service

You consume a web service in a Silverlight application in much the same way that you consume one in a full-fledged.NET application. The first step is to create a proxy class by adding a Visual Studio web reference.

Note Before you begin, you need to know the correct URL for your web service. When testing your application, Visual Studio loads the test web server at a randomly chosen port. To add a web reference, you need to know this port. To find out what it is, run your website just before you add the reference, copy the root URL, and add the service endpoint to the end (as in http://localhost:4198/ASPWebSite/TestService.svc). And don't worry—even though you use the dynamically chosen port number to add the web reference, you'll see how to set your Silverlight application so it can always find the right URL, even when the port number changes.

To add the web reference, follow these steps:

1. Right-click your Silverlight project in the Solution Explorer and choose Add Service Reference. The Add Service Reference dialog box will appear (see Figure 13-6).

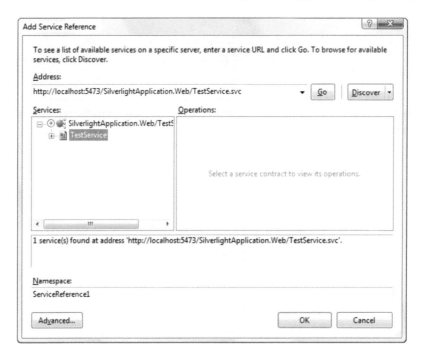

Figure 13-6. *Adding a service reference*

2. In the Address box, enter the URL that points to the web service and click Go. (Or, just click the Discover button to automatically find all the web services that are in your current solution.)

3. In the Namespace box, enter the C# namespace that Visual Studio should use for the automatically generated classes.

4. Click OK. Visual Studio will create a proxy class that has the code for calling the web service. To see the file that contains this code, select the Silverlight project in the Solution Explorer, click the Show All Files button, expand the Service References node and the Reference.svcmap node inside, and open the Reference.cs file.

When you perform this task, Visual Studio creates a *proxy class*—a class that you can interact with to call your web service. The proxy class is named after the original web service class—for example, Visual Studio will create a proxy class named TestServiceClient for the TestService shown earlier. The proxy class contains methods that allow you to trigger the appropriate web service calls, and it takes care of the heavy lifting (creating the request message, sending it in an HTTP request, getting the response, and then notifying your code).

Calling the Web Service

To use the proxy class, start by importing the namespace that you specified for the service reference in step 3. Assuming you used the namespace MyWebServer and your project is named MySilverlightProject, you'd need this statement:

```
using MySilverlightProject.MyWebServer;
```

In Silverlight, all web service calls must be asynchronous. That means you call a method to start the call (and send off the request).This method returns immediately. Your code can then carry on to perform other tasks, or the user can continue to interact with the application. When the response is received, the proxy class triggers a corresponding proxy class event, which is named in the form *MethodName*Completed. You must handle this event to process the results.

■ **Note** This two-part communication process means that it takes a bit more work to handle a web service call than to interact with an ordinary local object. However, it also ensures that developers create responsive Silverlight applications. After all, making an HTTP call to a web service can take as long as one minute (using the default timeout setting), so it's not safe to make the user wait. (And yes, Microsoft imposes this limitation to ensure *your* code can't give *its* platform a bad name.)

Here's how to call the TestService.GetServerTime() method shown earlier:

```
// Create the proxy class.
TestServiceClient proxy = new TestServiceClient();

// Attach an event handler to the completed event.
proxy.GetServerTimeCompleted += new
  EventHandler<GetServerTimeCompletedEventArgs>(GetServerTimeCompleted);

// Start the web service call.
proxy.GetServerTimeAsync();
```

To get the results, you need to handle the completed event and examine the corresponding EventArgs object. When generating the proxy class, Visual Studio also creates a different EventArgs class for each method. The only difference is the Result property, which is typed to match the return value of the method. For example the GetServerTime() method works in conjunction with a GetServerTimeCompletedEventArgs class that provides a DateTime object through its Result property.

When accessing the Result property for the first time, you need to use exception handling code. That's because this is the point where an exception will be thrown if the web service call failed—for example, the server couldn't be found, the web method returned an error, or the connection timed out.

Here's an event handler that reads the result (the current date and time on the server) and displays it in a TextBlock:

```
private void GetServerTimeCompleted(object sender,
    GetServerTimeCompletedEventArgs e)
{
    try
    {
        lblTime.Text = e.Result.ToLongTimeString();
    }
    catch (Exception err)
    {
        lblTime.Text = "Error contacting web service";
    }
}
```

Tip Even though web service calls are performed on a background thread, there's no need to worry about thread marshalling when the completed event fires. That's because the proxy class ensures that the completed event fires on the main user interface thread, allowing you to access the controls in your page without worry.

By default, the proxy class waits for one minute before giving up if it doesn't receive a response. You can configure the timeout length by using code like this before you make the web service call:

```
proxy.InnerChannel.OperationTimeout = TimeSpan.FromSeconds(30);
```

Configuring the Web Service URL

When you add a service reference, the automatically generated code includes the web service URL. As a result, you don't need to specify the URL when you create an instance of the proxy class.

However, this raises a potential problem. All web service URLs are fully qualified—relative paths aren't allowed. If you're using the test web server in Visual Studio, that means you'll run into trouble if you try to run your application at a later point, when the test web server has chosen a different port number. Similarly, you'll need to update the URL when you deploy your final application to a production web server.

You can solve this problem by regenerating the service reference, but it's usually easier to change the address dynamically in your code. To do so, you need to create a new Endpoint-Address object with the appropriate URL, and then pass that as a constructor argument when creating the proxy class.

For example, the following code ensures that the web service call always works, no matter what port number the Visual Studio test web server chooses:

```
// Create a new URL for the TestService.svc service using the current port number
EndpointAddress address = new EndpointAddress("http://localhost:" +
  HtmlPage.Document.DocumentUri.Port + "/ASPWebSite/TestService.svc");

// Use the new address to create a proxy object.
TestServiceClient proxy = new TestServiceClient(new BasicHttpBinding(), address);
```

You could use similar code to create a URL based on the current Silverlight page, so that the web service continues to work no matter where you deploy it, so long as you keep the web service and Silverlight application together in the same web folder.

Data Types

When creating a web service for use with Silverlight, you're limited to the core set of .NET data types—for example, strings, Boolean values, bytes, numeric data types, enumeration values, and DateTime objects. You can also use arrays and collections of any supported type, and custom classes, provided these classes use the DataContract and DataMember attributes to indicate that they can be serialized. Use DataContract on the class declaration and Data-Member on the individual properties (which must be public, writable, and use one of the previously discussed serializable data types). Additionally, your class must include a zero-argument default constructor.

Here's an example:

```
[DataContract]
public class Customer
{
    private string firstName;
    private string lastName;

    [DataMember]
    public string FirstName
    {
        get { return firstName; }
        set { firstName = value; }
    }

    [DataMember]
    public string LastName
    {
        get { return lastName; }
        set { lastName = value; }
    }
}
```

If you add a reference to a web service that uses the Customer class (either as a return type or parameter), Visual Studio will generate a similar Customer class definition in your Silverlight application, alongside the proxy class. You can then create Customer objects in the client and send them to the server, and vice versa.

You'll see a much more in-depth example of a web service that uses custom classes in Chapter 14, when you use data binding with a web service that returns data from a database.

Cross-Domain Web Service Calls

Silverlight allows you to make web service calls to web services that are a part of the same website with no restrictions. Additionally, Silverlight allows you to call web services on other web services *if* they explicitly allow it with a policy file.

In Chapter 17, you'll consider the implications this has when you're using third-party web services and downloading content on the web. But now, it's worth understanding how you can configure your web service to allow cross-domain callers. To make this possible, you must create a file named ClientAccessPolicy.xml, and place that in the root of your website (for example, in the c:\inetpub\wwwroot directory of an IIS web server). The ClientAccess-Policy.xml file indicates what domains are allowed to access your web service. Here's an example that allows any Silverlight application that's been downloaded from any web server to access your website:

```xml
<?xml version="1.0" encoding="utf-8"?>
<access-policy>
  <cross-domain-access>
    <policy>
      <allow-from>
        <domain uri="*"/>
      </allow-from>
      <grant-to>
        <resource path="/" include-subpaths="true"/>
      </grant-to>
    </policy>
  </cross-domain-access>
</access-policy>
```

When you take this step, third-party Silverlight applications will be able to call your web services and make arbitrary HTTP requests (for example, download web pages). Ordinarily, neither task would be allowed in a Silverlight application. (Desktop applications and server-side applications face no such restrictions—no matter what policy file you create, they will be able to do everything an ordinary user can do, which means they can download any public content.)

Alternatively, you can limit access to Silverlight applications that are running on web pages in specific domains. Here's an example that allows requests from Silverlight applications that are hosted at www.somecompany.com or www.someothercompany.com:

```xml
<?xml version="1.0" encoding="utf-8"?>
<access-policy>
  <cross-domain-access>
    <policy>
      <allow-from http-request-headers="*">
        <domain uri="http://www.somecompany.com" />
        <domain uri="http://www.someothercompany.com" />
```

```
      </allow-from>
      <grant-to>
        <resource path="/" include-subpaths="true"/>
      </grant-to>
    </policy>
  </cross-domain-access>
</access-policy>
```

You can use wildcards in the domain names to allow subdomains. For example, *.some-company.com allows requests from mail.somecompany.com, admin.somecompany.com, and so on.

Furthermore, you can selectively allow access to part of your website. Here's an example that allows Silverlight applications to access the services folder in your root web domain, which is presumably where you'll place all your cross-domain web services:

```
<?xml version="1.0" encoding="utf-8"?>
<access-policy>
  <cross-domain-access>
    <policy>
      <allow-from>
        <domain uri="*"/>
      </allow-from>
      <grant-to>
        <resource path="/services/" include-subpaths="true"/>
      </grant-to>
    </policy>
  </cross-domain-access>
</access-policy>
```

Note Instead of using clientaccesspolicy.xml, you can create a crossdomain.xml file. This file has essentially the same purpose, but it uses a standard that was first developed for Flash applications. The only advantage to using it is if you want to give access to Silverlight and Flash applications in one step. Compared to crossdomain.xml, clientaccesspolicy.xml is slightly more featured, because it allows you to grant access to just a specific part of your website (both standards allow you to limit requests based on the caller's domain). For more information about crossdomain.xml, see Chapter 17.

Using ASP.NET Platform Services

Ordinarily, WCF services don't get access to ASP.NET platform features. That means that even though ASP.NET is responsible for compiling your service and hosting it, your service can't use any of the following:

- Session state

- Data caching

- The authorization rules in the web.config file

- Provider-based features, such as authentication, membership, and profiles

In many cases, this makes sense, because WCF services are meant to be independent of the ASP.NET platform. In other words, it's dangerous to use ASP.NET-only features, because they limit your ability to move your service to other hosts, use other transport protocols, and so on. Although these considerations might not come into play with a Silverlight application, there's still a good philosophical basis for making your services as self-contained as possible.

Furthermore, some of the features really don't make sense in a web service context. Currently, there are a number of workarounds to get session state to work with WCF services. However, the session state feature fits awkwardly with the web service model, because the lifetime of the session is not linked to the lifetime of the web service or proxy class. That means a session could unexpectedly time out between calls. Rather than introduce these headaches, it's better to store state information in a database.

However, there are some scenarios where ASP.NET features can legitimately save a good deal of work. For example, you might want to build a service that uses in-memory caching if it's available. If it's not, the service can degrade gracefully, and get its information from another source (like a database). But if the in-memory cache is working and has the information you need, it can save you the overhead of requerying it or re-creating it. Similarly, there's a case to be made for using some of the ASP.NET provider-based features to give you easy user-specific authentication, role-based security, and storage, without forcing you to reimplement a similar feature from scratch.

To access ASP.NET features in a web service, you use the static Current property of the System.Web.HttpContext class. The HttpContext represents the HTTP environment that hosts your service. It provides access to key ASP.NET objects through its properties, such as Session (per-user session state), Application (global application state), Cache (the data cache), Request (the HTTP request message, including HTTP headers, client browser details, cookies, the requested URL, and so on), User (the user making the request, if authenticated through ASP.NET), and so on. ASP.NET developers will be familiar with these details.

The following example uses HttpContext to get access to the data cache. It caches a collection of Product objects so the database doesn't have to be queried each time the web method is called:

```
// This is the web service method.
public Product[] GetAllProducts()
{
    // Check the cache.
    HttpContext context = HttpContext.Current;

    if (context.Cache["Products"] != null)
    {
        // Retrieve it from the cache
        return (Product[])context.Cache["Products"];
    }
    else
    {
```

```
        // Retrieve it from the database.
        Product[] products = QueryProducts();

        // Now store it in the cache for 10 minutes.
        context.Cache.Insert("Products", products, null,
         DateTime.Now.AddMinutes(10), TimeSpan.Zero);

        return products;
    }
}

// This private method contains the database code.
private Product[] QueryProducts()
{ ... }
```

The actual caching feature (and other ASP.NET features) is outside of the scope of this book. However, this example shows how experienced ASP.NET developers can continue to use some of the features of ASP.NET when building a WCF service. To try out an example of ASP.NET caching in a web service, check out the downloadable examples for this chapter.

TWO-WAY COMMUNICATION

Ordinarily, web services use a fairly straightforward and somewhat limiting form of interaction. The client (your Silverlight application) sends a request, waits for a response, and then processes it. This is a distinctly one-way type of communication, as the client must initiate every conversation.

This model is no surprise, because it's based on the underlying HTTP protocol. Browsers request web resources, but websites can never initiate connections and transmit information to clients without first being asked. Although this model makes sense, it prevents you from building certain types of applications (such as chat servers) and implementing certain types of features (such as notification). Fortunately, there are several ways to work around these limitations in Silverlight:

- **Polling.** With polling, you create a client that connects to the server periodically and checks for new data. For example, if you want to create a chat application, you might create a chat client that checks the web server for new messages every second. The obvious problem with polling is that it's inefficient. On the client side, the overhead is fairly minimal, but the server can easily be swamped with work if a large number of clients keep bombarding it with requests.

- **Duplex services.** Silverlight includes a feature for creating duplex services, which allow two-way communication (meaning the server can contact your client when needed). Behind the scenes, duplex services are based on polling, but they implement it in a more efficient manner. The client's network request is left open but in an inactive state that doesn't hassle the server. It stays open until it times out, 90 seconds later, at which point the client connects again. Unfortunately, creating a duplex service involves a fair bit of boilerplate code to establish a custom binding. Furthermore, the duplex contract feature is provided for developer evaluation, and isn't recommended for real-world applications just yet. To see an example that uses a duplex service, read the article at http://msdn.microsoft.com/en-us/library/cc645027(VS.95).aspx.

> • **Sockets.** The most powerful option is to use sockets—low-level network connections. Sockets avoid HTTP altogether, in favor of the leaner and more efficient TCP. However, using sockets is complex, and it requires you to worry about issues like network timeouts, byte arrays, and user concurrency. If you're still interested, Chapter 17 provides a complete example with a messaging application that uses sockets.

The Last Word

In this chapter, you considered the widely different ways that ASP.NET features can interact with Silverlight code.

First, you considered how new ASP.NET server controls can render Silverlight content, whether it's a Silverlight application you've developed separately or a ready-made media playback page. This approach to Silverlight development is still evolving, and you'll see many more custom ASP.NET controls that create Silverlight content in the future.

Next, you started exploring Silverlight's web service support. You saw how you could build a web service that's hosted on the server, but accessible to the Silverlight client at any point over its lifetime. You'll build on this technique in Chapter 14, when you explore how you can use a web service to provide your Silverlight application with information extracted from a server-side resource, like a database.

CHAPTER 14

■■■

Data Binding

Data binding is the time-honored tradition of pulling information out of an object and displaying it in your application's user interface, without writing the tedious code that does all the work. Often, rich clients use *two-way* data binding, which adds the ability to push information from the user interface back into some object—again, with little or no code.

In this chapter, you'll learn how to use Silverlight data binding to display, format, and edit data. You'll see how to get information from a server-side using a web service, how to shape it with data templates, and how to format it with value converters. You'll even take a look at data filtering with Language Integrated Query (LINQ), and use Silverlight's newest and most high-powered data control, the DataGrid.

SILVERLIGHT DATA BINDING VS. WPF

If you've programmed with WPF, you'll find that Silverlight's data binding abilities are significantly scaled back. Though data binding is still a critical part of Silverlight programming (as it is a critical part of WPF programming), there are many data binding features that are available in WPF but missing from the Silverlight world. Here's a list that includes the most significant omissions:

- Silverlight doesn't allow you to bind one element to another element. Instead, all bindings are to data objects. (You could get around this using an intermediate object, but the added inconvenience means it's rarely worthwhile.)

- Silverlight omits several properties that WPF supports in data binding expressions, including RelativeSource, UpdateSourceTrigger, and the OneWayToSource BindingMode. In fact, Silverlight binding expressions use a slightly different syntax, so there's no way to reuse markup between WPF and Silverlight if it uses data binding.

- Silverlight doesn't support binding to the ADO.NET DataSet classes, because Silverlight doesn't include any part of ADO.NET.

- Silverlight does not include a CollectionView class for changing the way that a collection of objects is sorted and filtered.

- Silverlight doesn't support grouped data.

- Silverlight lacks custom validation rules and support for the IDataErrorInfo interface.

- Silverlight value converters can only act on one data property, not multiple ones.

- Silverlight doesn't allow you to create selectors that dynamically choose the right style or template for bound data.

- Silverlight doesn't include object providers for code-free data binding. (This feature was of limited use in WPF anyway, unless you needed a quick code-free way to bind XML data.)

- Silverlight doesn't allow you to define multiple, prioritized bindings, which would allow you to display a temporary value while waiting for information that takes longer to retrieve.

Some of these limitations cut out specialized features that WPF developers rarely use. Others remove significant features. However, it's interesting to note that Silverlight also adds one feature that's not found in WPF—a DataGrid control for displaying a highly optimized grid of data that's split into rows and columns.

Binding to Data Objects

At its simplest, data binding is a process that tells Silverlight to extract some information from a *source* object and use it to set a property in a *target* object. The target property must be a dependency property, and the target object must be a Silverlight element (technically, a class that derives from FrameworkElement). This makes sense—after all, the ultimate goal of Silverlight data binding is to display some information in your user interface. The source can be just about any data object, including the ones you create yourself.

Building a Data Object

The best way to try out Silverlight's data binding features is to create a simple data object. Using data binding expressions, you'll be able to display the data from your data object, without writing tedious data-display code.

A data object is simply a package of related information. Any class will work as a data object, provided it consists of public properties. (A data object can also have fields and private properties, but the information these members contain can't be extracted through a data binding expression.) Furthermore, if you want to the user to be able to modify a data object through data binding, its properties cannot be read-only.

Here's a simple data object that encapsulates the information for a single product in a product catalog:

```
public class Product
{
    private string modelNumber;
    public string ModelNumber
    {
```

```
        get { return modelNumber; }
        set { modelNumber = value; }
    }

    private string modelName;
    public string ModelName
    {
        get { return modelName; }
        set { modelName = value; }
    }

    private double unitCost;
    public double UnitCost
    {
        get { return unitCost; }
        set { unitCost = value; }
    }

    private string description;
    public string Description
    {
        get { return description; }
        set { description = value; }
    }

    public Product(string modelNumber, string modelName,
      double unitCost, string description)
    {
        ModelNumber = modelNumber;
        ModelName = modelName;
        UnitCost = unitCost;
        Description = description;
    }

    // A no-argument constructor allows you to create instances of this class
    // in XAML markup.
    public Product(){}
}
```

Displaying a Data Object with DataContext

Consider the simple page shown in Figure 14-1. It shows the information for a single product using several text boxes in a Grid.

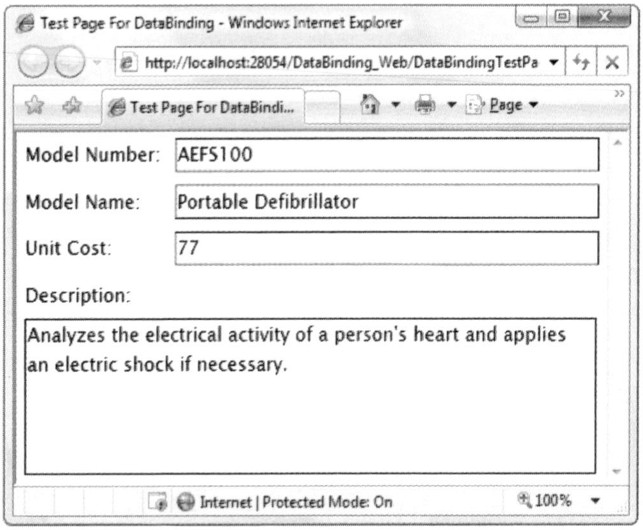

Figure 14-1. *Displaying data from a Product object*

To build this example, you need some code that creates the Product object you want to display. In this example, you'll use code to create a Product object using hard-coded details. Of course, in real life it's much more likely that you'll extract the data from another resource—such as a web service, an XML document, a file that's been downloaded from the Web (see Chapter 17), and so on. You'll explore a more realistic example that uses a full-fledged web service throughout this chapter, as you dig into data binding in more detail.

To display the information from a Product object, you can obviously resort to tedious data-copying code like this:

```
txtModelNumber = product.TextNumber;
```

This code is lengthy, error-prone, and brittle (for example, you'll probably need to rewrite it if you choose to use different display controls). Data binding allows you to move the responsibility for transferring the data from your C# code to your XAML markup.

To use data binding, you must set the target property using a *binding expression.* A binding expression is a markup extension (somewhat like the StaticResource extension you used in Chapter 2). It's delineated by curly braces, and always starts with the word *Binding.* The simplest binding expression that you can create requires just one more detail—the name of the property in the source object that has the data you want to extract.

For example, to access the Product.ModelNumber property, you use a binding expression like this:

```
{Binding ModelNumber}
```

And here's how you use it to set the Text property in a text box:

```
<TextBox Text="{Binding ModelNumber}"></TextBox>
```

Using this straightforward technique, it's easy to build the page shown in Figure 14-1, with its four binding expressions:

```
<Grid Name="gridProductDetails">
  <Grid.ColumnDefinitions>
    <ColumnDefinition Width="Auto"></ColumnDefinition>
    <ColumnDefinition></ColumnDefinition>
  </Grid.ColumnDefinitions>
  <Grid.RowDefinitions>
    <RowDefinition Height="Auto"></RowDefinition>
    <RowDefinition Height="Auto"></RowDefinition>
    <RowDefinition Height="Auto"></RowDefinition>
    <RowDefinition Height="Auto"></RowDefinition>
    <RowDefinition Height="*"></RowDefinition>
  </Grid.RowDefinitions>

  <TextBlock Margin="7">Model Number:</TextBlock>
  <TextBox Margin="5" Grid.Column="1"
    Text="{Binding ModelNumber}"></TextBox>
  <TextBlock Margin="7" Grid.Row="1">Model Name:</TextBlock>
  <TextBox Margin="5" Grid.Row="1" Grid.Column="1"
    Text="{Binding ModelName}"></TextBox>
  <TextBlock Margin="7" Grid.Row="2">Unit Cost:</TextBlock>
  <TextBox Margin="5" Grid.Row="2" Grid.Column="1"
    Text="{Binding UnitCost}"></TextBox>
  <TextBlock Margin="7,7,7,0" Grid.Row="3">Description:</TextBlock>
  <TextBox Margin="7" Grid.Row="4" Grid.Column="0" Grid.ColumnSpan="2"
    TextWrapping="Wrap" Text="{Binding Description}"></TextBox>
</Grid>
```

The binding expressions specify the name of the source property, but they don't indicate the source object. There are two ways that you can set the source object—by setting the Data-Context property of an element and by setting the Source property of a binding.

In most situations, the most practical approach is to set the DataContext property, which every element includes. In the previous example, you could set the DataContext property of all four text boxes. However, there's an easier approach. If an element uses a binding expression but has a null value for DataContext (which is the default), the element will continue its search up the element tree. This search continues until the element finds a data object or reaches the top-level container, which is the user control that represents the page. In the preceding example, that means you can save considerable effort by setting the DataContext property of the Grid. All the text boxes will then use the same data object.

Here's the code that creates the Product object and sets the Grid.DataContext property when the page first loads:

```
private void Page_Loaded(object sender, RoutedEventArgs e)
{
    Product product = new Product("AEFS100", "Portable Defibrillator", 77,
        "Analyzes the electrical activity of a person's heart and applies " +
        "an electric shock if necessary.");
    gridProductDetails.DataContext = product;
}
```

If you don't run this code, no information will appear. Even though you've defined your bindings, no source object is available, so the elements in your page will remain blank.

Tip Usually, you'll place all your bound controls in the same container, and you'll be able to set the Data-Context once on the container rather than for each bound element.

Storing a Data Object As a Resource

You have one other option for specifying a data object. You can define it as a resource in your XAML markup, and then alter each binding expression by adding the Source property.

For example, you could create the Product object as a resource using markup like this:

```
<UserControl.Resources>
  <local:Product x:Key="resourceProduct"
  ModelNumber="AEFS100"
  ModelName="Portable Defibrillator" UnitCost="77"
  Description="Analyzes the electrical activity of a person's heart and applies
an electric shock if necessary.">
  </local:Product>
</UserControl.Resources>
```

This markup assumes you've mapped the project namespace to the XML namespace prefix local. For example, if the project is named DataBinding, you would add this attribute to the UserControl start tag:

```
xmlns:local="clr-namespace:DataBinding"
```

To use this object in a binding expression, you need to specify the Source property. To set the Source property, you use a StaticResource expression that uses the key name of your resource:

```
<TextBox
 Text="{Binding ModelNumber, Source={StaticResource resourceProduct} }">
</TextBox>
```

Unfortunately, you'll be forced to specify the Source property in each data binding expression. If you need to bind a significant number of elements to the same data object, it's easier to set the DataContext property of a container. In fact, you can still use the StaticResource to set the DataContext property, which allows you to bind a group of nested elements to a single data object that's defined as a resource:

```
<Grid Name="gridProductDetails" DataContext="{StaticResource resourceProduct}">
```

Either way, when you define a data object as a resource, you give up a fair bit of freedom. Although you can still alter that object, you can't replace it. If you plan to retrieve the details for your data object from another source (such as a web service), it's far more natural to create the data object in code.

Incidentally, the Binding markup extension supports several other properties along with Source, including Mode (which allows you to use two-way bindings to edit data objects) and Converter (which allows you to modify source values before they are displayed). You'll learn about Mode in the next section, and Converter later in this chapter.

Editing with Two-Way Bindings

At this point, you might wonder what happens if the user changes the bound values that appear in the text controls. For example, if the user types in a new description, is the in-memory Product object changed?

To investigate what happens, you can use code like this that grabs the current Product object from the DataContext, and displays its properties in a TextBlock:

```
Product product = (Product)gridProductDetails.DataContext;
lblCheck.Text = "Model Name: " + product.ModelName + "\nModel Number: " +
  product.ModelNumber + "\nUnit Cost: " + product.UnitCost;
```

If you run this code, you'll discover that changing the displayed values has no effect. The Product object remains in its original form.

This behavior results because binding expressions use one-way binding by default. However, Silverlight actually allows you to use one of three values from the System.Windows.Data.BindingMode enumeration when setting the Binding.Mode property. Table 14-1 has the full list.

Table 14-1. *Values from the BindingMode Enumeration*

Name	Description
OneWay	The target property is updated when the source property changes.
TwoWay	The target property is updated when the source property changes, and the source property is updated when the target property changes.
OneTime	The target property is set initially based on the source property value. However, changes are ignored from that point onward. Usually, you'll use this mode to reduce overhead if you know the source property won't change.

■ **Note** When using two-way binding, the in-memory data object isn't modified until the text box loses focus. However, other elements perform their updates immediately. For example, when you make a selection in a list box, move the thumb in a slider, or change the state of a checkbox, the source object is modified immediately.

If you change one or more of your bindings to use two-way binding, the changes you make in the text box will be committed to the in-memory object as soon as the focus leaves the text box (for example, as soon as you move to another control or click a button).

```
<TextBox Text="{Binding UnitCost, Mode=TwoWay}"></TextBox>
```

Validation

When the Silverlight data binding system encounters invalid data, it usually ignores it. For example, consider the following list, which details the three types of errors that can occur when editing a two-way field:

- **Incorrect data type.** For example, a numeric property like UnitCost can't accommodate letters or special characters. Similarly, it can't hold extremely large numbers (numbers larger than 1.79769313486231570E+308).

- **Property setter exception.** For example, a property like UnitCost might use a range check and throw an exception if you attempt to set a negative number.

- **Read-only property.** This can't be set at all.

If you run into these errors, you're likely to miss them altogether. That's because the Silverlight data binding system doesn't give you any visual feedback. The incorrect value remains in the bound control, but it's never applied to the bound object.

To avoid confusion, it's a good idea to alert users to their mistakes as soon as possible. The easiest approach is to use two Binding properties, ValidatesOnExceptions and NotifyOnValidationError, which tell Silverlight to use error notification events. If you set ValidatesOnExceptions to true, you'll get a notification event if the property setter in your data object throws an exception. If you set both properties to true (which is the most common approach), you'll also catch the errors that occur in the data binding system, like failed data type conversions.

Here are these two properties applied to the binding for UnitCost:

```
<TextBox Margin="5" Grid.Row="2" Grid.Column="1" x:Name="txtUnitCost"
  Text="{Binding UnitCost, Mode=TwoWay, ValidatesOnExceptions=true,
NotifyOnValidationError=true}" ></TextBox>
```

When these properties are in place, the data binding system will fire a BindingValidationError event when an error occurs. BindingValidationError is a bubbling event, which means you can handle it where it occurs (in the TextBox) or at a higher level (such as the containing Grid). Handling errors where they occur gives you the opportunity to write targeted error-handling logic that deals separately with errors in different fields. Handling them at a higher level (as shown here) allows you to reuse the same logic for many different types of errors.

```
<Grid Name="gridProductDetails"
  BindingValidationError="Grid_BindingValidationError">
```

The final step is to actually do something when the problem occurs. Usually, you'll want to display some sort of error indicator, such as an error message or an error image next to the offending control. Optionally, you may want to restore the current value. The following example displays an error message and indicates the current value (see Figure 14-2). It also transfers focus back to the offending text box, which is a heavy-handed (but occasionally useful) technique.

```
private void Grid_BindingValidationError(object sender, ValidationErrorEventArgs e)
{
    // Display the error.
```

```
lblInfo.Text = e.Error.Exception.Message;
lblInfo.Text += "\nThe stored value is still: " +
    ((Product)gridProductDetails.DataContext).UnitCost.ToString();

// Suggest the user try again.
txtUnitCost.Focus();
}
```

Figure 14-2. *Pointing out a validation error*

The BindingValidationError event only happens when the value is changed and the control loses focus. If you don't reset the value in the text box, the incorrect value will remain on display, even though it isn't stored in the bound data object. You might allow this behavior so that users have another chance to edit invalid values.

Change Notification

In some cases, you may want to modify a data object after it's been bound to one or more elements. For example, consider this code, which increases the current price by 10%:

```
Product product = (Product)gridProductDetails.DataContext;
product.UnitCost *= 1.1;
```

Note If you plan to modify a bound object frequently, you don't need to retrieve it from the DataContext property each time. A better approach is to store it using a field in your page, which simplifies your code and requires less type casting.

This code won't have the effect you want. Although the in-memory Product object has been modified, the change won't appear in the bound controls. That's because a vital piece of infrastructure is missing—quite simply, there's no way for the Product object to notify the bound elements.

To solve this problem, your data class needs to implement the System.Component-Model.INotifyPropertyChanged interface. The INotifyPropertyChanged interface defines a single event, which is named PropertyChanged. When a property changes in your data object, you must raise the PropertyChanged event and supply the property name as a string.

Here's the definition for a revamped Product class that uses the INotifyPropertyChanged interface, with the code for the implementation of the PropertyChanged event:

```
public class Product : INotifyPropertyChanged
{
    public event PropertyChangedEventHandler PropertyChanged;
    public void OnPropertyChanged(PropertyChangedEventArgs e)
    {
        if (PropertyChanged != null)
          PropertyChanged(this, e);
    }

    ...

}
```

Now you simply need to fire the PropertyChanged event in all your property setters:

```
private double unitCost;
public double UnitCost
{
    get { return unitCost; }
    set {
        unitCost = value;
        OnPropertyChanged(new PropertyChangedEventArgs("UnitCost"));
    }
}
```

If you use this version of the Product class in the previous example, you'll get the behavior you expect. When you change the current Product object, the new information will appear in the bound text boxes immediately.

Tip If several values have changed, you can call OnPropertyChanged() and pass in an empty string. This tells Silverlight to reevaluate the binding expressions that are bound to any property in your class.

Building a Data Service

Although the examples you've seen so far have walked you through the basic details of Silverlight data binding, they haven't been entirely realistic. A more typical design is for your Silverlight application to retrieve the data objects it needs from an external source, such as a web service. In the examples you've seen so far, the difference is minimal. However, it's worth stepping up to a more practical example before you begin binding to collections. After all, it makes more sense to get your data from a database than to construct dozens or hundreds of Product objects in code.

In the examples in this chapter, you'll be relying on a straightforward data service that returns Product objects. You've already learned to create a WCF service (and consume it) in Chapter 13. Building a data service is essentially the same.

The first step is to move the class definition for the data object to the ASP.NET website. You must place the file that contains the code in the App_Code folder. The data object needs a few modifications—namely, the addition of the DataContract and DataMember attributes to make it serializable. Here's a partial listing of the code, which shows you the general outline you need:

```
[DataContract()]
public class Product : INotifyPropertyChanged
{
    private string modelNumber;

    [DataMember()]
    public string ModelNumber
    {
        get { return modelNumber; }
        set
        {
            modelNumber = value;
            OnPropertyChanged(new PropertyChangedEventArgs("ModelNumber"));
        }
    }

    private string modelName;

    [DataMember()]
    public string ModelName
    {
        get { return modelName; }
        set
        {
            modelName = value;
            OnPropertyChanged(new PropertyChangedEventArgs("ModelName"));
        }
    }
    ...
}
```

Note Even when you define the data object on the web server, you can still use the INotifyProperty-Changed interface to add change notification. When you add the web reference to your Silverlight application, Visual Studio will create a client-side copy of the Product class that preserves its public members and calls OnPropertyChanged().

With the data object in place, you simply need a web service method that uses it. The web service class is exceedingly simple—it provides just a single method that allows the caller to retrieve one product record. Here's the basic outline:

```
[ServiceContract(Namespace = "")]
[AspNetCompatibilityRequirements(RequirementsMode =
 AspNetCompatibilityRequirementsMode.Allowed)]
public class StoreDb
{
    private string connectionString =
      WebConfigurationManager.AppSettings["storeDbConnectionString"];

    [OperationContract()]
    public Product GetProduct(int ID)
    {
        ...
    }
}
```

The query is performed through a stored procedure in the database named GetProduct. The connection string isn't hard-coded—instead, it's retrieved through an application setting in the web.config file. Here's the section of the web.config file that defines the connection string:

```
<configuration>
  ...
  <appSettings>
    <add key="storeDbConnectionString"
     value="Data Source=localhost;Initial Catalog=Store;Integrated Security=True" />
  </appSettings>
  ...
</configuration>
```

The database component that's shown in the following example retrieves a table of product information from the Store database, which is a sample database for the fictional IBuySpy store included with some Microsoft case studies. You can get a script to install this database with the downloadable samples for this chapter (or you can use an alternative version that grabs the same information from an XML file).

In this book, we're primarily interested in how data objects can be bound to Silverlight elements. The actual process that deals with creating and filling these data objects (as well as other implementation details, such as whether StoreDb caches the data over several method calls, whether it uses stored procedures instead of inline queries, and so on) isn't our focus. However, just to get an understanding of what's taking place, here's the complete code for the data service:

```
[ServiceContract(Namespace = "")]
[AspNetCompatibilityRequirements(RequirementsMode =
 AspNetCompatibilityRequirementsMode.Allowed)]
public class StoreDb
{
    private string connectionString =
      WebConfigurationManager.AppSettings["storeDbConnectionString"];

    [OperationContract()]
    public Product GetProduct(int ID)
    {
        SqlConnection con = new SqlConnection(connectionString);
        SqlCommand cmd = new SqlCommand("GetProductByID", con);
        cmd.CommandType = CommandType.StoredProcedure;
        cmd.Parameters.AddWithValue("@ProductID", ID);

        try
        {
            con.Open();
            SqlDataReader reader = cmd.ExecuteReader(CommandBehavior.SingleRow);
            if (reader.Read())
            {
                // Create a Product object that wraps the
                // current record.
                Product product = new Product((string)reader["ModelNumber"],
                    (string)reader["ModelName"],
                    Convert.ToDouble(reader["UnitCost"]),
                    (string)reader["Description"]);
                return product;
            }
            else
            {
                return null;
            }
        }
        finally
        {
            con.Close();
        }
    }
}
```

Note Currently, the GetProduct() method doesn't include any exception handling code, so exceptions will bubble up the calling code. This is a reasonable design choice, but you might want to catch the exception in GetProduct(), perform cleanup or logging as required, and then rethrow the exception to notify the calling code of the problem. This design pattern is called *caller inform*.

Using the ADO.NET objects directly (as in this example) is the simplest, cleanest way to write the code for a data service. Another option is to use LINQ to SQL, which allows you to automatically generate data classes based on the structure of your database. (For more information about LINQ to SQL, consult a book like *Pro LINQ: Language Integrated Query in C# 2008* by Joseph C. Rattz, Jr. [Apress, 2007]). Generally, you won't use ADO.NET's disconnected data objects, such as the DataSet, because Silverlight does not include these classes and so cannot manipulate them.

Calling the Data Service

Figure 14-3 shows a page that lets the user retrieve the details about any product.

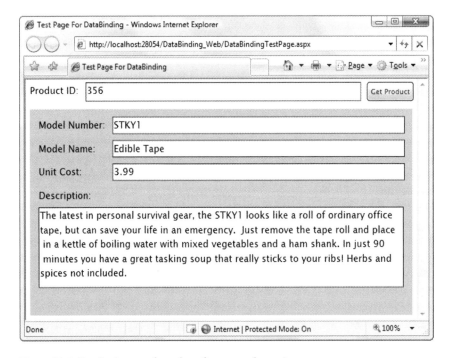

Figure 14-3. *Retrieving product data from a web service*

When the user clicks Get Product, this code runs:

```
private void cmdGetProduct_Click(object sender, RoutedEventArgs e)
{
    // Set the URL, taking the port of the test web server into account.
    EndpointAddress address = new EndpointAddress("http://localhost:" +
      HtmlPage.Document.DocumentUri.Port + "/DataBinding_Web/StoreDb.svc");
    StoreDbClient client = new StoreDbClient(new BasicHttpBinding(), address);

    // Call the service to get the Product object.
    client.GetProductCompleted += client_GetProductCompleted;
    client.GetProductAsync(356);
}
```

When the web service returns its data, you simply need to set the DataContext property of
the container, as in previous examples:

```
private void client_GetProductCompleted(object sender,
  GetProductCompletedEventArgs e)
{
    try
    {
        gridProductDetails.DataContext = e.Result;
    }
    catch (Exception err)
    {
        lblError.Text = "Failed to contact service.";
    }
}
```

If you want to allow the user to make database changes, you need to use two-way bindings (so the Product object can be modified), and you need to add a web service method that
accepts a changed object and uses it to commit databases changes (for example, an
UpdateProduct() method).

Binding to a Collection of Objects

Binding to a single object is quite straightforward. But life gets more interesting when you
need to bind to some collection of objects—for example, all the products in a table.

Although every dependency property supports the single-value binding you've seen so
far, collection binding requires an element with a bit more intelligence. In Silverlight, every
control that displays a list of items derives from ItemsControl. To support collection binding,
the ItemsControl class defines the key properties listed in Table 14-2.

Table 14-2. *Properties in the ItemsControl Class for Data Binding*

Name	Description
ItemsSource	Points to the collection that has all the objects that will be shown in the list.
DisplayMemberPath	Identifies the property that will be used to create the display text for each item.
ItemTemplate	Provides a data template that will be used to create the visual appearance of each item. This property acts as a far more powerful replacement for DisplayMemberPath.
ItemsPanel	Provides a template that will be used to create the layout container that holds all the items in the list.

At this point, you're probably wondering exactly what type of collections you can stuff in the ItemSource property. Happily, you can use just about anything. All you need is support for the IEnumerable interface, which is provided by arrays, all types of collections, and many more specialized objects that wrap groups of items. However, the support you get from a basic IEnumerable interface is limited to read-only binding. If you want to edit the collection (for example, you want to allow inserts and deletions), you need a bit more infrastructure, as you'll see shortly.

Displaying and Editing Collection Items

Consider the page shown in Figure 14-4, which displays a list of products. When you choose a product, the information for that product appears in the bottom section of the page, where you can edit it. (In this example, a GridSplitter lets you adjust the space given to the top and bottom portions of the page.)

To create this example, you need to begin by building your data access logic. In this case, the StoreDb.GetProducts() method retrieves the list of all the products in the database using the GetProducts stored procedure. A Product object is created for each record and added to a generic List collection. (You could use any collection here—for example, an array or a weakly typed ArrayList would work equivalently.)

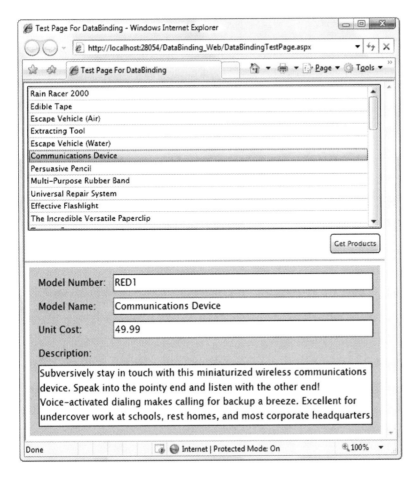

Figure 14-4. *A list of products*

Here's the GetProducts() code:

```
[OperationContract()]
public List<Product> GetProducts()
{
    SqlConnection con = new SqlConnection(connectionString);
    SqlCommand cmd = new SqlCommand("GetProducts", con);
    cmd.CommandType = CommandType.StoredProcedure;

    List<Product> products = new List<Product>();
    try
    {
        con.Open();
        SqlDataReader reader = cmd.ExecuteReader();
        while (reader.Read())
        {
```

```
                    // Create a Product object that wraps the
                    // current record.
                    Product product = new Product((string)reader["ModelNumber"],
                      (string)reader["ModelName"], Convert.ToDouble(reader["UnitCost"]),
                      (string)reader["Description"], (string)reader["CategoryName"]);

                    // Add to collection
                    products.Add(product);
                }
            }
            finally
            {
                con.Close();
            }
            return products;
        }
```

When the Get Products button is clicked, the event handling code calls GetProducts()
asynchronously:

```
private void cmdGetProducts_Click(object sender, RoutedEventArgs e)
{
    EndpointAddress address = new EndpointAddress("http://localhost:" +
      HtmlPage.Document.DocumentUri.Port + "/DataBinding_Web/StoreDb.svc");
    StoreDbClient client = new StoreDbClient(new BasicHttpBinding(), address);

    client.GetProductsCompleted += client_GetProductsCompleted;
    client.GetProductsAsync();
}
```

When the product list is received from the web service, the code stores the collection as a
member variable in the page class for easier access elsewhere in your code. It then sets it as
the ItemsSource for the list.

```
private Product[] products;

private void client_GetProductsCompleted(object sender,
  GetProductsCompletedEventArgs e)
{
    try
    {
        products = e.Result;
        lstProducts.ItemsSource = products;
    }
    catch (Exception err)
    {
        lblError.Text = "Failed to contact service.";
    }
}
```

This successfully fills the list with Product objects. However, the list doesn't know how to display a Product object, so it will simply call the ToString() method. Because this method hasn't been overridden in the Product class, this has the unimpressive result of showing the fully qualified class name for every item (see Figure 14-5).

Figure 14-5. *An unhelpful bound list*

You have three options to solve this problem:

- Set the DisplayMemberPath property of the list. For example, set this to ModelName to get the result shown in Figure 14-4.

- Override the Product.ToString() method to return more useful information. For example, you could return a string with the model number and model name of each item. This approach gives you a way to show more than one property in the list (for example, it's great for combining the FirstName and LastName property in a Customer class). However, it isn't a good fit when using a data service, because you'll need to modify the client-side version of the Product code. When you refresh the web reference, that code will be overwritten.

- Supply a data template. This way, you can show any arrangement of property values (and along with fixed text). You'll learn how to use this trick later in this chapter.

Once you've decided how to display information in the list, you're ready to move on to the second challenge: displaying the details for the currently selected item in the grid that appears below the list. To make this work, you need to respond to the SelectionChanged event and change the DataContext of the Grid that contains the product details. Here's the code that does it:

```
private void lstProducts_SelectionChanged(object sender, RoutedEventArgs e)
{
    gridProductDetails.DataContext = lstProducts.SelectedItem;
}
```

■**Tip** To prevent a field from being edited, set the IsReadOnly property of the text box to true or, better yet, use a read-only control like a TextBlock.

If you try this example, you'll be surprised to see that it's already fully functional. You can edit product items, navigate away (using the list), and then return to see that your edits were successfully committed. In fact, you can even change a value that affects the display text in the list. If you modify the model name and tab to another control, the corresponding entry in the list is refreshed automatically.

However, there's one quirk. Changes are only committed when a control loses focus. If you change a value in a text box and then move to another text box, the data object is updated just as you'd expect. However, if you change a value and then click a new item in the list, the edited value is discarded and the information from the selected data object is loaded. If this behavior isn't what you want, you can add code that explicitly forces a change to be committed. Unlike WPF, Silverlight has no direct way to accomplish this. Your only option is to programmatically send the focus to another control (if necessary, an invisible one) by calling its Focus() method. This commits the change to the data object. You can then bring the focus back to the original text box by calling its Focus() method. You can use this code when reacting to the TextChanged, or you can add a Save or Update button. If you use the button approach, no code is required, because clicking the button changes the focus and triggers the update automatically.

Inserting and Removing Collection Items

One limitation of the previous example is that it uses a fixed-sized array of Product objects. Thus, you can't insert new products or remove existing ones.

To solve this problem, you need to use a collection class instead. Your first instinct might be to use the standard List class. You can define it in your page like this:

```
List<Product> products = new List<Product>();
```

When the web service call finishes, you can add the array of items to the List collection with code like this:

```
products.Clear();
products.AddRange(e.Result);
```

Unfortunately, this doesn't solve the problem. You will be able to add and remove items in the collection. However, the bound list box won't pick up on the changes you make.

For example, imagine you add a Delete button that executes this code:

```
private void cmdDeleteProduct_Click(object sender, RoutedEventArgs e)
{
    products.Remove((Product)lstProducts.SelectedItem);
}
```

The deleted item is removed from the collection, but it remains stubbornly visible in the bound list.

To enable collection change tracking, you need to use a collection that implements the INotifyCollectionChanged interface. Most collections don't, including the List collection used in the current example. In fact, Silverlight includes a single collection that uses INotify-CollectionChanged: the ObservableCollection class.

To use the ObservableCollection class, begin by changing the collection you're storing in your page:

```
private ObservableCollection<Product> products =
  new ObservableCollection<Product>();
```

Unfortunately, the ObservableCollection class doesn't have the handy Range() method that the List class provides. That means you need slightly more long-winded code to copy the array of items into the ObservableCollection, as shown here:

```
products.Clear();
foreach (Product product in e.Result) products.Add(product);
```

Now, if you remove or add an item programmatically, the list is refreshed accordingly. Of course, it's still up to you to create the data access code that can commit changes like these permanently—for example, the web service methods that insert and remove products from the back-end database.

There's one other option. You can explicitly configure your web service reference to use ObservableCollection objects. The only limitation with this technique is that it will apply to *every* web method that returns a collection (or return an object with a collection property).

To make this change, select the Silverlight project in the Solution Explorer and click the Show All Files button. Then, expand the web reference node until you find the file named Reference.svcmap. Open this file, which contains XML configuration details, and look for the following element:

```
<CollectionMappings />
```

Now, replace it with this:

```
<CollectionMappings>
  <CollectionMapping
   TypeName="System.Collections.ObjectModel.ObservableCollection`1"
   Category="List" />
</CollectionMappings>
```

Now the generated client classes will always use ObservableCollection objects for their collections and arrays, regardless of what's actually used in the web service.

Binding to a LINQ Expression

One of Silverlight's many surprises is its support for Language Integrated Query, which is an all-purpose query syntax that was introduced in .NET 3.5.

LINQ works with any data source that has a LINQ provider. Using the support that's included with Silverlight, you can use similarly structured LINQ queries to retrieve data from an in-memory collection or an XML file. (The LINQ to SQL feature, which allows you to query information from a database, isn't included in Silverlight because Silverlight applications never get the opportunity to access a database.) And as with other query languages, LINQ allows you to apply filtering, sorting, grouping, and transformations to the data you retrieve.

Although LINQ is somewhat outside the scope of this chapter, you can learn a lot from a simple example. For example, imagine you have a collection of Product objects, named *products*, and you want to create a second collection that contains only those products that exceed $100 in cost. Using procedural code, you can write something like this:

```
// Get the full list of products.
List<Product> products = App.StoreDb.GetProducts();

// Create a second collection with matching products.
List<Product> matches = new List<Product>();
foreach (Product product in products)
{
    if (product.UnitCost >= 100)
    {
        matches.Add(product);
    }
}
```

Using LINQ, you can use the following *expression*, which is far more concise:

```
// Get the full list of products.
List<Product> products = App.StoreDb.GetProducts();

// Create a second collection with matching products.
IEnumerable<Product> matches = from product in products
        where product.UnitCost >= 100
        select product;
```

This example uses LINQ to Objects, which means it uses a LINQ expression to query the data in an in-memory collection. LINQ expressions use a set of new language keywords, including from, in, where, and select. These LINQ keywords are a genuine part of the C# language.

> **Note** A full discussion of LINQ is beyond the scope of this book. (For a detailed treatment, refer to the LINQ developer center at `http://msdn.microsoft.com/en-us/netframework/aa904594.aspx` or the huge catalog of LINQ examples at `http://msdn2.microsoft.com/en-us/vcsharp/aa336746.aspx`.)

LINQ revolves around the IEnumerable<T> interface. No matter what data source you use, every LINQ expression returns some object that implements IEnumerable<T>. Because IEnumerable<T> extends IEnumerable, you can bind it in a Silverlight page just as you bind an ordinary collection (see Figure 14-6):

```
lstProducts.ItemsSource = matches;
```

Unlike the List and ObservableCollection classes, the IEnumerable<T> interface does not provide a way to add or remove items. If you need this capability, you need to first convert your IEnumerable<T> object into an array or List collection using the ToArray() or ToList() method.

Here's an example that uses ToList() to convert the result of a LINQ query (shown previously) into a strongly typed List collection of Product objects:

```
List<Product> productMatches = matches.ToList();
```

> **Note** ToList() is an extension method, which means it's defined in a different class from the one in which it is used. Technically, ToList() is defined in the System.Linq.Enumerable helper class, and it's available to all IEnumerable<T> objects. However, it won't be available if the Enumerable class isn't in scope, which means the code shown here will not work if you haven't imported the System.Linq namespace.

The ToList() method causes the LINQ expression to be evaluated immediately. The end result is an ordinary collection, which you can deal with in all the usual ways. For example, you can wrap it in an ObservableCollection to get notification events, so any changes you make are reflected in bound controls immediately:

```
ObservableCollection<Product> productMatchesTracked =
  new ObservableCollection<Product>(productMatches);
```

You can then bind the productMatchesTracked collection to a control in your page.

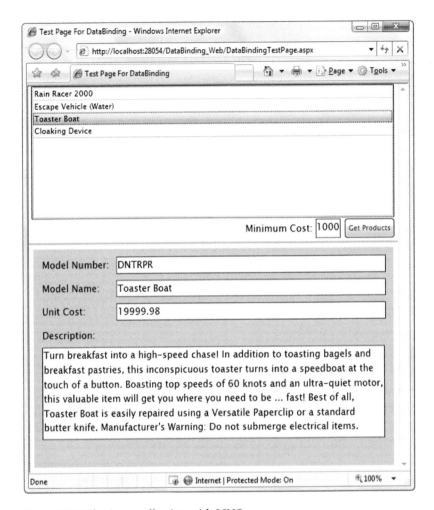

Figure 14-6. *Filtering a collection with LINQ*

Master-Details Display

As you've seen, you can bind other elements to the SelectedItem property of your list to show more details about the currently selected item. Interestingly, you can use a similar technique to build a master-details display of your data. For example, you can create a page that shows a list of categories and a list of products. When the user chooses a category in the first list, you can show just the products that belong to that category in the second list. Figure 14-7 shows exactly this example.

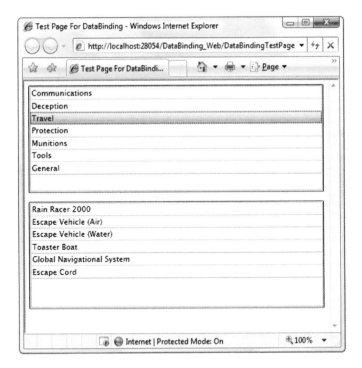

Figure 14-7. *A master-details list*

To pull this off, you need to have a *parent* data object that provides a collection of related *child* data objects through a property. For example, you could build a Category product that provides a property named Category.Products with the products that belong to that category. Like the Product class, the Category class can implement the INotifyPropertyChanged to provide change notifications. Here's the complete code:

```
public class Category : INotifyPropertyChanged
{
    private string categoryName;
    public string CategoryName
    {
        get { return categoryName; }
        set { categoryName = value;
            OnPropertyChanged(new PropertyChangedEventArgs("CategoryName"));
        }
    }

    private List<Product> products;
    public List<Product> Products
    {
        get { return products; }
        set { products = value;
            OnPropertyChanged(new PropertyChangedEventArgs("Products"));
```

```
        }
    }

    public event PropertyChangedEventHandler PropertyChanged;
    public void OnPropertyChanged(PropertyChangedEventArgs e)
    {
        if (PropertyChanged != null)
            PropertyChanged(this, e);
    }

    public Category(string categoryName, ObservableCollection<Product> products)
    {
        CategoryName = categoryName;
        Products = products;
    }
}
```

To use the Category class, you also need to modify the data access code that you saw earlier. Now, you'll query the information about products and categories from the database. The example in Figure 14-7 uses a web service method named GetCategoriesWithProducts(), which returns a collection of Category objects, each of which has a nested collection of Product objects:

```
[OperationContract()]
public List<Category> GetCategoriesWithProducts()
{
    // Perform the query for products using the GetProducts stored procedure.
    SqlConnection con = new SqlConnection(connectionString);
    SqlCommand cmd = new SqlCommand("GetProducts", con);
    cmd.CommandType = CommandType.StoredProcedure;

    // Store the results (temporarily) in a DataSet.
    SqlDataAdapter adapter = new SqlDataAdapter(cmd);
    DataSet ds = new DataSet();
    adapter.Fill(ds, "Products");

    // Perform the query for categories using the GetCategories stored procedure.
    cmd.CommandText = "GetCategories";
    adapter.Fill(ds, "Categories");

    // Set up a relation between these tables.
    // This makes it easier to discover the products in each category.
    DataRelation relCategoryProduct = new DataRelation("CategoryProduct",
        ds.Tables["Categories"].Columns["CategoryID"],
        ds.Tables["Products"].Columns["CategoryID"]);
    ds.Relations.Add(relCategoryProduct);
```

```
// Build the collection of Category objects.
List<Category> categories = new List<Category>();
foreach (DataRow categoryRow in ds.Tables["Categories"].Rows)
{
    // Add the nested collection of Product objects for this category.
    List<Product> products = new List<Product>();
    foreach (DataRow productRow in categoryRow.GetChildRows(relCategoryProduct))
    {
        products.Add(new Product(productRow["ModelNumber"].ToString(),
            productRow["ModelName"].ToString(),
            Convert.ToDouble(productRow["UnitCost"]),
            productRow["Description"].ToString()));
    }
    categories.Add(new Category(categoryRow["CategoryName"].ToString(),
        products));
}
return categories;
}
```

To display this data, you need the two lists shown here:

```
<ListBox x:Name="lstCategories" DisplayMemberPath="CategoryName"
  SelectionChanged="lstCategories_SelectionChanged"></ListBox>
<ListBox x:Name="lstProducts"  Grid.Row="1" DisplayMemberPath="ModelName">
</ListBox>
```

After you receive the collection from the GetCategoriesWithProducts() method, you can set the ItemsSource of the topmost list to show the categories:

```
lstCategories.ItemsSource = e.Result;
```

To show the related products, you must react when an item is clicked in the first list, and then set the ItemsSource property of the second list to the Category.Products property of the selected Category object:

```
lstProducts.ItemsSource = ((Category)lstCategories.SelectedItem).Products;
```

Note If you want to use change tracking with this example (so that product and category insertions and deletions show up in the bound lists), you need to use the ObservableCollection class in two places. First, you must treat the data returned by GetCategoriesWithProducts as an ObservableCollection. Second, each Category must use an ObservableCollection for its Products property. To implement this change, you don't need to change anything about the web service. Instead, you simply need to modify the Reference.svcmap file to use the ObservableCollection for all collections, as described in the previous section.

Data Conversion

In an ordinary binding, the information travels from the source to the target without any change. This seems logical, but it's not always the behavior you want. Often, your data source might use a low-level representation that you don't want to display directly in your user interface. For example, you might have numeric codes you want to replace with human-readable strings, numbers that need to be cut down to size, dates that need to be displayed in a long format, and so on. If so, you need a way to convert these values into the right display form. And if you're using a two-way binding, you also need to do the converse—take user-supplied data and convert it to a representation suitable for storage in the appropriate data object.

Fortunately, Silverlight allows you to do both by creating (and using) a *value converter* class. The value converter is responsible for converting the source data just before it's displayed in the target and (in the case of a two-way binding) converting the new target value just before it's applied back to the source.

Value converters are an extremely useful piece of the Silverlight data binding puzzle. They can be used in several useful ways:

- **To format data to a string representation.** For example, you can convert a number to a currency string. This is the most obvious use of value converters, but it's certainly not the only one.

- **To create a specific type of Silverlight object.** For example, you could read a block of binary data and create a BitmapImage object that can be bound to an Image element.

- **To conditionally alter a property in an element based on the bound data.** For example, you might create a value converter that changes the background color of an element to highlight values in a specific range.

In the following sections, you'll consider an example of each of these approaches.

Formatting Strings with a Value Converter

Value converters are the perfect tool for formatting numbers that need to be displayed as text. For example, consider the Product.UnitCost property in the previous example. It's stored as a decimal, and as a result, when it's displayed in a text box, you'll see values like 3.9900. Not only does this display format show more decimal places than you'd probably like, it also leaves out the currency symbol. A more intuitive representation would be the currency-formatted value $49.99, as shown in Figure 14-8.

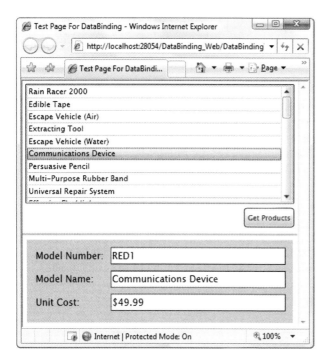

Figure 14-8. *Displaying formatted currency values*

To create a value converter, you need to take three steps:

1. Create a class that implements IValueConverter.

2. Implement a Convert() method that changes data from its original format to its display format.

3. Implement a ConvertBack() method that does the reverse and changes a value from display format to its native format.

Figure 14-9 shows how it works.

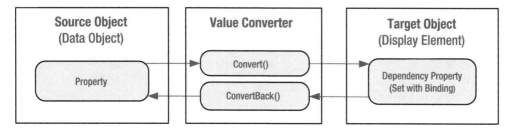

Figure 14-9. *Converting bound data*

In the case of the decimal-to-currency conversion, you can use the Decimal.ToString() method to get the formatted string representation you want. You simply need to specify the currency format string "C", as shown here:

```
string currencyText = decimalPrice.ToString("C");
```

This code uses the culture settings that apply to the current thread. A computer that's configured for the English (United States) region runs with a locale of en-US and displays currencies with the dollar sign ($). A computer that's configured for another local might display a different currency symbol. If this isn't the result you want (for example, you always want the dollar sign to appear), you can specify a culture using the overload of the ToString() method shown here:

```
CultureInfo culture = new CultureInfo("en-US");
string currencyText = decimalPrice.ToString("C", culture);
```

You can learn about all the format strings that are available in the Visual Studio help. However, Table 14-3 and Table 14-4 show some of the most common options you'll use for numeric and date values, respectively.

Table 14-3. *Format Strings for Numeric Data*

Type	Format String	Example
Currency	C	$1,234.50.Parentheses indicate negative values: ($1,234.50). The currency sign is locale-specific.
Scientific (Exponential)	E	1.234.50E+004.
Percentage	P	45.6%.
Fixed Decimal	F?	Depends on the number of decimal places you set. F3 formats values like 123.400. F0 formats values like 123.

Table 14-4. *Format Strings for Times and Dates*

Type	Format String	Format
Short Date	d	M/d/yyyy. For example: 10/30/2005
Long Date	D	dddd, MMMM dd, yyyy. For example: Monday, January 30, 2005
Long Date and Short Time	f	dddd, MMMM dd, yyyy HH:mm aa. For example: Monday, January 30, 2005 10:00 AM
Long Date and Long Time	F	dddd, MMMM dd, yyyy HH:mm:ss aa. For example: Monday, January 30, 2005 10:00:23 AM
ISO Sortable Standard	s	yyyy-MM-dd HH:mm:ss. For example: 2005-01-30 10:00:23
Month and Day	M	MMMM dd. For example: January 30
General	G	M/d/yyyy HH:mm:ss aa (depends on locale-specific settings). For example: 10/30/2002 10:00:23 AM

Converting from the display format back to the number you want is a little trickier. The Parse() and TryParse() methods of the Double type are logical choices to do the work, but ordinarily they can't handle strings that include currency symbols. The solution is to use an overloaded version of the Parse() or TryParse() method that accepts a System.Globalization.NumberStyles value. If you supply NumberStyles.Any, you'll be able to successfully strip out the currency symbol, if it exists.

Here's the complete code for the value converter that deals with price values like the Product.UnitCost property:

```
public class PriceConverter : IValueConverter
{
    public object Convert(object value, Type targetType, object parameter,
      CultureInfo culture)
    {
        double price = (double)value;
        return price.ToString("C", culture);
    }

    public object ConvertBack(object value, Type targetType, object parameter,
      CultureInfo culture)
    {
        string price = value.ToString();

        double result;
        if (Double.TryParse(price, NumberStyles.Any, culture, out result))
        {
            return result;
        }
        return value;
    }
}
```

To put this converter into action, you need to begin by mapping your project namespace to an XML namespace prefix you can use in your markup. Here's an example that uses the namespace prefix local and assumes your value converter is in the namespace DataBinding:

```
xmlns:local="clr-namespace:DataBinding"
```

Typically, you'll add this attribute to the <UserControl> start tag at the top of your markup.

Now, you simply need to create an instance of the PriceConverter class in the Resources collection of your page, as shown here:

```
<UserControl.Resources>
  <local:PriceConverter x:Key="PriceConverter"></local:PriceConverter>
</UserControl.Resources>
```

Then, you can point to it in your binding using a StaticResource reference, as shown here:

```
<TextBox Margin="5" Grid.Row="2" Grid.Column="1"
 Text="{Binding UnitCost, Mode=TwoWay, Converter={StaticResource PriceConverter}}">
</TextBox>
```

■**Note** Unlike WPF, Silverlight lacks the IMultiValueConverter interface. As a result, you're limited to converting individual values, and you can't combine values (for example, join together a FirstName and a LastName field) or perform calculations (for example, multiply UnitPrice by UnitsInStock).

Creating Objects with a Value Converter

Value converters are indispensable when you need to bridge the gap between the way data is stored in your classes and the way it's displayed in a page. For example, imagine you have picture data stored as a byte array in a field in a database. You could convert the binary data into a System.Windows.Media.Imaging.BitmapImage object and store that as part of your data object. However, this design might not be appropriate.

For example, you might need the flexibility to create more than one object representation of your image, possibly because your data library is used in both Silverlight applications and Windows Forms applications (which use the System.Drawing.Bitmap class instead). In this case, it makes sense to store the raw binary data in your data object and convert it to a BitmapImage object using a value converter.

■**Tip** To convert a block of binary data into an image, you must first create a BitmapImage object and read the image data into a MemoryStream. Then, you can call the BitmapImage.SetSource() method to pass the image data in the stream to the BitmapImage.

The Products table from the Store database doesn't include binary picture data, but it does include a ProductImage field that stores the file name of an associated product image. In this case, there's even more reason to delay creating the image object. First, the image might not be available depending on where the application's running. Second, there's no point in incurring the extra memory overhead storing the image unless it's going to be displayed.

The ProductImage field includes the file name but not the full URI of an image file. This gives you the flexibility to pull the image files from any location. The value converter has the task of creating a URI that points to the image file based on the ProductImage field and the website you want to use. The root URI is stored using a custom property named RootUri, which defaults to the same URI where the current web page is located.

Here's the complete code for the ImagePathConverter that performs the conversion:

```
public class ImagePathConverter : IValueConverter
{
    private string rootUri;
    public string RootUri
    {
        get { return rootUri; }
        set { rootUri = value; }
    }

    public ImagePathConverter()
    {
        string uri = HtmlPage.Document.DocumentUri.ToString();

        // Remove the web page from the current URI to get the root URI.
        rootUri = uri.Remove(uri.LastIndexOf('/'),
          uri.Length - uri.LastIndexOf('/'));
    }

    public object Convert(object value, Type targetType, object parameter,
      System.Globalization.CultureInfo culture)
    {
        string imagePath = RootUri + "/" + (string)value;
        return new BitmapImage(new Uri(imagePath));
    }

    public object ConvertBack(object value, Type targetType, object parameter,
      System.Globalization.CultureInfo culture)
    {
        throw new NotSupportedException();
    }
}
```

To use this converter, begin by adding it to the Resources. In this example, the RootUri property is not set, which means the ImagePathConverter defaults to the current application website:

```
<UserControl.Resources>
  <local:ImagePathConverter x:Key="ImagePathConverter"></local:ImagePathConverter>
</UserControl.Resources>
```

Now it's easy to create a binding expression that uses this value converter:

```
<Image Margin="5" Grid.Row="2" Grid.Column="1" Stretch="None"
 HorizontalAlignment="Left" Source=
 "{Binding ProductImagePath, Converter={StaticResource ImagePathConverter}}">
</Image>
```

This works because the Image.Source property expects an ImageSource object, and the BitmapImage class derives from ImageSource.

Figure 14-10 shows the result.

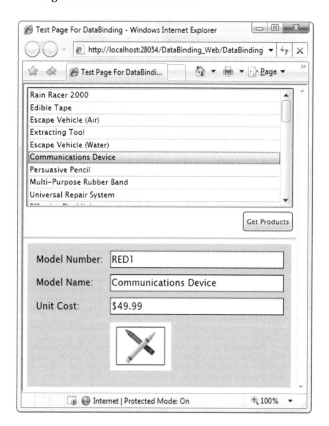

Figure 14-10. *Displaying bound images*

You might improve this example in a couple of ways. First, attempting to create a BitmapImage that points to a nonexistent file causes an exception, which you'll receive when setting the DataContext, ItemsSource, or Source property. Alternatively, you can add properties to the ImagePathConverter class that allow you to configure this behavior. For example, you might introduce a Boolean SuppressExceptions property. If set to true, you could catch exceptions in the Convert() method and return an empty string. Or, you could add a Default-Image property that takes a placeholder BitmapImage. The ImagePathConverter could then return the default image if an exception occurs.

Applying Conditional Formatting

Some of the most interesting value converters aren't designed to format data for presentation. Instead, they're intended to format some other appearance-related aspect of an element based on a data rule.

For example, imagine you want to flag high-priced items by giving them a different background color. You can easily encapsulate this logic with the following value converter:

```
public class PriceToBackgroundConverter : IValueConverter
{
    public double MinimumPriceToHighlight
    {
        get; set;
    }

    public Brush HighlightBrush
    {
        get; set;
    }

    public Brush DefaultBrush
    {
        get; set;
    }

    public object Convert(object value, Type targetType, object parameter,
      System.Globalization.CultureInfo culture)
    {
        double price = (double)value;
        if (price >= MinimumPriceToHighlight)
            return HighlightBrush;
        else
            return DefaultBrush;
    }

    public object ConvertBack(object value, Type targetType, object parameter,
      System.Globalization.CultureInfo culture)
    {
        throw new NotSupportedException();
    }
}
```

■**Tip** If you decide you can't perform the conversion, you can return the value Binding.UnsetValue to tell Silverlight to ignore your binding. The bound property (in this case, Background) will keep its default value.

Once again, the value converter is carefully designed with reusability in mind. Rather than hard-coding the color highlights in the converter, they're specified in the XAML by the code that *uses* the converter:

```
<local:PriceToBackgroundConverter x:Key="PriceToBackgroundConverter"
  DefaultBrush="{x:Null}" HighlightBrush="Orange" MinimumPriceToHighlight="50">
</local:PriceToBackgroundConverter>
```

Brushes are used instead of colors so that you can create more advanced highlight effects using gradients and background images. And if you want to keep the standard, transparent background (so the background of the parent elements is used), just set the DefaultBrush or HighlightBrush property to null, as shown here.

Now all that's left is to use this converter to set the background of some element, like the Border that contains all the other elements:

```
<Border Background=
  "{Binding UnitCost, Converter={StaticResource PriceToBackgroundConverter}}"
  ... >
```

In many cases, you'll need to pass information to a converter beyond the data you want to convert. In this example, the PriceToBackgroundConverter needs to know the highlight color and minimum price details, and this information is passed along through properties. However, there's one other alternative. You can pass a single object (of any type) to a converter through the binding expression, by setting the ConverterParameter property. Here's an example that uses this approach to supply the minimum price:

```
<Border Background=
  "{Binding UnitCost, Converter={StaticResource PriceToBackgroundConverter},
ConverterParameter=50}"
  ... >
```

The parameter is passed as an argument to the Convert() method. Here's how you can rewrite the earlier example to use it:

```
public object Convert(object value, Type targetType, object parameter,
  System.Globalization.CultureInfo culture)
{
    double price = (double)value;
    if (price >= Double.Parse(parameter))
        return HighlightBrush;
    else
        return DefaultBrush;
}
```

In general, the property-based approach is preferred. It's clearer, more flexible, and strongly typed. (When set in the markup extension, the ConverterParameter is always treated as a string.) However, in some situations you might want to reuse a single value converter for multiple elements, and you might need to vary a single detail for each element. In this situation, it's more efficient to use the ConverterParameter than to create multiple copies of the value converter.

Data Templates

A *data template* is a chunk of XAML markup that defines how a bound data object should be displayed. Two types of controls support data templates:

- Content controls support data templates through the ContentTemplate property. The content template is used to display whatever you've placed in the Content property.

- List controls (controls that derive from ItemsControl) support data templates through the ItemTemplate property. This template is used to display each item from the collection (or each row from a DataTable) that you've supplied as the ItemsSource.

The list-based template feature is actually based on content control templates. That's because each item in a list is wrapped by a content control, such as ListBoxItem for the List-Box, ComboBoxItem for the ComboBox, and so on. Whatever template you specify for the ItemTemplate property of the list is used as the ContentTemplate of each item in the list.

So, what can you put inside a data template? It's actually quite simple. A data template is an ordinary block of XAML markup. Like any other block of XAML markup, the template can include any combination of elements. It should also include one or more data binding expressions that pull out the information that you want to display. (After all, if you don't include any data binding expressions, each item in the list will appear the same, which isn't very helpful.)

The best way to see how a data template works is to start with a basic list that doesn't use them. For example, consider this list box, which was shown previously:

```
<ListBox Name="lstProducts" DisplayMemberPath="ModelName"></ListBox>
```

You can get the same effect with this list box that uses a data template:

```
<ListBox Name="lstProducts">
  <ListBox.ItemTemplate>
    <DataTemplate>
      <TextBlock Text="{Binding ModelName}"></TextBlock>
    </DataTemplate>
  </ListBox.ItemTemplate>
</ListBox>
```

When the list is bound to the collection of products (by setting the ItemsSource property), a single ListBoxItem is created for each Product. The ListBoxItem.Content property is set to the appropriate Product object, and the ListBoxItem.ContentTemplate is set to the data template shown earlier, which extracts the value from the Product.ModelName property and displays it in a TextBlock.

So far, the results are underwhelming. But now that you've switched to a data template, there's no limit to how you can creatively present your data. Here's an example that wraps each item in a rounded border, shows two pieces of information, and uses bold formatting to highlight the model number:

```
<ListBox Name="lstProducts" HorizontalContentAlignment="Stretch"
 SelectionChanged="lstProducts_SelectionChanged">
  <ListBox.ItemTemplate>
    <DataTemplate>
```

```
    <Border Margin="5" BorderThickness="1" BorderBrush="SteelBlue"
     CornerRadius="4">
      <Grid Margin="3">
        <Grid.RowDefinitions>
          <RowDefinition></RowDefinition>
          <RowDefinition></RowDefinition>
        </Grid.RowDefinitions>
        <TextBlock FontWeight="Bold"
         Text="{Binding ModelNumber}"></TextBlock>
        <TextBlock Grid.Row="1"
         Text="{Binding ModelName}"></TextBlock>
      </Grid>
    </Border>
  </DataTemplate>
  </ListBox.ItemTemplate>
</ListBox>
```

When this list is bound, a separate Border object is created for each product. Inside the Border element is a Grid with two pieces of information, as shown in Figure 14-11.

Figure 14-11. *A list that uses a data template*

Separating and Reusing Templates

Like styles, templates are often declared as a page or application resource rather than defined in the list where you use them. This separation is often clearer, especially if you use long, complex templates or multiple templates in the same control (as described in the next section). It also gives you the ability to reuse your templates in more than one list or content control if you want to present your data the same way in different places in your user interface.

To make this work, all you need to do is to define your data template in a resources collection and give it a key name (as described in Chapter 11). Here's an example that extracts the template shown in the previous example:

```
<UserControl.Resources>
  <DataTemplate x:Key="ProductDataTemplate">
    <Border Margin="5" BorderThickness="1" BorderBrush="SteelBlue"
     CornerRadius="4">
      <Grid Margin="3">
        <Grid.RowDefinitions>
          <RowDefinition></RowDefinition>
          <RowDefinition></RowDefinition>
        </Grid.RowDefinitions>
        <TextBlock FontWeight="Bold"
         Text="{Binding ModelNumber}"></TextBlock>
        <TextBlock Grid.Row="1"
         Text="{Binding ModelName}"></TextBlock>
      </Grid>
    </Border>
  </DataTemplate>
</UserControl.Resources>
```

Now you can use your data template using a StaticResource reference:

```
<ListBox Name="lstProducts" HorizontalContentAlignment="Stretch"
 ItemTemplate="{StaticResource ProductDataTemplate}"
 SelectionChanged="lstProducts_SelectionChanged"></ListBox>
```

■**Note** Data templates don't require data binding. In other words, you don't need to use the ItemsSource property to fill a template list. In the previous examples, you're free to add Product objects declaratively (in your XAML markup) or programmatically (by calling the ListBox.Items.Add() method). In both cases, the data template works in the same way.

More Advanced Templates

Data templates can be remarkably self-sufficient. Along with basic elements such as the TextBlock and data binding expressions, they can also use more sophisticated controls, attach event handlers, convert data to different representations, use animations, and so on.

For example, you can use a value converter in your binding expressions to convert your data to a more useful representation. Consider, for example, the ImagePathConverter demonstrated earlier. It accepts a picture file name and uses it to create a BitmapImage object with the corresponding image content. This BitmapImage object can then be bound directly to the Image element.

You can use the ImagePathConverter to build the following data template that displays the image for each product:

```
<UserControl.Resources>
  <local:ImagePathConverter x:Key="ImagePathConverter"></local:ImagePathConverter>
  <DataTemplate x:Key="ProductDataTemplate">
    <Border Margin="5" BorderThickness="1" BorderBrush="SteelBlue"
     CornerRadius="4">
      <Grid Margin="3">
        <Grid.RowDefinitions>
          <RowDefinition></RowDefinition>
          <RowDefinition></RowDefinition>
          <RowDefinition></RowDefinition>
        </Grid.RowDefinitions>
        <TextBlock FontWeight="Bold" Text="{Binding Path=ModelNumber}"></TextBlock>
        <TextBlock Grid.Row="1" Text="{Binding Path=ModelName}"></TextBlock>
        <Image Grid.Row="2" Grid.RowSpan="2" Source=
"{Binding Path=ProductImagePath, Converter={StaticResource ImagePathConverter}}">
        </Image>
      </Grid>
    </Border>
  </DataTemplate>
</UserControl.Resources>
```

Although this markup doesn't involve anything exotic, the result is a much more interesting list (see Figure 14-12).

Figure 14-12. *A list with image content*

■**Note** If there is an error in your template, you won't receive an exception. Instead, the control will simply be unable to display your data and will remain blank.

Changing Item Layout

Data templates and style selectors give you remarkable control over every aspect of item presentation. However, they don't allow you to change how the items are organized with respect to each other. No matter what templates and styles you use, the ListBox puts each item into a separate horizontal row and stacks each row to create the list.

You can change this layout by replacing the container that the list uses to lay out its children. To do so, you set the ItemsPanel property with a block of XAML that defines the panel you want to use. This panel can be any class that derives from System.Windows.Controls.Panel.

The following uses a horizontal StackPanel to arrange items in a single row from left to right:

```
<ListBox Margin="7,3,7,10" Name="lstProducts"
 ItemTemplate="{StaticResource ItemTemplate}">
  <ListBox.ItemsPanel>
    <ItemsPanelTemplate>
      <StackPanel Orientation="Horizontal"></StackPanel>
    </ItemsPanelTemplate>
  </ListBox.ItemsPanel>
</ListBox>
```

Silverlight doesn't include very many specialized layout containers, so this technique isn't terribly useful unless you also create one of your own. For example, you can create a layout container that wraps them from left-to-right over multiple rows (as described in Chapter 3), and then use that to power the layout of your list. Figure 14-13 shows an example.

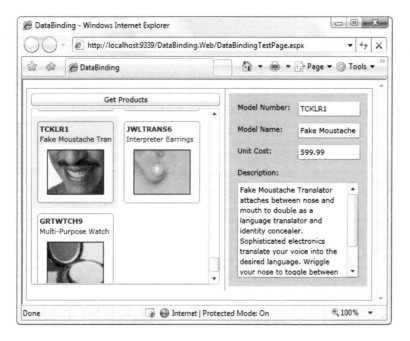

Figure 14-13. *Tiling a list*

The DataGrid

Silverlight leaves out many of WPF's more specialized list-based controls. Notably absent are the ComboBox, ListView, TreeView, Toolbar, and Menu. However, Silverlight does add one control that you won't find in WPF—the DataGrid.

The DataGrid is, at its name suggests, a data display control that takes the information from a collection of objects and renders it as a grid of rows and cells. Each row corresponds to a separate object, and each column corresponds to a property in that object.

The DataGrid adds a bit of much-needed versatility for dealing with data in Silverlight. Its advantages include the following:

- **Flexibility.** You use a column-based model to define exactly the columns you want to use, and supply the binding expressions that extract the data from the bound objects. The DataGrid also supports a few important tools you've already learned about: templates and value converters.

- **Customizability.** The appearance of the DataGrid can be radically altered using properties, along with headers and styles that format individual components of the grid. And if you're truly daring, you can give the entire DataGrid a new control template, complete with custom drawn visuals and animations.

- **Performance.** The DataGrid also boasts excellent performance with large sets of data because it uses *virtualization*, unlike any other Silverlight control. That means the DataGrid only retains in-memory objects for the data that's currently visible, not the entire set of data that's loaded. This reduces the memory overhead dramatically and allows it to practically hold thousands (or even millions) of rows. The only tradeoff is that the DataGrid is slightly slower when scrolling, because it needs to clear the current set of DataGridRow objects and load the information that corresponds to the new rows.

■**Note** To see the effect of the DataGrid's virtualization, compare the performance when you display a huge list of items (like the prime number list in Chapter 16) in a DataGrid and a simple ListBox. In any control but the DataGrid, performance is abysmal. Not only is memory wasted, but it takes an excruciatingly long amount of time to create all the visual elements that are needed for the super-long list.

Creating a Simple Grid

The DataGrid is defined in the familiar System.Windows.Controls namespace, but it's deployed in a different assembly from other Silverlight elements—the System.Windows.Controls.Data.dll assembly. By default, your Silverlight project won't have a reference to this assembly. However, as soon as you drag a DataGrid onto a page, Visual Studio will add the reference and insert a new namespace mapping, like the one shown here:

```
<UserControl xmlns:data=
  "clr-namespace:System.Windows.Controls;assembly=System.Windows.Controls.Data" ... >
```

This maps the DataGrid and its related classes to the namespace prefix *data*.

To create a quick-and-dirty DataGrid, you can use automatic column generation. To do so, you simply need to set the AutoGenerateColumns property to true (which is the default value), as shown here:

```
<data:DataGrid x:Name="gridProducts" AutoGenerateColumns="True">
</data:DataGrid>
```

Now you can fill the DataGrid as you fill a list control, by setting the ItemsSource property:

```
gridProducts.DataSource = products;
```

Figure 14-14 shows a DataGrid that uses automatic column generation with the collection of Product objects you've seen in previous examples. When using automatic column generation, the DataGrid uses reflection to find every public property in the bound data object. It creates a column for each property. To display non-string properties, the DataGrid simply calls ToString(), which works well for numbers, dates, and other simple data types, but won't work as well if your objects includes a more complex data object. (In this case, you may want to explicitly define your columns, which gives you the chance to bind to a subproperty, use a value converter, or apply a template to get the right display content.)

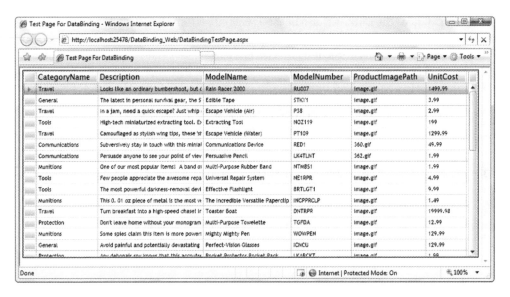

Figure 14-14. *A DataGrid with automatically generated columns*

Table 14-5 lists some of the properties that you can use to customize the basic display of the DataGrid. In the following sections, you'll see how to get fine-grained formatting control with styles and templates. You'll also see how the DataGrid deals with sorting and selection, and you'll consider many more properties that underlie these features.

Table 14-5. *Basic Display Properties for the DataGrid Enumeration*

Name	Description
RowBackground and AlternatingRowBackground	RowBackground sets the brush that's used to paint the background behind every row. If you set AlternatingRowBackground, alternate rows are painted with a different background color, making it easier to distinguish rows at a glance. By default, the DataGrid gives odd-number rows a white background and gives the alternating, even-numbered rows a light gray background.
ColumnHeaderHeight	The height (in pixels) of the row that has the column headers at the top of the DataGrid.
RowHeaderWidth	The width (in pixels) of the column that has the row headers. This is the column at the far left of the grid, which shows no data but indicates the currently selected row (with an arrow) and indicates when the row is being edited (with an arrow in a circle).
ColumnWidth	The default width of every column. If you define columns explicitly, you can override this width to size individual columns. By default, columns are 100 pixels wide.
RowHeight	The height of every row. This setting is useful if you plan to display multiple lines of text or different content (like images) in the DataGrid. Unlike columns, the user cannot resize rows.

Name	Description
GridlinesVisibility	A value from the DataGridGridlines enumeration that determines which gridlines are shown (Horizontal, Vertical, None, or All).
VerticalGridlinesBrush	The brush that's used to paint the grid lines in between columns.
HorizontalGridlinesBrush	The brush that's used to paint the grid lines in between rows.
HeadersVisibility	A value from the DataGridHeaders enumeration that determines which headers are shown (Column, Row, All, None).
HorizontalScrollBarVisibility and VerticalScrollBarVisibility	A value from the ScrollBarVisibility enumeration that determines whether a scrollbar is shown when needed (Auto), always (Visible), or never (Hidden). The default for both properties is Auto.

Resizing and Rearranging Columns

When displaying automatically generated columns, the DataGrid attempts to size the width of each column intelligently. Initially, it will make each column just wide enough to show the largest value that's currently in view (or the header, if that's wider).

Interestingly enough, the DataGrid attempts to preserve this intelligent sizing approach when the user starts scrolling through the data. As soon as you come across a row with longer data, the DataGrid widens the appropriate columns to fit it. This automatic sizing is one-way only, so columns won't shrink when you leave large data behind.

The automatic sizing of the DataGrid columns is interesting and often useful, but it's not always what you want. Consider the example shown in Figure 14-14, which contains a Description column that holds a long string of text. Initially, the Description column is made extremely wide to fit this data, crowding the other columns out of the way. In Figure 14-14, the user has manually resized the Description column to a more sensible size. (All the other columns are left at their initial widths.) Once a column has been resized, it won't exhibit the automatic enlarging behavior when the user scrolls through the data.

■**Note** Obviously, you don't want to force your users to grapple with ridiculously wide columns. To size columns right from the start, you need to define your columns explicitly, as described in the next section.

Ordinarily, users can resize columns by dragging the column edge to either size. You can prevent the user from resizing the columns in your DataGrid by setting the CanUserResize-Columns property to false. If you want to be more specific, you can prevent the user from resizing an individual column by setting the CanUserResize property of that column to false. You can also prevent the user from making the column extremely narrow by setting the Min-Width property of a column.

The DataGrid has another surprise frill that allows users to customize the column display. Not only can columns be resized, but they can also be dragged from one position to another. If you don't want users to have this reordering ability, set the CanUserReorderColumns property of the DataGrid or the CanUserReorder property of a specific column to false.

Defining Columns

Using automatically generated columns, you can quickly create a DataGrid that shows all your data. However, you give up a fair bit of control. For example, you can't control how columns are ordered, how wide they are, how the values inside are formatted, and what header text is placed at the top.

A far more powerful approach is to turn off automatic column generation by setting Auto-GenerateColumns to false. You can then explicitly define the columns you want, with the settings you want, and in the order you want. To do this, you need to fill the DataGrid.Columns collection with the right column objects.

Currently, the DataGrid supports three types of columns, which are represented by three different classes that derive from DataGridColumn:

- **DataGridTextColumn.** This column is the standard choice for most data types. The value is converted to text and displayed in a TextBlock. When editing the row, the TextBlock is replaced with a standard text box.

- **DataGridCheckBoxColumn.** This column shows a checkbox. This column type is used automatically for Boolean (or nullable Boolean) values. Ordinarily, the checkbox is read-only, but when editing the row, it becomes a normal checkbox.

- **DataGridTemplateColumn.** This column is by far the most powerful option. It allows you to define a data template for displaying column values, with all the flexibility and power you had when using templates in a list control. For example, you can use a Data-GridTemplateColumn to display image data, or use a specialized Silverlight control (like a drop-down list with valid values or a DatePicker for date values).

For example, here's a revised DataGrid that creates a two-column display with product names and prices. It also applies clearer column captions and widens the Product column to fit its data:

```
<data:DataGrid x:Name="gridProducts" Margin="5">
  <data:DataGrid.Columns>
    <data:DataGridTextColumn Header="Product" Width="175"
     Binding="{Binding ModelName}"></data:DataGridTextColumn>
    <data:DataGridTextColumn Header="Price"
     Binding="{Binding UnitCost}"></data:DataGridTextColumn>
  </data:DataGrid.Columns>
</data:DataGrid>
```

When defining a column, you will almost always set three details: the header text that appears at the top of the column, the width of the column, and the binding that gets the data. The header text is just as straightforward as it seems. The column width is a bit more sophisticated. If you don't want automatic column sizing, stick with a hard-coded pixel width. If you do want automatic sizing, you can use one of three special values: SizeToCells (widen to match the largest displayed cell value), SizeToHeader (widen to match the header text), or Auto (widen to match the largest displayed cell value or the header, whichever is larger). When using SizeToCells or Auto, the column may be widened while you scroll, which is either a handy convenience or an annoying distraction, depending on your perspective.

The most important detail is the binding expression that provides the right information for the column. This approach is a bit different than the list controls you considered earlier. List controls include a DisplayMemberPath property instead of a Binding property. The Binding approach is more flexible—it allows you to incorporate a value converter without needing to step up to a full template column. For example, here's how you would format the UnitCost column as a currency value (see Figure 14-15):

```
<data:DataGridTextColumn Header="Price" Binding=
  "{Binding UnitCost, Converter={StaticResource PriceConverter}}">
</data:DataGridTextColumn>
```

Of course, this assumes you've created an instance of the PriceConverter in the UserControl.Resources collection and given it the key name PriceConverter, as demonstrated earlier.

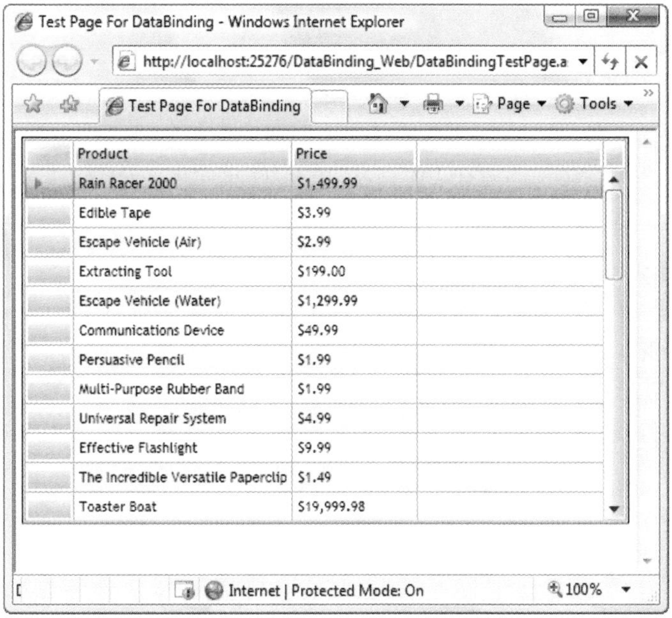

Figure 14-15. *Setting the header text and formatting column values*

Tip You can dynamically show and hide columns by modifying the Visibility property of the corresponding column object. Additionally, you can move columns at any time by changing their DisplayIndex values.

The Product class doesn't include any Boolean properties. If it did, the DataGridCheck-BoxColumn would be a useful option.

As with the DataGridTextColumn, the Binding property extracts the data—in this case, the true or false value that's used to set the IsChecked property of the CheckBox element inside. The DataGridCheckBoxColumn also adds a property named Content that allows you to show optional content alongside the checkbox. Finally, the DataGridCheckBoxColumn includes an IsThreeState property that determines if the checkbox supports the "undetermined" state as well as the more obvious checked and unchecked states. If you're using the DataGridCheck-BoxColumn to show the information from a nullable Boolean value, you might set IsThree-State property to true. That way, the user can click back to the undetermined state (which shows a lightly shaded checkbox) to return the bound value to null.

The DataGridTemplateColumn uses a data template, which works in the same way as the date template features you explored with list controls earlier. The only different in the Data-GridTemplateColumn is that it allows you to define two templates—one for data display, and one for data editing, which you'll consider shortly. Here's an example that uses the template data column to place a thumbnail image of each product in the grid (assuming you've added the ImagePathConverter value converter to the UserControl.Resources collection):

```
<data:DataGridTemplateColumn>
  <data:DataGridTemplateColumn.CellTemplate>
    <DataTemplate>
      <Image Stretch="None" Source=
        "{Binding ProductImagePath, Converter={StaticResource ImagePathConverter}}">
      </Image>
    </DataTemplate>
  </data:DataGridTemplateColumn.CellTemplate>
</data:DataGridTemplateColumn>
```

Figure 14-16 shows the result.

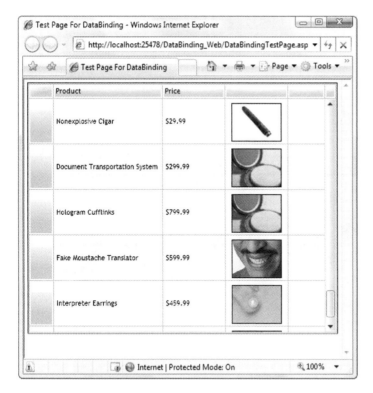

Figure 14-16. *A DataGrid with image content*

Formatting and Styling Columns

You can format a DataGridTextColumn as you format a TextBlock element, by setting the
Foreground, FontFamily, FontSize, FontStyle, and FontWeight properties. However, the Data-
GridTextColumn doesn't expose all the properties of the TextBlock. For example, there's no
way to set the very used Wrapping property if you want to create a column that shows multiple
lines of text. In this case, you need to use the ElementStyle property instead.

Essentially, the ElementStyle property allows you to create a style that will be applied to
the element inside the DataGrid cell. In the case of a simple DataGridTextColumn, that's a
TextBlock. (In a DataGridCheckBoxColumn, it's a checkbox, and in a DataGridTemplate-
Column, it's whatever element you've created in the data template.)

Here's a simple style that allows the text in a column to wrap:

```
<data:DataGridTextColumn Header="Description" Width="400"
 Binding="{Binding Description}">
  <data:DataGridTextColumn.ElementStyle>
    <Style TargetType="TextBlock">
      <Setter Property="TextWrapping" Value="Wrap"></Setter>
    </Style>
  </data:DataGridTextColumn.ElementStyle>
</data:DataGridTextColumn>
```

In order to see the wrapped text, you'll need to expand the row height. Unfortunately, the DataGrid can't size itself as flexibly as Silverlight layout containers can. Instead, you're forced to set a fixed row height using the DataGrid.RowHeight property. This height will apply to all rows, regardless of the amount of content they contain. Figure 14-17 shows an example with the row height set to 70 pixels.

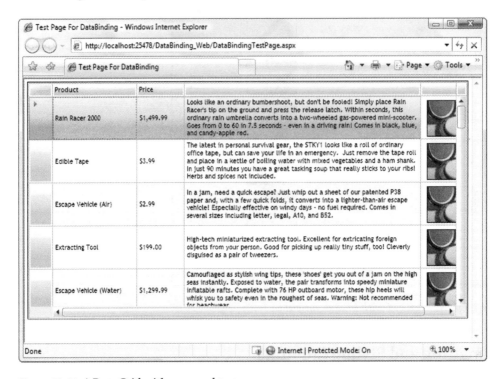

Figure 14-17. *A DataGrid with wrapped text*

■ **Tip** If you want to apply the same style to multiple columns (for example, to deal with wrappable text in several places), you can define the style in the Resources collection, and then refer to it in each column using a StaticResource.

You can use EditingElementStyle to style the element that's used when editing a column. In the case of the DataGridTextColumn, the editing element is the TextBox control. You can also use various properties of the DataGrid to style various other parts of the grid. Table 14-6 has the full story.

Table 14-6. *Style-Based DataGrid Properties*

Property	Style Applies To...
ColumnHeaderStyle	The TextBlock that's used for the column headers at the top of the grid
RowHeaderStyle	The TextBlock that's used for the row headers
CornerHeaderStyle	The corner cell between the row and column headers
RowStyle	The TextBlock that's used for ordinary rows (rows in columns that haven't been expressly customized through the ElementStyle property of the column)

Formatting Rows

By setting the properties of the DataGrid column objects, you can control how entire columns are formatted. However, in many cases it's more useful to flag rows that contain specific data. For example, you might want to draw attention to high-priced products or expired shipments. You can apply this sort of formatting programmatically by handling the DataGrid.LoadingRow event.

The LoadingRow event is a powerful tool for row formatting. It gives you access to the data object for the current row, allowing you to perform simple range checks, comparison, and more complex manipulations. It also provides the DataGridRow object for the row, allowing you to format the row with different colors or a different font. However, you can't format just a single cell in that row—for that, you need a DataGridTemplateColumn and IValue-Converter.

The LoadingRow event fires once for each row when it appears on screen. The advantage of this approach is that your application is never forced to format the whole grid—instead, the LoadingRow fires only for the rows that are currently visible. However, there's also a downside. As the user scrolls through the grid, the LoadingRow event will be triggered continuously. As a result, you can't place time-consuming code in the LoadingRow method unless you want scrolling to grind to a halt.

There's also another consideration—virtualization. To lower its memory overhead, the DataGrid reuses the same DataGrid objects to show new data as you scroll through the data. (That's why the event is called LoadingRow rather than CreatingRow.) If you're not careful, the DataGrid can load data into an already-formatted DataGridRow. To prevent this from happening, you must explicitly restore each row to its initial state.

In the following example, high-priced items are given a bright orange background (see Figure 14-18). Regular price items are given the standard white background.

```
// Reuse brush objects for efficiency in large data displays.
private SolidColorBrush highlightBrush = new SolidColorBrush(Colors.Orange);
private SolidColorBrush normalBrush = new SolidColorBrush(Colors.White);

private void gridProducts_LoadingRow(object sender, DataGridRowEventArgs e)
{
    // Check the data object for this row.
    Product product = (Product)e.Row.DataContext;
```

```
    // Apply the conditional formatting.
    if (product.UnitCost > 100)
    {
        e.Row.Background = highlightBrush;
    }
    else
    {
        // Restore the default white background. This ensures that used,
        // formatted DataGrid object are reset to their original appearance.
        e.Row.Background = normalBrush;
    }
}
```

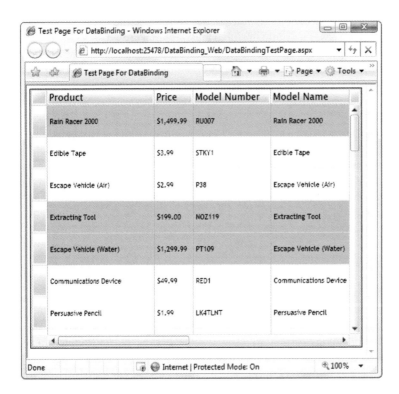

Figure 14-18. *Highlighting rows*

Remember, there's another option for performing value-based formatting. You can use an IValueConverter that examines bound data and converts it to something else. This technique is especially powerful when combined with a DataGridTemplateColumn column. For example, you could create a template-based column that contains a TextBlock, and bind the TextBlock.Background property to an IValueConverter that sets the color based on the price. Unlike the LoadingRow approach shown previously, this technique allows you to format just the cell that contains the price, not the whole row. For more information about this technique, refer back to the "Applying Conditional Formatting" section earlier in this chapter.

■**Tip** The formatting you apply in the LoadingRow event handler only applies when the row is loaded. If you edit a row, this LoadingRow code won't fire (at least not until you scroll the row out of view and then back into sight).

Row Details

The DataGrid also supports row details—an optional, separate display area that appears just under the column values for a row. The row details area adds two things that you can't get from columns alone. First, the row details area spans the full width of the DataGrid and isn't carved into separate columns, which gives you more space to work with. Secondly, the row details area can be configured so it appears only for the selected row, allowing you to tuck the extra details out of the way when they're not needed.

Figure 14-19 shows a DataGrid that uses both of these behaviors. The row details area shows the wrapped product description text, and it's only shown for the currently selected product.

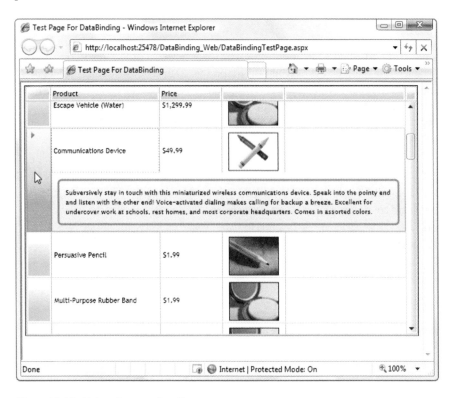

Figure 14-19. *Using the row details area*

To create this example, you need to first configure the display behavior of the row details area by setting the DataGrid.RowDetailsVisibility property. By default, this property is set to Hidden, which means the row details area is never shown. However, you can set it to Visible or VisibleWhenSelected (the option used in this example).

Next, you need to define the content that's shown in the row details area by setting the DataGrid.RowDetailsTemplate property. In this case, the row details area uses a basic template that includes a TextBlock that shows the full product text and a Border element that wraps it:

```
<data:DataGrid.RowDetailsTemplate>
  <DataTemplate>
    <Border Margin="10" Padding="10" BorderBrush="SteelBlue" BorderThickness="3"
      CornerRadius="5">
      <TextBlock Text="{Binding Description}" TextWrapping="Wrap" FontSize="10">
      </TextBlock>
    </Border>
  </DataTemplate>
</data:DataGrid.RowDetailsTemplate>
```

Other options include adding controls that allow you to perform various tasks (for example, getting more information about a product, adding it to a shopping list, editing it, and so on).

Selection

As with an ordinary list control, the DataGrid allows the user to select individual items. You can react to the SelectionChanged event when this happens. To find out what data object is currently selected, you can use the SelectedItem property. If you want the user to be able to select multiple rows, set the SelectionMode property to Extended. (Single is the only other option and the default.) To select multiple rows, the user must hold down the Shift or Ctrl key. You can retrieve the collection of selected items from the SelectedItems property.

■Tip You can set the selection programmatically using the SelectedItem property. If you're setting the selection to an item that's not currently in view, it's a good idea to follow up with a call to the Data-Grid.ScrollIntoView() method, which forces the DataGrid to scroll forward or backward until the item you've indicated is visible.

Sorting Rows

The DataGrid features built-in sorting as long as you're binding a collection that implements IList (such as List<T> and ObservableCollection<T>). If you meet this requirement, your Data-Grid gets basic sorting for free.

To use the sorting, the user simply needs to click a column header. Clicking once sorts the column in ascending order based on its data type (for example, numbers are sorted from 0 up and letters are sorted alphabetically). Click the column again, and the sort order is reversed. An arrow appears at the far right side of the column header, indicating that the DataGrid is sorted based on the values in this column. The arrow points up for an ascending sort and down for a descending sort. (When you click a column more than once, the arrow flips with a quick animation effect.)

Users can sort based on multiple columns by holding down Shift while they click. For example, if you hold down Shift and click the Category column followed by the Price column, products will be sorted into alphabetical category groups, and the items in each category group will be ordered by price.

It's possible to exercise some control over the DataGrid sorting process, depending on how much effort you're willing to make (and how much code you're willing to live with). Here are your options:

- **SortMemberPath.** Every column provides the SortMemberPath property, which allows you to specify the property in the bound data object that's used for sorting. If Sort-MemberPath isn't set, the column is sorted using the bound data, which makes perfect sense. However, if you have a DataGridTemplateColumn, you need to use SortMember-Path because there's no Binding property to provide the bound data. If you don't, your column won't support sorting.

- **ICollectionView.** It's beyond the scope of this chapter, but you can create a custom class that implements ICollectionView and provides sorting. You can then bind an instance of that class to the DataGrid.

- **A custom template.** If you don't like the arrows that indicate when a sort order has been applied (or you want to add a glitzier animation), you need to use the Data-Grid.ColumnHeaderStyle property to apply a new template. You'll find three key states: Unsorted State (when no sorting is applied), SortedAscending State (when the column is first sorted), and SortedDescending State (when the column header is clicked twice, and the sort order is reversed). Customize these to plug in your own visuals.

Freezing Columns

A frozen column is a column that stays in place at the left size of the DataGrid, even as you scroll to the right. Figure 14-20 shows how a frozen Product column remains visible during scrolling. Notice how the horizontal scrollbar only extends under the scrollable columns, not the frozen columns.

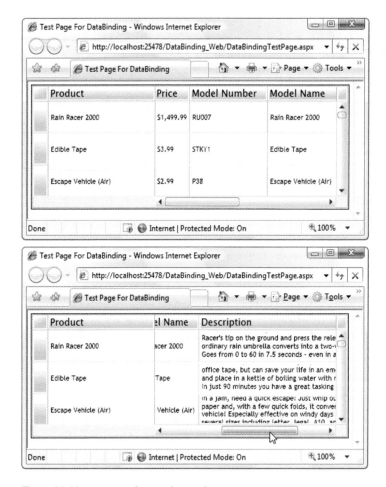

Figure 14-20. *Freezing the Product column*

Column freezing is a useful feature for very wide grids, especially when you want to make sure certain information (like the product name or a unique identifier) is always visible. To use it, you simply need to set the IsFrozen property of the column to true:

```
<data:DataGridTextColumn Header="Product" Width="175" IsFrozen="True"
 Binding="{Binding ModelName}"></data:DataGridTextColumn>
```

There's one catch. Frozen columns must always be on the left side of the grid. So if you freeze one column, it must be the leftmost column; if you free two columns, they must be the first two on the left, and so on.

The Last Word

This chapter took a thorough look at data binding. You learned how to create data binding expressions that draw information from custom objects and how to push changes back to the source. You also learned how to use change notification, bind entire collections of data, and get your records from a web service. Finally, you considered Silverlight's surprisingly capable all-in-one data control, the DataGrid.

CHAPTER 15

Isolated Storage

Silverlight code isn't permitted to write to arbitrary locations on the file system (or read from them). Obviously, if this ability *were* possible, it would break the web browser's secure sandbox model. However, Silverlight applications that need to store data permanently still have an option. They can use a feature called *isolated storage*.

Isolated storage gives you access to a small segment of hard disk space, with certain limitations. For instance, you won't know exactly where your files are being stored. You also won't be able to read the files left by another Silverlight application or recorded for another user. In essence, isolated storage provides carefully restricted, tamperproof file access for applications that need to store permanent information on the local computer—usually so this information can be retrieved the next time the user runs the application. In this chapter, you'll learn how to create files in isolated storage and write and read data. You'll see how to store miscellaneous data, application settings, and entire objects. You'll also learn how to request more isolated storage space for your application, and you'll consider one alternative that *does* give you the ability to read the data from an ordinary file that's not in isolated storage—provided the user explicitly allows it.

Understanding Isolated Storage

Isolated storage provides a virtual file system that lets you write data to a small, user-specific and application-specific slot of space. The actual location on the hard drive is obfuscated (so there's no way to know exactly where the data will be written beforehand), and the default space limit is a mere 1MB (although you can request that the user grant you more).

Essentially, isolated storage is the Silverlight equivalent of persistent cookies in an ordinary web page. It allows small bits of information to be stored in a dedicated location that has specific controls in place to prevent malicious attacks (such as code that attempts to fill the hard drive or replace a system file).

The Scope of Isolated Storage

With isolated storage, a unique storage location is created for every combination of user and application. In other words, the same computer could have multiple isolated storage locations for the same location, assuming each one is for a different user. Similarly, the same user could have multiple isolated storage locations, one for each Silverlight application. Isolated storage isn't affected by browser, so a Windows user switching from Internet Explorer to Firefox would get the same isolated storage location in both browsers.

Note Data in one user's isolated store is restricted from other users (unless they are Windows adminis-
trators).

The critical factor that gives a Silverlight application its identity is the URL of the XAP file.
That means:

- Different XAP files on the same web server and in the same folder will still have different isolated stores.

- If you host the website on different domains, each instance will get its own isolated
  store.

- If you create different test pages that use the same application at the same location,
  they'll share the same isolated storage.

- If you rename the XAP file (or the folder that it's in), you'll get a new isolated store.

- If you change the GUID, version, or other assembly metadata for your Silverlight application, you'll keep the same isolated store.

- If you replace a Silverlight application with another application that has the same XAP
  file name, it will acquire the previous application's isolated store.

What to Put in Isolated Storage

Isolated storage is a great way to store small amounts of non-essential information. Good
choices include user-specific details, user preferences, and information about recent user
actions. Isolated storage is also a great temporary storage. For example, imagine you create a
Silverlight application that allows a user to fill out a multipart form (over several pages) and
then send it to a web service, where it will be stored permanently. Each time the user moves
from one part of the form to the next, you could save the current data to isolated storage.
Then, when the user completes the operation and successfully submits the data to the web
service, you could delete it. This commonsense approach prevents the user from losing data if
the application can't contact the web service (because the network isn't working) or the user
accidentally restarts the application (for example, by clicking the browser's Back button). Your
application can check for the temporary data on startup, and give the user the option of
reloading that data.

Isolated storage is persistent—unlike the browser cache, it never expires and it's not
removed if the user chooses to explicitly delete temporary Internet files. However, isolated
storage isn't a good storage place for important documents, as they're never backed up, easily
deleted, and even more easily lost (for example, if the user changes accounts or computers).
Furthermore, isolated storage generally isn't a good place to cache resources (for example,
external bitmaps and media files). It may seem tempting, but isolated storage is intended to
be a limited-size storage location for data, not a handcrafted replacement for HTTP caching.

Using Isolated Storage

Isolated storage is quite easy to use because it exposes the same stream-based model that's used in ordinary .NET file access. You simply use the types in the System.IO.IsolatedStorage namespace, which are a core part of the Silverlight runtime.

File Management

Silverlight creates isolated stores automatically. To interact with an isolated store, you use the IsolatedStorageFile class. You get the IsolatedStorageFile object for the current user and application by calling the static IsolatedStorageFile.GetUserStoreForApplication() method, as shown here:

```
IsolatedStorageFile store =
  IsolatedStorageFile.GetUserStoreForApplication();
```

The IsolatedStorageFile class name is somewhat misleading, because it doesn't represent a single file. Instead, it provides access to the collection of files in the isolated store. The methods that the IsolatedStorageFile class provides are similar to the file management methods you can use through the File and Directory classes in a full-fledged .NET application. Table 15-1 lists the methods you can use.

Table 15-1. *File Management Methods for IsolatedStorageFile*

Method	Description
CreateDirectory()	Creates a new folder in the isolated store, with the name you specify.
DeleteDirectory()	Deletes a folder from the isolated store.
CreateFile()	Creates a new file with the name you supply, and returns an IsolatedStorageFileStream object that you can use to write data to it.
DeleteFile()	Deletes a file from the isolated store.
Remove()	Removes the isolated store, along with all its files and directories.
OpenFile()	Opens a file in the isolated store, and returns an IsolatedStorageFileStream that you can use to manipulate it. Usually, you'll use this method to open an existing file for reading, but you can supply different FileMode and FileAccess values to create a new file or overwrite an existing file.
FileExists()	Returns true or false depending on whether the specified file exists in the isolated store. You can use an overloaded version of this method to look in a specific subfolder or match a file with a search expression (using the wildcards ? and *).
DirectoryExists()	Returns true or false depending on whether the specified folder exists in the isolated storage location.
GetFileNames()	Returns an array of strings, one for each file in the root of the isolated store. Optionally, you can use an overloaded version of this method that accepts a single string argument. This argument allows you to specify a subfolder you want to search or a search expression (using the wildcards ? and *).

Continued

Table 15-1. *Continued*

Method	Description
GetDirectoryNames()	Returns an array of strings, one for each subfolder in the root of the isolated store. Optionally, you can use an overloaded version of this method that accepts a single string argument. This argument allows you to get subfolders in a specific directory or specify a search expression (using the wildcards ? and *).

Writing and Reading Data

Using the methods in Table 15-1, you can create files and use streams to write and read data. Of course, you're unlikely to deal with the IsolatedStorageFileStream class directly, unless you want to read and write your data one byte at a time. Instead, you'll use one of the more capable classes from the System.IO namespace that wrap streams.

- If you want to write data to ordinary text strings, use the StreamWriter and StreamReader. You can write the data in several pieces and retrieve it in line-by-line or in one large block using StreamReader.ReadToEnd().

- If you want to write data more strictly (and somewhat more compactly), use the BinaryWriter and BinaryReader. When retrieving data, you'll need to use the data type. (For example, you must use the BinaryReader.ReadInt32() method to retrieve an 32-bit integer from the file, the BinaryReader.ReadString() to read a string, and so on.)

The following example gets the current isolated store, creates a new file named date.txt, and writes the current date to that file as a piece of text:

```
// Write to isolated storage.
try
{
    using (IsolatedStorageFile store =
        IsolatedStorageFile.GetUserStoreForApplication())
    {
        using (IsolatedStorageFileStream stream = store.CreateFile("date.txt"))
        {
            StreamWriter writer = new StreamWriter(stream);
            writer.Write(DateTime.Now);
            writer.Close();
        }
        lblStatus.Text = "Data written to date.txt";
    }
}
catch (Exception err)
{
    lblStatus.Text = err.Message;
}
```

Retrieving information is just as easy. You simply need to open the IsolatedStorage-FileStream in read mode:

```
// Read from isolated storage.
try
{
    using (IsolatedStorageFile store =
      IsolatedStorageFile.GetUserStoreForApplication())
    {
        using (IsolatedStorageFileStream stream = store.OpenFile("date.txt",
          FileMode.Open))
        {
            StreamReader reader = new StreamReader(stream);
            lblData.Text = reader.ReadLine();
            reader.Close();
        }
    }
}
catch (Exception err)
{
    // An exception will occur if you attempt to open a file that doesn't exist.
    lblStatus.Text = err.Message;
}
```

In this example, you'll find the date.txt file in a path in this form:

```
C:\Users\[UserName]\AppData\LocalLow\Microsoft\Silverlight\is\[Unique_Identifier]
```

There are several automatically generated folder names tacked onto the end of this path. Here's an example of a dynamically created path that Silverlight may use for isolated storage:

```
C:\Users\matthew\AppData\LocalLow\Microsoft\Silverlight\is\sid3dsxe.u1y\lstesiyg.ezx
\s\atkj2fb5vjnabwjsx2nfj3htrsq1ku1h\f\date.txt
```

If you're curious, you can get the path for the current isolated store using the Visual Studio debugger. Simply hover over the IsolatedStorageFile object while in break mode, and look for the m_AppFilesPath variable, as shown in Figure 15-1.

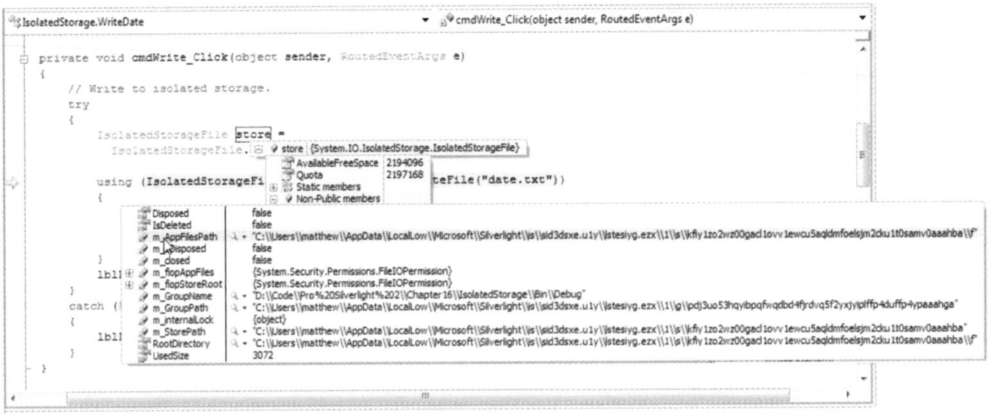

Figure 15-1. *Finding the isolated storage location*

Fortunately, you don't need to worry about the directory structure. You can check for files and retrieve from isolated storage using the methods of the IsolatedStorageFile, such as Get-FileNames() and OpenFile().

Note Notably, Silverlight does not obfuscate the names of files in isolated storage. That means if the user knows the file name, the user can perform a file search to find the file.

Requesting More Space

Initially, each Silverlight application gets 1MB of space in its isolated store. You can examine the IsolatedStorageFile.AvailableFreeSpace property to find out how much free space is remaining.

If your application needs more space, there is an option you can use: the IsolatedStorage-File IncreaseQuotaTo() method. When you call this method, you request the number of bytes you want. Silverlight then shows a message box with the current number of bytes the application is using in isolated storage (*not* the current quota limit), and the new requested amount of space. The dialog box will also show the URL of the Silverlight application (or file:// if you're running it locally).

Figure 15-2 shows an example where the application currently has no files stored in isolated storage, and is attempting to increase the limit to 1MB. If the user clicks Yes to accept the request, the quota is increased and the IncreaseQuotaTo() method returns true. If the user clicks No, the request is denied and IncreaseQuotaTo() returns false.

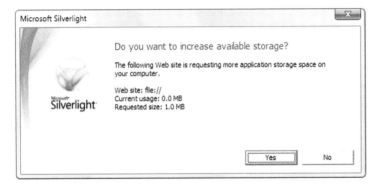

Figure 15-2. *Asking to increase the isolated store quota*

There are two considerations that limit how you can use IncreaseQuotaTo():

- You must use it in an event handler that reacts to a user action (for example, a button click). If you attempt to use it elsewhere—say, when a page loads—the call will be simply ignored. This is a security measure designed to prevent users from inadvertently accepting large quotas if the confirmation dialog suddenly steals the focus.

- You must request a value that's higher than the current quota. Otherwise, you'll receive an exception. That means you can't use the IncreaseQuotaTo() method to ensure that there's a certain level of free space—instead, you need to explicitly check whether you have the required amount of space.

You can determine the current quota size by checking the IsolatedStorageFile.Quota property. You can find the amount of space that remains in the isolated store using the IsolatedStorageFile.AvailableFreeSpace property. (It therefore follows that you can calculate the amount of space you're using in isolated storage by calculating IsolatedStorageFile.Quota – IsolatedStorageFile.AvailableFreeSpace.)

Here's an example of the IncreaseQuotaTo() method in action:

```
using (IsolatedStorageFile store = IsolatedStorageFile.GetUserStoreForApplication())
{
    // In an application that writes 1000 KB files, you need to ask for an increase
    // if there is less than 1000 KB free.
    if (store.AvailableFreeSpace < 1000*1024)
    {
        if (store.IncreaseQuotaTo(
          store.Quota + 1000*1024 - store.AvailableFreeSpace))
        {
            // The request succeeded.
        }
        else
        {
            // The request failed.
            lblError.Text = "Not enough room to save temporary file.";
```

```
            return;
        }
    }

    // (Write the big file here.)
}
```

The preceding example uses a calculation to request an exact amount of space. The potential problem with this approach is that every time you need a bit more space, you'll need to present the user with a new request. To avoid these constant requests, it makes sense to request an amount of space that's comfortably above your immediate needs.

There's an easy way to find out how much isolated space storage has been allocated to every Silverlight application that you've ever used. To do so, you must first browse to a page with Silverlight content. Right-click the Silverlight content region and choose Silverlight Configuration. A tabbed dialog box will appear that displays information about the current version of Silverlight, allows you to control whether updates are installed automatically, and allows you to enable or disable media content that uses Digital Rights Management (DRM) licensing.

To review the isolated storage quotas for various applications, click the Application Storage tab. There you'll see a list of all the Silverlight 2 applications that the current user has run and that use isolated storage (see Figure 15-3). Next to each application is information about its maximum space quota and the current amount of space used.

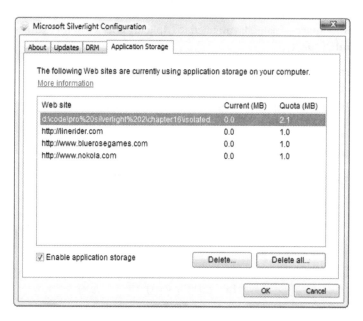

Figure 15-3. *Reviewing the isolated stores of different applications*

The Application Storage tab gives you the only way to remove isolated storage. Simply select the application and click Delete. When you do so, two things happen—all the files in isolated storage for that application are removed, and the quota is reset to the standard 1MB.

Note There's no way to lower the isolated storage quota of an application without removing the current contents of its isolated store. You can also do this programmatically using the IsolatedStorageFile.Remove method.

Storing Objects with the XmlSerializer

As you've already seen, you can write to files in isolated storage using the same classes you use for ordinary file access in a .NET application, such as StreamWriter and BinaryWriter. To read from them, you use the corresponding StreamReader and BinaryReader classes. Although this approach gives you the most direct control over your files, it's not the only option.

The XmlSerializer provides a higher-level alternative that allows you to serialize and deserialize objects rather than write and read individual pieces of data. The XmlSerializer works by converting a live object into a stream of bytes, which you can push out to any stream. The XmlSerializer can also perform the reverse trick, and convert a stream of bytes into an object instance. To use the XmlSerializer, you need to add a reference to the System.Xml.Serialization.dll assembly, which will be included in the XAP file for your compiled application.

The XmlSerializer can't work with every class. In fact, XmlSerializer has two nonnegotiable requirements:

- The class you want to serialize must have a public no-argument constructor. This is the constructor that the XmlSerializer will use when deserializing a new instance.

- The class you want to serialize must be made up of public settable properties. The XmlSerializer will read these properties (using reflection) when serializing the object, and will set them (again using reflection) when restoring it. Private data will be ignored, and any validation logic that you place in your property procedures—for example, requiring one property to be set before another—is likely to cause a problem.

If you can live with these limitations, the advantage is that the XmlSerializer gives you a clean, concise way to store an entire object's worth of information.

Ideally, the classes you use to store information with XmlSerializer will be simple data packages with little or no functionality built in. Here's a simple Person class that's serialized in the next example you'll consider:

```
public class Person
{
    public string FirstName { get; set; }
    public string LastName { get; set; }
    public DateTime? DateOfBirth { get; set; }

    public Person(string firstName, string lastName, DateTime? dateOfBirth)
    {
        FirstName = firstName;
        LastName = lastName;
```

```
            DateOfBirth = dateOfBirth;
    }

    public Person() { }
}
```

Figure 15-4 shows a test page that uses the XmlSerializer and the Person class. It allows the user to specify the three pieces of information that make up a Person object, and then store that data in isolated storage. Person files are named using the first name, last name, and extension .person, as in JoeMalik.person. The list on the left of the page shows all the .person files in isolated storage, and allows the user to select one to view or update its data.

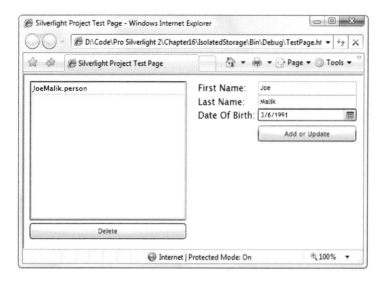

Figure 15-4. *Storing person objects*

Building this example is easy. First, you need an instance of the XmlSerializer that's customized to use the Person class and is available to all your event handling code:

```
private XmlSerializer serializer = new XmlSerializer(typeof(Person));
```

When the user clicks the Add button, the current information in the two text boxes and the DatePicker control is used to build a Person object, and that Person object is serialized to isolated storage.

```
private void cmdAdd_Click(object sender, RoutedEventArgs e)
{
    Person person = new Person(txtFirstName.Text, txtLastName.Text,
        dpDateOfBirth.SelectedDate);

    using (IsolatedStorageFile store =
        IsolatedStorageFile.GetUserStoreForApplication())
    {
```

```
    // The CreateFile() method creates a new file or overwrites an existing one.
    using (FileStream stream = store.CreateFile(
      person.FirstName + person.LastName + ".person"))
    {
        // Store the person details in the file.
        serializer.Serialize(stream, person);
    }

    // Update the list.
    lstPeople.ItemsSource = store.GetFileNames("*.person");
  }
}
```

When the user clicks one of the person files in the list, the data is retrieved from isolated storage:

```
private void lstPeople_SelectionChanged(object sender, SelectionChangedEventArgs e)
{
    if (lstPeople.SelectedItem == null) return;

    using (IsolatedStorageFile store =
      IsolatedStorageFile.GetUserStoreForApplication())
    {
        using (FileStream stream = store.OpenFile(
          lstPeople.SelectedItem.ToString(), FileMode.Open))
        {
            Person person = (Person)serializer.Deserialize(stream);
            txtFirstName.Text = person.FirstName;
            txtLastName.Text = person.LastName;
            dpDateOfBirth.SelectedDate = person.DateOfBirth;
        }
    }
}
```

And finally, if the Delete button is clicked, the selected person file is removed from the isolated store altogether:

```
private void Delete_Click(object sender, RoutedEventArgs e)
{
    if (lstPeople.SelectedItem == null) return;

    using (IsolatedStorageFile store =
      IsolatedStorageFile.GetUserStoreForApplication())
    {
        store.DeleteFile(lstPeople.SelectedItem.ToString());
        lstPeople.ItemsSource = store.GetFileNames("*.person");
    }
}
```

Storing Application Settings

A common pattern with isolated storage is to load it when the application starts (or as needed), and then save it automatically when the application ends and the Application.Exit event fires. Silverlight has a higher-level class that allows you to implement this pattern to store miscellaneous pieces of information (typically, application settings). This class is IsolatedStorageSettings.

The IsolatedStorageSettings class provides two static properties, both of which hold collections of information that you want to store. The most commonly used collection is IsolatedStorageSettings.ApplicationSettings, which is a name-value collection that can hold any items you like. Behind the scenes, the ApplicationSettings class uses the XmlSerializer to store the information you add.

To add an item, you simply need to assign it with a new string key name. Here's an example that stores the date under the key name LastRunDate:

```
IsolatedStorageSettings.ApplicationSettings["LastRunDate"] = DateTime.Now;
```

And here's an example that stores a Person object under the key name CurrentUser:

```
IsolatedStorageSettings.ApplicationSettings["CurrentUser"] = new Person(...);
```

Retrieving it is just as easy, although you'll need to cast the object to the right type:

```
DateTime date = (DateTime)
    IsolatedStorageSettings.ApplicationSettings["LastRunDate"];
Person person = (Person)IsolatedStorageSettings.ApplicationSettings["CurrentUser"];
```

You can also use the Contains() method to check whether a key exists in the Application-Settings collection, and the Remove() method to delete an existing piece of information.

The ApplicationSettings class stores all the information it contains automatically when the Silverlight application shuts down (for example, when the user navigates to a new page). Thus, the information will be present in the ApplicationSettings collection the next time the user runs the application.

Although the ApplicationSettings collection is really just a nicety that simplifies what you can already do directly with isolated storage, the IsolatedStorageSettings class provides another feature that's a bit different. The IsolatedStorageSettings.SiteSettings collection works much like the ApplicationSettings collection—for example, it's an untyped collection that can hold any type of serializable data—with a twist. It's scoped to the current website domain. That means that any Silverlight applications running at that domain will have access to these settings. However, these applications are still user-specific. You might choose to use SiteSettings when you are developing a group of Silverlight applications and you want some personalization information to be shared by all of them.

Reading Local Files with OpenFileDialog

Although Silverlight applications aren't allowed to access the file system directly, there's one backdoor you can use to read a file that's on the local file system. That backdoor is the Open-FileDialog class.

The OpenFileDialog allows you to show the ordinary Open File dialog box. Once the user chooses a file, it's then made available to your application for reading only. No restrictions are placed on the OpenFileDialog, so it's possible for the user to choose any file. However, there's no way for you to access any file without the user explicitly choosing it and clicking Open, which is considered to be a high enough bar for security.

To use the OpenFileDialog, you first create a new instance and then set the Filter and FilterIndex properties to configure what file types the user will see. The Filter determines what appears in the file type list.

You need to indicate the text that should appear in the file type list, and the corresponding expression that the OpenFileDialog box will use to filter files. For example, if you want to allow the user to open text files, you might show the text "Text Files (*.txt)" and use the filter expression *.txt to find all files with the .txt extension. Here's how you would then set the Filter property:

```
OpenFileDialog dialog = new OpenFileDialog();
dialog.Filter = "Text Files (*.txt)|*.txt";
```

You use the | (pipe) character to separate the display text from the filter expression in the filter string. If you have multiple file types, you string them one after the other, separated by additional pipe characters. For example, if you want to allow the user to see different types of images, you might write the filter string like this:

```
dialog.Filter = "Bitmaps (*.bmp)|*.bmp|JPEGs (*.jpg)|*.jpg|All files (*.*)|*.*";
```

You can also create a filter expression that matches several file types, by separating them with semicolons:

```
dialog.Filter = "Image Files(*.bmp;*.jpg;*.gif)|*.bmp;*.jpg;*.gif";
```

Once you've configured the OpenFileDialog, you then show the dialog box by calling ShowDialog(). The ShowDialog() method returns a DialogResult value that indicates what the user selected. If the result is true, the user picked a file and you can go ahead and open it.

```
if (dialog.ShowDialog() == true)
{ ... }
```

The file is exposed through the OpenFileDialog.File property, which is a FileDialogFileInfo object. The FileDialogFileInfo is a relatively simply class that exposes just three useful members: a Name property that returns the file name, an OpenRead() method that returns a FileStream in read-only mode, and an OpenText() method that creates the FileStream and returns a StreamReader for it.

```
if (dialog.ShowDialog() == true)
{
    using (StreamReader reader = dlg.File.OpenText())
    {
        string data = reader.ReadToEnd();
    }
}
```

Obviously, the OpenText() method is a good shortcut if you're dealing with text data, and the OpenRead() method is a better choice if you need to create a BinaryReader or use the FileStream.Read() method directly to pull out a block of bytes.

Tip The OpenFileDialog also supports multiple selection. Simply set OpenFileDialog.Multiselect to true before you call ShowDialog(). Then, retrieve all the selected files through the OpenFileDialog.Files property.

One interesting way to use the OpenFileDialog is to copy a selected file from the local hard drive to isolated storage, so it can be manipulated by the application later on. Here's an example that performs this trick:

```
OpenFileDialog dialog = new OpenFileDialog();
dialog.Filter = "All files (*.*)|*.*";
dialog.Multiselect = true;

// Show the dialog box.
if (dialog.ShowDialog() == true)
{
    // Copy all the selected files to isolated storage.
    using (IsolatedStorageFile store =
      IsolatedStorageFile.GetUserStoreForApplication())
    {
        foreach (FileDialogFileInfo file in dialog.Files)
        {
            using (Stream fileStream = file.OpenRead())
            {
                // Check for free space.
                if (fileStream.Length > store.AvailableFreeSpace)
                {
                    // (Cancel the operation or use IncreaseQuotaTo().)
                }

                using (IsolatedStorageFileStream storeStream =
                    store.CreateFile(file.Name))
                {
                    // Write 1 KB block at a time.
                    byte[] buffer = new byte[1024];
                    int count = 0;
                    do
                    {
                        int count = fileStream.Read(buffer, 0, buffer.Length);
                        if (count > 0) storeStream.Write(buffer, 0, count);
                    } while (count > 0);
                }
```

```
                }
            }
        }
    }
}
```

The Last Word

In this chapter, you saw how Silverlight allows you to access the local hard drive, but with careful restrictions in place. First, you took a thorough look at isolated storage, the obfuscated, space-limited storage location that you can use to store miscellaneous data, serialized objects, and application settings. Then, you saw how you can use the OpenFileDialog to retrieve information from a user-selected file anywhere on the hard drive. These two features give Silverlight applications an impressive balance of safety and performance, ensuring malicious applications can't tamper with local files or read sensitive data but legitimate software can store details from one user session to the next.

CHAPTER 16

■ ■ ■

Multithreading

One of Silverlight's least expected surprises is its support for *multithreading*—the fine art of executing more than one piece of code at the same time. It's a key part of the full .NET Framework, and a commonly used feature in rich client applications built with WPF and Windows Forms. However, multithreading hasn't appeared in the toolkit of most browser-based developers, and it's a notably absent from both JavaScript and Flash.

The second surprise is how similar Silverlight's threading tools are to those in the full .NET Framework. As with ordinary .NET programming, Silverlight developers can create new threads with the Thread class, manage a long-running operation with the BackgroundWorker, and even submit tasks to a pool of worker threads with the ThreadPool. All of these ingredients are closely modeled after their counterparts in the full .NET Framework, so developers who have written multithreaded client applications will quickly find themselves at home with Silverlight. And while there are some clear limitations—for example, you can't control thread priorities with Silverlight code—these issues don't stop Silverlight threading from being remarkably powerful.

In this chapter, you'll begin by taking a look at the lower-level Thread class, which gives you the most flexible way to create new threads at will. Along the way, you'll explore the Silverlight threading model and the rules it imposes. Finally, you'll explore the higher-level BackgroundWorker class, which gives you a conveniently streamlined, practical way to deal with background tasks.

Understanding Multithreading

When you program with threads, you write your code as though each thread is running independently. Behind the scenes, the Windows operating system gives each thread a brief unit of time (called a *time slice*) to perform some work, and then it freezes the thread in a state of suspended animation. A little bit later (perhaps only a few milliseconds), the operating system unfreezes the thread and allows it to perform a little more work.

This model of constant interruption is known as *preemptive multitasking*. It takes place completely outside the control of your program. Your application acts (for the most part) as though all the threads it has are running simultaneously, and each thread carries on as though it's an independent program performing some task.

Note If you have multiple CPUs or a dual-core CPU, it's possible that two threads will actually execute at once, but it's not necessarily likely—after all, the Silverlight plug-in, other applications and services, and the client's operating system can also compete for the CPU's attention. Furthermore, the high-level tasks you perform with a programming platform like Silverlight will be translated into many more low-level instructions. In some cases, a dual-core CPU can execute more than one instruction at the same time, meaning a single thread can keep more than one CPU core busy.

The Goals of Multithreading

Multithreading increases complexity. If you decide to use multithreading, you'll need to code carefully to avoid minor mistakes that can lead to mysterious errors later on. Before you split your application into separate threads, you should carefully consider whether the additional work is warranted.

There are essentially three reasons for using multiple threads in a program:

- **Making the client more responsive.** If you run a time-consuming task on a separate thread, the user can still interact with your application's user interface to perform other tasks. You can even give the user the ability to cancel the background work before it's complete. By comparison, a single-threaded application will lock up the user interface when it performs time-consuming work on the main thread.

- **Completing several tasks at once.** On its own, multithreading doesn't improve performance for the typical single-CPU computer. (In fact, the additional overhead needed to track the new threads decreases it slightly.) However, there are certain tasks that can involve a high degree of latency, like fetching data from an external source (web page, database, or a file on a network), or communicating with a remote component. While these tasks are underway, the CPU is essentially idle. Although you can't reduce the wait time, you can use the time to perform other work. For example, you might send requests to three web services at the same time to reduce the total time taken, or you might perform CPU-intensive work while waiting for a call to complete.

- **Making a server application scalable.** A server-side application needs to be able to handle an arbitrary number of clients. Depending on the technology you're using, this might be handled for you (as it is if you're creating an ASP.NET web application). In other cases, you might need to create this infrastructure on your own—for example, if you're building a socket-based application with the .NET networking classes, as demonstrated in Chapter 17. This type of design usually applies to .NET-based server applications, not Silverlight applications.

In this chapter, you'll explore an example where multithreading makes good sense—dealing with a time-consuming operation in the background. You'll see how to keep the application responsive, avoid threading errors, and add support for progress notification and cancellation.

■Tip The CPU is rarely the limiting factor for the performance of a Silverlight application. Network latency, slow web services, and disk access are more common limiting factors. As a result, multithreading rarely improves overall performance, even on a dual-core CPU. However, by improving responsiveness, it can make an application "feel" much more performant to the user.

The DispatcherTimer

In some cases, you can avoid threading concerns altogether using the DispatcherTimer class from the System.Windows.Threading namespace. The DispatcherTimer was used in Chapter 9 to power the bomb-dropping animations in a simple arcade game.

The DispatcherTimer doesn't offer true multithreaded execution. Instead, it triggers a periodic Tick event on the main application thread. This event interrupts whatever else is taking place in your application, giving you a chance to perform some work. However, if you need to frequently perform small amounts of work (for example, starting a new set of bomb-dropping animations every fraction of a second), the DispatcherTimer works as seamlessly as actual multithreading.

The advantage of the DispatcherTimer is that the Tick event always executes on the main application thread, thereby sidestepping synchronization problems and the other headaches you'll consider in this chapter. However, this behavior also introduces a number of limitations. For example, if your timer event handling code performs a time-consuming task, the user interface will lock up until it's finished. Thus, the timer doesn't help you make a user interface more responsive, and it doesn't allow you to collapse the waiting time for high-latency operations. To get this functionality, you need the real multithreading discussed in this chapter.

However, clever use of the DispatcherTimer can achieve the effect you need in some situations. For example, the DispatcherTimer is a great way to periodically check a web service for new data. As you learned in Chapter 13, all web service calls are asynchronous, and are carried out on a background thread. Thus, you could use the DispatcherTimer to create an application that periodically downloads data from a slow web service. For example, it might fire every five minutes and then launch the web service call asynchronously, allowing the time-consuming download to take place on a background thread.

■Note The name of the DispatcherTimer refers to the *dispatcher*, which controls the main application thread in a Silverlight application. You'll learn more about the Dispatcher in this chapter.

The Thread Class

The most straightforward way to create a multithreaded Silverlight application is to use the Thread class from the System.Threading namespace. Each Thread object represents a separate thread of execution.

To use the Thread class, you being by creating a new Thread object, at which point you supply a delegate to the method you want to invoke asynchronously. A Thread object can only point to a single method. This signature of this method is limited in several ways. It can't have a return value, and it must have either no parameters (in which case it matches the Thread-Start delegate) or a single object parameter (in which case it matches the Parameterized-ThreadStart delegate).

For example, if you have a method like this:

```
private void DoSomething()
{ ... }
```

you can create a Thread that uses it like this:

```
ThreadStart asyncMethod = new ThreadStart(DoSomething);
Thread thread = new Thread(asyncMethod);
```

Once you've created the Thread object, you can start it on its way by calling the Thread.Start() method. If your thread accepts an object parameter, you pass it in at this point.

```
thread.Start();
```

The Start() method returns immediately, and your code begins executing asynchronously on a new thread. When the method ends, the thread is destroyed and cannot be reused. In between, you can use a small set of properties and methods to control the thread's execution. Table 16-1 lists the most significant.

Table 16-1. *Members of the Thread Class*

Property	Description
IsAlive	Returns true unless the thread is stopped, aborted, or not yet started.
ManagedThreadId	Provides an integer that uniquely identifies this thread.
Name	Enables you to set a string name that identifies the thread. This is primarily useful during debugging, but it can also be used to distinguish different threads. Once set, the Name property cannot be set again.
ThreadState	A combination of ThreadState values, which indicate whether the thread is started, running, finished, and so on. The ThreadState property should only be used for debugging. If you want to determine if a thread has completed its work, you need to track that information manually.
Start()	Starts a thread executing for the first time. You cannot use Start() to restart a thread after it ends.
Join()	Waits until the thread terminates (or a specified timeout elapses).
Sleep()	Pauses the current thread for a specified number of milliseconds. This method is static.

Note Seasoned .NET programmers will notice that the Silverlight version of the Thread class leaves out a few details. In Silverlight, all threads are background threads, you can't set thread priorities, and you have no ability to temporarily pause and then resume a thread. Similarly, although the Thread class includes an Abort() method that kills a thread with an unhandled exception, this method is marked with the Security-Critical attribute, and so can only be called by the Silverlight plug-in, not by your application code.

The challenge of multithreaded programming is communicating between the background thread and the main application thread. It's easy enough to pass information to the thread when it starts (using parameters). But trying to communicate with the thread while it's running, or trying to return data when it's complete, are two more difficult tasks. You may need to use locking to ensure that the same data isn't accessed on two threads at once (a cardinal sin of multithreaded programming) and marshalling to make sure you don't access a user interface element from a background thread (an equally bad mistake). Even worse, threading mistakes don't result in compile-time warnings and don't necessarily lead to clear, showstopper bugs. They may cause subtler problems that only appear under occasional, difficult-to-diagnose circumstances. In the following sections, you'll learn how to use a background thread safely.

Marshalling Code to the User Interface Thread

Much like .NET client applications (for example, WPF applications and Windows Forms applications), Silverlight supports a *single-threaded apartment* model. In this model, a single thread runs your entire application and owns all the objects that represent user interface elements. Furthermore, all these elements have *thread affinity*. The thread that creates them owns them, and other threads can't interact with them directly. If you violate this rule—for example, try to access a user interface object from a background thread—you're certain to cause an immediate exception, lock up, or a subtler problem.

To keep your application on an even keel, Silverlight uses a *dispatcher*. The dispatcher owns the main application thread and manages a queue of work items. As your application runs, the dispatcher accepts new work requests and executes one at a time.

Note The dispatcher is an instance of the System.Windows.Threading.Dispatcher class, which was introduced with WPF.

You can retrieve the dispatcher from any element through the Dispatcher property. The Dispatcher class includes just two members—a CheckAccess() method that allows you to determine if you're on the correct thread to interact with your application's user interface, and a BeginInvoke() method that allows you to marshal code to the main application thread that the dispatcher controls.

Tip The Dispatcher.CheckAccess() method is hidden from Visual Studio IntelliSense. You can still use it in code; you just won't see it in the pop-up list of members.

For example, the following code responds to a button click by creating a new System.Threading.Thread object. It then uses that thread to launch a small bit of code that changes a text box in the current page.

```
private void cmdBreakRules_Click(object sender, RoutedEventArgs e)
{
    Thread thread = new Thread(UpdateTextWrong);
    thread.Start();
}

private void UpdateTextWrong()
{
    // Simulate some work taking place with a five-second delay.
    Thread.Sleep(TimeSpan.FromSeconds(5));

    txt.Text = "Here is some new text.";
}
```

This code is destined to fail. The UpdateTextWrong() method will be executed on a new thread, and that thread isn't allowed to access Silverlight objects. In this case, the problem is undetected—the operation simply has no effect. However, it's possible that on certain platforms and in combination with other actions an exception or more serious error may occur.

To correct this code, you need to get a reference to the dispatcher that owns the TextBox object (which is the same dispatcher that owns the page and all the other Silverlight objects in the application). Once you have access to that dispatcher, you can call Dispatcher.BeginInvoke() to marshal some code to the dispatcher thread. Essentially, BeginInvoke() schedules your code as a task for the dispatcher. The dispatcher then executes that code.

Here's the corrected code:

```
private void cmdFollowRules_Click(object sender, RoutedEventArgs e)
{
    Thread thread = new Thread(UpdateTextRight);
    thread.Start();
}

private void UpdateTextRight()
{
    // Simulate some work taking place with a five-second delay.
    Thread.Sleep(TimeSpan.FromSeconds(5));

    // Get the dispatcher from the current page, and use it to invoke
    // the update code.
```

```
    this.Dispatcher.BeginInvoke((ThreadStart) delegate()
        {
            txt.Text = "Here is some new text.";
        }
    );
}
```

The Dispatcher.BeginInvoke() method takes a single parameter—a delegate that points to the method with the code you want to execute. This could be a method somewhere else in your code, or you can use an anonymous method to define your code inline (as in this example). The inline approach works well for simple operations, like this single-line update. However, if you need to use a more complex process to update the user interface, it's a good idea to factor this code into a separate method.

■ **Note** The BeginInvoke() method also has a return value, which isn't used in the earlier example. Begin-Invoke() returns a DispatcherOperation object, which allows you to follow the status of your marshalling operation and determine when your code has actually been executed. However, the DispatcherOperation is rarely useful, because the code you pass to BeginInvoke() should take very little time.

Remember, if you're performing a time-consuming background operation, you need to perform this operation on a separate thread and *then* marshal its result to the dispatcher thread (at which point you'll update the user interface or change a shared object). It makes no sense to perform your time-consuming code in the method that you pass to BeginInvoke(). For example, this slightly rearranged code still works but is impractical:

```
private void UpdateTextRight()
{
    // Get the dispatcher from the current page.
    this.Dispatcher.BeginInvoke((ThreadStart) delegate()
        {
            // Simulate some work taking place.
            Thread.Sleep(TimeSpan.FromSeconds(5));

            txt.Text = "Here is some new text.";
        }
    );
}
```

The problem here is that all the work takes place on the dispatcher thread. That means this code ties up the dispatcher in the same way a non-multithreaded application would.

Creating a Thread Wrapper

The previous example shows how you can update the user interface directly from a background thread. However, this approach isn't ideal. It creates complex, tightly coupled applications that mingle the code for performing a task with the code for displaying data. The result is an application that's more complex, less flexible, and difficult to change. For example, if you change the name of the text box in the previous example, or replace it with a different control, you'll also need to revise your threading code.

A better approach is to create a thread that passes information back to the main application and lets the application take care of the display details. To make it easier to use this approach, it's common to wrap the threading code and the data into a separate class. You can then add properties to that class for the input and output information. This custom class is often called a *thread wrapper*.

Before you create your thread wrapper, it makes good sense to factor out all the threading essentials into a base class. That way you can use the same pattern to create multiple background tasks without repeating it each time.

We'll examine the ThreadWrapperBase class piece by piece. First of all, the ThreadWrapperBase is declared abstract so that it can't be instantiated on its own. Instead, you need to create a derived class.

```
public abstract class ThreadWrapperBase
{ ... }
```

The ThreadWrapperBase defines two public properties. Status returns one of three values from an enumeration (Unstarted, InProgress, or Completed). ID returns an automatically generated unique ID, which is useful for tracking the task when several are underway at once.

```
// Track the status of the task.
private StatusState status = StatusState.Unstarted;
public StatusState Status
{
    get { return status; }
}
```

The ThreadWrapperBase wraps a Thread object. It exposes a public Start() method which, when called, creates the thread and starts if off:

```
// This is the thread where the task is carried out.
private Thread thread;

// Start the new operation.
public void Start()
{
    if (status == StatusState.InProgress)
    {
        throw new InvalidOperationException("Already in progress.");
    }
    else
    {
        // Initialize the new task.
        status = StatusState.InProgress;
```

```
        // Create the thread and run it in the background,
        // so it will terminate automatically if the application ends.
        thread = new Thread(StartTaskAsync);
        thread.IsBackground = true;

        // Start the thread.
        thread.Start();
    }
}
```

The thread executes a private method named StartTaskAsync(). This method farms the work out to two other methods—DoTask() and OnCompleted(). DoTask() performs the actual work (calculating the prime numbers). OnCompleted() fires a completion event or triggers a callback to notify the client. Both of these details are specific to the particular task at hand so they're implemented as abstract methods that the derived class will override:

```
private void StartTaskAsync()
{
    DoTask();
    status = StatusState.Completed;
    OnCompleted();
}

// Override this class to supply the task logic.
protected abstract void DoTask();

// Override this class to supply the callback logic.
protected abstract void OnCompleted();
```

This completes the ThreadWrapper. Now you need to create a derived class that uses it. The following section presents a practical example with an algorithm for finding prime numbers.

Creating the Worker Class

The basic ingredient for any test of multithreading is a time-consuming process. The following example uses a common algorithm for finding prime numbers in a given range called the *sieve of Eratosthenes*, which was invented by Eratosthenes himself in about 240 BC. With this algorithm, you begin by making a list of all the integers in a range of numbers. You then strike out the multiples of all primes less than or equal to the square root of the maximum number. The numbers that are left are the primes.

In this example, I won't go into the theory that proves the sieve of Eratosthenes works or show the fairly trivial code that performs it. (Similarly, don't worry about optimizing it or comparing it against other techniques.) However, you will see how to perform the sieve of Eratosthenes algorithm on a background thread.

The full code for the FindPrimesThreadWrapper class is available with the online examples for this chapter. Like any class that derives from ThreadWrapperBase, it needs to supply four things:

- Fields or properties that store the initial data. In this example, that's the from and to numbers that delineate the search range.

- Fields or properties that store the final data. In this example, that's the final prime list, which is stored in an array.

- An overridden DoTask() method that does the actual operation. It uses the initial data and sets the final result.

- An overridden OnCompleted() method that raises the completion event. Typically, this completion event will use a custom EventArgs object that supplies the final data. In this example, the FindPrimesCompletedEventArgs class wraps the from and to numbers and the prime list array.

Here's the code for the FindPrimesThreadWrapper:

```
public class FindPrimesThreadWrapper : ThreadWrapperBase
{
    // Store the input and output information.
    private int fromNumber, toNumber;
    private int[] primeList;

    public FindPrimesThreadWrapper(int from, int to)
    {
        this.fromNumber = from;
        this.toNumber = to;
    }

    protected override void DoTask()
    {
        // Find the primes between fromNumber and toNumber,
        // and return them as an array of integers.
        // (See the code in the downloadable examples.)
    }

    public event EventHandler<FindPrimesCompletedEventArgs> Completed;
    protected override void OnCompleted()
    {
        // Signal that the operation is complete.
        if (Completed != null)
            Completed(this,
                new FindPrimesCompletedEventArgs(fromNumber, toNumber, primeList));
    }
}
```

It's important to note that the data that the FindPrimesThreadWrapper class uses—the from and to numbers, and the prime list—are not exposed publically. This prevents that information from being accessed by the main application thread while it's being used by the background thread, which is a potentially risky scenario that can lead to data errors. If you wanted to make the prime list available, the best approach is to add a public property. This property would then check the ThreadWrapperBase.State property, and only return the prime list if the thread has completed its processing.

A far better approach is to notify the user with a callback or event, as with the completion event demonstrated in the thread wrapper. However, it's important to remember that events fired from a background thread continue to execute on that thread, no matter where the code is defined. That means that when you handle the Completed event, you will still need to use marshalling code to transfer execution to the main application thread before you attempt to update the user interface or any data in the current page.

■**Note** If you really do need to expose the same object to two threads that might use it at the same time, you'll need to safeguard the access to that object with locking. As in a full-fledged .NET application, you can use the lock keyword to obtain exclusive access to an in-memory object. However, locking complicates application design and raises other potential problems. It can slow performance, because other threads must wait to access a locked object, and it can lead to deadlocks if two threads are trying to achieve locks on the same objects.

Using the Thread Wrapper

The last ingredient is a Silverlight sample application that uses the FindPrimesThreadWrapper. Figure 16-1 shows one such example. This page allows the user to choose the range of numbers to search. When the user clicks Find Primes, the search begins, but it takes place in the background. When the search is finished, the list of prime numbers appears in a DataGrid.

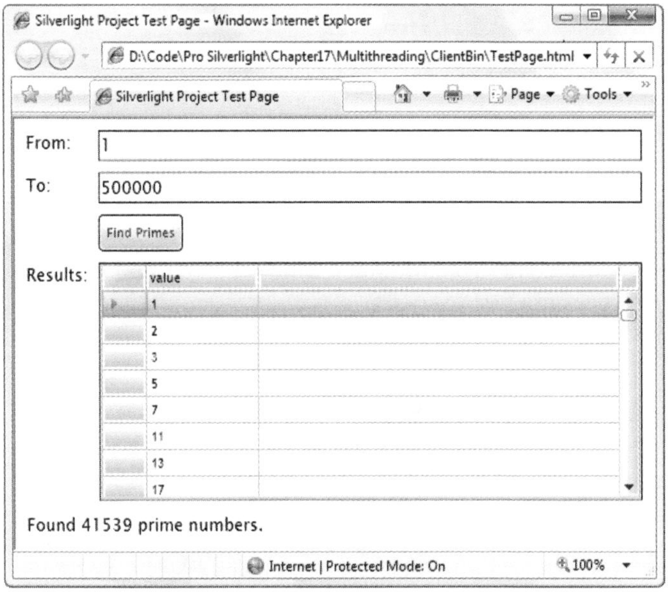

Figure 16-1. *A completed prime number search*

The code that underpins this page is straightforward. When the user clicks the Find Primes button, the application disables the button (preventing multiple concurrent searches, which are possible but potentially confusing to the user) and determines the search range. Then it creates the FindPrimesThreadWrapper, hooks up an event handler to the Completed event, and calls Start() to begin processing.

```
private FindPrimesThreadWrapper threadWrapper;

private void cmdFind_Click(object sender, RoutedEventArgs e)
{
    // Disable the button and clear previous results.
    cmdFind.IsEnabled = false;
    gridPrimes.ItemsSource = null;

    // Get the search range.
    int from, to;
    if (!Int32.TryParse(txtFrom.Text, out from))
    {
        lblStatus.Text = "Invalid From value.";
        return;
    }
    if (!Int32.TryParse(txtTo.Text, out to))
    {
        lblStatus.Text = "Invalid To value.";
        return;
    }

    // Start the search for primes on another thread.
    threadWrapper = new FindPrimesThreadWrapper(from, to);
    threadWrapper.Completed += threadWrapper_Completed;
    threadWrapper.Start();

    lblStatus.Text = "The search is in progress...";
}
```

When the task is in process, the application remains remarkably responsive. The user can click other controls, type in the text boxes, and so on, without having any indication that the CPU is doing additional work in the background.

When the job is finished, the Completed event fires and the prime list is retrieved and displayed:

```
private void threadWrapper_Completed(object sender, FindPrimesCompletedEventArgs e)
{
    FindPrimesThreadWrapper thread = (FindPrimesThreadWrapper)sender;

    this.Dispatcher.BeginInvoke(delegate()
        {
            if (thread.Status == StatusState.Completed)
```

```
    {
        int[] primes = e.PrimeList;
        lblStatus.Text = "Found " + primes.Length + " prime numbers.";
        gridPrimes.ItemsSource = primes;
    }

    cmdFind.IsEnabled = true;
    cmdCancel.IsEnabled = false;
  }
);
}
```

Note This example uses the DataGrid to display the prime list, because it's an extremely long list. Other approaches, such as adding the numbers to a list box or combining them into a string and displaying them in a scrollable text block, are extremely slow—in fact, the memory overhead and time delay is greater than what's required for the actual prime number processing. The DataGrid doesn't suffer the same problem because it uses *virtualization*, which means it only creates objects for the items that are currently visible, rather than attempting to hold the entire collection of items in memory at once.

Cancellation Support

Now that you have the basic infrastructure in place, it takes just a bit more work to add additional features like cancellation and progress notification.

For example, to make cancellation work, your thread wrapper needs to have a field that, when true, indicates that it's time to stop processing. Your worker code can check this field periodically. Here's the code you could add to the ThreadWrapperBase to make this a standard feature:

```
// Flag that indicates a stop is requested.
private bool cancelRequested = false;
protected bool CancelRequested
{
    get { return cancelRequested; }
}

// Call this to request a cancel.
public void RequestCancel()
{
    cancelRequested = true;
}

// When cancelling, the worker should call the OnCancelled() method
// to raise the Cancelled event.
public event EventHandler Cancelled;
```

```
protected void OnCancelled()
{
    if (Cancelled != null)
      Cancelled(this, EventArgs.Empty);
}
```

And here's a modified bit of worker code in the FindPrimesThreadWrapper.DoWork()
method that makes periodic checks (about 100 of them over the course of the entire operation) to see if a cancellation has been requested.

```
int iteration = list.Length / 100;

if (i % iteration == 0)
{
    if (CancelRequested)
    {
        return;
    }
}
```

You also need to modify the ThreadWrapperBase.StartTaskAsync() method so it recognizes the two possible ways an operation can end—by completing gracefully or by being
interrupted with a cancellation request:

```
private void StartTaskAsync()
{
    DoTask();
    if (CancelRequested)
    {
        status = StatusState.Cancelled;
        OnCancelled();
    }
    else
    {
        status = StatusState.Completed;
        OnCompleted();
    }
}
```

To use this cancellation feature in the example shown in Figure 16-1, you simply need to
hook up an event handler to the Cancelled event, and add a new Cancel button. Here's the
code that initiates a cancel request for the current task:

```
private void cmdCancel_Click(object sender, RoutedEventArgs e)
{
    threadWrapper.RequestCancel();
}
```

And here's the event handler that runs when the cancellation is finished:

```
private void threadWrapper_Cancelled(object sender, EventArgs e)
{
    this.Dispatcher.BeginInvoke(delegate() {
        lblStatus.Text = "Search cancelled.";
        cmdFind.IsEnabled = true;
        cmdCancel.IsEnabled = false;
    });
}
```

Remember, Silverlight threads cannot be halted with the Abort() method, so you have no choice but to request a polite stop that the worker code is free to honor or ignore.

The BackgroundWorker

So far, you've seen the no-frills approach to multithreading—creating a new System.Threading.Thread object by hand, supplying your asynchronous code, and launching it with the Thread.Start() method. This approach is powerful, because the Thread object doesn't hold anything back. You can create dozens of threads at will, pass information to them at any time, temporarily delay them with Thread.Sleep(), and so on. However, this approach is also a bit dangerous. If you access shared data, you need to use locking to prevent subtle errors. If you create threads frequently or in large numbers, you'll generate additional, unnecessary overhead.

One of the simplest and safest approaches is the System.ComponentModel.BackgroundWorker component that was first introduced with .NET 2.0 to simplify threading considerations in Windows Forms applications. However, the BackgroundWorker is equally at home in Silverlight. The BackgroundWorker component gives you a nearly foolproof way to run a time-consuming task on a separate thread. It uses the dispatcher behind the scenes and abstracts away the marshalling issues with an event-based model.

As you'll see, the BackgroundWorker also supports two frills: progress events and cancel messages. In both cases the threading details are hidden, making for easy coding. It ranks as the single most practical tool for Silverlight multithreading.

■**Note** The BackgroundWorker is perfect if you have a single asynchronous task that runs in the background from start to finish (with optional support for progress reporting and cancellation). If you have something else in mind—for example, an asynchronous task that runs throughout the entire life of your application or an asynchronous task that communicates with your application while it does its work—you'll need to design a customized solution that uses the threading features you've already seen.

Creating the BackgroundWorker

To use the BackgroundWorker, you begin by creating an instance in your code and attaching the event handlers programmatically. If you need to perform multiple asynchronous tasks, you can create your BackgroundWorker objects when needed and store them in some sort of collection for tracking. In the example described here, just one BackgroundWorker is used, and it's created in code when the page is first instantiated.

Here's the initialization code that enables support for progress notification and cancellation and attaches event handlers to the DoWork, ProgressChanged, and RunWorker-Completed events:

```
private BackgroundWorker backgroundWorker = new BackgroundWorker();

public BackgroundWorkerTest()
{
    InitializeComponent();

    backgroundWorker.WorkerReportsProgress = true;
    backgroundWorker.WorkerSupportsCancellation = true;
    backgroundWorker.DoWork += backgroundWorker_DoWork;
    backgroundWorker.ProgressChanged += backgroundWorker_ProgressChanged;
    backgroundWorker.RunWorkerCompleted += backgroundWorker_RunWorkerCompleted;
}
```

Running the BackgroundWorker

The first step to using the BackgroundWorker with the prime number search example is to create a custom class that allows you to transmit the input parameters to the Background-Worker. When you call BackgroundWorker.RunWorkerAsync(), you can supply any object, which will be delivered to the DoWork event. However, you can supply only a single object, so you need to wrap the to and from numbers into one class, as shown here:

```
public class FindPrimesInput
{
    public int From
    { get; set; }

    public int To
    { get; set; }

    public FindPrimesInput(int from, int to)
    {
        From = from;
        To = to;
    }
}
```

To start the BackgroundWorker on its way, you need to call the BackgroundWorker.Run-WorkerAsync() method and pass in the FindPrimesInput object. Here's the code that does this when the user clicks the Find Primes button:

```
private void cmdFind_Click(object sender, RoutedEventArgs e)
{
    // Disable this button and clear previous results.
    cmdFind.IsEnabled = false;
    cmdCancel.IsEnabled = true;
    lstPrimes.Items.Clear();

    // Get the search range.
    int from, to;
    if (!Int32.TryParse(txtFrom.Text, out from))
    {
        MessageBox.Show("Invalid From value.");
        return;
    }
    if (!Int32.TryParse(txtTo.Text, out to))
    {
        MessageBox.Show("Invalid To value.");
        return;
    }

    // Start the search for primes on another thread.
    FindPrimesInput input = new FindPrimesInput(from, to);
    backgroundWorker.RunWorkerAsync(input);
}
```

When the BackgroundWorker begins executing, it fires the DoWork event on a separate thread. Rather than create this thread (which incurs some overhead), the BackgroundWorker borrows a thread from the runtime thread pool. When the task is complete, the Background-Worker will return this thread to the thread pool, so it can be reused for another task. The thread pool threads are also used for the asynchronous operations you've seen in other chapters, such as receiving a web service response, downloading a web page, and accepting a socket connection.

■**Note** Although the thread pool has a set of workers at the ready, it can run out if there are a large number of asynchronous tasks underway at once, in which case the later ones will be queued until a thread is free. This prevents the computer from being swamped (say, with hundreds of separate threads), at which point the overhead of managing the threads would impede the CPU from performing other work.

You handle the DoWork event and begin your time-consuming task. However, you need to be careful not to access shared data (such as fields in your page class) or user interface objects. Once the work is complete, the BackgroundWorker fires the RunWorkerCompleted event to notify your application. This event fires on the dispatcher thread, which allows you to access shared data and your user interface, without incurring any problems.

Once the BackgroundWorker acquires the thread, it fires the DoWork event. You can handle this event to call the Worker.FindPrimes() method. The DoWork event provides a DoWorkEventArgs object, which is the key ingredient for retrieving and returning information. You retrieve the input object through the DoWorkEventArgs.Argument property and return the result by setting the DoWorkEventArgs.Result property.

```
private void backgroundWorker_DoWork(object sender, DoWorkEventArgs e)
{
    // Get the input values.
    FindPrimesInput input = (FindPrimesInput)e.Argument;

    // Start the search for primes and wait.
    // This is the time-consuming part, but it won't freeze the
    // user interface because it takes place on another thread.
    int[] primes = Worker.FindPrimes(input.From, input.To);

    // Return the result.
    e.Result = primes;
}
```

Once the method completes, the BackgroundWorker fires the RunWorkerCompleted-EventArgs on the dispatcher thread. At this point, you can retrieve the result from the RunWorkerCompletedEventArgs.Result property. You can then update the interface and access page-level variables without worry.

```
private void backgroundWorker_RunWorkerCompleted(object sender,
  RunWorkerCompletedEventArgs e)
{
    if (e.Error != null)
    {
        // An error was thrown by the DoWork event handler.
        MessageBox.Show(e.Error.Message, "An Error Occurred");
    }
    else
    {
        int[] primes = (int[])e.Result;
        foreach (int prime in primes)
        {
            lstPrimes.Items.Add(prime);
        }
    }
}
```

```
    cmdFind.IsEnabled = true;
    cmdCancel.IsEnabled = false;
    progressBar.Width = 0;
}
```

Notice that you don't need any locking code, and you don't need to use the Dispatcher.Begin-Invoke() method. The BackgroundWorker takes care of these issues for you.

Tracking Progress

The BackgroundWorker also provides built-in support for tracking progress, which is useful for keeping the client informed about how much work has been completed in a long-running task.

To add support for progress, you need to first set the BackgroundWorker.WorkerReports-Progress property to true. Actually, providing and displaying the progress information is a two-step affair. First, the DoWork event handling code needs to call the Background-Worker.ReportProgress() method and provide an estimated percent complete (from 0% to 100%). You can do this as little or as often as you like. Every time you call ReportProgress(), the BackgroundWorker fires the ProgressChanged event. You can react to this event to read the new progress percentage and update the user interface. Because the ProgressChanged event fires from the user interface thread, there's no need to use Dispatcher.BeginInvoke().

The FindPrimes() method reports progress in 1% increments, using code like this:

```
int iteration = list.Length / 100;
for (int i = 0; i < list.Length; i++)
{
    ...

    // Report progress only if there is a change of 1%.
    // Also, don't bother performing the calculation if there
    // isn't a BackgroundWorker or if it doesn't support
    // progress notifications.
    if ((i % iteration == 0) &&
      (backgroundWorker != null) && backgroundWorker.WorkerReportsProgress)
    {
        backgroundWorker.ReportProgress(i / iteration);
    }
}
```

Once you've set the BackgroundWorker.WorkerReportsProgress property, you can respond to these progress notifications by handling the ProgressChanged event. However, Silverlight doesn't include a progress bar control, so it's up to you to decide how you want to display the progress information. You could simply display the progress percentage in a TextBlock, but it's fairly easy to build a basic progress bar out of common Silverlight elements. Here's one that uses two rectangles (one for the background, and one for the progress meter) and a TextBlock that shows the percentage in the center. All three elements are placed in the same cell of a Grid, so they overlap.

```
<Rectangle x:Name="progressBarBackground" Fill="AliceBlue" Stroke="SlateBlue"
 Grid.Row="4" Grid.ColumnSpan="2" Margin="5" Height="30" />
<Rectangle x:Name="progressBar" Width="0" HorizontalAlignment="Left"
 Grid.Row="4" Grid.ColumnSpan="2" Margin="5" Fill="SlateBlue" Height="30" />
<TextBlock x:Name="lblProgress" HorizontalAlignment="Center" Foreground="White"
 VerticalAlignment="Center" Grid.Row="4" Grid.ColumnSpan="2" />
```

To make sure the progress bar looks right even if the user resizes the browser window, the following code reacts to the SizeChanged event and stretches the progress bar to fit the current page:

```
private double maxWidth;

private void UserControl_SizeChanged(object sender, SizeChangedEventArgs e)
{
    maxWidth = progressBarBackground.ActualWidth;
}
```

Now you simply need to handle the BackgroundWorker.ProgressChanged event, resize the progress meter, and display the current progress percentage.

```
private void backgroundWorker_ProgressChanged(object sender,
 ProgressChangedEventArgs e)
{
    progressBar.Width = (double)e.ProgressPercentage/100 * maxWidth;
    lblProgress.Text = ((double)e.ProgressPercentage/100).ToString("P0");
}
```

It's possible to pass additional information beyond just the progress percentage. The ReportProgress() method also provides an overloaded version that accepts two parameters. The first parameter is the percent done, and the second parameter is any custom object you wish to use to pass additional information. In the prime number search example, you might want to pass information about how many numbers have been searched so far or how many prime numbers have been found. Here's how to change the worker code so it returns the most recently discovered prime number with its progress information:

```
backgroundWorker.ReportProgress(i / iteration, i);
```

You can then check for this data in the ProgressChanged event handler, and display it if it's presents:

```
if (e.UserState != null)
    lblStatus.Text = "Found prime: " + e.UserState.ToString() + "...";
```

Figure 16-2 shows the progress meter while the task is in progress.

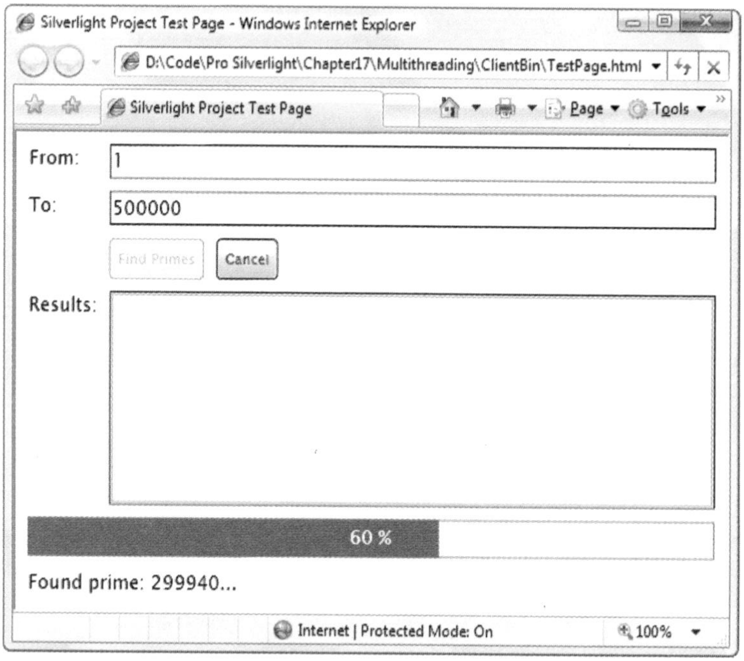

Figure 16-2. *Tracking progress for an asynchronous task*

Supporting Cancellation

It's just as easy to add support for canceling a long-running task with the BackgroundWorker. The first step is to set the BackgroundWorker.WorkerSupportsCancellation property to true.

To request a cancellation, your code needs to call the BackgroundWorker.CancelAsync() method. In this example, the cancellation is requested when a Cancel button is clicked:

```
private void cmdCancel_Click(object sender, RoutedEventArgs e)
{
    backgroundWorker.CancelAsync();
}
```

Nothing happens automatically when you call CancelAsync(). Instead, the code that's performing the task needs to explicitly check for the cancel request, perform any required cleanup, and return. Here's the code in the FindPrimes() method that checks for cancellation requests just before it reports progress:

```
for (int i = 0; i < list.Length; i++)
{
    ...
    if ((i % iteration) && (backgroundWorker != null))
    {
        if (backgroundWorker.CancellationPending)
        {
```

```
            // Return without doing any more work.
            return;
        }

        if (backgroundWorker.WorkerReportsProgress)
        {
            backgroundWorker.ReportProgress(i / iteration);
        }
    }
}
```

The code in your DoWork event handler also needs to explicitly set the DoWorkEvent-Args.Cancel property to true to complete the cancellation. You can then return from that method without attempting to build up the string of primes.

```
private void backgroundWorker_DoWork(object sender, DoWorkEventArgs e)
{
    FindPrimesInput input = (FindPrimesInput)e.Argument;
    int[] primes = Worker.FindPrimes(input.From, input.To,
      backgroundWorker);

    if (backgroundWorker.CancellationPending)
    {
        e.Cancel = true;
        return;
    }

    // Return the result.
    e.Result = primes;
}
```

Even when you cancel an operation, the RunWorkerCompleted event still fires. At this point, you can check whether the task was cancelled and handle it accordingly.

```
private void backgroundWorker_RunWorkerCompleted(object sender,
  RunWorkerCompletedEventArgs e)
{
    if (e.Cancelled)
    {
        MessageBox.Show("Search cancelled.");
    }
    else if (e.Error != null)
    {
        // An error was thrown by the DoWork event handler.
        MessageBox.Show(e.Error.Message, "An Error Occurred");
    }
    else
    {
```

```
        int[] primes = (int[])e.Result;
        foreach (int prime in primes)
        {
            lstPrimes.Items.Add(prime);
        }
    }
    cmdFind.IsEnabled = true;
    cmdCancel.IsEnabled = false;
    progressBar.Value = 0;
}
```

Now the BackgroundWorker component allows you to start a search and end it prematurely.

The Last Word

In this chapter, you saw two powerful ways to incorporate multithreading into a Silverlight application. Of course, just because you can write a multithreaded Silverlight application doesn't mean you should. Before you delve too deeply into the intricacies of multithreaded programming, it's worth considering the advice of Microsoft architects. Because of the inherent complexity of deeply multithreaded code, especially when combined with dramatically different operating systems and hardware, Microsoft's official guidance is to use multithreading sparingly. Certainly, you should use it to move work to the background, avoid long delays, and create more responsive applications. However, when possible it's better to use the straightforward BackgroundWorker than the lower-level Thread class. And when you need to use the Thread class, it's better to stick to just one or two background threads. It's also a good idea to set your threads up to work with distinct islands of information, and thereby avoid locking complications and synchronization headaches.

■■■

CHAPTER 17

Networking

Like most software, Silverlight applications need to interact with the outside world to get relevant, current information. You've already seen one tremendously useful way to pull information into a Silverlight application—using WCF services, which allow Silverlight applications to retrieve data from the web server by calling a carefully encapsulated piece of .NET code. However, WCF services won't provide all the data you need to use. In many situations you'll want to retrieve information from other non-.NET repositories, such as REST web services, RSS feeds, and ordinary HTML web pages.

In this chapter, you'll learn about this other side of the Silverlight networking picture. You'll pick up the techniques you need to download data from a variety of different non-.NET sources, and convert it to the form you need. On the way, you'll also learn how to process XML data with the remarkable XDocument class and LINQ to XML. Finally, you'll wrap up the chapter by considering an even more ambitious task—using Silverlight's socket support to build a basic messaging application.

Note The networking examples in this chapter assume you're using a solution with an ASP.NET test website, as described in Chapter 1. You need to use a test website both to build simple web services and to use Silverlight's downloading features, which aren't available when you launch a Silverlight application directly from your hard drive.

Interacting with the Web

In Chapter 6, you saw how you can use the WebClient class to download a file from the Web. This technique allows you to grab a resource or even a Silverlight assembly at the exact point in time when an application needs it.

The WebClient isn't just for downloading binary files. It also opens some possibilities for accessing HTML pages and web services. And using its bigger brother, WebRequest, you gain the ability to post values to a web page. In the following sections, you'll see a variety of approaches that use these classes to pull information from the Web. But before you begin, you need to reconsider the security limitations that Silverlight applies to any code that uses HTTP.

Cross-Domain Access

If you've ever created a web page using Ajax techniques, you've no doubt used the XML-HttpRequest object, which allows you to perform web requests in the background. However, the XMLHttpRequest object imposes a significant limitation—namely, the web page can only access web resources (HTML documents, web services, files, and so on) that are on the same web server. There's no direct way to perform a cross-domain call to fetch information from another website.

Silverlight imposes almost exactly the same restrictions in its WebClient and WebRequest classes. The issue here is security. If a Silverlight application could call other websites without informing the user, it opens up the possibility for phishing attacks. For example, if a user is currently logged on to a service like Hotmail, a malicious Silverlight application could quietly retrieve pages that provide the user's Hotmail data. There are some possible changes that could stave off these attacks—for example, linking user credentials to their source URLs—but these would require a fairly significant change to the way browsers work.

However, Silverlight isn't completely restrictive. In fact, it borrows a trick from Flash to allow websites to opt-in to cross-domain access through an XML policy file. When you attempt to download data from a website, Silverlight looks on that website for a file named clientaccesspolicy.xml (which you learned to create in Chapter 13). If this file isn't present, Silverlight looks for a file named crossdomain.xml. This file plays the same role, but was originally developed for Flash applications. The end result is that websites that can be accessed by Flash applications can also be accessed by Silverlight applications.

The clientaccesspolicy.xml or crossdomain.xml file must be stored in the web root. So, if you attempt to access web content with the URL www.somesite.com/~luther/services/CalendarService.ashx, Silverlight will check for www.somesite.com/clientaccesspolicy.xml and then (if the former is not found) www.somesite.com/crossdomain.xml. If neither of these files exists, or if one exists but it doesn't grant access to the domain of your Silverlight application, your application won't be able to access any content on that website. Often, companies that provide public web services will place them on a separate domain to better control this type of access. For example, the photo-sharing website Flickr won't allow you to access http://www.flickr.com, but it will allow you to access http://api.flickr.com.

Tip Before you attempt to use the examples in this chapter with different websites, you should verify that they support cross-domain access. To do so, try requesting the clientaccesspolicy.xml and crossdomain.xml files in the root website.

In Chapter 13, you learned what the clientaccesspolicy.xml file looks like. The cross-domain.xml file is similar. For example, here's a crossdomain.xml file that allows all access (which you'll find on the Flickr website `http://api.flickr.com`):

```
<?xml version="1.0"?>
<!DOCTYPE cross-domain-policy SYSTEM
  "http://www.macromedia.com/xml/dtds/cross-domain-policy.dtd">
<cross-domain-policy>
  <allow-access-from domain="*" />
</cross-domain-policy>
```

On the other hand, the Twitter social networking website uses its clientaccesspolicy.xml file to allow access to just a few domains, which means your Silverlight code won't be able to retrieve any of its content:

```
<?xml version="1.0"?>
<!DOCTYPE cross-domain-policy
  SYSTEM "http://www.macromedia.com/xml/dtds/cross-domain-policy.dtd">
<cross-domain-policy>
  <allow-access-from domain="*.twitter.com" />
  <allow-access-from domain="*.discoveringradiance.com" />
  <allow-access-from domain="*.umusic.com" />
  <allow-access-from domain="*.hippo.com.au" />
  <allow-access-from domain="*.ediecareplan.com" />
  <allow-access-from domain="*.yourminis.com" />
  <allow-access-from domain="*.korelab.com" />
  <allow-access-from domain="*.zoozoom.com" />
</cross-domain-policy>
```

If you need to access web content from a website that doesn't allow cross-domain access, there's just one option. You can build a server-side proxy. To implement this design, you must create an ASP.NET website that includes a web service, as you learned to do in Chapter 13. Your web page will be allowed to call that service, because it's on the same website (and even if it isn't, you'll simply need to add your own clientaccesspolicy.xml file alongside the web service). Your web service can then access the website you want, and return the data to your page. This works, because the web service is allowed to call any website, regardless of the cross-domain access rules. That's because web services run on the server, not the browser, and so they don't face the same security considerations. Figure 17-1 compares this arrangement to the more straightforward direct downloading approach.

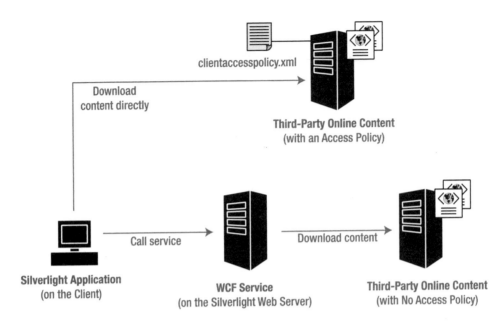

Figure 17-1. *Downloading web content in Silverlight*

Creating a server-side proxy requires a bit more work, but it's an acceptable solution if you need to retrieve small amounts of information infrequently. However, if you need to make frequent calls to your web service (for example, you're trying to read the news items in an RSS feed on a server that doesn't allow cross-domain access), the overhead can add up quickly. The web server will end up doing a significant amount of extra work, and the Silverlight application will wait longer to get its information because every call goes through two delays—first, the web page's request to the web service, and second, the web service's request to the third-party website.

Now that you understand the rules that govern what websites you can access, you're ready to start downloading content. In this chapter, you'll learn how to manipulate several different types of content, but you'll start out with the absolute basic—ordinary HTML files.

HTML Scraping

One of the crudest ways to get information from the Web is to dig through the raw markup in an HTML page. This approach is fragile, because the assumptions your code makes about the structure of a page can be violated easily if the page is modified. However, in some circumstances, HTML scraping is the only option. In the past, before websites like Amazon and eBay provided web services, developers often used screen scraping techniques to get price details, sales rank, product images, and so on.

In the following example, you'll see how HTML screen scraping allows you to pull information from the table shown in Figure 17-2. This table lists the world's population at different points in history, and it's based on information drawn from Wikipedia.

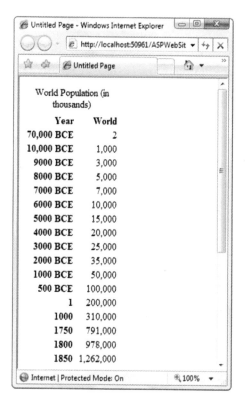

Figure 17-2. *A plain HTML page*

The information in the table has a structure in this format:

```
<table>
  <tr>
    <th>Year</th>
    <th width="70">World</th>
  </tr>
  <tr>
    <th>70,000 BCE</th>
    <td>2</td>
  </tr>
  <tr>
    <th>10,000 BCE</th>
    <td>1,000</td>
  </tr>
  <tr>
    <th>9000 BCE</th>
    <td>3,000</td>
  </tr>
  ...
</table>
```

The WebClient gives you the ability to download the entire HTML document. It's then up to you to parse the data.

In Chapter 6, you learned to use the WebClient.OpenReadAsync() method to download a file from the Web as a stream of bytes. You then have the flexibility to read that stream using a StreamReader (for text data) or a BinaryReader (for binary information). In this example, you can use the OpenAsync() method and then use a StreamReader to browse through the page. However, the WebClient provides a shortcut for relatively small amounts of text content—the DownloadStringAsync() method, which returns the results as a single string. In this example, that string includes the HTML for the entire page.

Figure 17-3 shows a simple Silverlight page that allows you to query the table from Figure 17-2 for information. The user enters a year. The code then searches the web page for a matching cell, and returns the population number from the next column. No attempt is made to interpolate values—in other words, if the indicated year falls between values in the table, no result is returned.

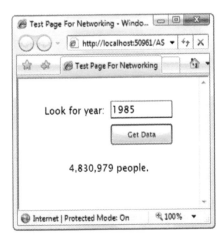

Figure 17-3. *Querying an HTML page with WebClient*

When the user clicks the Get Data button, a new WebClient object is created. The DownloadStringAsync() method is called with the appropriate website address:

```
private void cmdGetData_Click(object sender, RoutedEventArgs e)
{
    WebClient client = new WebClient();
    Uri address = new Uri("http://localhost:" +
        HtmlPage.Document.DocumentUri.Port + "/ASPWebSite/PopulationTable.html");

    client.DownloadStringCompleted += client_DownloadStringCompleted;
    client.DownloadStringAsync(address);
}
```

> **Tip** When starting an asynchronous operation like this one, it's also a good time to update the user inter-
> face with some sort of status message. For example, you could display the text "Contacting web service" in
> a TextBlock.

And here's the code that receives the results:

```
private void client_DownloadStringCompleted(object sender,
    DownloadStringCompletedEventArgs e)
{
    string pageHtml = "";

    try
    {
        pageHtml = e.Result;
    }
    catch
    {
        lblResult.Text = "Error contacting service.";
        return;
    }
    ...
```

When reading the Result property, an exception will be thrown if the web request failed—
for example, if the specified web page couldn't be found, or it doesn't allow cross-domain
access. For this reason, exception handling code is required.

It takes a bit more work to coax the information you want out of the HTML string. Although
you could manually step through the string, examining each character, it's far easier to use
regular expressions. Regular expressions are a pattern-matching language that's often used to
search text or validate input. Using the ordinary methods of the String class, you can search
for a series of specific characters (for example, the word "hello") in a string. Using a regular
expression, however, you can find any word in a string that is five letters long and begins with
an "h".

The full .NET Framework includes classes for working with regular expressions, and Silverlight borrows the same model.

REGULAR EXPRESSION BASICS

All regular expressions are made up of two kinds of characters: literals and metacharacters. *Literals* represent a specific defined character. *Metacharacters* are wildcards that can represent a range of values. Regular
expressions gain their power from the rich set of metacharacters that they support.

Two examples of regular expression metacharacters include \s (which represents any whitespace
character) and \d (which represents any digit). Using these characters, you can construct the following
expression, which will successfully match any string that starts with the numbers 333, followed by a single

whitespace character and any three numbers. Valid matches include 333 333, 333 945, but not 334 333 or 3334 945.

```
333\s\d\d\d
```

You can also use the asterisk (*) and plus (+) signs to represent repeated characters. For example 5+7 means "one or more 5 characters, followed by a single 7." The number 57 matches, as does 555557. You can also use the brackets to group together a subexpression. For example, (52)+7 would find match any string that starts with a sequence of 52. Matches include 527, 52527, 52552527, and so on. The * character is similar to the + character, but it allows zero or more matches, while the + requires at least one match.

You can also delimit a range of characters using square brackets. [a-f] would match any single character from "a" to "f" (lowercase only). The following expression would match any word that starts with a letter from "a" to "f", contains one or more letters, and ends with "ing"—possible matches include acting and developing.

```
[a-f][a-z]+ing
```

This discussion just scratches the surface of regular expressions, which constitute an entire language of their own. However, you don't need to learn everything there is to know about regular expressions before you start using them. In fact, many programmers simply look for useful prebuilt regular expressions on the Web. Without too much trouble, you can find examples for e-mails, phone numbers, postal codes, and more, all of which you can drop straight into your applications. For reference, you can look at the list of key regular expression metacharacters provided at the end of this section, in Table 17-1. To learn more about regular expressions, you might be interested in a dedicated book like the excellent *Mastering Regular Expressions* by Jeffrey Friedl (O'Reilly, 2006).

In this example, you need to find scraps of HTML in this form:

```
<th>500 BCE</th><td>100,000</td>
```

Here, the year in the <th> element is the lookup value, which is provided by the user. The number in the following <td> element is the result you want to retrieve.

There are several ways to construct a regular expression that does the trick, but the cleanest approach is to use a *named group*. A named group is a placeholder that represents some information you want to retrieve. You assign the group a name, and then retrieve its value when you need it. Named groups use this syntax:

```
(?<NamedGroupName>MatchExpression)
```

Here's the named group used in this example:

```
(?<population>.*)
```

This named group is named population. It uses .* as its expression, which is just about as simple as a regular expression can get. The period (.) matches any character except a new line. The asterisk (*) indicates that there can be zero, one, or more occurrences of this pattern—in other words, the population value can have any number of characters.

What makes this named group useful is its position inside a larger regular expression. Here's an example that's very similar to the final expression used in this example:

```
<th>1985</th>\s*<td>(?<population>.*)</td>
```

If you break this expression down piece by piece, it's relatively straightforward. First, this regular expression looks for the column with the year value 1985:

```
<th>1985</th>
```

That can be followed by zero or more whitespace characters (spaces, lines, hard returns, and so on), which are represented by the \s metacharacter:

```
<th>1985</th>\s*
```

Then, the <td> tag for the next column appears, followed by the value you want to capture (the population number), in a named group.

```
<th>1985</th>\s*<td>(?<population>.*)
```

Finally, the closing </td> tag represents the end of column and the end of the expression.

The only difference in the final version of this expression that the code uses is that the year is not hard-coded. Instead, the user enters it in a text box, and this value is inserted into the expression string:

```
string pattern = "<th>" + txtYear.Text + "</th>" + @"\s*" + "<td>" +
    "(?<population>.*)" + "</td>";
```

Once you have the regular expression in place, the rest of the code is easy. You simply need to create a Regex object that uses the expression, and pass in the search string to the Regex.Match() method. You can then look up your group by name, and extract the value:

```
    ...
    Regex regex = new Regex(pattern);
    Match match = regex.Match(pageHtml);
    string people = match.Groups["population"].Value;
    if (people == "")
        lblResult.Text = "Year not found.";
    else
        lblResult.Text = match.Groups["population"].Value + " people.";
}
```

This isn't the most elegant way to get information from the Web, but it demonstrates how the WebClient can work as a straightforward tool for reading HTML and other text sources on the Web. This behavior becomes even more useful when you begin to dabble in web services that use REST, as described in the following sections.

Table 17-1. *Regular Expression Metacharacters*

Character	Rule
*	Represents zero or more occurrences of the previous character or subexpression. For example, a*b matches aab or just b.
+	Matches one or more occurrences of the previous character or subexpression. For example, a+b matches aab but not a.
( )	Groups a subexpression that is treated as a single element. For example, (ab)+ matches ab and ababab.
{m}	Requires m repetitions of the preceding character or group. For example, a{3} matches aaa.
{m, n}	Requires n to m repetitions of the preceding character or group. For example, a{2,3} matches aa and aaa but not aaaa.
|	Either of two matches. For example, a|b matches a or b.
[ ]	Matches one character in a range of valid characters. For example, [A-C] matches A, B, or C.
[^]	Matches a character that is not in the given range. For example, [^A-C] matches any character except A, B, and C.
.	Matches any character except newline.
\s	Matches any whitespace character (like a tab or space).
\S	Matches any non-whitespace character (like a tab or space).
\d	Matches any digit character.
\D	Matches any character that is not a digit.
\w	Matches any alphanumeric character (letter, number, or underscore).
^	Represents the start of the string. For example, ^ab can only find a match if the string begins with ab.
$	Represents the end of the string. For example, ab$ can only find a match if the string ends with ab.
\	Indicates that the following character is a literal (even though it might ordinarily be interpreted as a metacharacter). For example, use \\ for the literal \ and use \+ for the literal +.

REST and Other Simple Web Services

Recently, there's been a resurgence of simple web services—web services that avoid the detailed SOAP protocol and the complexity of the WS-* standards. Simple web services will never replace SOAP-based web services, because they don't provide solutions for the real challenges of distributed processing, such as routing, transactions, and security. However, their clean, stripped-down structure makes them an ideal choice for building public web services that need to be compatible with the broadest range of clients possible. Many top-notch websites (like Amazon, eBay, and Google) provide REST-based and SOAP-based interfaces for their web services.

SOAP VS. REST

So what are the differences between SOAP, REST, and other web service standards? All web services pass messages over HTTP. However, there are differences in the way information is presented, both when it's passed to the web service and when it's returned from the web service.

Full-fledged SOAP web services place their data into a specific XML structure—a SOAP document. SOAP can be verbose, which means it's more work to construct a SOAP message on a platform that doesn't have built-in SOAP support. (Silverlight is an example of a platform that does have built-in SOAP support, which is why you simply need to add a web reference to a SOAP service in order to use it, rather than construct the XML you need by hand.) SOAP also provides some significant advantages—it uses strongly typed data, and it's highly extensible thanks to SOAP *headers* (separate pieces of information that can be passed along with a message but aren't placed in the actual message body). SOAP headers are a key extensibility point that other SOAP-based standards use.

Non-SOAP web services have simpler ways to pass in information. Input values can be supplied in the URL (in which cased they're tacked on to the end as query string parameters), or supplied as a combination of name-value pairs in the message body. Either way, there's less overhead, but no real type checking. The web service response might use plain string data or XML.

Simple web services that return HTML documents are often described as using XML over HTTP. Simple web services are often also described as REST services, but in truth REST is a philosophical idea rather than a concrete standard. The fundamental idea behind REST (representational state transfer) is that every URL represents a unique object rather than a mere method call. The different HTTP verbs represent what you want to do with it (for example, you use an HTTP GET to retrieve the object and HTTP POST to update it). Most web services that describe themselves as REST-based don't completely adhere to this idea, and are actually just simple non-SOAP web services.

In this section, you'll see how to consume a simple web service that returns plain text data. Later in this chapter, you'll go a bit further and consider a simple web service that returns XML.

Earlier, you looked at a simple page that included a table with world population numbers throughout history. If you wanted to convert this to a simple web service, you might write a simple bit of web code that receives a year and writes out the relevant population figure. The requested year could be supplied through a query string argument (in an HTTP GET request) or posted to your page (with an HTTP POST request). The strategy you choose will determine whether the client must use the WebClient or the somewhat more complex WebRequest class. The WebClient is enough for an ordinary HTTP GET request, while only the WebRequest allows your Silverlight code to post a value.

You can build your simple web service using ASP.NET, but you need to avoid the full web form model. After all, you don't want to return a complete page to the user, with unnecessary elements like <html>, <head>, and <body>. Instead, you need to create what ASP.NET calls an *HTTP handler*.

To do so, right-click your ASP.NET website in the Solution Explorer and choose Add New Item. Then choose the Generic Handler template, supply a name, and click Add. By default, HTTP handlers have the extension .ashx. In this example, the handler is called Population-Service.ashx.

All HTTP handlers are code as classes that implement IHttpHandler, and they need to provide a ProcessRequest() method and an IsReusable property getter. The IsReusable property simply indicates whether your HTTP handler can, once created, be reused to handle more than one request. If you don't store any state information in the fields of your class, you can safely return true.

```
public bool IsReusable
{
    get { return true; }
}
```

The ProcessRequest() method does the actual work. It receives an HttpContext object through which it can access the current request details and write the response. In this example, ProcessRequest() checks for a posted value named year. It then checks if the year string includes the letters, and gets the corresponding population statistic using a custom method called GetPopulation (which isn't shown). The result is written to the page as plain text.

```
public void ProcessRequest (HttpContext context)
{
    // Get the posted year.
    string year = context.Request.Form["year"];

    // Remove any commas in the number, and excess spaces at the ends.
    year = year.Replace(",", "");
    year = year.Trim();

    // Check if this year is BC.
    bool isBc = false;
    if (year.EndsWith("BC", StringComparison.OrdinalIgnoreCase))
    {
        isBc = true;
        year = year.Remove(year.IndexOf("BC" , StringComparison.OrdinalIgnoreCase));
        year = year.Trim();
    }

    // Get the population.
    int yearNumber = Int32.Parse(year);
    int population = GetPopulation(yearNumber, isBc);

    // Write the response.
    context.Response.ContentType = "text/plain";
    context.Response.Write(population);
}
```

On the client side, you need to use the WebRequest class from the System.Net namespace. To make this class available, you need to add a reference to the System.Net.dll assembly, which is not included by default.

The WebRequest requires that you do all your work asynchronously. Whereas the Web-Client had one asynchronous step (downloading the response data), the WebRequest has two—creating the request stream, and then downloading the response.

To use WebRequest, you first need to create a WebRequest object, configure it with the correct URI, and then call BeginGetRequestStream(). When you call BeginRequestStream(), you supply a callback that will write the request to the request stream, when it's ready. In this example, that task falls to another method named CreateRequest().

```
private string searchYear;

private void cmdGetData_Click(object sender, RoutedEventArgs e)
{
    Uri address = new Uri("http://localhost:" +
    HtmlPage.Document.DocumentUri.Port + "/ASPWebSite/PopulationService.ashx");

    WebRequest request = WebRequest.Create(address);
    request.Method = "POST";
    request.ContentType = "application/x-www-form-urlencoded";

    // Store the year you want to use.
    searchYear = txtYear.Text;

    // Prepare the request asynchronously.
    request.BeginGetRequestStream(CreateRequest, request);
}
```

There's one other detail in this code. Before calling BeginGetRequestStream(), the code copies the search year from the text box into a private field named searchYear. This technique serves two purposes. First, it ensures that the CreateRequest() callback can access the original search value, even if the user is somehow able to edit the text box before the CreateRequest() code runs. More importantly, this technique avoids threading headaches. Because the Create-Request() callback runs on a background thread (not the main application thread), it can't directly access the elements in the page. As you saw in Chapter 16, you can work around this problem using Dispatcher.BeginInvoke(). However, copying the search year sidesteps the problem altogether.

Typically, Silverlight will call your CreateRequest() method a fraction of a second after you can BeginGetRequestStream(). At this point, you need to write the posted values as part of your request. Often, web services use the same standard for posted values as HTML forms. That means each value is supplied as a named value pair, separated by an equal sign, and multiple values are chained together with ampersands (&), as in FirstName=Matthew&Last-Name=MacDonald. To write the data, you use a StreamWriter.

```
private void CreateRequest(IAsyncResult asyncResult)
{
    WebRequest request = (WebRequest)asyncResult.AsyncState;

    // Write the year information in the name-value format "year=1985".
    Stream requestStream = request.EndGetRequestStream(asyncResult);
```

```
StreamWriter writer = new StreamWriter(requestStream);
writer.Write("year=" + searchYear);

// Clean up (required).
writer.Close();
requestStream.Close();

// Read the response asynchronously.
request.BeginGetResponse(ReadResponse, request)
}
```

Once you've written the request, you need to close the StreamWriter (to ensure all the data is written) and then close the request stream. Next, you must call BeginGetResponse() to supply the callback that will process the response stream when its available. In this example, a method named ReadResponse() does the job.

To read the response, you use a StreamReader. You also need error-handling code at this point, to deal with the exceptions that are thrown if the service could not be found. If the response uses XML, it's also up to you to parse that XML now.

```
private void ReadResponse(IAsyncResult asyncResult)
{
    string result;
    WebRequest request = (WebRequest)asyncResult.AsyncState;

    // Get the response stream.
    WebResponse response = request.EndGetResponse(asyncResult);
    Stream responseStream = response.GetResponseStream();

    try
    {
        // Read the returned text.
        StreamReader reader = new StreamReader(responseStream);
        string population = reader.ReadToEnd();
        result = population + " people.";
    }
    catch (Exception err)
    {
        result = "Error contacting service.";
    }
    finally
    {
        response.Close();
    }
    ...
```

As with the callback for BeginGetRequestStream(), the callback for BeginGetResponse() runs on a background thread. If you want to interact with an element, you need to use

Dispatcher.BeginInvoke() to marshal the call to the foreground thread. Here's the code that does the trick:

```
...
// Update the display.
Dispatcher.BeginInvoke(
  delegate()
  {
      lblResult.Text = result;
  });
}
```

Ironically, calling a simple web service is more work in Silverlight than calling a SOAP-based web service, because Silverlight can't generate any code for you. This is part of the drawback with simple web services—although they are easier to call, they aren't self-describing. That means they lack the low-level documentation details that allow development tools like Visual Studio to generate some of the code you need.

Processing Different Types of Data

So far, you've seen how to retrieve ordinary text data from the Web, whether it's from a static file or dynamically generated by a web service. You've also seen how to search through that text if it contains HTML markup. However, both plain text and HTML are limited from a programming point of view, because they're difficult to parse. More often, you'll deal with more complex structured data. Web services that return structured data usually adopt a standardized format, such as ordinary XML, SOAP messages, or JSON. Silverlight supports all three formats, and you'll see how to use them in the following sections.

XML

Many simple web services return their data in XML. When consuming this sort of service, you need to decide how to process the XML.

Silverlight includes several options for dealing with XML:

- **XmlWriter and XmlReader.** These classes offer a barebones approach for dealing with XML, with the fewest features. Using them, you can write or read XML content one element at a time.

- **XmlSerializer.** This class allows you to convert a live object into an XML representation, and vice versa. The only limitation is that the XML is forced to adhere to the structure of the class.

- **XDocument.** This class is the foundation of LINQ to XML. It allows you to transform XML objects (and back), but it gives you far more flexibility than XmlSerializer. Using the right expression, you can filter out just the details you want and change the structure of your content.

So which is the best one to use? The XmlReader and XmlWriter offer the lowest-level approach. For example, to read an XML document with XmlReader, you need to loop through all the nodes, keeping track of the structure on your own, and ignoring comments and whitespace. You're limited to travelling in one direction (forward). If you want just a single node, you're still forced to read through every node that occurs before it in the document. Similarly, when writing a document you need to write all the elements sequentially, relying on the order of your statements to generate the right structure. You also need to explicitly write the start and end tag for each element that contains nested elements.

Generally, most Silverlight applications are better off using the higher-level XmlSerializer and XDocument classes. The only exception is if you need to deal with a huge amount of XML and you want to avoid the overhead of loading it all into memory at once. In this case, the bit-by-bit processing the XmlWriter and XmlReader might be required.

Between XmlSerializer and XDocument, XmlSerializer is a reasonable option if you're in complete control of the data format—in other words, you've created the class you want to serialize and you don't need to conform to a specific XML format. However, XDocument provides much more flexibility, giving you the ability to look at XML as a collection of elements or transform it into a collection of objects. It's particularly useful when consuming someone else's XML—for example, when retrieving data from a web service.

■**Note** Silverlight doesn't include a class that uses the XML DOM model (such as the XmlDocument class you can use in .NET). If you want to perform in-memory XML processing, you'll be better off with the more streamlined and efficient XDocument.

In the next section, you'll see how to use XDocument to parse the data that's returned from a web service, and to create an XML document to send to a web service. If you have a specialized scenario that requires the XmlWriter, XmlReader, or XmlSerializer, you'll find that they work much the same way as in the full .NET Framework.

Services That Return XML Data

Flickr is an image-sharing website that provides REST-like services. You supply your parameters by tacking query string arguments onto the end of the URL. The Flickr web service returns a response in XML.

Figure 17-4 shows an example that allows the user to supply a search keyword, and then displays a list of images that are described with that keyword on Flickr.

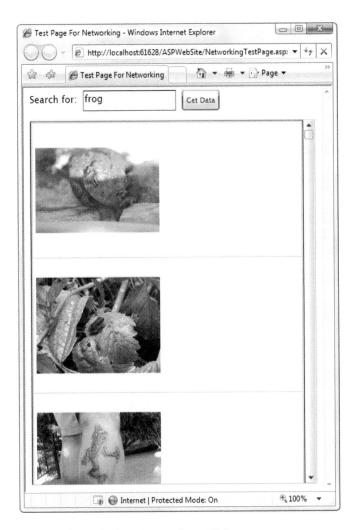

Figure 17-4. *Retrieving pictures from Flickr*

In this example, the Flickr request includes the following query string arguments: method (indicates the type of operation being performed), tags (the search keywords), perpage (the number of results you want to retrieve), and api_key (a unique ID that allows you to get access to Flickr's service). There are many more arguments that you can use to fetch multiple pages of results, apply sorting, filter by dates, and so on. To get more information and get your own free API key, visit http://www.flickr.com/services/api.

Tip Flickr provides several different ways to call its web services. Although the simple REST approach is used here to demonstrate how to deal with XML in a Silverlight application, if you're building a practical Silverlight application that uses Flickr, you'll find it easier to use the SOAP interface, and let Visual Studio generate some of the code for you.

Here's what the request used in Figure 17-4 looks like:

```
http://api.flickr.com/services/rest/?method=flickr.photos.search&tags=frog&
api_key=...&perpage=10
```

Because all the input parameters are passed in through the URL, there's no need to post anything, and you can use the simpler WebClient instead of WebRequest. Here's the code that builds the Flickr request URL and then triggers an asynchronous operation to get the result:

```
private void cmdGetData_Click(object sender, RoutedEventArgs e)
{
    WebClient client = new WebClient();
    Uri address = new Uri("http://api.flickr.com/services/rest/?" +
      "method=flickr.photos.search" + "&tags=" +
      HttpUtility.UrlEncode(txtSearchKeyword.Text) +
      "&api_key=..." + "&perpage=10");

    client.DownloadStringCompleted += client_DownloadStringCompleted;
    client.DownloadStringAsync(address);
}
```

Here, the static HttpUtility.UrlEncode() method ensures that if there are any non-URL-friendly characters in the search string, they're replaced with the corresponding character entities.

The result is retrieved as a single long string, which contains XML in this format:

```
<?xml version="1.0" encoding="utf-8" ?>
<rsp stat="ok">
  <photos page="1" pages="1026" perpage="100" total="102577">
    <photo id="2519140273" owner="85463968@N00" secret="9d215a1b8b" server="2132"
    farm="3" title="He could hop in, but he couldn't hop out" ispublic="1"
    isfriend="0" isfamily="0" />
    <photo id="2519866774" owner="72063229@N00" secret="05bccd89cd" server="2353"
    farm="3" title="Small Frog on a Leaf" ispublic="1" isfriend="0" isfamily="0" />
    ...
  </photos>
</rsp>
```

To parse this information, the first step is to load the entire document into a new XDocument object. The XDocument class provides two static methods to help you out: a Load() method for pulling content out of an XmlReader, and a Parse() method for pulling content out

a string. When the WebClient.DownloadStringCompleted event fires, you use the Parse()
method:

```
XDocument document = XDocument.Parse(e.Result);
```

Once you have the XDocument object, you can use one of two strategies to extract the
information you need. You can move through the collections of elements and attributes in the
XDocument, which are represented as XElement and XAttribute objects. Or, you can use a
LINQ expression to retrieve the XML content you want and convert it into the most suitable
object representation. The following sections demonstrate both approaches.

■**Note** To use the XDocument class and LINQ to XML, you must add a reference in your Silverlight project
to the System.Xml.Linq.dll assembly.

Navigating Over an XDocument

Every XDocument holds a collection of XNode objects. The XNode is an abstract base class.
Other more specific classes, like XElement, XComment, and XText, derive from it, and are used
to represent elements, comments, and text content. Attributes are an exception—they are not
treated as separate nodes, but simple name-value pairs that are attached to an element.

Once you have a live XDocument with your content, you can dig into the tree of nodes
using a few key properties and methods of the XElement class. Table 17-2 lists the most useful
methods.

Table 17-2. *Essential Methods of the XElement Class*

Method	Description
Attributes()	Gets the collection of XAttribute objects for this element.
Attribute()	Gets the XAttribute with the specific name.
Elements()	Gets the collection of XElement objects that are contained by this element. (This is the top level only—these elements may in turn contain more elements.) Optionally, you can specify an element name, and only those elements will be retrieved.
Element()	Gets the single XElement contained by this element that has a specific name (or null if there's no match).
Nodes()	Gets all the XNode objects contained by this elements. This includes elements and other content, like comments.

There's a critically important detail here—the XDocument exposes nested elements
through methods, not properties. This gives you added flexibility to filter out just the elements
that interest you. For example, when using the XDocument.Elements method, you have two
overloads to choose from. You can get all the child elements (in which case you would supply
no parameters) or get just those child elements that have a specific element name (in which
case you would specify the element name as a string).

In the Flickr example, the top-level element is named <rsp>. Thus, you can access it like this:

```
XElement element = document.Element("rsp");
```

Of course, what you're really interested in is the <photos> element inside the <rsp> element. You could get this in two steps:

```
XElement rspElement = document.Element("rsp");
XElement photosElement = element.Element("photos");
```

or even more efficiently in one:

```
XElement photosElement = document.Element("rsp").Element("photos");
```

To get the <photo> elements inside the <photos> element, you use the Elements() method (because there are multiple matching elements). You don't need to specify the name <photos>, because there isn't any other type of element inside:

```
IEnumerable<XElement> elements =
  document.Element("rsp").Element("photos").Elements();
```

All the information you need is in the attributes of each <photo> element. To get the Flickr image (which you can then display using the Image element), you need to construct the right URL, which involves combining several pieces of information together in the right format.

```
private void client_DownloadStringCompleted(object sender,
  DownloadStringCompletedEventArgs e)
{
    XDocument document = XDocument.Parse(e.Result);

    // Clear the list.
    images.Items.Clear();

    // Examine each <photo> element.
    foreach (XElement element in
      document.Element("rsp").Element("photos").Elements())
    {
        // Get the attribute values and combine them to build the image URL.
        string imageUrl = String.Format(
          "http://farm{0}.static.flickr.com/{1}/{2}_{3}_m.jpg",
          (string)element.Attribute("farm"),
          (string)element.Attribute("server"),
          (string)element.Attribute("id"),
          (string)element.Attribute("secret")
        );

        // Create an Image object that shows the image.
        Image img = new Image();
```

```
        img.Stretch = Stretch.Uniform;
        img.Width = 200; img.Height = 200;
        img.Margin = new Thickness(10);
        img.Source = new BitmapImage(new Uri(imageUrl));

        // Add the Image element to the list.
        images.Items.Add(img);
    }
}
```

■Tip The easiest way to get the actual value out an XAttribute or XElement object is simply to cast it to the desired type. In the previous example, all the attributes are treated as string values.

You've already seen how to use the Element() and Elements() methods to filter out elements that have a specific name. However, both these methods only go one level deep. However, the XDocument and XElement classes also include two methods that search more deeply: Ancestors() and Descendants(). The Ancestors() method finds all XElement objects contained by the current element, at any depth. The Descendants() method finds all the XElement objects that contain the current element, again at any level. Using Ancestors(), you can rewrite this statement from the earlier code block:

```
foreach (XElement element in
  document.Element("rsp").Element("photos").Elements())
```

like this:

```
foreach (XElement element in document.Descendants("photo"))
```

The XDocument and XElement classes are a small miracle of efficiency. If you take a closer look at them, you'll find many more members for navigation. For example, you'll find properties for quickly stepping from one node to the next (FirstNode, LastNode, NextNode, PreviousNode, and Parent) and methods for retrieving sibling nodes at the same level as the current node (namely, the ElementsAfterSelf() and ElementsBeforeSelf() methods). You'll also find methods for manipulating the document structure, which you'll consider later in this chapter.

Querying an XDocument with LINQ

As you've seen, it's easy to use methods like Element(), Elements(), and Ancestors() to reach into an XDocument and get the content you want. However, in some situations you want to transform the content to a different structure. For example, you might want to extract the information from various elements and flatten it into a simple structure. This technique is easy if you use the XDocument in conjunction with a LINQ expression.

As you learned in Chapter 14, LINQ expressions work with objects that implement IEnumerable<T>. The XDocument and XElement classes include several ways for getting

IEnumerable<T> collections of elements, including the Elements() and Descendants() methods you've just considered.

Once you place your collection of elements in a LINQ expression, you can use all the standard LINQ operators. That means you can use sorting, filtering, grouping, and projections to get the data you want.

Here's an example that selects all the <photo> elements in an XML document (using the Descendants() method), extracts the most important attribute values, and sets these as the properties of an object:

```
var photos = from results in document.Descendants("photo")
             select new
             {
                 Id = (string)results.Attribute("id"),
                 Farm = (string)results.Attribute("farm"),
                 Server = (string)results.Attribute("server"),
                 Secret = (string)results.Attribute("secret")
             };
```

This technique uses the standard LINQ feature of *anonymous types*. Essentially, this expression generates a collection of a dynamically defined type that includes the properties you've specified.

The C# compiler creates the class definition you need. Because you don't have a reference to this class definition in your code, you need to use the var keyword when defining the photos collection. However, the code is still strongly typed because the class really does exist—it's just generated automatically at compile time. Elsewhere in your code, you can loop over the photos collection and interact with the properties of the dynamically generated type to build Image elements, as you saw earlier:

```
foreach (var photo in photos)
{
    url = string.Format("http://farm{0}.static.flickr.com/{1}/{2}_{3}_m.jpg",
        photo.farm, photo.server, photo.id, photo.secret);
    ...
}
```

This technique of mapping a portion of an XML document to new class is called *projection*. Often, projection is combined with anonymous types for one-off tasks, when you don't need to use the same grouping of data elsewhere in your application. However, it's just as easy to use a projection to create instances of a custom class. In fact, you'll need to use this approach if you plan to perform data binding with the newly generated objects.

To see how this works, it helps to consider an alternative way to build the example that's shown in Figure 17-4. Instead of manually constructing each Image element, you can define a data template that will take bound objects, extract the URL information, and use it in an Image element:

```
<ListBox x:Name="images">
  <ListBox.ItemTemplate>
    <DataTemplate>
      <Image Stretch="Uniform" Width="200" Height="200"
```

```
        Margin="5" Source="{Binding ImageUrl}"></Image>
    </DataTemplate>
  </ListBox.ItemTemplate>
</ListBox>
```

To make this work, you need a custom class that provides an ImageUrl property (and may include other details). Here's the simplest possibility:

```
public class FlickrImage
{
    public string imageUrl { get; set; }
}
```

Now you can use a LINQ expression to create a collection of FlickrImage objects:

```
var photos = from results in document.Descendants("photo")
             select new FlickrImage
             {
                 imageUrl =
                 String.Format(
                    "http://farm{0}.static.flickr.com/{1}/{2}_{3}_m.jpg",
                    (string)results.Attribute("farm"),
                    (string)results.Attribute("server"),
                    (string)results.Attribute("id"),
                    (string)results.Attribute("secret"))
             };
images.ItemsSource = photos;
```

This approach requires the least amount of code, and provides the most streamlined solution.

XDOCUMENT AND NAMESPACES

The XDocument class has a particularly elegant way of dealing with namespaces. You simply add the namespace before the element name, wrapped in curly braces. For example, if you want to find the <photos> element in the namespace http://www.somecompany.com/PhotoMarkup, you would change this:

```
XElement photosElement = element.Element("photos");
```

to this:

```
XElement photosElement = element.Element(
  "{http://www.somecompany.com/PhotoMarkup}photos");
```

To clean up this code, you should use the XNamespace class, as shown here:

```
XNamespace ns = "http://www.somecompany.com/DVDList";
XElement photosElement = element.Element(ns + "photos");
```

> This way, you simply need to define the namespace once and you can reuse it whenever you need to refer to an element in that namespace. You can use the same name-changing approach when creating elements that you want to place in a particular namespace. Just remember that most XML-based languages place elements in namespaces, but don't take the same step with attributes. Because the elements are already scoped to a specific namespace and the attributes are attached to an element, it's not considered necessary to specifically place the attributes in the same namespace.

Services That Require XML Data

Simple web services often allow you to supply all the input parameters through query string arguments. However, query string arguments are limited by the rules of web browser URIs. They can only be so long, and they're hard-pressed to represent structured data.

For that reason, web services that need more detailed data usually accept some form of XML. SOAP (described next) is one example. Non-SOAP web services often use a basic standard called XML-RPC. For example, Flickr provides an XML-RPC interface for its image search. To use it, you post an XML request in this format:

```
<methodCall>
  <methodName>flickr.photos.search</methodName>
  <params>
    <param>
      <value>
        <struct>
          <member>
            <name>tags</name>
            <value><string>value</string></value>
          </member>
          <member>
            <name>api_key</name>
            <value><string>...</string></value>
          </member>
        </struct>
      </value>
    </param>
  </params>
</methodCall>
```

You can add additional parameters by adding more <member> elements. For example, you could add the optional perpage parameter, as in the previous examples.

To use an XML-RPC service (or any web service that requires an XML request message), you need to send the XML document in the body of an HTTP POST. That means you need the higher-powered WebRequest class rather than WebClient.

To construct the XML message, you can use simple string concatenation. This works well if you need to set just a single detail. (Just remember to use HttpUtility.HtmlEncode() to escape characters like the angle brackets, which would otherwise be interpreted as XML.) However, string concatenation is also fragile, because you won't be notified of any errors if your XML is invalid. (Instead, your web service call will fail.) Another option is to construct the XML document using the XDocument classes (XDocument, XElement, XAttribute, XComment, XDeclaration, and so on). The code you need is refreshingly clean and concise code.

All the XDocument classes provide useful constructors that allow you to create and initialize them in one step. For example, you can create an element and supply text content that should be placed inside using code like this:

```
XElement element = new XElement("Price", "23.99");
```

The code savings become even more dramatic when you consider another feature of the XDocument—its ability to create a nested tree of nodes in a single code statement. Here's how it works. The XDocument and XElement classes include constructors that take a parameter array for the last argument. This parameter array holds a list of nested nodes.

Note A *parameter array* is a parameter that's preceded with the params keyword. This parameter is always the last parameter, and it's always an array. The advantage is that users don't need to declare the array—instead, they can simply tack on as many arguments as they want, which are grouped into a single array automatically. String.Format() is an example of a method that uses a parameter array. It allows you to supply an unlimited number of values that are inserted into the placeholders of a string.

Here's an example that creates an element with an attribute and two nested elements:

```
XElement element = new XElement("photo",
  new XAttribute("src", "http://www.someplace.com/someimage.jpg")
  new XElement("tag", "horse"),
  new XElement("tag", "plow")
);
```

This code creates XML markup like this:

```
<photo src=" http://www.someplace.com/someimage.jpg">
  <tag>horse</tag>
  <tag>plow</tag>
</photo>
```

You can extend this technique to create an entire XML document. For example, here's the complete code that creates an XML-RPC request for a Flickr image search, using the search keywords in a text box:

```
XDocument document = new XDocument(
    new XElement("methodCall",
        new XElement("methodName", "flickr.photos.search"),
        new XElement("params",
            new XElement("param",
```

```
                    new XElement("value",
                        new XElement("struct",
                            new XElement("member",
                                new XElement("name", "tags"),
                                new XElement("value",
                                    new XElement("string",
                                        HttpUtility.HtmlEncode(txtSearchKeyword.Text))
                                )
                            ),
                            new XElement("member",
                                new XElement("name", "api_key"),
                                new XElement("value",
                                    new XElement("string", "...")
                                )
                            )
                        )
                    )
                )
            )
        )
    )
);
```

One nice detail about using the XDocument to create XML content is the way the indenting of the code statements mirrors the nesting of the elements in the XML document, allowing you to quickly take in the overall shape of the XML content.

Once the XML content has been created, you can save it to a TextWriter using the XDocument.Save() method or convert it to a string using ToString(). When using the XDocument with the WebRequest class, you need to write it to the request stream using a StreamWriter, as shown here:

```
StreamWriter writer = new StreamWriter(requestStream);
writer.Write(document.ToString());
```

When you call the Flickr image search through XML-RPC, you'll also get an XML-RPC response. To get the photo information you used earlier, you simply need to call Http-Utility.HtmlDecode() on the message and then use LINQ to XML to filter out the <photo> elements. For the complete code, see the downloadable examples for this chapter.

Note You've now learned how to read and create XML with XDocument. These techniques are useful when dealing with XML-based web services, but they also come in handy if you need to work with XML in other scenarios (for example, if you have a locally stored file in isolated storage that has XML content). If you dig into the XDocument and XElement classes, you'll find they have many more elements that make it easy to modify XML documents after you've created them. Not only can you set the value of any element or attribute, you can also use methods for inserting, removing, and otherwise manipulating the XML tree of nodes, such as Add(), AddAfterSelf(), AddBeforeSelf(), RemoveNodes(), Remove(), ReplaceWith(), and so on.

Services That Return SOAP Data

As you learned in Chapter 13, Silverlight works seamlessly with .NET web services. These web services send SOAP-encoded data. SOAP is a form of XML, so it's technically possible to use Silverlight's XML processing (for example, the XDocument class) to create request messages and parse response messages, as in the previous sections. However, it's far easier to use the Visual Studio web reference feature.

What you may not know is that the same technique applies to any SOAP-based web service. In other words, you can add references to SOAP-based services that are not built in .NET. In fact, Silverlight has no way of distinguishing between the two, and no way of knowing what code powers the service its calling.

When you add a web reference to any SOAP-based web service, Visual Studio will create the proxy class you need, complete with asynchronous methods and events for each web method in the web service. For more information, see Chapter 13.

Services That Return JSON Data

JavaScript Object Notation (JSON) is an object notation syntax that's sometimes used as a lightweight alternative to JavaScript. It was used more heavily in Silverlight 1.0. However, although Silverlight 2.0 is more at home with SOAP, JSON is still supported. You just need to go to a little more work to deserialize JSON data to an object representation.

In practice, the only time you'll need to use the JSON serializer is when consuming a web service that returns JSON data, and provides no SOAP alternative. (If the web service returns JSON or simple XML, it's up to you whether you prefer the JSON approach or the XDocument.) To make matters even more interesting, Silverlight actually provides two distinct ways to parse JSON data. You can deserialize it with the JSON deserializer, as the next example demonstrates, or you can use LINQ to JSON, which works in much the same way as LINQ to XML. Although this chapter doesn't discuss LINQ to JSON, you can get more information in the Silverlight SDK documentation (or read a quick review at http://blogs.msdn.com/mikeormond/archive/2008/08/21/linq-to-json.aspx).

Before you can deal with JSON data, you need to add references to three additional assemblies: System.Runtime.Serialization.dll, System.ServiceModel.dll, and System.Service-Model.Web.dll.

Deserializing JSON is a lot like deserializing XML with the XmlSerializer class. The first requirement is to have a suitable class that matches the structure of your JSON data. You can then use the DataContractJsonSerializer class to convert instances of this class into JSON data, and vice versa.

For example, Yahoo! provides a JSON interface for its image search service (described at http://developer.yahoo.com/search/image/V1/imageSearch.html). It returns data that looks like this:

```
{"ResultSet":{
  "totalResultsAvailable":"957841",
  "totalResultsReturned":10,
  "firstResultPosition":1,
  "Result":[
    {
      "Title":"tree_frog.jpg",
```

```
        "Summary":"Red-Eyed Tree Frog",
        "Url":"http:\/\/www.thekidscollege.com\/images\/animals\/redeyetree_frog.jpg",
        ...
    },
    {
        "Title":"tree_frog_large-thumb.jpg",
        "Summary":"Before I came back in though I got another shot of the frog.",
        "Url":"http:\/\/www.silveriafamily.com\/blog\/john\/treefrog.jpg",
        ...
    }
  ]
}}
```

The data is in name-value pairs, which is grouped into classes using curly braces, {}, and into arrays using square brackets, []. To model the data shown here with classes, you need a class for each individual search result (named Result in the JSON), a class for the entire result set (named ResultSet in the JSON), and a top-level class that holds the search result set. You can give these classes any name you want, but the property names must match the names in the JSON representation exactly, including case. Your classes don't need to include properties for details that you don't want to retrieve—they can be safely ignored.

Here are the classes you need. The property names (which are based on the JSON representation) are highlighted.

```
public class SearchResults
{
    public SearchResultSet ResultSet;
}


public class SearchResultSet
{
    public int totalResultsAvailable { get; set; }
    public int totalResultsReturned { get; set; }
    public SearchResult[] Result { get; set; }
}


public class SearchResult
{
    public string Title {get; set;}
    public string Summary { get; set; }
    public string Url { get; set; }
}
```

Now you can use these classes to deserialize the results of a search. It's a two-step affair. First, you create an instance of the DataContractJsonSerializer, specifying the type you want to serialize or deserialize as a constructor argument:

```
DataContractJsonSerializer serializer =
  new DataContractJsonSerializer(typeof(SearchResults));
```

Then you can use ReadObject() to deserialize JSON data or WriteObject() to create it.

```
SearchResults results = (SearchResults)serializer.ReadObject(jsonData);
```

Figure 17-5 shows a sample Silverlight page that searches for images by keyword.

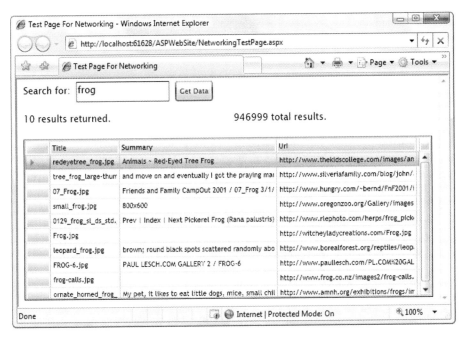

Figure 17-5. *Searching for images with Yahoo!*

Here's the code that underpins this page:

```
private void cmdGetData_Click(object sender, RoutedEventArgs e)
{
    WebClient client = new WebClient();
    Uri address = new Uri(
      "http://search.yahooapis.com/ImageSearchService/V1/imageSearch?" +
      "appid=YahooDemo&query=" + HttpUtility.UrlEncode(txtSearchKeyword.Text) +
      "&output=json");

    client.OpenReadCompleted += client_OpenReadCompleted;
    client.OpenReadAsync(address);
}
```

```
private void client_OpenReadCompleted(object sender, OpenReadCompletedEventArgs e)
{
    DataContractJsonSerializer serializer =
      new DataContractJsonSerializer(typeof(SearchResults));
    SearchResults results = (SearchResults)serializer.ReadObject(e.Result);

    lblResultsTotal.Text = results.ResultSet.totalResultsAvailable +
      " total results.";
    lblResultsReturned.Text = results.ResultSet.totalResultsReturned +
      " results returned.";
    gridResults.ItemsSource = results.ResultSet.Result;
}
```

RSS

RSS (Really Simple Syndication) is an XML-based format for publishing summaries of frequently updated content, such as blog entries or news stories. These documents are called *feeds*. Client applications called RSS readers can check RSS feeds periodically, and notify you about newly added items.

.NET 3.5 introduced classes that support the RSS 2.0 or Atom 1.0 formats. Silverlight borrows these same classes, allowing you to read feed information without tedious XML-parsing code. These classes are defined in the System.ServiceModel.Syndication namespace, and to get access to them you need to add a reference to the System.ServiceModel.Syndication.dll assembly.

When using RSS, it's important to remember that you're limited by the cross-domain rules explained at the beginning of this chapter. Obviously, if you try to access a feed on a web server that doesn't allow cross-domain access, you'll get an error. However, feeds also contain links. For example, a typical feed item will contain a summary and a link that points to the full page for the corresponding blog entry or news item. If you attempt to download the page at this location, you'll also need to be sure it's on a web server that allows cross-domain access.

There's one other issue to consider. The items in an RSS feed usually point to full-fledged HTML pages. However, even if you download this HTML content, there's no way to display it in its properly formatted form in the Silverlight content region. A better approach is to show it on another part of the current HTML page—for example, just below the Silverlight control. Figure 17-6 shows an example that combines a Silverlight page that displays feed items (on top) with an ordinary HTML <iframe> element, which shows the page that corresponds to the currently selected item.

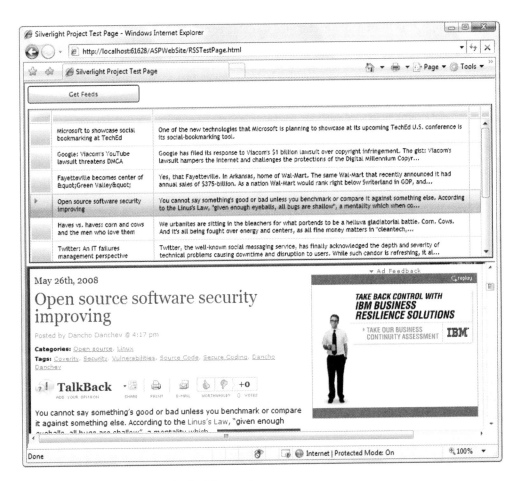

Figure 17-6. *Browsing an RSS feed with news items*

Creating this example is surprisingly straightforward. First, you need a feed URI. This example uses the URI http://feeds.feedburner.com/ZDNetBlogs, which points to blogged news items on the high-tech website ZDNet. Feeds are simply XML documents, and you can download them easily using the familiar DownloadStringAsycn() or OpenReadAsync() methods. The latter is more efficient, because the entire XML document doesn't need to be held in memory at once as a string.

```
private void cmdGetData_Click(object sender, RoutedEventArgs e)
{
    WebClient client = new WebClient();
    Uri address = new Uri("http://feeds.feedburner.com/ZDNetBlogs");
    client.OpenReadCompleted += client_OpenReadCompleted;
    client.OpenReadAsync(address);
}
```

When reading the response, you can load the XML content into a SyndicationFeed object. The SyndicationFeed class includes various properties that describe details about the feed, such as its author, its last update, a summary of what the feed is about, and so on. The most important detail is the Items property, which holds a collection of SyndicationItem objects. It's the SyndicationItem objects that are shown in the Grid in Figure 17-6.

```
private void client_OpenReadCompleted(object sender, OpenReadCompletedEventArgs e)
{
    try
    {
        XmlReader reader = XmlReader.Create(e.Result);
        SyndicationFeed feed = SyndicationFeed.Load(reader);
        gridFeed.ItemsSource = feed.Items;
        reader.Close();
    }
    catch (Exception err)
    {
        lblError.Text = "Error downloading feed.";
    }
}
```

To display the information from each SyndicationItem object, you need to pull the right information out with custom binding expressions. Useful properties include Authors, Title, Summary, and PublishDate, each of which is returns a different type of syndication object (all of which are defined in the System.ServiceModel.Syndication namespace). The example in Figure 17-6 uses the title and summary information:

```
<my:DataGrid>
  <my:DataGrid.Columns>
    <my:DataGridTextColumn Binding="{Binding Title.Text}"
      ElementStyle="{StaticResource DataGridWrapStyle}" />
    <my:DataGridTextColumn Width="400"
      Binding="{Binding Summary.Text, Converter={StaticResource HtmlCleanUp}}"
      ElementStyle="{StaticResource DataGridWrapStyle}" />
  </my:DataGrid.Columns>
</my:DataGrid>
```

The DataGrid also uses a custom style for text wrapping (as described in Chapter 14), and a custom value converter to remove the HTML tags from the summary and shorten it if it exceeds a certain maximum number of characters. (To see the custom value converter, refer to the downloadable code examples for this chapter.)

When an item is clicked in the DataGrid, the following event handler grabs the corresponding SyndicationItem object and examines the Links property to find the URI that points to the full web page with the full story. It then uses a dash of HTML interoperability (as described in Chapter 12) to point an <iframe> to that page.

```
private void gridFeed_SelectionChanged(object sender, EventArgs e)
{
    // Get the selected syndication item.
    SyndicationItem selectedItem = (SyndicationItem)gridFeed.SelectedItem;

    // Find the <iframe> element on the page.
    HtmlElement element = HtmlPage.Document.GetElementById("rssFrame");
    // Point the <iframe> to the full page for the selected feed item.
    element.SetAttribute("src", selectedItem.Links[0].Uri.ToString());
}
```

Sockets

So far, you've focused exclusively on retrieving information over HTTP. And even though HTTP was developed for downloading simple HTML documents in the earliest days of the Internet, it also works surprisingly well as a transport mechanism for XML documents and the request and response messages used to interact with web services.

That said, HTTP isn't without a few significant drawbacks. First, HTTP is a high-level standard that's built on Transmission Control Protocol (TCP). It will never be as fast as a raw network connection. Second, HTTP uses a request model that forces the client to ask for data. There's no way for the server to call back to the client if new information arrives. This limitation means that HTTP is a poor choice for everything from real-time Internet games to stock monitoring. If you need to go beyond these limitations in order to build a certain type of application, you'll need to step up to a rich client platform (like WPF), or use Silverlight's support for *sockets*.

Understanding Sockets and TCP

Strictly speaking, sockets are nothing more than endpoints on a network. They consist of two numbers:

- **IP address.** The IP address identifies your computer on a network or the Internet.

- **Port.** The port number corresponds to a specific application or service that's communicating over the network.

The combination of two sockets—one on the client that's running the Silverlight application, and one on a web server that's running a server application—defines a connection, as shown in Figure 17-7.

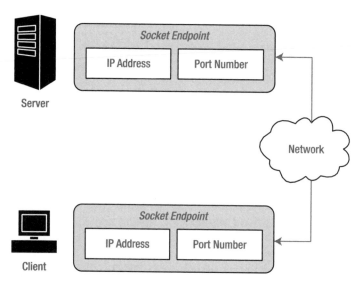

Figure 17-7. *A socket-based connection*

■**Note** Port numbers don't correspond to anything physical—they're simply a method for separating different application endpoints on the same computer. For example, if you're running a web server, your computer
will respond to requests on port 80. Another application might use port 8000. Essentially, ports map the network communication on a single computer to the appropriate applications. Silverlight allows you to open
connections using any port in the range 4502–4532.

Silverlight supports *stream sockets*, which are sockets that use TCP communication.
TCP is a connection-oriented protocol that has built-in flow control, error correction, and
sequencing. Thanks to these features, you won't need to worry about resolving any one of the
numerous possible network problems that could occur as information is segmented into
packets, and then transported and reassembled in its proper sequence at another computer.
Instead, you can simply write data to a stream on one side of the connection, and read it from
the stream on the other side.

To create a TCP connection, your application must perform a three-stage handshaking
process:

1. First, the server must enter listening mode by performing a passive open. At this point,
   the server will be idle, waiting for an incoming request.

2. A client can then use the IP address and port number to perform an active open. The
   server will respond with an acknowledgment message in a predetermined format that
   incorporates the client sequence number.

3. Finally, the client will respond to the acknowledgment. At this point, the connection is
   ready to transmit data in either direction.

In the following sections, you'll use Silverlight to build a socket client and .NET to build a socket server. The result is a simple chat application that allows multiple users to log in at the same time and send messages back and forth. Figure 17-8 shows two of these instances of the client engaged in conversation.

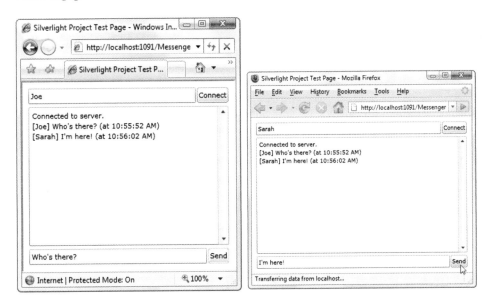

Figure 17-8. *A socket-based chat client*

Implementing this solution takes a fair bit of networking code. However, the result is well worth it, and takes you far beyond the bounds of ordinary HTML pages.

The Policy Server

Before you can even think about designing a socket server, you need to develop something else—a policy server that tells Silverlight what clients are allowed to connect to your socket server.

As you saw earlier in this chapter, Silverlight won't allow you to download content or call a web service if the domain doesn't have a clientaccesspolicy.xml or crossdomain.xml file that explicitly allows it. A similar restriction applies to your socket server. Unless it provides a way for the client to download a clientaccesspolicy.xml file that allows remote access, Silverlight will refuse to make a connection.

Unfortunately, providing the clientaccesspolicy.xml file for a socket-based application takes a bit more work than providing it with a website. With a website, the web server software can hand out the clientaccesspolicy.xml file for you, as long as you remember to include it. With a socket-based application, you need to open a socket that clients can call with their policy requests, and you need to manually write the code that serves it. To perform these functions, you must create a policy server.

As you'll see, the policy server works in much the same way as the messaging server—it just has a simpler range of interactions. Although you can create the policy server and messaging server separately, you can also combine them both in one application, as long as they're listening for requests on different threads. In this example, you'll begin with a simple policy server and then enhance it to be a messaging server.

To create a policy server, you need to begin by creating a .NET application. Although you can use any type of .NET application to serve as a policy server, a simple command-line Console application is the most common choice. (Once you've perfected your server, you might choose to move the code to a Windows service, so it can run quietly in the background at all times.)

The Policy File

Here's the policy file that the policy server provides:

```xml
<?xml version="1.0" encoding="utf-8" ?>
<access-policy>
  <cross-domain-access>
    <policy>
      <allow-from>
        <domain uri="*"/>
      </allow-from>
      <grant-to>
        <socket-resource port="4502-4534" protocol="tcp"/>
      </grant-to>
    </policy>
  </cross-domain-access>
</access-policy>
```

This policy file establishes three rules:

* It allows access on all ports from 4502 to 4532, which is the full range supported by Silverlight. To change this detail, modify the port attribute in the <socket-resource> element.

* It allows TCP access through the protocol attribute in the <socket-resource> element.

* It allows callers from any domain. In other words, the Silverlight application that's making the connection can be hosted on any website. To change this detail, modify the uri attribute in the <domain> element.

To make life easy, this policy is included in the policy server project. That way, the policy server simply needs to find the file on the hard drive, open it, and return the contents to the client.

The PolicyServer Classes

The policy server's functionality resides in two key classes. The first class, PolicyServer, is responsible for waiting and listening for connections. When a connection is received, it's handed off to a new instance of the second class, PolicyConnection, which then sends the policy file. This two-part design is common in network programming, and you'll see it again with the messaging server.

When the PolicyServer class is created, it loads the policy file from the hard drive and stores it in a field, as an array of bytes:

```
public class PolicyServer
{
    private byte[] policy;
    public PolicyServer(string policyFile)
    {
        // Load the policy file.
        FileStream policyStream = new FileStream(policyFile, FileMode.Open);
        policy = new byte[policyStream.Length];
        policyStream.Read(policy, 0, policy.Length);
        policyStream.Close();
    }
    ...
```

To start listening, the server application must call PolicyServer.Start(). This creates a TcpListener, which waits for requests. The TcpListener is configured to listen on port 943, because Silverlight reserves this port for policy servers. (As you'll see, when Silverlight applications make policy files requests, they automatically send them to this port.)

```
    ...
    private TcpListener listener;

    public void Start()
    {
        // Create the listener.
        listener = new TcpListener(IPAddress.Any, 943);

        // Begin listening. This method returns immediately.
        listener.Start();

        // Wait for a connection. This method returns immediately.
        // The waiting happens on a separate thread.
        listener.BeginAcceptTcpClient(OnAcceptTcpClient, null);
    }
    ...
```

To accept any pending connections, the policy server calls BeginAcceptTcpClient(). Like all the BeginXxx() methods in .NET, this method returns immediately and starts the real work on a separate thread. This is an important detail for a networking application, because it allows you to handle multiple policy file requests at the same time.

Note Newcomers to network programming often wonder how they can handle more than one simultaneous request, and they sometimes assume that multiple server reports are required. This isn't the case—if it were, a small set of applications could quickly exhaust the available ports. Instead, server applications handle multiple requests with the same port. This process is almost completely transparent because the underlying TCP architecture in Windows automatically identifies messages and routes them to the appropriate object in your code. Connections are uniquely identified based on four pieces of information: the IP address and server port, and the IP address and client port.

Each time a request is make, the OnAcceptTcpClient() callback is triggered. That callback then calls BeginAcceptTcpClient() again to start waiting for the next request on *another* thread, and then gets to the real work of dealing with the current request:

```
...
public void OnAcceptTcpClient(IAsyncResult ar)
{
    if (isStopped) return;
    Console.WriteLine("Received policy request.");

    // Wait for the next connection.
    listener.BeginAcceptTcpClient(OnAcceptTcpClient, null);

    // Handle this connection.
    try
    {
        TcpClient client = listener.EndAcceptTcpClient(ar);
        PolicyConnection policyConnection = new PolicyConnection(client,
          policy);
        policyConnection.HandleRequest();
    }
    catch (Exception err)
    {
        Console.WriteLine(err.Message);
    }
}
...
```

Each time a new connection is received, a new PolicyConnection object is created to deal with it. The task of serving the policy file is handled by the PolicyConnection class, which you'll consider in the next section.

The final ingredient in the PolicyServer class is a Stop() method that stops waiting for requests. The application can call this if it's shutting down:

```
...
    private bool isStopped;
    public void Stop()
    {
        isStopped = true;
        try
        {
            listener.Stop();
        }
        catch (Exception err)
        {
            Console.WriteLine(err.Message);
        }
    }
}
```

To start the policy server, the Main() method of the server application uses this code:

```
static void Main(string[] args)
{
    PolicyServer policyServer = new PolicyServer("clientaccesspolicy.xml");
    policyServer.Start();
    Console.WriteLine("Policy server started.");

    Console.WriteLine("Press Enter to exit.");
    // Wait for an enter key. You could also wait for a specific input
    // string (like "quit") or a single key using Console.ReadKey().
    Console.ReadLine();

    policyServer.Stop();
    Console.WriteLine("Policy server shut down.");
}
```

The PolicyConnection Classes

The PolicyConnection class class has a simple task. When created, it stores a reference to the policy file data. Then, when the HandleRequest() method is called, it accesses the network stream for the new connection and attempts to read from it. If all is well, the client will have sent a string that contains the text "<policy-file-request/>". After reading that string, the client writes the policy data to that stream, and closes the connection.

Here's the complete code:

```
public class PolicyConnection
{
    private TcpClient client;
    private byte[] policy;
```

```
public PolicyConnection(TcpClient client, byte[] policy)
{
    this.client = client;
    this.policy = policy;
}

// The request that the client sends.
private static string policyRequestString = "<policy-file-request/>";

public void HandleRequest()
{
    Stream s = client.GetStream();

    // Read the policy request string.
    byte[] buffer = new byte[policyRequestString.Length];

    // Only wait 5 seconds. That way, if you attempt to read the request string
    // and it isn't there or it's incomplete, the client only waits for 5
    // seconds before timing out.
    client.ReceiveTimeout = 5000;
    s.Read(buffer, 0, buffer.Length);

    // Send the policy. (Optionally, you could verify that the policy request
    // contains the content you expect.)
    s.Write(policy, 0, policy.Length);

    // Close the connection.
    client.Close();

    Console.WriteLine("Served policy file.");
}
}
```

You now have a complete, fully functioning policy server. Unfortunately, you can't test it yet. That's because Silverlight doesn't allow you to explicitly request policy files. Instead, it automatically requests them when you attempt to use a socket-based application. And before you build a client for that socket-based application, you need to build the server.

The Messaging Server

Although you can create the messaging server as a separate application, it's tidier to place it in the same application as the policy server. Because the policy server does its listening and request-handling work on separate threads, the messaging server can do its work at the same time.

Like the policy server, the messaging server is broken into two classes: MessengerServer, which listens for requests and tracks clients, and MessengerConnection, which handles the interaction of a single client. To see the full code, refer to the downloadable examples for this chapter. In this section, you'll just explore the differences between the policy server and messaging server.

First, the messaging server performs its listening on a different port. As described earlier, Silverlight allows socket-based applications to use any port in a limited band from 4502 to 4532. The messaging server uses port 4530:

```
listener = new TcpListener(IPAddress.Any, 4530);
```

When the messaging server receives a connection request, it performs an extra step. As with the policy server, it creates an instance of a new class (in this case, MessengerConnection) to handle the communication. Additionally, it adds the client to a collection so it can keep track of all the currently connected users. This is the only way you can allow interaction between these clients—for example, allowing messages to be sent from one user to another. Here's the collection that performs the tracking, and a field that helps the server give each new client a different identifying number:

```
private int clientNum;
private List<MessengerConnection> clients = new List<MessengerConnection>();
```

When the client connects, this code creates the MessengerConnection and adds the client to the clients collection:

```
clientNum++;
Console.WriteLine("Messenger client #" + clientNum.ToString() + " connected.");

// Create a new object to handle this connection.
MessengerConnection clientHandler = new MessengerConnection(client,
  "Client " + clientNum.ToString(), this);
clientHandler.Start();

lock (clients)
{
    clients.Add(clientHandler);
}
```

Because there's the possibility that several clients will be connecting at once, this code locks the clients collection before adding the client. Otherwise, subtle threading errors could occur when two threads in the messaging server attempt to add a new client (or perform a different task with the clients collection) at the same time.

When the messaging server is stopped, it steps through this complete collection and makes sure every client is disconnected:

```
foreach (MessengerConnection client in clients)
{
    client.Close();
}
```

You've now seen how the basic framework for the messaging server is designed. However, it still lacks the message-delivery feature—the ability for one client to submit a message that's then delivered to all clients.

To implement this feature, you need two ingredients. First, you need to handle the message submission in the MessengerConnection class. Then, you need to handle the message delivery in the MessengerServer class.

When a MessengerConnection object is created and has its Start() method called, it begins listening for any data:

```csharp
public void Start()
{
    try
    {
        // Listen for messages.
        client.Client.BeginReceive(message, 0, message.Length,
          SocketFlags.None, new AsyncCallback(OnDataReceived), null);
    }
    catch (SocketException se)
    {
        Console.WriteLine(se.Message);
    }
}
```

The OnDataReceived() callback is triggered when the client sends some data. It reads one byte at a time, until it has all the information that the client has sent. It then passes the data along to the MessengerServer.Deliver() method, and begins listening for next message:

```csharp
public void OnDataReceived(IAsyncResult asyn)
{
    try
    {
        int bytesRead = client.Client.EndReceive(asyn);

        if (bytesRead > 0)
        {
            // Ask the server to send the message to all the clients.
            server.DeliverMessage(message, bytesRead);

            // Listen for more messages.
            client.Client.BeginReceive(message, 0, message.Length,
              SocketFlags.None, new AsyncCallback(OnDataReceived), null);
        }
    }
    catch (Exception err)
    {
        Console.WriteLine(err.Message);
    }
}
```

> **■Note** When a message is received, the Messenger assumes that message is entirely made up of text that needs to be delivered to other recipients. A more sophisticated application would allow more complex messages. For example, you might serialize and send a Message object that indicates the message text, sender, and intended recipient. Or, you might use a library of string constants that identify different commands—for example, for sending messages, sending files, querying for a list of currently connected users, logging off, and so on. The design of your messaging application would be the same, but you would need much more code to analyze the message and decide what action to take.

The DeliverMessage() method walks through the collection of clients and calls each one's ReceiveMessage() method to pass the communication along. Once again, threading issues are a concern. But locking the entire collection isn't ideal, because the delivery process could take some time, particularly if a client isn't responding. To avoid any slowdowns, the Deliver-Message() code begins by creating a snapshot copy of the collection. It then uses that to deliver its message.

```
public void DeliverMessage(byte[] message, int bytesRead)
{
    Console.WriteLine("Delivering message.");

    // Duplicate the collection to prevent threading issues.
    MessengerConnection[] connectedClients;
    lock (clients)
    {
        connectedClients = clients.ToArray();
    }

    foreach (MessengerConnection client in connectedClients)
    {
        try
        {
            client.ReceiveMessage(message, bytesRead);
        }
        catch
        {
            // Client is disconnected.
            // Remove the client to avoid future attempts.
            lock (clients)
            {
                clients.Remove(client);
            }
        }
```

```
            client.Close();
        }
    }
}
```

The MessengerConnection.ReceiveMessage() method simply writes the message data back into the network stream, so the client can receive it:

```
public void ReceiveMessage(byte[] data, int bytesRead)
{
    client.GetStream().Write(data, 0, bytesRead);
}
```

The final change you need is to modify the startup code so that the application creates and starts both the policy server and the messaging server. Here's the code, with additions in bold:

```
static void Main(string[] args)
{
    PolicyServer policyServer = new PolicyServer("clientaccesspolicy.xml");
    policyServer.Start();
    Console.WriteLine("Policy server started.");

    MessengerServer messengerServer = new MessengerServer();
    messengerServer.Start();
    Console.WriteLine("Messenger server started.");

    Console.WriteLine("Press Enter to exit.");
    // Wait for an enter key. You could also wait for a specific input
    // string (like "quit") or a single key using Console.ReadKey().
    Console.ReadLine();

    policyServer.Stop();
    Console.WriteLine("Policy server shut down.");

    messengerServer.Stop();
    Console.WriteLine("Messenger server shut down.");
}
```

Figure 17-8 showed what happens when two clients begin talking to each other through the socket server. Figure 17-9 shows the back end of the same process—the messages that appear in the Console window of the socket server while the clients are connecting and then interacting.

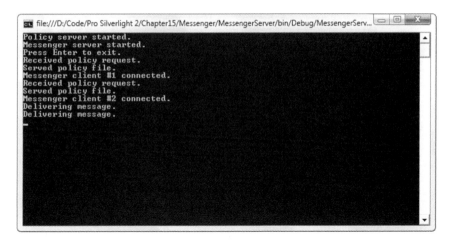

Figure 17-9. *The policy and messaging server*

The Messenger Client

So far, you've focused exclusively on the server-side .NET application that powers the messaging server. Although this is the most complex piece of the puzzle, the Silverlight socket client also requires its fair share of code.

The messaging client has three basic tasks: to connect to the server, to send messages, and to receive and display them. The actual code is similar to the socket server, but requires slightly more work. That's because Silverlight doesn't have a TcpClient class, but forces you to use the lower-level Socket class instead.

To use the socket class, you use three asynchronous methods: ConnectAsync(), Send-Async(), and ReceiveAsync(). All three of these methods require a SocketAsyncEventArgs object. This object stores a reference to the socket (in the UserToken property) and the remote connection (in the RemoteEndPointProperty). It also provides a Completed event that fires when the appropriate operation is finished. To perform any task with a socket in Silverlight, you must create and configure a SocketAsyncEventArgs object and then pass it to one of the asynchronous Socket methods.

Connecting to the Server

The first task in the messaging client is to establish a connection when the user clicks the Connect button. Here's what happens:

```
// The socket for the underlying connection.
private Socket socket;

private void cmdConnect_Click(object sender, RoutedEventArgs e)
{
    try
    {
        if ((socket != null) && (socket.Connected == true)) socket.Close();
```

```
    }
    catch (Exception err)
    {
        AddMessage("ERROR: " + err.Message);
    }

    DnsEndPoint endPoint =
      new DnsEndPoint(Application.Current.Host.Source.DnsSafeHost, 4530);
    socket = new Socket(AddressFamily.InterNetwork,
      SocketType.Stream, ProtocolType.Tcp);

    SocketAsyncEventArgs args = new SocketAsyncEventArgs();
    args.UserToken = socket;
    args.RemoteEndPoint = endPoint;
    args.Completed +=
      new EventHandler<SocketAsyncEventArgs>(OnSocketConnectCompleted);
    socket.ConnectAsync(args);
}
```

Most of these details are fairly straightforward. If the socket is already opened, it's closed. Then, a DnsEndPoint object is created to identify the location of the remote host. In this case, the location of the remove host is the web server that hosts the Silverlight page, and the port number is 4530. Finally, the code creates the SocketAsyncEventArgs, and attaches the OnSocketConnectCompleted() event to the Completed event.

Note Remember, unless you specify otherwise, the client's port is chosen dynamically from the set of available ports when the connection is created. That means you could create a client that opens multiple connections to the same server. On the server side, each connection would be dealt with uniquely, because each connection would have a different client port number.

You'll notice that the code uses a custom method named AddMessage() to add information to the message list. This method takes the extra step of making sure it's running on the user interface thread. This is important, because AddMessage() may be called during one of the client's asynchronous operations.

```
private void AddMessage(string message)
{
    Dispatcher.BeginInvoke(
      delegate()
      {
          lblMessages.Text += message + "\n";
          // Scroll down to the bottom of the list, so the new message is visible.
          scrollViewer.ScrollToVerticalOffset(scrollViewer.ScrollableHeight);
      });
}
```

When the client's connection attempt finishes, the OnSocketConnectCompleted() event handler runs. It updates the display and reconfigures the SocketAsyncEventArgs object, wiring the Completed event to a new event handler. It then begins listening for messages.

```
private void OnSocketConnectCompleted(object sender, SocketAsyncEventArgs e)
{
    if (!socket.Connected)
    {
        AddMessage("Connection failed.");
        return;
    }

    AddMessage("Connected to server.");

    // Messages can be a maximum of 1024 bytes.
    byte[] response = new byte[1024];
    e.SetBuffer(response, 0, response.Length);
    e.Completed -=
      new EventHandler<SocketAsyncEventArgs>(OnSocketConnectCompleted);
    e.Completed += new EventHandler<SocketAsyncEventArgs>(OnSocketReceive);

    // Listen for messages.
    socket.ReceiveAsync(e);
}
```

To listen for a message, you must create a buffer that will receive the data (or at least a single chunk of that data). The messaging client creates a 1024-byte buffer, and doesn't attempt to read more than one chunk. It assumes that messages will not be greater than 1024 bytes. To prevent potential errors, the messaging application should enforce this restriction as well. One good safety measure is to set a MaxLength property of the text box where the user enters new messages.

Sending Messages

The messages in the chat application are slightly more detailed than simple strings. Each message includes three details—the text, the sender's chosen name, and the sender's time when the message was submitted. These three details are encapsulated in a custom Message class:

```
public class Message
{
    public string MessageText {get; set;}
    public string Sender {get; set;}
    public DateTime SendTime {get; set;}

    public Message(string messageText, string sender)
    {
        MessageText = messageText;
        Sender = sender;
```

```
        SendTime = DateTime.Now;
    }

    public Message() { }
}
```

To send a message, the user enters some text and clicks the Send button. At this point, you need to create a new SocketAsyncEventArgs object. (Remember, the first one is still in use, waiting to receive new messages on a background thread.) The new SocketAsyncEventArgs object needs to store the buffer of message data. To create it, you begin by constructing a Message object. You then serialize that message object to a stream with the XmlSerializer, convert it to a simple byte array, and finally add it to the SocketAsyncEventArgs object using the BufferList property, as shown here:

```
private void cmdSend_Click(object sender, RoutedEventArgs e)
{
    if ((socket == null) || (socket.Connected == false))
    {
        AddMessage("ERROR: Not connected.");
        return;
    }

    SocketAsyncEventArgs args = new SocketAsyncEventArgs();

    // Prepare the message.
    XmlSerializer serializer = new XmlSerializer(typeof(Message));
    MemoryStream ms = new MemoryStream();
    serializer.Serialize(ms, new Message(txtMessage.Text, txtName.Text));
    byte[] messageData = ms.ToArray();
    List<ArraySegment<byte>> bufferList = new List<ArraySegment<byte>>();
    bufferList.Add(new ArraySegment<byte>(messageData));
    args.BufferList = bufferList;

    // Send the message.
    socket.SendAsync(args);
}
```

Unfortunately, because the Socket class in Silverlight works at a lower level than the TcpClient in .NET, you don't have the straightforward stream-based access to the network connection that you have on the server side.

■**Tip** You can write any type of data you want to the server, in any form. You certainly don't need to use the XmlSerializer. However, serialization gives you a simple way to pass along a bundle of information as an instance of some class.

Receiving Messages

When a message is sent to the client, the other SocketAsyncEventArgs object fires its Completed event, which triggers the OnSocketReceive() event handler. At this point, you need to deserialize the message, display it, and then wait for the next one.

```
private void OnSocketReceive(object sender, SocketAsyncEventArgs e)
{
    if (e.BytesTransferred == 0)
    {
        AddMessage("Server disconnected.");
        try
        {
            socket.Close();
        }
        catch { }
        return;
    }

    try
    {
        // Retrieve and display the message.
        XmlSerializer serializer = new XmlSerializer(typeof(Message));
        MemoryStream ms = new MemoryStream();
        ms.Write(e.Buffer, 0, e.BytesTransferred);
        ms.Position = 0;
        Message message = (Message)serializer.Deserialize(ms);

        AddMessage("[" + message.Sender + "] " + message.MessageText +
            " (at " + message.SendTime.ToLongTimeString() + ")");
    }
    catch (Exception err)
    {
        AddMessage("ERROR: " + err.Message);
    }

    // Listen for more messages.
    socket.ReceiveAsync(e);
}
```

This completes the messaging client. To experiment with the complete solution, try out the downloadable code for this chapter.

Note There are a number of refinements you could make to polish up the messaging application. You've already considered how you could replace the simple message-passing mechanism on the server side with more complex logic that recognizes different types of messages and performs different operations. Other changes you might want to implement include managing user interface state (for example, disabling or enabling controls based on whether a connection is available), intercepting the application shutdown event and politely disconnecting from the server, allowing users to deliver to specific people, adding identify authentication, and informing newly connected clients about how many other people are currently online. With all that in mind, the messaging application is still an impressive first start that shows how far a Silverlight application can go with direct network communication.

The Last Word

In this chapter, you saw a wide range of Silverlight networking features. You learned how to use them to do everything from directly downloading HTML files to calling simple XML-based web services to building an entire messaging system based on socket communication. Along the way, you considered several techniques for parsing different types of information, including regular expressions (to search HTML), LINQ to XML (to process XML), and serialization (to save or restore the contents of an in-memory object). These techniques can come in handy in a variety of situations—for example, they're just as useful when you need to manage information that's stored on the client computer in isolated storage.

Index

■Special Characters

$ character, 542
* (asterisk), 540, 542
[ ] (square brackets), 542, 560
[^] character, 542
^ character, 542
{ } (curly braces), 560
{m, n} character, 542
{m} character, 542
| character, 542
+ character, 542
= operator, 9
- (dashes), 200–202
. (period), 540, 542
( ) character, 542
\ character, 542

■A

Abort( ) method, 513, 523
Absolute sizes strategy, 64
AcceptsReturn property, 150, 335
ActiveX controls, 20
ActualHeight property, 62
ActualWidth property, 62, 250
adaptive streaming, 301
Add Service Reference dialog box, 426
AddHistoryItem( ) method, 401–402
AddMessage( ) method, 578
Address box, 426
AdRotator control, 421
alignment
    content, 138
    StackPanel, 58–59
AlignmentX property, 228
AlignmentY property, 228
AlternatingRowBackground property, 478
alternative content, 20
Ancestors( ) method, 553

animation
    bomb dropping game
        bomb user control, 270–271
        counting bombs and cleaning up,
            277–279
        dropping bombs, 272–275
        intercepting bombs, 275–277
        main page, 268–270
        overview, 267–268
    brushes, 262–263
    controlling playback, 255–257
    encapsulating
        base class, 281–282
        overview, 279
        page transitions, 279–280
        wipe transition, 282–284
    frame rate, 257–258
    frame-based, 285–288
    key frame, 263–266
    lifetime of, 252–254
    overview, 243, 244
    properties
        By, 251
        Duration, 251–252
        From, 249–251
        overview, 249
        To, 251
    rules of, 244–245
    simultaneous, 254–255
    starting
        with code, 248–249
        with event triggers, 247–248
    Storyboard class, 246–247
    transforms, 259–262
Animation class, 245–246
anonymous types, 554
App class, 22, 168, 383
App_Code folder, 445

M

You Need the Companion eBook

Your purchase of this book entitles you to buy the companion PDF-version eBook for only $10. Take the weightless companion with you anywhere.

We believe this Apress title will prove so indispensable that you'll want to carry it with you everywhere, which is why we are offering the companion eBook (in PDF format) for $10 to customers who purchase this book now. Convenient and fully searchable, the PDF version of any content-rich, page-heavy Apress book makes a valuable addition to your programming library. You can easily find and copy code—or perform examples by quickly toggling between instructions and the application. Even simultaneously tackling a donut, diet soda, and complex code becomes simplified with hands-free eBooks!

Once you purchase your book, getting the $10 companion eBook is simple:

❶ Visit **www.apress.com/promo/tendollars/**.

❷ Complete a basic registration form to receive a randomly generated question about this title.

❸ Answer the question correctly in 60 seconds, and you will receive a promotional code to redeem for the $10.00 eBook.

2855 TELEGRAPH AVENUE | SUITE 600 | BERKELEY, CA 94705

Offer valid through 5/24/09.